SAFETY OF COMPUTER CONTROL SYSTEMS 1992 (SAFECOMP'92)

Computer Systems in Safety-critical Applications

Proceedings of the IFAC Symposium,
Zürich, Switzerland, 28 - 30 October 1992

Edited by

HEINZ H. FREY

ABB Transportation Systems Ltd,
Zürich, Switzerland

Published for the

INTERNATIONAL FEDERATION OF AUTOMATIC CONTROL

by

PERGAMON PRESS

OXFORD • NEW YORK • SEOUL • TOKYO

UK	Pergamon Press Ltd, Headington Hill Hall, Oxford OX3 0BW, England
USA	Pergamon Press, Inc., 660 White Plains Road, Tarrytown, New York 10591-5153, USA
KOREA	Pergamon Press Korea, KPO Box 315, Seoul 110-603, Korea
JAPAN	Pergamon Press Japan, Tsunashima Building Annex, 3-20-12 Yushima, Bunkyo-ku, Tokyo 113, Japan

First edition 1992

Library of Congress Cataloging in Publication Data

A catalogue record for this book is available from the Library of Congress

British Library Cataloguing in Publication Data

A catalogue record for this book is available from the British Library

ISBN 0-08-041893-7

These proceedings were reproduced by means of the photo-offset process using the manuscripts supplied by the authors of the different papers. The manuscripts have been typed using different typewriters and typefaces. The lay-out, figures and tables of some papers did not agree completely with the standard requirements: consequently the reproduction does not display complete uniformity. To ensure rapid publication this discrepancy could not be changed: nor could the English be checked completely. Therefore, the readers are asked to excuse any deficiencies of this publication which may be due to the above mentioned reasons.

The Editor

Printed in Great Britain

IFAC SYMPOSIUM ON SAFETY OF COMPUTER CONTROL SYSTEMS 1992 (SAFECOMP'92)

Computer Systems in Safety-critical Applications

Sponsored by
International Federation of Automatic Control (IFAC)

Co-sponsored by
International Federation for Information Processing (IFIP)
- Technical Committee TC10

Organized and Supported by
European Workshop on Industrial Computer Systems (EWICS)
- Technical Committee on Safety, Security and Reliability
Swiss Federation for Automatic Control (SGA)
ABB Transportation Systems Ltd, Zürich, Switzerland
Austrian Computer Society (OCG)
Swiss Association for the Promotion of Quality (SAQ)
Centre for Software Reliability, Newcastle-Upon-Tyne, UK
The British Computer Society, London, UK

International Programme Committee

H.H. Frey (CH)   (Chairman)
R. Bloomfield (UK) (EWICS TC7 Chairman)
K. Asmis (CDN)
S. Bologna (I)
L. Boullart (B)
G. Dahil (N)
B.K. Daniels (UK)
W. Ehrenberger (G)
K. Frühauf (CH)
R. Genser (A)
J. Gorski (PL)
S.L. Hansen (DK)
K. Kanoun (F)
H. Kirrmann (CH)

F. Koornneef (NL)
J.L. de Kroes (NL)
R. Lauber (G)
J.F. Lindeberg (N)
L. Motus (RUSSIA)
J.M.A. Rata (F)
F. Redmill (UK)
M. Rodd (UK)
B. Runge (DK)
G.H. Schildt (A)
E. Schoitsch (A)
B. Sterner (S)
A. Toola (SF)
G. Vuilleumier (CH)

National Organizing Committee
H.H. Frey   (Chairman)
J. Frey
K. Frühauf
H. Kirrmann
R. Messerli

PREFACE

Computer systems controlling and monitoring industrial processes and applied in various ways in critical missions are commonplace in today's world. Even the use of computers in life-critical applications is generally accepted, provided that appropriate technology and project management are used and certain principles and guidelines are carefully observed by specifically trained and experienced engineers. Significant changes in technology, the increased use of computer systems and experience have led to the development of these principles and have helped create guidelines in the key areas of system and software engineering in safety-critical applications.

This book represents the proceedings of the IFAC Conference on Computer Systems in Safety-critical Applications held in Zürich, Switzerland, 28-30 October 1992. This conference continues the series of SAFECOMP conferences and workshops which have been held since the first SAFECOMP in 1979. SAFECOMP'92 is the 10th in the series. The conference is now held annually. The initiator of the SAFECOMP events is EWICS TC7, the European Workshop on Industrial Computer Systems TC on Safety, Security and Reliability. EWICS TC7 was founded in 1974 in Zürich under the name of Purdue Europe.

SAFECOMP'92 advances the state of the art, reviews experiences of the past years, considers the guidance now available and identifies the skills, methods, tools and technologies required as we move toward the 21st century.

The great response to the Call for Papers for this conference clearly indicates the ever-growing importance of computer systems where safe and highly reliable operation is required and shows the increased interest on the part of industry, system operators and authorities. I must thank all the authors whose work makes the technical level of the conference a high one as well as the International and National Organizing Committees and their staffs and the co-sponsors whose support have made it possible to hold SAFECOMP'92.

Heinz H. Frey

CONTENTS

SPECIFICATION

SYSTEMS AND COMPONENTS

DISTRIBUTED SYSTEMS

ISSUES OF TEST AND EVALUATION IN RAILWAY APPLICATIONS

ISSUES OF CERTIFICATION IN AVIONICS APPLICATIONS

ANALYSIS

ISSUES OF INTRUSION

DEVELOPMENT

ISSUES OF SECURITY

EVALUATION

VERIFICATION

A CASE STUDY IN THE ANALYSIS OF SAFETY REQUIREMENTS

Glenn Bruns
Stuart Anderson

Laboratory for Foundations of Computer Science
Computer Science Department, University of Edinburgh
Edinburgh EH9 3JZ, UK

Abstract. We show how formal methods can be used to assist in developing requirements of a safety-critical system. The approach is to express the requirements in temporal logic, and then to develop a process model satisfying the requirements. The existence of such a model ensures the requirements are consistent, and also helps in their validation.

Keywords. Safety; computer software; concurrency; formal methods; temporal logic.

INTRODUCTION

The literature on the application of mathematical methods to the construction of safety-critical systems has tended to assume the requirements analysis is given; concentrating on proving properties of specifications (Atkinson and Cunningham, 1991) or of implementations (Bruns and Anderson, 1991). Here we explore the use of such methods in formulating the safety requirements for systems. Requirements analysis is an open-ended task but we believe that by using formally expressed properties and models of the system we can support important verification and validation activities in the requirements stage.

In this paper we explore the use of temporal logic and process algebra in carrying out the requirements analysis for a component designed for use in a railway interlocking system. We begin by developing the service and safety requirements of the component. We are then faced with the questions: Is a system with these properties feasible? How well does a system with these properties meet our informal notion of the system? We answer these by constructing a system with the properties, thereby verifying the consistency of the properties and providing a simple "simulation" model of a system which satisfies these properties. We focus on the detection of failures in a low-speed communication link, but the approach taken here could be applied to all the service and safety requirements. An important feature of the approach is the discovery/refinement of requirements necessitated by the process of building a model which satisfies the chosen properties.

BACKGROUND

The overall function of British Rail's Solid State Interlocking (SSI) (Cribbens, 1987) is to adjust, at the request of the signal operator, the settings of signals and points in the railway to permit the safe passage

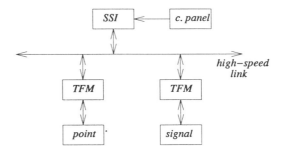

Fig. 1: Solid State Interlocking

of trains. "Safe", in this context, means that the system is designed to protect the signal operator from inadvertently sending trains along routes that could lead to a collision or derailment. The entire BR network is controlled by many SSI's, each responsible for one sub-network.

Figure 1 depicts an SSI and the devices it controls. Safe commands issued from the control panel are allowed to effect signals and points via messages sent over a high-speed communication link to track-side functional modules (TFM's).

One of the safety-related features of the SSI is its pattern of communication with the TFM's. Instead of sending signal or point commands only as needed, the SSI sends a message of the form ⟨*TFM address, state*⟩ to each attached TFM about once every second, indicating the intended current device state. These messages are sent in a predefined cyclic pattern, called a *major cycle*, one TFM after another. After sending a message, the SSI waits at most a few milliseconds for the addressed TFM to respond with the current state of the device. This scheme allows failures of the TFM's and the communication link to be detected quickly, and forces devices that have autonomously changed state to re-

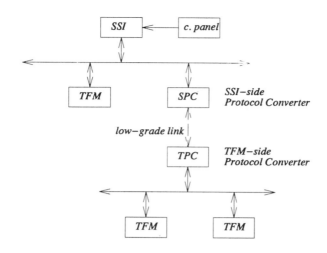

Fig. 2: The Slow-scan System

turn to their proper state.

In some sections of the BR network, many miles of track lie between TFM's, making the cost of the high-speed link prohibitive. A cheaper low-speed link cannot be directly adopted because it could not support the bandwidth needed for the TFM command cycling scheme. On the other hand, dropping the scheme would endanger system safety and force changes to the SSI and TFM communication protocols. A proposed solution is to reduce the needed bandwidth by designing a pair of protocol converters, one at each end of a low-speed link (see Figure 2). The SSI-side protocol converter (SPC) accepts TFM commands, and responds immediately to the SSI just as a TFM would, but only sends commands along the low-speed link occasionally. The TFM-side protocol converter (TPC) sends a command to each attached TFM once every second. Responses from the TFM's are occasionally sent by the TPC to the SPC, in order to update the SPC's device status information. This arrangement of low-speed link (also called a *low-grade link*, or LGL) and protocol converters is called a *slow-scan* system. The requirements we describe here and the constructed model are broadly in line with those reported in(Taleb and Gurney, 1990).

Clearly the slow-scan system must differ from a high-speed link in a manner observable to an external observer. For a safety analysis we do not require slow-scan to possess all the properties of a high-speed link but we should require that properties sufficient to guarantee the safety of the system should hold for slow-scan. In addition we should expect some (suitably diminished) level of service from the system.

SAFETY CONSIDERATIONS

Taken on its own, slow-scan cannot be considered safety-critical, since it does not directly control physical devices. However, by first looking at the safety-critical properties of the train routing system as a whole, and then working through the levels of the system, it is possible to obtain derived safety requirements of slow-scan. There is not room here to present

such a hierarchical safety analysis. We will simply observe that the primary safety requirements the SSI must guarantee are: *timely and error-free delivery of commands* and *timely detection of failures*.

The SSI can satisfy these requirements if a high-speed link is used. The bandwidth of the link and error coding of messages ensures that the first requirement is met. The TFM-command cycling scheme ensures the second is met. Both requirements are threatened by slow-scan.

In this study we focus on the ability of the LGL to meet the second requirement. In the next section we develop properties which if they are satisfied by an implementation of slow-scan will guarantee that slow-scan faults will evoke the same behaviour in the overall system as a failure of the high speed data highway.

REQUIREMENTS ANALYSIS

In requirements analysis we are interested in expressing all the required properties of the system in a precisely stated form. In this section we demonstrate the use of a temporal logic to express such properties. The models underlying the temporal logic are labelled transition systems, also referred to as *processes*. These systems describe the behaviour of real-world systems as states, plus actions that effect state changes. Thus, in describing properties of systems, we are interested in expressing the ability of a system to carry out (or fail to carry out) certain sequences of actions.

In slow-scan we are certainly interested in six actions which should be visible to the outside world (overbars are used to denote output actions):

comm-in: an input action which occurs when slow-scan receives an command from the SSI

comm-out: an output action which occurs when the TPC generates a command intended for a remote TFM

status-in: an input action which occurs when a remote TFM generates a status input to the TPC

status-out: an output action which occurs when the SPC generates a status output to the SSI

fail: an output action which occurs when some internal failure occurs in slow-scan

det: an output action which occurs when slow-scan has detected a failure

In some ways this list of actions can be seen as a "black box" description of slow-scan. The actions carry no information of the contents of the messages, they just indicate they occur — since we are interested primarily in safety we have no need for additional detail. In addition we have no idea of the sequences of these actions which the system might allow. The goal of requirements analysis to develop properties of the sequences of actions of the system.

To compress the presentation of the process of developing properties we focus on a single one, that of the requirement for timely error-detection.

Formalising Safety Properties

The requirement has two components. Informally we can state these properties as follows:

- After a low-grade link failure, slow-scan will eventually detect the failure and stop responding to the SSI and TFM.

- No false alarms occur.

We use the modal mu-calculus (Kozen, 1983) in a slightly extended form (Stirling, 1989) as our temporal logic. The syntax of the mu-calculus is as follows, where L ranges over sets of actions and Z ranges over variables:

$$\phi ::= \neg\phi \mid \phi_1 \wedge \phi_2 \mid [L]\phi \mid Z \mid \nu Z.\phi$$

Informally, the formula $\neg\phi$ holds of a process P if ϕ does not hold of P. The formula $\phi_1 \wedge \phi_2$ holds of P if both ϕ_1 and ϕ_2 hold of P. The formula $[L]\phi$ holds of P if ϕ holds for all processes P' that can be reached from P through the performance of action $\alpha \in L$. The formula $\nu Z.\phi$ is the greatest fixed point of the recursive modal equation $Z = \phi$, where Z appears in ϕ. Some intuition about fixed point formulas can be gained by keeping in mind that $\nu Z.\phi$ can be replaced by its "unfolding": the formula ϕ with Z replaced by $\nu Z.\phi$ itself. Thus, $\nu Z.\psi \wedge [\{a\}]Z = \psi \wedge [\{a\}](\nu Z.\psi \wedge [\{a\}]Z) = \psi \wedge [\{a\}](\psi \wedge [\{a\}](\nu Z.\psi \wedge [\{a\}]Z)) = \ldots$ holds of any process for which ψ holds along any execution path of a actions.

The operators $\vee$, $\langle\alpha\rangle$, and μ can be defined as duals to existing operators (where $\phi[\psi/Z]$ is the property obtained by substituting ψ for free occurrences of Z in ϕ):

$$\phi_1 \vee \phi_2 \stackrel{\text{def}}{=} \neg(\phi_1 \wedge \phi_2)$$
$$\langle L\rangle\phi \stackrel{\text{def}}{=} \neg[L]\neg\phi$$
$$\mu Z.\phi \stackrel{\text{def}}{=} \neg\nu Z.\phi[\neg Z/Z]$$

Informally $\langle L\rangle\phi$ holds of a process that can perform an action in L and thereby evolve to a process satisfying ϕ. As with $\nu Z.\phi$, the formula $\mu Z.\phi$ can be understood through unfolding, except here only finitely many unfoldings can be made. Thus, $\mu Z.\psi \vee \langle\{a\}\rangle Z$ holds of a process that can evolve to a process satisfying ψ after finitely many occurrences of action a.

These additional abbreviations are also convenient (where L ranges over sets of actions, and Act is the set of CCS actions):

$$[\alpha_1,\ldots,\alpha_n]\phi \stackrel{\text{def}}{=} [\{\alpha_1,\ldots,\alpha_n\}]\phi$$
$$[-]\phi \stackrel{\text{def}}{=} [Act]\phi$$
$$[-L]\phi \stackrel{\text{def}}{=} [Act - L]\phi$$

The booleans are defined as abbreviations: $\mathtt{tt} \stackrel{\text{def}}{=} \nu Z.Z$, $\mathtt{ff} \stackrel{\text{def}}{=} \neg\mathtt{tt}$. An example using these abbreviations is $\langle a, b\rangle\mathtt{tt}$, which holds of processes that can perform either an a or a b action. As another exam-

ple, the formula $\mu Z.\langle-\rangle\mathtt{tt} \wedge [-]Z$ holds of deadlock-free processes.

Before considering specific properties of slow-scan we present two more abbreviations that often make it possible to avoid the fixed-point operators:

$$[L]^*\phi \stackrel{\text{def}}{=} \nu Z.\phi \wedge [L]Z$$
$$\langle L\rangle^*\phi \stackrel{\text{def}}{=} \mu Z.\phi \vee \langle L\rangle Z$$

Informally, $[L]^*\phi$ holds if ϕ always holds along all paths composed of actions in the set L. For example, the absence of deadlock can be written $[-]^*\langle-\rangle\mathtt{tt}$ — in every state some action is possible. The dual operator $\langle L\rangle^*\phi$ holds of processes having a finite execution path composed of actions from L leading to a state in which ϕ holds.

We are ready now to formalise the two important slow-scan properties. Recall the first property:

> After a low-grade link failure, slow-scan will eventually detect the failure and stop responding to the SSI and TFM.

There are two distinct parts to this property: a) failures are eventually detected, and b) after detection eventually no responses are made to the TFM's or SSI. In formalizing the first part, we have the idea "after a $\overline{fail}$ action occurs then eventually a $\overline{det}$ action occurs". Care needs to be taken here with the notion of eventuality, however, because the modal mu-calculus has no "built-in" notion of time — we only have actions. To capture the notion of eventuality in this informal statement of the property we need the idea that there is some time frame which is (approximately) the same at either end of slow-scan. In order to capture this we introduce a new output action called $\overline{tick}$ which indicates the passage of time in this time frame. Any process which satisfies the safety properties given below should also ensure that $\overline{tick}$ indicates the passage of time at *both* ends of slow-scan.

The next step is therefore to define an abbreviation for the property "if tick actions continue to occur then eventually action α will occur":

$$even(\alpha) \stackrel{\text{def}}{=} \mu Z.[-\overline{tick}, \alpha]^*[\overline{tick}]Z$$

A reasonable translation of this formula to English is "action α must eventually occur if tick actions continue to occur". A useful and closely-related abbreviation captures the property "property ϕ must eventually hold if tick actions continue to occur".

Part of the formalisation of our property is that failure will eventually be detected after a failure has occurred. To express the eventuality of detection we use the formula: $even(\overline{det})$.

Now we can formalise "after $\overline{fail}$ occurs then eventually a $\overline{det}$ action occurs":

$$failures\text{-}detected \stackrel{\text{def}}{=} [-\overline{fail}]^*[\overline{fail}]even(\overline{det})$$

A potential pitfall is that *failures-detected* is vacuously true if a failure never occurs. So, for example, a deadlocked process satisfies the formula. The formula is also vacuously true of processes in which tick actions do not continue to occur. So the process that performs action $\overline{fail}$, then $\overline{tick}$, and then deadlocks also satisfies the formula. To ensure that the slow-scan model does not satisfy failures-detected in one of these ways, we can write two more formulas:

$$failures\text{-}possible \stackrel{\text{def}}{=} \langle - \rangle^* \langle \overline{fail} \rangle \texttt{tt}$$

$$can\text{-}tick \stackrel{\text{def}}{=} [-]^* \langle - \rangle^* \langle \overline{tick} \rangle \texttt{tt}$$

The formula *failures-possible* says that there is some execution path containing the action $\overline{fail}$. The formula *can-tick* says that, from every state, there is some execution path containing the action $\overline{tick}$. Note that *can-tick* is stronger than the property we need: "$\overline{tick}$ can occur infinitely often after a $\overline{fail}$ action".

To complete the formalization of the first property, we need to also express the second part: "after detection eventually no responses are made to the TFM's or SSI". Using the auxiliary formula *silent*, the property can be expressed as follows:

$$silent \quad \stackrel{\text{def}}{=} \quad [-]^* \overline{[comm\text{-}out, status\text{-}out]} \texttt{ff}$$

$$eventually\text{-}silent \quad \stackrel{\text{def}}{=} \quad [-]^* \overline{[det]} even(silent)$$

The property *silent* expresses that no occurrence of actions $\overline{comm\text{-}out}$ or $\overline{status\text{-}out}$ is ever possible. The first property of interest is thus fully captured by the conjunction of *failures-detected*, *eventually-silent*, *failures-possible*, and *can-tick*.

The second property, "a failure is detected only if a failure has actually occurred", is much simpler to express:

$$no\text{-}false\text{-}alarms \stackrel{\text{def}}{=} [-\overline{fail}]^* \overline{[det]} \texttt{ff}$$

While carrying out requirements analysis of a safety-critical system one must also develop a *service requirement* which characterises the minimum level of service required from the system. In validating that the safety properties are consistent one must only consider processes which satisfy this service requirement. For example, in the process control area a shutdown interlocking which always shuts the system down is certainly safe but is unacceptable. For lack of space we omit the development of the service requirement for slow-scan which would amount to requiring that commands and status information are transmitted in the absence of failures. (The model of slow-scan to be developed has this property.)

A MODEL OF SLOW-SCAN

Having formulated our safety requirements we must now verify that the requirements are consistent. To do this we build a simple model of slow-scan and check that all the required properties are satisfied. Furthermore, to give confidence in the feasibility of implementation, we build a model with a component structure that reflects the hardware components of slow-scan. The model is also useful in validating the requirements because we have a model which can be used to simulate the behaviour of the system.

Our notation for describing the behaviour of processes is CCS (Milner, 1989). We will give only a brief and informal overview of CCS here.

Processes are described in CCS by terms for which the only possible behaviour is to perform *actions*, which are either names ($a,b,c,...$), co-names ($\overline{a}$, $\overline{b}$, $\overline{c},...$), or the special action τ. The reason for having both names and co-names is that, as we will see, processes composed in parallel can synchronise if one of them can perform action a and the other can perform action $\overline{a}$.

Process terms have the following syntax, where L ranges over sets of actions and f ranges over functions from actions to actions:

$$P ::= 0 \mid a.P \mid P_1 + P_2 \mid P_1 \mid P_2 \mid P \backslash L \mid P[f]$$

The term 0 denotes the nil process, which can perform no actions. The operator . expresses sequential action. The process $a.P$ can perform the action a and thereby become process P. The operator + expresses choice. If P_1 can perform a and become P_1', then so can $P_1 + P_2$, and similarly for P_2. The operator $\mid$ expresses parallel execution. If process P_1 can perform a and become P_1', then $P_1 \mid P_2$ can perform a and become $P_1' \mid P_2$, and similarly for P_2. Furthermore, if P_1 can perform a and become P_1', and P_2 can perform $\overline{a}$ and become P_2', then $P_1 \mid P_2$ can perform τ and become $P_1' \mid P_2'$. The operator $\backslash$ expresses the restriction of actions. If P can perform a and become P', then $P \backslash L$ can only perform a to become $P' \backslash L$ if $a \notin L$. Finally, $P[f]$ expresses the relabelling of actions. if P can perform a and become P', then $P[f]$ can perform $f(a)$ and become $P'[f]$. A relabelling function f has the property that $f(\tau) = \tau$, and $f(\overline{a}) = \overline{f(a)}$.

The idea of repetition is captured by allowing recursive process definitions of the form $P \stackrel{\text{def}}{=} E$, where P is a process constant and E is a process term possibly containing P. For example, the process defined by $P \stackrel{\text{def}}{=} a.P + b.0$ has the possibility of performing either a or b, and continues to have this possibility as long as action a is performed. Once action b is performed, the process terminates.

The set of actions that can be eventually performed by a process is called its *sort*. For example, the sort of $P \stackrel{\text{def}}{=} a.P + b.0$ is $\{a, b\}$.

We are now ready to develop a CCS model of slow-scan. The model will have process components that model the behaviour of the LGL, SPC, TPC, and a clock. Figure 3 shows a flow diagram of the model.

The low-grade link is modelled as a pair of simple unidirectional links that operate independently:

$$LGL \quad \stackrel{\text{def}}{=} \quad Comm[c2/in, c3/out, c3_u/out_u] \mid$$
$$Comm[s2/in, s3/out, s3_u/out_u]$$

$$Comm \quad \stackrel{\text{def}}{=} \quad in.Comm' + \overline{out_u}.Comm +$$
$$\overline{fail}.Comm''$$

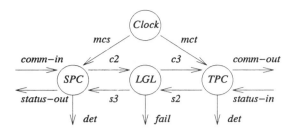

Fig. 3: Flow diagram for the slow-scan model

$$Comm' \stackrel{\text{def}}{=} in.\overline{fail}.Comm'' + \overline{out}.Comm + \overline{fail}.Comm''$$

$$Comm'' \stackrel{\text{def}}{=} in.Comm'' + \overline{out_u}.Comm''$$

A link can receive and buffer a message. The output actions $\overline{out}$ and $\overline{out_u}$ model the delivery of a message and the signalling that no message is available, respectively. Note that messages are modelled simply as content-less "pulses". A link can fail if its buffering capacity is exceeded, or if its communication medium is broken. After a failure occurs, a link can continue to accept messages, but will never deliver messages.

To satisfy the safety requirements, the protocol converters must detect LGL failures. The method used in the model is to have each protocol converter send a message periodically over the LGL, at the same time maintaining a count of messages sent since an LGL message has been received. If the count ever exceeds a limit, then an LGL failure must have occurred. This strategy works because the LGL never outputs messages after a failure.

The CCS model of the SPC is as follows:

$$SPC(i) \stackrel{\text{def}}{=} comm\text{-}in.\overline{status\text{-}out}.SPC(i)$$
$$+\overline{c2}.SPC(i)$$
$$+mcs.\overline{c2}.(\text{if } i > n \text{ then } \overline{det}.SPCF$$
$$\text{else } SPC(i+1))$$
$$+s3.SPC(0) + s3_u.SPC(i)$$

$$SPCF \stackrel{\text{def}}{=} comm\text{-}in.SPCF + s3.SPCF$$
$$+s3_u.SPCF + mcs.SPCF$$

Two new notational features have been introduced here: parametrised actions and conditional statements. The process term $SPC(i)$ can be regarded as shorthand for the indexed process constant SPC_i. A term of the form **if** b **then** P_1 **else** P_2 behaves as process P_1 if the boolean expression b evaluates to true, or as the process P_2 if b evaluates to false.

The SPC accepts commands from the SSI, responds to the SSI with TFM status information, and sometimes sends a command over the LGL. Also, the SPC receives TFM status information over the LGL. In this new model, the SPC is guaranteed to send a message over the LGL at least once after each message from the clock (action mcs). Also, if n mcs actions occur without the receipt of a message from the TPC, then the SPC enters failure mode, in which it never again sends messages to the SSI or LGL. Of course, a more detailed model would contain a mechanism by

which the SPC could exit failure mode.

The TPC model is similar in form. Here commands are received over the LGL and sent to the TFM, while status information is received from the TFM and sent over the LGL:

$$TPC(i) \stackrel{\text{def}}{=} \overline{comm\text{-}out}.status\text{-}in.TPC(i)$$
$$+\overline{s2}.TPC(i)$$
$$+mct.\overline{s2}.(\text{if } i > n \text{ then } \overline{det}.TPCF$$
$$\text{else } TPC(i+1))$$
$$+c3.TPC(0) + c3_u.TPC(i)$$

$$TPCF \stackrel{\text{def}}{=} status\text{-}in.TPCF + c3.TPCF$$
$$+c3_u.TPCF + mct.TPCF$$

Note that both protocol converters stop sending messages after a failure is detected. This causes detection of an LGL failure in one protocol converter to be eventually detected by the other protocol converter.

The clock process sends a message to each protocol converter after each clock tick:

$$Clock \stackrel{\text{def}}{=} \overline{tick}.\overline{mcs}.\overline{mct}.Clock$$

The clock process embodies the assumption that the protocol converters proceed roughly in synchrony. Rather than constructing such a process we could have developed our properties using the clock ticks at the sender and receiver ends of the medium and required synchrony between the two ticks. The existence of the clock process is also justified by the need for a physical clock in an implementation so that the TPC can send TFM messages every major cycle.

The complete model of the slow-scan with LGL failure detection:

$$SS \stackrel{\text{def}}{=} (SPC(0) \mid LGL \mid TPC(0) \mid Clock)\backslash$$
$$\{c2, c3, c3_u, s2, s3, s3_u, mcs, mct\}$$

CHECKING SAFETY PROPERTIES

Now that we have constructed a simple model of slow-scan motivated by its safety and service properties we can begin to check the formalised requirements for consistency. Since the slow-scan model has a finite and reasonably small state space (of 3842 states), the Concurrency Workbench (Cleaveland et al., 1989) can be used to check whether the properties formulated in Section hold of the model.

The complexity of some of the properties means that they cannot practically be checked directly with the Workbench. For each such property, checking was made of a smaller model derived from the slow-scan model by hiding actions not relevant to the property. Then, by using a technique (Bruns, 1991) that cannot be described here because of space, the property was shown by hand to hold of the full model if and only if it held of the smaller model. In what follows, we will write that a property was checked *indirectly* if this technique was used, and checked *directly* if the Workbench alone was sufficient.

Recall that the first property of interest involved detection of LGL failures. The property *failures-detected* was checked indirectly and shown to hold. The properties *failures-possible* and *can-tick* were also shown to hold, the first directly and the second indirectly.

The property *eventually-silent*, which holds if slow-scan eventually stops performing output actions after a failure is detected, could not practically be checked even indirectly. The property is expensive to check because after any $\overline{det}$ action a complicated eventuality property must be shown to hold.

The second property, *no-false-alarms*, expresses that failures cannot be detected before they occur. This property could be checked directly, but was found not to hold. It fails to hold because the action $\overline{fail}$ occurs after a failure, not simultaneously with it. A failure can be detected, and the corresponding action $\overline{det}$ can occur, between the moment of failure and the moment action $\overline{fail}$ occurs.

Knowing that *no-false-alarms* fails to hold, other questions become interesting, such as "can both protocol converters signal detection of failure before $\overline{fail}$ occurs?", and "if a failure is detected before $\overline{fail}$ occurs, must $\overline{fail}$ eventually occur?". The formula *detects-before-failure* expresses the property that two $\overline{det}$ actions can occur before a $\overline{fail}$ action:

$$detects\text{-}before\text{-}failure \stackrel{\mathrm{def}}{=} \langle -\overline{fail}\rangle^*\langle\overline{det}\rangle\langle -\overline{fail}\rangle^*\langle\overline{det}\rangle \mathtt{tt}$$

This property was checking indirectly and shown not to hold. However, it was shown that two $\overline{fail}$ actions *can* occur before any $\overline{det}$ actions occur.

The two following formulas express the idea that $\overline{det}$ and $\overline{fail}$ are related by property "if a $\overline{fail}$ occurs before a $\overline{det}$, then eventually a $\overline{det}$ will occur, and conversely":

$$even\text{-}detect \stackrel{\mathrm{def}}{=} [-\overline{fail},\overline{det}]^*[\overline{fail}]even(\overline{det})$$
$$even\text{-}fail \stackrel{\mathrm{def}}{=} [-\overline{fail},\overline{det}]^*[\overline{det}]even(\overline{fail})$$

Note that the property *failures-detected* is slightly stronger than *even-detect*; the former property requires that $\overline{det}$ occurs after $\overline{fail}$ even if $\overline{det}$ occurred before $\overline{fail}$. These properties were checked indirectly and shown to hold.

In summary, we have verified that LGL failures are detected in our slow-scan model. To ensure that this property is meaningful we have also shown that in all states the clock can continue to tick, and that it is possible for such failures can occur. However, we have not verified that slow-scan will eventually stop performing output actions after an LGL failure is detected by either protocol converter. The failure of *no-false-alarms* requires either a revision of the model or the requirement. In a large project the modelling and requirements process would proceed hand-in-hand and we could expect to see such decisions resolved by considering which matched the real-world situation most accurately.

CONCLUSIONS

We hope that this paper illustrates how the formalisation of properties and models of systems can be used to provide support for requirements analysis. In the course of constructing requirements it is hard to formulate a small collection of important properties. We believe that the approach outlined here in which properties and models are developed hand-in-hand provides a promising means of developing requirements. An important factor in this is the availability of automated tools for checking properties of systems. In this case-study we used the Concurrency Workbench and even our simple models required a fairly large number of states. Work is in progress which should facilitate the verification of several difficult slow-scan properties; we hope to extend the scope and effectiveness of this technique.

Acknowledgements

We would like to thank Colin Stirling for discussions and comments, and Ian Mitchell, Chris Gurney, and others at British Rail Research, Derby, for their help. This work was supported by SERC grant "Mathematically-Proven Safety Systems", IED SE/1224.

REFERENCES

Atkinson, W. and Cunningham, J. (1991). Proving properties of a safety-critical system. *Software Engineering Journal*.

Bruns, G. (1991). Verifying properties of large systems by abstraction. To be submitted for publication.

Bruns, G. and Anderson, S. (1991). The formalization and analysis of a communications protocol. In Lindeberg, J., editor, *Proceedings of SAFECOMP '91*.

Cleaveland, R., Parrow, J., and Steffen, B. (1989). The concurrency workbench: A semantics based tool for the verification of concurrent systems. Technical Report ECS-LFCS-89-83, Laboratory for Foundations of Computer Science, University of Edinburgh.

Cribbens, A. (1987). Solid-state interlocking (SSI): an integrated electronic signalling system for mainline railways. *IEE Proceedings*, 134(3).

Kozen, D. (1983). Results on the propositional mu-calculus. *Theoretical Computer Science*, 27:333–354.

Milner, R. (1989). *Communication and Concurrency*. Prentice Hall International.

Stirling, C. (1989). An introduction to modal and temporal logics for CCS. In Yonezawa, A. and Ito, T., editors, *Concurrency: Theory, Language, and Architecture*. Springer Verlag. Lecture Notes in Computer Science, volume 391.

Taleb, F. and Gurney, C. (1990). Requirements analysis final report slow scan SSI project. Technical Report ELS-DOC-4826, British Rail Research.

Computer-Aided Specification and Verification of Process Control Software

Bernd Krämer and Wolfgang Halang
Fachbereich Elektrotechnik
FernUniversität Hagen
Postfach 940, D-5800 Hagen, Germany

Abstract

This article presents a rigorous system development process promoting formal specifications of functional requirements of process control software. These specifications provide the grounds for specification-based testing of abstract designs and computer-assisted proofs of the conformance of program code to its requirements. Specifications are formulated in the algebraic specification language OBJ. The pertinent OBJ3 environment is used as a proof checker performing all clerical work related to correctness proofs. To illustrate the design and validation method, the specification and control program for a simple function block is provided and a few properties and assumptions about its functional behavior are proved.

Keywords: Programmable controllers, computer-aided system design, algebraic specification techniques, verification, software tools.

Our society increasingly relies on computer-based systems for control and automation functions in safety-critical applications. Examples of application domains are (air) traffic control, patient monitoring, or process and production line control. A specific class of computer-based systems are programmable logic controllers (PLCs) intended to replace traditional hard-wired switching networks based on relay or discrete electronic logic. PLCs are typically used for binary and sequence control, process supervision, data acquisition, signal processing, or for communications and other tasks closely related to industrial processes. Their advantages over pure hardware solutions are flexible adaptation to necessary modifications of the controlled processes just by re-programming instead of re-wiring and high information processing capabilities. These advantages are, however, partly outweight by the increasing complexity of the control software and a lack of sound methods to thoroughly understand, specify, design, implement, maintain, and assess properties of such systems. Other than hardware, software does not wear out and environmental circumstances cannot cause software faults. Rather all software errors are design or programming errors which cannot be detected solely program testing, peer reviews or other, mostly informal methods prevailing in software development practice. As a consequence, licensing authorities are extremely reluctant in approving safety-critical systems whose behavior is exclusively program controlled.

To overcome these obstacles, we developed a formal method for designing and validating PLC programs which strongly depends on the use of formal specification, verification, and specification-based testing methods. Requirements and design specifications are expressed in the algebraic specification language OBJ [1]. OBJ allows the language user to construct modular specifications of functional units that are encapsulated as abstract data types. The pertinent OBJ3 environment [2] contains an interpreter supporting specification testing and formal verification. We employ the proof techniques developed in [3] to verify the consistency between critical requirements and the corresponding design specification. In this validation activity OBJ3 acts as a proof checker performing all clerical work, while the system developer designs and directs the proofs. To gain further confidence about the adequacy of a given specification, formal proofs of correctness are supplemented by specification testing, which is based on term rewriting techniques [4] and OBJ's underlying order-sorted equational logic. Our approach aims at a substantial enhancement of the reliability of individual PLCs, in particular, their functional correctness with respect to formal requirements. With conventional PLC development methods relying on informal or semi-formal requirements and designs programmed directly in terms of ladder diagrams [5] or Structured Text (a Pascal-like procedural programming language), a rigorous verification of the correctness of a PLC program (with respect to the intended requirements) is impossible because the expectations about program behavior are not expressed formally.

This work extends the graphical design method and prototype tool described earlier [5]. The tool supports the function block language currently under standardization by the IEC [6], where each function blocks is a software abstraction of some PLC. The tool allows the system developer to identify suitable instances in a library of reusable function blocks and 'wire' them together to more complex automation programs. Based on a high-level Petri net model of function blocks which includes algebraic interface specifications, our prototype tool is able to exploit analysis functions of an existing net tool to verify the consistency of the design and determine dynamic properties of process control programs under the assumption that function blocks in the library are proven correct. Petri net models of PLCs have been proposed independently of our work in [7] to verify PLC-based software by means of a Petri net tool similar to ours.

The paper is structured as follows. First we briefly describe the steps, intermediate results, and underlying techniques of our formal PLC development process. In Section 2 we introduce a simple example of a data supervision module and develop formal requirements specifications from an informal problem definition. In Section 3 some aspects of a design specification for this example are sketched and formally related to the previously specified requirements. Finally the design specification is developed into a program that is decorated with assertions about the intended programs behavior. These assertions are formally verified using again OBJ3.

1 Formal Development Process

The PLC development process we propose consists of seven steps illustrated in Fig. 1. Feedback loops representing repetitions of previous steps due to unsatisfactory results are omitted. The first step is concerned with the solicitation of function block requirements and their formalization in terms of OBJ. At the moment we confine ourselves to functional requirements as the formalization of non-functional requirements, such as safety, reliability, or performance, and associated verification techniques are subject to ongoing research.

Formalized requirements represent prescriptions for the second step in which the designer constructs a formal interface specification of the function block under consideration. Interface speci-

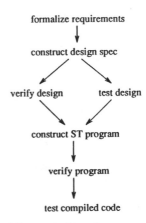

Figure 1: Development steps

fications capture the functionality of a function block and provide a black box view of its behavior and provide the basis for verifying the conformance of the design with critical functional requirements. This step is extremely simplified because design and requirements specification are expressed in the same formal notation, namely OBJ.

Independently from the design verification step, which compares two abstract models of the intended or reconstructed reality, it often useful to test the design specification with selected input data to gain further confidence about the adequacy of a design. Algebraic specifications such as OBJ designs can be tested by rewriting a term into its normal form. In this way, the behaviour of the system to be developed can be observed and evaluated in early development phases to correct design errors before further expensive development steps are taken [8]. In comparison to program testing, specification testing has the additional advantage of testing whole classes of programs rather than exactly one instance of an entire class of possible implementations.

If both design verification and testing produce acceptable results, the design is developed into a program in terms of Structured Text (ST), another language in the family of IEC standard PLC languages. An important part of this step is the decoration of the program with so-called verification conditions (VCs). They represent assertions about program behavior. The validity of the assertions then has to be proved, manually or with the aid of a theorem prover. VCs can be derived automatically from the design specification or the program itself by means of VC generators. They rely on logical deduction systems consisting of a set of axioms and deduction rules that map a given set of well-formed formulae into a set of well-formed formulae. We employ classical Hoare style proof rules for program verification [9]. Hoare's technique allows us to verify the partial correctness of a program S with respect to assertions P and Q that may or may not be satisfied by the variables occurring in S. A decorated expression of the form $\{P\}S\{Q\}$ informally means that, if the assertion P holds before the execution of S, then the assertion Q holds when the execution of S terminates.

The whole development process is concluded by testing the code into which the ST program is compiled using an off-the-shelf compiler. In this step the design specification can be used to generate suitable test data [10].

It is obvious that, compared to a conventional development process where the focus is on program development and program testing only, some extra effort is necessary to develop and validate formal requirements and design specifications and formally verify associated programs. But this effort is justified by a number of reasons. Standard function blocks will be used in hundreds or thousands of control programs and their correct operation is often crucial to satisfy hard safety and reliability requirements. A formal development process provides more certainty about the logical consistency between specification and program for all possible input data. It helps gaining deeper insight into a problem at hand and reduces the costs for error detection in later stages of development and for maintenance. Formal interface specifications enhance the systematic reuse of function blocks and verified interface specifications extend the reuse of function blocks to the reuse of their associated proofs.

2 An Example and its Formal Requirements

The following problem is taken from a function block performing process data supervision in process control software used in chemical industry. The functionality and behavior of this function block, called **check**, may be stated informally as follows:

There are eight inputs DIGX, XB, XE, CF, UL, LL, LAE, and UAE, and four outputs X, UA, LA, and COND. The function block transforms a digitised and normalized signal DIGX, which an external AD converter produced from analogue raw data, into a measuring value of type integer provided on output X. To compute this value, measuring range limits XB and XE are used as integer parameters. If a channel fault CF is indicated, the most recent OK value is delivered. The inputs UL and LL define an upper and lower limit at which an alarm is raised via output UA or LA, respectively, provided that input UAE or LAE, respectively, is active. Output COND produces a notification about check's processing state. It is encoded as an integer value:

1 indicates a channel fault, 2 means that the upper limit was exceeded by the measuring value, and 3 means that the measuring value remained under the lower limit. Error notifications are ordered according to this priority.

Before we can formally state functional requirements, i.e., requirements about system inputs and constraints on these inputs, functions performed, and outputs it produces, we have to translate the concepts of the problem domain into appropriate constructs of the chosen specification formalism OBJ. The notion of type associated with inputs and outputs of function block **check** immediately translates into the notion of abstract data type and functional behavior can be described by OBJ operations. For example, we might associate type Boolean with binary valued inputs and outputs, use Bit sequences to represent digitised data, and employ integers to model measuring and range values of instruments.

The interface of a function block is made precise by viewing names of inputs and outputs as abbreviations for access functions to typed data that can be observed on inputs and outputs of **check**. To make the distinction between a port name such as **X** and the value it denotes in a certain state of computation explicit, we use lower case letters **x** when we refer to the value on **X**. As input data are read synchronously in each computation step, we model inputs as vectors of sort **Input** to come up with the following type constraints of input functions:

$$\text{digx} \quad : \quad \text{Input} \; \text{->} \; \text{Bits} \; . \tag{1}$$

and output functions:

$$\text{cond} \quad : \quad \text{Input} \; \text{->} \; \text{Int} \; . \tag{2}$$

Such type constraints can be easily checked by a simple type checker and will not be further considered. More interesting is the following requirement for output **COND** for arbitrary inputs **I**:

```
cond(I)=0 if not cf(I) and not ua(I)
                and not la(I)
cond(I)=1 if cf(I)}
cond(I)=2 if not cf(I) and ua(I)
cond(I)=3 if not cf(I) and not ua{}(I)
                and la(I)
```

Similarly further requirements can be formulated to complete the first step of our sample development process. Instead we proceed to the next step and demonstrate the task of design specification and verification in the following section.

3 Design Specification, Verification, and Testing

The design specification to be developed will give meaning to those operations of function block **check** that compute its outputs. Once these functions are abstractly defined we can apply specification verification techniques to verify that no ambiguities, incompletenesses, and inconsistencies resulting from design errors and oversights exist. Additionally, we can apply term rewriting techniques to enhance the user's or designer's confidence in a design by testing the design specification.

For the given set of inputs of function block **check**, the following definition of auxiliary function **input** and of **check**'s input functions can be generated automatically:

```
vars   Cf Uae Lae  :  Bool.
...
eq     digx(input(Digx, Xb, Xe, . . .)) = Digx.
...
eq     input(cf(I), digx(I), . . . , lae(I)) = I.
```

This is not the case, however, for the output functions defining the intended behaviour of a function block. Their definition requires a careful interpretation of the problem statement and sufficient knowledge about the problem domain. Two examples are given below:

```
eq   ua(I)  =  (ul(I) < x(I))  and  uae(I).
cq   x(I)   =  xb(I)  +  bi(digx(I)) *
               (xe(I) − xb(I)) if not cf(I).
```

Informally, the first equation states that **ua(I)** is true if and only if both the value of **x(I)** exceeds the upper range limit **ul(I)** and input **uae(I)** is **true**. The second definition reflects our knowledge about normalization of measuring values and employs an auxiliary operation **bi** which maps bit sequences into their corresponding number value.

A graphical illustration of a complete black box abstraction for function block **check** is depicted in Figure 2. What we wanted to show here is that OBJ allows the user to specify such software components independently of any concrete representation of data and without reference to any particular implementation of operations. A further important asset of this formalism is its unique semantics and the underlying equational calculus which admits proving theorems and equations from specifications and deriving terms from terms using equations as rewrite rules (called reduction rules in OBJ3). In the sequel we apply proof techniques developed in [3] to formally verify that our design specification satisfies the requirements stated earlier and, if necessary, further propositions about conjectured properties of the

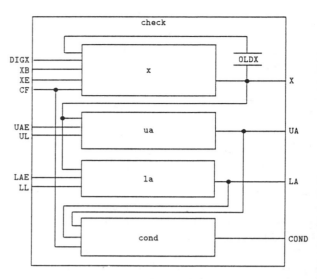

Figure 2: Abstract functionality of function block **check**

design. These requirements or propositions are expressed as equational theorems in OBJ. The goal of a proof is to conclude the theorem in question from the given specification and a set of premisses, which are again equations. A proof consists of a sequence of rewrite steps using premisses and specification equations. OBJ3 is used to perform routine work automatically, and the modularity concepts of the language help structuring user directed proofs in modules and hierarchies.

The application of OBJ3 is illustrated below with excerpts of corresponding protocols of a session in which we verify the correctness of function **x** with respect to the following requirement:

$$0 \leq x(I) = \mathtt{true} \ \mathtt{if} \ xb(I) \ \leq \ xe(I)$$

using structural induction over the bit sequences provided via input **digx**. As the requirement to be verified is expressed as a conditional equation, we must assume the condition is true. Hence we assert:

```
obj CHECK-BEHAV is using CHECK-VARS .
  eq Xb <= Xe = true .
  eq 0 <= Oldx = true .
endo
```

and attempt to verify the base cases with |**digx(I)**| = 1 for some arbitrary **Bit B** and **cf(I) = true** or **false**. The first case is trivial:

```
OBJ> reduce 0 <= x(input(B,Xb,Xe,true,
                   Uae,Ul,Lae,Ll,Oldx)) .
result Bool: true
```

because **x(input(B,Xb,Xe,true,...))** reduces to **Oldx**, for which the condition holds by input assumption. For **cf(I) = false** reduction yields:

```
OBJ> reduce 0 <= x(input(B,Xb,Xe,false,
                      Uae,Ul,Lae,Ll,Oldx)) .
result Bool: 0 <= Xb + bi(B) * (Xe - Xb)
```

The resulting expression cannot be further reduced, because `Xb`, `Xe`, and `xB` are constants whose structure is unknown but would be necessary to be known in order to use equations of `INT`. But due to the input assumption `Xb <= Xe`, we can conclude that `Xe - Xb` is a natural number, say `m`. Further we know that `bi(B)` is a natural number, say `n` and, hence, the product `n * m` is a natural number. Owing to the fact that `0 <= M + N` holds for two arbitrary natural numbers `M` and `N`, the base case is verified and we can assert:

$$Xb + 1 * (Xe - Xb) = Xe$$

After asserting the induction assumption, the induction step yields

```
OBJ> reduce x(input(B Digx,...)) .
result Bool: true
```

for `cf(I) = false`.

Other properties and output functions are treated similarly.

As OBJ specifications are executable, the design specification can also be taken as a prototype of the function block `check` to validate its functioning under specific application conditions. Simple tests of function `bi` are shown in the following session protocol:

```
OBJ> reduce bi(1 0 1) .
result Nat: 5
OBJ> reduce bi(0) .
result Nat: 0
```

4 Program Verification

The goal of program verification is to verify a program in a finite number of steps by applying appropriate proof rules to the statements of that program. For example, for a conditional statement

$$S = \text{IF } C \text{ THEN } S_1 \text{ ELSE } S_2 \text{ FI}$$

with pre-condition P and post-condition R we can derive pre- and post-conditions for S_1 and S_2 by means of the usual rule for conditional statements [9]:

$$\{P \text{ and } C\} \quad S_1 \quad \{R\} \qquad (3)$$
$$\{P \text{ and not } C\} \quad S_2 \quad \{R\} \qquad (4)$$

If we can find proofs for Assertions 3 and 4, we also have a proof for $\{P\}S\{R\}$. In the stepwise

proof we proceed as follows: Start from the post-condition and follow the program path in backward direction. For each statement S on this path an appropriate proof rule is applied to transform the post-condition of this statement into a weakest pre-condition. This pre-condition is then the post-condition of the preceding statement. That is, we derive pre- and post-conditions for the statements constituting `check` using appropriate proof rules to end up with an ST program whose individual statements are decoration with VCs.

To give an example, a section of an ST program intended to implement the design specification of `check`, in particular, function `cond`, is shown below. Local VCs derived from the precondition `true` and some postcondition `T` corresponding to the requirement for output `cond` are also given:

```
{CF or UA or LA}
IF CF
   THEN COND := 1
   ELSE
        {(CF or UA or LA) and not CF}
        IF UA
           THEN COND := 2
           ELSE
                {(CF or UA or LA) and
                 not CF and not UA}
                IF LA
                   THEN COND := 3
                FI
                {T}
        FI
        {T}
FI;
{T}
```

The conditions to verified for this piece of program are then:

```
((CF or UA or LA) and CF) implies T{COND/:
((CF or UA or LA) and not CF and UA)
        implies T{COND/2}
((CF or UA or LA) and not CF and not UA
        and LA) implies T{COND/3}
```

where the expression `TCOND/1` denotes the same as condition `T` except that variable `COND` in `T` is substituted by expression 1. The proof of the conditions boils down to term reduction in OBJ3 using an OBJ specification not given here:

```
OBJ> reduce ((CF or UA or LA) and CF)
            implies T{COND/1} .
reduce in PROG-VERIFICATION :
   (CF or UA or LA) and CF
        implies T{COND/1}
rewrites: 206
result Bool: true
```

11

With the proof of all verification conditions generated for program **check**, the whole program is proved correct with respect to its requirements and design specifications.

5 Conclusion

We have presented the capabilities and advantages of formal specification and validation techniques for the development of high quality PLC programs. Our emphasis was on the functional correctness of elementary function blocks that will be used as standard building blocks in numerous process control applications and, therefore, justify the extra effort necessary to obtain guaranteed quality criteria. It should have become clear that manual proofs of verification conditions, even for relatively simple programs as they occur in function block design, are tedious and error prone. We have argued that algebraic specification techniques, and OBJ in particular, provide an efficient and computer supported way of constructing and validating formal specifications of software requirements and designs.

References

[1] K. Futatsugi, J.A. Goguen, J.P. Jouannaud, and J. Meseguer. Principles of OBJ2. In Conf. 12th Annual ACM Symposium on *Principles of Programming Languages*, pages 52–66, Louisiana, New Orleans, 1985.

[2] J.A. Goguen and T. Winkler. Introducing OBJ3. TR SRI-CSL-88-9, SRI International, August 1988.

[3] J.A. Goguen. OBJ as a theorem prover with applications to hardware verification. TR SRI-CSL-88-4R2, SRI International, August 1988.

[4] D.W. Pessen. Ladder-Diagram design for programmable controllers. *Automatica*, 3(25):407–412, 1989.

[5] W. Halang and B. Krämer. Achieving high integrity of process control software by graphical design and formal verification. *Software Engineering Journal*, 7(1):53–64, 1992.

[6] TC 65: Industrial Process Measurement International Electrotechnical Commission and Working Group 6, Subcommittee 65A. Standards for programmable controllers, working draft. December 1988.

[7] J. Lilius and P. Östergard. On the verification of programmable logic controller programs. In Preprints of 12th Intern. Conference on *Application and Theory of Petri Nets*, pages 310–328, 1991. Pergamon Press.

[8] R.A. Kemmerer. Testing formal specifications to detect design errors. *IEEE Transactions on Software Engineering*, SE-11(1):32–43, 1985.

[9] C.A.R Hoare. An axiomatic basis for computer programming. *Communications of the ACM*, 12(10):576–580, 1969.

[10] P. Jalote and M. Caballero. Automated testcase generation for data abstraction. In Proc. *compsac 88*, pages 205–210, Chicago, October 1988.

The Redundancy Specification in Configuration Languages

Pierre BILAND & Anne-Marie DEPLANCHE

Laboratoire d'Automatique de Nantes
ECN, 1 rue de la Noë, 44072 NANTES Cedex 03, France
E-mail : BILAND@LAN01.ENSM-NANTES.FR
Telephone: (33)-40-37-25-92   Fax : (33)-40-74-74-06

Abstract

By separating the structural configuration issues from functional component actions, configuration languages provide a support for flexibility. The aim of the paper[1] is to show that in addition they offer a good basis for the development of fault-tolerant modules. After a description of the principles of configuration languages, with Conic®[2] examples, some expressions to be integrated in configuration languages in order to specify redundancy in software components are proposed. This approach provides the programmer with an uniform framework for the development of fault-tolerant programs, so that he can select the redundancy he wants to affect to every application component, while being released from the redundancy runtime monitoring. Unlike other approaches, this proposal, owing to modularity and hierarchical composition capacities offered by configuration languages, allows to implement selective software fault-tolerance. The principles described in this model have been implemented and tested in the Conic® environment for distributed systems.

Keywords : Configuration, Redundancy, Software development, System failure and recovery, Control systems, Programming languages, Real time computer systems, Software Fault-Tolerance, Conic® Language

---

[1] This paper is part of a research project supported by the "Ministère de la recherche et de la Technologie" of France.

[2] Conic® is computer software developed by the Department of Computing, Imperial College, London.

INTRODUCTION

Description, building and evolution of sophisticated computer applications is made easier by the explicit separation of the system structure considered as a components set and their logical interconnections "programming in the large", and the functional description of every one of their components "programming in the small, (De Remer, 1976). Several proposals were made with this model. As a general rule, they use a configuration language and their relevant tools, that permits modularity, reuseability, and nested configuration. They provide an uniform framework for an accurate specification of systems configuration.

Due to their critical nature, some computer based applications require techniques for fault-tolerance to be implemented. Fault-tolerance can be provided at different levels. One can make use of hardware-based solutions, or relies on software operating structures for the fault-tolerant features. In the latter case, so that fault-tolerance be application-tailored, fault-tolerance specifications have to be combined with the configuration ones. Thus programmers need environments that effectively support the development of fault-tolerant programs.

This paper presents our attempt in integrating software fault-tolerance considerations in constructive approaches based on configuration languages. Our challenge is to provide a flexible fault-tolerance while not imposing an overhead on those parts of the system which do not require it : at application configuration time, the application designer can choose which modules he wishes to make fault-tolerant and to which degree. Thus application can be made incrementally fault-tolerant on a service-by-service basis, while program implementation, readability and maintenance are not greatly complicated. The paper proposes some expressions to be integrated in configuration languages in order to specify redundancy in software components. A variety of redundancies for software fault-tolerance are supported in a structured way thanks to the encapsulation properties of configuration languages.

This approach provides the programmer with an uniform framework for the development of fault-tolerant programs, so that he can select the most suitable fault-tolerant mechanism he wants to affect to an application component, while being released from the redundancy runtime monitoring.

The first section of this paper is a presentation of the principles and purposes of configuration languages, based on an example in the Conic® configuration language (Kramer, 1985, 1989). The second section describes the main techniques of software fault-tolerance and tries to define a model of redundant frameworks providing software fault-tolerance. Expressions allowing to build redundant structures by encapsulating basic components are introduced in the third section.

The fourth section presents the implementation of the approach in Conic®.

THE CONFIGURATION LANGUAGES

The interest of configuration languages is to avoid loosing overall system structure and links between various modules inside the modules themselves, by distinguishing two activities, each one with its typical language : "programming in the small", which refers to the design of primitive modules by use of an algorithmic language and "programming in the large", which designs a system from a set of components and their interconnections and requires a configuration language.

If interested, the reader can find a presentation of various configuration languages in Biland (1991a) and in Deplanche (1992).

As a general rule, an application developed with a configuration language consists of a hierarchical composition of modules (Fig. 1.), each one implementing one or more functions required by the application. Primitive modules are described using an algorithmic language, whereas composite modules are described in configuration language in terms of instances of components and their logical interconnections.

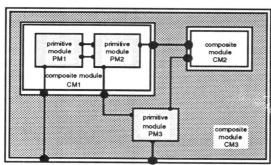

Fig. 1. Hierarchical composition of modules

Every primitive or composite module is a black box with a well-defined interface, that defines the points at which interactions with other components occur. These interaction points are called ports. The configuration language permits to describe a composite module as a configuration specification that identifies the module types from which the composite module will be designed, declares the instances of these types which will exist in the composite module and describes the interconnection of the instances by the links between their ports.

Example of a primitive module in Conic® environment

In Conic® environment primitive module is called "task module". It is defined by an interface and a functional part described in Conic® programming language that is an extension to ISO Pascal. The task module interface is specified by declaring typed entryports and exitports. The main extension provided to ISO Pascal is the inclusion of message communication primitives.

For example consider (Fig. 2.) the module CTRDURATION used in the monitoring of a manufacturing process (Biland, 1991b). Its function is to compute the consistency of a liquid and to deduce from it the duration of the gate-valve opening for the matrix filling up. When activated through a signal received at the port START, the module reads three temperature sensors T1, T2, T3 and one atmospheric

pressure sensor AP. From these physical data, the module computes the duration and sends the result through port END.

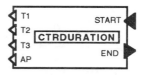

```
task module CTRDURATION;
entryport START:signaltype;
exitport T1, T2, T3, AP :signaltype reply real;
        END:real;
var TEMPE1, TEMPE2, TEMPE3, PRESSURE : real;
function CONSISTANCE(T1, T2, T3, AP:real) : real;
begin
    ...
end;
begin
    loop
        select
            receive signal from START
            =>  send signal to T1 wait TEMPE1;
                send signal to T2 wait TEMPE2;
                send signal to T3 wait TEMPE3;
                send signal to AP wait PRESSURE;
                send CONSISTANCE(TEMPE1,
                TEMPE2,TEMPE3,PRESSURE) to END;
        end;
    end;
end.
```

Fig. 2. A Conic® task module

Example of composite module in Conic® environment

In the Conic® environment, a composite module is called a "group module".The descriptive syntax of the group module interface is the same as that of the task module interface. For example, consider (Fig. 3.) the group module GUNIT1, a component of production manufacturing unit monitoring. It encapsulates the module CTRDURATION which calculates the gate-valve opening duration and the module CTRLOADER, which opens or shuts the gate-valve by sending a signal through its ports BPOUTON and BPOUTOFF. Before opening the gate-valve, the module CTRLOADER "requests" the module CTRDURATION in order to know the duration of the opening. For this purpose it sends a signal through its port REQUEST and receives the duration through its port DURATION.

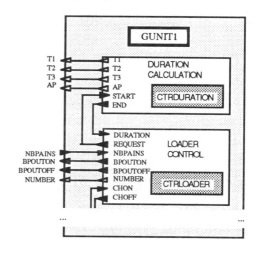

```
group module GUNIT1;
entryport NBPAINS:integer;
...
exitport T1,T2,T3,AP:signaltype reply real;
        BPOUTON,BPOUTOFF: signaltype;
        NOMBRE : signaltype reply integer;
...
use CTRDURATION;
    CTRLOADER;
...
create CTRDURATION;
       CTRLOADER;
...
link CTRDURATION.T1 to T1;
     CTRDURATION.T2 to T2;
     CTRDURATION.T3 to T3;
     CTRDURATION.AP to AP;
     CTRDURATION.END to CTRLOADER.DURATION;
     CTRLOADER.REQUEST to CTRDURATION.START;
...
end;
```

Fig. 3. A Conic® group module

Configuration languages and fault-tolerance

Configuration languages aim at providing flexibility and are accompanied in most cases by dynamic configuration. Flexibility is the capacity to modify and incrementally extend a system; it is an essential advantage for critical computer applications. Systems need to evolve as human needs, technology and the application environnment change. In general, these changes cannot be predicted at the time the system is designed, therefore the system must be flexible enough to allow for arbitrary, incremental changes. The dynamic configuration permits unpredicted change or system extension without interrupting the processing of those parts of the system which are not directly affected. System flexibility infers fault-tolerance capacities : dependability constraints may be evolutive, i.e. not etablished by the component type, but by its current context. It will be able to substitute a component for a version with more capacity of error detection, to map the most critical components at the most reliable sites, or to create (instantiate) components with a variable number of replications. However, to our knowledge, there has been very little researches about fault-tolerant attributes specification in configuration languages today.

A selective hardware fault-tolerance has been studied in Conic® environment (Loques, 1986). Reconfiguration is used to recover from station failures by providing further standby modules to replace failed ones. Two redundancy types (cold- and hot-standby) are supported. Cold standby modules are created and activated by the system in order to replace failed modules, but no state information is preserved. Hot standby modules do preserve information and provide transparent recovery from failure.

An environment for developing fault-tolerant software is proposed in Purtilo (1991). The environment supports in uniform manner, the execution of programs using different techniques for software fault-tolerance, N-versions programming and recovery blocks. It allows versions to be written in different programming languages and executed on different machines.

SOFTWARE FAULT-TOLERANCE

Computer systems able to tolerate physical faults have been an industrial and commercial reality for some years. Tolerance to design faults has also, although on a much more reduced scale, become a reality.

Design faults are a source of common-mode failures. Such failures defeat fault-tolerance strategies based on strict replication (thus intended to cope with physical faults). Software fault-tolerance aimed at providing service continuity necessitates design diversity.The software fault-tolerance is based on two redundancy types : check redundancy by acceptance test and functional redundancy by two most well documented techniques, the recovery blocks (RB) (Randell, 1975; Anderson, 1981) and the N-version programming (NVP) (Chen, 1978), and more recently the N-self-checking programming (NSCP) (Laprie, 1987). Functional redundancy is built up 1) from the existence of at least two variants of a component, produced through a design diversity approach from a common service specification, 2) from a decider aimed at providing a result (supposed to be) error-free. The hardware fault-tolerance architecture equivalent to RB, NVP and NSCP are passive dynamic redundancy, static redundancy and active dynamic redundancy. In the following paragraphs, we shall try to define a model of redundant frameworks providing software fault-tolerance.

Elementary task

Task is a black box. After being activated by its environment, it must react to deliver a specified service expressed in terms of functional and timing constraints. Functional constraints concern output value : does it belong to validity field? Timing constraints place conditions on task output issue: is the output interval of time respected?

Check redundancy by acceptance test : SC structure

In check redundancy by acceptance test, the component has an error detection mechanism which checks the delivered service and reacts by indicating its possible failure. This mechanism is a simple acceptance test on task output value.

Recovery blocks : RB structure

In RB structure, the variants (two at least) are called alternates and the decider is an acceptance test, which is applied sequentially to the alternates results. If the results of the first alternate do not meet the acceptance test, the secondary alternate is executed and so on until the end of redundancy or until the output value is accepted. The structure delivers a failure signal or a valid output, as required. RB structure can use self-checking components as alternates. In this case, if the component produces a failure signal, the system executes the following alternate without the acceptance test being performed.

RETRY structure

RETRY structure is a specific case of RB structure in the context of intermittent faults. It only uses one component variant, but its failure involves the re-execution of the same variant until the output value is accepted or the redundancy stops. Redundancy level is defined as the maximum number of component re-executions before the structure failure has been acknowledged.

N-Version programming : NVP structure

In NVP structure, the variants are called versions and the decider performs a vote based on the results of all versions. The versions are executed at the same time. If a majority of results are in the same validity field, NVP structure delivers a valid output; if not, it produces a failure signal. To mask n faults, 2n+1 versions are needed, otherwise the structure allows error detection but not masking. NVP structure can use self-checking components as versions. In this case, the vote only applies to the versions which did not deliver a failure signal.

N-Self-checking programming : NSCP structure

In NSCP structure, variants are self-checking components. They are executed in parallel. One component is considered as being acting (i.e., it produces a result) while the other components remain "hot" spares. Upon failure of the acting component a spare becomes acting and delivers a result, and so on until the redundancy or the failure signal stops. The decider is a simple switch of component results. NSCP structure as other redundant structures produces a valid output or a failure signal.

THE SPECIFICATION OF REDUNDANT STRUCTURES

As indicated at the end of paragraph "Configuration languages and fault-tolerance", there is no research, to our knowledge, about software fault-tolerance in configuration languages, except [Pur 91]. If some configuration languages aim at developing fault-tolerant applications among other things, they leave this fault-tolerance responsibility to the programmer complicating significantly the implementation, readability and maintenance of programs. Yet it seems possible to introduce, into configuration languages, expressions which would allow to build redundant structures by encapsulating basic components. In return, and because functional features of application may be not implicitly assumed, the programmer will have to select which system parts should be made fault-tolerant. Then he will have to declare the fault-tolerance techniques to be implemented, and to supply basic components for redundancy, since this functional side cannot be treated automatically. In particular, the programmer must provide the acceptance test function in case of RB or RETRY structure, and the vote function in case of NVP structure, because their algorithms are closely connected to the type of developed application. All redundant structures lead to define self-checking components. We apply here the model of redundancy structuring proposed in Deplanche (1989).

Basic components of a redundant structure

In this paper, the basic components of a redundant structure are the several variants of a component involved in a functional or check (in this case, there is only one variant) redundancy. Basic components may be themselves a redundant structure, any redundant structure can be a basic component of a redundant structure at upper level. A basic component is a primitive or a composite module, with an interface comprising two or three ports : one input port allowing for task activation, one output port allowing for signaling task completion, and possibly a second output port for indicating any failure (So this component is a self-checking component). For understanding we shall call the activation port START, the task end port END and the failure port ALARM. The data type sent or received through END, START or ALARM ports depends on the data supported by the module at the activation time and on the expected results. They may be simple signals, scalars or more

complex data structures. The ALARM port may be able to provide specific failure data.

The fault-tolerant modules

We propose to introduce composite modules dedicated to fault-tolerance and to call them "fault-tolerant modules". They may be of SC, RB, RETRY, NVP, NSCP types depending on the various types of redundant structures. Whatever the redundancy type to be used, a fault-tolerant module encapsulates all basic modules involved in redundancy and one primitive module which manages redundancy. We call this module RM (redundancy manager). In the following paragraphs, we set out the elements needed to describe a fault-tolerant module, according to type SC and RB, and the simplified (It gives neither all states, nor all possible transitions) state graph of the corresponding redundancy manager. The description of fault-tolerant modules of types RETRY, NVP, NSCP are in Biland (1992).

The basic components are set out as self-checking components and subject to maximum execution duration, that is not strictly obliged. If these characteristics don't exist, the diagrams of fault-tolerance box and the graph of the corresponding redundancy manager are simplified and are deduced from this presentation.

SC type fault-tolerant modules

The description of SC type faut-tolerant module is limited to 1) the identification of it basic component, 2) the possible definition of a maximum execution duration before the failure acknowledgment by the RM, 3) the definition of the function which provides the acceptance test of basic component output. This test function will be implemented in the redundancy manager.

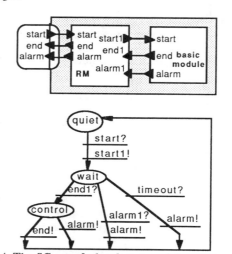

Fig. 4. The SC type fault-tolerant module and the state graph[3] of its redundancy manager.

RB type fault-tolerant modules

The description of RB type fault-tolerant modules is limited to 1) the identification of the n structure basic components, 2) the possible definition of a maximum

---

3 Understandings in the graphs :
P? indicates that the transition has been passed over if a message is received through port P.
P! indicates that the transition has been passed over with the spontaneous sending of a message through P.

execution duration of the redundant structure, 3) the definition of the function which provides the acceptance test on basic component output.

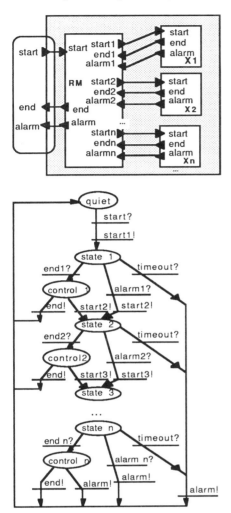

Fig. 5. The RB type fault-tolerant module and the state graph[3] of its redundancy manager.

REDUNDANCY SPECIFICATION IN CONIC®

This section describes the implementation of the previous approach in Conic®. The purpose is, on the one hand, to extend expression capacities of the configuration language Conic® to fault-tolerant modules definition, and, on the other hand, to construct and manage automatically, in Conic® self-context, various modules involved in redundancy. We have chosen the Conic® language because it is an appropriate development framework and it is presently the only available configuration language we know.

We have implemented fault-tolerant modules in Conic® as "fault-tolerant modules" with SC, RB, RETRY, NVP, or NSCP types. At the compilation time of an application described in Conic®, all fault-tolerant modules are treated by a preprocessor (Fig. 6.) that generates automatically 1) a group module encapsulating basic module(s) and redundancy manager, 2) a task module implementing the redundancy manager which corresponds to the redundancy type selected by the programmer. The group module and the task module so generated are also treated normally by the Conic® compiler to obtain executable objects.

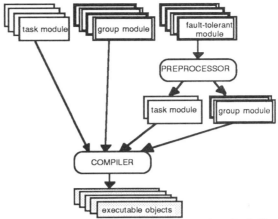

Fig. 6. The preprocessor and the compiler Conic®

The figure 7 display the fault-tolerant module structure. The fault-tolerant module header allows for the definition of its identification and type. As Conic® rules, the FT_MODULE_id must be followed , in all cases, by formal parameters allowing to define, at instantiation time, internal constants of encapsulated modules.

Several MODULE_TYPE are recognized : SC, RB, RETRY, NVP, NSCP. The MODULE_TYPE may be followed by keyword "timeout" with maximum fault-tolerant module execution duration. As Conic® rules, this parameter can be an immediate value or defined at instantiation time. In case of a RETRY module, the MODULE_TYPE must be followed by the value of the maximum basic module reexecution number, parameter of integer type.

The fault-tolerant module interface statement complies with Conic® rules, it could be built-up automatically by the preprocessor, but to make the description of the application clearer, it is better to keep its description inside the source program.

The USE part allows to list identifiers of various basic modules. In case of SC or RB or RETRY, the USE part is followed by the statement of the function that implements the acceptance test of encapsulated modules outputs. This function has an argument of the same type as module port END, it returns boolean true if result is accepted. In case of NVP, the USE part is followed by the statement of the function that implements the vote between various basic modules output. This function has two arguments per basic component, and one extra argument where the function puts the output value, that is the result of vote if it is possible to conclude. The first argument by component is the output value sent by the component, the second is boolean, true if the component has really replied, false if the component has sent alarm signal or has sent nothing.

```
/* module identification*/
fault-tolerant module FT_MODULE_id [(parameters)] :
        MODULE_TYPE [nb-max]
                    [timeout EXECUTION_TIME];
/* module interface*/
...
/* list of various basic modules */
use MODULE_id  [,MODULE_id ];
/* function of acceptance test or vote */
...
/* end of module description */
end.
```

Fig. 7. The fault-tolerant module structure.

17

Example of RB fault-tolerant module

A fault-tolerant module specifying RB structure is described below (Fig. 8.). The maximum structure execution duration is TIMEOUT1. The structure needs n alternates called X1, X2, ..., Xn and one function ACCEPT that implements acceptance test.

```
fault-tolerant  module  FTX  :  RB  timeout
TIMEOUT1;
/* declaration of interface */
entryport      START : ... ;
exitport       END : ... ;
               ALARM : ... ;
/* declaration  of alternates*/
use X1, X2, ..., Xn;
/* declaration of acceptance test function */
function ACCEPT(RESULT: ... ):boolean;
begin
        ...
end;
end.
```

Fig. 8. The fault-tolerant module FTX.

The preprocessor generates the group module FTX (Fig. 9.) and the task module GR_FTX, implementing the redundancy manager , whose state graph is described before.

```
group module FTX(TIMEOUT1:integer);
/* declaration of interface */
entryport START : ... ;
exitport END : ... ;
exitport ALARM : ... ;
/* declaration of used module-types */
use X1, X2, ...Xn,GR_FTX;
/* instantiation of used modules */
create X1, X2,..,Xn, GR: GR_FTX(TIMEOUT1);
/* interconnection of interface of encapsulating module
to interface of redundancy manger */
link START to GR.START;
    GR.END to END;
    GR.ALARM to ALARM;
/* interconnection of interface of redundancy manger to
interface of every one alternate*/
link    GR.START1 to X1.START;
        X1.END to GR.END1;
        X1.ALARM to GR.ALARM1;
link    GR.START2 to X2.START;
        X2.END to GR.END2;
        X2.ALARM to GR.ALARM2;
...
link    GR.STARTn to Xn.START;
        Xn.END to GR.ENDn;
        Xn.ALARM to GR.ALARMn;
```

Fig. 9. The group module FTX generated by the preprocessor.

CONCLUSION

In large systems, it may be infeasible to have multiple versions of the entire system, and it is desirable to have the capability of supporting faul-tolerance for only some critical modules of the system. In such a case, only those modules need to be replicated. Our approach allows fault-tolerance to be supported for modules embedded in a larger program in a natural and flexible manner. In this paper, we have shown that it was possible to integrate specifications of redundancy in view of software fault-tolerance into configuration languages, because of their modularity and hierarchisation capacities. The implementation of our proposal in Conic® language has pointed-out its generic nature. Now it has to be further experimented and possibly refined. We intend to extend the attractive aspects of this approach in order to take into account physical faults as well. Other fault-tolerance specifications will have to be supported such as specifications of reconfiguration after a degradation of the computing system. The dynamic configuration capabilities of configuration languages, such as REX's ones (Magee, 1990), will have to be explored. They will also make possible to integrate mapping and resources specifications.

REFERENCES

Anderson, T., and P.A. Lee (1981). Fault tolerance : principle and practice, Englewoods Cliffs, New Jersey, Prentice Hall, 1981

Biland, P., and A.M. Deplanche (1991a). Langages de Configuration pour les Systèmes Temps-réel Répartis, Report 91-05 / LAN-ECN

Biland, P. (1991b).Le développement du système de contrôle d'un procédé de fabrication dans le langage CONIC, Mémoire de D.E.A. - LAN-ECN

Biland, P., and A.M. Deplanche (1992). La spécification de la redondance dans les langages de configuration, Report 92-06 / LAN-ECN

Chen, L., and A. Avizienis (1978). N-version programming : a fault tolerance approach to reliability of software operation", FTCS 8, Toulouse, pp 3/9

Deplanche, A.M., and J.P. Elloy (1989). Architecture Tolérant les Fautes pour les Systèmes de Contrôle Temps-réel, Séminaire Franco-Brésilien, Florianopolis- SC, Brasil

Deplanche, A.M. (1992). Configuration des applications réparties : quelques approches, Report 92-03 / LAN-ECN

Kramer, J. and J. Magee (1985). Dynamic Configuration for Distributed Systems, IEEE Trans. on Soft. Eng., Vol. 11, N° 4, pp 424-436

Kramer, J., J. Magee and M. Sloman (1989). Constructing Distributed Systems in Conic, IEEE Trans. on Soft. Eng., Vol. 15, N° 6, pp 663-675

Laprie, J.C., J. Arlat, C. Beounes, K. Kanoun and C. Hourtolle (1987). Hardware- and software- fault tolerance : definition and analysis of architecturals solutions, FTCS 17, Pittsburgh, pp 116-121

Loques, O.G. and J. Kramer (1986). Flexible fault tolerance for distributed computer systems, IEE Proceedings, Vol. 133, Pt. E, N°6, pp 319-332

Magee, J., J. Kramer, M. Sloman and N. Dulay (1990). An Overview of the REX Software Architecture, 2nd IEEE Workshop on Future Trends of Distributed Computing Systems, Le Caire, pp 396-402

Purtilo, J.M. and P. Jalote (1991). An Environment for Developing Fault-Tolerant Software, IEEE Trans. on Soft. Eng., Vol 17, N° 2, pp 153-159

Randell, B. (1975). System structure for software fault tolerance, IEEE Trans. on Soft. Eng., vol SE1, n°2, pp 220-232

De Remer, F. and H.H. Kron (1976). Programming-in-the-Large Versus Programming-in the Small, IEEE Trans. on Soft. Eng., vol. SE-2, N° 2, pp 80-86

Specifying, Designing and Rapid Prototyping Computer Systems with Structured Petri Nets

Christof Ebert, Institute for Control Engineering and Industrial Automation.
University of Stuttgart, Pfaffenwaldring 47, W-7000 Stuttgart 80, F.R.Germany.
e-mail: ebert@irp.e-technik.uni-stuttgart.dbp.de

Abstract:

The paper describes the use of structured Petri nets for specifying, designing and rapid-prototyping real-time software for reliability related automation systems. High order Petri nets can be applied to problems of automation domains, such as dynamic and embedded systems with timing requirements, parallelism, dataflow, and non-determinism of events controlling such systems. The structured development of these real-time systems and their evaluation for reliability is illustrated with guidelines for a hierarchical top-down design. Problems resulting from software/hardware interaction and their formalization with Predicate transition Petri nets are discussed. This new structured technique for the application of such PrT-nets supports the real-time simulation of sufficiently refined specifications that can be used as a system prototype for customer presentations and also for reliability assessment.

Keywords: executable specification, Petri nets, process control, structured design, system design.

1. The Development of Real-Time Systems

You may forget some critical factors, but they won't forget you.

Alvin Toffler, The Third Wave

The development of any concurrent or embedded software system is a complex task. The main source of difficulty is the large number of subtle and often unexpected interactions that can occur among the various parts of such a system. Real-time systems have the property that past and present events, both external and internal, change their behavior. These changes are more difficult to understand and hence to describe in a specification than the production of a specific output value from a computation when the corresponding inputs change. The fundamental idea underlying the event-based perspective in specifying concurrent systems is that their behavior can be viewed as sequences of events. These events can be of arbitrary complexity, depending on the systems characteristics of interest. The specification of a concurrent system is primarily based on two sets of event sequences: the set representing the desired behaviors of the system and the set representing the possible behaviors of the system as it is interacting with its environment.

To ensure completeness of the specification it is necessary to combine the two sets without any contradictions. Almost all familiar event-based representations for concurrent systems consist of the following four components:

states of the system, events that may change states, transitions caused by events and showing how events change states, and actions that are caused by events and might belong to states.

Literature on system design techniques includes a vast amount of different methods to specify software systems. Most methods focus on distinct aspects of the development process (certain parts of the process, distinct objects and their relations, etc.) and therefore they are only useful for distinguished application areas. Research in suitable representations of distributed or real-time computer systems has primarily focused on distributed programming languages. Such languages have been developed for expressing direct communication or synchronisation and communication via shared variables between processes. Design methods and languages have been created by extending such programming languages, still incorporating ideas such as communicating sequential processes, monitors or distributed processes.

In requirements specification, common techniques such as SA or JSD emphasize activities and data flow, however, they are difficult to be applied to real world domains such as industrial automation because of the lack of adequately formalizing parallelism and behavior [YaTs86]. Real-time extensions of some requirements analysis techniques, such as SA-RT or statecharts seem to be suitable, however, they usually offer different views on the same model, thus being difficult to understand when developing large systems [Goma86]. Petri nets and their modifications have also been used for modeling and representing distributed or real-time systems [Maio85, Pete81, Reis88].

Because of the problems with representing data flows with typical state transition nets, variations of such nets have been introduced [EbOs91, Genr87, Mura89, YaCa83]. Some of these extensions were just mentioned in research papers and disappeared later because of lacking tool support for editing and simulating the nets. With the advent of high resolution graphic workstations used during the software engineering process newer techniques with tool support based on high Petri nets are now available. Some of them are used intensively for the analysis and design of real-time software systems [DGGK87, OEM90].

In this paper we will present an analysis and design technique based on higher Petri nets. Our approach is based on the ideas of modular design and functional decomposition as they have been formulated by Parnas and others [YaTs86].

2. Using Petri Nets in Software Engineering

The complete description of both computer control and external behavior requires a model of these interacting subsystems. To analyze and prove the correctness of all components of automation domains it is extremely useful if their descriptions and specifications take advantage of the same formal technique. Petri nets provide such a formal description technique because their general concepts can be applied to software and hardware components on the one hand, and to human interactions on the other hand. In order to give an idea of how to use Petri nets in the course of system design, we will describe the process of applying such nets in this chapter. The relevant aspects of system design with Petri nets, as well as some analysis techniques will be introduced and discussed, however, more detailed descriptions are provided elsewhere [Mura89, Pete81, Reis88].

One of the most fundamental principles of Petri nets is that the two basic types of components in real systems, being either "*active*" or "*passive*", are used for formal description. "*Passive*" components are denoted as places and can be interpreted as state elements, conditions, model domains, channels, or products. Their "*active*" counterparts are denoted as transitions and might represent events, facts, dependencies, specifications, or production activities. These two types are represented as circles or boxes, respectively. A Petri net graph is a collection of the two types of nodes connected by directed arcs. Places can be marked by tokens that can "*fire*" transitions by removing tokens from their input places and adding tokens to their output places.

High order Petri nets combine these features with dataflow mechanisms. We selected so-called *predicate-transition nets* (*PrT-nets*) that permit dataflow via inscriptions of arcs connecting places (predicates) and transitions. Simulation and animation are based on the following firing rules: When data tokens are available, the arc conditions and the guard of all input predicates are evaluated and the output predicates are checked for

spaces for tokens. When these conditions are fulfilled the transition may fire. After firing, all input data tokens are consumed and output tokens are sent to appropriate output predicates.

These high order Petri nets are used for developing and executing specifications of real-time systems. The proposed technique permits a systematic approach for capturing requirements by executing the specification, a formal notation for expressing them, and different tools to assist in their validation. The advantages of this formal basis are the elimination of ambiguities during requirements analysis and the support to analyze, visualize and verify the specification early in the life cycle. Especially the application of Petri nets as an efficient formalism for specifying concurrent systems as well as user interfaces seems to be valuable for early and intensive user demonstrations and customer negotiations. The workstation based tools that have been used provide the kind of environment needed to accomodate frequent changes and experimentations necessary during the specification and prototyping process.

Large problems require methods for dividing them into smaller and less complex subproblems. It is hence impossible to describe large systems' specifications with Petri nets without a method for partitioning them. The theory of hierarchical refinement of Petri nets has already been described [Genr87]. The structuring elements are modules or agencies that are illustrated as shaded boxes representing a number of elements of the next lower level of the hierarchy. An agency has the characteristics of a transition on its level of appearance. It might be nested, thus allowing several levels of hierarchical refinement. Such refinements can be defined top-down or bottom-up.

High order Petri nets can be applied to problems of automation domains, such as dynamic and embedded systems with timing requirements, parallelism, dataflow, and nondeterminism of events controlling such systems [Genr87]. Their advantages are founded upon a precise definition. Thus, they can be analyzed and executed. Execution can be simulated by moving tokens with data sets through the nets, hence supporting rapid prototyping and user-oriented validation of correct functionality and behavior. Applying high order Petri nets to the analysis and design of real-time software systems supports the graphical representation of both control flows and data flows in one single graph [EbOs91, YaCa83].

3. Structured Petri Nets

Our experiences with applying higher Petri nets to requirements specification in industrial projects show that the whole development process consists of several steps up to an executable specification that can eventually be transformed to programming code. The requirements analysis and system design modeling process thus consists of the following steps:

1. Abstract the *problem* as much as possible, find main parts. Result: a few main parts which can eventually be represented by a single predicate or transition.

2. Model the main relations between these parts.

3. Execute the net and check it; add necessary elements to enable simulation. These elements can be either additional subnets or Input/Output elements that allow to visualize net states and to stimulate the net with events.

4. Improve the model; verify and *measure* it; look for potential conflicts and invariants, *calculate complexity measures* [EbOs91] and reduce net complexity. Result: understandable and maintainable abstract model.

5. Validate the model (together with customer). Result: Approved, correct, abstract model, approved test sequences.

6. Repetition: apply the same strategy to the parts beginning at step 1 and construct recursively the complete system. Petri net models for system analysis are terminated when the externally observable activities and concepts of the real-time system are specified and planned. Such models for preliminary and detailed design are terminated when they are sufficiently detailed for implementation. Ideas concerning structures, flows, etc. for later phases of the development process may be included and mentioned as comment parts connected to appropriate objects.

For generating a Petri net model that is easy to understand we enhanced these basic techniques by additional requirements towards structured modeling. These observations eventually lead to the following guidelines for structured Petri nets:

❏ A top level net models the complete environment including the technical process, the real-time computer system and the user interface. These three parts are distinguished components of the complete automation system that must not be mixed. Communication and interactions of these main parts is therefore clearly defined. Each of them is constituted by a single transition with arcs to places that model the interfaces between the components (Fig. 1). Hence, interfaces are already defined and described on the top level.

❏ Since we are mainly interested in modeling and designing the real-time computer system, we will further concentrate on this component. Because the hierarchical top-down approach seems to be most suitable for system modeling or design, we will divide individual functional units and thus create top level modules for the software system (Fig. 2). Good modularity is especially important in design because of the ability to perform changes in a short time and to eventually reuse parts of components.

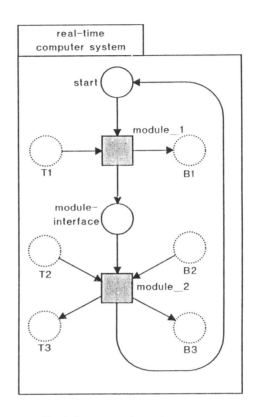

Fig. 2: Real-time computer system.

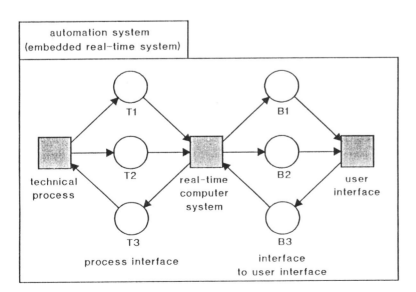

Fig. 1: Automation system (embedded real-time system).

❏ To ensure robust interfaces the number of arcs entering or leaving a module (on any level) should be minimized. The problem with using too many arcs is that they might have different semantic meanings. Arcs can be used for control flow, data flow, or synchronization. We hence emphasize to distinguish among these three meanings by assigning data names (arc inscriptions) to the arcs in case of modeling data flows, while control flows and synchronization arcs have no labels. Remember that human beings tend to think linear, thus being sometimes unable to detect and understand synchronization mechanisms between parallel running tasks and modules or distributed processes immediately (Fig. 3).

❏ The use of multiple subviews of the same net element, mainly modules, is prohibited. Subviews tend to hide control flows because different places can be connected with the same module in several subviews of this module.

❏ For consistency of the net description and to permit automatic code generation from the refined net it is necessary to use distinct net structures. These elementary nets permit the modeling of all different control flows and synchronization constructs of real-time software. Some of these structures are illustrated in Fig. 4.

❏ Data flow should be modeled via interfaces on the top levels between modules and via labeled arcs (thus transporting distinct data tokens) inside modules. Communication of modules that are not

connected with arcs might be realized with global data elements.

❏ Initial marking of transitions with tokens is permitted only for the entry point of the net and for *exclusive*-constructs where tokens are used as semaphors for synchronization. This restriction again is necessary for a unique transformation to a real-time programming language.

❏ The results of different design levels may be used to demonstrate the behavior of the real-time system. The simulation of Petri net models permit the identification of performance bottlenecks. By placing tokens in a distribution that is typical for distinct critical situations it is also possible to simulate the dynamic behavior in these situations, and to provide insight about which aspects of the behavior are not acceptable and why. Of course it is the designer's *and* the user's responsibility to ensure that all demanded requirements are fulfiled and to judge upon the behavior and the consequences of the requirements' interpretation.

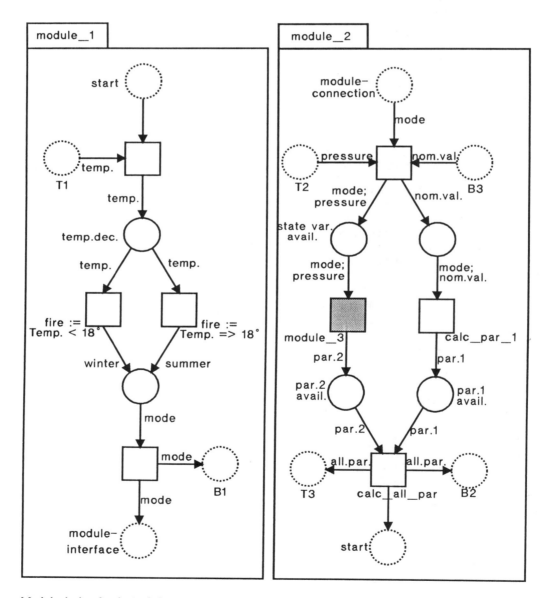

Fig. 3: Module design for the real-time computer system

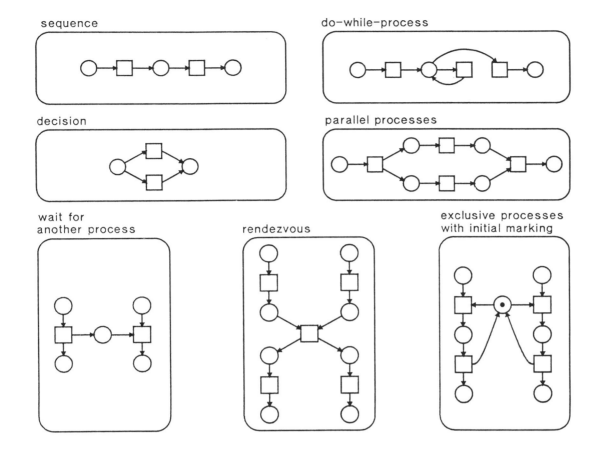

Fig. 4:   Elementary structures for Petri net modeling

As a result of this process you will eventually obtain a complete specification that is both executable, thus allowing complete simulation, and it is able to be transformed to source code. By appropriate structuring of the net it is possible to transform parts of it to a real-time parallel environment (control tasks) and other parts to a user interface generator.

4. Summary

A method for applying high order Petri nets in a structured fashion has been introduced. The method supports the analysis and design of real-time systems. An example of the top-level architectural design of a real-time system is presented for better understanding of the suggested structured techniques. Guidelines that were found during the application to real-time projects are presented to provide deeper insight in the use of higher Petri nets in engineering real-time software. The proposed strategy is suggesting a structured top-down approach.

Experiences with projects showed that the main disadvantage of top-down proceeding - e.g. to select unsuitable main parts - is compensated by the advantage of early simulation and analysis of the communication between main parts before refining them. For large real-time software systems, more experiences are necessary to determine the amount of detail the complete net models should

incorporate. Of course, the halting rules for modeling are influenced by the degree of separating design from programming issues and by the prerequisites of automatic code generation from the refined net models.

5. Acknowledgements

I would like to thank Marc Repnow and Klaus Bramkamp for their comments on the feasibility of the described methods. I am especially indepted to the research of Heinz Oswald and many discussions with him. The development and test of the techniques described in this article has been supported by the Petri net tools SPECS (Landis & Gyr, Zug, Switzerland) and PACE (Grossenbacher, St. Gallen, Switzerland). I would like to thank the DFG for the financial support of this ongoing research project.

Bibliography

[DGGK87]   Dähler, J., P. Gerber, H.-P. Gisiger und A. Kündig: A Graphical Tool for the Design and Prototyping of Distributed Systems. In: *ACM SIGSOFT Software Engineering Notes*, vol. 12, no. 3, S. 25 - 36, Jul. 1987.

[EbOs91]   Ebert, C. and H. Oswald: Complexity Measures for the Analysis of Specifications of (Reliability Related) Computer Systems. In: *Proc. of the IFAC SAFECOMP*, Pergamon Press, London, 1991.

[Genr87]   Genrich, H.: Predicate/Transition Nets. In: *Petri Nets: Central Models and Their Properties*. Editors: W. Brauer, W. Reisig and R. Rozenberg, p. 18 - 68. Springer Verlag, Heidelberg, 1987.

[Goma86]   Gomaa, Hassan: Software Development of Real-Time Systems. *Communications of the ACM*. Vol. 29, No. 7, pp. 657 - 668, July 1986.

[Maio85]   Maiocchi, M.: The Use of Petri Nets in Requirements and Functional Specification. In: *System Description Methodologies. D. Teichroew and G. David, ed.* Elsevier Science Publishers B.V., North Holland, NL, 1985.

[Mura89]   Murata, T.: Petri Nets: Properties, Analysis and Applications. *Proceedings of the IEEE*, Vol. 77, No. 4, pp. 541 - 580, 1989.

[OEM90]   Oswald, H., R. Esser und R. Mattmann: An Environment for Specifying and Executing Hierarchical Petri Nets. In: *Proc. of the 12. Int. Conf. on Software Engineering*, IEEE Comp. Soc. Press, Washington, DC, USA, 1990.

[Pete81]   Peterson, J. L.: Petri Net Theory and the Modeling of Systems. Prentice-Hall, Englewood Cliffs, NJ, USA, 1981.

[Reis88]   Reisig, W.: Embedded System Description Using Petri Nets. In: *Embedded Sytems. A. Kündig, R. E. Bührer and J. Dähler, ed.* p. 18 - 62. Springer Verlag, Heidelberg, 1988.

[YaCa83]   Yau, S. S. and M. U. Caglayan: Distributed Software Design Representation Using Modified Petri Nets. *IEEE Transactions on Software Engineering*. Vol. SE-9, No. 6, pp. 733 - 745, Nov. 1983.

[YaTs86]   Yau, S. S. and J. J.-P. Tsai: A Survey of Software Design Techniques. *IEEE Transactions on Software Engineering*, Vol. SE-12, No. 6, pp. 713 - 721, June 1986.

Appendix:

The proposed development technique with PrT-nets is embedded in the complete development process according to Fig. 5. We have based this complete process on the well-known waterfall model that also permits prototyping.

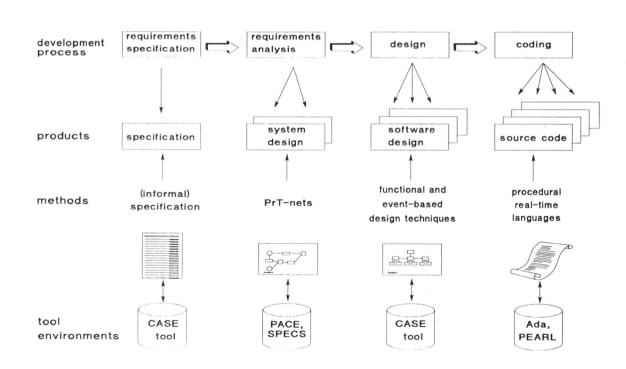

Fig. 5:   The underlying model for the software development process

A SAFETY SYSTEM FOR CLOSE INTERACTION BETWEEN MAN AND ROBOT

ALBERT-JAN BAERVELDT
Institute of Robotics, ETH Zurich
CH-8092 Zurich, Switzerland

Abstract. The question of robot *safety* becomes increasingly important as future robots will be required to share their working area with humans in order to achieve a fruitful *cooperation* between man and robot. This paper presents a new safety system which allows such a close interaction. The safety system consists basically of two modules. One module has the task to localize people inside the working area and provide the robot with an appropriate behavior pattern in order to avoid situations endangering the operator. This module uses a camera and computer vision techniques to obtain the location of the operator. The other module has to prevent a robot runaway, which can be defined as an unexpected robot motion due to a failure of robot hardware or software. Our runaway protection system measures the acceleration of the robot arm by means of three orthogonal accelerometers. An emergency stop is initiated if the difference between measured and expected acceleration exceeds a certain limit.

Keywords. Robots; safety; man-machine systems; intelligent machines; image processing.

INTRODUCTION

The requirements for robots are increasing, as they tend to be used for tasks which are more demanding than simple repetitive handling. The often-declared ultimate goal for intelligent machines, namely its complete autonomous behavior, will in reality rarely be technically or economically feasible, or even desirable. This is emphasized by the fact that current developments seem to concentrate more and more on teleoperation, rather than on autonomous robots. There is another property that appears to be much more important than autonomy: for difficult tasks our working environment usually stipulates an interaction between the robot and the human operator in order to guide the machine to deal with exceptional situations. The way in which such a cooperative interaction is performed may be defined as the true "intelligence" of a machine (Schweitzer, 1991).

We thus focus our attention on the development of a robot as an interactive and cooperating machine. This conception has led to the project "Cooperating Robot", concerned with the development of a robot able to cooperate with a human being in an unstructured environment (Vischer, 1992).

In our project, the robot has to share its working area with humans. In such environments safety considerations are very important. Accidents resulting in injury of people or the damage of expensive machinery including the robot itself must be prevented. Traditionally, robots have been caged or fenced to prevent human injuries, with the aim to keep humans out of the robot workspace by physical barriers. This approach is no longer feasible when we allow a human operator in the workspace of the robot in order to achieve a true cooperation.

This paper presents a new safety system which allows a close interaction between man and robot. The two major tasks of the safety system are: The detection and localization of people inside the working area and the detection and control of robot runaways. When people are detected in the working area the robot system reacts to the intrusion by slowing down the robot speed or stopping the robot motion. This behavior of the robot is only safe if it is guaranteed that the robot follows the given commands. Therefore a robot runaway-detection system is needed. In the case of any erroneous motion of the robot arm, the system shuts off the robot with an emergency stop.

THE HUMAN LOCALIZATION SYSTEM

Among the existing techniques used to detect a person are passive infrared sensors, pressure-sensitive floor mats, ultrasonic sensors, capacitance sensors, light curtains and computer vision systems. Some of these techniques are only able to detect the presence of a human being in a certain area but are not suitable to locate the intruder (Helander, 1990). We aimed at a sensor system which is also able to locate the intruder so that, eventually, our robot system is able to avoid a human being by changing its path. In the future the use of mobile robots equipped with a robot arm for both industrial and domestic applications is projected to increase. Therefore our sensor system should be applicable to these mobile systems as well. After a thorough evaluation of the sensors mentioned above, we decided to employ a computer vision system to detect and locate a human being, because it is a very flexible and powerful sensor. The major problem with computer vision is the huge amount of data which must be processed. This may lead to very slow response times. We tried to overcome this problem by employing dedicated hardware.

The vision algorithms, which were implemented on a commercially available dataflow-machine (Data Cube), aim at the detection of *moving* objects and thus only extract *changes* in the camera picture (Fischer and Voutsis, 1991). It is possible to simply use the difference in grey level of a reference and the current image to detect such changes. This simple method has the disadvantage that it also detects changes in the illumination of the scene. To overcome this disadvantage we combined this simple method with the so-called shading algorithm of Skifstad and Jain (1989) for our application. This method concentrates on changes in the texture of the surfaces on the image and is almost independent of the illumination. The system is able to provide the position of the intruder every 20 milliseconds. The performance during the international robot exhibition "Industrial Handling 92" in Zurich has shown that this system effectively detects and locates an intruder in the working area of our robot system under varying lighting conditions.

Once the intruder has been detected and located by the vision system, there are different alternatives for the behavior of the robot. The behavior should comply with the *three laws of robotics* formulated by the science fiction writer Isaac Asimov (1950).

1) A robot may not injure a human being, or, through inaction, allow a human being to come to harm.

2) A robot must obey orders given by human beings, except where such orders would conflict with the First Law.

3) A robot must protect its own existence as long as such protection does not conflict with the First or Second Law.

We implemented three different behaviors. If there is no human being in the working area of the robot, the robot is allowed to perform its task with maximum speed. This is called the *automatic mode*. If there is a human being in the working area, but at a safe distance to the robot arm, the speed is limited to a certain value. To anticipate safety hazards, the operator should be able to perceive and react adequately to robot-arm movements. It is therefore

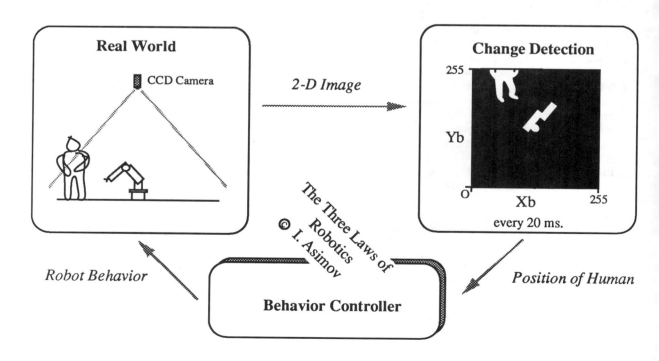

Fig. 1. Basic structure of the human localization system

important that the speed of the robot be not too high. Several experiments have been performed to quantify the perception of safe speeds by human subjects (Helander 1990, Karwowski and others 1987). Based on their results we limited the speed to 200 mm/s when human beings are in the working area. This is called the *cooperation mode*. If the intruder comes too close to the robot arm the movement is stopped. This is called the *stop mode*. Another behavior which is not yet implemented would be to change the robot's path in order to avoid the intruder.

To describe the human-robot interface which uses a speech recognition and synthesis system as well as the orders which can be given to the robot, would be beyond the scope of this paper. The reader is referred to Baerveldt (1992) for this topic.

The human localization system sends the appropriate mode to the robot controller as well as to the runaway detection system which stops the robot immediately in the case of an erroneous movement.

THE RUNAWAY PROTECTION SYSTEM

The term *"robot runaway"* designates an unexpected robot motion due to a failure of robot hardware or software. Mostly because of the resulting high *kinetic energy* of the robot arm, runaways are dangerous and should be prevented at all times. Runaways can occur for a multitude of reasons, such as encoder faults, software bugs and faulty cables (Ramirez, 1988). To be able to understand what kind of failures can lead to a runaway and how they can effectively be detected, a short description of current industrial robot controllers is given below.

Current industrial robot controllers

In current industrial-robot controllers each joint is treated as an independent servo mechanism. The controller of the PUMA robot, which we used for our project, consists of one main processing unit and six joint controller modules, each with a slave processor, a joint encoder, a digital-to-analog converter (DAC) and a current amplifier. The control structure is hierarchically arranged. The top level consists of the *master* CPU which serves as a supervisor. The lower level includes six *slave* processors, one for each degree of freedom. Other types of robot controllers may use a single slave processor to control several joints instead of only one, but the control structure is basically the same.

The master CPU handles several tasks, such as on-line user interaction, interpretation and execution of user made robot programs, communication with external devices and sensors, as well as trajectory planning which executes the robot's movements prescribed by the user program. The final output of the trajectory planning consists of the new desired joint positions for all joints at a fixed clock interval.

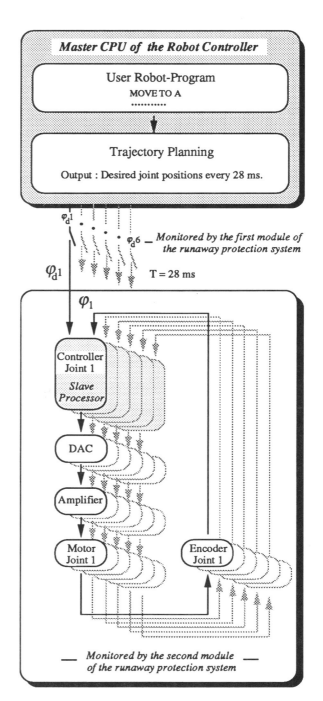

Fig.2. Hierarchical structure of an industrial robot controller.

Based on the actual joint position provided by the encoder, the slave processors control their specific joints, trying to follow the generated set points from the master CPU. The period of one clock cycle is typically between 10 and 50 milliseconds (28 milliseconds for the PUMA). This is illustrated in Fig. 2.

Based on this hierarchic control structure, all possible failures which may result in a robot runaway can be divided in *two* main classes:

1. The desired joint positions generated by the master CPU may not correspond to positions specified in the user program. This happens when the

master CPU has a hardware malfunction or there is a software bug.

2. Something may go wrong in one of the joint control loops, causing the specific joint not to follow the desired joint position commanded by the master CPU.

Current robot controllers can detect these failures to some extent. Especially defects of the second class can be detected fairly well by monitoring the error between the desired and the actual position of each joint. When this so-called *envelope error* exceeds a certain threshold, an emergency stop of the robot is initiated. Many failures of the second class, such as a malfunction of the digital-to-analog converter, cause the envelope error to exceed the given threshold.

Design of the runaway-protection system

For our project "Cooperating Robot", where a close interaction between man and robot is needed, the built in safety measurements of the robot controller are not sufficient. In order to reduce the probability of a runaway to an acceptable level, *redundancy* in the sensor information and the control hardware is required (Weck and Kohring, 1990). An encoder failure, for example, leads to a runaway, which usually cannot be detected with an envelope error check since this method relies on correct encoder information. Only with a second redundant sensor will an encoder failure be detected for certain. Redundancy is also needed in the computer system itself, which performs the envelope error check. In order to obtain this redundancy we decided to develop a safety system employing a separate computer board. We divided the safety system into two main modules corresponding to the two main failure classes, which were described in the previous chapter.

Safety module for monitoring the master controller

One module supervises the desired joint positions generated by the master CPU. A principal solution would be a fully redundant master controller for the robot, i.e. the first module of the safety system would be a copy of the original master CPU of the robot controller fed with the same user robot-program. The output, the desired joint positions, of both systems could be compared. As soon as these differ, an emergency stop is generated. The drawback of this approach is that the safety system only detects malfunctions of the hardware as the software is a copy of that running on the master controller. To be able to detect possible software bugs, an independent second software for the safety module must be developed which performs the same task as the master controller. This would be an excessively high expense, especially as the safety module would then be only applicable to one type of robot controller.

Therefore, we decided to monitor the generated joint positions of the master controller on the safety computer without any knowledge about the user robot program (Hüsler, 1990). From the joint positions, the arm speed and acceleration can be derived. Those values can be monitored to determine whether they are outside the range of normal conditions, like Kilmer and others (1985) did for their watchdog safety computer. In our case we feed this safety module with the appropriate mode dictated by the human localization system to specify the normal range of conditions: maximum speed (470 mm/s) for the automatic mode, reduced speed (200 mm/s) for the cooperation mode and no motion for the stop mode (see Fig. 3).

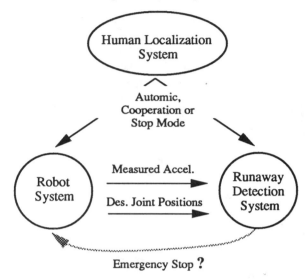

Fig. 3. Overview of the final safety system

Safety module for monitoring the joint controllers

The second module monitors the joint control loop and checks whether the desired joint positions are followed correctly (see Fig. 2). In this module it is assumed that the desired joint positions generated by the master CPU and monitored by the first module of the safety system are correct and correspond to the desired movement specified in the user program. As only the movements resulting from a runaway of the three main joints are of potential danger, we decided to monitor those three joints only, and to neglect the three wrist joints.

Our approach, which is described in detail in Baerveldt and Vischer (1991), is to measure the accelerations of the robot arm close to the end-effector by means of three orthogonal accelerometers. An emergency stop is initiated if the difference between *measured* and *expected* acceleration exceeds a certain limit. The expected accelerations are derived from the *desired joint positions* generated by the master CPU every clock cycle (see also Fig. 3).

The idea to use accelerometers for runaway detection is not new. Bennekers and Teal (1988) also used a triaxial accelerometer to detect robot runaways. They assumed that the considered robot is only used for tasks where it moves on a pre-programmed and therefore predictable path. They sampled the measured accelerations for this specified cycle of motion. They called this the reference signal. After this "acquisition mode" the robot switched to "protection mode". In this mode the measured acceleration was compared with the stored reference signal. A mismatch of those two signals generated an emergency stop.

The main disadvantage of this approach is that the robot motion has to be known in advance to be able to obtain the reference signal. As robots are more frequently controlled on-line, for instance by a vision system or other sensors, this requirement is increasingly not met. Also in the case where a human operator teaches the robot with a joystick or a teach-pendant the robot motion is not known in advance. This situation is common industrial practice, where a close interaction between robot and operator is often inevitable. As we derive the expected accelerations from the desired joint positions, our method is also applicable to these tasks, where the robot's path is of arbitrary and unpredictable shape.

Another feasible approach would be to mount a *second encoder* at each joint and then use an additional redundant computer system to check the envelope error related to this encoders. A drawback of this approach, however, is that a second encoder might be difficult to mount at the joints, if the robot manufacturer did not provide the necessary mounting space. Besides being rather inexpensive and small, accelerometers have the advantage of being easy to mount on a robot arm. Our resulting runaway protection system can thus be easily applied to any existing (industrial) robot.

CONCLUSION

Inherent *safety* will play a major role in future robot systems as robots will be required to share their working area with humans in order to achieve a productive cooperation. Until now national safety authorities do not allow such a close interaction. They prescribe physical barriers around the robot, such as cages and fences, in order to separate man and robot. We developed an inherent robot safety system which could allow a *close interaction* between man and robot. The system employs a camera to *locate* a human being in the workspace of the robot. This information is used to avoid situations endangering the operator by slowing down the robot arm speed or stopping the robot. In this case unexpected robot motions due to *failures* of hardware or software, i.e. a robot runaway, must absolutely be detected to initiate an emergency stop. Therefore we developed a new concept for robot runaway detection. The tests have shown this system to effectively detect a runaway, providing a short reaction time and good sensitivity.

ACKNOWLEDGEMENTS

I would like to thank Patrick Almy, Erhard Hüsler, Rolf Fischer and Nicola Voutsis as well as the members of the Cooperating Robot project for their valuable contributions to this paper.

REFERENCES

Asimov, I. (1950). I, *Robot*. Doubleday & Co., Inc., New York, 1950.

Baerveldt, A.J. and D. Vischer (1991). A Runaway Protection System for Robots Based on Acceleration Measurements. *IFAC/IFIP/ IMACS-Symposium on Robot Control*, SYROCO'91, Vienna, 1991.

Baerveldt, A.J. (1992). Cooperation between Man and Robot: Interface and Safety. Submitted to the *IEEE Int. Workshop on Robot and Human Communication*, Tokyo, Sept. 1992.

Bennekers, B. and H. Teal (1988). Robot runaway protection system. *IEEE Int. Conf. on Robotics and Automation*, 1988, pp. 1474-1476.

Fischer, R. and N. Voutsis (1991). *Ein Visionsystem zur Erkennung des Menschen*. Report, Institute of Robotics, ETH Zürich, Switzerland.

Helander, M.G. (1990). Ergonomics and safety considerations in the design of robotics workplaces: a review and some priorities for research. Int. *Journal of Ind. Ergonomics*, Elsevier, Vol. 6, 1990, pp. 127-149.

Hüsler, E. (1990). *Watchdog für einen Industrieroboter*. Diplom-Thesis, Institute of Robotics, ETH Zürich, Switzerland.

Karwowski, W., T. Plank, H.R. Parsaei and M. Rahimi (1988). Human perception of the maximum safe speed of robot motions. *Proc. of the human factors society*, 31st annual meeting, 1987.

Kilmer, R.D., H.G. McCain, M. Juberts and S.A. Legowik (1985). Safety computer design and implementation. In Bonney, M.C. and Y.F. Yong (Ed.), *Robot Safety*, IFS (Publications) Ltd and Springer Verlag, pp. 141-160.

Ramirez, C. A. (1988). Safety of Robot. In Dorf R.C. (Ed.), *International Encyclopedia of Robotics*, Wiley, Vol. 3, pp. 1419-1428.

Schweitzer, G. (1991). The robot as an intelligent interactive machine. *Mechatronics*, Vol. 1, No. 4, 1991, pp. 525-533.

Skifstad, K. and R. Jain (1989). Illumination independent change detection for real world image sequences. *Computer Vision, Graphics and Image Processing*, Vol. 46, 1989, pp. 387-399.

Vischer, D. (1992). Cooperating Robot with Visual and Tactile Skills. *IEEE International Conference on Robotics and Automation*, Nice, 1992.

Weck, M. and A. Kohring (1990). *Sicherheitsaspekte bei der Ansteuerung von Industrieroboterachsen*. Schriftenreihe der Bundesanstalt für Arbeitsschutz, Fb 627, Germany, 1990.

A SIMPLE STRONGLY-FAIL-SAFE CIRCUIT USED AS BASIC CELL FOR DESIGNING SAFETY ARCHITECTURES

S.NORAZ - M.PRUNIER

Merlin Gerin
Safety and Electronic Systems (SES) Department
38050 Grenoble Cedex, France

Abstract .   As part of critical application used in railways transportation, space, chemical and nuclear industries, the processing part which controls the actuators of the electromechanical part is realized with fail-safe circuits. But these give use to the following problems:
- Complexity of design in case of redundant solutions, done till now, which require conventionnal fail-safe circuits.
- Necessity of off-line test sequences in case of non redundant solutions involving "strongly-fail-safe" circuits.

This paper aims to provide a practical solution using "strongly-fail-safe" circuit for designing dependable computer systems aimed at critical processes.The goal is to make use of such systems easier, to avoid the drawbacks generated by off-line test phase and to obtain the best "cost-safety" compromise.

First of all, we introduce the scheme of a "strongly-fail-safe" basic cell without any off-line test equipments. The advantage is to obtain a "strongly-fail-safe" circuit which requires few components.

Then, we suggest an architecture of a "strongly-fail-safe majority voted output" circuit designed from the "strongly-fail-safe" basic cell. The reliability, the safety and the availability of this "majority voted output" mechanism is evaluated.

In conclusion a triple modular redundancy computer system including this last mechanism is compared with well known dependable computer systems. The good results obtained show that such a solution may meet a wide range of safe applications because of its low complexity and its fitness to be easily implemented.

Keywords. Fail-safe circuits, "Strongly-fail-safe" circuits, majority voted output mechanism, Dependable computer systems.

1- INTRODUCTION

Most of digital fail-safe systems aimed for control of critical applications have been developed by using conventional fail-safe techniques, well approved but not suited to realize today's complex computer systems.

At SAFECOMP'89 conference, The MERLIN GERIN's Safety and Electronic Systems Department has proposed practical schemes (NOR 89) of "strongly-fail-safe" circuits to be easily implemented and used in existing critical processes architectures designs. But these solutions have a major shortcoming because they include off-line test mechanisms requested during defined test phase modes for which a part of the application is shut off.

In this paper we first set out a simple "strongly-fail-safe" circuit without inherent fault detection mechanisms. Then from this basic cell, called "Compact Secure Interface (CSI)", we show how to obtain easily a "Strongly-fail-safe majority voted output" component, a voter as those usually used in computing architectures aimed for critical applications. Finally, and for information only, we compare a triple modular redundancy (TMR) computer system including this "majority voted output" circuit with well known TMR or redundant computer systems.

2- FAIL-SAFE CIRCUITS

In this paragraph, we shall recall the main ideas of the generalized theory of fail-safe systems (NIC 89).

2.1 Fail-safe circuits : basic definition

Mine and Koga (MIN 67) gave the first formal definition of conventional fail-safe circuits. But it may be presented in a quite different way as following:

Definition D$\emptyset$: A single output circuit G is fail-safe with respect to his input space X, with respect to the fault set F and with respect to "0" (or "1") if :
$\forall x \in X, \forall f \in F, G(x,f) = G(x,\emptyset)$
$\qquad$ or $G(x,f) = $ "0" (or "1").
where $G(x,\emptyset)$ denotes the correct function and $G(x,f)$ denotes the function under fault f.

In this definition the state "0" (resp."1") of binary output is considered to be safe and the state "1" (resp."0") non-safe.

However the concept of safe and non-safe states may be extended to output spaces having any number of states. In this case, the more general definition of fail-safe systems is the restricted definition D1 usually used when developing practical fail-safe implementation techniques for circuits.

Definition D1 : A system G is fail-safe with respect to a fault set F, an input space X and a safe output space Os if :

$$\forall \, a \in X, \, \forall \, f \in F, \, G(a,f) = G(a,\emptyset)$$
$$\text{or} \quad G(a,f) \in Os.$$

Here Os is the set of the safe output words that never involves a dangerous situation in the system, even if these output words occur erroneously. All other words compose the non-safe output space On.

2.2 The "strongly-fail-safe" property

In most fail-safe systems the occurrence of the erroneous outputs belonging to the normal operation output space will not involve fault detection. So suppose a system is fail-safe according to the definition D1 with respect to a fault set F. If a fault f1 in F occurs in the system then it is ensured that it never produces non-safe erroneous output and the safety is ensured.

However if the system is used a long time after the occurrence of the first fault a second fault f2 may occur. The combined fault [f1, f2] may not belong to F and the fail-safe property could be lost. Therefore in a fail-safe system some mechanism is needed to quickly detect the occurrence of a fault avoiding the use of service delivered from the faulty system for a long time after the fault occurrence.

This requirement, the self testing property, is ensured during a special mode (off-line mode) for systems which have not inherent fault detection mechanisms, while the normal operation mode (on-line mode) may be sufficient for systems with inherent fault detection mechanisms (output coding).

Definition D2 : A circuit is totally fail-safe (TFS) if it is fail-safe and self-testing.

In a fail-safe circuit the fact that several erroneous outputs can be produced before fault detection is not a drawback as far as these outputs are safe states. This required goal is called the totally fail-safe goal.

Totally fail-safe circuits will achieve the TFS goal under the following hypothesis :

Hypothesis H1' :
a) faults occur one by one,
b) between the occurrence of two faults a sufficient time elapses so that the circuit is sufficiently exercised by means of the fault detection modes.

"Strongly-fail-safe" circuits (definition D3) are the most general class of circuits allowing to achieve the TFS goal under hypothesis H1'.

Definition D3 : A circuit G is "strongly-fail-safe" with respect to a fault set F if for each fault $f \in F$ either :
a) G is totally fail-safe or,
b) G is fail-safe and if a new fault in F occurs, for the obtained multiple fault, case a) or b) is true.

Now we discuss the possibility of designing "strongly-fail-safe" systems without the use of fault detection mechanisms. The following theorem gives the necessary and sufficient condition for the existence of such systems.

Theorem 1 : A system G which has not fault detection capabilities is "strongly-fail-safe" with respect to a fault set F if and only if G is fail-safe with respect to F*.
In which for a given fault set F, F* is the set of multiple faults made up of faults belonging to F.

A common technique used for computer systems aimed for critical applications is to use more than one computing element generating results by their combined operation. An odd number such as three is usually chosen, allowing the combined result, called the "majority-voted output", to be generated by the majority vote of individual results.

This method does not make the system completely free of failure points. In particular, separating out the computing elements of the system into several units and combining their result by majority vote still leaves the system with a single point of failure, the majority vote mechanism itself.

In this way, there is a need for majority-voted output systems which are not subject to a single point of failure able to bring the entire system to a halt or to be the source of a catastrophic event.

This is the topic of the following sections in which we propose, the implementation of a "strongly-fail-safe" circuit by using coding techniques and aimed to design a dependable "strongly-fail-safe majority voted output" mechanism.

3 - DESIGN OF A "STRONGLY-FAIL-SAFE" BASIC CELL

For most critical applications using fail-safe systems where each binary output drives a critical function, as electromechanical engine (actuators), what is needed is to obtain signals that are individually fail-safe. A convenient way to code such signals is to use frequency coding. That is to say a range of frequencies represents the non safe state (says "1" state) and any other electrical state represents the safe state (says "0" state).
In practice, many existing fail-safe systems use binary signals with frequency coding (FUT 88).

What we are looking at is to make a device, for specific needs, by using frequency coding technique in such a way that, regarding its inputs/output, the device is "strongly-fail-safe" according to the definition D3.

3.1 Functional description

To do this we propose in figure 1 the basic cell whose principle is laid down below.

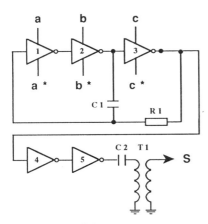

Inverters 1, ..., 4 : NMOS inverters.
Inverter 5 : Power CMOS inverter.

Fig.1 A basic cell designing with coding techniques.

The device, called "Compact Secure Interface" (CSI), is built with an odd number (3) of logic gates (inverters) performing a dynamic circuit and a suitable transformer part. Its functional inputs correspond to the power supply inputs of the first three NMOS inverters The two others, the NMOS one and the CMOS one, are respectively used to improve the signal to squares and amplify them in order to drive the transformer correctly.

For a voltage coded binary ("1" = 5v, "0" = 0v) input signals a, a*, .. , c, c*, code words are those for which a* = .. = c* = ¬a = .. = ¬c.
That is to say, from these words, the CSI generates a frequency coded output signal on S.
In one case, a* = .. = c* = ¬a = .. = ¬c = "0" (defined as "action code word"), the output signal is a frequency signal Fø corresponding to the "1" non safe state.
In the other case, a* = .. = c* = ¬a = .. = ¬c = "1" (defined as "non action code word"), due to the fact that all the logic gates are supplied, the output signal is a normal low level voltage corresponding to the "0" safe state.

For non code words consistent with :
∃ (i, i*) = (0,0) or (1,1), i ∈ {a, b, c}, the output signal of the CSI is in the "0" safe state.

3.2 "Strongly-fail-safe" property

By construction and by the use of power supply inputs of its logic gates, we can ensure that the above depicted cell is fail-safe according to the definition Dø with respect to a predicted single fault set F likely to occur in a logic gate, transformer, capacitor, resistor, ...
Indeed on a demonstration model, we have made a fault injection test sequence including each kind of the predicted single fault set F done in figure 2.

Component	Fault
Switch of any inverter	"Stuck at" one input
	"Stuck at" zero input
	Open circuited input
	Short between gate/drain
	Short between gate/source
	Short between drain/source
	Open circuited source
	Open circuited drain
Transformer	Opened line
Capacitor	Opened and shorted
Resistor	Opened and shorted
Connection	Opened line

Fig.2 Predicted single fault set F.

Each time, we have checked that the behavior of the circuit is consistent to the Dø basic definition (Fig 3).

Injected predicted single fault f	Coded binary input signal		
	Action code word	Non action code word	No code words
No fault	⊓⊔⊓ 150KHZ	—	—
Opened Capacitor C1	⊓⊔⊓ 300KHZ	—	—
Shorted resistor R1	⊓⊔⊓ 280KHZ	—	—
Shorted capacitor C2	⊓⊔⊓ 150KHZ	—	—
Open circuited input of the NMOS of CMOS inverter	Uncertain behavior ⊓⊔⊓ or —	—	—
Open circuited source of the PMOS of CMOS inverter	Uncertain behavior ⊓⊔⊓ or —	—	—
All other single faults	—	—	—

Fig.3 Results of the single fault injection test sequence.

In the same way and for any predicted combined fault f" = f x f' (f and f' belonging to the above predicted single fault set F), the result shows that the fail-safe property is maintained (Fig 4).

Injected predicted combined fault	Coded binary input signal		
	Action code word	Non action code word	No code words
No fault	⊓⊔⊓ 150KHZ	—	—
Short between gate/drain of the switch of the NMOS inverter 4 and Short between gate/source of the NMOS of CMOS inverter 5	⊓⊔⊓ 150KHZ	—	—
Open capacitor C1 and shorted resistor R1	⊓⊔⊓ 300KHZ	—	—
All other combined faults	—	—	—

Fig.4 Results of the combined fault injection test sequence.

We analysed the behavior of the CSI under single and multiple faults with SPICE simulator. We obtained the same results that the fault injection test sequences on the demonstration model.

Therefore, according to theorem 1, the CSI is "strongly fail-safe" with respect to any predicted single fault which may occur.

3.3 Valuation of the estimated failure rate

First of all we consider the non safe failure rate λ_{ns} of the CSI as the failure rate of the failures modes which lead its output S to the "1" non safe state when its functional inputs are "non action code word" or non code words.
As well its safe failure rate λ_S is the failure rate of the failures modes for which its output S is in the "0" safe state whatever its functional inputs may be.

Due to its "strongly-fail-safe" property, the estimated non safe failure rate of the CSI, performing the safety is :
$\lambda_{ns}CSI < 10^{-9}\ h^{-1}$.

Its estimated safe failure rate, performing the reliability and availability, is obtained in adding up the estimated failures rates (CNET 86 reliability review) of all the components. That is to say, with a pessimistic hypothesis, all the single failure which may occur in the CSI lead its output S to the "0" safe state.
With the following estimated reliability data :
$\lambda_{gate}\quad = \lambda_G = 1,15 * 10^{-6}\ h^{-1}$,
$\lambda_{capacitor}\quad = \lambda_C = 2,28 * 10^{-8}\ h^{-1}$,
$\lambda_{transformer}\ = \lambda_T = 1,00 * 10^{-7}\ h^{-1}$,
$\lambda_{resistor}\quad = \lambda_R = 2,26 * 10^{-8}\ h^{-1}$,
the safe failure rate $\lambda_S CSI$ is:
$\lambda_S CSI \quad \leq 3\lambda_G + 2\lambda_C + \lambda_T + \lambda_R$.
$\qquad\qquad \leq 3,62 * 10^{-6}\ h^{-1}$.

Now, such a cell is used as a basic block in order to design a "Strongly-fail-safe majority voted output" circuit.

4 - A STRONGLY-FAIL-SAFE "MAJORITY VOTED OUTPUT" CIRCUIT

4.1 Functional description

Assuming that we have three identical Totally Self Checking (NIC 88) processing systems A, B, C doing the same tasks at the same time and delivering the same data. In order to design a TMR computer system, we use "majority voted output Si" circuits as the one given in figure 5 where each single output Si must be used for the safe drive of a critical function.

The "majority voted output (MVO) Si" circuit depicted down includes three CSI as this done in section 3. For each interface, a signal adaptator device and a diode, required for the vote function, are added.
Regarding from the processing systems, (a1,a1*),.., (ai,ai*),.., (an,an*), (CA,CA*), are the data delivered by the processor A, (b1,b1*),.., (bi,bi*),.., (bn,bn*),

(CB,CB*), the data delivered by the processor B, and, (c1,c1*),.., (ci,ci*),.., (cn,cn*), (CC,CC*), the data delivered by the processor C with :
$\forall\ i \in \{1,..., n\}$, $ai* = bi* = ci* = \neg ai = \neg bi = \neg ci$, and,
$\forall\ I \in \{A, B, C\}$, $CI* = \neg CI = "0"$.

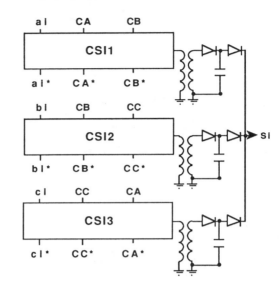

Fig.5 The "majority voted output Si" circuit.

The pair (CI,CI*) is the double rail encoded watch dog signal of the processing system I, $I \in \{A, B, C\}$. It indicates for each processor I if that processor has failed and its data is no longer valid.

The functional truth table of the "majority voted output Si" circuit, which attempts to form its majority output from (ai,ai*), (bi,bi*), (ci,ci*) valid data only, is shown in figure 6 with :
$A = ai * CA$, $B = bi * CB$ and $C = ci * CC$.

The obstructed squares are impossible cases because of the correlation $K = ki * CK$, with $K = A, B, C$ and $k = a, b, c$.

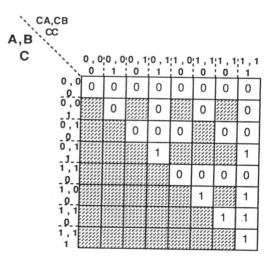

Fig.6 Truth table of the depicted "majority voted output Si" circuit.

4.2 "Strongly-fail-safe" property

As shown in figure 4, the "majority voted output Si" circuit is made from three subcircuits including both "strongly-fail-safe" CSI and some components used to achieve the "vote" function.

We verified by fault injection test sequence on a demonstration model that the voting element is fail-safe according to the definition Dø with respect to any predictable single fault set F (done in section 3.2) likely to appear in any subcircuit (CSI and components required for the vote function).

In the same way, we can ensure that if a new predicted fault f ∈ F occurs, in the same subcircuit or in another one, for the combined fault the "majority voted output Si" circuit does not lose its fail-safe property. Therefore (Theorem 1), the "majority voted output Si" circuit is "strongly-fail-safe" with respect to any predicted fault which may occur.

4.3 Valuation of the estimated failure rate

Due to its "strongly-fail-safe" property, the "majority voted output Si" circuit has an estimated non safe failure rate $\lambda_{ns}MVO < 10^{-9}\ h^{-1}$ according to the fault hypothesis.

The graph (Fig 7) performing the "majority voted output Si" behavior, with regard to exponentially distributed variables, allows to determine the analytic expression of its reliability: $R_{MVO}(t)$ or the availability $A_{MVO}(t)$.

Then, $R_{MVO}(t) = \exp - (3\ \lambda_{sub} * t)$
$$- 3 \exp - (2\ \lambda_{sub} * t)$$
$$+ 3 \exp - (\ \lambda_{sub} * t)$$

With :
$\lambda_{sub} = \lambda_{CSI} + \lambda_{capacitor} + 2\lambda_{diode}$
$= 3,86 * 10^{-6}\ h^{-1}$

Note that,
$1 - R_{MVO}(t) \cong 8 * 10^{-4}$ with t = 18 months.

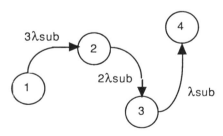

$\lambda_{sub} = \lambda_{CSI} + \lambda_{capacitor} + 2\lambda_{diode}$.

State 1 : The structure operates correctly.
State 2 : 1 among 3 subcircuits has failed.
State 3 : 2 among 3 subcircuits has failed, the remaining subcircuit ensures the "2/2" function.
State 4 : Failed state, all the subcircuits are out of order.

Fig.7 Behavior graph of the "majority voted output Si".

So, because of its non safe failure rate, this mechanism is efficient from the safety point of view, it is not the same from the availability point of view in case of widely available requirements. Therefore, to improve this last measure, the only way consists in making use of the "majority voted output" circuit so that it can be checked on-line.

In the next paragraph, we briefly describe this purpose.

4.4 MVO circuit and availability

So that the "majority voted output" circuit can be tested on-line, its output value, corresponding to the standby status of the function which it controls should be the unsafe state (Si = "1" = 5v).

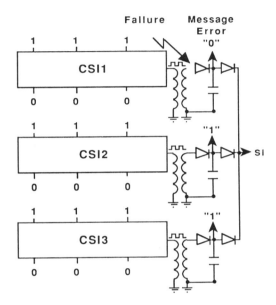

Fig 9 An on-line tested "majority voted output Si" circuit

In this case, the function downstream to the "majority voted output Si" should operate with voltage loss. So, during the standby status each part involving a CSI circuit and the added components are accessed. Then, if an output of one part changes to a safe state, following a failure, it can be immediately signaled (monitoring each output by a message error). This is the only way to act on the availability of the assembly (Fig 9).

If the "majority voted output circuit" is used as depicted before, its behavior under fault is pictured in figure 10.

The results of the reliability and availability assessmentss show that, over one year period, the non safe failure rate of the "majority voted output" circuit ($\lambda_{ns}MVO$) and the safe one ($\lambda_{s}MVO$) are :

$\lambda_{ns}MVO \quad < 10^{-9}\ h^{-1} \quad$ (Safety) and,
$\lambda_{s}MVO\ (t) \quad < 10^{-9}\ h^{-1} \quad$ (Availability)
$t \leq 1$ year
consequently to exponentially distributed variables.

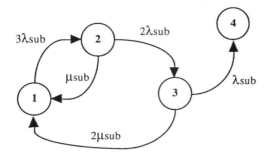

λsub $= \lambda$CSI $+ \lambda$capacitor $+ 2\lambda$diode.

μsub $= \dfrac{1}{T}$ with T = 1 h.

State 1 : The 3 subcircuits operate correctly.
State 2 : 2 among 3 subcircuits operate, the other one is under repair because of a hardware fault.
State 3 : Only one subcircuit operates and ensures the 2/2 "vote", the other ones are under repair because of a hardware fault.
State 4 : Failed state, all the subcircuits are out of order.

Fig 10 Behavior graph of the on-line available "majority voted output Si" circuit

5 - WHICH SOLUTION FOR WHICH PROBLEM ?

The next scheme (Fig 11) is only given for information. It is used to compare various dependable architectures but not to actually obtain the features of each one. Moreover, the failure rate of each processing unit is the same for the duplex, triplex or non redundant architectures.

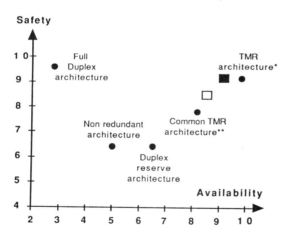

* May not be spoilt in full duplex architecture
* • May be spoilt in full duplex architecture

■ TMR architecture including "majority voted output" circuit which may be spoilt in full duplex architecture

☐ TMR architecture including "majority voted output" circuit which may be spoilt in full duplex architecture and in non redundant too.

Fig 11 Comparative board for some well known architectures

We carry over the x-axis and the y-axis respectively $\lambda_{A(t)}$ (A(t) is the availability) and $\lambda_{S(t)}$ (S(t) is the safety) where the first value corresponds to the

transition rate to the unavailable state and the second one, the transition rate to the unsafe state. These transition rates are given for a determined time.

It is interesting to note that a TMR architecture including a "strongly-fail-safe majority voted output" circuit which may be degraded in full duplex system may be a very attractive solution. Because first it has about the same features with a non degradable TMR system. On the other hand and from a safety point of view, with such a solution the results are a little worse than a full duplex architecture and better than common TMR systems which may be in full duplex system.

From an availability point of view, our solution is better than full duplex architecture and in the same order for the common degradable (full duplex) TMR systems.
solution is better than full duplex architecture and in the same order for the common degradable (full duplex) TMR systems.

What is interesting to note is that a TMR At last, it is easy to show that such a solution is better than a TMR system using "strongly-fail-safe majority voted output" circuit which may be not only in full duplex architecture but in non redundant architecture too.

6 - CONCLUSION

In order to safely drive electromechanical actuators in critical applications, a well known method consists in using fail-safe techniques. But on the one hand an important drawback of conventional fail-safe circuits is that they require redundant solutions which involve complex designs. On the other hand, in the case of "strongly-fail-safe" circuits made till now, off-line test mechanisms may involve too much material which is not "cost-safety" in keeping with a better compromise .

In this paper a practical alternative of these solutions, well adapted to industrial needs, is given. Firstly by giving the scheme of a "strongly-fail-safe" basic cell without off-line test equipments and made with few components. Secondly by designing an architecture of a "strongly-fail-safe majority voted output" circuit from basic cells. The good results obtained for reliability as well as for availability, the low complexity of its architecture and its fitness to be easily implemented, and to be easily modified for special needs, show that this "vote" hardware function is able to meet a wide range of safe and available applications with a good "cost/dependability" compromise.

7 - REFERENCES

[FUT 88] FUTSUHARA K., SUGIMOTO N., MUKAIDO M. "Fail-safe logic elements having upper and lower thresholds and their application to safety control" The 18th Int. Symp. on Fault-Tolerant Computing, Tokyo, June 1988.

[MIN 67] MINE H., KOGA Y. "Basic properties and a construction method for fail-safe logical systems" IEEE Trans. Elec. Comp., June 1967.

[NIC 88] NICOLAIDIS M.
          "A Unified Built In Self Test Scheme : UBIST"
          The 18th Int. Symp. on Fault-Tolerant Computing,
          Tokyo, June 1988.

[NIC 89] NICOLAIDIS M., NORAZ S., COURTOIS B.
          "A generalized theory of fail-safe systems"
          The 19th Int. Symp. on Fault-Tolerant Computing,
          Chicago, June 1989.

[NOR 89] NORAZ S., NICOLAIDIS M., COURTOIS B.
          "VLSI implementation for control of critical systems"
          SAFECOMP'89, Vienna, December 1989.

A SINGLE-CHIP COMPUTER FOR ROBUST VARIABLE-STRUCTURE CONTROL OF LARGE-SCALE SAFETY-CRITICAL SYSTEMS

Norman E. Gough
University of Wolverhampton, School of Computing and Information Technology
Wulfruna Street, Wolverhampton, WV1 1SB, Great Britain

Wolfgang A. Halang
University of Groningen, Department of Computing Science
P. O. Box 800, 9700 AV Groningen, The Netherlands

Abstract: This paper describes the specification and design of a low-cost advanced microcomputer controller suitable for use in large-scale process control systems in safety-critical applications. Accurate and robust decentralized control at a local level is achieved by a variable-structure controller with state observer. A suitable specification for a general-purpose microcontroller based on a RISC architecture is given, including the control procedure and its formal correctness proof. The proposed chip has fully integrated peripherals and may be connected via a network to a higher-level coordinating computer, permitting design, verification and downloading of control parameters. Interconnecting several microcontrollers, facilitates implementation of a two-level supervisory control strategy.
Keywords: microcomputer-based control, variable-structure control, robustness, safety

INTRODUCTION

Recent trends in data acquisition and control are characterised by a move towards intelligent digital sensors connected to distributed controllers using local area networks (Burd and Dorey, 1984). In addition to overcoming the many problems associated with transmission of low-level analogue signals over large distances, this offers considerable potential for the design of advanced control systems involving interconnected local controllers, coordinated by global controllers. It has the practical advantage of allowing local controls to be designed and implemented independently to achieve local requirements such as accuracy and integrity, and then supplementing the system with higher-level controls to implement heat and mass balance, global coordination, optimization etc. In addition, distributed systems possess a high degree of fault tolerance, ensuring that local computer failures do not result in overall system failure as in centralized control systems. In safety-critical situations such as hazardous areas in petroleum refineries, this offers scope for implementing robust control algorithms to overcome the disadvantages of conventional control.

The paper is organized as follows: In section 2, a general variable-structure control methodology is presented which achieves robust sliding-mode control of a multivariable (multi-input multi-output, MIMO) system expressed as a state-variable model. In order to achieve distributed control, the model is then disassociated in section 3, by ignoring the interactions between subsystems, and a simplified decentralized (single-input single-output, SISO) design procedure results. Section 4 then considers the supervisory procedure required to coordinate the local controls through a two-level approach. The local microcontroller specification is next considered in section 5. Section 6 outlines the proposed microcontroller implementation and the formal correctness proof used to verify the control software is detailed in section 7. The paper concludes with a discussion on the design and its potential applications.

VARIABLE-STRUCTURE CONTROL

Consider a large-scale process requiring the implementation of m control loops that may interact dynamically with one another. Modern multivariable control system design methods for a process with n states are based on the availability of an approximate state-variable model, linearized at a nominal operating point

$$\dot{x}(t) = Ax(t) + Bu(t), \quad x \in R^n \; u \in R^m \quad (1)$$
$$y(t) = Hx(t), \qquad y \in R^m \quad (2)$$

with a continuous negative feedback control

$$e(t) = r(t) - y(t), \quad e, \, r \in R^m \quad (3)$$
$$u(t) = -Ke(t) \quad (4)$$

where y, r and e are the controlled, reference and error signal vectors, u is the input vector, x the state vector and A, B, H and K are real matrices of appropriate dimension. Unfortunately, this requires accurate estimation of all states to achieve the best control, and is often highly sensitive to structural and parametric uncertainty: Basic assumptions such as plant linearity, model structure and parameters, rarely hold for any length of time, and changes in operating level, load or disturbances invalidate the design, with consequent loss in accuracy and integrity, often resulting in instability. Since this affects other parts of large-scale control schemes through interacting paths, the global effect of a single controller deterioration may have far-reaching consequences for safety.

Various approaches to the problem have been investigated, including self-tuning regulation and robust linear design. The former has encountered problems with stability, whilst the latter tends to result in conservative (inaccurate) controls. In contrast, this paper proposes a discontinuous control strategy of variable structure (VS) in which K is switched according to the control law

$$u(t) = -Kx(t) = -(K_o + dK)x(t) \qquad (5)$$

where dK is a matrix of discontinuous incremental gains and K_o is a constant gain component (Itkis, 1976; Utkin, 1976). The gains are chosen to ensure that the state trajectory x(t) moves towards a set of hyperplanes s_i passing through the origin of the state space defined by the vector

$$s = Cx(t), \ s \in R^{n-m} \qquad (6)$$

where C is a real, constant matrix. When the state trajectory hits a hyperplane, it can be forced to slide along it and eventually move along the intersection of the planes towards the set-point. The reachability and hitting the hyperplane are both guaranteed if

$$K_{ij} = \begin{cases} F_{ij} & \text{if } s_i^T x_j(t) > 0 \\ G_{ij} & \text{if } s_i^T x_j(t) \leq 0 \end{cases} \qquad (7)$$

for all i, j and the required F and G parameters are easily computed (Gough and coworkers, 1972, 1982, 1984). Furthermore, the system in sliding mode behaves as if it has the equivalent continuous control

$$u_{eq}(t) = -(CB)^{-1}CAx(t) \qquad (8)$$

and the reduced-order dynamic model

$$\dot{x}(t) = [I - B(CB)^{-1}C]Ax(t) = A_{eq}x(t) \qquad (9)$$

It is known that the stability of the sliding mode is ensured provided that all eigenvalues of A_{eq} have negative real part. Furthermore, using projector theory, it can be shown that the projector $B(CB)^{-1}C$ has a range equivalent to the range of B, which is equivalent to the null space of its complement (El-Ghezawi, Zinober and Billings, 1983; White, 1986). Hence any disturbance vector in the range of B is assigned to the null space of the sliding mode, and therefore does not affect it. In particular, if the system model

is expressed in a canonical (Companion) form, then the sliding mode is completely insensitive to variations such as changes in A or B (Draxenovic, 1969). Furthermore, under fairly mild conditions, the system is still insensitive if implemented as a sampled-data (computer) control (Opitz, 1986). Thus the robustness properties of VS control make it ideally suited to the requirement of maintaining a stable and accurate tracking control, despite modelling errors and plant variations that inevitably arise in practice.

Various strategies for designing suitable hyperplanes have been reviewed by Gough and coworkers (1989), including eigenvalue-eigenvector assignment (Dorling and Zinober, 1986) and minimisation a quadratic performance index of the form:

$$J = 1/2 \int_0^t (x^T Qx + u^T Ru)dt \qquad (10)$$

where real weighting matrices Q and R are chosen to place emphasis on certain states and control signals. However, because of the difficulty of visualising hyperplanes, choosing meaningful specifications, and ensuring that the sliding conditions are not violated, it may be reasonably concluded that the MIMO VS design and implementation would be unacceptably complex in industrial practice. VS controls are more likely to be used if there is a simplified methodology based on a single hyperplane.

DECENTRALIZED CONTROL STRATEGY

Variable-structure control may be applied more easily if the problem is viewed as a large-scale, decentralized control application (Khurana and coworkers, 1986; Mathews and deCarlo, 1988). In this work, we replace the multivariable model by the decomposition proposed by Siljak and Sundareshan (1976):

$$\dot{x}(t) = Ax(t) + Bu(t) + Hx(t) \qquad (11)$$

$$A = diag(A_1, \ldots, A_m), \ B = diag(B_1, \ldots, B_m)$$

$$H = diag(H_1, \ldots, H_m) \text{ and } u = u^\ell + u^g$$

where the superscripts ℓ, g denote "local" and "global" respectively. The ith local subsystem is then of the form

$$\dot{x}_i = A_i x_i + B_i u_i^\ell + B_i u_i^g + H_i x \qquad (12)$$

and ignoring the interactions, this becomes the simple decentralized (SISO) VS control problem

$$\dot{x}_i = A_i x_i + B_i u_i^\ell, \ u_i^\ell = -K_i x_i \qquad (13)$$

It is now easier to design and visualise the hyperplane. Each control loop is assigned a dedicated VS controller, designed to be robust in the face of local variations using the algorithm (Gough and Ismail, 1972)

$$\text{if } x_i Cx < 0 \text{ then} K_i > (A^T C)_i / BC$$

$$\text{else } K_i < (A^T C)_i / BC \qquad (14)$$

40

TWO-LEVEL COORDINATING CONTROL

If the neglected interacting terms in (12) are strong, the accuracy of the local control will be reduced and it becomes necessary to introduce a global control u_i^g into each loop to ensure that

$$B_i u_i^g + H_i x = 0 \qquad (15)$$

Hence, using the generalised inverse,

$$\begin{aligned} u_i^g &= -(B^T B)_i^T B_i^T H_i x \\ \text{or} \quad u_i^g &= -B_i^{-1} H_i x \end{aligned} \qquad (16)$$

if B is square and non-singular. Note that (16) requires the use of the full state vector and hence its implementation may be an excessive transmission and computational burden. In practice however, an approximation to (16), such as a steady-state version, will help to reduce overheads and ameliorate the effect of interaction to some extent. Furthermore, transmitting information about local states to the supervisory computer is not essential, since knowledge of the control signals u_i and outputs y_i is sufficient to allow reconstruction the state vector. Since this machine has greater power and requires the information in any case, in order to compute the performance criterion (10), the additional computational burden is not unreasonable. Thus, a two-level coordinating control is proposed that requires transmission of local control signals and outputs to the supervisory machine, and global control signals to the microcomputers.

Finally, we note that implementation of the coordinating control must not violate local controller integrity. Fortunately, because of the robustness properties of each local VS controller, good design should ensure that bounded errors in the global controls will not compromise this. A practical safeguard would require the supervisory machine to check this before switching to global coordination.

VARIABLE-STRUCTURE MICROCONTROLLER

The proposed microcontroller is connected to an appropriate sensor, an actuator and a suitable data highway. It operates in a discrete mode by sampling and converting the measured variable $y_i(k)$ at instant k with a sampling period T. Thus equations (1-16) should now be interpreted in a discrete state framework. The controller estimates the states, computes the gain of the required local control signal $u_i^\ell(k)$ using a discrete scalar version of (7) and sends it via a convertor and hold to the actuator.

On initialization, the discrete model parameters for A, B, K_o, dK, the local set-point $r_i(0)$ and the global control $u_i^g(0)$ are downloaded to the microcontroller via the highway. The first component of the error signal $e(0) = r_i(0) - y_i(0)$ is then determined using state x_1 only, giving rise initially to output control only. At this stage it is important to ensure that the

state trajectory, based on incomplete state information, is directed towards a hyperplane to ensure hitting. However, as k evolves, a simplified observer is used to build up the state estimates, including those of the sensor and actuator, thus providing full VS control without additional intervention:

$$x(k+1) = A^* x(k) + B^* u^*(k) \qquad (17)$$

where $A^* = A - K_e H$, $B^* = (K_e|B)$ and $u^{*T} = (y^T|u^T)$. It is well known that suitable choice of the observer gain matrix K_e, such that the eigenvalues of A^* are within the unit disc, will give asymptotic convergence of the state estimates. The procedure for implementing a 5th-order observer comprising a second-order disturbance model, second-order time delay and convertor integration has been described previously (Halang, Gough and Srai, 1991) and is not repeated here.

In addition, the microcontroller sends the measured variable $y_i(k)$ and local control signal $u_i^\ell(k)$ to a supervisory computer via a bidirectional UART and data highway. The higher-level machine then reconstructs the state vector, computes the global control signals using (16), and downloads them to the microcontrollers. The global coordinator may also be assigned the task of computing the performance measure (10) on a local and global basis, determining optimal hyperplanes, and updating the microcontroller parameters in the event of changes in operating level etc.

IMPLEMENTATION

The general-purpose SISO VS microcontroller is to be implemented using a dedicated chip. Because only simple arithmetic and if-statements are required, a RISC architecture is adopted which has only six instructions (load and store, two floating-point arithmetic operations, and two comparison operations with implied branching). Since the chosen state formulation has sparse matrices, matrix multiplication is performed as a linear code sequence which eliminates all superfluous multiplications by zero. Looping and subroutine linking are also avoided and only floating-point numbers are stored in RAM. The architecture provides a CPU, program address counter, an accumulator for 32 bit wide floating-point operations, a 116-word program ROM for 9-bit words (addressed by 7 bits) and a 43-word RAM for 32 bit data (addressed by 6 bits). A timer is derived from the system clock. The concept of memory mapping was applied in order to simplify the instruction set.

The chip specification has fully integrated peripherals, including an integrating ADC based on counting impulses from a voltage-to-frequency convertor (Halang, 1987), and a DAC. 20 bits are provided in the counter, the remaining 12 bits of the memory-mapped register being hardwired to a constant. Conversion from binary to floating point is then performed using only one floating point subtraction. The integration time is chosen to be equal to one program cycle length, yielding optimal smoothing and noise supression, even at fast sampling rates. The chip is interfaced using a standard V24 connector.

Since the communication requirements are modest, elaborate protocols can be avoided by using asynchronous data transmission, and hence a fully-integrated bidirectional UART is included for inter-processor communication, using an appropriate subset of the RS-232C standard. Data are received in units of 4 bits. For output, each 4-bit group is expanded into ASCII code words, setting the three most significant bits to 011 and adding a parity bit. Serial output operation commences when data has been written from the accumulator to its memory-mapped register following a store instruction.

Initialization of the chip is implemented as a 4-state machine: After power is attached, data is expected from the UART. On receipt of 8-bit ASCII characters the upper three bits and parity are discarded, the remaining 4 bits are placed in the memory mapped output register, and a flag is set. The register is then read out and its contents transferred to RAM location 0. This repeats until 43 locations are filled, thus providing the initial values for the calculation. On receipt of the next string of 8 characters, the program counter is set to zero, the ADC and DAC convertors are enabled with counter reset to zero, and the timer is started. ADC impulses are counted until the timer marks the end of the first cycle, when the output is latched and the counters reset. Program execution commences and is suspended on completion. A check is then made for overflow of a modulo 116 counter, which indicates the next cycle is due and automatically transfers progam control to the beginning of the routine. Further details were given previously by Halang, Gough and Srai (1991).

The VS chip is required to update the control signal u in real time using an assembler routine based on the program given below. Arguments passed to the program correspond to parameters required by the observer-controller chip. To ensure the integrity of the system, we concentrate here on verification of the control program.

FORMAL CORRECTNESS PROOF

To prove the correctness of the variable-structure control algorithm considered in this paper, we make use of Hoare-triples having the form $\{ P \} \ S \ \{ Q \}$ where S is a statement with predicate P as its precondition and predicate Q as its post-condition. When knowing the pre- and the post-conditions, statement S can be formally proven correct by applying the predicate calculus of Dijkstra and Feijen (1984).

For the proof, we depart from a transformed version of our algorithm, which was modified to yield higher efficiency:

```
procedure designu (A:mat; b,c,dk,x:vec);
var i : integer; bdotc : real;
```

```
begin { PRE }
  i:=1; u:=0; bdotc:=dot(b,c);
  { P }
  if dot(c,x) * bdotc < 0
    then while i ≤ N do { INV1 ∧ i ≤ N }
    begin
      if x[i] < 0
        then u:=u + (dot(A[i],c)/bdotc + dk[i]) * x[i]
        else u:=u + (dot(A[i],c)/bdotc − dk[i]) * x[i];
      i:= i + 1
    end
    else while i ≤ N do { INV2 ∧ i ≤ N }
    begin
      if x[i] < 0
        then u: = u + (dot(A[i],c)/bdotc − dk[i]) * x[i]
        else u: = u + (dot(A[i],c)/bdotc + dk[i]) * x[i];
      i: = i + 1
    end
end { POST };
```

Since there is a division by $b \cdot c$, this expression may not be zero. We exclude the possibility that $x[j] * c \cdot x$ vanishes, because $k[j]$ is then not defined. Finally, N must be greater than zero for the calculation to be not empty. Hence, the pre-condition reads as:

$PRE \equiv$
$(\forall j : 0 < j \leq N : c \cdot x * x[j] \neq 0)$
$\wedge (\forall j : 0 < j \leq N : dk[j] > 0)$
$\wedge b \cdot c \neq 0$
$\wedge N > 0$

The program should accomplish the correct calculation of the vector u according to the given conditions on the model's sliding mode. So the post-condition should read:

$POST \equiv$
$((c \cdot x * b \cdot c < 0 \wedge u = (\sum j : 0 < j < N+1 \wedge x[j] < 0$
$: ((A^T c)_j / b \cdot c + dk[j]) * x[j])$
$+ (\sum j : 0 < j < N + 1 \wedge x[j] > 0$
$: ((A^T c)_j / b \cdot c − dk[j]) * x[j]))$
$\vee (c \cdot x * b \cdot c > 0 \wedge u = (\sum j : 0 < j < N+1 \wedge x[j] < 0$
$: ((A^T c)_j / b \cdot c − dk[j]) * x[j])$
$+ (\sum j : 0 < j < N + 1 \wedge x[j] > 0$
$: ((A^T c)_j / b \cdot c + dk[j]) * x[j])))$
$\wedge bdotc = b \cdot c \wedge$

From this post-condition, the following invariants can be derived:
$INV1 \equiv$
$c \cdot x * b \cdot c < 0$
$\wedge u = (\sum j : 0 < j < i \wedge x[j] < 0$
$: ((A^T c)_j / b \cdot c + dk[j]) * x[j])$
$+ (\sum j : 0 < j < i \wedge x[j] > 0$
$: ((A^T c)_j / b \cdot c − dk[j]) * x[j])$
$\wedge 0 < i \leq N + 1$
$\wedge bdotc = b \cdot c$
$\wedge (\forall j : 0 < j \leq N : dk[j] > 0 \wedge x[j] \neq 0)$

$INV2 \equiv$
$c \cdot x * b \cdot c > 0$
$\wedge u = (\sum j: 0 < j < i \wedge x[j] < 0$
$: ((A^T c)_j / b \cdot c − dk[j]) * x[j])$

42

$+ (\sum j : 0 < j < i \wedge x[j] > 0$
$: ((A^T c)_j / b \cdot c + dk[j]) * x[j])$
$\wedge 0 < i \leq N+1$
$\wedge \; bdotc = b \cdot c$
$\wedge (\forall j : 0 < j \leq N : dk[j] > 0 \wedge x[j] \neq 0)$
In both repetitions, we choose the variant function to be: $vf = N+1-i$.

In order to prove the program's correctness, a condition will be derived that holds before the outer if-statement. Consequently, this will result in the proof of this if-statement's correctness consisting of the following two parts:

```
{ P ∧ dot(c,x) * bdotc < 0 }
while i ≤ N do { INV1 ∧ i ≤ N }
begin if x[i] < 0
then u:=u + (dot(A[i],c)/bdotc + dk[i]) * x[i]
else u:=u + (dot(A[i],c)/bdotc - dk[i]) * x[i];
i:=i+1
end
{ POST }
```

The proof of the first while-loop's correctness consists of four parts:
a. $P \wedge dot(c,x) * bdotc < 0 \Rightarrow INV1$
b. `{ INV1 ∧ i ≤ N ∧ vf=VF }`
   ```
   if x[i]<0
   then u:=u + (dot(A[i],c)/bdotc + dk[i]) * x[i]
   else u:=u + (dot(A[i],c)/bdotc - dk[i]) * x[i];
   i:=i+1
   { INV1 ∧ vf<VF }
   ```
c. $INV1 \wedge i \leq N \Rightarrow vf \geq 0$
d. $INV1 \wedge \neg (i \leq N) \Rightarrow POST$

```
{ P ∧ dot(c,x) * bdotc ≥ 0 }
while i ≤ N do { INV2 ∧ i ≤ N }
begin if x[i]<0
then u:=u + (dot(A[i],c)/bdotc - dk[i]) * x[i]
else u:=u + (dot(A[i],c)/bdotc + dk[i]) * x[i];
end
{ POST }
```

Also the proof of the second while-loop's correctness consists of four parts:
e. $P \wedge dot(c,x) * bdotc \geq 0 \Rightarrow INV2$
f. `{ INV2 ∧ i ≤ N ∧ vf=VF }`
   ```
   if x[i]<0
   then u:=u + (dot(A[i],c)/bdotc - dk[i]) * x[i]
   else u:=u + (dot(A[i],c)/bdotc + dk[i]) * x[i];
   i:=i+1
   { INV2 ∧ vf<VF }
   ```
g. $INV2 \wedge i \leq N \Rightarrow vf \geq 0$
h. $INV2 \wedge \neg (i \leq N) \Rightarrow POST$

Parts *a* and *e* in this proof represent a deduction of P. Having established the validity of the predicates *a* through *h*, the proof reduces to show that it holds:

`{ PRE } i:=1; u:=0; bdotc:=dot(b,c) { P }`

The proof is rather lengthy and has to be omitted here for lack of space. For full details we refer to Gerlach and Frauenfelder (1992).

DISCUSSION AND CONCLUSION

A design has been given for a general-purpose, low-cost decentralized VS controller implemented on a single chip using a simple RISC architecture. Only 1376 bits of RAM and 1071 bits of ROM need to be accommodated, enabling high-speed realization using a gate array with only several thousand gates. Such chips could be realized in 2 micrometer CMOS technology featuring low power consumption, battery back-up supply, and high reliability in rugged environments (high temperature, radiation). It is thus feasible to package them with sensors and include fibre optic transmission, virtually eliminating signal transmission problems.

For application in safety-related environments, the controller must be highly dependable. Therefore, its software may not contain any errors which, for software, are inherently design errors with a permanently latent presence. Accordingly, we subjected our variable-structure control algorithm to a formal correctness proof method, viz., predicate calculus. For a subroutine of the considered size, the method turned out to be feasible. It is questionable, however, whether much larger programs can be verified in the same way, because of the effort necessary and due to the fact that the rather lengthy proof process is quite error-prone in itself.

It is envisaged that in many applications where feedback loop dynamic interactions are small, the microcontroller may be used in a stand-alone configuration, initialized and tested using a portable programming device connected to the serial port. The controller can compensate for sensor time-delay and model disturbance dynamics. By virtue of the formally-verified program and the robustness of the control algorithm, once set-up correctly, the device should give safe operation under normal operating conditions, even in the face of considerable uncertainty. Clearly, the integrity of the control cannot be guaranteed under adverse conditions: On initialization, or when large changes in set-point or operating level arise, control of the initial trajectory before sliding mode is reached lacks robustness. However, since these large changes can either be anticipated in advance, or are detectable, careful external monitoring could diagnose the problem in safety-critical applications. In addition, it should be noted that although large sampling periods and pure time delays in a loop do not invalidate the proposed VS design, the consequent "spreading out" of the sliding region reduces the accuracy of control attainable.

In practice, due to the advisability of monitoring loop performance for reasons of safety, the microcontroller capability has been extended by providing a data link to a supervisory computer. In addition to facilitating algorithm design and parameter down-loading capability, the supervisory computer can also compensate for interactions between loops using the two-level coordinating algorithm decribed here. Again, although the robustness properties of the sliding modes can accommodate global bounded uncertainties, adverse conditions are possible that could violate the sliding mode. For example, incorrect computation of the coordinating control could compromise the safety of the local controls. Thus it is recommended that the global control signals are constrained in terms of allowable magnitude and rate of change. It should also be stressed that the integrity of the entire system requires that the local controls should remain stable in the event of a loop failure i.e. the plants under consideration should be open-loop stable.

The communication requirements for global coordination are relatively modest and could be handled by any appropriate LAN. However, in view of recent developments in standardization of digital communications for instrumentation, it is expected that the coordinated system could be enhanced by implementing either the 39 kbit/s Fielbus/H1 or 1 Mbit/s Fieldbus/H2 standards (Lindner, 1990). In the past, VS control has been applied to diverse systems, such as manoeverability control of spacecraft and VSTOL aircraft, interconnected syncronous machines and robotics. Fabrication of a robust microcontroller chip could be expected to result in decentralized control applications in chemical and pertroleum industries. It would also be applicable to SCADA applications and has been tested successfully in the simulation of building energy control, and river pollution control in which in-stream biochemical oxygen demand and dissolved oxygen are regulated in separate reaches of a river (Gough and coworkers, 1988, 1992).

ACKNOWLEDGEMENT

The authors would like to thank NATO for a grant in support of this work.

REFERENCES

Burd, N.C. and Dorey, A.P.(1984). Intelligent transducers. *J. Micrcomputer Appl.*, 7, 87-97.

Dijkstra, E.W., and W.H.J. Feijen (1984). *Een methode van programmeren*. Academic Service, The Hague.

Dorling, C.M. and Zinober, A.S.I. (1986). Two approaches to hyperplane design in multivariable variable-structure control systems. *Int. J. Control*, 44, 1, 65-82.

Draxenovic, B. (1969). The invariance conditions in variable structure systems. *Automatica*, 5, 3, 287-295.

El-Ghezawi, O.M.E., Zinober, A.S.I. and Billings, S.A. (1983). Analysis and design of variable-structure systems using a geometric approach. *Int. J. Control*, 38, 3, 657-671.

Gerlach, J., and S. Frauenfelder (1992). *Formal correctness proof of a variable-structure control algorithm*. Internal report, Department of Computing Science, University of Groningen.

Gough, N.E. and Ismail, Z.M. (1972). Computer-aided design of variable-structure control systems. *Int. J. Control and Computers*, 10, 3, 71-75.

Gough, N.E. and Ismail, Z.M. (1982). Computer-aided design of multivariable variable structure control systems. *Proc. IASTED Conf. on Control Systems*, Paris.

Gough, N.E., Ismail, Z.M. and King, R.E. (1984). Analysis of variable structure systems with sliding modes. *Int. J. Sys. Sci.*, 15, 4, 401-409.

Gough, N.E., Leach, M.J. and Srai, M.S. (1988). Use of variable structure controls in energy management. *Proc. Sixth Int. Conf. on Systems Eng.*, Coventry Polytechnic, UK.

Gough, N.E., Dimirovski, G.M., Srai, M.S. and Icev, Z.A. (1989). A survey of variable structure control systems. *Proc. ETAI'89 Conf.*, Ohrid YU.

Gough, N.E., Dimirovski, G.M., Abul-Huda, B. and Srai, M.S. (1992). Application of decentralized variable-structure techniques to river pollution control. *Int. J. Control and Computers* (in press).

Halang, W.A. (1987). A voltage-to-frequency convertor design without inherent linearity error suitatble for bipolar operation. *Computer Standards and Interfaces*, 6, 221-224.

Halang, W., Gough, N.E. and Srai, M.S., (1991). Single-chip implementation of a real-time variable structure controller. *Proc. 1st IFAC Workshop on Algorithms and Architectures for Real-Time Control*, Bangor, U.K.

Itkis, U. (1976). *Control Systems of Variable Structure*. New-York: Wiley.

Khurana, H., Ahson, S.I. and Lamba, S.S. (1986). Variable-structure control system design for large scale systems. *IEEE Trans. on Sys. Man and Cybern.*, 16, 4, 573-576.

Lindner, K.-P. (1990). Fieldbus - a milestone in field instrumentation technology. *Measurement and Control*, Vol.23, 272-277.

Matthews, G.P and deCarlo, R.A. (1988). Decentralized tracking for a class of interconnected nonlinear systems using variable structure control. *Automatica*, 24, 2, 187-193.

Opitz, H.-P. (1986). Robustness properties of discrete-variable structure controllers. *Int. J. Control*, 43, 3, 1003-1014.

Siljak, D.D. and Sundareshan, M.K. (1976). A multilevel optimisation of large-scale dynamic systems. *IEEE Trans. on Autom. Control*, AC-21, 79-84.

Utkin, I.V. (1976). *Control Systems of Variable Structure*, Toronto: Wiley and Sons.

White, B.A. (1986). Range-space dynamics of scalar variable-structure control systems. *Proc. IEE*, 133, Pt.D, 1, 35-41.

A VIEW on COMPUTER SYSTEMS and their RELIABILITY in JAPAN

Takeshi Natsume   IBM Japan Ltd., System Quality Center,   JAPAN

Yoshiko Hasegawa   Furukawa INFOTECH Ltd.   Planning,   JAPAN

Astruct. Tremendous growth of computer systems application for any industries is still continuing and these systems are migrating as a key function within public, or generic, or national service area - that is banking on lines sytem, transportation system, global network systems, information service system in governments and performance enhancements in industries are also developing and examining. Despite of these business and technical trend, which means these system configuration including hardware and software with special maintenance and its support, are becoming so much complexity beyond power of human management some estimations and requirements as for safety of computers systems are not emphasized in contractions, introduction of the system, and system design also exception of special applications. Social impacts, confusion, and loss are easily assumed in such environment when systems are failed to performed with duration for system recovery. Here typical systems in Japanese industries are described from the view points of system performance and system failures through last several years and majority. Issues on system dependability and safety are discussed through these data and authors' experience.

Keyword. system down; system dependability; system safety; social impact; Quality management system; system quality of service; configurations; configuration management;

1. General view of computer systems in Japan

11. Information based on survey data   By the Minister of International Trade and Industry in Japan (MITI), we can recognize tremendous growth in computer application in current Japanese industry such indexes as follows: - Computer system installation rate: investment cost per employees - Software implementation rate : purchased cost per employees - Communication network system popularization rate : investment cost per employees - Growth of on-line terminals for the governments administration - Growth of on-line terminals for the local administration. Refer to FIG 1. to FIG 6.

12. The government treatment   The government has many strategic action plans for promotion of computer industries in Japan through the year. Two of them are pointed out as significant factors for the sound growth of Japanese computer industries from a view point of reliability and maintainability, and safety, that is, 1) Guideline on Safety and its counter measures of computer systems in 1977 and revised in 1984. Here safety was defined as, Disaster from natural incident, system failure caused by configured components, procedural violation of operations, failed operations, scattered lost alter and disrupt of data, - To prevent these factors and to minimize the effect by these factors on cost and rapid action for recovery time of system and here term system noted here is include configured all hardware software components, network sub-system, I/O equipments and their facilities. and the guideline also affected the area of power facilities, computer rooms and its conditions, data facilities, air conditioning facilities, and procedures for system operations. The other one is an act of special industrial promotion programme in 1978. Aid for the programme was offered around 60 billion yen at that time currency through 5 years. The remarkable mention of the act is that reliability objectives by equipments are addressed for new developed computer

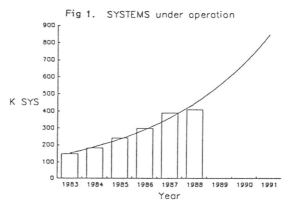

Fig 1.   SYSTEMS under operation

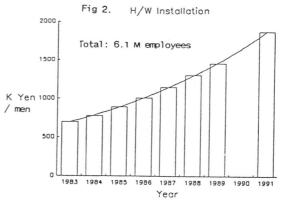

Fig 2.   H/W Installation

Total: 6.1 M employees

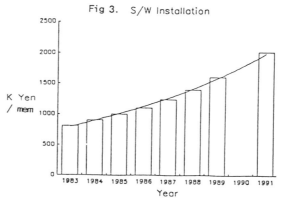

Fig 3.   S/W Installation

machines as return for this aids such as MTBF of DISK
Drive having memory capacity of 10MB must be more than
2k hrs, one of magnetic tape drivers must be more than
1.8k hrs, and failure rate of CPU itself per a gate
must be less than 5 FIT and MTBF of office computer
system must be more than 8k hrs and so on.

We can believe such public objectives for reliability
of computer systems and their equipments and
facilities promoted effectively growth of computer
engineering and its techniques, and business itself.
This is a typical Japanese way for management of
promotion programme which is not yet documented but
effectively functioning way for the natives in time
being. That means integrated harmonized managements
system for the projects which is consisted on soft
management by governments or an equivalent group,
median management by industrial groups, and severe
management and control for process.

13. The committee for safety technology of computer
systems   Additionally MITI was sponsored the
committee for safety technology of computer systems
which had aimed to develop generic guidelines for the
industries for six years since 1981. Annual technical
reports are available as study results of task teams
which consist of professors form University, system
engineers or equivalent from major computer
manufacturers, ones from typical representative user
of conputer system. Standardization of this guideline
as JIS, a national standard failed but these reports
for six years were remained results as useful and
valuable references which was reflecting state of the
arts as is.

2. Dependability and system performance

21. Definition of dependability and complexity
IEC/TC56 (International Electrotechnical Commutations
No. 56 - Titled Reliability and Maintainability) was
renamed as DEPENDABILITY in 1990. That phenomena
looks like reflecting technical trend of worldwide
industries' growth on significant complexity of
computer systems and/or world wide network system.
When we consider such complex systems which are
dependable by other components' factors of the system
due to beyond the managements power by current the
most possible technical skills, this term is useful
and cute but no any needless term for traditional
reliability engineers such as components. Careful use
is requesting for this term for eliminating confusion
and loss by using it. Here Dependability is used by
definition of IEC/TC55 glossary IEC50 (191) despite of
reliability and maintainability as : Collective
term used to describe the availability performance and
its influencing factors - reliability performance,
maintainability and maintenance support performance.
For better understanding of this term, we shall
introduce the concept of Quality of Service based on
carrying out of objective mission of the system as a
subject or as an item.

22. Definition of safety performance
Additionally a term of SAFETY is also used as related
concept of dependability as follows; characteristics
of a system on freedom against danger, injury and

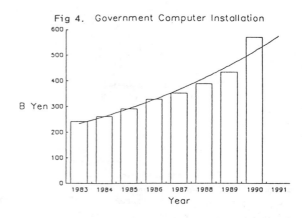

Fig 4. Government Computer Installation

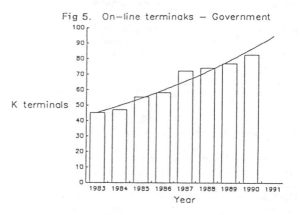

Fig 5. On-line terminaks – Government

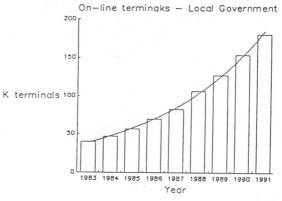

On-line terminaks – Local Government

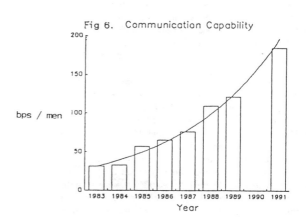

Fig 6. Communication Capability

damage by natural incidents and loss by dependability, and data loss and security for data/information, dependability by faulty operations and maintenance activities under defined maintenance support. Accordingly we can use distingushly these terms as different level of concept as SAFETY ⊇ DEPENDABILITY for items of repairable system ⊇ RELIABILITY for items non-repairable system.

3. Typical system configuration and maintenance supports

31. Averaged large computer system For conveniences of statistics of computer systems, classification of somputer systems is done by investment costs as
- Large system   (L)   more   than   250M¥
- Middle system (M)   250N¥   to   100M¥
- Small system   (S)   100M¥   to   40M¥
- Work station   (W)   Less than   40M¥

Ratio by latest average share of investment by year is L:M:S:W = 1:2:6:61. The latest business size is about 2.7k systems for L in total and also about 1000 billion yen for L installation cost.

32. A model of integration system and complexity There are major eight on-line banking systems which are typical stable complexity in Japanese banking industry. These average sizes of complexity are shown with estimation as,

H/W components
  4xCPU + 600xDISK drive + 8xCCP + 3500xterminals
    + 6xI/O + 2xCVCF
  note: CPU (Central processing Unit)
      CCP (Communication controller products)
      CVCF (Constant voltage constant frequency
          controller)

S/W components
  Typical configuration is as follows;
MVS, VM, IMS, NETVIEW, VTAM, NCP, JCCP, SAIL, DB2, TIMES, TSO, MERVA, user application programs (20k programms) - 12PPs + APs

around total 9MLOC + 2GB address space + 16TB data space

Such complexity looks like an alive organized body by factors as; - Many engineering changes are applying through life - System configuration is continuously changing - Components of the system are replaced and reallocated by time and by case - Daily modification and enhancements for user applications - Daily S/W maintenance activities - correction and modification - Death and Birth phenomena on bugs within software integration - Sudden faulty operation or natural disaster - Rare Criminal data damage due to system down - system down by dependable factors which are not able to manage for prevention such disasters as public power supply system down, communication line incidents, and unexpected noises or unknown factors against stable system operations, and unbelievable down of fault tolerant system.   Refer to FIG 7.

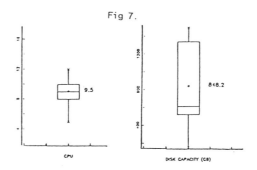

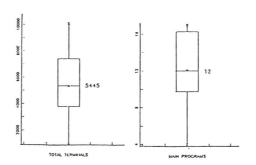

Fig 7.

4. Status of computer system down - system dependability
Information through mass media from such as journals, newspapers, amd engineering news and papers are not intensive reports on facts as same as intangible information with their sensitivities through experience, but it may not be introspective to assume that these facts are reflecting technical trend or engineering level like a sampling of facts or phenomena based on the facts.

41. Data from journal
Nikkei COMPUTER, this is one of major journal of computer industries in Japan is continuing special note on failed case study of system installation and system down in Japanese industries since 1981. By the intangible data from these note, we can see the facts that faulty and defective incidents are repeated through the year. No any facts on time dependent factors are found through the data. Major reasons can be shown as follows; - The business such as system integration, and its development and introduction are not mature to manage by contract between suppliers and purchasers.   - No adequate engineering methods and technical support tools are provided for such developments at current technical level and business environments.   - Definition of requirements for systems integration such as system complexity looks like not to be able to develop by suppliers by themselves and also purchasers. - Defects from human factors are also introduced by combinations of multiple products and/or project which are controlling under different management system with their style.

It is considerable that major detractors of these situation are to introduce uncontrollable small softhouses for cost reduction and to have system declaring that are not matured for operation and also technical viewpoint for saving workload of genuine systems engineers. This may be unavoidable business requirements for forcing to accept for business growth and needs. - Moreover these situation, documentation and authorization under formalized management systems are not established yet as a common management tools for such complexity.

42. Data from others survey
The latest survey data from 1992 Computer Report expresses a view of status of performance of average computer system in Japan industry ; 87% of total computer systems have experience of system failures or trouble and area of that majors causes are reported as follows; Hardwares, Software, User application, Operation, change of configuration and so on.
The other survey report from banking industries association are shown as; System down and major causes. Refer to FIG 8.

43. Data through experience in computer manufacturers
Toward significant progress of computer technologies, and software applications, system dependability are keeping also to continuous improvements by reducing elments for input/output points by components integrations, and fault tolerance skills and technologies based on cost reduction and combination of high reliability components, that is system failures are also improving from around 0.6/month/system to 0.05 beyond ten years regardless system complexity and technologies.
However area % of causes are almost same as User application programmers are covering around 40% of total failures. Keeping of freedom for design and development of software products are contributing higher productivities and expansion of functions meanwhile complexity of their systems are growing and sometimes beyond the limitation of human management power. Additionally business of systems integration which means combination of many sort of software components designed under different types of quality management system look like to breed potential system failure points. Moreover such complexity are not able to verify by any circumstances in state of the arts. There are no adequate methods for such verification and risk assessment based on sample verification which means just a part of coverage for the mulithread of complexity.

Data through experience in computer users Every user and their experts of the such complex system know well this difficulty and unavoidable behaviors for continuous business requirements, enhancements and modification based on rapid business growth and also undefinable their requirements and they are feeling everytime fear on occurrence of system down and its impacts by unavailability of the system without assurance and/or confidence of system operations.

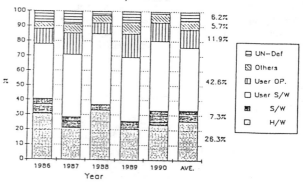

Fig 8. Incidents by cause

Data from in formal system auditing checklist They have system audit and registration system in Japan. Major focusing points in the checklist are reflecting current criticality of the system troubles for normalized prevention of any troubles. In this checklist, proper trouble shooting plan and preventive actions to such foreseened cases are requested to be assessed intensively in system design activities and all systems jointed to the other operations for maintenance as one of criteria of system auditing.

5. Issues on discussion on computer system safety

51. Through actual case   Cost reduction and shortening turn around time of design of a system are business needs for competition in time being. Almost case they don't mention about dependability assessment in design phase and also maintenance phase in any cases. The two discussion points are considered as main detractors in the most worst case ; one is shortage of proper system engineers (SE) in the industries because of unbalance between rapid business enlargements and multiple installation of system, and supply for SE from institutes, the other is growing system integration by connectability and portability between different systems. In the former case, true system requirements and overall system design involving system expansion plan through the years are not definitely specified between supplier and a purchaser and in the condition of such indistinct specification they have started design of the system which are in almost case delivery of the system is concretely fixed by the reason of business. Meanwhile verification and validation for such integration system are not completely executed due to set-up test environments in supplier's facility or equivalents due to much complex system elements which are incorporated by central CUP elements, network subsystem and its equipments, disk memory subsystem, area network workstation terminals, I/O equipments and OS packaging and its utilities, application programmes and so on. Actual environment test and stress tesst for critical load of system may not be impossible for

completely execution. Even if verification test for overall system integration in some proper test coverage are performed, no any confidence by the results of the any tests cannot obtained through test results and estimations. Additionally configuration managements for such different products under different quality managements may be over limitation of human managements that is not found until system clash and affection of business impacts occurred under normal operation as a rare case.

52. Suggestion for future needs There are no typical solution for these issues, which are considered from the viewpoints of difficulty. Through the discussion on such environments and situation of system installation and integration, several solutions to be considered against such technical and economical unmatured conditions are suggested for next steps for our study.

Modelling of typical integration system considering life cycle costing and configuration managements based on assumption of economic growth and expansion of system by defined sizes and changes.

Verification test methods with assessment of optimized system test multipaths.

Modelling of management system for development of the integration system such as suggested system through requirements definition and maintenance/operation process.

And to resolve issues by these suggestions, a task team which are membered by academies, industries and users under the government or international public bodies by that is, soft managements such as sponcer. And here it shall be emphasized for prompt investigation and managemets supports that one of very important points is to own jointly any data and information related to the system integtation through manufacturers and its ownner for recognization and better understanding on the such situation and their issues.

Reference

1. 通産省 告示 602 1978-12-21 情報産業振興
   臨時措置法 － Government act No.602
   Special act for promotion of information
   industries
2. 官報 1981-08-01 コンピュータシステムの安全対策基準の
   改訂について Government news － 1981-08-01
3. MITI コンピュータシステムの高信頼性技術に関する調査研
   究報告書 1987/88/89/90
   Technical report of safety and reliability of
   computer system 1987, 1988, 1989, 1990 by MITI
4. 情報化白書 1988/89/90/91 -日本情報処理開発協会
   White report on computerization － Japan DPE
   development association 1988, 1989, 1990,
   1991, 1992
5. S/W Quality Control － A view of quality control
   and issues for large scale S/W 1989 S/W QC
   special task symposium
6. J C Laprie 1985 Dependable computing and fault
   tolerance
7. IEC/TC56 document 56(S)305 － A new title, a new
   scope, and a strategic policy statement for
   IEC/TC56 1990
8. IEC 50 (IEV191) Terminology 1990-12
9. NIKKEI Computer 1981 － 1992 動かぬコンピュータ
   special note on unoperable computer system
   from 1981 through 1992
10. システム監査基準解説書 － チェックリスト 日本情報処理開発協会
    Reference book on system auditing － Checklist of
    system auditing 1991.

A GENERIC FAILURE MODEL FOR DISTRIBUTED SYSTEMS

Francis Tam and Ranjib Badh

School of Computing
Staffordshire University
Blackheath Lane, Stafford ST18 0AD United Kingdom

JANET: cdtfpt@uk.ac.stafpol.cr83

Abstract This paper discusses the need for classifying failure semantics in distributed systems. It argues that a generic description is essential for the understanding and unification of the varying concepts used. A failure model based on the layering structure is proposed. The architectural framework, failure representation and faults classification for this model are explained. The concepts of Virtual and Actual Failures are introduced and the model's properties are highlighted. Three applications are presented to illustrate its usefulness in supporting the structuring of fault tolerant distributed systems.

Keywords distributed systems, failure model, fault tolerance, reliability, safety

INTRODUCTION

With the advent of computing and communications technology, distributed systems are being deployed in wide ranging applications from provision of general purpose computing environment to sophisticated real time control systems. In most cases, the stringent requirement of maximum reliability, availability, safety and dependability of these systems imply that they have to continue to operate in a 'reasonable' way even if there is a partial failure. The fact that distributed systems are capable of surviving from failures, and any system that can tolerate failures must be distributed, has led to the incorporation of fault tolerance capabilities as a norm rather than exception.

Fault tolerance techniques seek to intervene and defend against faults from causing system failure. A typical fault tolerant system carries out the detection of faults and the recovery to normal operation as internal functions. As such, the representation of faults in a system is fundamentally important. Throughout this paper we do stress that fault tolerance is advocated as a complement to fault avoidance, which attempts to prevent introducing faults into the system in the first place, for constructing a safe and reliable system. Typical fault avoidance techniques are formal methods, quality control and validation. Discussions of these techniques are outside the scope of this paper.

It is observed that the level of fault tolerance requirement relates to factors like the diverse effects of failures, models of fault tolerant computations supported by the underlying hardware, cost and performance of the final system. Without a commonly agreed failure model, it would be difficult, if not impossible to communicate what one has to tolerate! Another observation is that the current development efforts on support for programming distributed fault tolerant applications tend to be too specific and dissimilar. This again boils down to the lack of a common failure model. A case in point is the study of MVS software defects (Sullivan and Chillarege 1991), a specific representation of failure behaviour and classification, and without some basic modification is of little use to other systems.

It is believed that failure manifestation and the cause of them could be represented systematically. This results in a number of well defined failure classes, for example a file server crash, together with the faults that cause such a failure. In this way, precise faults can be specified and appropriate counter actions can be expressed during system development.

DISTRIBUTED SYSTEM STRUCTURE

In practice there are a wide variety of structures and components used in distributed systems. It is therefore impossible to consider all these variations in this paper. Instead, a general and simplified structure based on (Sloman and Kramer 1987) is used to illustrate our ideas.

Figure 1 shows the architectural layers of a distributed system. Notice that the Application Software and Distributed Operating System (DOS) service layers are distributed over all the nodes while the lower layers are local to a station. A brief explanation of each layer's functionality follows:

Application Software

This layer contains the software which provides the services to the end users, for example an electronic fund transfer system. The application is usually decomposed into modules after which they are distributed across the network of computing stations. This layer makes use of the services provided by the DOS underneath.

Distributed Operating System Service

This layer is responsible for coordinating the use of shared resources and to provide system wide services, such as file servers, remote program execution and mailing.

Shared Resource

This layer administers system wide resources, for example files for a mail server.

Local Resource Management

This layer manages resources such as local file system and memory management. Combining services at this layer with the Kernel's form what is known as the traditional centralised operating system.

Station Kernel

A minimum kernel which handles task scheduling, protection and interprocess communications.

Station Hardware

Typical devices such as processors, memory and network interfaces.

Communications System

The communications system is local to each station. It provides the services required for transporting systems and application messages to and from stations. Note that each of the four local layers has access into the communications system which consists of a number of layers itself.

THE MODEL

The failure model is based on the layering concept, which is used by almost all distributed system designs to reduce complexity. A system is partitioned into functional levels. Each level has a few **entities**, that is either a software module or hardware component, which may fail in a certain way. Within each entity there are fault **classes**. Together they form a hierarchical representation of failures in the system as a whole.

Architectural Framework

The failure model, shown in fig. 2, is organised into a set of functional layers, where each layer represents the hardware and/or software services provided by that layer. A layer (N) implements its services by employing the use of a set of services provided to it by a layer (N-1), and in turn, provides its services to a layer (N+1). An interface between the two layers defines the means by which the higher layer uses the services provided by the lower one.

What we obtain in effect is a hierarchically distributed service-user and service-provider model, where an entity providing a layer (N) service is labelled a service-provider and a layer (N+1) entity requiring that service is labelled a service-user, a client of the layer (N) service-provider. Furthermore, the layer (N) service-provider may be a service-user itself, employing the services of service-providers at layer (N-1) to implement its services. Therefore, at one level of abstraction a module may be labelled a service-provider and at another level of abstraction that same module may be labelled a service-user.

Notice that a layer (N) service-provider depends upon the provision of services from layer (N-1) in the provision of its services, which may in turn depend on the services of a layer (N-2) in the provision of its services and so forth up to the atomic layer, the hardware layer.

Representation of Failures

In this model we concentrate on representing the failure of layer entities to provide their services to their clients and on representing the effects these failures exhibit within a system.

A service-provider failure can be formally defined as:

> 'the failure of the service-provider to provide its service to its client in the specified manner'

Two possible causes of a service-provider failure have been identified and represented formally.

A layer (N) service-provider may fail to provide a layer (N) service to a layer (N+1) client due to one of the following two reasons:

i) Due to the failure of a layer (N-1) service-provider to provide it with a service in the specified manner, or

ii) due to a stand alone failure of the layer (N) service provider.

Let us use an application layer module failure as an example to illustrate the representation of failures and the subsequent tracing of their cause.

An application layer module failure occurs when the module fails to provide its client with a specified service in the specified manner. Because the module depends upon the services of a set of DOS layer modules in the provision of its services, which in turn depend upon the services of a set of Shared Resource layer modules in the provision of their services, and so forth, the failure of the module could be the result of the failure to be provided with the required service from one of the DOS layer modules, which could in turn be the result of the failure to be provided with the required service from a Shared Resource layer module and so forth up to the failure of the provision of a hardware layer service.

Alternatively, the application software layer module may have failed as a result of the failure of the internal workings of the module, which has nothing to do with the services the module is being provided by lower layers. Note that the ultimate cause of any failure will be a stand alone service-provider failure, either at the hardware layer or in one of the proceeding layers. However this failure is only observed as a service failure by other modules using it.

The Concept of Virtual and Actual Failures

Within our model we have classified two failure types, Virtual and Actual (or Real) failures, in order to distinguish the representation of the ultimate cause of a failure from the representation of its effects, and to distinguish the faulty service-providers within a system from the non faulty ones.

We will use the simple example depicted in fig. 3 to illustrate the representation of these failure types. The figure shows how a module z at the highest level (level 3) in the systems hierarchy, is dependent upon the service(s) of a module y at level 2 in the provision of its service(s), which in turn is dependent upon the service(s) of module x at the lowest level (level 3) in the provision of its service(s). As a consequence of this dependency relationship the stand alone failure of module x will result in the failure of modules y and z.

When module x fails we give a classification of failures as follows. We say that module x has suf-

fered an Actual Failure, module y has experienced an Actual Service Failure which has led to its Virtual Failure. And we say that module z has experienced a Virtual Service Failure which has led to its Virtual Failure.

Therefore an Actual service-provider failure is observed as an Actual Service failure at the next level of abstraction, and causes a Virtual service-provider failure at that level of abstraction. And a Virtual service-provider failure is observed as a Virtual service failure at the next level of abstraction, and causes a Virtual service-provider failure at that level of abstraction. In effect we obtain two observable failure types, Virtual and Actual Service Failures, and we obtain two service-provider failure types, Actual and Virtual service-provider failures.

In the above scenario the ultimate cause of module z's failure is the stand alone failure of module x, hence its Actual failure classification. While the effects are the failures of modules y and z, hence their Virtual failure classification. And the module which holds the ultimate responsibility for the failure is the one which is classified as being faulty, module x in this case. Although modules y and z have failed they are not classified as being faulty because the only thing stopping them from functioning in their specified manner is their dependency upon the services of modules x and y.

In essence Actual and Virtual failure classifications allow us to distinguish the real failures within a system from their consequences. For example the real failure within the above scenario is the failure of module x and its consequences are the failures of modules y and z.

It is observed that Virtual failures are quite easily recovered from by employing duplicate or alternate services offered by other modules. For example the Virtual failures of modules y and z can be recovered from by simply employing the alternate services offered by module p at level 3, however the actual failure of module x is more complicated to recover from, for example backward error recovery, state restoration and fault treatment may be required.

Failure Propagation and Failure Masking

This very simple yet powerful model presents us with two desirable properties for the representation, communication and control of failures. They are failure propagation and failure masking.

Failure propagation The concept that we have been discussing above is more formally referred to as failure propagation, where the failure of a component residing at a lower layer is propagated to components residing at higher layers, through the dependency relationship.

As a failure is propagated to higher levels of abstraction the failure itself is also abstracted, hence the triangular representation of the failure model.

Failure masking Rather than propagating a failure and its effects we may elect to contain the failure within a layer. In effect we attempt to offer the specified service in the specified manner at all times. This concept is more formally referred to as failure masking.

For example in our model we could mask lower level service-provider failures from higher level ones, by adopting replication and alternate service access strategies. The incorporation of module p into level 3 in the example is entirely the decision of the designer of that layer. Similarly, this philosophy is applied to all other layers within the system.

Classification of Faults

Within each layer, faults characterised by (Ezhilchelvan and Shrivastava 1986) are used for the classification. They consist of:

Timing fault
A component produces a correct result either too early or too late. This is apparently related to the current system loading.

Timely fault
A component produces an incorrect result within the real-time interval.

Omission fault
A component fails to produce a result at all. This could be extended to describe a crash.

Commission fault
A component does not work according to specification. Clearly, it covers the above three types of fault and implies design faults as well.

Given this classification, designer of a component or module can then incorporate counter actions against one or more of these faults at each level, depending on the fault tolerance requirement of the system.

Arriving at a suitable classification of faults is not a trivial task due to its inherent conflicting goals. It is not realistic to specify what component is expected to be used in each level, at best, a possible set of candidates could be listed. This, however, is thought to be too vague and can end up as the initial problem of not having a concrete definition of faults at all. At the other end of the spectrum, one would like the classification as general and flexible as pos-

sible.

The advantage of adopting this classification for each layer is mainly a balanced combination of rigour and flexibility. The secondary benefit comes from its generic characteristics which can be applied to both hardware and software components.

DISCUSSIONS

In this paper, we have taken the fundamental concepts such as service, server and the 'depends' relation (Cristain 1991) further and integrated them into a layered structure. It must be emphasized that the failure model itself does not provide any fault tolerance capabilities, nor does it solve any reliability and availability problems directly. It was developed to provide a framework for the understanding of faults and a better integration of fault tolerance into a distributed system. The model as it stands only contains conceptual description and one of the future investigations would be to formalise these concepts.

In the following sections, three applications of the model are outlined in order to demonstrate its usefulness. Moreover, they form a basis for a qualitative analysis of the model and an indication of some possible future developments.

Testbed for Developing Fault Tolerant Distributed Applications

An integrated development and testbed environment to aid determination of the level of fault tolerance required. The testbed is envisaged to facilitate specification of failure behaviour and responses using the failure model, testing of fault tolerant actions by means of appropriate software fault injection techniques (Barton and colleagues 1990) and evaluation of candidate solutions based on cost and performance. All these services aim to provide a balanced and predictable implementation of the final system.

Safety Critical Systems

The failure model can be turned round and used as a safety framework. Classification of safety level of a system is now possible. As an illustration, the safety level of a system can be specified by stating a certain class(es) of fault in a particular entity at a specific level should not be present. Equally, this framework could be used by safety assessors, in a similar fashion, to verify and subsequently certify a system.

Distributed Programming Language Design

A study conducted by (Badh 1992) on language support for programming fault tolerant distributed systems concluded that existing language tools are either too specific for a particular type of application, or simply inadequate in a certain respect. The languages for this study were chosen in such a way that they establish a combination of application and system programming oriented approaches, as well as similar and distinct syntax. Interested readers are referred to this report for a detailed analysis. As a result, it is believed that development of control structures to express the corresponding fault tolerant actions for those failure classes would be a uniform approach. An analogy in traditional sequential programming is a **while** construct for expressing an **iteration**. Furthermore, these control structures could be implemented as a set of generic primitives, forming a coordination language (Gelernter and Carriero 1992) to any host language, in order to maximise their adaptability in new application domains.

CONCLUSIONS

The proposed failure model attempts to unify the varying concepts used in developing fault tolerant distributed applications, in particular, it forms a framework for the representation, communication and control of failures. The layering structure of this model allows for easy integration of fault tolerance capabilities into existing distributed system designs. The Virtual and Actual failure concepts enable designers to distinguish real failures within a system from their consequences, therefore, facilitating the analysis and subsequent construction of the error detection, damage confinement and assessment, error recovery and fault treatment phases of a fault tolerant system. The model exhibits two desirable properties, namely failure propagation and failure masking, which aid structuring of fault tolerant distributed systems. Applications of this model have been used to illustrate its usefulness. This is an important area of development given that there is an ever increasing demand for reliable, safe and dependable computing systems.

REFERENCES

Badh, R. (1992). Language support for programming fault tolerant distributed systems. *MSc Dissertation*. School of Computing, Staffordshire University.

Barton, J., E. Czeck, Z. Segall and D. Siewiorek (1990). Fault injection experiments using FIAT. *IEEE Transactions on Computers*, Vol C-39 No 4, 575-582.

Cristain, F. (1991). Understanding fault-tolerant distributed systems. *Communications of the ACM*, Vol 34 No 2, 56-78.

Ezhilchelvan, P. and S. Shrivastava (1986). A characterization of faults. *Proceedings of 5th Symposium on Reliability in Distributed Software and Data Base Systems*, 215-222.

Gelernter D. and N. Carriero (1992). Coordination languages and their significance. *Communications of the ACM*. Vol 35 No 2, pp 96-107.

Sloman, M. and J. Kramer (1987). *Distributed Systems and Computer Networks*. Prentice Hall. pp 20-32.

Sullivan, M. and R. Chillarege (1991). Software defects and their impacts on system availability - a study of field failures in operating systems. *Digest of 21st International Symposium on Fault Tolerant Computing*, 2-9.

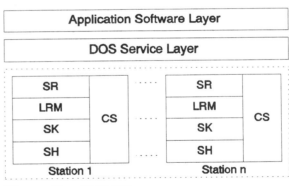

SR:	Shared Resources.
LRM:	Local Resource Management.
SK:	Station Kernel.
SH:	Station Hardware.
CS:	Communications System.

Fig. 1. Architectural layers of a distributed system.

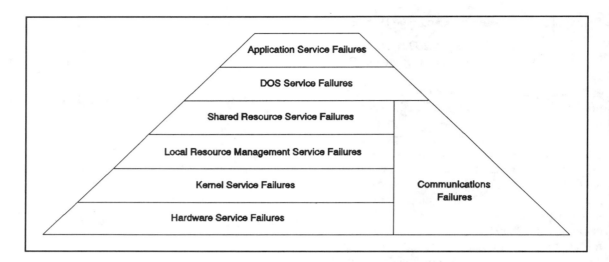

Fig. 2. The failure model.

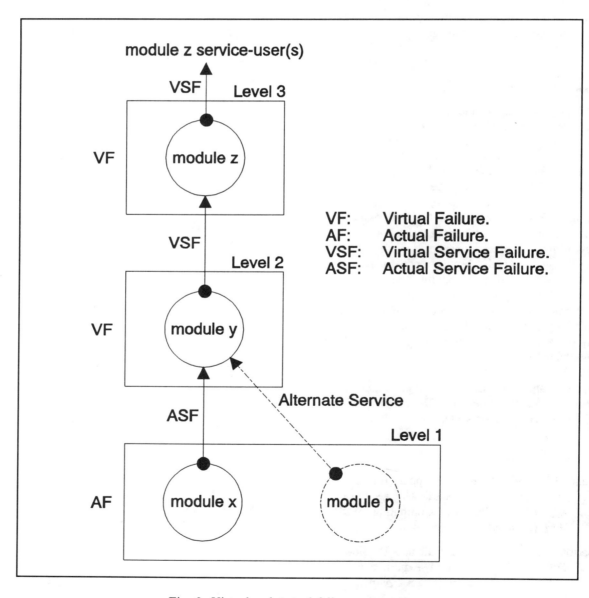

Fig. 3. Virtual and Actual failure propagation.

RECOVERY IN DISTRIBUTED SYSTEMS FROM SOLID FAULTS

Makhlouf ALIOUAT

Computing Science Institute, University of Constantine Route de Ain el Bey 25000 ALGERIA

Abstract. Our study is dealing with recovery processes in a distributed environment in case of solid fault like transient or permanent. The recovery mechanism we presented can be based on one of several strategies (six) where some of them involve saving information messages exchanged between cooperating application processes. This exhaustive number is system-dependant. The strategies are examined with respect to propagation recovery through processes in order to prevent the fastidious well known domino effect problem. The considered framework is a system composed of a set of autonomous physical stations (nodes) having each one a local system; and some of them are predisposed to relay potential failing ones in case of permanent fault. The whole system can still in service until the end of the application; this gives the system a non-stop operating cycle.
A simulation of a fault tolerant mechanism based upon one of the proposed strategies has been experimented, and the obtained results are convincing.

Keywords. recovery, distributed systems, transient permanent fault tolerance, domino effect

I. INTRODUCTION

Meeting requirements of dependability in crucial applications has led to eborate techniques to improve design of fault tolerant systems which can be able to maintain specified services in spite of fault occurrences. The developed techniques can be dedicated to cope with hardware faults, software faults or both. They are essentially based on two fundamental and complementary approaches: - backward error recovery (Anderson,1981; Gregory, 1989;Horning,1974;Kim,1989;Tamir,1991) and - forward error recovery (Campbell,1983; Cristian, 1982;Melliar,1977).

Based on the identification and the accurate knowledge of the error, Forward Error Recovery (FER) copes with the failure in correcting erroneous system state by acting on the damaged part. This action needs beforehand an accurate assessment of damages inflicted to the system. Backward Error Recovery (BER) is independent towards assessment and prediction of damages caused by a fault. It is more general since it does not depend on applications. So, recovery from an error is then accomplished in considering that the corrupted system state cannot be corrected when removing or isolating that error. Then it is more convenient to restore an old state (presumed error free) prior to the fault occurrence from which restarting of the failed system takes place.

Designing a recovery mechanism, particularly in a concurrent processes system, implies to take into account the more complex problem of error propagation resulting from information exchanges between processes. So, if interprocess communications are not well coordinated according to the establishment of recovery points, BER approach can be exposed to an uncontrolled recovery propagation which can degenerate into domino effect (Randell, 1975).

Restarting of distributed applications must take place from a Recovery Line (RL) and the way according to which this RL is determined, constitutes a characteristic of a recovery mechanism. Two policies are usable: (1) Static determination: where the recovery line is established during writting

of programs like in conversation scheme (Randell 1975; Tyrrell,1986) and (2) dynamic determination: where the RL is determined automatically during a recovery operation.

Another characteristic is the relationship existing between application programmer and a recovery mechanism. The latter one can be transparent (Kim, 1990; Tam;1991;Woo,1981) if it is based on BER approach, or entirely integrated into application if it is issued from FER approach. In the latter case, the programmer must take into account the fault tolerance problem when writting his application.

A recovery mechanism is also distinguishable with regard of the fault type which can handle: i.e, can it handle software fault? hardware fault? or both? In case of hardware fault, can it handle transient fault, permanent fault or both? Exception handling and more generally FER approach is dedicated to tolerate essentially software faults, while BER fits as well on software faults as on hardware faults. However, if BER approach is fitting on hardware faults, more particularly in permanent ones, the recovery of these faults always require some redundancy in hardware components. Based on their inherent and intrinsic redundancy and on their large availability, distributed systems provide an appropriate environment to improve capabilities of fault tolerance, and thus are suitable framework to render them non-stop systems.

The aim of the present study consists in processes recovery in distributed environment in case of hardware faults (transient or permanent). Many error recovery strategies based on BER approach are presented. The used framework is a distributed system consisting of a set of Autonomous stations or nodes having every one a local system where interprocess exchanges are message-based. The particularity of this work is: (1) Handling together transient or permanent faults without requiring special architecture unlike for instance in (Kop,1990 Tam,1991). The provided recovery strategies are system level based and may be usable in numerous existing systems with a transparent manner. (2) The perturbations (time overhead resulting from recovery operation are partially avoided by a conservation of information messages (compensation), or completely when (in addition) some easily feasible criteria, which prevent forward propagation (D7) between processes, hold. (3) No constraint on processes communications or recovery points creation is imposed. This total freedom provides an important result of the present proposal which has not gave more attention in other papers, more particularly for preventing the well known domino effect problem. Furthermore, when the recovery blocks scheme is integrated in our strategies, the complexity will be certainly increased, but the resultant recovery mechanism realized will be of general purpose (handling of hardware faults as well as software ones). This combination is actually under study. This paper is organized as follows. After a given set of appropriate definitions in section II, we present, in section III, many basic recovery strategies. Each strategy is studied with regard to system perturbation (overhead) in case of error recovery from transient or permanent fault. In order to get minimal system perturbation values, we combine, in section IV, the positive aspects of basic strategies to form two mixed ones. In section V, we give an unformal strategies comparison, while section VI describes a simple implementation to point out one of mixed strategies feasibility. A conclusion is given in section VII.

II. DEFINITIONS

Before detail of the study, some preliminary definitions (Ali,1985) are needed.

D1: A recovery point (RP) is the moment where the activity of a process is temporarily suspended to save the current state for restoring it later in case of error. The period of activity between two consecutive RP is called the Recovery Region (RR).
Remark: For the sake of implementation each RR can be associated to reception or emission of message(s). So, we need to characterize it as an RR which receives or sends message(s) with an Identifier Receiving Recovery Region (IRRR) or Identifier Emitting Recovery Region (IERR).

D2: An RP is said to be active if it is the most recently established one. We call Restart Recovery Point (RRP), an RP chosen to restart an execution of a process involved in a recovery operation. Let RPi and RPj belong to process Pi, RPi is said to be dominant of RPj if RPi is created before RPj (notation: RPi < RPj).

D3: For every pair (RPp, RPq) of recovery points, such that RPp belongs to process P and RPq to Q, RPp is said to be a Direct Propagator (DP) of RPq (noted RPp -> RPq) if and only if : one message at least flows from the recovery region identified by RPp in P to the recovery region identified by RPq in process Q. Conversely RPq is said to be a Direct Dependent (DD) of RPp. In the same way, RPp is said to be an Indirect Propagator (IP) of RPq (noted RPp-/-> RPq) if and only if: - either RPp is a DP of RPq, - or (recursively), there exists RPs belonging to process S such that: RPp is a DP of RPs and, RPs or any other recovery point of S, successor to RPs, is an IP of RPq. Conversely, RPq is called an Indirect Dependent (ID) of RPp.

D4: A Dependents List (DL) of a process P, is the set of dependents of all RP's belonging to P at instant t. A sub_list of DL associated to a given RP of P is called an Immediate Dependents List (IDL) of that RP. In the same way, the set of DP of all RP's belonging to P is called Propagators List (PL) of P. the DP's of a given RP which belong to P represent an Immediate Propagators List (IPL) of that RP.

D5: A coherent state of a system (or Recovery Line : RL) is a state defined by a set of RP, each one represents a communicating process. They form together a "barrier" which stops any recovery propagation.

D6: A Definite Invocation (DI) of a process is an invocation for a recovery where the called process must roll back to RRP supplied in received invoca-

tion message. As opposed to DI, a Random Invocation (RI) is one where the RRP of the invocated process P is determined in accordance with the RRP of the calling process indicated in received invocation message.

D7: An information message is said to be revoked if it is erroneous, or if it is correct but its use causes problems. A message is said to be indispensable if it is required for a re-execution of the recovered process. A backward propagation is a propagation of recovery generated by a process Pj to reach Pi in order to recreate for Pj at least one indispensable message. A forward propagation issued from Pj to reach Pk is a recovery propagation subsequent to reception by Pk of one revoked message at least, sent by Pj.

D8: A recovery propagation is said to be of level n (n > 0) if it reaches n different processes from the initiator process of this propagation. In the same way, a recovery propagation is said to be of order p (p > 0) relatively to process Pi, if the length of roll back executed by Pi is p recovery regions.

D9: A recovery graph (RG) associated to process Pi (1≤i≤N) is a graph which describes exchanges between Pi and its partners Pj (i≠j, 1≤j≤N). An RG contains information needed by a recovery operation like DL and PL lists. for instance, each Recovery point List (RpL) element Bi in fig. 2 (see appendix) contains: A contex pointer (CTX), a list pointer to DL or IDL, and a list pointer to PL or IPL. The DL list of process B (or its most dominant RP), is <A1, D1, C2>, its PL list is <C1,A2>. The DL list of recovery point B2 is <C2>, its PL is <A2>. while B1 is dominant, then B2's DL is included in B1's DL, it is the same for their PL.
Remark: a garbage collector algorithm is used to minimize the size of an RG each time a new recovery line is reached (erasing of inaccesible recovery points) but, due to the lack of space we cannot discuss it here, refer to (Ali,1986).

III. BASIC STRATEGIES

Several strategies for recovery from transient or permanent faults have been studed; but due to the resticted paper space, only few of them are examined below and the others are merely introduced (For more details refer to (Ali,1986)).

1. Strategy A: *Every Potential failing Node (PFN) saves the messages that it receives.*

2. Strategy B: *Every message received by a PFN is saved and conserved by its producer in sending node.*

3. Strategy C: *No saving messages is required.*

4. Strategy D: *Every message received by a PFN is picked up and saved by the corresponding recovery node.*

5. Strategy AB: *Every message received and saved in a PFN is also saved in the sending node.*

6. Stategy AD: *Every message received and saved in a PFN is captured and saved by the associated recovery node.*

Before developing some strategies, we first look into the principle of a recovery operation, the needed hypotheses, and how to avoid a forward propagation of roll_back (D7).

1. Recovery Principles

A recovery operation is the action taken by an appropriate mechanism to enable a failing system to recover a correct state from which re-execution is resumed. The faults we consider are hardware (transient or permanent), and the distinction between them is complex (indeed impossible). So, when detected, a fault is firstly considered as transient (except the case where a processor becomes suddenly unserviceable) and handled as such. It is considered as permanent one after several vain trials. Usually, processing of transient faults is accomplished in two stages: detection, and recovery; but permanent faults need four: detection, diagnosis and hard reconfiguration (

switching to spare component), soft reconfiguration (selecting an efficient process context), and recovery. We assume available below all means for detection (for instance: self-checking components: in this case, the diagnosis step may be omitted), and hard reconfiguration algorithm like in (Banerjee,1990). To avoid any ambiguity in recovery operation, the following hypotheses are applied. H1: the error latency is scarcely presumed nil except where otherwise stated. H2 : no error happens during a recovery operation. H3: Transmission system is reliable.

With H1 and following criteria, all messages sent before error are considered correct, then no propagation of roll-back to partners of a failing process is needed. H1, particularly, depends on the error detection method, like concurrent detection by means of self-checking logic. The criteria defined below, when satisfied, allow forward propagation to be avoided.

criterion 1: When received, a message is recognized to be useful for the execution of the receiving process, or harmful because it results from a roll-back of the issuing process and must be ignored (the message has been already consumed during previous reception).

criterion 2: The recovery processor (the one on which rolls back a failing process) is able to recognize the message already sent during a normal execution of a process P and avoids the reemission of the same message when P is rolling back after error.

criterion 3: After a process roll_back, all messages are resent but without causing any perturbation in receiving processes, i.e. the actions generated by those messages are idempotent. It is intended that the non respect of criteria 1,2 is merely due to the unuse of the associated algorithms. In the sequel, we consider criteria 1, 2 to be held. Then the coherent system state (i.e. RL) is reached in only one roll back per process. A distributed algorithm (Aliouat 1986), initiated by a recovery processor, enables to know all RP's of processes represented in the RL; after this, a recovery message (definite invocation : D6) is sent to every concerned process.

2. Strategy A

In this strategy, *every Potential Failing Node (PFN) saves the messages that it receives.* In order to see what happens and how each type of hard fault is handled, strategy A is successively examined according to transient fault, permanent fault and finally both integrated in the same handling algorithm.

2.1. Transient fault.
Their occurrences may lead to an alteration of the internal environment of the affected process Pi ′ and possibly, by "contamination", to its partners Pj's. This contamination takes place when Pj's partners have consumed at least a revoked message (D7) produced by Pi. To correct this abnormal system functioning, Pi and Pj's must suspend their current execution and resume from a recovery line. Since the new execution is submitted to the same events as during the first one, particulary, the necessity to re-use the same information, this is accomplished by means of locally saved messages in the potential failing node.

With hypothesis H1 and satisfaction of precedent criteria 1 or 2, recovery operation is achieved without any perturbation of partners Pj (no contamination). Then, the recovery of any failing process takes place in the original failing node, since the latter is not affected by any irreversible physical damage.

2.2. Permanent fault.
Contrary to what happens in case of transient fault, the damaged node is now unable to reach execution of its process Pi, then recovery is achieved in another functional node called Recovery Node (RN) associated to the

first one. The RN may be a spare node in case of non degradable overall system, in which original architecture topology is preserved, or in one of the active nodes with degradable performance (modified topology). All information saved in the failing node are lost and the only recovery information available on the RN are: the code of failing process Pi and one RP at least. To resume execution of Pi, the recovery processor must impose the backward propagation to all partners Pj to recreate indispensable messages for Pi. Forward propagation inherent to messages sent previously by Pi, is avoided by criteria 1 and 2. We now examine what information are needed to the mechanism which may adopts this recovery strategy.

2.3. Required information.
In order to respect criterion 1, it is necessary for every process to keep information relative to received messages, (in particular, the serial number of each message, the identifier of the sender). For the criterion 2, saving of serial number of each sent message and identifier of its receiver process is needed.

In case of unsatisfied criteria 1 or 2, it is important to propagate the recovery from the failing process Pi to every partner Pj which has received from Pi one revoked message at least. This action is achieved by means of information which identify the exchanges established between Pi and Pj's. Those information are found in the DL list (D4) of the recovery graph (D9). Thereby, a protocol between processes is needed, so when a process receives a message, it sends to its sender the Identifier of Receiving Recovery Region (IRRR). Thus with DL list, a recovery processor is able to designate to each partner Pj of the failing process Pi, an RRP (D2) from which restart can be done (definite invocation D6). The information required to handle permanent faults, and available on each recovery node, are: the code of process and one or several contexts associated to RP of that process. The structure of a message may carry additional information to be used by the recovery mechanism; for instance, message number, the Identifier of the Emission Recovery Region (IERR), required to built the PL list (D4) of recovery graph. As an example of RG for process B depicted in fig. 1, see fig. 3 in appendix. After that, we develop below an algorithm of recovery operation for every case previously specified.

2.4. Recovery operation.
The criteria 1 or 2 are satisfied (no forward propagation is possible).

2.4.1. Case of Transient Fault:
After detection of the error, the recover processor RPri restarting the failing process Pi, performs the following recovery algorithm.
1 - RPri uses as Restart Recovery Point (RRP) the active RP of Pi. Since no forward propagation is possible, there is no return of propagation to Pi reaching a dominant RP (D2) of RRP;
2 - RPri restores the state of Pi corresponding to RRP;
3 - RPri resumes execution of Pi.
In this case, only a single context of RP is needed to save for each process of the system, and moreover, criterion 2 may be preferably satisfied.

2.4.2. Case of Permanent Fault:
The failing node is recognized as such, diagnosis and hard reconfiguration are supposed realized. Because of lack of RG of Pi, the Recovery Processor RPri initiates a random invocation (D6) to cause backward propagation of every Process Pj, partner of Pi, such that : RPj ∈ Pj and RPj->RRP, i.e RPj is a direct propagator (D3) of RRP of failing process Pi. The following algorihm is then executed.
1) Emission, to every process/node, of a random invocation message which contains the RRP of failing process Pi. This RRP is the active RP of

Pi (the RL is determined according to a progressive roll back principle).
2) After sending the invocation message, RPri restores a state of Pi associated to RRP, and resumes execution of Pi.
3) As soon as an invocation message is received, the receiver processor RPrj determines if there is one of its processes Pj such that : RPj ∈ Pj and RPj -> RRP, if several RPj may exist, then only the dominant one is selected.
4) Deletion of all possible successors of RPj.
5) Restoration of Pj state corresponding to RPj.
6) Resumption of Pj. The concerned processor RPri must satisfy criterion 2, and only information message needed by Pi are resent.

2.4.3. Case of the Two Types of Faults:
One of the aims in this study is to recover from solid faults, whatever their type. Then when detected, a fault is firstly handled as a transient one; it is considered as a permanent after many vain attempts to recover from it. The algorithms in 2.4.1 and in 2.4.2 are then applied.

2.5. Perturbations and roll-back length.
The concern of a recovery mechanism is tightly related to its cost (overhead incurred), then the difficulties resulting from its design is more relevant to efficiency than to the error recovery aspect. Therefore it is important to consider the strategy according to a determining factor inherent to recovery operation cost represented by the domino effect.
Avoidance of any propagation in transient fault, gives the strategy optimal perturbation values, thus the factors of propagation (D8) are: level n = 0 and order p = 1.
Generally, with any type of solid fault, strategy A is exempt from domino effect. Indeed, the latter one can only be caused by backward propagation, but while only a single permanent fault is considered at time, any process Pj reached by a backward propagation cannot propagate the latter (since indispensable messages are locally available for failing process Pi). Then there is no possibility of creating a cycle of backward propagation, and the absence of a cycle implies absence of a domino effect. Therefore the level of propagation is: n ≤ m where m is the number of direct propagator processes of Pi.

2.6. Conclusion. The strategy A is particularly attractive for recovery of transient faults. However permanent faults may create situation of unnegligible system penalization during recovery operation. Since the occurrence frequency of these permanent faults is definitely lower than the one of transient fault (≈10 % for the former and ≈90 % for the latter, (Siewiorek, 1982), this does not represent an handicap. Nevertheless, an improvement to handle this class of faults is devoted to the strategy B.

IV. COMBINED STRATEGIES

Since these strategies are combined from the two basic ones, a summary description of each one is given below.

1. Strategy AB

Every message received and saved in potential failing node is also saved in the sending node (in message producers).
This strategy is a combination of strategy A and strategy B. The essential aim of this grouping is to make the best possible use of those two strategies in order to limit more and more (indeed suppress) the recovery perturbations. Indeed, as regards to transient faults, strategy A is the most interesting one, but permanent faults are less well handled than the former ones. This "inadequacy" may be compensated for by the positive aspect of strategy B where permanent faults are well

handled. For this purpose, strategy AB is designed to make indispensable messages to be saved in producer nodes and in the receiving ones. In other words each node saves both sent and received messages. The recovery algorithm is combined from the one which handles transient fault (in strategy A), and permanent fault (in strategy B). This association gives a sure advantage to the strategy where recovery propagations are notably reduced. This is done at the detriment of the overhead resulting from management of saved messages. Note that, this overhead is proportional to the interactivity degree of processes. The data structure adopted to represent required information must comply with grouping strategies A and B. This must allow the local re-use of saved messages, and supply recovery processor with indispensable messages, respectively in case of transient or permanent fault.

1.1. Recovery operation. As may be the case, in transient or permanent fault the recovery algorithm in strategy AB is derived respectively from strategy A and strategy B.

1.2 Perturbations and roll-back length.
Two important results are reached:
1) the perturbations are optimum so, level n = 0 and order p = 1. 2) a single context corresponding to the active RP, is saved for any process. It should be noted that the strategy fits particularly the systems where the processes interactions are asymmetrical (for instance system with many producers and a single consummer).

2. Strategy AD

Every message received and saved in Potential Failing Node is captured and saved by the corresponding Recovery Node.
With duplication of message saving, in both potential failing node and recovery node, we gather advantages of basic strategy A and D, relatively to handling transient faults and permanent ones. So, it results from this association two fondamental characteristics, namely:
- no transfer of indispensable message takes place during a recovery operation, then neither penalization of processes other the failing one; and no tendency to increase the activity of transmission system is incurred.
- complete isolation of safe processes opposite to the failing one. Consequently a single context is saved for each process.
While overhead incurred from message management is proportional to the intercommunication of processes, the former may be unnegligible. However, a separate procesor may be dedicated to perform this management.

3. Recovery Operation

While strategy AD is combined from strategies A and D, the recovery information required are: a recovery graph as described in strategy A, and a data structure inherent to a recovery node like one defined in strategy D. The recovery algorithm is formed by the one defined in strategy A for transient fault, combined to which given in strategy D relatively to permanent fault.

4. Perturbation and Roll-backs Length

Strategy AD is the most optimal one so, we state: level n = 0, order p = 1.

V. COMPARISON OF STRATEGIES

After strategies have been studied, it is obvious to compare them for determining which strategy fits better to a given application. While it is impossible to claim to elaborate a "universal" strategy independent on applications, because the incurred overhead may be unacceptable (for real time applications) or solely the specification of the latter ones cannot be guaranted, then it is of great interest to characterize each strategy towards other ones. Therefore, to make comparaison, it is necessary to define criteria related to hardware and/or software system requirements for which a strategy may be adopted. These requirements may be relative to : - physical nodes like: resource limitation (memory space, transmission capabilities, availability factor in the system, degradable topology or not).

- application: overhead inducted in the application when implementing a selected strategy.

However, due to the random behaviour of processes in exchanging messages and creating RP's, it is difficult to make formal comparaison, so some affirmations below are empirical. Under these considerations, and while the number of comparaison criteria to be stated may be important, we only retain four of them which appear to comply better the reaching aim. The criteria we consider, though empirical, are as follows: C1: Trend to generate an interprocesses perturbation during a recovery operation. If possible, the roll back propagation can be quantified in term of level n and order p.

C2: Overhead incurred by an application due to the preparing of the environment required by a recovery mechanism which adopts a given strategy.

C3: Trend to increase message traffic in distributed system during recovery actions.

C4: Trend to require more memory space (this space includes data structures and saving space due to messages and RP's). Then, we can informally state (Aliouat, 1986):

$$C1AB \approx C1AD < C1D \approx C1B < C1A < C1C$$
$$C2C < C2B \approx C2A \approx C2D < C2AB \approx C2AD$$
$$C3AD \leq C3AB < C3A \leq C3D \approx C3B < C3C$$
$$C4AD \approx C4AB < C4C < C4B \approx C4D \leq C4A$$

VI. IMPLEMENTATION

Our first simple application was experienced in three workstations on each one is running a process. One of the three processes say P has to determine prime numbers in [1,N] interval and sends them to the others (Q,R) for usage (the prime numbers are also displaying in P screen). Q and R are doing other things where the generated numbers are consumed. Each workstation has an associated recovery one. A transient fault was simulated in executing an interruption handler, while a permanent one is simulated in switching off the P/workstation. In the first case, the process P redisplays the prime numbers previously determined in the active recovery region showing then the strategy principle. The strategy used in this feasability is AD. In the second case, the failed process P is recovered on its recovery workstation(Q); the displaying of prime numbers is resumed at point its was interrupted previously. The recovery workstation screen is divided in two windows where one part shows scrolling of resumed prime numbers and the second part shows the result of process Q. The progression of Q and R are not affected. A second switching off of Q/node has led to R/node to support P,Q,R continuation but the given response time was heavy. The obtained results are then to confirm our ideas. Our actual work consists in implementing a recovery mechanism based on AD strategy in a real application in a local network.

VII. CONCLUSION

Recovery strategies in distributed system in case of hardware faults have been presented. They handle both transient and permanent faults. This can allow the crucial application programs to have a nonstop execution despite solid failures. Generally, the avoidance of situation of important system penalization (undoing a great deal computation in case of error) is obtained from a control of propagation. This imposes on concurrent processes to respect some constraints. These constraints are relative either to their communications or setting of their recovery points. This control is achieved in our strategies, partially by means of saving messages, or completely by additional feasible criteria. Then the processes liberty is preserved. The strategies (notably AD, AB) are very attractive in the sense that they are domino effect free, and also, only a single recovery point is saved for each process. The aim of the strategies exhaustivity is to cope with a great class of systems, may be endowed with fault tolerance capabilities.

It is noteworthy that to improve more and more reliability, it is necessary to take into account both hardware and software faults. So, we are actually incorporating the recovery blocks technique in the proposed strategies in order to reach a more general recovery mechanism.

VII. REFERENCES

Aliouat, M. (1986) Reprise de processus en environnement distribué après occurrences de pannes matériel. *Docteur ingenieur Thesis* 1986, INPG grenoble.

Aliouat, M., B. Courtois (1985). Recovery processes in distibuted environment after transient or permanent faults. *Research report N°601, IMAG TIM3 lab.* Grenoble.

Anderson, T., P.A. Lee (1981). Fault-tolerance Principles and Practice, *Prenctice Hall ed.*

Banerjee,P. and others (1990). Algorithm-based fault tolerance on a hypercube multiprocessor. *IEEE trans. on computers.* vol. 89, n°9.

Barigazzi, G. (1983). Application transparent setting Recovery points. *FTCS 13*

Cristian, F. (1982). Exception Handling and Software Fault Tolerance. *IEEE trans. On computers*, C.31 pp 531-539.

Gregory, T.S., J.C. Knight. (1989). On the provision of B.E.R in production Programming Languages. *FTCS 19.*

Horning, J.J. and others. (1974). A program structure for error detection and recovery. *Lecture note computer sciences,16 springer verlag ed.*

KIM K.H, S.M. Yang. (1989). Performance Impact of Look-Ahead Execution in the Conversation Scheme. *IEEE Trans. On Computers*, vol. 38.

KIM, K.H., J.H. You. (1990). A Highly Decentralized Implementation Model for the Programmer Transparent Coordination (PTC) Scheme for Cooperative Recovery. In *FTCS 20.*

Kopetz, H., and others. (1990). Tolerating transient faults in MARS. *FTCS 20.*

Melliar Smith, P.M, B. Randell. (1977). The role of programmed exception handling. *Sigplan Notices* 12, 3, 1977.

Randell, B. (1975). System structure for software fault tolerance. *IEEE Trans. soft. Eng.*SE 1,2 pp 220-232.

Russell D.L. (1980). State Restoration in systems of communicating processes. *IEEE Trans. soft. Eng.* SE 6(2) pp 183-194.

Siewiorek, D.P., R.S Swarz (1982). The theory and practice of reliable system design *Digital press ed.*

Tamir, Y. and others.(1991). The UCLA Mirror Processor: A Building Block for Self-Checking Self-Repairing Computing Nodes. *FTCS 21.*

Tyrrell, A. M., D. J. Holding.(1986). Design of Reliable Software in Distributed Systems Using the Conversation Scheme. *IEEE trans. on Soft. Eng.*, Vol. SE, n°.

Wood W.G. (1981). A decentralized Recovery control protocol. In *FTCS 11* pp 159-164

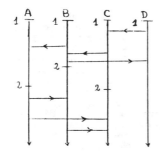

Fig. 1. Example of communicating processes

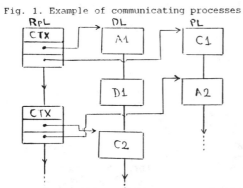

Fig. 2. Recovery Graph of process B in fig. 1.

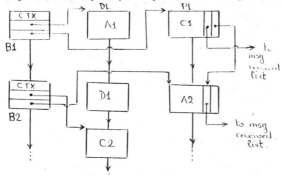

Fig. 3. RG of process B in fig. 1. for Strategy A

FAULT TOLERANCE BY A DISTRIBUTED SOFTWARE CONTROL FOR A HIGH RELIABILITY

Emmanuelle RENAUX
LETI (CEA - Technologies Avancées)
DSYS - CEN / G - 85X - 38041 GRENOBLE CEDEX
email : renaux@leti.cea.fr ; tel : 76-88-37-45

CRAN - LARA (Laboratoire d'Automatique et de Recherche Appliquée)
Parc Robert Bentz - 54500 VANDOEUVRE LES NANCY

Abstract. The perfect computer has not still been built and fault do occur. Fault tolerance, based on redundancy, is a good way of making dependable computers. This paper describes a fault tolerant system that provides availability and high reliability by units replication, fault masking and correction. In this system, the control is distributed, implemented by software. This control uses the results of the well known diagnosable PMC model, proposed by Preparata, Metze and Chien. And more, from its ability to have important exchanges throughputs on high speed dedicated links, it allows to check the consistency not only of results computed by the replicated application processors but also of the software programs, and the parameters kept in application memory. This fault tolerant system gives a level of reliability equivalent to the soundness of the cache memory.

Keywords. dependability, reliability, redundancy, software development

INTRODUCTION

The perfect computer has not still been built and faults in both hardware and software do occur. Some systems therefore need to be able to compute correctly even with their presence and regardless of their source (hard or soft ?). Fault tolerance, based on redundancy, is a good way of making dependable computers.

This paper describes a fault tolerant system that provides availability and high reliability by units replication, fault masking and correction. However, in this system, only the faults that occur in hardware and by extension their effects in the software are considered. Indeed, the hardware fault occurrence results mainly in errors of two types :
• the program sequence is correct but the final results are wrong,
• the program sequence is modified and the specified algorithm is no longer executed. Then it provides either erronous results or nothing.
To tolerate software faults, a number of independently designed programs that perform the same function must be developped. Here, the control is performed on the same applicative part that is replicated. This control is based on the data values and report of comparison which are exchanged.

HARDWARE CONFIGURATION

System architecture

Taking into account the continuous error-free operation and doing tests independant of application field, the degree of redundancy has to be at least equal to three (more than one to provide redundancy, at least two to detect a failure and at least three to detect and locate the failed unit). Thereby the chosen architecture is a variation of the common fault masking configuration nMR (n Modular Redundancy) where n modules perform each treatment concurrently. In a traditional nMR arrangement, they would send their results to a hardware voter. It would select the output corresponding to the majority vote of these n modules, thus masking any failure in one of them.

In the chosen configuration, for avoiding the system to be vulnerable to its voter failure, this one is replicated. Rather to use several hardware implemented voters like for example in Fault Tolerant Multi-Processor (FTMP) system (Hopkins, 1978), voting is executed in software with modules exchanging data values. This technique does not require additional specific hardware and it provides flexibility that would be more difficult to reach with hardware implementation : dynamic management of acceptance criteria, possibility to have levels of validity and not only a control on absolute values. And more, the software vote can be relatively independant of the application. Other systems, as SIFT (Wensley and others, 1978) or more recently VOTRICS (Theuretzbacher, 1986), have already chosen this software approach , but limitations in the speed of transfer imply a small amount of data exchanges and synchronization needs between computers are a source of troubles.

Now, we are speaking about the characteristics that we want the part of control (fault tolerance unit) to have :
• redundancy of degree three. Most of systems that have a degree of redundancy superior to three use three units in correct fonctionnement and keep the last one(s) as a back-up to replace the failed unit.
• fault tolerance management by software approach ;
• data exchanges and need of synchronisation between the concurrent units ;

• important throughput on high speed link. The fault tolerant system has to hold this property for controlling quickly all the memory cells and so being able to reduce error latency. This property is all the more benefic because the transient and intermittent faults are much more frequent than the permanent faults. A large percentage of these two types of faults (more than 50%) are due to memory chips (Madeira and co-workers, 1989). This implies that most of the faults will cause errors in memories and these errors have to be quickly detected.

As conclusion of the hardware configuration paragraph, a general view of the fault tolerant system architecture is shown in fig. 1.

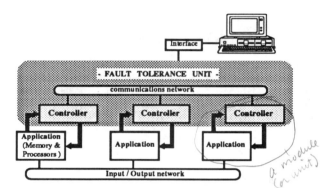

Fig. 1. General overview of the system architecture

The controller is the manager of these dependability functions :
• inter-unit communication and synchronization,
• data voting and fault masking,
• error/fault detection and handling,
• isolation of faulty unit and reconfiguration.

SOFTWARE IMPLEMENTED CONTROL

Description of the distributed voting schema

The voting schema (represented in fig. 2) consists of three parts :

1- Sending and reception of data to be controlled
When the controller receives the information that the application processor has produced some results, it transfers, to its own memory, all the data stored in the application memory. Then it sends them to its one way neighbour. In the same way, it receives data from its another neighbour.

2- Comparison of the data stored in the controller memory
Once the controller has two series of data (its own and those received from its neighbour), it makes the comparison.

Remark. The same method (sending of results and comparison) is used by others ring system, as for example in (Obac Roda, 1982).

3- Sending and reception of reports of comparison
After the comparison, the controller returns the result

of matching to all its neighbours.

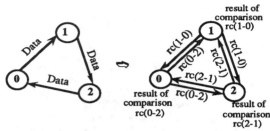

Sending results   Sending results of comparison

Fig. 2. Schema of the distributed software voting

The different fault tolerance characteristics that can be achieved by the use of this distributed schema are described below.

Faulty unit detection and localization

We call a module or unit the set composed of an application processor and its controller.
The method for the faulty unit detection and its localization is based on the well-known PMC diagnosable model, proposed by Preparata, Metze and Chien (1967). Here, the test that each unit performs to evaluate another one is a comparison. The report is "ok" if there is no discordance between the compared results, else "error".

If one fault appears, according to the type of this fault, there is either one or two reports of matching indicating a discordance (fig. 3).
• In the first case (two reports of matching equal to error), the faulty unit is the one which send and receive a report of comparison indicating an error.
• In the second case, it is more difficult to designate with assurance which unit is faulty. Is it the unit that is pointed by the arc at the value error or those at the origin of this arc ?

In the general case, to determine which unit is faulty, we use the results of the diagnosable PMC model. The sequence composed by the outcomes of comparison performed by the controllers is analysed. The failed module (represented in the color grey in the fig. 3) is pointed out by the oriented sequence "x-ok-error" where x represents ok or error.

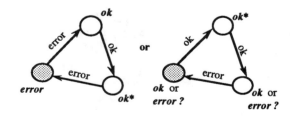

Fig. 3. Localization of the faulty unit

This figure is simplified : it is represented as if each controller sent its result of comparison only to the unit that has given it its data to control. However with only these specific reports of matching it illustrates, by analogy, the fault - test relation digraph introduced by the PMC model.

To give each controller the possibility to qualify the working state of all the system units (faulty and fault-free units localization), the report of matching is sent to all the neighbours and not only to the one which has sent its data, cf fig. 3.

Under the assumption that the occurrence of Byzantine faults (Lamport, 1982) is negligible which means the same report of comparison is sent to the neighbours, this voting schema allows each controller to have a consistent view of the working state of all the modules of the network. Classically a minimun of four processors is required to really guarantee interactive consistency, in the single fault case (Pease, 1980).

Availability of service

When a failed unit has been accused, the two others units should be fault free. But according to the type of the fault, as for exemple if a controller returns a wrong report of comparison (equal to error), a unit can be accused faulty unjustly. Thereby, at each control, the system is able to give one fault-free unit with assurance, after analysis of the sequence of results of matching. It is indicated in the fig. 4 by "ok*". If the outputs are not redundant, this unit shoud give its results. It is important to ensure the user the availability of the service.

Fault handling

The module judged faulty corrects itself : it modifies its own data with those received from its neighbour. It is proved that a good module never changes its results with faulty ones.

This fault correction is done so long as the fault is considered as transient. Indeed, in opposition to a permanent fault that does not disappear once it occurs, the effects of transient faults can often be masked by trying again the operation which failed before.

Isolation and reconfiguration

Isolation. If the same unit is accused to be faulty several times running, it has to be isolated. This is necessary to avoid the whole system to be unreliable if a second unit becomes defectuous. Indeed if this unit produces the same wrong results than the another failed unit, the majority vote will select these results and discard the good ones. Reliability is no more warranted.

The direction of sending results is modified at each control to ensure that the unit pointed failed by the oriented sequence composed by the different reports of comparison is really defectuous and not accused unjustly by a controller doing an erronous comparison. So one time it is "judged" by one controller and the following time by the other one. If one module then another one are indicated faulty by the third in turn, then it is this third unit that performs badly the comparison and has to be isolated. So it is always the true faulty unit which will be isolated.

Reconfiguration.

When a faulty unit is isolated, this means that the two others units stop communicating with it and the system will go on working in a duplex structure.

If there is either one or two reports of the comparison equal to error, two cases are possible dependent of the degree of dependability tolerated. In the first one, additional tests are executed to determine the faulty unit. So the good unit can go on working but there is no more fault tolerance because no redundancy. In the second case, the system has to be halt "properly".

TIME AND COMMUNICATION CONSTRAINTS

Time consideration

This voting schema makes a decision on the validity of the different data but the time the module takes to answer has to be considered as well. Indeed, it is important to avoid a controller waiting indefinitely for results coming from its application processor or from its neighbour because this would lock all the control system. And more solving time constraints is absolutely necessary for real time applications.

So specific mechanisms have been studied and validated.

Watchdog timer. It is one method to detect when no result is produced or communicated in a given time : a fault will be signaled when the timer goes off.

However with the use of timeouts, two problems appear. The first is to well define how long the timeout has to be set. It is essential not to take it too short so that a fault is signaled even if there is no fault, and not too long so that there is an important fault detection latency. The second problem is to determine when starts the timer.

Watchdog timers are used to discover the occurrence of two types of faults :
• omission fault, where no result is produced by the application processor ;
• timing fault, where the results are given too early or too late.

Timers implementation. The controller has to be general and so independent of application. Consequently the time to perform a treatment (of the application) is unknown.

The first idea is to set a timer when the controller receives neighbouring results. But if these results are received earlier because the neighbouring application processor is defectuous, the timer will go off. Then it will signal a fault that should not exist and no result are going to be produced. Thereby only two series of data are available for the control procedure. Unfortunately, there is a high probability that the results produced earlier are wrong and it would be difficult to determine what are the correct data.

The second idea is that the watchdog timer starts when a controller (whom its application processor has not yet finished its treatment) has received the information telling it that its two neighbours have already finished their treatment. Thereby a controller has to indicate to its neighbours when its application part has finished to compute. Thus, the chosen solution is the following : when a controller receives the information that its application processor has produced some results, it sends concurrently :

• these data to its one way neighbour ;
• a message indicating to its another neighbour the end of its treatment.
So the timer has to be set when a controller received these two kinds of information : a set of data from one neighbour and a message from its another one.
The lenght of this timeout corresponds at the possible desynchronisition that can exist between the different modules because of the serial loading or the time needed to correct the execution code of one of them..

Communication failure

However, the use of time guard is not sufficient to solve problems due to a communication failure. If the system halts during a transfer, as a part of data has been already received, the timer could not be more selected and the system will be unable to continue... So special considerations are required to the handling of communication failure. The controller must recognize that such failure has occured.

In relation with these problems (time constraints and communication failure), the distibuted voting schema has been improved : it has been a little modified to tolerate and handle these specific faults.

IMPLEMENTATION AND VALIDATION

Controller architecture

Taking into account the characteristics requested for the fault tolerance unit and to validate all the software concept described in the next paragraph, we have chosen a modular architecture made of a transputer associated with a fast exchange unit (fig. 4) as controller.

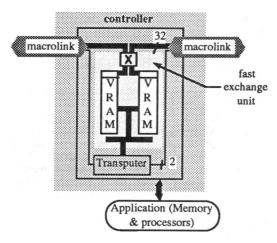

Fig. 4. Network communication structure

This controller structure allows to speed up the exchanges between units and to use occam, the appropriate language of transputer. This language and its associated primitives are well adapted for a lot of reasons :
• occam is closer to the language machine,
• the easiness of parallel programming and

development,
• the synchronization of several concurrent processes or processors by data exchange,
• the means of measuring and sharing time,
• its unvaluable constructs PAR and ALT...

Macrolink is the name given to the association of :
• a transputer asynchronous serial link for its synchronisation mechanism,
• VRAM (Video RAM) synchronous parallel link for its high througput.
Macrolink is bidirectional as a transputer link and allows an important exchange throughput (40 Mb/s), faster than communication by transputer link (2 Mb/s). This dedicated high speed interface unit is as well defined as the mother board of the architecture ATILA (Pirson, 1990) and has been developped in our laboratory.

A general ovierview of the fault tolerant architecture with this controller structure is given fig. 5.

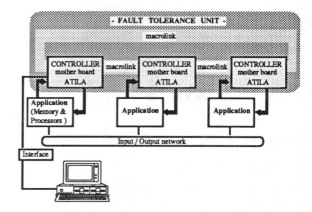

Fig. 5. Fault tolerant system architecture

Solving time constraints and handling communication failure

With the use of occam language, the timeout is easily implemented due to the ALT construct (fig. 6).

```
VAL waiting_lengh IS 1000:
TIMER clock :
INT timenow :
SEQ
    clock ? timenow
    ALT
        from_ another_system ? message
            --- action
        clock ? AFTER timenow PLUS waiting_lengh
            --- error detection
```

Fig. 6. Example of an alternative construct in occam with a timeout on the inputs

When a link failure occurs during a transfer, the process performing the alternative is already in the guard "from_another_system ? message" (cf fig. 6). Then the timer guard could not be more selected. So special inter-process communication protocols have been developped to allow the controller to recognize this kind of failure and cancel the appointment managing any occam exchange. The communicating processes (transmitter and receiver) must not be in a deadlock state waiting for a message or its end. To provide this feature we use predefined procedures (Sheperd, 1987), such as "InputOrFail" and "OutputOrFail". Link failure can be detected by a timeout on communication or signaled via a message on a specific internal soft channel.

Examples :
InputOrFail.t (CHAN c, ()BYTE message, TIMER clock, INT s_t, BOOL aborted)   (1)
OuputOrFail.t (CHAN c, ()BYTE message, CHAN kill, BOOL aborted)   (2)

The comunication is detected as having failed if :
• in the case (1), the time measured by the timer clock is after the specified time s_t,
• in the case (2), any message is received on the specific channel kill.
In these two cases, the link failure is signaled by the boolean variable aborted which is set true, false otherwise.

Once the failure is detected and the involved processes have stopped trying to establish a communication, the link hardware must be reinitialised. To identify that the link has been set up the processors regularly check the link and try to exchange any message. It is necessary to ensure that they attempt to communicate at the same time.

The use of the structure occam-transputer seems to be well suitable to implement the fault tolerance techniques and to solve the different constraints described before. Therefore some problems (such as a correct communication restart after reconnection of the link and resynchronisation) have not still been resolved.

CONCLUSION

This system provides high reliability by fault masking and from its ability to have fast exchanges of important data flow, it could be used to repeatedly check the consistency of high data volumes in the redundant units. The software implemented control is distributed, and the voting algorithm is performed in parallel with the application tasks thus reducing the overhead due to fault tolerance.

Implemented with three modules, the voting schema gives experiments full of promise. This schema could be extended to a higher number of redundant components to detect more complex faults, for example Byzantine faults. Therefore, in this case, the ring network would not be more well suitable.

Possible applications of such a system and all the associated concepts could be used in error tolerance in computers in spacecraft control, industrial process, autonomous mobile robotics, hostile environment, ...

REFERENCES

Hopkins, A.L., T. Basil Smith III, and J.H. Lala (1978). FTMP - A Highly Reliable Fault-Tolerant Multiprocessor for Aircraft. *Proc. IEEE*, 66(10), 1221-1239.

Lamport, L., R. Shostak, and M. Pease (1982). The Byzantine generals problem. *ACM Transactions on Programming Languages and Systems*, 4(3), 382-401.

Madeira, H., B. Fernandez, M. Rela and J.G. Silva (1989). The fault-tolerant architecture of the SAFE system. *Microprocessing and Microprogramming*, 27, 705-712.

Obac Roda, V. and O.J. Davies (1982). Aspects of fault tolerant ring structures. *IEEE Colloquium on Microprocessor Applications Requiring High Integrity and Fault Tolerance*, IEEE digest 1982/67, London.

Pease, M., R. Shostak, and L. Lamport (1980). Reaching agreement in the presence of faults. *Journal of the Association for Computing Machinery*, 27(2), 228-234.

Pirson, A. (1990). Conception et simulation d'architectures parallèles pour le traitement d'images. Ph.D. thesis, National Polytechnic Institute of Grenoble

Preparata, F.P., G. Metze, and R.T. Chien (1967). On the connection assignment problem of diagnosable systems. *IEEE Transactions on Electronic Computers*, 16(6), 848-854.

Sheperd, R. (1987). Extraordinary use of transputer links. Technical note1, inmos

Theuretzbacher, N. (1986). 'VOTRICS' : Voting Triple Modular Computing System. International Symposium on Fault-Tolerant Computing, 16, 144-150.

Wensley, J.H., L. Lamport, J. Goldberg, M.W. Green, K.N. Levitt, P.M. Melliar-Smith, R.E. Shostack and C.B. Weinstock. (1978). SIFT : design and analysis of a fault tolerant-computer for aircraft control. *Proc. IEEE*, 66(10), 1240-1255.

THE VERIFICATION SUPPORT ENVIRONMENT VSE

Dr. Baur and T. Plasa, GPP mbH, 8024 Oberhaching, Germany
P. Kejwal, Dornier GmbH, 7990 Friedrichshafen 1, Germany
R. Drexler, W. Stephan, W. Reif, A. Wolpers, University of Karlsruhe, Germany
D. Hutter and C. Sengler, University of Saarbrücken, Germany
E. Canver, University of Ulm, Germany

Abstract   The VSE (Verification Support Environment) is a first approach to integrate the methods of formal specification and verification into an existing and industrially approved CASE tool. Safety/security-critical software systems (or parts of) can be developed within the VSE under the guidance of a formal design method, based on the principles of modularization and refinement. VSE support covers the whole development process, starting with fairly abstract *security models* down to the concrete system implementation (which is formally correct w. r. t. its specification, due to the VSE development method). For that purpose, the VSE system integrates an appropriate formal specification language (VSE-SL) and universitary resp. industrially approved components for specification and verification into a single, ready to use software development environment.
The VSE project is a national promoted project, initiated and sponsored by the BSI (Bundesamt für Sicherheit in der Informationstechnik).

Keywords   computer applications; formal verification; modeling; reliability; safety; software engineering; specification languages

INTRODUCTION

Nowadays, industry, commerce and public administration are increasingly dependent on the smooth and correct function and continuous availability of technical and information systems based on software components.

This rises the need for adequate methods and tools for the development and evaluation of these systems in order to guarantee the compliance with the safety and security requirements appropriate to the respective risk in different operational environments.

The Verification Support Environment VSE is an attempted answer to this problem. It is an unique approach, to combine the benefits of a CASE environment with the methods and tools for formal specification and verification.

GOALS OF THE VSE

The VSE will be the prototype of an industrially usable software system, consisting of ready to use specification and verification tools, embedded in a common development environment. Its suitability will be examined in realistic and close to practice case studies.

For the realization of the Verifiction Support Environment, the following objectives are pursued:

- Provision of a specification component to identify user requirements and categorize them accor-

ding their criticality

- Support for the definition and analysis of safety / security models

- Different problem oriented specification concepts

- Concepts for dividing a problem into abstraction levels

- Verification in parallel to the development, controlled by a verification management system

- Identification of the links between requirements, safety/security model and program specification

- Automated generation of source code out of the program specification

WHY USING FORMAL METHODS ?

Software Engineering nowadays is conceptually described by a wide range of development methods and supported by a variety of software-tools (CASE tools). Most of the existing CASE tools use pure informal or semi-formal methods in the development process. Their basic concept is to avoid committing errors by a constructive approach (analysis and design methods, tool support, automatic documentation, code generators, configuration management etc.).

The second concept is to detect and remove all those errors, which could not be avoided by performing tests on the analysis, design and program descriptions.

On one hand it is commonly agreed that this approach will improve the quality of a system to be developed. On the other hand this is only a tendency that cannot be formally measured. Although there are several concepts for a systematic and complete testing, there is no way to assert the overall correctness of software by pure testing alone. All this cannot be the sole basis for the certification of a system.

The solution to this problem is the use of formal specification and formal verification. Formal methods use mathematical descriptions (stated in a formal specification language) to establish models both of the security and safety requirements of the software system. Furthermore, they use an appropriate logic calculus to prove the correctness of the mathematical models as well as the compliance between formal models of the system and the concrete system itself. The advantage of this method is -among others-, that the assertions obtained from formal verification are valid in a mathematical sense.

Since concrete software systems usually are of great complexity, formal system descriptions must be broken down into smaller pieces by modularisation and refinement principles, just as in conventional software engineering.

As a disadvantage of the pure formal methodology is considered the loss of a more "practical" view of things that designers usually get from an informal oriented system description. So the optimal development strategy should use a combination of both formal and informal methods. This integration principle is one of the main features underlying the VSE-philosophy.

FORMAL DEVELOPMENT METHODS AND TOOLS IN THE VSE

The VSE offers an integrated software engineering environment with informal and formal methods. This means, that it delivers both the conceptual frame and the appropriate tools for formal specification and verification in every phase of the life cycle of a software system.

The methods and tools are as follows:

Requirements Analysis

The initial system requirements are described at first informally in an industrial approved way by means of a requirements specification tool. Requirements can then be categorized according to their safety/security relevance and stated in terms of the VSE-specific formal specification language VSE-SL (see below). This defines the *security model* of the system.

Formalization of System Specification

System components that are not safety or security related are developed in a conventional way by means of a design specification language, which supports a wide range of development methods.

For the security relevant system components, the VSE offers a *formal* development method. Formal development involves the design of a *structured* formal specification, the refinement of the individual components of this specification, and proofs of the correctness of these refinements. Structured specifications add horizontal structure to the system design, while the refinement steps add vertical structure.

The use of structured specifications breaks a system down into several pieces that can be developed independently. Furthermore, the method supports design by stepwise refinement: intermediate layers of specifications may be introduced to bridge the gap between the rather abstract specification of a system (e.g. a booking system) and the structures found in the implementation environment (like arrays or database entries) in manageable steps.

The highest level of the vertical structure is given by the security model of the system, the lowest level by the target language (for which Ada has been chosen within the VSE). Together, these principles enforce and encourage a highly modular system design. Apart from its well known advantages, this is a "must" for making verification possible at all.

Since flexibility is especially important when using formal methods, the VSE is not restricted to a single method of modeling the world: systems may be described as abstract data types (see Reif, 1991; Wirsing, 1990) as state based systems (see Rushby, 1991), or as a suitable combination of both. The integration of further techniques is possible.

Formal Verification

While formal specification of a system is usually considered as an advantage in itself, it does not ensure a correct *implementation* of the system. The correspondence between a specification and its implementation can be shown by a formal verification.

While verification of the entire program against the specification of the entire system is prohibitive (due to the complexity of the objects involved), a verification of the individual vertical refinements with respect to their import (the specifications they are based upon) and their export (the specification which they implement) *is* possible.

On the implementation side, the vertical structure of a system's specification is reflected in the programs which link two levels of abstraction. These programs are considered as "abstract programs" in the sense that they do not operate on data structures like arrays, but rather on structures described in intermediate specifications (like "booking systems", "employee lists" etc.).

In the VSE system development method, the correctness of each refinement (consisting of import specifications, a collection of programs and an export specification) is formally verified within a logical calculus. The proof obligations are created automatically, the proofs are done either automatically or interactively by the VSE prover components. Since the verification is as modular as the system design, the verification of a refinement step is independent of the implementation of its import specification, and any two refinement steps can be verified independently. As a result, development and verification can proceed in parallel. Overall, the entire process is controlled by a verification management system.

Implementation

The implementation of the final system is done by automatic generation of the source code. The source description for the generated code is built from the *abstract programs* that realize the links between the formal abstraction levels. Due to the VSE development and verification methods, the resulting code is formally correct w. r. t. the system specification.

VSE SYSTEM STRUCTURE

The VSE System consists of several levels or components, which run under a unique graphical user interface, as indicated in Fig. 1.

The VSE components are made up by three existing software tools, which will be integrated into a unique system. Due to the integration, each tool will be

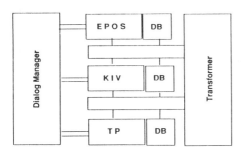

Fig. 1: VSE Sytem Structure

adapted and enhanced to establish the overall VSE-functionality. The basis for formal specification is given by the VSE-SL, a VSE specific formal specification language.

In the following sections, the main features of the different components will be described.

EPOS

The CASE-Tool EPOS is the VSE platform for specification, development management and integrated data management in the VSE System. Among others, it is used for informal and formal requirements analysis, formal specification and abstract programming. It also contains an integrated verification management

system, which keeps track of the *verification status* of the development items.

EPOS (Engineering and Project Management Oriented Specification System) is a software tool system designed for computer support of development and project management activities (see Lempp, 1986). Its aim is to release experts, engaged in software/hardware projects, from tedious routine work, enabling them to spend more time on development activities.

Some of the various objectives of the EPOS System are:

- Homogeneous computer support in all phases of a project

- Integrated computer support for development, project management and product management

- Support for various development methods

- Automatic, up to date generation of documentation, according to documentation standards

- Automatic code generation and code feedback (tracing)

The EPOS system is built up by the following items:

- Specification languages for requirement engineering, system specification and project management

- The EPOS project database for storage of all data described by the specification languages

- Several software tool systems for the evaluation of the EPOS project database (error analysis, design method support, documentation system, code generation system, management support)

Development of the EPOS System including the installation, service and maintenance, is carried out by GPP (Gesellschaft für Prozessrechnerprogrammierung mbH), Oberhaching near Munich. Today, EPOS is used world-wide in thousands of installations. It has been used by industry, governmental agencies, research institutes and universities since 1980.

For the integration into the VSE-System, EPOS is - among others- enhanced by a "formal component" to enable formal specification in the VSE specification language (VSE-SL).

Embedded Formal Specification Language VSE-SL

All formal specifications are stated in terms of a general purpose specification language, named VSE-SL. VSE-SL is a strongly typed language based on first-order predicate logic, enriched by features for modeling state-dependent behaviour. Requirements of safety-critical systems may be expressed in an appropriate manner.

Specifications in VSE are organized around units; a unit may contain a first-order theory, an abstract data type or an abstract state machine. Units are the basic blocks in VSE-SL, from which large specifications are built. They are the means of modularizing a system by the principles of horizontal structuring, vertical refinement, and generic features.

A unit may be parameterized by types, functions and predicates, and constraints may be stated on the parameters; this generates proof obligations for each instantiation of the generic specification unit, but on the other side, enhances the reusability of specifications.

The basis for VSE-SL is first-order typed predicate logic; the primitives of the logic – sorts, functions, predicates, variables, and first order connectives – are explicitly provided in the language. However, because of several extensions, VSE-SL is rather a specification language than just merely a logic. One extension has a pure syntactic character and mainly deals with names, their visibility, and features for overloading operators. Other extensions implicitly introduce axioms into the specification, like pre-defined data types, and again others affect the class of models described by the specification; for example constructors describe only generated models.

VSE-SL provides features for modeling state based systems; these are the primitives *state object* and *operation*. State objects correspond to variables in a procedural programming language, e.g. Ada. Operations cause a state change and thus may affect the values of state objects; they correspond to procedures in conventional programming languages.

A major aspect of VSE-SL is its support for structures, with respect to both, horizontal decomposition and vertical hierarchy. The specification of a system may be structured by composing specification units at the same level of abstraction (horizontal structure). The vertical hierarchy is expressed by the relation between successive levels of abstraction and refinements. A refinement step employs a mapping, which links successive abstraction levels, and an implementation stated in terms of an abstract programming language, which in turn uses specifications written in VSE-SL.

This methodology favors the top-down development of a system, resulting in a hierarchy of abstraction levels, reaching from the requirement specification to the specification of the executable code and primitive data types.

KIV

As mentioned above, the VSE supports the modeling of systems in a variety of ways (abstract data types, state based systems etc.). This raises the need for a matching set of tools to support the corresponding correctness proofs. Within the VSE, the KARLSRUHE INTERACTIVE VERIFIER (KIV) serves the needs of proving correctness of programs wrt. their specification.

Architecture of the KIV system. The KIV system realizes a *shell* for implementing different verification methods on a common logical basis (see Heisel, 1990). This design combines the flexibility required for the various specification methods, a mechanism to ensure the

correctness of the implemented verification methods, and the option for future enhancements.

To achieve these goals, the KIV system follows the paradigm of *tactical theorem proving* (see Gordon, 1989), which combines a powerful logical basis with a programming language designed for manipulating proofs. This allows to build a layered system which can be adapted to several needs.

On the lowest level, the built-in logic can be tailored for a specific verification method. This also involves a "reduction" of the tailored version to the built-in logic, and to be successful this task requires expertise with the built-in logic. On the next level, proof tactics are formed from the extended logic. This requires some experience with logic as well. These two lower levels will not be directly accessible within VSE.

The third level combines tactics and heuristics to form proof strategies, and adds a user interface. The user interface hides most technical details from the end user of the VSE system, and consequently using proof strategies requires only marginal knowledge of the particular built-in logic. However, it *does* require the ability to perform some formal reasoning, but the use of the system in courses at the university has shown that computer science students master the proof strategies fairly quick.

Integration into the VSE. Following this way, most of the well known verification methods have been realized within the KIV system. Also, a number of program synthesis methods, where programs are developed starting from the specification, have been integrated. The important feature for the VSE is that the KIV system supports the modularized specification of systems described earlier. There is a special proof strategy for modular verification which performs the proofs necessary to show the correctness of a refinement step.

For the VSE, the management of proofs within the KIV system will be integrated into the VSE's verification management. This includes the possibility of multiuser operation, keeping track of changes to programs (after all, since mistakes are only human, the first attempt to verify a refinement step will usually fail), and tools to analyse, store and document proofs.

Enhancements. Proof strategies are usually *interactive*, in the sense that the "key steps" in the proof are initiated by the user, and the system performs the routine proof steps. Key steps are, for example, the formulation of loop invariants or induction hypotheses, or the selection of the next reduction step out of a choice offered by the system. The actual degree of automation that can be reached currently lies between 80 and 95%. A degree of 95% may sound impressive, but it should be noted that a correctness proof for a refinement step may easily require several ten thousand proof steps.

There are several ways in which this degree of automation can be increased. One of these is to use a better theorem prover to determine properties of the import specification of a module. The integration of the theorem prover described below is expected to result in further improvements. Another major source of improvement will be the experience gained with the VSE case studies, which will result in enhancements of the existing proof strategies within the KIV system.

While formal verification may be expensive, the remarkable results we have already achieved show that formal verification is possible with today's (hard- and software) technology.

The Theorem Prover

Proving the correctness of programs w. r. t. their specification within KIV results in a bundle of (first order) predicate logical formulas which have to be deduced from the specification. The more these formulas can be proven automatically the more the degree of automation in the KIV system increases. Hence within VSE, this task is handled by a specialized automated theorem prover.

The heart of this theorem prover is the INKA-system (Biundo, 1986) which is an inductive theorem prover based on resolution and paramodulation. Resolution is the best known calculus to handle full first-order predicate logic automatically. The calculus is guided by elaborated strategies based (like the KIV system) on the paradigm of tactical theorem proving.

The theorem proving component has to be capable of several techniques:

Mathematical induction is required for reasoning about objects containing repetition, e.g. lists of numbers. Induction proofs are characterised by the application of so called *induction rules*, of which the simplest and best known example is an induction rule on natural numbers: To prove a formula

$$\forall x : nat \; P(x)$$

we have to prove both formulas:

$$P(0) \; \text{and} \; \forall x : nat \; P(x) \rightarrow P(x+1)$$

Within VSE similar and other rules are available for every kind of recursively defined data structure, e.g. list of numbers, integers, trees, etc. In fact, applying induction rules creates infinitely many branching points in search space. Hence, the theorem prover has to be guided by sophisticated heuristics selecting an appropriate induction rule to get rid of the combinatorical explosion. There are other heuristics which contain the knowledge how to prove typically base cases or induction steps (Hutter (1989)).

Within VSE some data structures - integer, sets or arrays - and functions - $+, *, \cup$, etc. - operating on these data structures are predefined. This opens up the ability to incorporate highly specialized deduction tools and strategies for dealing with these data structures and operations. A typical example is a built-in semi decision procedure for Presburger Arithmetic (handling integers with $+, -$).

THE VSE PROJECT

It is the objective of the VSE-project to create an integrated software development tool (VSE-tool) to generate security-relevant program systems, which can be proved to be correct.

The VSE is in development by a consortium of industrial companies and institutes (Dornier, GPP, University of Karlsruhe, University of Saarbrücken and University of Ulm) under contract of the BSI (Bundesamt für Sicherheit in der Informationstechnik).

The project organization is shown by Fig. 2.

The individual components (KIV, theorem prover, formal specification language) will be integrated into the EPOS software development environment.

Industrial relevance and usefulness of the VSE-tool will be proved in the course of the project by means of comprehensive case studies based on industrial projects.

These case studies shall cover all aspects of the definition of the VSE-tool requirements, mainly a wide spectrum of the IT security criteria. Additionally, the case studies shall reveal strong and weak points of the VSE-tool and of all components. The features to be determined are, for example, the degree of automation, termination, run time behavior and efficiency. Above all, the case studies shall show, to which extent the user is supported by the VSE-tool.

VSE PROJECT ORGANISATION		
· **Commissioner:** Bundesamt fuer Sicherheit in der Informationstechnik (BSI)		
. **Projectpartners**	**(Location**	**Responsibility)**
- Fa. Dornier	Friedrichshafen	project management and case studies
- Fa. GPP	Muenchen	integration of components into EPOS
- University	Karlsruhe	interactive verification system (KIV)
- University	Ulm	specification language
- University	Saarbruecken	theorem provers
. **Duration:** 3 1/2 years (February 91 - July 94)		
. **Hardware-Platform:** SUN SPARCstation .... , UNIX		

Fig. 2: Project Organisation

For the selection from a great number of industrial case studies which have already been conducted or are currently in preperation, mainly the following criteria were taken as a basis:

- Suitability, extent, and complexity of the case studies

- Relation to reality

- Security requirements

- Assessment of current methods and components

- Development activities required

REFERENCES

Biundo, S., B. Hummel, D. Hutter, C. Walther (1986).
The Karlsruhe Induction Theorem Proving System.
Proceedings 8th Conference on Automated Deduction.
Springer LNCS, Vol 230.

Heisel, Reif, Stephan (1990). Tactical Theorem Proving in Program Verification. *Proceedings 10th International Conference in Artificial Intelligence.* Springer
LNCS, Vol 449.

Hutter (1989). Complete Induction. In K.H. Bläsius
and H.-J. Bürckert (Ed.), *Deduction Systems in Arti-
fical Intelligence*, Ellis Horwood. 1989 Chap 7.

Gordon, Milner, Wadsworth (1979). Edinburgh LCF.
Lecture Notes in Computer Science, 78. Springer Verlag, Berlin.

Lempp, P. (1986). Development and Project Management Support with the Software Engineering Environment EPOS. In I. Sommerville (Ed.), *Intl. Conf.
Software Eng. Environments.* Lancaster, Great Britain.

Reif (1991). *Correctness of Specifications and Generic Modules.* PhD thesis, Universität Karlsruhe. In
Deutsch.

Rushby, von Henke, Owre (1991). *An Introduction
to Formal Specification and Verification Using EHDM.*
SRI International, Menlo Park, California.

Wirsing (1990). Algebraic Specification. In J. van
Leeuwen (Ed.), *Handbook of Theoretical Computer
Science*, Vol. B, Formal Models and Semantics. Else-
vier Science Publishers B.V.. pp 675–788.

DESIGN AND PLANNING IN THE DEVELOPMENT OF SAFETY-CRITICAL SOFTWARE WITH ADA

J. Prorok, K. Bührer, U. Ammann, K. Vit

Oerlikon-Contraves AG
Department S-EI
Schaffhauserstrasse 580
CH-8052 ZÜRICH, Switzerland

Abstract A study carried out for the European Space Agency by Oerlikon-Contraves recommends 30 approaches for improving the safety of software to be developed in Ada; recommendations are also made against the use of a further 21 approaches. Of particular significance among the recommendations are an Ada Language coding guideline, recommendations for the use of object-oriented design approaches, disciplined management practices, and early consideration of testing requirements and testability. Most of the recommended approaches are either entirely or substantially carried out in early phases of a software development project. In particular, in order to be in the position of being able to avoid "dangerous" practices at a later stage, it is necessary to plan ahead, and design-out the opportunities for such practices early on. A proper appreciation of the planning and design of safety-critical software is thus essential for a satisfactory project outcome.

Keywords safety, software engineering, software development, programming languages, program testing, real-time computer systems

The work reported here was carried out under contract to the European Space Agency (Contract No. 9202/90/NL/JG "Procedure for Developing Safety Critical Software in Ada"). The opinions expressed in this paper are those of the authors and not necessarily those of the European Space Agency.

INTRODUCTION

The European Space Agency (ESA) expects to use software for the implementation of safety-critical functions on the Columbus and Hermes projects. Both these projects have adopted the Ada Language for all software development, and while it is expected that the use of Ada will have a positive effect on software quality as well as productivity, it is a particular concern that Ada be used in such a way that the *safest* possible software is produced.

Oerlikon-Contraves has considerable experience both in the development of mission-critical systems as well as in the use of the Ada Language. Consequently, ESA commissioned Oerlikon-Contraves to carry out a Study with the goal of recommending a procedure for the development of safety-critical software using Ada. The Final Report for this Study (Oerlikon-Contraves, 1991) recommends 30 approaches for use in the development of safety-critical software. The applicability of each of the recommended approaches over the course of the development life-cycle has been identified, and (as might be expected) the Study showed that particular attention must be paid to planning and design. Of the 30 approaches recommended, 20 require execution (to have begun) by the end of the architectural design phase, while specific preparation and/or planning activities will have been required for a further 6. The need to give adequate consideration to so many different issues at an early stage of a project imposes a strain on managers and designers, and implies greater risk for the project, since more funds will be used up before the success of the project can be judged.

The manager of a safety-critical software development project has three basic ways of ensuring that critical failures will not occur during software missions:
a) error avoidance,
b) software testing, and
c) fault tolerance.

ERROR AVOIDANCE

The total (and guaranteed) avoidance of errors during development would be a worthy goal to achieve, but despite the serious efforts made up to now in this direction, is not a practical proposition in an industrial environment. Nevertheless, enough is known about software development that techniques which help reduce the making of errors can be defined and applied.

Project Management

One of the first tasks of the software project manager is to select the techniques whose application is most likely to bring positive results, and to see to it that the development team has the means to apply them effectively.

Configuration Management Configuration management is a discipline which is accepted in the hardware world, and even the most hardened software individualists are prepared to concede that some configuration management is necessary on a software project. The importance of software configuration management is recognised within the Ada Language by the inclusion of both a library concept, as well as the notion of obsolescence of compilation units, within the definition of the language. Nevertheless, on any but the smallest projects, the software manager would be well advised to provide tools to support the demands which configuration management places on developers (Tichy, 1989).

The importance of configuration management for most projects is as a means of coordinating the team (Babich, 1986) so that the work of each individual fits into the work of the team as a whole, thus maintaining a reasonable level of productivity. The absence of effective configuration management promotes the breakdown of coordination and discipline, leading to chaos, which would certainly be detrimental to the safety characteristics of the product being developed.

However, laying aside the coordination aspects of configuration management, software configuration management's key role in safety-critical projects is in ensuring that the product which is delivered to the customer is really the one the customer expects, fulfilling all the specified requirements, and being the result of the approved development process; in particular, configuration management will provide the traceability between the delivered product and the requisite successful verification and validation steps.

The means to provide this configuration auditing capability must be laid down at an early stage by establishing rules and procedures for configuration identification and control.

Quality Assurance The manager of a team developing an obviously safety-critical application may be at an advantage in motivating his team to work under a regime of strict quality assurance compared with his colleague on a conventional project, who may have difficulty in convincing his team that all the prescribed formality of the development process is really necessary.

Nevertheless, the manager of the safety-critical software development project must still ensure that the pre-conditions for carrying out the development of safety-critical software are met, namely that:
a) the software development process has been defined and adequately documented, and in particular that
b) the criteria for assessing each kind of work result are defined and documented;
c) the quality assurance team has been set-up, and allocated enough resources and independence to allow them to carry out their functions adequately;
d) the software development project has enough resources to do justice to the requirements of the prescribed development process.

Unless requirements (a) and (b) are fulfilled by adopting the quality management scheme from an already existing organisational context, a substantial investment of time and money will first need to be made to develop the requisite infra-structure preceding the product development itself. It is thus difficult to imagine a newly created organisation being equipped with the necessary capabilities.

On the other hand, an organisation which has undertaken such an investment can expect to obtain official certification (e.g. ISO9001, AQAP-13, etc.) which can reassure prospective customers of its competence and commitment in this area.

Review Practices A key element in any team software effort is "ego-less" development, by which software parts do not "belong" to individuals but instead are developed by the whole team, or at least groups within the team. This is a means of putting diversity of thinking to good use, allowing constructive team efforts to achieve results superior to those that a single individual could be expected to attain. Consistent with the ego-less developer concept, and an important mechanism supporting it, is the extensive conduct of reviews throughout a project.

Although much of the reviewing activity will be carried out in the course of the development work, all the way through to final testing and installation, there are two aspects of reviewing which concern the planning and design phases in particular.

Firstly, the conduct of reviews should follow adequately established guidelines, concerning
a) the form of each kind of review (walkthroughs, inspections, private reviews, life-cycle phase reviews, etc.), in particular concerning

b) the criteria for acceptance or rejection of work results (see above), and

c) the use of appropriate kinds of review according to circumstances.

It may be possible to inherit such guidelines from an encompassing organisation, but it is still often necessary to tune them to the specific work results of a particular project.

Secondly, the importance of thorough reviewing of the work done early in a project must be emphasised. Because it is exactly at this stage that the understanding of the nature of a product is at its weakest, so is it necessary that the various fledgling concepts held by individuals in the team must be put down in black and white and subjected to the constructive criticism of peers in the team. Not only must the need to carry out reviews be defined in the software development process, but resources (i.e. in particular developer time) must be allowed for performing these reviews.

Stability of the Environment The reliability and safety of the software product directly depends on the correctness of core development tools such as the Ada compiler, linker and run-time system (the "APSE" tools). Even well tested and widely used APSEs contain bugs, and new APSE versions may introduce new problems besides removing known ones. It is by no means correct to conclude that a validated APSE is also a fault-free APSE: validation is concerned much more with program portability than with APSE correctness. The selection of a suitable APSE should be carried out well in advance of a project, usually by an evaluation team established just for the purpose. No universally accepted criteria for the evaluation of APSEs for safety-critical software development yet exist, but the most reasonable approach is to ask the supplier for evidence of reliability and maturity of his product. An APSE could also provide special features to support the development of safety-critical software, such as safe implementation of access types, garbage collection, unlimited task stacks or extended compile--time checks; no Ada implementation currently supports any of these features, however.

Nevertheless, all commercially available software products, including Ada development tools, undergo considerable evolution over their lifetime. As any significant modifications of the development environment may disrupt or delay the flow of a project and may thus have a generally negative impact on the quality of the application software, project management is well advised to keep the development environment as stable as possible. For safety-critical software this is not enough, however.

Modification of the APSE tools may have a very serious impact on the quality of the application software, in ways which the developers may not normally be aware of. For the development of safety-critical software, APSEs must be frozen as soon as formal testing starts. Unfortunately, freezing an APSE will on most computer systems require the freezing of the underlying operating system (because APSE and operating system are tightly integrated), and hence freezing of most development tools on that computer system. In many cases this will make the frozen computer system unusable for other projects and other users. It thus turns out that freezing an APSE usually means exclusive reservation of an entire computer system, maybe even including peripherals, for a single project, which requires considerable funds and early managerial preparations.

Training and Experience Under normal circumstances, a project manager will not expect to have an ideally trained set of staff made available to him, and will seek to undertake training on account of the project, in the methods, languages, and tools to be used on the project. For safety-critical projects, additional training in specialised methods and safety standards, preferably leading to professional certification of individuals, should be undertaken for a certain number of team members, certainly of the key persons in the team.

On the other hand, the manager will seek to make maximum use of the capabilities available in an organisation, even if these are not allocated full-time to his project. Experts should be available throughout the life of a project to deal with problems or queries about the design of the product, or even more importantly on the correct use of the development methods and tools. Because of the relative complexity of the Ada Language and its compilers, experts with knowledge of the workings of Ada compiler systems can not only advise on optimal and safe ways of using the language, but can be very useful in solving problems encountered in its usage. Nevertheless, the greatest benefits are obtained when an expert has a degree of involvement in a project, best achieved by assigning him with certain project responsibilities.

Software Design

Ada Coding Rules The focus of attention for the study was the Ada language itself. The ways in which developers can misuse the language to produce unsafe software, as well as the so-called language "uncertainties" were analyzed; 58 rules for the safe use of the Ada language were formulated and presented in the form of an Ada coding guideline. Even though the coding guideline appears to be directed at the detailed design and coding of the application software, about half of the rules actually aim at mistakes committed in earlier development phases, in particular at faults within the architectural design.

The Ada programming language has the power to implement almost any design, no matter how inappropriate the design may be. However, in doing so, the software developer may be forced to make assumptions (for example concerning task scheduling) which do not hold, or to use constructs such as global variables, busy loops or passive synchronization, which are generally considered as "bad programming style", and which not only reduce the general quality of the software but also pose a serious and direct threat to software reliability and safety.

It has in the past been remarked that Ada is one of the best specified languages yet to have been put into widespread use, despite a number of reports which have identified specification weaknesses (e.g. Wichmann, 1989). Even though such "uncertainties" could cause an Ada program to be erroneous, they are mostly intended to be there and should not be regarded as a shortcoming of the language; they are a safety problem only if particular language features are used in an inadequate way. Such misuse of Ada features is - as already mentioned - often the result of an incorrect design, or a design which does not take into account Ada as the implementation language. Software implementation problems due to Ada uncertainties should always alert the development team to the existence of faults lurking somewhere in the design of the system.

A number of organisations which use Ada for safety- or mission-critical software have decided to restrict the programmer in the range of language constructs available to him. This is however a very questionable approach as not only do the suggested subsets usually not exclude the constructs most threatening to safety (e.g. global variables), but they typically prohibit the use of some language constructs which actually improve the safety of the Ada software (e.g. tasks for interrupt handling). The key issue here is that it is not the language features by themselves which pose safety problems but their mode of usage or the context in which they are used. Restrictions imposed by coding rules must thus always be flexible, still allowing the programmer to use Ada in a natural and straightforward way, taking full advantage of the power of the language. The static analysis of Ada source code to verify the absence of unsafe constructs was found to be an approach with considerable potential, but in practice marred by the inability of currently available analysers to cope with the full extent of the language.

Object-Oriented Development Considerable attention was paid to the use of object-oriented approaches to software development, as this is considered to be the natural way of designing reliable software, and is well supported by the Ada language. Not only does object-oriented analysis and design help to avoid coding mistakes, but it also provides a convenient basis for fault detection and fault tolerance mechanisms.

Object-oriented development differs from other, purely functionally- or purely data-oriented approaches in that functions and data are considered as inseparable elements which together constitute objects. Object-oriented analysis and design methods are thus clearly more powerful and more flexible than purely functionally- or data-oriented approaches, which are largely superseded. The key to high software quality, in particular reliability and safety, is an adequate decomposition of the application system into objects. However, analysis and decomposition of a software system into objects is currently not well understood and poorly supported by methods and tools. Most object-oriented analysis techniques are based on intuitive selection of candidate objects and the iterative investigation of relationships between these objects. More support and tools are available for object-oriented design, and at least one systematic and well documented methodology, HOOD, exists.

Any object-oriented decomposition approach will eventually identify 3 types of objects: Actors (which only require operations), Servers (which only suffer operations) and Agents (which both require and suffer operations). It has been found that the highest level of software quality is achieved if Agent objects are systematically avoided during system analysis and design, and throughout software production. The well known quality defects of functionally decomposed software illustrate this conclusion: functional decomposition usually produces an overwhelming number of Agent objects.

Another negative aspect of the use of Agents is their tendency to sequentialise the execution of essentially independent software tasks, thus creating real-time constraints which are not related to any software or system requirements. Hard real-time constraints found in embedded software may thus often result from an inappropriate software design and not from stringent requirements. A software developer asking himself: "What should a software task do if it overruns its execution deadline ?" may already be trapped on the wrong line of thought. Instead, he should ask himself: "How should the software be structured so that no task *need* meet an execution deadline ?!" The latter question will probably lead to a better design, which is also more suitable for implementation in Ada, and will eventually result in the production of higher quality software. Nevertheless, there will always be a small part of the software which has to satisfy real-time constraints imposed by the system requirements, but in general these parts can be kept very small indeed.

SOFTWARE TESTING

Despite all attempts at error avoidance during development, and the knowledge that design features have been incorporated into a product so that it can tolerate failures if they should occur, no responsible software developer should be prepared to release critical software without first conducting rigorous testing. Unfortunately, while "design for testability" is standard practice among hardware developers, software developers rarely consider the need, let alone the details of testing, at an early stage.

Careful design using an object-oriented approach, plus careful analysis of software concurrency, not only help reduce the incidence of errors but can be useful in allowing a structural framework for testing to be defined. However, in the final analysis, there seems to be little alternative to the use of personnel with considerable experience of software testing and integration, as soon as possible during design, in order to ensure that it will be possible to perform reasonable tests on the software at a later phase of the project. This need is particularly highlighted in the case of systems which include heavy use of fault-tolerance features.

At the level of detail design and coding, restrictions on the complexity of individual software units, coupled with requirements to achieve a high test coverage of paths, lead designers and programmers to choose simpler, and usually more testable implementations for their units. This can be brought home even more forcefully to designers/programmers if they themselves are required to design tests (which meet the testing requirements) for their individual software units !

Testing Strategies

A sound structural framework for testing is one which allows progressive testing to be carried out during the integration of the software product. A convenient approach is to follow the software build process and test successively larger software units before they are cemented together within the system. While white-box testing should be enforced at the level of individual units, it is unlikely to remain practical as the level of integration increases, so that black-box testing against specifications becomes more and more important. However, black-box testing is limited by the quality of the specifications against which tests are carried out, which again puts the emphasis on writing good specifications in the first place. Furthermore, specifications need also take into consideration unforeseen situations and illegal inputs in order to be adequate for testing purposes.

In general, a wide range of testing techniques should be applied, extending even to random test generation, so as to achieve the best possible coverage of the software. Unfortunately, no reliable guide for when to stop testing is available, and this decision must ultimately be made on the basis of the SW Project or Test Manager's intuition.

Regression Testing

When errors are detected and changes are made in the software to correct them, these changes also invalidate the results of tests carried out previously. Although a judicious scheme for making releases of successively more mature software versions can help restrain costs, in the final analysis, the need to provide 100% regression testing leads the testing activity to be a major budget item in the software development project. Failure to make due allowance for this in the budgeting will lead to cost overruns or an inadequately tested product.

FAULT TOLERANCE

As the third option in the three-pronged attack on software defects, inclusion of mechanisms in the software itself which can dynamically deal with failures, is a powerful means of complementing the other two options for the case where a defect does, after all, remain in the released software, and is activated during a mission. Moreover, this class of options can often fit-in well with the hardware fault tolerance and detection mechanisms which are standard on critical systems.

As in the hardware world, the number of design choices open to the software designer can be very large, and a decision must be made early on, on the kind of fault tolerance approaches to be used.

Most hardware fault tolerance mechanisms imply considerable penalty in increased complexity (fault detection mechanisms less so), and the software area has its analogues (e.g. N-Version Programming, in which the added complexity seems as likely to introduce new problems as it is of solving existing ones, Eckhardt, 1991). As a rule, software fault tolerance mechanisms which do not immediately lead to a significant increase in complexity should be given preference.

Furthermore, the inflexibility of approaches such as fall-back recovery (Leveson, 1983), or the simplistic nature of the safety-net or similar approaches, should be taken into consideration, particularly for complex hard real-time systems, before such approaches are adopted for use in a product design.

Exceptions

A key element in the implementation of effective fault tolerant software is Ada's "exception" concept, which effectively provides a second plane of control for dealing with exceptional situations. Successful use of exceptions, however, requires that designers:

a) have a clear understanding of how Ada exceptions work, in particular in conjunction with the use of tasks;
b) decide what is to be considered "exceptional" and what merely constitutes testing of unusual conditions;
c) take the use of exceptions into consideration early on in the design activities, preferably incorporating the use of exceptions into the design of "objects" in an object-oriented development approach.

Assertions

No less important is the extensive use of assertions at all levels of the software, in order to verify the validity of the assumptions underlying particular operations, before attempting to carry these out. The use of assertions requires designers to reflect on the meaning of the operations they are designing, which after a little practice not only becomes second nature, but also has the effect of eliminating errors at source. Included here are checks on the plausibility of data, which can be used to avoid processing internal data or sensor readings which have become corrupted in some way. The failure of an assertion to hold during execution of a program is conveniently used to trigger an exception, which leads to an appropriate recovery action.

Forward Recovery

The physical nature of most real-time systems almost invariably allows them to tolerate a measure of transient failures without losing stability or irrevocably entering dangerous states; the periodic nature of most such systems conveniently allows processing of a cycle to be abandoned and further processing to continue with a new cycle, possibly with some clearing-up operations carried out in the mean time. An understanding of the physical characteristics of the system, and of its limitations, allows designers to determine the capability of the system to absorb transient failures within acceptable levels of performance, but again requires careful study of system characteristics at an early stage.

While local recovery actions, which attempt to repair failures close to their occurrence, may be feasible, as the level at which a failure has to be handled becomes more remote from the point of occurrence, so it becomes more likely that an action abandoning current operations in progress will have to be taken, and a forward recovery carried out.

CONCLUSIONS

Oerlikon-Contraves' experience in the development of mission-critical real-time embedded Ada software has allowed it to make a number of recommendations to the European Space Agency concerning the best approaches to be used for producing safety-critical Ada software. The recommendations, both positive and negative, reflect the pragmatic approach taken in the conduct of the Study.

The effectiveness of some of the available techniques is controversial, and indeed, it seems likely that in some cases, the potential for improvement is outweighed by a real risk of associated degradation. Furthermore, in a real industrial situation, safety notwithstanding, cost and schedule constraints and the unavailability of specialised resources result in only those approaches being considered which are complementary and most likely to be effective in yielding improvements in safety.

It becomes clear that not only is additional effort required throughout all phases of development, but that unless careful attention is paid to a number of planning and design issues early on during development, an expensive as well as an unsafe product will result.

REFERENCES

Babich W.A. (1986). *Software Configuration Management: Coordination for Team Productivity.* Addison-Wesley.

Eckhardt D.E. and co-workers (1991). An experimental evaluation of software redundancy as a strategy for improving reliability. *IEEE Trans. on Software Engineering*, SE-17, 692-702.

Leveson N.G. (1983). Software Fault Tolerance: the case for forward recovery. *Proceedings of the 4th AIAA Computers in Aerospace Conference, Hartford, Oct. 1983.*

Oerlikon-Contraves (1991). *Procedure for Developing Safety-Critical Software in Ada - Final Report.* (Internal ref. CU 441 005 AVA).

Tichy W. (1989). Tools for software configuration management. in *Proceedings of the International Workshop on Software Version and Configuration Control, Grassau, Jan. 1988.* Ed. J. Winkler, Teubner.

Wichmann B.A. (1989). Insecurities in the Ada programming language, *UK National Physical Laboratory Report DITC 137/89.*

THE MYTHICAL MEAN TIME TO FAILURE

A.K.Bissett

School of Computing & Management Sciences,
Sheffield City Polytechnic,
100 Napier Street, Sheffield S11 8HD, England

Abstract. As software engineering has emerged as a discipline in its own right, its practitioners have often borrowed methods and techniques from other engineering fields. These techniques have proved useful in the past, and the expectation has been that they would have a similar utility when applied to software.

The peculiar nature of software sometimes invalidates such an approach. This paper develops a critique of the use of the Mean Time To Failure (MTTF) metric with software, and discusses some of the implications for software reliability.

Keywords. Software engineering; software reliability; software reliability growth models

INTRODUCTION

It is both desirable and possible to engineer software, but appropriate methods must be found for this task, taking into account the particular nature of software. Methods which work in other engineering disciplines may not transfer meaningfully to software, given the different nature of the artefacts involved.

Fred Brooks (1975) has argued famously that the concept of the man-month, used as a unit of production effort, is dangerously misleading when employed in the context of large software engineering projects. He labelled this metric as "mythical" when employed in the software development context.

Another metric which has often been used in assessing the reliability of software is the Mean Time To Failure (MTTF) measure (Conte, Dunsmore and Shen, 1986; Musa, Iannino and Okumoto, 1987; Rook, 1990). MTTF is the expected value of the time between the occurrence of failures. MTTF may be regarded as the inverse of failure intensity, which is itself the number of failures per unit time. Failures are the manifestations of faults contained in the software.

This paper takes issue with the application of the MTTF concept to software. The MTTF metric is a tool which appeals to engineers, especially as it works very well in the engineering of physical artefacts which have well-understood and equally physical failure modes. In the software field it could be used to argue for compliance with a reliability figure such as the "less than 10^{-9} failures per hour of operation" required for safety-critical aerospace software (Levenson, 1991; Moser and Melliar-Smith, 1990). Many authors have expressed doubts concerning the appropriateness of using MTTF with software, but they have not presented a full analysis as to precisely why there might be a problem. In this paper we attempt to develop a fuller analysis.

Other doubts have been expressed concerning the accuracy with which very low failure rates, such as the figure for aerospace software mentioned above, can be estimated (Levenson, 1991). We show that, however such figures may be arrived at, certainly MTTF is a poor basis for their calculation.

We argue that from the viewpoint of software reliability, the MTTF value is, to borrow Brook's term, somewhat mythical.

AN INAPPROPRIATE TRANSFER

There is a crucial misconception at the heart of the use of MTTF with software, a misconception based on the very nature of the engineered artefact. We may distinguish four roots of unreliability in any system, be it hardware or software. These are design faults, implementation faults, replication faults, and fatigue faults.

The MTTF approach used with hardware is aimed at the likelihood of failure due to faults introduced in replication activities, or later due to in-service wear and tear (fatigue). In other words, the hardware system is assumed to have been designed and specified correctly. A statistical sampling approach, based on assumptions of randomness and independence of fault distribution, is an appropriate way to handle these kinds of failures. Thus MTTF assumes a physical artefact, whereas in fact software is primarily logical in nature. The physical realisation of software is "accidental", to employ another of Brook's (1987) terms, and can be ignored from a reliability viewpoint. The code may happen to be embodied as a file of binary on disk, or blocks of binary in RAM, or, assuming a reliable translator, as a file of text, but the particular physical embodiment does not affect the reliability of the software when it is executed.

Once a program is fault free, it is always fault free. If it contains faults, it will always remain potentially unreliable. Faults introduced by the replication of a program are vanishingly small, given modern storage technology. Fatigue faults, of course, are non-existent for software. Provided that software is not altered, it does not degrade in the way that physical artefacts are prone to do during their operational life. Thomas (1988) puts the distinction between hardware and software very succinctly: "...software is totally reliable (in the sense that it will continue to display the same functionality it had when it was first designed)."

To summarise the discussion so far, we can say that for physical engineered artefacts, replication and fatigue faults are at least as significant as design and implementation faults, whereas for software artefacts, design and implementation errors are everything, and replication errors are nothing - they can be safely discounted to the point of being ignored. Furthermore, fatigue errors simply do not exist.

Because of the different nature of faults in hardware and software, it is not appropriate to treat on a probabilistic basis the issue of when a program will fail. It will either fail given the "right" combination of circumstances, or else it will not. Certainly, faults which are introduced during the software development process will have the potential to manifest themselves as failures once the software is in operation. But there is nothing random about the way in which they will appear. They will manifest themselves in a logical and indeed entirely deterministic fashion - "...software does not exhibit random failures" (Thomas, 1988).

Moreover, it is doubtful that even the way in which faults are introduced by the design process can meaningfully be described as "random", especially given the bespoke nature of most software.

The basic mistake has been to try to apply an essentially physical measure to an essentially logical entity. Now let us examine in detail how the MTTF is practically derived, in order to follow through the consequences of this misapplication.

Initially the MTTF value is derived empirically, from testing the software. There are well-known problems involved in the testing of software - quality of test data, test data's "realism" compared to real operation, and Dijkstra's famous dictum that testing can only prove the presence, as opposed to the absence, of faults. These problems can, in principle, be ameliorated by measuring failure intensity of the system as it is in actual use. (This may not of course be feasible in actuality because of the expensive or dangerous consequences of failures). Let us allow that it is possible, then, to measure a fairly representative failure intensity/MTTF. However, this measured value of MTTF should be treated with extreme caution. It is a poor predictor of reliability. Unforseen circumstances during execution of the "live" system are always possible, and unless the software and its environment are trivially simple, testing is unlikely to have exercised all the possibilities. Testing is an imperfect science, and consequently any values such as MTTF derived from it are themselves necessarily imperfect.

The measured MTTF figure is used, wrongly, we argue, in more or less sophisticated ways to predict future reliability of the software. The more sophisticated predictive approaches involve the use of reliability growth models.

THE RELIABILITY GROWTH APPROACH

Different definitions of software reliability are possible. For example, Sommerville (1989) says that "reliability is a measure of how well the sofware provides the services which it is supposed to". Moser and Melliar-Smith (1990) simply use the term to refer to the absence of failures. The reliability growth approach prefers to define reliability in relation to time: software reliability is "the probability of failure-free operation of a program for a specified time in a specified environment" (Musa, Iannino and Okumoto, 1987). The predictive implication of this definition is worth noting.

We have seen that the measured MTTF figure has its limitations. The MTTF figure is extrapolated beyond its measured value by using the reliability growth approach. This is an empirical, pragmatic approach to assessing system and component reliability which once again is posited on the probability of the entity failing in a random manner. This suggests that the predictive MTTF value derived from reliability growth modelling should be treated with even more caution than the measured MTTF value.

Reliability growth works in an essentially simple way. The software system is exercised. Failures are observed due to faults in the software. The number of failures per unit time of operation is counted to give a failure intensity figure. Faults in the software are repaired, and the software run again to see the effect of the repairs on the failure rate. The failure intensity is extrapolated using a probabilistic model. This suggests that the failure rate can be related to the number of error repairs performed. The software can now be released to service on the basis that either the likely failure rate is known, or that an adequate number of error repairs has been performed and, by extrapolation, the likely failure rate is at an acceptable level for the kind of service envisaged (Csenki, 1991a, 1991b).

CRITIQUE OF RELIABILITY GROWTH APPROACH

We next present a more detailed critique of how the reliability growth approach treats the results of the measured MTTF.

Fault Independence in the Models

Most of the reliability growth models assume that faults will manifest themselves independently. At the root of this assumption is the view of software as being stateless. This is a very big and quite unjustified assumption. Faults very often have a combinatorial effect or propagate further faults.

No-fault Repairs

Following on from the view that faults will manifest themselves in an independent fashion is the assumption that repairing the errors which caused those faults can be performed in an independent fashion. There is a further assumption here that error repairs will not introduce further errors. Some reliability growth models attempt to capture the unfortunate real experience that repairing a fault often introduces further faults by adding a random component (Csenki, 1991b; Rook, 1990). This is not convincingly realistic since, as argued previously, there is nothing random about fault manifestation.

Faults Equally Likely

Another aspect of the fault-independence assumption is that all faults are equally likely to manifest themselves as failures. Sommerville (1989) points out that different use patterns will exercise different parts of the software. As mentioned above, this shortcoming can in principle be moderated by measuring failure intensity *in situ*, in the live operating environment. However, we are still confronted with the fact that faults will not be executed with equal regularity. This is another over-simplification in the reliability growth model.

Failures Modes Ignored

The causes of failures in hardware entities are generally well understood. For example, "stuck at one" faults in digital logic circuits, fatigue in load-bearing metal structures, power transmission lines being struck by lightning, and so forth. These effects may often be calculated, or in other ways handled (eg. by allowing for "worst-case scenarios"), without the need to resort to probability.

However, when MTTF is applied to software, the failure modes of software are not taken into account. For example, the likelihood of "out by one" errors in a WHILE loop is not discriminated for. From a reliability model view, all program statements carry equal weight and are equally likely to be a source of random failure. This is in sharp contrast to the empirical results from using a metric such as McCabe's Cyclomatic Complexity measure (1976). McCabe's results show that the complexity, and therefore the maintainability, and indirectly the reliability, of different program structures vary considerably.

Lack of Failure Effect Discrimination

MTTF does not take into account the differing effects of failures, for example, whether the software immediately "crashes" and stops executing, or whether a subtler effect takes place, resulting at some difficult-to-quantify later time in corrupted data, or indeed subsequent delayed "crash". Again with reference to hardware, a failure is usually immediate and obvious in its effects. The situation with software failure, however, is much more variable in its effects.

Thus MTTF prediction is based on a rather blunt instrument for software, namely reliability growth models, which regard all failures as being independent, and equal in importance and likelihood.

If MTTF is based on an inappropriate transfer of hardware techniques to the software context, and if its predictive models are unconvincing, then what view of software failure assessment should we take? To continue this investigation, let us look more closely at the specific nature of software. We will try to present a view which does not do such violence to the essential nature of software.

CRAFT vs. SCIENCE vs. ENGINEERING

Much software production in the past has been a craft activity, that is, the individual skills and intuition upon which it has relied are only partially reproducible. The development is based upon small-scale activity. Whilst this may have been more or less adequate for small scale systems, large systems are required to be engineered - that is, based upon sound, rigorous, reproducible methods, techniques, and tools, and constructed by teams of people. This kind of engineering enterprise is informed by science, which is formal, objective, and comparatively abstract. Engineering is science applied to a practical task.

If we are uncertain about the validity of empirical methods such as the use of the MTTF metric, perhaps we can turn to computer science to inform us about its applicability (or otherwise). What view of programs does computer science give us?

What is a Program?

As Brooks (1975) argues, software, in distinction to hardware entities, is an intangible logical construct akin to "pure thought-stuff". Given that any non-trivial program is a complex, human-constructed artefact, it is natural that a program can be defined as many different things. A commonly-used definition is that a program is a general solution to a set of specific problem instances. Another view is that it is a function, mapping from an input space to an output space. Alternatively, it may be viewed as an algorithm expressed in machine-readable form.

However, three further views are especially relevant to this discussion:-

(1) The MTTF view, that a random failure can occur in a program. This, as we have seen, is not well-founded, since there is nothing random about a program. At the very least the code must be syntactically correct in order to be put into operation. A piece of randomly-generated text (produced, say, by ten thousand monkeys sitting at keyboards), would not meet even this elementary criterion. However, this last (syntactical) consideration leads us to a second view:-

(2) The program is a formal object within a formal system. A formal system, be it a part of mathematics or a programming language, consists of axioms, an alphabet out of which strings can be constructed, production rules, and theorems. The program statements are productions ("theorems") within a Post production system (Brady, 1977; Krishnamurthy, 1983). We could call this view "Type A theorems". These theorems are well-formed formulae (strings constructed from the axioms using the production rules) without any particular meaning attached to them. This takes us a little way further on towards understanding the nature of software, but we need to introduce an interpretation to the formal system to understand its meaning. Moving on from the syntactical view of "Type A theorems" to a more semantically-based one, let us consider the work of Floyd, Hoare and Manna on associating assertions with programs:-

(3) The Floyd-Hoare-Manna inductive assertion technique for proving some of the properties of a program uses a series of assertions in predicate calculus attached to program statements (Brady, 1977; Krishnamurthy, 1983). Thus the interpretation being placed upon the Post production system is given by predicate logic - logical truth or falsity. Each assertion describes the properties of parts of the program. The assertions taken together form a proof concerning the behaviour of the whole program. Thus the program itself has the nature of a theorem, but in mechanically executable form. Let us refer to programs seen from this viewpoint as "Type B theorems".

Implications for Programs

Given the insight that a program may be viewed as a theorem in the "Type B" sense, then what deductions may be made concerning program reliability and program failure? What does the figure which has been given the name "MTTF" actually mean?

Our concept of "Type B" theorems has the same meaning as that of a theorem in mathematics. Let us examine a very simple and familiar theorem: that of Pythagoras. We pose the question: what is meant by the MTTF of Pythagoras' Theorem?

This is not quite such a stupid question as it initially seems. It is possible to imagine situations where Pythagoras' Theorem, although self-sufficient and correct in itself, in the abstract, could fail in implementation or application.

Pythagoras' Theorem may be stated as:- "In a right-angled triangle, the sum of the squares of the lengths of the sides containing the right angle is equal to the square of the hypotenuse, ie. $a^2 = b^2 + c^2$, where a is the length of the side opposite the right angle" (Daintith and Nelson, 1989).

Let us collect together the situations where this seemingly inviolable theorem could be caused to fail:-

(1) The first situation which could result in failure is when the theorem is applied to a figure which is not a right-angled triangle. The figure to which it is applied might be a three-sided entity where the length of sides 2 and 3 added together are less than the length of side 3. Alternatively, the theorem might be applied to a triangle which is not right-angled. In program terms this corresponds to attempting to run the program using an invalid data set. This situation is likely to be caused by poor requirements analysis - Pythagoras' Theorem was not what was required at all. (Perhaps we are actually going to be dealing with squares, not triangles, all along).

(2) The second case in which the theorem could fail is when the data is valid but an incorrect calculation takes place, due to a mental slip on the part of our geometrician. In program terms this is equivalent to a faulty implementation of the programming language (via its compiler) or the execution of the code (via faulty hardware).

(3) A third case could arise because the person performing the calculation based upon Pythogoras' Theorem is working with a faulty specification of what squaring or adding numbers means. This is no different in principle from case (2) above.

Notice that none of these three failure categories has a sensible interpretation in probabilistic terms for the mechanised version (program). The first case - applying the theorem to invalid data - can be guarded against in the program version by building into it input validation sequences. This means that the program is "stronger" than the abstract theorem, in this sense; the preconditions for its correct application can be automatically enforced.

The second and third cases can be eliminated for the program by providing ourselves with a reliable translator and hardware.

Perhaps it is helpful at this stage to make the distinction between internally caused faults and externally caused faults. The program itself, faults and all, is a deterministic object. As Hoare (1969) puts it: "...all the properties of a program and all the consequences of executing it in any given environment can, in principle, be found out from the text of the program itself by means of purely deductive reasoning." How the program may be used (or misused !), what will be in its external environment, is outside the control of the software constructor. The best we can do is to work to a precise specification of the given environment. For dependable applications we can build in robustness by means of input data validation and

exception handling routines, thoroughness in the requirements and overall system analysis, N-version programming, fault-tolerant strategies, formal verification, and other such techniques as surveyed by Levenson (1991).

MTTF REVISITED

If programs have the nature of theorems, then what does MTTF actually express in software terms? We can surmise that typical fault rates occur in the development of software, depending on the "difficulty" of the project, its number of novel characteristics, the nature of the programming language, etc. Note, however, that this fault rate is emphatically not the same thing as predicted Mean Time To Failure. It is an indirect, unquantified, indication of the unreliability of the software, but no more than that.

The "MTTF" measure is in fact an indirect measure of how good the developer's requirements capture, specification, coding, compilers, maintenance etc. are. In other words, what the MTTF figure actually expresses is a measure of the quality of the software developer's methods, including the efficacy of the maintenance. It is not a realistic, direct, metric of the reliability of the software. Any statements about the literal MTTF of an engineered system which contains software are merely statements of intent - desirable goals which the developer would like to attain.

CONCLUSION

Whilst MTTF has its uses in hardware engineering, where failure modes of the artefacts are "randomisable" and can be ascribed to replication or fatigue faults, it is not appropriate to apply this concept to software. Unlike hardware, software is not significantly susceptible to replication faults and is completely unaffected by fatigue faults.

Programs are, effectively, theorems. If there is a fault - any fault - in the software, then the whole construction, the whole theorem, is strictly unreliable. The probabilistic paradigm which underpins the MTTF approach is not appropriate given this view of the nature of software. Software does not exhibit random failures.

What is actually being expressed in the MTTF approach is an approximate measure of the quality of the development and maintenance methods used on the project.

Accordingly, we concur with one of the admirably judicious conclusions put forward by Levenson [6], namely that we could use such techniques to demonstrate that a level of reliability has not been achieved (rather than to support an argument that it has).

A further area in which MTTF can be useful is in pragmatic project management, where it could be used to predict test and maintenance effort in a known development environment.

Employing MTTF values as a reliability predictor, whether based on reliability growth models or not, should be treated with great caution. We must detach the "MTTF" figure from any time-quantified prediction of software failure rate. Indeed, we have argued that it is impossible to arrive at any such figure with confidence given its empirical basis.

The reliability of software should be assessed on the basis of its correctness, rather than attempting to predict that it will not fail within quantified time limits.

We have argued that we need appropriate methods for describing and developing software, methods which treat the software in accordance with its true nature.

A move away from the MTTF view of software reliability is therefore recommended, and what should be utilised is a view which regards the program as being akin to the (animatable) embodiment of a theorem. This suggests that attention should continue to be paid to specification and verification techniques. If the software is correct in respect of its specification, then this will have direct consequences for its reliability.

ACKNOWLEDGMENTS

Robin Whitty of the Centre for Systems and Software Engineering at South Bank Polytechnic, and Attila Csenki of the Department of Computer Science and Applied Mathematics at Aston University kindly supplied the author with useful references. The author is also grateful to the participants of the Fourth European Workshop on Dependable Computing held in Prague, April 1992, for their comments on an earlier presentation of this work.

REFERENCES

Brady, M. (1977). *The Theory of Computer Science: A Programming Approach*. Chapman and Hall, London.

Brooks, F. (1975) The Mythical Man-Month. Addison-Wesley, Reading, Mass.

Brooks, F. (1987). No silver bullet. *IEEE Computer*, April 1987. 10-19.

Conte, S.D., H.E.Dunsmore, and V.Y.Shen (1986). *Software Engineering Metrics and Models*. Benjamin/ Cummings, Menlo Park.

Csenki, A. (1991a). Statistical software failure prediction: basics. *Computing*, 27th June, 1991.

Csenki, A. (1991b). Statistical software failure prediction: advanced modelling. *Computing*, 4th July, 1991.

Daintith, J., and R.D.Nelson (Eds.) (1989). *The Penguin Dictionary of Mathematics*. Penguin Books, London.

Hoare, C.A.R. (1969). An axiomatic basis for computer programming. *Comm. ACM*, 12, 10, October 1969. 576-583.

Krishnamurthy, E.V. (1983). *Introductory Theory of Computer Science*. Macmillan, London.

Levenson, N.G. (1991). Software safety in embedded computer systems. *Comm. ACM*, 34, 2, February 1991, 34-46.

McCabe, T.J. (1976). A complexity measure. *IEEE Trans. Software Eng.*, SE-2, 1976. 308-320.

Moser, L.E. and P.M. Melliar-Smith (1990). Formal verification of safety-critical systems. *Software-Practice & Experience*, 20(8), August 1990, 799-821.

Musa, J.D., A.Iannino, and K.Okumoto (1987). *Software Reliability: Measurement, Prediction, Application*. McGraw-Hill, New York.

Rook, P. (Ed.) (1990). *Software Reliability Handbook*. Elsevier Science Publishers, London.

Sommerville, I. (1989). *Software Engineering*, 3rd Edition. Addison-Wesley, London.

Thomas, M. (1988). *Should We Trust Computers ?* BCS/Unisys Annual Lecture, BISL, Swindon.

PRACTICAL FORMAL METHODS FOR PROCESS CONTROL ENGINEERING

Clive Fencott and **Colin Fleming**
School of Computing and Mathematics
University of Teesside
Cleveland TS1 3BA UK
phone 44642 342680 fax 44642 230527.

Chris Gerrard
Gerrard Software Macclesfield Cheshire UK

Abstract. We document the application of formal methods to the specification and verification of the type of process control typically used in safety critical systems. We discuss the use of an executable subset of the formal specification language OBJ to model and verify systems utilising Programmable Logic Controllers (PLCs) prior to hardware implementation. We specify a stand alone PLC, a common instruction sub-set, and a complete "test engine" combining all the main elements of a PLC, ie. I/O/program scan + Program + IO-History. The method integrates with existing techniques for the development of PLC programs which we specify by an abstract data type which models ladder logic. Examples are presented to demonstrate the practicality of the approach and the benefits to be gained from testing such systems in software. The role of such techniques in an industrial safety critical context are discussed, both from the point of view of systems implementation and maintenance. In conclusion we outline current work focusing on hand held tool support, additional formal verification methods, and the application of the technique to systems development within safety standards.

Keywords. Process control engineering, formal methods, PLCs, OBJ, rapid prototyping, ladder logic, integrated methods.

Introduction

Microprocessor based systems are increasingly being used as mechanisms for real time process control. Such sytems require high degrees of correctness to be cost effective as well as being, in addition, safety critical in a large number of cases. Much recent interest has been devoted to standards for the development and certification of such systems with the emphasis on the demonstration of correctness and safety. Formal methods are commonly viewed as a possible means of establishing such demonstrations whilst at the same time presenting practical problems for their general adoption into industrial practice.

The integration of structured and formal specification techniques is increasingly seen as a possible solution to this problem (Fencott, Lockyer and Taylor). In this paper we present such an approach to the utilisation of formal methods in a very common class of industrial process control systems which make use of Programmable Logic Controllers (PLCs) (Swainston). PLC based systems have been the predominant digital real-time control mechanism for many years and, indeed, will continue to offer the process control engineer significant advantages over PCs, and the like, for many years to come.

A major problem with many formal description techniques is that the only verifiation techniques available are structured walkthroughs and formal proofs. Walkthroughs are common practice but time consuming and inefficient. Certainly, formal proofs of necessary system properties have to be part of any realistic safety standard but are not a practical proposition for any but a few specialist staff. However, all process control engineers will be conversant with verification by testing and for this reason, and others to be made clear, we have chosen to work with executable formal specification langugages (Alexander and Jones). In the longer term the use of such techniques will allow process control engineers to interact with formal specifications of PLC based systems much in the same way as data processing personel interact with relational databases, themselves formally specified, through query languages such as SQL which are also quite formal.

The formal technique used here is OBJEX (Gerrard) which is an executable subset of the widely used formal specification lanuage OBJ Goguen. In this paper we will primarily be concerned with the practical implications of our approach rather than a detailed discussion of the formalisms involved. Fleming (1991) gives a detailed account of the formal specifiation and test results.

Overview

In this section we will take a general view of the formal specification of a stand alone PLC and the means by which a process control engineer would interact with it. Our system comprises three basic components which are the PLC itself, the user program, and the I/O history.

The PLC component consists of an evaluation engine which mimics the I/O and program scans, in conjunction with a status table with which it interacts. The I/O history specifies the future input values to be read in the input scan and records the values given by successive ouput scans. Programs in our system are expressed by means of an abstract data type whose operators and syntax closely resemble PLC ladder logic.

The OBJ object dependencies for the top level of the specification are given in the following diagram where Observers is a basic interface to the system which allows users ot structure test results

in a simple manner. Buffer lists specifies the status table and I/O datatypes.

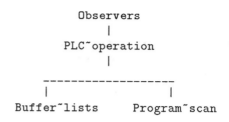

To interact with the system a user would first of all develop a program in ladder logic in the normal way using engineering drawings, schematics, interlocking charts, wiring diagrams, and so on. The result would be a program in PLC ladder logic which can be readily translated into the syntax required by our ADT. Having specified the required program the user must next provide a suitable instantiation of the status table upon which the program when interpreted by the evaluation engine will operate. This declaration will again be derived from the design already generated and consists of the number of bits in the status table together with the name and form of each bit, eg. whether they are inputs, outputs, flags, or timers etc. In this way we can specify status tables of any configuration.

To test the program two further things are required, an initialisation of the status table and a sequence of bit patterns for the successive input scans. Having supplied the necessary program and data the user runs the whole thing through the interpreter. In the simplest current configuration this will generate a sequence of output bit patterns. It is left to the user to check them against the input patterns to judge the correctness or otherwise of the behaviour exhibited. It is also possible to specify the output patterns in advance and let the machine establish their correlation with the actual values generated.

Notice that in all this process the user has not had to modify or understand the formal specification of the PLC animator. As long as the user is familiar with the workings of any standard PLC they will be able to use the animator. Having given a brief overview of the workings of the system we now proceed to describe the specification of certain essential components in more detail.

Ladder Logic

Of obvious interest to process control engineers will be the instruction set for our prototype PLC.

Most PLCs can be programmed in a variety of ways whether diagramatically or by means of simple programming languages but the majority allow the use of PLC ladder logic which is well understood by process control engineers and it is this we have chosen to specify as our basic instruction set. We will begin by example with a very simple program in ladder logic followed by it's formal equivalent expressed as defined in OBJ. The system has three inputs and three outputs detailed in the following table:

Bit No.	Device
I1	start/stop switch
I2	safety gate switch
I3	emergency stop button
Q1	fan
Q2	fan ON indicator
Q3	fan OFF indicator

and it's behaviour is given by the following ladder diagram:

```
      I1      I2      I3      Q1
|-----] [-----] [-----]/[-----()-----|
|                               |
|     Qi                       Q2     |
|-----] [--------------------()-----|
|                               |
|     Q1                       Q3     |
|----]/[--------------------()-----|
```

in which rung 1 turns the fan on or off depending on the state of the input switches and button and rungs 2 and 3 switch the indicator light on or off depending on whether the fan is running or not.

To formally specify this it was decided to treat the diagramming conventions of ladder logic as operator symbols to be defined in OBJ and thus make the formal specification match the diagrams very closely. The OBJ specification of the above thus becomes;

```
I1][ ----I2][----I3]/[---- - ----Q1 {}
Q1][ ---- - ----                 Q2 {}
Q1]/[---- - ----                 Q3 {} !
```

which is in fact a single OBJ expression constructed from the following operators;

```
_][       examine ON
_]/[      examine OFF
_{}       output
_----_    AND
-         empty rung
_-----_   results in
!         empty program
```

The OBJ object dependencies for program specification are given by the following diagram;

```
        Programs
           |
        Full~rungs
           |
        Rung~front
           |
        Instruction
           |
         Bit~id
```

Of course, most PLC manufactures provide other basic instructions such as OR which we have not at present implemented due to it being expressible in terms of AND and]/[. In our system flags and markers can be treated as extra bits within the status table. In addition we have specified instructions which represent timers and counters, and the ability to reset them.

Finally, in this section, it is worth pointing out that no defining equations are necessary at this level because all evaluation is carried out by the OBJ specificaton for the PLC itself.

Test-engine

Having briefly discussed the specification of ladder logic based PLC programs we now turn to the test-engine which models the behaviour of the PLC. Basically the test-engine takes a program specified in OBJ ladder logic together with a sequence of input bit patterns and returns a sequence of output bit patterns. This is accomplished by initialising and maintaining a correct status table. As with ladder logic the status table is specified by an OBJ object which models an appropriate data structure containing the information required for a status table. This information consists of the state, form, and name of each bit in the table. However, to further model a typical PLC system we separate user ids for bits from their internal names and require the user to define the mapping. An initialisation of the basic example from the previous section would be:

```
OBJ identifying/bits
OPS
bit1,bit2,...,bit6: -> bit
I1,I2,I3,Q1,Q2,Q3 : -> id~bit
EQNS
```

89

```
bit~id(bit1) = I1
form(bit1)   = input
...
bit~id(bit4) = Q3
form(bit4)   = ouput
...
JBO
```

This declaration establishes the number of bits in the status table and their form. The object dependencies which accomplish this mechanism are;

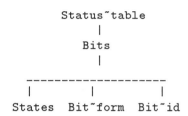

```
           Status~table
                |
              Bits
                |
        --------------------
        |       |          |
     States Bit~form  Bit~id
```

We now have to initialise the status table. The state of an individual bit is simply ON or OFF while the bit form allows the user to specify the bit as an input, output, flag, timer, or counter. The specification of the initialised status table for our example system will thus be:

```
OBJ Table1 / Identifying Status~table
OPS
 table1 : -> table
EQNS
 table =
 [bit1.OFF]val{0}[bit2.ON]val{0}
 [bit3.OFF]val{0}[bit4.OFF]val{0}
 [bit5.OFF]val{0}[bit6.ON]val{0} @
JBO
```

The table assigns a state value, ON or OFF, for each bit and sets the initial counter values. In this case no bits are declared counters and the default of 0, which will not be used is set for each. The symbol @ represents the empty status table. When the system starts the fan is not running and the indicator light is off. The safety gate switch is on but the emergency button is off.

To prototype this simple system we finally have to specify some input sequences of bit patterns for the designated input bits. To do this similar data-type to the status table is constucted which simply records bit ids and their new values.

Bottle Labeller

We now present a larger example specification for a bottle labelling system. Although not safety critical it does require responding to simple error situations in an appropriate manner. We present the formal specification and an outline of its development to illustrate the fact that it was derived using standard industrial techniques.

The system consists of a main feed which delivers bottles to a labelling machine. A return feed connects to the main feed to deliver bottles which have erroneously not been labelled. After labelling, bottles pass through a checking station which performs various tasks. First of all a sensor checks that each bottle has a label and either sends it down the return feed if it has not or sends it out down the main feed if it has. The checking station also keeps a tally of unlabelled bottles. If more than one bottle in ten escapes labelling then an alarm is sounded which has to be manually reset at the labelling station. This is to ensure the labelling station does not become swamped with bottles.

The necessary inputs and outputs are given in the following table

I/O	Description
I1	Bottle sensor
I2	Label sensor
I3	Returning bottle sensor
I4	Manual reset button
Q1	Direction changer
Q2	Alarm lamp
C1	Bottle counter
C2	Unlabelled bottle counter

In addition to three input bits and two ouput bits the status table this time has to make use of two counters, one for bottles entering the system and one for the unlabelled bottles. The analysis for this system follows a normal pattern of specifying boolean expressions to represent the basic interlocking of the system and then using boolean algebra to transform expressions involving OR and to reduce inter rung dependencies by introducing flags and os on. In OBJ the resulting program expression is as follows:

```
I1] [---- - ----     C1 ctr 10{}
I2] [----I1][ ---- - ----    F1{}
F1] [---- - ----     C2 ctr 2{}
Q1] [----I3]/[---- - ----    F3{}
F3]/[----F1]/[ - ----     F4{}
f4]/[---- - ----             Q1{}
C11] [----C2]/[---- - ----F5{}
F5]/[----I4]/[---- - ----F6{}
F6]/[---- - ----             F2{}
```

```
C1] [----C2] [---- - ----    Q2{}
F2] [---- - ----          C1 rst {}
F2] [---- - ----          C2 rst {} !
```

Anyone familiar with ladder logic should be able
to understand the above specification with little
difficulty. At Teesside this program together with
suitable test data has been animated and the results show the PLC would function as required if
implemented and installed using the formal specification data. A full description of this and other
test examples is given in Fleming (1991).

System Evaluation

To date the PLC rapid prototype has been applied to a number of small but realistic control
problems such as the automatic car wash, simple
traffic lights, and the bottle labeller. Initially,the
main objective hase been to establish the correctness of the overall PLC specification rather than
the general applicability of the system in an industrial context. However, even these small test
systems have demonstrated the practical potential for this approach.

In use the system compares very favourably
with PLC test rigs for the given specifications.
The complete specification is not small and test
runs can entail high numbers of rewrites. Timing
tests have shown the system to have performed
1.3 million rewrites in 50 minutes in response to
a small set of input patterns for the bottle labeller
on a Sun sparc slc with 8Mbs of ram. One great
advantage of the system is that a large number of
test cases may be programmed into very small input sequences involving major state changes over
a small number of PLC cycles. The length of time
taken to evaluate an imput pattern is thus not at
present significant. Sometimes, indeed, the density of the activity in the prototypes can present
problems which would not occur in an implementation because of the large number of extra intermediate cycles which would be involved.

Major system errors may be tested for and eliminated before the construction of a test rig is considered. At present this involves the process control engineer in learning the necessary notations
for expressing programs and test data but because
these have been designed to resemble ladder logic
and are based around familiar boolean algebra we
do not believe this to be a great problem. Even
in it's present implementation with no specific interface for control engineers the system seems to
be of potential benefit.

We briefly catalogue advantages and disadvantages as we currently see them:

Advantages

- Integration of existing methods with formal
  techniques.

- Common platform for control engineers and
  formal methods specialists.

- Formal approach to existing control systems
  by translation from existing programs into
  OBJ.

- Rapid prototyping of systems generates confidence in specifications prior to formal proofs
  if required.

- Easier to comply with upcoming safety standards which stipulate formal methods.

- Internal view of controller, eg. status table
  histories etc. makes detection of undesirable
  behaviours easier.

Limitations and Disadvantages

- Size of status table limited to 50 bits by the
  software at present.

- Only logical AND and NOT used at present.
  Commercial PLCs always provide OR as well
  as other constructs such as jumps etc.

- Timing between formal prototypes and PLC
  implementations not compatible.   Scaled
  down times used.

- Control engineers still have some additional
  formal notations to learn.

- Models only a very basic PLC. The specification needs to be customised to model commercially available products.

- Models only single stand alone PLC.

Current Work

We are currently working to improve the existing system and to extend the range of formal
techniques avaiable. In relation to the former
it has been shown that many of the additional
programming constructs required such as jumps,
non-retentive timers, and basic arithmetic operations may be easily added to the present system.

We expect the limitations on the size of the status table to be eliminated in the near future.

An interesting application of these techniques which we have already alluded to is in the fields of reverse engineering and maintenance. We are looking at versions of the prototyper which can be ported to the same hardware that is used by PLC programmers so that rapid prototyping of maintenance changes may be made before altering an existing running system. In particular we are looking to port the software to intrinsically safe hand held machines to achieve a genuinely portable formal methods tool for the control engineer.

In terms of formal techniques we are working in two directions. First of all we are using the formal description technique LOTOS (Bolognesi and Brinksma) to model distributed systems involving multiple PLCs which interact with monitor and alarm stations, a very common industrial application solution. This work is well advanced and makes use of the same formal specifications of ladder logic and status tables etc. so that individually specified and prototyped PLCs may be combined into a distributed system with little extra work. The second area of work concentrates on a temporal logic of status tables which will allow formal proofs of safety properties to be constucted for compliance with safety standards.

Conclusions

We have used an executable formal specification language to specify and prototype basic stand alone PLC systems and are beginning to demonstrate the usefulness of this approach. PLCs are heavily used in process control and general real-time systems many of which are considered safety critical by evolving safety standards. The rapid prototyping technique we have described provides a means for compliance with such safety standards as well as greatly enhancing the efficiency of the development process for PLC based systems.

References

Alexander, H. & Jones, V. (1990) *Software engineering and prototyping using Metoo.*Prentice Hall.

Bolognesi, T. & Brinksma, E. (1989) *Introduction to the formal specification language LOTOS.* The formal description technique LOTOS, Edited by van Eijk, Vissers & Diaz. Elsavier.

Fencott, P., Lockyer, M. & Taylor, P. (1992) *The integration of structured and formal methods for real-time system specification.* 5th International conference on putting into practice methods and tools for information systems design. Nantes.

Fleming, C. (1991) *Application of the formal language OBJ to programmable logic controller specifications and program development.* MSc. dissertation. University of Teesside.

Gerrard, C. (1991) *ObjEx - An invitation.* Gerrard Software, Macclesfield, England.

Goguen, J.A. & Tardo, J. (1979) *An introduction to OBJ: a language for writing and testing software systems.* IEEE Specifications of Reliable Systems.

Swainston, F. (1991) *A systems approach to programmable controllers.* Newnes. London.

FORMAL METHODS AND SOFTWARE SAFETY

J. P. Bowen

Oxford University Computing Laboratory, Programming Research Group,
11 Keble Road, Oxford OX1 3QD, UK
Email: <Jonathan.Bowen@comlab.ox.ac.uk>

V. Stavridou

Department of Computer Science, Royal Holloway and Bedford New College,
University of London, Egham Hill, Egham, Surrey TW20 0EX, UK
Email: <victoria@cs.rhbnc.ac.uk>

Abstract. The safety of software is becoming increasingly important as computers pervade control systems on which human life depends. Whilst hardware has become significantly more reliable over the years, the same cannot be said of software. This has become more complex and methods to ensure its correctness have been slow in development. One approach is to mathematically verify software in such systems. This paper investigates the industrial use of these techniques, their advantages and disadvantages, and the introduction of standards and their recommendations concerning formal methods in this area. The cost of safety is also considered.

Keywords. Safety; reliability; system integrity; standards; education; digital systems; computer software; formal languages; industrial control; software engineering.

INTRODUCTION

Safety can be defined as the freedom from exposure to danger, or the exemption from hurt, injury or loss; but in most situations, the major concern is the *degree* of safety and therefore safety is a subjective measure which makes safety provision and measurement extremely difficult and contentious tasks.

Safety concerns in computer systems are even more confusing. Such systems consist of many subcomponents which are tightly coupled and have highly complex interactions. The binding of application to operating system to architecture is a prime example of a tightly coupled system. When such a system is further embedded in larger a system, the probability of failure quickly approaches unity. The most effective means to avoid accidents during a system's operation is to eliminate or reduce dangers *during* the design and development of a system, not afterwards when system complexity becomes overwhelming. We strongly believe, that *safety must be designed in a system and dangers must be designed out*. We also feel that software and hardware safety are inextricably intertwined and must be considered as a whole with special attention to the interfaces.

Despite these considerable problems, the added versatility and flexibility afforded by digital systems has proved too tempting for many designers and users of safety-critical systems, and insufficiently validated software is often used. However implemented, we require that safety-critical systems are dependable. There are four approaches to achieving system dependability: fault removal, tolerance, avoidance and forecasting. It is commonly agreed that a combination of these approaches must be used in order to achieve maximum dependability. Different approaches have varying degrees of effectiveness, although this is an area of contention between the champions of each method. Formal methods are a fault avoidance technique which can increase dependability by removing errors at the requirements, specification and design stages of development.

Software safety standards are likely to provide a motivating force for the use of formal methods, and it is vital that realistic approaches are suggested in emerging and future standards to ensure effective application of such techniques.

This paper briefly discusses safety-critical systems, examines the use of formal methods as a possible technique for increasing safety and reliability, and surveys some standards in this area. The objective of the paper is to provide information on the current safety issues, particularly with regard to software, as reflected by a number of current and emerging standards and to examine ways in which formal methods technology can and has been used to improve system safety. This is a fast moving area in which rapid change is the norm; therefore, this paper should be seen as representative snapshot rather than as a comprehensive and definitive guide.

INCREASING DEPENDABILITY WITH FORMAL METHODS

It is often said that the use of formal techniques in the production of systems should be viewed as a means of delivering enhanced quality rather than establishing correctness. This difference of perception is crucial. Formal methods can deliver correctness – that is adherence to some requirements – and therefore enhanced quality; but correctness is not the end of the story. Correctness involves two or more models of a system (designer intentions and software/hardware system), where the models bear a tentative but uncheckable and possibly imperfect relation to both the user requirements and the final implementation. Even under the best possible circumstances, when we have an accurate interpretation of the requirements, at best we can assert that the model of the implementation satisfies these requirements. Whether the system will work satisfactorily *in situ* also depends on factors ranging from communication, training, and behaviour to the performance of mechanical, electrical and chemical components both within the system and its operational environment.

Formal methods are characterized by a number of levels of use and these provide different levels of assurance for the software developed by such methods. At a basic level, they may simply be used for system specification. The development process itself is informal but benefits are still gained since many bugs can be removed by formalizing and discussing the system at an early stage. The next level of use is to apply formal methods to the development process, using a design calculus allowing stepwise refinement of the specification to an executable program. At the most rigorous level, the whole process of proof may be mechanized. Hand proofs or design inevitably introduce errors for all but the simplest systems. Checking the process by computer reduces the possibility of error, although it never eliminates it since the program that does the checking may itself be incorrect. In addition, it is always possible that the basic underlying axioms may themselves be inconsistent.

Despite the present inadequacies, safety-critical software is the one application domain where the added confidence of mechanical proofs may be justifiable if feasible, even though the development cost of such an approach is high.

AREAS OF APPLICATION OF FORMAL METHODS

Some examples of current formal methods research work are given in this section. An example of a suggested overall approach to project organization using formal methods is provided by Ravn and Stavridou (1991).

Requirements capture

Accurate requirements capture is very important in the design of any system. A mistake at this stage will be carried through the entire development process and will be very expensive to correct later. Studies have shown that a modification in service can cost up to 1,000 times more than a modification at the requirements stage. There is now a considerable interest in this aspect of design in the formal methods community. For safety-critical systems, timing is often of great importance. This has proved to be a difficult area to formalize in a practical way. However research in this area is gathering momentum (e.g., using the

Duration Calculus developed by Zhou ChaoChen *et al.* (1991)).

Design

The design process refines a specification down to a program using (possibly) provably correct transformations or some other kind of rigorous refinement method. In general this must involve input from the engineer since there are many programs that meet a particular specification. Most formal methods until now have not considered the problem of timing issues in these transformations, partly because of its intractability. However research is active in this area.

Compilation

Compilers produce code that it is notoriously difficult to analyze, particularly as far as timing aspects are concerned. They themselves may be unreliable and introduce an extra unknown into the development process. The development of the compiler needs to be as strictly controlled as the development of the high-level safety-critical code itself. Recent research has demonstrated that it is possible to verify compiling specifications elegantly and even produce a rapid prototype compiler that is very close to the original specification in the form of a logic program as in Hoare *et al.* (1990). Other related research is investigating methods to verify a real compiler, including the bootstrap process, but significant barriers remain before such an approach can become viable in practice.

Programmable hardware

Programmable Logic Controllers (PLCs) are often used in process control and work has been undertaken to formalise the design process for these devices (Halang and Krämer, 1992). Another relatively new digital hardware technology, which may be of interest to safety-critical engineers who currently use embedded computer systems, is the *Field Programmable Gate Array* (FPGA). Hardware compilers from high-level programming languages down to a '*netlist*' of components are now being produced (Page and Luk, 1991), and it seems a realistic goal that such compilers could be formally proved correct. This is a promising research area for the 1990s and it is foreseen that programmable hardware will be used increasingly during the coming years. Formal verification of the overall system will be simplified since the high-level program is related directly to gate-level hardware without the complexity of an intermediate instruction set.

Documentation

An important part of a designed system is its documentation, particularly if subsequent changes are made. Formalizing the documentation leads to less ambiguity and thus less likelihood of errors. In the case of safety-critical systems, timing issues become significant and methods for documenting these are especially important. Formal methods provide a precise and unambiguous way of recording expected/delivered system functionality and can therefore be used as a powerful documentation aid. The normal expectation would be that the system documentation contains both the requirements and the system specification in a suitable formal notation, accompanied where appropriate with English narrative.

TABLE 1 Applications of formal methods to safety-critical systems.

Application	Notation	Specification	Verification	Machine Support [1]
Aviation	STP/EHDM	●	●	●
	Spectool/Clio	●	●	●
Railway systems	B	●	●	
Nuclear power plants	VDM	●		●
Medical systems	HP-SL & Z	●		

The latter is particularly important for conveying information on system aspects which are not formally specified for various reasons.

Human-Computer Interface

The human-computer interface (HCI) is an increasingly significant part of most software systems. In safety-critical systems, it is even more important that the interface is both dependable and ergonomically sound.[2] Formalizing HCI in a useful manner is a difficult task since the problem has widely divergent facets such as task allocation and cognition, but progress is being made in categorizing features of interfaces that may help to ensure their reliability. Investigation of human errors and how computers can help to avoid them is now being undertaken in a formal context (Harrison, 1992).

EXAMPLES OF USE

Safety-critical systems make up a minority of industrial applications using formal methods. Despite the fact that such systems have the most to gain potentially, industry is wisely cautious in adopting new untried techniques in this area. The following sections give an overview of some sectors and significant projects involved in the development of safety-critical systems that have used formal methods over the past few years. In general the results have been successful, but comments concerning individual cases are included below. Table 1 summarizes these experiments.

Aviation

An early example of the application of formal methods to a real life system, was the SIFT project, which probably represents the most substantial US experiment in the safety-critical sector. SIFT is an aircraft control computer which was commissioned by NASA in the mid-seventies. The design of the voting software was formally verified and SIFT was found to be a very reliable system. Although this was a successful research exercise it was a failure as far as subsequent actual deployment of the processor was concerned.

More recently, NASA commissioned work involving the application of formal methods to support fault tolerance in digital flight control systems (DFCS). It appears that NASA has found this line of investigation

fruitful and preferable to experimental quantification of software reliability (Butler and Finelli, 1991).

Railway systems

The SACEM system controls the speed of all trains on the RER Line A in Paris. The SACEM software consists of 21,000 lines of Modula-2 code. 63% of the code is deemed as safety-critical and has been subjected to formal specification and verification (Guiho and Hennebert, 1990). The specification was done using Abrial's B language and the proofs were done manually using verification conditions for the code. The validation effort for the entire system (including non safety-critical procedures) was of the order of 100 man years and therefore, this experiment represents a substantial investment in formal methods technology.

Nuclear energy

Rolls-Royce and Associates have been applying formal methods (mainly VDM) to the development of software for safety-critical systems, and nuclear power stations in particular, for a number of years (Hill, 1991). This approach has proved very successful and has produced the following conclusions:

- The main problem is the system as a whole, rather than the software alone.

- A combination of modern techniques, including formal methods, can help in the development of safety-critical software, even though their scope may be limited at present.

- Improvements in time-scales, costs and quality are possible in practice using such techniques.

A comparison of cost-effectiveness of different methods has been made. Using formal methods has doubled the specification and analysis stage, but eliminated the redevelopment stage. Since the latter can be of the order of half the costs whereas the former is a much smaller percentage, the overall saving is up to half the cost.

Medical systems

A number of medical instruments have life critical functionality and require a high degree of dependability. Two Hewlett-Packard divisions have used formal specification in order to enhance the quality of a range of cardiac care products. In both cases the formal notation used was HP-SL (Bear, 1991).

Deaths due to software in medical equipment have been documented elsewhere (e.g., the Therac 25 radiotherapy machine, where the dosage editor was poorly designed) and as a result others are also resorting to

---

[1] A ● under a column heading indicates whether a particular activity was undertaken as part of the project. The machine support heading indicates whether machine support was used in this particular case for either specification or verification or both, *not* whether a method is supported by tools.

[2] Witness, for example, the HCI issues surrounding the fly-by-wire A320 Airbus. Some pilots have consistently criticized the ergonomics of the cockpit instrument layout which they have identified as a possible contributing factor to the pilot errors which have caused several crashes so far.

TABLE 2 Summary of software-related standards.

Country	Body	Sector	Name	FMs content	FMs mandated	Status (June 1992)	Year
US	DoD	Defence	MIL-STD-882B	No	N/A	Standard	1985
			MIL-STD-882C	Likely	?	Draft	1992
US	RTCA	Aviation	DO-178A	No	N/A	Guideline	1985
			DO-178B	Yes	?	Draft	1992
Europe	IEC	Nuclear	IEC880	No	N/A	Standard	1986
UK	HSE	Generic	PES	No	N/A	Guideline	1987
Europe	IEC	Generic	IEC65A WG9	Yes	No	Draft	1989
			IEC65A 122	Yes	No	Proposed	1991
Europe	ESA	Space	PSS-05-0	Yes	Yes	Standard	1991
UK	MoD	Defence	00-55	Yes	Yes	Interim	1991
US	IEEE	Generic	P1228	No	No	Draft	1992
UK	RIA	Railway	(IEC-related)	Yes	Yes	Draft	1991
Canada	AECB	Nuclear	–	Yes	?	Draft	1991

TABLE 3 Cost of saving a life.

Hazard	Safety measure	Cost (in 1985)
Car crashes	Mandatory seat belts	$500
Cervical cancer	Screening	$75,000
Radiation	Reduce exposure & leaks	$75,000,000
Toxic air	Reduce emissions	$5,880,000,000

formal techniques in this area. Jacky (1991) discusses formal specification and verification issues regarding a clinical cyclotron control system which is under development at the University of Washington Hospital Cancer Treatment Center.

SAFETY STANDARDS

Until recently very few standards were concerned specifically with software in safety-critical systems. Often software quality standards such as the ISO9000 series have been used instead since these were the nearest relevant guidelines. Now a spate of standards in this area have been or are about to be issued. Many standards do not mention a formal approach specifically although most are periodically updated to incorporate new ideas.

The software engineering community became acutely aware of the introduction of formal methods in standards in the late 1980s and particularly since the introduction of the UK MoD DefStan 00-55. Although, the debate on the exact formal methods content of standards like 00-55 is bound to continue, we feel that there are certain aspects such as formal specification which *cannot* sensibly be ignored by standardizing bodies.

Table 2 summarizes the recommendations concerning the use of formal methods in a number of software safety standards. The selection is somewhat eclectic, but demonstrates the range of areas and organizational bodies that are involved. An overview of current standards concerned with software safety with an American slant is provided by Wright and Zawilski (1991).

The US and Europe are the major sources of software safety standards and research in this area. In

Canada, the AECB and Ontario Hydro are producing stands relating relation to the nuclear industry. Standards Australia is recommending adoption of the IEC Draft Document 65A WG9. Interestingly, or perhaps inevitably, information on activity in this area in Japan seems to be hard to obtain. A full list of standards mentioned in this paper, and more information on their recommendations concerning formal methods, is included in Bowen and Stavridou (1992).

THE COST OF SAFETY

The cost of safety is determined, ultimately, by what people are willing to pay. Table 3 illustrates the wide range of amounts of money spent on trying to save a human life in some situations. Although various methods for calculating the objective cost of safety have been proposed, the problem is largely unresolved. One cannot ever be certain, when an accident *does not* occur, whether it is because of the safety devices or because the system was designed "well enough" so that the safety devices are superfluous. On the other hand, when accidents *do* occur, the penalties for ignoring software safety can be very severe.

The overall system safety cost includes a multitude of factors and components. We concentrate on the cost of software defects for the *producer* of the software; some of these will affect safety and others will not. We will attempt to estimate how much it costs to eliminate software defects at large since the proportion of safety-critical defects to benign ones cannot be quantified for all systems. Note that, we do not take into account the liability costs incurred by producers of safety-critical software that has failed causing accidents.

Software defect costs can be investigated using a number of approaches. Ward (1991) uses data focused on

TABLE 4 Software defect cost summary for a typical HP software project.

Code size:	75 KNCSS[3]
Software Test Phase:	6 Months
Prerelease Defects:	110
Software Rework "Waste":	$165,000 ($1,500 per defect)
Profit Loss Due to Rework:	$1,000,000 (Approximately $9,000 per defect)
Total Cost of Software Defects:	$1,165,000
Cost per Corrected Defect:	**$10,500**

TABLE 5 Software defect avoidance cost summary for a formally verified system.

Code size:	21 KNCSS
Software Validation Phase:	70 man years
Number of Defects Avoided:	30 (defect density as in Table 4)
Total Cost of Defects:	$10,920,000 (52 weeks per man year, $75 per eng. hour)
Cost per Avoided Defect:	**$364,000**

the cost per prerelease software defect that is found and fixed during the integration through to the release phases of project development. The calculation of the cost is based on the formula

Software defect cost =
    Software defect rework cost + Profit loss

Based on data obtained from an extensive software project database maintained at the Hewlett-Packard Waltham Division for product releases over the past five years, Ward has produced software defect costs for typical software projects as shown in Table 4. These figures are based on the assumptions that each defect requires 20 engineering hours to find and fix, a cost of $75 per engineering hour and a 1,000 unit customer base of a $20,000 product with a 15% profit margin. The profit loss factor is quantified using the model of new product development in Reinertsen (1983).

The above figures give us an approximation to cost of software defects in projects where current practice is used. We are interested in arriving at a similar cost approximation when fault avoidance techniques, and in particular formal methods, are used. we base our calculations on the SACEM railway system mentioned earlier. If we assume that the system is bespoke, there is no profit loss associated with late delivery and we can therefore base our calculations solely on engineering hours required to avoid defects. In order to make the comparison with the Hewlett-Packard data meaningful, we assume the same defect density (in other words 1·46 defects per KNCSS). The figures are shown in Table 5. Although our figures are very rough approximations and they are based on a single set of data, it would appear that the cost per defect avoided is substantially larger than that required for development without formal methods; in this case by over an order of magnitude.

The high cost may be due to the cost of training, which could be amortized over several projects if formal methods is adopted on a permanent basis. Other substantial industrial examples (e.g., Hill (1991)) have demonstrated that formal methods *can* be the most cost-effective technology if used in an appropriate manner. In particular, full verification may not be fea-

sible in many cases, but can be helpful for the most critical parts of an application; formal *specification* alone may be more appropriate for the rest of the system, with *rigorous* rather than formal development of the implementation.

Such conflicting evidence on the cost-effectiveness of formal methods makes the need for proper deployment and quantification of the technology even more pressing. It is hoped that an international ongoing study of the industrial applications of formal methods by Ted Ralston *et al.* will help shed light on this issue.

CONCLUSIONS

The subject of software safety has profound technical, business, professional and personal aspects for the individuals who research, develop, sell, use and rely upon computer controlled systems. So it is hardly surprising that the introduction of a technology such as formal methods in this context is accompanied by vigorous if not heated debate. What is at stake ranges from substantial industrial investment, to 'closed shop' interests, professional pride in the job and ultimately to our very lives. The arguments surrounding the value and use of formal methods for safety-critical systems are a prime example of the potential for controversy.

The complexity of critical systems is rising as more and more functionality is provided by software solutions. The gap between the dependability requirements and what we can achieve in terms of delivering and measuring such dependability is huge. We believe that, on the evidence of past experiments, formal methods technology deployed in conjunction with other techniques can help narrow this gap. The factors that diminish the effectiveness of formal methods in this context are:

- Some aspects of the technology, such as formal specification, have been widely used and are relatively well understood. Other practices, however, such as machine-supported theorem proving, have not benefited from real-world use and are correspondingly less well developed.

---

[3] Thousands of lines of non-comment source statements.

- Formal methods can be expensive when compared with traditional defect removal techniques. It is naive to assume that "money is no object" given that the cost of safety is highly subjective, varies from system to system even within the same sector and depends on the perception and the politics of risk.[4] Clearly the cost-effectiveness of formal methods will need to be established on a case by case basis.

- Although it is accepted that the use of formal methods increases dependability margins, we cannot measure by how much. In fact, even if we could, we would not be able to measure global dependability since we do not know how to combine formal methods assurance with metrics collected from other techniques such as fault tolerance.

In spite of these problems, we feel that *mature* formal methods can and should be used to produce safer software because benefits can be obtained without wholesale adoption. The mere act of writing a formal specification, for instance, can help to clarify system design and requirements; it can be used to improve or simplify a design; it can even be used to produce a rapid prototype in order to evaluate the projected system behaviour. However, in the context of safety-critical systems, it is profoundly important to recognize the limitations of any technology. Formal methods cannot do much, for example, in a chaotic software production environment.

If the issues surrounding the applicability of formal methods to critical systems are so complicated, it is hardly surprising that educational provision and standardization are equally complex matters. Currently, there is no universally agreed curriculum for safety critical software professionals. On the contrary, there is a plethora of standards and this domain is beginning to look surprisingly similar to the state of the art in formal methods; too many standards that are not industrially used and assessed.

In this paper, we have tried to present an objective account of the state of the art of formal methods as reflected by recent industrial practice and standardization activities. In our opinion, the areas that need to be addressed in the future are research, technology, education/accreditation and standardization for the use of formal methods in the development of safety-critical software.

ACKNOWLEDGEMENTS

The European ESPRIT Basic Research Action **ProCoS** project (BRA 3104) and the UK Information Engineering Directorate **safemos** project (IED3/1/1036) provided financial support.

Many people have helped by supplying advice, information, papers, standards and feedback which have been used as input to this survey; a full list is included in Bowen and Stavridou (1992).

---

[4]For instance, the MoD in the UK places different criticality on the importance of saving a life threatened by military aircraft in flight depending on whether the individual is a civilian, a pilot in flight at peace time and a pilot in flight at war time.

REFERENCES

Bear, S. (1991). An overview of HP-SL. In Prehn, S., and Toetenel, W.J. (Eds.), *VDM '91, Formal Software Development Methods*, Springer-Verlag, *Lecture Notes in Computer Science* **551**, pp. 571–587.

Bowen, J.P., and Stavridou, V. (1992). Safety-critical systems, formal methods and standards. Technical Report PRG-TR-5-92, Oxford University Computing Laboratory, UK. Submitted to *Software Engineering Journal*.

Butler, R.W., and Finelli, G.B. (1991). The infeasibility of experimental quantification of life-critical software reliability. Proc. ACM SIGSOFT '91 Conference on Software for Critical Systems, *Software Engineering Notes*, ACM Press, **16**(5), pp. 66–76.

Guiho, G., and Hennebert, C. (1990). SACEM software validation. *Proc. 12th International Conference on Software Engineering*, IEEE Computer Society Press, pp. 186–191.

Halang, W.A., and Krämer, B. (1992). Achieving high integrity of process control software by graphical design and formal verification. *Software Engineering Journal*, **7**(1), pp. 53–64.

Harrison, M.D. (1992). Engineering human error tolerant software. In Nicholls, J.E. (Ed.), *Z User Workshop, York 1991*, Springer-Verlag, Workshops in Computing. To appear.

Hill, J.V. (1991). Software development methods in practice. *Proc. 6th Annual Conference on Computer Assurance*, (COMPASS).

Hoare, C.A.R., He Jifeng, Bowen, J.P., and Pandya, P.K. (1990). An algebraic approach to verifiable compiling specification and prototyping of the ProCoS level 0 programming language. In Directorate-General of the Commission of the European Communities (Ed.), *ESPRIT '90 Conference Proceedings*,, Kluwer Academic Publishers B.V., pp. 804–818.

Jacky, J. (1991). Verification, analysis and synthesis of safety interlocks. Technical Report 91-04-01, Department of Radiation Oncology RC-08, University of Washington, Seattle, WA 98195, USA.

Page, I., and Luk, W. (1991). Compiling Occam into field-programmable gate arrays. In Moore, W., and Luk, W. (Eds.), *FPGAs*, Oxford Workshop on Field Programmable Logic and Applications. Abingdon EE&CS Books, 15 Harcourt Way, Abingdon OX14 1NV, UK, pp. 271–283.

Ravn, A.P., and Stavridou, V. (1991). Project organisation. In Ravn, A.P. (Ed.), *Embedded, Real-time Computing Systems*, Vol. I, ESPRIT BRA 3104, Provably Correct Systems, ProCoS, Draft Final Deliverable. Chap. 8. To appear, Springer-Verlag, *Lecture Notes in Computer Science*, 1992.

Reinertsen, D.G. (1983). Whodunit? The search for the new product killers. *Electronic Business*, July 1983.

Ward, W.T. (1991). Calculating the real cost of software defects. *Hewlett-Packard Journal*, October 1991, pp. 55–58.

Wright, C.L., and Zawilski, A.J. (1991). Existing and emerging standards for software safety. The MITRE Corporation, Center for Advanced Aviation System Development, 7525 Colshire Drive, McLean, VA 22102-3481, USA.

Zhou ChaoChen, Hoare, C.A.R., and Ravn, A.P. (1991). A calculus of durations. *Information Processing Letters*, **40**(5), pp. 269–276.

OBJECT REPRESENTATION
OF THE OPERATIVE ENVIRONMENT

M. Mekkaoui & K. Ouriachi
LIRRF UA CNRS 1118
Université de Valenciennes
F-59326 Valenciennes cedex

ABSTRACT:

This paper presents a new model of knowledge representation, that will constitute a basic for the implementation of a language of representation and manipulation of knowledge in artificial vision. These concepts are inspired by different approaches based on object notion: object oriented languages, frame-based knowledge representation, actor language , and abstract type of data. This language may be a powerful tool for the resolution of artificial vision applications.

keyword:

knowledge representation, Abstract type of data, object oriented langages, frame, actor.

1 INTRODUCTION:

The need of automatizing the image processing appeared in several fields mainly in the field of the industrial robotic, where the robot owes to be able to adapt itself to the environment. The vision is, the favoured mode of knowledge among others, allowing the possibility to acquire in required times, in function of action to realize, the pertinent parameters to help the command of the robot.

The objective of this work is to study the model of knowledge representation to dedicate to the robot-vision, by constructing the formal specification of all problems aspects of the real world inherent to the execution of the operative task. Such result can't be attained if all characteristic properties of the manipulated object in the problem statement are expressed precisely in this description.

-The objective of data specification is twice:

1°/To formulate, in terms of object oriented model, a representation of operative space objects: each object is considered like an instance.

2°/To structure, these data using powerful abstract mechanism based on a componential aggregation (hierarchical structural), such mechanism allows to formalize a process of refinement which is expressed, at each level of abstraction in terms of intermediate sub-object aggregate. The link between the class of object and the classes of sub-objects is expressed with the help of constructors of classes.

Once a level of abstraction is reached, we note that is frequently have to apply treatment of different natures to the same object. Also is it desirable to present this object in the same manner?, meaning that to give a uniform representation.

In fact, the temptation is great, to extract from the canonical representation several sub-representations. Each of these sub-representation is function of treatment applied to the object, from this a horizontal abstraction mechanism called functional aggregation ensue.

2 PROPOSED MODEL:

The proposed model encompasses tools that allow to describe, in abstract and structured manner, objects properties, using an object oriented approach.

This model is based on componential aggregation and on functional aggregation.

2.1 CLASS AND OBJECT:

Main idea is that all objects having common properties are regrouped in the same abstract entity : the class.

The class represents an abstract type implementation, the instance a concretesation of this type.

Hence, a class may be intuitively defined as:

-A data collection,

-And a set of operations to handler this data

2.1.1 EXAMPLE:

Let an object nominate "CYL" declared as follows:

declare object

begin

cyl **kind-of** cylinder

end

cylinder class is declared by:

class cylinder **is**

attributes

begin

radius : real;

height : real;

end

methods

begin

moving(x, y, z);

localizing(x);

end;

-the radius and height designate structural attributes of object "CYL"

-"x", "y" et "z" designate the position of the object "cyl". They are the descriptive attributes,

-moving(x,y,z) and localizing(x) represent two function associated

with the object "cyl" of class or of "cylinder" type.

From this example we can derive a syntax of an atomic object and an atomic class.

-Syntax of an instruction to declare an atomic object:

dec-object-ato> ::= **declare**

object <bloc-declaratif>

<bloc-declaratif> ::= **begin**

{<dec-object>;} <dec-object>

end

<dec-object> ::= <id-object>

kind-of <id-class>

-syntax of an instruction to declare an atomic class is:

<dec-class> ::= **class** <id-class> **is**

<bloc-dec-attr>

<bloc-dec-op>

<bloc-dec-attr> ::= **attributes**

begin

{<dec-attr>;} <dec-attr>

end

<bloc-dec-op> ::= **methods**

begin

{<dec-op>;} <dec-op>

end

<dec-attr>::=<id-attr>: <class-attr>;

<class-attr> ::= integer/real/ string

/ boolean

<dec-op> ::= <id-op> (<list-arg>)

<bloc-dec-arg>

<bloc-op>

<list-arg> ::= {<arg>};} <arg>

<bloc-dec-arg> ::= **begin**

{<dec-objet>;} <dec-objet>

end

<bloc-op>::=**corp** method <id-op>

is <bloc-implantation>

<bloc-implantation> ::= **begin**

{<app-op>;} <app-op>

end

to clarify this syntax we take an example:

declare object

begin

es **kind-of** stairs;

wa **kind-of** wall;

end

stairs class is:

class stairs **is**

attributes

begin

id-stairs : string;

nb-step : integer;

leng-step : real;

heig-step : real;

end

```
methods
    begin
        climb-step ( x) ;
        count-step( x);
        top-step (x);
        butom-step (x);
    end
```
wall class is :
```
class wall is
    attributes
        begin
        id-wall : string;
        higt-wall : real;
        dist-wall: real*real;
        end

    methods
        begin
        avoid ( x);
        evaluate-dis(cyl, wa);
        end
```

To illustrate an instruction of method we take "evaluate-dis(cyl,x)" method which has an objective evaluation of the distance between the object "cyl" of cylinder class and the object "wa" of wall class.

```
evaluate-dis (cyl ,wa)
        begin
    cyl : cylinder;
    wa : wall;
        end

corp method evaluate-dis is
        begin
        position (cyl);
        position (wa);
        distance (cyl,wa);
        end
```

2.2 COMPONENTIAL AGGREGATION:

Inheritance concept in object oriented languages is founded on a conceptual hierarchy based on the "is-a" relation, which is made out by the abstraction/concretesation relation.

Comparatively, componential aggregation represents a structural hierarchy between one class of object and a collection of others classes of objects; it is made out with the "is-part" relation.

The main of this concepts is to introduce a strong abstraction mechanism, enabling us to represent a complex object with an aggregation of sub-objects without having to give implementation details of these sub-objects.

2.2.1 ABSTRACT CLASSES BUILDING:

As defined, componential aggregation represents a structural hierarchy based on decomposition of each non atomic object of a particular class into sub-objects of others classes.

In order to express this objects relation, we use a set of operations on a kind of classes called classes constructors.

2.2.1.1 CARTESIAN PRODUCT CONSTRUCTOR:

Let n classes h_i $1 \le i \le n$ belonging to domain H of classes; cartesian product class of classes h_i, noted :

$$h_{pc} = PROD(h_1, h_2, ..., h_n)$$

where the PROD operator is called constructor of cartesian product class; its syntax is as follows:
```
PRODUCT <id_class>
            <liste_class_arg>
<liste_class_arg>::= begin
{<id_class>;} <id_class>;
            end
```

To illustrate this definition, let's consider the composit object in (Fig.2) which represent a valve; we way declare this object class using the cartesian product of constructor.
```
        product valve
            begin
screw, screw, screw, screw,
enclosure, joint, rivet, strip, plate,
sheet
            end
```
In this same way the general syntax of the instruction declaration of the object of product class is:
```
<id-object> kind-of <id-class>
```
The following two instruction:
-valve_1 kind-of valve
-valve_1=(v1,v2,v3,v4,e1,

j1,r1,r2,i1,i2,p1,f1)

Mean that v1, v2, v3, v4 are instances of "screw" class, e1 of

"enclosure" class, j1 of "joint" class, r1, r2, of "rivet" class, i1, i2 of "strip" class, p1 of "plate" class, f1 of "sheet" class.

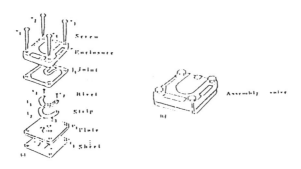

Fig.2   VALVE

2.2.1.2 CONSTRUCTOR OF DISJOINT UNION CLASS:

let n classes h_i $1 \leq i \leq n$; the disjoint UNION class of classes h_i, noted , $h_{un} = UNION(h_1, h_2,...,h_n)$

The general syntax is:
union <id_class> <liste_class_arg>
<liste_class_arg>::=**kind-of**
{<id_class>;} <id_class>;
        end-kind

In the same way the general syntax of the instruction declaration of an instance of an union class is :
    <id-object> **kind-of** <id-class>

As illustrate, let's take the example of "obstacle" class constructed such that:
    union obstacle
        kind-of
    stairs; wall; inclined-plane;
        end-kind

is used to declare an object called "obstacle_1" it has to be overcome by the mobile robot.
    obstacle_1 **kind-of** obstacle
    Using an object constructor noted "< >un" of the union class, we can write: obstacle_1=<stairs_1, wal_1, inclined_plane_1>$_{un}$

to access to the sub-object "stairs_1" we have to call on an operator noted "< >$_{sel}$": <stairs : obstacle_1>$_{sel}$.

likewise, for the sub-object "wall_1" we apply:
    <wall : obstacle_1>$_{sel}$

2.2.1.3 CONSTRUCTOR OF COMPOSITION CLASS:

let n classes h_i $1 \leq i \leq n$; the constructor composition class of classes h_i, noted ,
    $h_{co} = comp(h_1, h_2,...,h_n)$

The general syntax of declaration instruction of composition class is:
composition   <id_class>
            <liste_class_arg>
    <liste_class_arg>::= **kind-of**
    {<id_class>;} <id_class>;
            end-kind
In the same way , the general syntax of declaration of a composition class instance:
    <id-object> **kind-of** <id-class>

To illustrate this type of constructor we take an example of piece called "piston" composed of a "bore", and of a "cylinder", the two located in "enclosure", we propose to describe this piece by constructing the piston class with the help of the constructor "comp":

    composition piston
            begin
    cylinder; enclosure; bore;
            end
to declare an instance of this class: w **kind-of** piston

2.2.1.4 GENERALISATION:

let a class h_j, which class generalize h_j is the class $h_g = $ Gen (h_j) where "Gen" is the constructor of the generalized class, we say that the class h_g is a generalisation of h_j if and only if all the instances of h_j are instances of h_g.

To show this let's consider three classes their attributes as follows:

        class screw is
            begin
        length, diameter : real;
            end

```
class flat-screw is

    begin
length, diameter : real;
thickness : real;
    end

class round-screw is

    begin
length, diameter : real;
radius : real;
    end
```

the class "screw" is generalisation of two classes "flat-screw" and "round-screw

2.2.1.5 SPECIALISATION:

Let us class h_j, the class which specialize h_j is the class $h_s = \mathrm{spe}(h_j)$, the class h_s is a specialisation of h_j, if and only if all instances of h_s are also instances of h_j, for example:

```
flat-screw   = spe(screw)
round-screw  = spe(screw)
```

3.3 FUNCTIONAL AGGREGATION:

The notion of function aggregation is issued from the idea of associating to each sub-representation of the canonical representation a treatment to be applied to the object.

To formalize the idea we introduce the notion of horizontal abstraction and function specification.

2.3.1 NOTION OF HORIZONTAL ABSTRACTION:

The idea is to compose the canonical representation of the object in an aggregate of sub-representation in function of processing we will apply to the object. his decomposition allows justly to infer pertinent properties from the set of all the object properties (Fig.3)

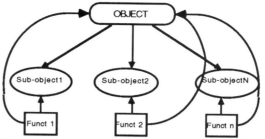

Fig. 3 NOTION OF AGGREGATION FUNCTIONAL

2.3.2 NOTION OF FUNCTIONAL SPECIALIZATION:

Generally, at a high level of abstraction, we observe that we are often brought to apply treatments of different natures on the same object. Is this object seen in he same way?. That is, is its representation uniform?.

We are tempted to give several representations and classify them according to the functions applied to the declared object in statement.

As an illustration, let us take the example of a task expressed as a function TAKE(W), where w is the object declared as follows:

   w   **kind-of**   coffee-maker

The class coffee-maker can be expressed by composition of classes: "shape", "cover", "handle", "pouring"; using the constructor of class composition.

    composition coffee-maker
       begin
  shape; cover; handle; pouring;
       end

Using the object constructor "$< >_{ag}$", we can construct the canonical representation of object w: $R_c(w) = <w_1, w_2, w_3, w_4>_{ag}$ from the sub-objects declared as follows:

    w_1 **kind-of** shape
    w_2 **kind-of** cover
    w_3 **kind-of** handler
    w_4 **kind-of** pouring

To make the robot hold the cafe-maker, the relevant data are the pertinent properties of sub-object w3 that is, its position (x, y, z : real) and its orientation angle (alpha : real).

2.3.3 SUB-OBJECT ACCESS OPERATOR:

Let w an object of class $h = (h_1, h_2, \ldots h_n)$, its canonical representation is defined using the n-uple: $R_c(w) = <w_1, w_2 \ldots, w_n>_{ag}$.

To access to different sub-representations $R_1(w)$, ..., $R_n(w)$ associated respectively to function $f_1, \ldots, f_n$, we resort systematically to an operator of access to the sub-object noted "< >rp" defined as:

$$<w : fp> = wp$$

Taking the previous example $<w : take> = w3$, the robot has only the useful information for la realisation the task "TAKE COFFEE-MAKER"

3 CONCLUSION

In the field of the vision we are face to great quantity of informations that must be structured and handled. For this, we suggested, in this paper, the basic principles of knowledge representation model for the vision. This model is the foundation of knowledge representation language in the field of "ROBOT-VISION".

REFERENCES :

1. D.G. Bobrow and T. Winograd, "An overview of KRL a knowledge representation language", vol. 1, cognitive Science, 77.

2. B. Carre, "Méthodologie orientée objet pour la représentation des connaissances: concepts de point de vue, de représentation multiple et évolutive d'objet" Thèse L.I.F.L, Univ. Lille1, Janv 89.

3. R. Ducourneau and J. Quinqueton, "YAFOOL: encore un langage objet à base de frame", Rapport technique n°72, INRIA, Jul 86.

4. J. Ferber, "MERING: un langage d'acteurs pour la représentation et la manipulation des connaissances", Thèse D.I.; Univ. Paris VI, Dec. 83.

5. C. Hewitt and B. Smith, "A plasma primer", Publication MIT, sept. 75.

6. M. Mekkaoui "implantation des structures de base d'un langage de représentation et manipulation des connaissances pour un systeme robot-vision" Rapport DEA Uni. valenciennes, 90

7. M. Minsky, "A framework for representing knowledge", The psychologie of computer vision, Mc graw-hill, 75.

8. K. Ouriachi "Contribution à la specification formelle des tâches opératoires: outils en vue d'une approche fonctionnelle basée sur l'agregation des données" These d'Etat , Univ. Valencienes, 91

9. S. E. Palmer, "Hierarchical structure in perceptual representation", Cognitive Science 9, 441-474, 74.

10 A. Ravishankar Rao and R. Jain, "Knowledge Representation and control in computer vision systems", SPRING 88, I.E.E.E. EXPERT, PP. 64-79, 88

11. F. Rechenmann, P. Fontaille and P. Uvietta, "Shirka: manuel d'utilisation", Rapport technique, INRIA-ARTEMIS, Grenoble, 89.

12. C. Roche and J. P. Laurent, "Les approches objets et le langage LRO2", T.S.I.; vol.8, N°1,89.

13. C. Roche, "Les systemes objets", Seminaire, micoud, Fev 90.

MARKOVIAN MODELS FOR CLASSIFICATION OF FAULTS
IN MANUFACTURING SYSTEMS

Zineb ABAZI Laboratoire d'Automatique de Grenoble (E.N.S.I.E.G.)

B.P. 46 - 38402 Saint Martin d'hères, France. Tél (33) 76 82 64 15

E.mail abazi @lag.grenet.fr.

ABSTRACT : This paper presents a method based on the Markov process to classify any faults which can affect the described system. The proposed method allows to model and evaluate the occurrence probability of these faults. One defines a new failure model which is able to take into account all faults. The resolution of this model gives the classification of the faults by their occurence probability. This paper also presents reduction rules that can be applied when the fault-free markovian model contains numerious states. Thanks to the reduction rules, for n faults, the classification is made by solving only once the (2n+1) Markov chain.

KEYWORDS : Dependability, Safety, Modeling, Markov chain, Classification.

I- INTRODUCTION

All manufacturing systems can be modeled by markovian models, one only has to know the various functioning modes of the system. The best way to provide for emergencies, is to take into account possible faults which can appear at the modeling level. This work focuses on the classification of these faults. Numerous works on this subject deal with different approaches based for example on the Petri nets controllers (Leveson, 1987 and Zhou, 1989). Markov processes with discrete state space over continuous time are good models for many stochastic systems, especially those applied to the safety, reliability or maintenance fields. In our research, this mathematical calculation tool is used. Analytic methods are adopted that highlight the set of faults which can affect the studied system. However, some of these faults require a long time to occur and therefore can be considered as unlikely. This is the reason why it is important to classify them by their occurrence probability.

To evaluate the occurrence probability we use a kind of discret Markov chain called "Absorbing Markov Chain". The first proposed model called the "failure model" is defined, with three states Markov chain (Abazi, 1989 - 1991). The first state represents the system when it is functioning correctely, the second state represents the system when it is malfunctioning. This state is reached when a failure occurs. The third state is the absorbing state which correspond to the detection state. This absorbing state is reached when the fault is detected.

With this failure model, each fault needs an associated failure model in order to calculate the occurrence probability. For the classification it is nessary to solve markov system for each fault . Therefore, n faults require to construct and solve n markovian systems.

In order to decrease the number of states of the model to be constructed, we develop at first a method which allows to obtain a model with a minimum number of states. The model describes all functioning modes of the system and is called the "compact model". From the compact model, one deduces a new failure model called the "compact failure model" which is able to take into account all faults and classify them by their occurrence probabilities. We have introduced a general modeling approach. For n faults, the compact failure model is constructed by associating one absorbing state to each fault to be studied and the classification is then made by solving only once the (2n+1) Markov chain which includes all possible faults. For a given length the classification is obtained by comparison with the stationnary probability of each absorbing state.

This paper is organised as follows : In section II, a markovian model is proposed with the reduction algorithm. Section III concerns the construction of the compact failure model. Before concluding, in section IV an example of the compact model and the compact failure model deduced for an application of chemical manufacturing are given along with some results. This example is first presented in section II and will be used to illustrate the different steps of the proposed method throughout the paper.

II-MARKOVIAN MODEL FOR THE FAULT-FREE SYSTEM

The behavior of all manufacturing systems can be represented by a set of states. The system may be operational or unoperational. This is expressed as two "macro states" Markov model shown in fig. 1. The system is in the macro-state RF when it is in the right functioning. It can stay in this state or move to macro-state WF which represents the system in the wrong functionning (this state include the system unoperational or under repair). The average probability a (resp. b) of transition RF → WF (resp. WF → RF) depends on different functioning mode of the system and then requires a more accurate representation. In fact, a macro-state RF (resp. WF) represents the set of states interconnected corresponding to the behavior of the system in a right functioning (resp. wrong functioning), then each macro-states substitutes for several states. The set of states which represents the different functionning modes is called the initial model.

The complexity of the initial model (state number) increases with the number of functioning mode of the system and may stay high. Then one goes on to reduce the state number in the macro-state by using different rules given below.

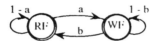

Fig.1 Markov chain describing the general behavior of a fault-free system

Example of chemical manufacturing : The aim is to conceive a reliable chemical manufacturing which manipulate the chlorine where the rate must not exceed a fixed norme. In order to control the rate of chlorine, this system has two principal functioning modes : purifing mode and confining mode. When functioning normal the system is in the purifing mode but when an abnormal rate of chlorine is detected the system is changed to the confining mode. In both these modes it is necessary to start up various pumps.

Before system can be started, an initialisation is required and various test (test mode) are made on some critical elements.

Then, this application can be modeled by a Markov chain with five states as shown in fig. 2 where M_0 is the initialisation state, M_1 is the state corresponding to the mode test, M_2 correspond to start up the pump and states M_3, M_4 are respectively states for the purifing mode and confining mode.

II-1. Reduction algorithm

The whole reduction algorithm is an iterative process requiring several steps as shown in fig.2. Starting with the basic model where all functioning mode are described, one constructs a succesion of model called compact-model (C-models), with progressive decrease of the state number. The model obtained at the end of the ith step denoted C-model(i) is deduced from C-model(i-1) by creating one or several new macro states and the first model acts as C-model(0). The iteration may stoped when the C-model(i-1) is irreducible if no macro-state can be created from it.

From now on, the general term "state" will indifferently designate kind of state (simple or macro). Definitions 1, 2 and 3 hold for all presented models.

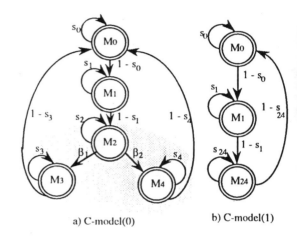

a) C-model(0)   b) C-model(1)

Fig.2 Markovian model for the chemical application :
  a) C-model(0) : five states markov chain;
  b) C-model(1): three states markov chain (after reduction).

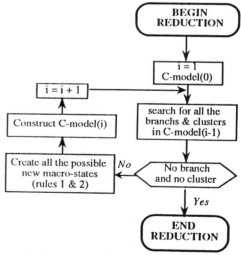

Fig.3 Compact modeling : reduction algorithm

Definition 1.

A state i *precedes* (resp.*follows*) a state j ≠ i if there is a transition i → j (resp.j → i).

❏

Definition 2.

A *branch* $b_{g,h}$ is a string {g-...-h} of consecutive states with at most one loop included in it.

❑

Fig. 4-a shows a branch $b_{1,j}$ = {1-...-j} and a loop {i -...-x - i }. As several states follow state q, the string {1 -...- x - q} is not a branch any more.

Definition 3.

A *cluster* $c_{g,h}$ is a group {g; ...; h} of states such that :

1) each state $j \neq g \in c_{g,h}$ is preceded by and only by state g; state g precedes no other state;

and 2) all states $j \neq g \in c_{g,h}$ precede a same state q and only this one.

❑

Fig 4-b shows a cluster $c_{1,x}$. Two types of grouping are possible to create macro-states as shown in fig.4-c.

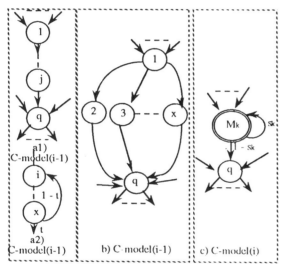

Fig. 4 Creation of macro-states in C-model(i)

Reduction rules

C-model(i) is constructed from C-model(i-1) by substitution of :

Rule 1 : one macro-state for each branch in C-model(i-1);

Rule 2 : one macro-state for each cluster in C-model(i-1).

❑

Example. In fig.5, three step are useful to reach the irreducible C-model thanks to the reduction rules : in the C-model(0), there are a loop {3, 5, 8, 3} and a cluster {4; 6; 7}; macro-states M_a and M_b respectively take their places in the C-model(1). In the second step, only one cluster {6; M_a; M_b} is reducible to a macro-state M_c; one obtains the C-model(2) in which the whole state form a branch. Step 3 leads then to the irreducible and minimum C-model(3) with a single macro-state M_d from rule 1.

II-2. *Construction of C-model(i)*

The transition probabilities in C-model(i) are deduced from the ones in C-model(i-1). They are unchanged between states which are not grouped in a new state. For each macro-state M_j created in the C-model(i), one has to calculate: Pr[$M_j \rightarrow M_j$] and Pr[$M_j \rightarrow q$] (see fig.4). For this purpose, one parameter s_y is associated with each state y :

$\rightarrow s_y$ = Pr[$y \rightarrow y$] called reduction coefficient.

If y is a simple state, s_y = 0 by construction. For each step i (i $\geq$ 1) one evaluates this parameter for the macro-state created in C-model(i). Theorems 1 and 2 given bellow, will allow to calculate the reduction coefficient from the ones associated with states of C-model(i-1). By construction, the transition probabilities in fig. 4c are given by the parameter s_j associated with M_j, so that :

Pr[$M_j \rightarrow M_j$] = s_j and Pr[$M_j \rightarrow q$] = 1 - s_j.

Definition 4.

A macro-state M_j is *s-equivalent* with the branch or the cluster of X states it substitutes for (fig. 4) if and only if :

$$Pr[Mi /i] = \sum Pr[y/i-1], y \in \{1, ..., X\} \qquad (1)$$

A C-model (i-1) and C-model(i) are s-equivalent if each new macro-state in C-model(i) verify equality (1)

❑

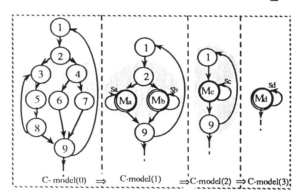

Fig.5 Construction of successive C-models

Theorem 1.

A macro-state M_j given by reduction rule 2 is s-equivalent with a cluster $c_{1,x}$ (fig.4b,c) if and only if :

$$s_k = \frac{s_1 + \sum_{i=1}^{X} \frac{\beta_i}{1 - s_i}}{1 + \sum_{i=1}^{X} \frac{\beta_i}{1 - s_i}} \qquad (2)$$

with β_i = Pr[1 $\rightarrow$ i] ; i = states which precede the state 1 of C-model(i-1);

and s_i = Pr[i $\rightarrow$ i] ; i = states include in the cluster of C-model(i-1),, (i = 2,...X).

❑

107

For a branch $b_{1,j}$ or a loop $l_{i,x}$ (fig. 4a-c), the value of s_k which ensures the s-equivalence with M_j is given by theorem 2. Theorems 1 and 2 are formally proven in (Abazi,1992).

Theorem 2.

2.1- A macro-state M_j given by reduction rule 1 is s-equivalent with a loop $l_{i,x}$ (fig.4a,c) if and only if :

$$s_{ix} = \frac{1 - s_x - t}{1 - s_x} \cdot \frac{1}{\sum_{j=i}^{x} \frac{1}{1 - s_j}} \qquad (3)$$

with $s_j = Pr[j \rightarrow j]$; j = states include in the loop C-model(i-1).

2.2- A macro-state M_j given by reduction rule 1 is s-equivalent with a branch $b_{1,j}$ (fig.4a,c) if and only if :

$$s_k = 1 - \frac{1}{\sum_{i=1}^{j} \frac{1}{1 - s_i}} \qquad (4)$$

with $s_i = Pr[i \rightarrow i]$; i = state include in the branch of C-model(i-1).

$\sqcup$

Example : The theorem 1 is illustrated by the chemical manufacturing described in section II. For this example (see fig.2a), the cluster $c_{2,4} = \{M_2; M_3; M_4\}$ is reducible to a macro-state M_{24} in C-model(1) as shown in fig.2-c. The associated reduction coefficient s_{24} is then calculated thanks to the theorem 1. For M_{24}, theorem 1 gives $s_{24} = 0.827$ with : $s_1 = 0.1$; $s_2 = 0.1$; $s_3 = 0.8$; $s_4 = 0.5$; and $\beta_1 = 0.8$; $\beta_2 = 0.1$.

Table 1 gives the stationary probabilities of the two models (before and after reduction). These numerical results confirm the s-equivalence between the two models. The stationary probabilities after the reduction are obtained with an error less than 10^{-4}.

States	Station. proba. C-model(0)	Station. proba. C-model(1)
M_0	0,126759	0,126719
M_1	0,140848	0,140797
M_2	0,140851	
M_3	0,563375	0,732486
M_4	0,028168	

Table 1 : Stationary probabilities .

III- MARKOVIAN MODEL FOR THE FAILED SYSTEM

To describe the failed system, a model wich take into account all faults which can affect the system is proposed. As the behavior of the system depends on the faults, for each fault, a model is constructed. However, for n faults, the faulty system is the markovian model containing (2n+1) states such that (see fig.6):

- one state RF represents the fault-free system it is the compact model obtained by applying the reduction algorithm (see section II-1).

- n states WF_i (i = 1,...,n) representing the behavior of the system when the fault f_i occurs. States WF_i are compact models obtained also by applying the reduction formulas given below.

- n absorbing states associated to each WF_i which are reached when a fault f_i is detected.

The transition probability to move from RF to one of states WFi depends on the fault. The resolution of the (2n+1) markov system gives the stationary probability for each state. The classification of fault is then made by comparing the probability of each absorbing state.

III- 1 Construction of the compact failed model

The failed model is constructed from the initial model (C-model(0)) of the system where different functioning modes are represented. For a fault f_i which affect a set of states S_i, the system is modeled by associating absorbing state D_i and then the reduction formulas given by the theorem 3 is applied to obtain the reduction coefficient associted to the macro state WF_i and the probability to move from WF_i to the absorbing state D_i.

According to the faults to be detected, one can move from one state of the initial model to the detection state. Then one need to define other kind of model to reduce as shown in fig.7 which represents the general case of reduction. For a given fault f_i, one set of states F_i is associated such that :

F_i : {states $\in$ initial model which can detect f_i}. If the set of states S={ states $\in$ initial model}, $S \supset F_i$.

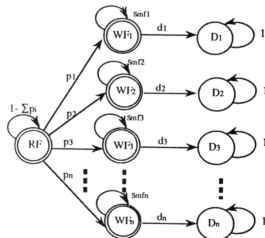

Fig.6 The general representation of the compact failed model.

The average probability z_i is associated to the transition from one state of F_i to the absorbing state D. Theorem 3 given bellow, allows to calculate the coefficient d_i to move

108

from the state WF_i to the absorbing state D_i and the coefficient s_{mi} to remain in the state WF_i.

Theorem 3.

The C-model(i-1) and the C-model(i) are equivalent (fig.7a-b) if and only if :

$$s_{mi} = 1 - \frac{1 - s_1}{1 + \sum_{k=2}^{n} \frac{\prod_{j=1}^{k-1} \alpha_j}{1 - s_k}} \tag{5}$$

and

$$d_i = \frac{z_1 + \sum_{k=2} z_k \cdot \frac{\prod_{j=1}^{k-1} \alpha_l}{1 - s_k}}{1 + \sum_{k=2}^{n} \frac{\prod_{j=1}^{k-1} \alpha_j}{1 - s_k}} \tag{6}$$

$s_i = Pr[\, i \rightarrow i\,]$; $i \in S$ of C-model(i-1) with S is set of states of C-model(i-1) and $z_i = 0$ if $i \notin F_i$. ⌐

For n faults , the classification is made up by comparing the stationary probabilities of state D_i knowing that : $\sum_{i=1}^{n} Pr[D_i] = 1$.

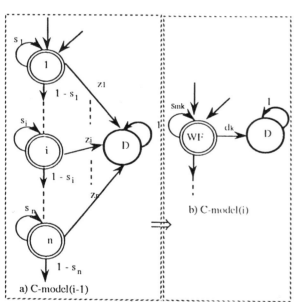

a) C-model(i-1)

b) C-model(i)

Fig. 7 General case of reduction states $\{1,....n\} \in F_i$.

III- 1 Failed model for the chemical manufacturing

Let us consider three faults f1, f2 and f3 such that :

- f_1 is a fault which can appear when the mode test is executed,

- f_2 is a fault which can appear at the start up of the pumps,

- f_3 is a fault which can appear in the purifing mode, that is to say, when an abnormal rate of chlorine is detected.

In this example, sets S and F_i (i=1,...4) are :

S = {M0, M1, M2, M3, M4}

and F1 ={M1}, F2 ={M2}, F3 ={M3}, F4 ={M4}.

To illustrate the method, the calculation is detailed only for a fault f_1. The compact failed model obtained is given in fig 8.

For the fault f_1, the theorem 3 is applied and reduction coefficients s_{m1} , d_1 are calculated.

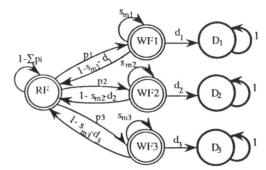

Fig.8 Chemical application : Compact failed model

The resolution of the compact failed model obtained (fig.8), gives the stationary probability given in the table 2. This result enables us to classify the fault according to the occurence probabilities by comparing probabilities of states D_1, D_2 and D_3 in the failed compact model.

From results given in table 2, it can be said for this example that a fault f_3 can be revealed before the fault f_1 and f_2 by the fact that : $Pr[D_3] > Pr[D_1] > Pr[D_2]$.

States	Stationary probabilites
RF	0,003080
WF_1	0,000651
WF_2	0,000959
WF_3	0,002061
D_1	0,194677
D_2	0,183410
D_3	0,615208

Table 2 : Stationary probabilities for the compact failed model

These results are obtained knowing that f_1, f_2 and f_3 has the same probability to appear ($p_1 = p_2 = p_3 = 10^{-2}$). For other probabilities p_i, the same fault classification is obtained.

CONCLUSION

This first fault classification allows to study closely the confining mode of the system. The same method is applied to classify all faults which can affect the system in this mode. When the system is in the confining mode, the chlorine is directed to the neutralisation column. This configuration is made by actuating specific valves which direct the chlorine flux to the column. This functioning mode is modeled by a markovian model. The compact model is deduced by applying theorems 1 and 2. The compact failed model is then constructed. The resolution of the compact failed model, thanks to the reduction algorithm and theorems 3, gives a classification of the faults studied. The obtained results in this maner enables us to say that a fault in a valve can be revealed before other faults (sensors). In order to increase the reliability involved in manufacturing with chlorine, this study strongly suggest the duplication of all valves used to direct the chlorine to the neutralisation column.

At the present time, a complete routine to computerize the method is developed. It take into account the modeling tasks. Starting with the transition matrix which correspond to the C-model(0), the routine gives the successive C-model(i) then, for any faults in the described system, it deduce the transition matrix for the failed model. The computation of the transition matrix gives the stationary probabilities of each states with the fault classification.

References

Abazi, Z and Thevenod P (1989), Modelisation compact en vue du test aléatoire de cartes à microprocesseur: calcul de la longueur de test; revue Traitement du signal. (T.S) vol.6, n°1, pp 69-80, 1989.

Abazi (1992) Un model compact pour la classification des fautes, Internal Repport LAG 92-102, June 1992.

Abazi, Z and Peter T (1991), Classification of critical events in systems described by grafcet using the markov process Safety of computer control systems 1991 IFAC (SAFECOMP'91), Norway 1991, pp 101-106.

Kemeni, J.G. and Snell, J.L. (1960) Finite Markov chains; New-York : Van Nostrand.

Leveson, N.G. and Stolzy J.L.(1987) Safety analysis using Petri nets IEEE Trans.Soft.Eng., vol.SE-23, n°3, pp 386-397.

Peter, T. (1990). Sûreté de fonctionnement: Modelisation par chaîne de Markov d'un système decrit par grafcet. D.E.A. Automatique, Productique et theorie des systèmes.

Zhou,M. and Di Cesare, F.(1989) Adaptative design of Petri net controllers for error recovery in automated manufacturing systems. Rensselaer Polytechnic Institute, Troy. New York, 31p.

LOGIC MODELLING OF DEPENDABLE SYSTEMS

John Murdoch

School of Computer Studies, The University of Leeds, Leeds LS2 9JT, England

Danny Pearce

The Turing Institute, 36 North Hanover St, Glasgow, Scotland

Nigel R Ward

British Aerospace (Space Systems) Ltd, Gunnels Wood Road, Stevenage, SG1 2AS, England

Abstract. One approach to achieving fault tolerance in a complex engineered system is to include within it an automated Fault Management (sub)System (FMS), in addition to conventional monitoring by human operators. The FMS assists in ensuring an appropriate response to component failures by generating commands to switch system resource usage, control mode, redundancy etc on the basis of sensor data. The specification of the required logical behaviour of the FMS must be derived from a consideration of the total system behaviour in the nominal case and under failure assumptions and should be compatible with operational procedures demanded from human operators. This typically leads to significant levels of complexity due to the proliferation of possible system states. A recently developed computer-based tool, called Integrated Fault Management Environment (IFME), addresses this problem. IFME provides a graphical interface for specifying hierarchical system structure, interdependencies and logical behaviours. The defined logical system model may then be subjected to various analyses supported by the toolset, including batch-type and interactive simulation, diagnostic rule induction, Failure Mode Effects Analysis (FMEA) and operations procedures design. The logic (or qualitative) modelling approach is evaluated and placed in the context of conventional systems and control engineering techniques.

Keywords. Safety; Dependability; Fault tolerance; Computer control

INTRODUCTION

A variety of fault avoidance and fault tolerance techniques are available for the development of dependable systems (Laprie, 1989). A frequently-used approach in the fault tolerance category is to arrange for the system itself to automatically correct for failure events, for example by switching in redundant units. We call such an automated subsystem a Fault Management System (FMS). Monitoring and control by human operators is often still required however, particularly when system failure carries a high level of risk.

Unfortunately, FMSs, usually implemented in software on general purpose microprocessors, are themselves potentially complex systems and subject to faults both in design and of physical origin. Furthermore they are products of the system design activity and therefore embody assumptions about failure modes and effects. Similar difficulties arise in the design of operations procedures which naturally have to be compatible with the automated systems.

This paper addresses the problem of designing FMSs and operations procedures, focussing on the requirements specification of fault management logic. A systems perspective is adopted, that is to say, FMS requirements are considered to be derived from the design of a containing system. An approach based on the modelling of the logical (or qualitative) behaviour of the containing system is discussed. Two aspects are explored; firstly a context for developing FMS and operations specifications, based on a particular view of systems and dependability; secondly, a recently-developed prototype toolset, aimed at supporting the logic modelling approach. The strengths and weaknesses of this approach are evaluated and set in the context of general systems engineering. Communications satellite systems are used to furnish examples, but it is hoped that the discussion is of wider interest.

PHYSICAL SYSTEMS OF INTEREST

Systems under consideration are complex, engineered artifacts, designed by multi-disciplinary teams of engineers using a variety of modelling and analysis techniques. We are particularly interested in systems, such as vehicles and process control applications, which exhibit both dynamical and logical behaviour. Logical behaviour is predominantly, although not exclusively, associated with embedded computing elements in, for example, control applications. Complexity arises by virtue of the number of components involved and the number and variety of interactions between them. While good engineering practice strives to minimise complexity in design, some applications demand a level of functionality and performance which necessarily entails complex solutions. Difficulties in design and validation arise when a complex system is required to be highly dependable. We are interested in systems in which dependability is achieved, in part, by two means; an automated Fault Management System and human operator monitoring and control (Figure 1).

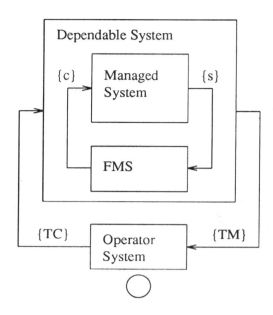

Fig. 1 Systems of interest have an automated FMS which monitors a set {s} and controls a set {c} of logical state variables. A human operator monitors a set {TM} of telemetred state variables and controls a set {TC} of telecommanded state variables.

For example, communications satellites are designed today with on-board FMSs which seek to maintain communications services in the event of single unit failures and, if this is not possible, to at least place the satellite in a safe configuration awaiting intervention from ground. Such intervention is provided by spacecraft operations teams who maintain round-the-clock monitoring and control services via telemetry and telecommand links. They are provided with operations plans to cover nominal and contingency situations and, not infrequently, call on back-up expertise from manufacturers and others to assist in fault diagnosis and correction.

DEPENDABILITY

Dependability is defined (Laprie, 1989) as that characteristic of a system which permits justifiable reliance to be placed on the services it delivers. This definition involves two systems; the dependable system itself and the system which is placing reliance on it. We view dependability therefore as a property of a system as viewed across an interface, with some specified (two-way) interaction implied. It is closely related to the notion of predictability. The services provided across an interface are predictable if they conform with the interface specification. The two key aspects of dependability are therefore (1) the accuracy, completeness etc of the interface specification and (2) the probability that the system meets the specification across the specified interface. The specification should include statements about the "user" side of the interface, defining the inputs to which the system of interest has to respond dependably. We may wish to focus attention on a subset only of the full specification, for example, the safety

requirements. The level of dependability required across an interface will be determined by the risk associated with unpredictable behaviour. Top-down Fault Tree Analysis is one technique to support the propagation of risk within the system. Dependability is usually considered as an external attribute of a system, that is as a feature which is observable by users. However, dependability can be extended to internal interfaces, corresponding to a view of systems as assemblies of mainly separate subsystems which place reliance on mutually provided services. It is assumed that a system can be made more dependable by identifying critical interfaces and by specifying in more detail and with greater rigour the behaviours and constraints on each side.

System modelling is a valuable approach to improving the rigour with which interfaces are specified and for testing the implied interactions between modules. However a clear distinction has to be drawn between system models and physical reality. The approach described below addresses the modelling of systems to support FMS and operations specifications. However, not all physical failure events nor fault propagation paths will be predicted at the design stage. There is no formal solution to this problem - all we can do is improve the quality of professional practice and employ development processes which support the accumulation of design experience. This does not remove the need to analyse specifications and designs early in the development lifecycle, on the basis of postulated fault conditions.

SYSTEM MODELLING

In general systems terms, systems of interest may be modelled as a hierarchy of interdependent subsystems and components, working together to achieve desired emergent properties (IEE, 1992). The recursive nature of this approach allows us to consider emergent properties at various levels in the subsystem hierarchy, the emergent properties at one level being used by the next higher level and so on. We informally consider such levels of decomposition as being separated by "horizontal" interfaces (Figure 2). We can also think of the system, at a particular level, as being partitioned into separate "sibling" systems, which interact with each other to achieve the emergent behaviour of that level. Interfaces between such sibling systems are informally classified as "vertical" interfaces.

Viewed in this way, a system comprises a set of objects which interact with each other by a variety of means. Some of these interactions will be the result of explicit design, that is, they are purposively arranged to achieve desired emergent properties. Other interactions will be by-products of the design, and will become important in the propagation of the effects of failure events. Dependability considerations may be applied to both horizontal and vertical interfaces.

The Attitude and Orbit Control Subsystem (AOCS) of a satellite, for example, has as its principal emergent behaviour the maintenance of spacecraft orientation within specified angular limits. We view this as a horizontal interface, since the behaviour is a product of the entire AOCS, not of any individual component. However, viewed from the AOCS system level, two constituent components, for example a momentum wheel unit and a wheel drive electronics unit, share a vertical interface.

The modelling of engineered systems rests heavily on the concept of state, that is, a condition of the system which remains unchanged unless some event or process occurs. The state of a system can be viewed at various levels of abstraction. In the systems of interest, it is useful to distinguish between "dynamical state variables" and "logical state variables". The former are the customary state variables associated essentially with energy storage mechanisms in the physical system. They are continuous functions of time and their evolution is modelled by sets of first order differential equations, with coefficients embodying the constraints of basic physics and of the design.

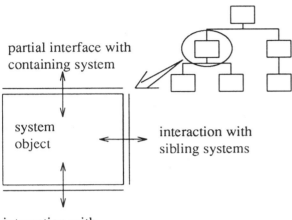

partial interface with
containing system

system
object

interaction with
sibling systems

interaction with
emergent properties
of contained systems

Fig. 2 A module within the decomposition of a system interacts with sibling systems at the same level and contributes to emergent properties used at the next higher level.

The latter are state variables which are not continuous functions of time (at the level of abstraction under consideration) and are not associated with energy storage mechanisms of the system. However, such logical variables do undergo time evolution, governed by interactions dictated by the design. For example, the velocity and acceleration of a satellite are dynamical state variables, whereas the open/closed status of latching valves within the propulsion subsystem are logical state variables. Typically, the dynamical and logical state variables of such a system will undergo parallel evolution in time, interacting in various ways. In certain cases, we can think of the logical state variables as being abstracted from the dynamical variables across a horizontal interface.

LOGIC MODELLING

The logic modelling of an engineered artifact developed here models a system as a set of interconnected modules, where interactions between modules are restricted to qualitative variables. Emphasis is therefore being placed on the logical state variables of the system, although dynamical variables can be treated approximately. The approach is similar to finite state machine models which have been developed in software engineering, for example Modecharts (Jahanian, 1988) and the Requirements State Machine approach (Jaffe, 1990). The qualitative modelling of dynamical variables is derived from the "naive physics" approach in the field of artificial intelligence. Each object is assigned a set of states, divided into nominal and fault

states, a behaviour which specifies the input-to-output mapping and timing information. An object which receives an input from another will typically change state and produce output signals to further objects.

It is possible to apply the model at various levels of abstraction. At a low level, the logical state of an embedded processor is described by the current contents of all memory registers and of the program counter. It is this kind of state which is represented in formal specification languages such as Z (Spivey, 1988). At a higher level, a state might represent a particular configuration of program control. In control engineering, the conventional state vector of lumped-parameter systems represents dynamical state variables and would not be well modelled by the approach discussed here. However, control modes, representing sets of control laws to invoke in response to qualitative stimuli, would be amenable to the logic modelling approach.

FMS SPECIFICATION

Suppose that across some interface in a system design the services are provided with an inadequate dependability compared with a dependability requirement derived from risk analysis. The designer may choose to introduce a FMS which monitors the provided services and, if the interface specification (or a subset) is violated, initiates corrective action. The corrective action may require inclusion in the design of redundant units or other measures. We do not address the nature of these resources but rather focus on the FMS as a device which responds to and stimulates logical state transitions in the containing system. It is assumed that dynamical state variables are converted to logical variables in the monitoring process. The FMS and contingency operations procedures are viewed as a means of enforcing compliance with interface specifications during system operation.

FMS specification is based on the identification of likely failure modes, or at least non-compliant behaviours, at critical interfaces. This task involves human judgement which we do not attempt to automate. However, we do address the complexity which arises due to the logical implications of postulated behaviours within a design. Usually a variety of failure modes have to be postulated in order to generate the required confidence in delivered services. Complexity in diagnosis, arising from practical constraints on the number of monitored state variables, and in recovery action increases rapidly as more reliance is placed on the FMS.

Logic modelling provides assistance with integrating the logical specification of the FMS within the behaviour of the containing system. Logic modelling provides: (1) a structured representation of the logical behaviour of the design, comprising the containing system and the FMS, for use throughout the system development lifecycle, (2) a means of testing the logical specification of the FMS against the behaviour of the containing system and its postulated failure modes, (3) a means of testing diagnosability of failure modes, given sets of monitored state variables, (4) a means of propagating the effects of failures across the network of modelled interactions between system modules, (5) a means of deriving exact diagnostic rules automatically using rule induction techniques.

OPERATIONS SPECIFICATION

The operation of critical systems is a crucial consideration in achieving dependability. The human interface presents special difficulties associated with cognition (not pursued here) and the open nature of human behaviour. It is not always possible to predict how a system will be used. This is both a weakness and a strength, for although such interfaces have to be designed to accommodate a range of possible operator behaviours, the flexibility of human response can correct for system behaviours which were unforeseen in design. Here we focus on the design of contingency procedures harmonised with automated FMS functions.

There are usually two kinds of operations required; a fast failure detection followed by rapid appropriate action and "off-line" fault diagnosis and repair. In the case of space systems, these functions are integrated into a single operations control centre because of the rather limited scope for maintenance. The logic model of a system can be used to develop and test operational procedures to meet rapid response requirements. As in the FMS case, such diagnostic and recovery procedures are necessarily based on fault states and effects predicted during system design. The logic model also provides assistance to operators in the case of unforeseen system behaviour. The model provides a structured representation of the current understanding of the system and can be updated as operational experience is accumulated. Of particular usefulness is an accurate model of the logical behaviour of the FMS which, in the event of anomalous system behaviour, has to be included in the fault diagnosis task.

A LOGIC MODELLING TOOL

A software tool, called Integrated Fault Management Environment (IFME), has been developed (Ward, 1991) to explore the practical use of logic modelling in industrial projects. The development has been motivated largely by needs in the space industry, but there is little in the toolset which is specific to space systems. IFME supports the development of a logic (or qualitative) model of a physical system for use as a central resource throughout the lifecycle of an engineering project. The software consists of a number of tools.

The Model Construction and Interactive Simulation Tool allows the user to build and edit hierarchical, interconnected networks of components as discussed above. A graphical interface provides all the construction, viewing and editing functions at any level in the model hierarchy (Figure 3). Components at the lowest level in the hierarchy are assigned behaviours, which comprise a specification of the input-to-output mapping, of internal nominal and fault states and of response times. Component behaviours may be entered either in a simple procedural language or as a truth table. One component communicates with another by a message sent along a specified connection between ports on the two components, after Davis (Davis, 1984).

A discrete event simulation approach is used in which the model time proceeds from the current event to the next scheduled event (ie the time step is not fixed). At each time step, messages are passed between the components and the consequences of all messages and behaviours associated with the current time step are modelled through the system, before the simulation moves to the next event. Messages for each object are queued on a FIFO basis. The

messages carry boolean and qualitative variables, the latter representing for example "high", "medium" and "low" values as approximations to dynamical state variables.

At any stage during model construction, the user may perform an interactive simulation of the model, for example to investigate the effects of postulated fault events on the system. Pop-up windows are used to display the status of state variables of interest. A simulation can be run step-by-step or to a set break point. IFME also supports non-interactive simulation in which large numbers of simulation runs can be performed to investigate the effects of faults. A Failure Modes Effects Analysis (FMEA) Tool accesses batch simulation data and generates FMEA output in conformance with MIL/STD/1629 (Figure 4). A Rule Induction Tool (Pearce, 1988) accesses the same data and generates sets of diagnostic rules, presented either in the form of rules (IF <system state> THEN <diagnosis>) or in decision tree form. If desired, these rules may be incorporated in the system model to represent FMS behaviour and/or operational procedures. A Recovery Assistant Tool allows procedures for recovering from faults to be tested on the logic model.

The IFME toolset is implemented as follows. Model construction and simulation via the direct manipulation of graphics is provided using the graphical interface tool "HyperNeWS", developed by the Turing Institute. HyperNeWS uses SUN Microsystem's PostScript windowing system, NeWS. IFME then uses a text-based intermediate model representation in order to translate from the PostScript graphical representation to an executable simulation model. The intermediate model uses SGML, permitting automatic translation into a variety of target forms. SGML, an ISO standard for document interchange, has been selected for the intermediate representation because it provides a user-definable grammar, allowing one-to-one mapping between graphical elements and grammar constructs.

Finally, IFME exploits an SGML parser/translator called "TOLK", also developed by the Turing Institute, which uses grammar-based translation rules to translate SGML documents to any required format. Currently, IFME translates to source code for the C++ programming language; other target languages have been considered and would be straightforward to implement. The C++ code is compiled and linked with a small, application-independent simulator shell program (also written in C++), to form the executable model. The C++ language was chosen for its execution speed and object-orientated capabilities.

The IFME tools currently run on SUN Microsystem platforms but are portable across many hardware and software systems.

ASSESSMENT OF LOGIC MODELLING

Early versions of the IFME tools were used in a study for the European Space Agency (Ward, 1992) which demonstrated the applicability of qualitative modelling to support the design of an on-board FMS for a satellite. A model of the AOCS of an existing satellite (OLYMPUS F1) was built, consisting of 60 objects, at 4 hierarchical levels. Connections between components in the model number over 200 and over 70 monitor points are used to define a complete system state. Results have been sufficiently encouraging to attract funding from the UK Defence Research Agency for the development of a prototype operations support system for a military communications satellite (SKYNET 4). IFME has also been used to model a data bus, a fuel subsystem and a canopy release system for a military aircraft and a hydrocarbon process in the oil industry.

It appears that a qualitative treatment of dynamical variables gives adequate fidelity in some applications, analogous with the qualitative nature of human diagnostic reasoning. However the coarse discretisation associated with the approach makes it difficult to model dynamic processes, ruling out accurate treatment of faults and propagation of effects which involve dynamical variables. For example, the failure of a heater element of the thermal control subsystem of a satellite will result in a thermal distribution difficult to predict with a qualitative model. The combined use of dynamical and qualitative models appears necessary to accurately model fault effects across logical and dynamical interactions.

A further question relating to model accuracy is the treatment of time. In IFME, although inter-module path delays can be modelled, and module behaviours can be timed and delayed, there remain some approximations in the handling of simultaneous messages. The treatment of timing is adequate for the level of abstraction for which we have used the tool, but would be inadequate for stringent real time applications. However, this is not a necessary shortcoming of the logic modelling approach, only a limitation on the IFME implementation.

Given these limitations, the logic modelling approach offers some considerable benefits. Firstly, because of the simplified model (over dynamical simulations), it is possible to perform large numbers of simulations in reasonable CPU time. For example, 10,000 simulation runs were performed in 60 minutes on a Sparcstation 1+ for the AOCS model described above. This makes it feasible to investigate large numbers of postulated failure cases or larger models. Secondly, the logic modelling approach supports analyses which are not possible by other means, for example, the automatic derivation of exact diagnostic rules using rule induction algorithms. Thirdly, a separate representation of logical aspects of system behaviour focusses attention on these systems aspects which experience has shown are difficult to manage over the development lifecycle.

It is generally not possible to simulate all possible combinations of faults in a system because of the combinatorial explosion in numbers of cases. However, the treatment of single faults or two fault cases is more tractable, and conforms with common design practice. The logic modelling approach is open to the same criticism as software testing, in that residual failure modes may remain after extensive simulation. On the other hand, logic modelling provides structured and complementary support to the human design task in the analysis of complex designs.

CONCLUSIONS

The logic modelling of dependable systems has been discussed, focussing on its use in the specification of FMS and operations logic. A contextual view of systems and dependability has been described, indicating an underlying method for fault management design. Dependability has been associated with interface specifications, both internal and external to the system and system modelling has been viewed as a means of increasing the probability that systems meet their specifications across system interfaces. A particular exploratory toolset (IFME) has been described as a representative approach. Although involving approximations in the treatment of dynamical state variables and in the treatment of some timing issues (in the IFME implementation), the logic modelling approach has been found to furnish a practical means through which dependability can be improved throughout a complex system.

Further development should examine optimum combinations of logic and dynamical modelling allowing more complete failure modes analysis for certain kinds of system. Practical needs may argue for a separation of concerns, maintaining distinct models of dynamic and logical behaviour, with looser sharing of results, perhaps. A further line of enquiry is the combination of logic modelling with mathematically formal methods. For particularly critical modules, formal proofs of correctness of behaviour (against specifications) and of timing may be required. The logic modelling approach would provide a link between mathematically formal representations and wider systems engineering.

ACKNOWLEDGEMENTS

The IFME Project was supported under DTI/SERC Project 1561 and developed collaboratively by BAe (Space Systems) Ltd, The Turing Institute, AEA Technology and BAe (Military Aircraft) Ltd. John Murdoch is funded under a Royal Society/SERC Industrial Fellowship, on secondment from BAe (Space Systems) Ltd.

REFERENCES

Davis, R (1984). Diagnostic reasoning based on structure and behaviour. Artificial Intelligence, 24, 347-410.

IEE (1992). Draft Guide to the Practice of System Engineering, (Third Draft), IEE Professional Group M5, March 1992

Jaffe, M S (1990), Leveson, N G, Heimdahl, M, Melhart, B. Software requirements analysis for real-time process-control systems. Tech Rep 90-04, Univ Cal, Irvine.

Jahanian, F (1988) and Stuart, D A. A method for verifying properties of Modechart specifications. Proc. Real Time Systems Symposium 1988, Huntsville AL, 12-21.

Laprie, J C (1989). Dependability: a unifying concept for reliable computing and fault tolerance. Ch 1 in Anderson, T. (ed) Dependability of resilient computers, BSP Professional Books.

Pearce, D (1988). The induction of fault diagnosis systems from qualitative models. Proc. 7th National Conference on Artificial Intelligence (AAAI88), 353-357, St Paul, Minnesota.

Spivey, J M (1988). Understanding Z. Cambridge University Press, 1988

Ward, N R (1991). An integrated fault management environment (IFME). ESA WPP-025, Procs. Workshop on Artificial Intelligence and Knowledge-Based Systems for Space, ESTEC, Noordwijk, Netherlands.

Ward, N R (1992). AOCS Software Assessmant. ESTEC Contract 7802/88/NL/MAC, Final Report.

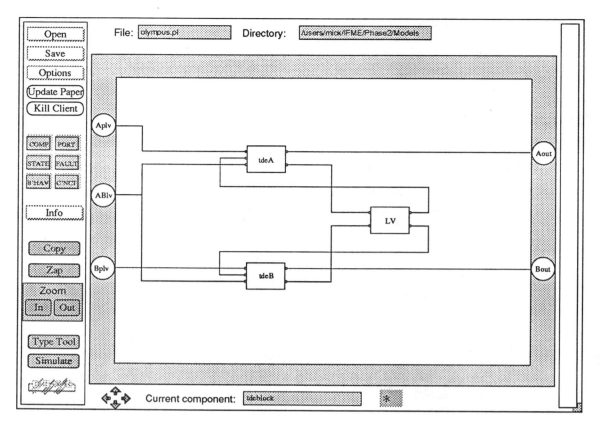

Fig. 3 Example screen layout during model construction using the IFME tools.

```
FMECA Assistant    Read File    Filters    FMECA    Sort FMECA    Summary

+------------------------------------------------------------------------------+
|                        FAILURE EFFECTS SUMMARY LIST                          |
+------------------------------------------------------------------------------+
|       Model: exproc                          Simulation: orbit               |
+------+--------+----------+---------------------------------+-----+-----+-----------+------+
| No.  | Item   | Block    | Failure Effects                 | Obs | Mon | Contributed | Fail |
|      |        |          |                                 |     | Grp | By          | Rate |
+------+--------+----------+---------------------------------+-----+-----+-----------+------+
|  1   | asA    | ceu in Aocs | Sun angle is maximum         |     |     | Failure  2 | 1.0E-06 |
|      |        |          |   In dynamics in Aocs :         |     |     |           |      |
|      |        |          |     theta is H instead of MINS  |  4  |  3  |           |      |
|      |        |          |     phi is H instead of S       |  4  |  3  |           |      |
|      |        |          | smmSWA finished in Sun Lock mode|     |     |           |      |
|      |        |          | In sasA in Aocs :               |     |     |           |      |
|      |        |          |   phi is H instead of S         |  4  |  3  |           |      |
|      |        |          |   theta is H instead of MINS    |  4  |  3  |           |      |
|      |        |          | In sasB in Aocs :               |     |     |           |      |
|      |        |          |   phi is H instead of S         |  4  |  3  |           |      |
|      |        |          |   theta is H instead of MINS    |  4  |  3  |           |      |
|      |        |          | In smmSWA in smmA in ceu in Aocs :|   |     |           |      |
|      |        |          |   theta is ? instead of MINS    |  8  |  3  |           |      |
|      |        |          |   alpha_a is H instead of S     |  8  |  3  |           |      |
|      |        |          |   beta_a is H instead of MINS   |  8  |  3  |           |      |
|      |        |          |   sp_b is FALSE instead of TRUE |  8  |  3  |           |      |
|      |        |          |   sp_a is FALSE instead of TRUE |  8  |  3  |           |      |
|      |        |          |   alpha_b is H instead of S     |  8  |  3  |           |      |
|      |        |          |   beta_b is H instead of MINS   |  8  |  3  |           |      |
|      |        |          |   phi is ? instead of S         |  8  |  3  |           |      |
+------+--------+----------+---------------------------------+-----+-----+-----------+------+
|  2   | asA    | ceu in Aocs | sasA sees small sun angle    |     |     | Failure  5 | 2.0E-06 |
|      | asA    | ceu in Aocs |   In sasA in Aocs :           |     |     | Failure  8 |      |
|      |        |          |     phi is MINS instead of S    |  4  |  3  |           |      |
|      |        |          |     theta is S instead of MINS  |  4  |  3  |           |      |
|      |        |          | sasB sees small sun angle       |     |     |           |      |
|      |        |          |   In sasB in Aocs :             |     |     |           |      |
|      |        |          |     phi is MINS instead of S    |  4  |  3  |           |      |
|      |        |          |     theta is S instead of MINS  |  4  |  3  |           |      |
|      |        |          | Sun angle is small              |     |     |           |      |
|      |        |          |   In dynamics in Aocs :         |     |     |           |      |
|      |        |          |     theta is S instead of MINS  |  4  |  3  |           |      |
+------+--------+----------+---------------------------------+-----+-----+-----------+------+
```

Fig. 4 Example output of the FMEA tool of IFME.

INTEGRATION OF SOFTWARE RELIABILITY PREDICTIONS TO ACHIEVE MODELLING FAULT TOLERANCE

F. Saglietti

Institute for Safety Technology (IST)
Gesellschaft für Anlagen- und Reaktorsicherheit (GRS) mbH
Forschungsgelände D-8046 Garching Germany

Abstract. A considerable number of reliability growth models has been proposed to evaluate software dependability. Each of them provides an inference rule from past failure data on the present and future behaviour; they are based on different assumptions, some of which are only realistic for particular application classes and unprovable at present. Also for this reason none of the models has ever shown to be the absolutely best: its accuracy varies from an application to another and cannot be predicted a priori. Although it may be easy to identify the worst models in a given case by means of absolute quality measures quantifying the departure of prediction from reality, the identification of the best one is particularly difficult, as the goodness of fit values may be time-variant. Thus even an experienced model user may encounter considerable difficulties in making up his mind when selecting the most promising modelization for the specific situation considered. In order to simplify the decision phase, allowing the use of evaluating tools also to appliers non-familiar with the underlying modelling theories, we suggest to automatize the model choice, by selecting deterministically the estimation value considered to be most reliable. The intention of this contribution is to study two particular strategies integrating different predictions, which have been suggested in literature, in particular with respect to their sensitivity to model-behavioural changes, identifying the most critical and most suitable situations to be treated by each of them.

Keywords. Computer software; software engineering; program testing; failure detection; reliability theory; probability; Bayes methods; modeling.

Acknowledgement. The investigations reported have been sponsored in part by the Commission of the European Communities under the ESPRIT program (subitem Software Technology, projects REQUEST and DARTS): the author thanks for the support.

DIVERSITY CONCEPT FOR SOFTWARE RELIABILITY PREDICTIONS

It is a well-known fact that the problem of estimating and predicting software reliability has not been solved yet in a satisfactory way. The high, continuously increasing number of existing models meant to provide an inference rule from past failure data on the present and future failure behaviour are based on different assumptions, which seem to be partly unrealistic and anyway unprovable at present.

Moreover, no one of these models has shown to be the relatively best among them: in fact, their success and accuracy varies from an application to another and thus cannot be predicted a priori with any confidence.

In particular, it is quite easy to identify the worst models in a given case by means of *absolute* quality measures quantifying the departure of the prediction from reality; on the contrary, the identification of the best one is particularly difficult as *relative* quality measures to compare models may not allow a simple and unique interpretation, their trend possibly varying with time.

This critical situation shows a strong parallelism with the achievement of software fault-tolerance by developing different versions intended to perform the same specified service: analogously, we are here provided with "diverse" reliability predictions and have thus to develop a sound strategy in order to obtain the best possible information on the basis of more possibly diverging outputs.

Due to the similarity described, we may adopt a general decision mechanism as the one suggested by Anderson (1986) and shown in Fig. 1.

In our case, the diverse reliability estimations $R_1,...,R_n$ resulting from n different software reliability growth models, will first be *filtered* by:

- identifying the results $R_1,...,R_n$,
- improving single predictions by a process of recalibration. An adaptive procedure is decribed by Brocklehurst (1987), Brocklehurst and others (1989),
- applying fixed criteria for the acceptance or the rejection of each single result. This may be done by evaluating absolute quality measures for the departure of the prediction from reality (e.g. the so-called u- and y-plots presented by Keiller and others (1983)),
- passing the final subset of results $\{r_1,...,r_m\}$ to the next step *(arbiter)*, which will consist of:

- receiving them,
- determining a single result derived from all values received calculating a set of weights $\{w_1,...,w_m\}$ or
- raising the alarm if this cannot be done,
- outputting the value:

$$\sum_{i=1}^{m} w_i \, r_i$$

The intention of this paper is to study the role of the arbiter by means of two particular examples suggested in literature. The second section will present a combination of predictions based on *Bayesian inference*, whereas the third one will introduce an alternative by weighting the results according to a *Likelihood maximization* procedure.

The subsequent chapter will finally compare both adjudicators, in particular with respect to their sensitivity to model-behavioural changes, trying to identify the most critical and most suitable situations to be treated by each of them.

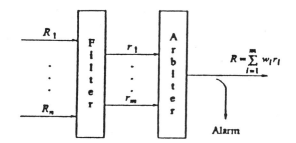

Fig. 1: The two-step adjudicator structure
from Anderson (1986)

BAYESIAN INFERENTIAL APPROACH

The linear combination of predictions presented in this section was suggested by Edwards (1984) for any reliability application involving modelling uncertainty concerning the choice of distribution. It is based on a Bayesian procedure to obtain a weighted average over a series of possible models M_i ($i \in \{1,...,m\}$).

On the basis of past observed times between failures $t_1,...,t_{n-1}$, each model M_i results in an own reliability prediction $R_i(t)$, representing the probability of surviving time t:

$$R_i(t) = P_i(T_n \geq t), \; i \in \{1,...,m\},$$

where T_n denotes the time from the latest to the next failure and P_i the approximated probability obtained by model M_i.

The Bayesian procedure consists then of an inference rule taking into account the failure data and the single predictions as well as the prior probabilities $P(M_i)$, $i \in \{1,...,m\}$, measuring our confidence in a given model (assuming there is exactly one correct among them).

On the basis of these inputs this approach will imply a final prediction value $R(t) = P(T_n \geq t)$, as sketched in fig. 2.

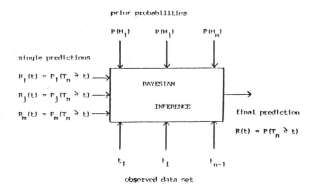

Fig. 2: Bayesian inferential approach

In details, the Bayesian inference procedure expresses the final reliability value as a linear combination of single model predictions weighted by the conditional probability of each model being the only correct one for the data D considered, i.e:

$$P(T_n \geq t) = \sum_{i=1}^{m} P(T_n \geq t \mid M_j) \cdot P(M_j \mid D)$$

$$= \sum_{i=1}^{m} P_j (T_n \geq t) \cdot P(M_j \mid D)$$

The posterior probability $P(M_j \mid D)$ itself may be obtained by means of the ratio

$$P(M_j \mid D) = L_j \cdot P(M_j) / \sum_{k=1}^{m}(L_k \cdot P(M_k))$$

where L_i denotes the likelihood function of model M_i on data set D.

Different strategies may be applied to define the prior probabilities $P(M_i)$:

- in case of prior ignorance, a rational way would be to assign an equal probability to each model, i.e. $P(M_i) = 1/m$ $\forall \; i \in \{1,...,m\}$;

- in case of sufficient experience with particular models, these priors may be continuously adjourned to identify higher suitability for given application classes or testing phases;

- in case of u- and y-plots of previous predictions having significant KS-distances at a given percentage level, the corresponding models may be ignored by setting their prior confidence on zero, i.e. $P(M_i) = 0$.

In the special case of only two alternative models A and B, i.e. m = 2, we obtain, assuming indifference among them:

$$R_x = x \cdot R_A + (1 - x) \cdot R_B,$$

where

$$x = L_A / (L_A + L_B).$$

Here R_A and R_B obviously stand for the reliability results obtained using model A resp. B. L_A and L_B similarly represent their both likelihood functions, i.e. the product of the modelled probability density functions f_A resp. f_B evaluated at the observed inter-failure times t_i:

$$L_A = \prod_{i=1}^{n-1} a_i, \; \text{where } a_i = f_A(t_i)$$

$$L_B = \prod_{i=1}^{n-1} b_i, \; \text{where } b_i = f_B(t_i)$$

This particular model resulting in value R_x is the one defined by Littlewood (1989) as $(A+B)_1$. We keep in the following this notation in order to permit a consistent comparison with the alternative possibility presented in the next section.

LIKELIHOOD MAXIMIZATION APPROACH

Another way of combining two model outputs R_A and R_B into a single result

$$R_y = y \cdot R_A + (1 - y) \cdot R_B$$

has been proposed by Littlewood (1988) by defining the weight y to be the value maximizing the resulting likelihood function, i.e.:

$$\max_{w} \prod_{i=1}^{n-1} (w \cdot a_i + (1 - w) \cdot b_i) = \prod_{i=1}^{n-1} (y \cdot a_i + (1 - y) \cdot b_i)$$

This combination of models A and B has been denoted $(A+B)_2$.

As remarked by Littlewood (1989), the mathematical computation involved by this procedure may be considerably heavy.

In order to be later able to carry out a comparison as detailed as possible between both combinations just presented, we will here make use of some elementary analytical methods and algebraic transformations to get a deeper insight into the conditions to be fulfilled by the maximum y.

118

We denote by f(w) the function to be maximized, i.e.:

$$f(w) = \prod_{i=1}^{n-1} (w \cdot a_i + (1 - w) \cdot b_i)$$

with derivative

$$f'(w) = \sum_{i=1}^{n-1} (a_i - b_i) \cdot \prod_{\substack{j=1 \\ j \neq i}}^{n-1} (w \cdot (a_j - b_j) + b_j)$$

The theory of extreme values yields:

$$f(y) > 0, \ f'(y) = 0 \Rightarrow f'(y) / f(y) = 0$$

It has to be remarked that the previously introduced linear combination R_y only makes sense if $y \in [0,1]$, whereas the last equation just given by the analytical method may not be fulfilled within the unitary interval.

In this case, the weight has to be chosen as the next one among the interval boundary values $\{0,1\}$ reflecting the fact that one of both models is decisively better than the other one.

Anyway, assuming now the non-degenerate case with comparably adequate models, we have just seen that the determination of the maximum value is equivalent to the solution of the following equation:

$$h(y) = 0, \text{ with}$$

$$h(y) = f'(y) / f(y) = \sum_{i=1}^{n-1} (1 / (y + c_i)),$$

where c_i represents a relative measure of difference between a_i and b_i:

$$c_i = b_i / (a_i - b_i).$$

The improbable case $a_i = b_i$ for some i can be excluded as it would only contribute as a scalar multiplication (independent from y) to the overall product given by function f.

Then the optimal weight y is determined by finding the zero value of the monotonically decreasing function h, e.g. by means of numerical algorithms as the bisective technique or Newton's iterative method.

This procedure allows a different interpretation of the combinatorial concept than the Bayesian one: rather than assuming one of both models to be the correct one and trying to identify it probabilistically by measuring its prequential likelihood, we may consider here both of them to be inaccurate to a certain extent. In case that they deviate from reality in opposite directions (one being optimistic, the other pessimistic), a weighted composition optimizing the prequential likelihood should be expected to be preferable.

COMPARISON OF BOTH APPROACHES

Some differences between both strategies have already been remarked with respect to two aspects.

The first one regards the effort involved by the numerical evaluation of the weight defined. The computations required by Bayesian inference are particularly simple concerning only a quotient of two prequential likelihoods. The second approach, on the other hand, considers in principle the prequential likelihood for any possible positive combination of models A and B, determining the maximal among them. This obviously results in a computationally heavier algorithm, which may nonetheless be justified with respect to further aspects to be compared.

The cost difference is a direct consequence of the already mentioned diverging concepts of "combination": the Bayesian technique assumes correctness to lie *among* A and B, whereas the likelihood maximization method considers it as being *between* A and B. Both interpretations can be graphically represented by the following Fig. 3.

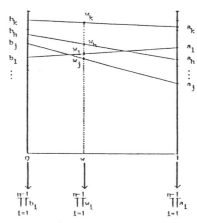

Fig. 3: Graphical difference between both combinations

For each model a vertical unitary segment stands for the axis of the density function values at the observed times, i. e. a_i resp. b_i.

The Bayesian technique considers for each axis the multiplication of all values reported on it and compares both products by determining their quotient.

Thus, due to multiplicative commutativity, this method does not distinguish any order in the factors a_i resp. b_i, but considers the past goodness-of-fit of each model as a whole without being able to identify any time-varying relation between A and B.

The alternative approach, on the other hand, takes into account the space between both vertical axis as well, by regarding for each pair (a_i, b_i) the line linking the corresponding points.

Considering for each weight w on the horizontal axis the values $w_1,...,w_{n-1}$ given by intersecting those lines with the vertical through w, the optimal weight is then chosen as the one maximizing the product

$$\prod_{i=1}^{n-1} w_i$$

In particular, this graphical representation shows that also in this case the absolute order of the sequences (a_i) resp. (b_i) is neglected, but their relative ordering is here decisive for the final result.

In other words, although actual time-dependence cannot be identified by neither of both approaches, the latter one is able to take into account a step-by-step comparison of the prediction goodness of the models.

In the extreme case, we may think of identical sets of values $\{a_i; 1 \leq i \leq n-1\}$ and $\{b_i; 1 \leq i \leq n-1\}$ occurring, however, in such an order that model A is always better than model B, apart from one exception, as sketched in the following Fig. 4.

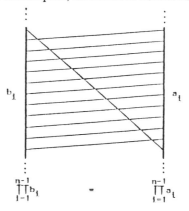

Fig. 4: Different prediction systems
with equal likelihood function

The only outlier may for example be due to an early prediction based on insufficient or unrepresentative failure data rather than to a model inadequacy.

Anyway, even in case of a large number of predictions supporting the superiority of one model, the Bayesian inferential method will ignore this evidence, weighting equally both of them (i.e. $x = 0.5$), while the maximization of the prequential likelihood will give more confidence to the generally better model, expecting in the future the same behaviour that was most often observable during the past (i.e. $y > 0.5$).

In order to analyze in more detail the differences between both techniques, we suggest to study the sensitivity of each method with respect to the latest weight and to the relative difference in the prediction goodness of the models.

To be more precise, we will consider the iterated process of determining a sequence of weights by taking into account, at each step, a new observed failure time.

Let w represent the presently chosen weight combining models A and B on the basis of $t_1,...,t_{n-1}$. Then, as soon as a new failure has occurred after time t_n, a new weight n(w) will be determined in order to adjourn the combination approach with regard to the additional information available.

Thus it will be interesting to study for each of both approaches, how much the new weight n(w) depends on the previous weight w as well as on the goodness of present and past model predictions.

Let the sequence (q_i) denote the quotient of such goodness values, i.e.:

$$q_i := a_i / b_i \quad i \geq 1$$

Then we will determine for each of both approaches the sensitivity function s with

$$n(w) = s(w; q_i,...,q_n)$$

For the Bayesian inferential method the weight x was defined as:

$$x = \prod_{i=1}^{n-1} a_i / (\prod_{i=1}^{n-1} a_i + \prod_{i=1}^{n-1} b_i)$$

This yields by simple algebraic transformations:

$$n(x) = x \cdot q_n / (1 + x \cdot (q_n - 1))$$

In particular, being Bayesian the sensitivity function s depends in this case only on x and q_n, completely ignoring the past quotients $q_1,...,q_{n-1}$ of prediction accuracies. This means that once we have determined a model combination, the next iteration step will shift the present weight with regard to the most recent comparison of goodness predictions, but without taking into account the previous ones.

The sensitivity of the Likelihood maximization approach, on the contrary, cannot be exactly expressed in such a simple form, due to the implicit expression of the weight y as solution of a numerical equation.

For this reason we will make use of a first order approximation of n(y):

$$k'(y) \cong (k(y) - k(n(y))) / (y - n(y)) \text{ where}$$

$$k(w) = \sum_{i=1}^{n} (1 / (w + c_i)) \quad \forall w$$

$$\Rightarrow k(n(y)) = 0, \quad k(y) = 1 / (y + c_n)$$

$$\Rightarrow n(y) \cong y - (1/k'(y)) \cdot ((q_n - 1)/(y \cdot (q_n - 1) + 1))$$

A common property of both sensitivity expressions of n(x) and n(y) results in the particular case of two almost equally good predictions, where both approaches will not change their present weight, in other words:

$$q_n \cong 1 \Rightarrow n(x) = x, \quad n(y) = y$$

If one of both predictions is, on the contrary, very poor compared with the other (as for $q_n \approx 0$), Bayesian inference will ignore that model in the future, whereas the maximization technique will take also into account the past model behaviour. This inflexibility of the Bayesian inferential approach is strongly connected with its complete insensitivity to model-behavioural changes once a weight has been localized very near the elements 0 or 1. In fact, we easily note:

$$x \cong 0 \Rightarrow n(x) \cong 0$$

$$x \cong 1 \Rightarrow n(x) \cong 1,$$

so that after rejection of one of both predictors, this approach does not allow to reconsider it in spite of its improved predictive accuracy.

The technique maximizing the likelihood function, on the other hand, permits to integrate at each step past and adjourned information, even for so far poor models, e.g.:

$$y \cong 0 \Rightarrow n(y) \cong -(1/k'(0)) \cdot (q_n - 1) = \sum_{i=1}^{n} (1/c_i^2)(q_n - 1)$$

The overweight given by Bayesian inference to the latest accuracy quotient q_n may also lead to an abrupt shift of a weight towards one of both extreme points of the unitary interval, e.g.:

$$x = 1/2 \Rightarrow n(x) = q_n / (1 + q_n) \rightarrow \begin{cases} 0 \text{ for } q_n \rightarrow 0 \\ 1 \text{ for } q_n \rightarrow \infty \end{cases}$$

whereas the alternative approach would alleviate this excessive reaction:

$$y = 1/2$$

$$\Rightarrow n(y) = (1 - (1/k'(1/2)) \cdot 4 \cdot (q_n - 1)/(q_n + 1))/2$$

$$\rightarrow \begin{cases} (1 + 4/k'(1/2))/2 \text{ for } q_n \rightarrow 0 \\ (1 - 4/k'(1/2))/2 \text{ for } q_n \rightarrow \infty \end{cases}$$

These abstract considerations may help to understand and interpret the following example presented by Littlewood (1988) and based on data from Musa (1979). It combines the Jelinski-Moranda (JM) - and the Littlewood-Verrall (LV) - models by means of both approaches, as shown in Fig. 5.

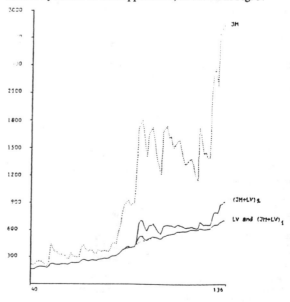

Fig. 5: Median predictions for Musa data set from Littlewood (1989)

The JM-model is known to behave optimistically on this particular data set, in opposition to the pessimistic LV-model. Thus the non-trivial combination $(JM+LV)_2$ of both models can achieve a real improvement as results from Table 1.

120

Model	KS distances	
	u-plot	y-plot
JM	.189	.126
LV	.145	.107
$(LV+JM)_1$	.145	.105
$(LV+JM)_2$	.134	.076

TABLE 1 KS-distances for u- and y-plots
from Littlewood (1989)

The alternative $(JM+LV)_1$, on the contrary, gives very small weights to JM from the beginning and thus, according to our theoretical analysis, throughout all the range of predictions.

CONCLUSIONS

On the whole, the comparing study proposed may be summarized in the following aspects:

- In case of an expected time-varying accuracy relation between alternative models, the maximization technique allows a higher flexibility with regard to behavioural changes, requiring, however, a major computational effort.

- On the contrary, if each problem class considered may be expected to be associated to a particular, but unknown failure distribution represented by one of several models, then it will be more promising (and moreover more economic) to make use of Bayesian inference in order to identify the most suitable model for the occurring distribution family.

REFERENCES

Abdel-Ghaly, A.A., Chan, P.Y., Littlewood, B. (1986). Evaluation of Competing Software Reliability Predictions. IEEE Transactions on Software Engineering, SE-12, pp. 950-967.

Anderson, T. (1986). A Structured Decision Mechanism for Diverse Software. Proc. Fifth Symp. on Reliability in Distributed Software and Database Systems, Washington, DC, USA, IEEE Comput. Society Press.

Brocklehurst, S. (1987). On the Effectiveness of Adaptive Software Reliability Modelling. Centre for Software Reliability, The City University, London.

Brocklehurst, S., Chan, P.Y., Littlewood, B., Snell, J. (1989). Recalibrating Software Reliability Models. Centre for Software Reliability, The City University, London.

Dawid, A.P. (1984). Statistical theory: the prequential approach. Journal of the Royal Statistical Society, A, 147, pp. 278 - 292.

Edwards, G. (1984). A Bayesian Procedure for Drawing Inferences from Random Data. Reliability Engineering 9, pp. 1 - 17, Elsevier Applied Science Publisher.

Keiller, P.A., Littlewood, B., Miller, D.R., Sofer, A. (1983). Comparison of Software Reliability Predictions. Digest 13th International Symposium on Fault-Tolerant Computing (FTCS-13), pp. 128-134, IEEE Computer Society Press.

Littlewood, B. (1988). Forecasting Software Reliability. Centre for Software Reliability, The City University, London.

Littlewood, B. (1989). Private communication.

Musa, J.D. (1979). Software Reliability Data. Data Analysis Centre for Software, Rome Air Development Center, Rome, NY.

Musa, J.D., Iannino, A., Okumoto, K. (1987). Software reliability: Measurement, Prediction and Application, McGraw-Hill, New York.

FUNCTIONAL SPECIFICATION OF VITAL COMPUTER SOFTWARE FOR HIHG-SPEED MAGLEV SYSTEMS

K. Jopke

Institut für Regelungs- und Automatisierungstechnik, Technische Universität Braunschweig, Germany

R. Knigge

Siemens AG, Bereich Verkehrstechnik, Braunschweig, Germany

E. Schnieder

Institut für Regelungs- und Automatisierungstechnik, Technische Universität Braunschweig, Germany

Abstract. The system design method of Ward and Mellor is used to describe the functional behaviour of the control and protection system of the high-speed maglev train TRANSRAPID. This operation control system has to control (ATC) and to protect (ATP) many vehicles. A simulation has already been run successfully at Siemens in Braunschweig. A substantial problem is to obtain the proof of the ATP (Automatic Train Protection) of the whole system on the functional level already. In Germany, this proof with regard to safety has to be passed at the TÜV (Technical Supervision Association). The implementation model which contains the functional behaviour is the only object which can be tested against the program code by the experts. The experts who are verifying the system should get a clearly structured specification which allows him to understand the correct relations between the program code and the implementation model. In particular, the real time aspect with regard to the method of Ward and Mellor and guidelines made to interpret the system description will be considered.

Keywords. Control system design; Describing functions; Real time computer systems; Safety proof; Software engineering; System analysis; Train control and protection.

INTRODUCTION

The German high-speed maglev system TRANSRAPID is a unique solution for the challenge of high-speed and efficient ground transportation systems. The operation of this advanced high-speed transportation system with operational speeds of more than 400 km/h and braking distances of several kilometres can only be managed by a fully automated operation control system, which provides all functions and facilities for protection, control and traffic guidance as well as their intercommunication (Gückel, Schnieder, 1988). Especially the protection tasks must completely be performed by technical devices without any assistance of human operators.

The protection consists of several tasks which are responsible for
- vehicle (position and speed detection, monitoring, headway protection, emergency target braking
- vehicle propulsion system monitoring and cut-off
- route safety (route locking, route proving and route release function)
- track points proving (track points operation, reversal, delocking, locking and proving function)
- safeguarding of data transmission

All in all they guarantee a safe vehicle mission if
1) the protection tasks are functionally correct
2) implemented without failure

3) carried out by a highly reliable thus fail-safe operating facility

Protection functions for the maglev system, i.e. all protection tasks which are carried out by vital computer systems and supported by a specially designed operation control system for vital computers are implemented by high level computer programs. The components of such a vital computer system are described by Frank (1991).

Following the assumption that the vital computer system guarantees a highly reliable and fail-safe operation by its fault-tolerant design, only the safe behaviour of the software system must be guaranteed. This implies either the principle of a deversion programming or an a priori failureless software! In the current application the latter principle has been chosen in accordance to the well anticipated rules and guidelines for protection systems in railway signalling. The total development of the software system for protection tasks must fulfil inordinately high demands.

In general, the demands must state the following specific requirements:
- transparency (modularisation)
- correctness (of the tasks specification)
- consistency
- proof of (functional) safety

The following constructional elements and development method assure this a priori correctness of the complete programming system.

1) Model of correct multi-level machines
   basis machine: fault-tolerant hardware
   core machine: modular operating system core (Input-Output interface)
   shell machine: modular shell interface (I/O driver, timing, multitasking, interrupt, memory administration)
   periphery machine: modular application programs

2) Software developing environment
   - High level programming languages for all machine levels
   - Validated compiler
   - Strict program development guidelines
   - Structured programming technique

3) Structured and computer-assisted software engineering
   - Phase model, development processing plan
   - Special design methodology

- Formalized description applied once during the initial design phases
- Tool utilization for design, documentation and analysis during all phases
- Accompanying quality control
- On-line tests - computer assisted

SPECIFICATION METHOD

Scope of Application

In order to fulfill these high requirements imposed on the protection tasks of automation systems the respective tasks were specified according to the system design method for real time systems by Ward and Mellor (1985). The designed tasks were implemented in the target hardware via a high level language (Pascal-86) and a validated compiler. The software runs on the base of a real time operation system specifically adapted to this application, on fail-safe computers designed for railway signalling tasks.

During the design phases of these automation systems, experts have already been evaluating their first results (design-accompanied expert report). Thus in the early design phases, documentation required for safety proof could already be adapted accordingly thanks to detailed discussions. Another advantage of a methodical system design as to designer teams and cooperation between designer and expert is that all of them are mastering the same descriptive language, thus making the design processes easier.

Method

The system design method by Ward and Mellor (1985) contains means of description for the different design phases. In this paper, the Structured Analysis with Real Time Expenditure shall be discussed only. In the system design, the Entity-Relationship Diagram, the Essential Model (SA) and the Nassi-Shneidermann-Diagrams (in the programming process) were also applied.

In the following, the transition from a global system representation to an examplary detail problem shall be presented. Fig. 1 shows a part from a possible maglev train system, which is not very abstract yet. The ATC and ATP systems are located on the vehicle and along the track on decentralized equipments. Fig. 2 shows a formalized description of a decentralized OCS-Subsystem wherein the single processes represent fail-safe 2v3-computers for transmission, protection, and control tasks.

Task Control

Before presenting the use of control processes and their related state-transition-diagrams in an example, Fig. 3 shall demonstrate how the operation system for the OCS-computer applied here controls the tasks in principle. At first a task is in its basic state ("terminated"). As the automation system starts up each task is set in the "ready" state. Then the tasks are called in their priority assignment and set in the "computing" state (in doing so, system variables are set). After having computed the task initiation each task finally takes on the "waiting" state.

The system designer or the programmer can only control the tasks between the two states "waiting" and "ready". Thus he can only determine whether the task shall compute or not! The operation system then calls the task if no other prior task is "computing" at that moment. In order to ensure operation of the automation system, control tasks make sure that the system consistency is always kept in and that no task is blocking the computer for too long. Thus two task states result for the user, i.e.

1. "waiting"
2. "active" = "ready" or "computing"

Fig. 4 shows three tasks with altogether two data inputs and three data outputs respectively as well as internal data flows. Here memories were encapsulated because of their insignificance in this consideration. Without any supplementary information the transformation graph does not show how the control process shall run in detail. Each data flow represents also a control flow because the receiving task must always react on the input data flow. For this reason, control flows going to the control process were left out because this fact has been defined once. The control flows shall only demonstrate which tasks are controlled. If Tasks 1 and Task 3 were the only ones which existed the control process would not be necessary because the causal reference would be sufficiently demonstrated by the data flows (with control effect).

The following definition underlines the distinction betwenn data and event of a flow:

$$Input_x = Data_{ix} + Event_{ix}$$

This means that an input flow possesses both data and event with control effect. This is worth in analogy to output flows.

Interpretation

The transformation graph in Fig. 4 shall represent those tasks which have been priority-assigned (shown as p = x within the task). If the priorities are left out the following consideration is simplified by the fact that the inputs I_x are no more functioning if another task is already active. The following definitions for the data flows are provided to explain the mode of interpretation:

1. All inputs I_x can provoke reaction of the control process at any time
2. All internal connections O_{xy} (x = source, y = sink) only provoke reaction if Task x has just been "computing"
3. All outputs O_x are leading to the "waiting" state

Thus, by taking into consideration the priorities, results the state-transition diagram in Fig. 5, which will be abbreviated in the following by "STD". In this application the highest priority has the lowest number. Furthermore means the state "computing" in Fig. 5 that the considered task shall compute. In case of a called task with a higher priority the task will obtain the state "ready". For further testing of the STD, linkage between states and events is represented in Fig. 6 by a Mealy machine. The horizontal line in Fig. 6 represents states and the vertical line events. Within the Mealy machine, the respective states resulting from the linkage of one state and one event are set up.

The Mealy machine can be subdivided into three blocks as follows:
1. Behaviour on input flows
2. Behaviour on internal flows
3. Behaviour on output flows

Because of the fact that the tasks are self-terminating (according to Ward and Mellor they are only triggered), the third group does not give very relevant information. The second group describes the internal handling of the tasks. In this case, partial results are transmitted which are not necessarily required because these tasks can also be controlled externally (via I_x). Due to the fixed priorities of the tasks (see the first group), Task 2 and Task 3 can be interrupted while being in the "computing" state by the first task or, in one case, also by the second task.

Definitions and Guidlines

The following definitions and guidelines were made during the developmnet accompanied examination.

1) A Flow contents Data and Events
$$I_x = D_{ix} + E_{ix}$$
$$O_x = D_{ox} + E_{ox}$$

2) A Task is terminated...
   a) ...regular by producing an output (following state: "waiting")
   b) ...irregular because there exist a higher priority (following state: "ready")

3) Control processes and flows are only hints for a further description

4) Every control process leads to a state transition diagram (parallel description)

5) A transformationgraph describes the data portion of the flows

6) A state transition diagram describes the control portion of the flows (event)

7) A task is labeled with its priority ($p = x$)

EVALUATION

All these considerations include the fact that the comprehension of a task control can only be provided in an adequate manner if the output data flows O_x and O_{xy} are concretely named, and if the tasks are described textually for any person (eg. experts, owners) who did not participate in the design process.

The guidelines for the specification of the OCS, which were worked out together, are leading to a system documentation which represents the base for the safety proof on the functional level. Due to the early cooperation with the experts the following design processes were very much simplified because the experts did already know the method of Ward and Mellor and were operating with the corresponding tools. Thus specifications of any design stadium could be transmitted to the experts for test purposes via diskettes.

Yet it must be admitted that the method of Ward and Mellor does not provide a mathematical base for automatic analysis. Also simulation is only possible with a simple representation, i.e. by marking the data processes (tasks). Dynamic analyses with respect to deadlocks, reachabilities of states

and other aspects are provided by Petri-Nets which were proposed by Petri (1962).

All in all it can be said that, with special regard to expert reports, the design process of a highly complex system with high safety requirements can be accelerated by a methodical procedure which is consequently carried out. This acceleration is especially due to the better information exchange between the designer and the expert who talk and understand the same language when a design method shall be applied.

REFERENCES

Frank, W. (1991). Die Zukunft elektronischer Stellwerke. *ETR Eisenbahntechnische Rundschau, Vol. 40,* 575 - 584.

Gückel, H., E. Schnieder (1988). *International Symposium on research and new technologies in transport and traffic. Betriebsleittechnik für Magnetschnellbahnen.* Hamburg

Petri, C. A. (1962). *Kommunikation mit Automaten.* Schriften des Institutes für Instrumentelle Mathematik, Bonn.

Ward, P. T. and S. J. Mellor (1985). *Structured development for real time systems,* Vol. I- III. Prentice-Hall, Englewood Cliff, New Jersey.

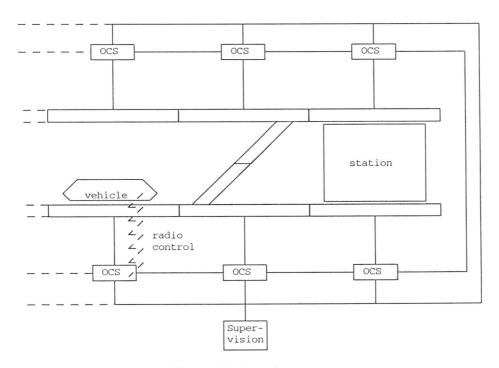

Fig. 1 Maglev train system

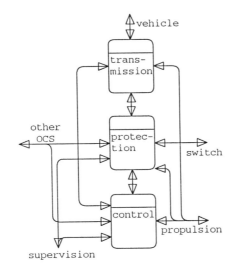

Fig. 2 OCS - Control and protection

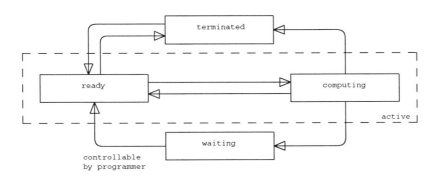

Fig. 3 Task states

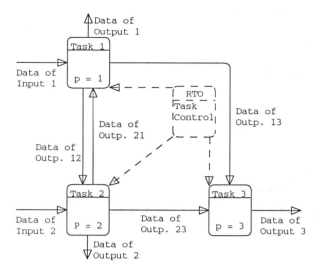

Fig. 4 Transformation Graph

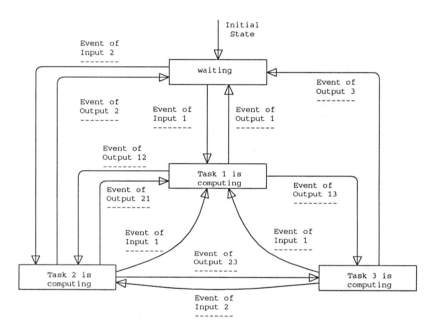

Fig. 5 State Transition Diagram

	E_{I1}	E_{I2}	E_{O12}	E_{O13}	E_{O21}	E_{O23}	E_{O1}	E_{O2}	E_{O3}
waiting	Task 1	Task 2							
Task 1 is computing			Task 2	Task 3			wait-ing		
Task 2 is computing	Task 1				Task 1	Task 3		wait-ing	
Task 3 is computing	Task 1	Task 2							wait-ing
	Block 1 (Inputs)		Block 2 (Internal Outputs)				Block 3 (Outputs)		

Priorities (see Block 1): p (Task 1) > p (Task 2) > p (Task 3)

Fig. 6 Mealy Machine

128

PROVING SAFETY OF A RAILWAY SIGNALLING SYSTEM INCORPORATING GEOGRAPHIC DATA

Michael Ingleby and Ian Mitchell,
British Rail Research, London Road,
Derby DE24 8YB , England.

Abstract Solid State Interlocking (SSI), a computer-based railway signalling system, is used extensively by British Rail and also by other railway administrations. An interlocking is implemented as a generic program, the same for all areas, together with a geographic database which serves as a detailed map of the track and signalling equipment in a specific area of control. We formally model SSI behaviour as that of a finite state automaton with next-state and output functions defined by geographic data. Safety of interlocking is modelled as a family of predicates of state, and a proof strategy based on mathematical induction is designed for showing that safety predicates remain invariant over an indefinite number of cycles. The strategy allows for a mixed approach to proof: high-level hand proof of lemmas relating to the transitivity of safety, and lower-level mechanized proof of detailed steps. The formal model also lends itself to investigation of the safety of behaviour patterns in the environment controlled by an interlocking. A pattern of is a subset of input sequences, and the automaton *connects* this to a set of states which remain invariant under such input. This connection is shown to induce topologies into state-space and into the environment.

Keywords Railway signalling, geographic data, rigorous proof strategy, safety-transitivity, mathematical induction, finite state automaton, Galois connections, topological spaces.

INTRODUCTION

Solid State Interlocking (SSI) is the control system developed by British Rail to manage route-setting, points movement, signal indication and train detection in an area of the permanent way. It consists of a replicated microprocessor control centre linked to trackside functional modules (TFM's). These detect trains on track sections, illuminate and extinguish signal lamps, and activate the hydraulic pumps and valves which move points. All communications links, trackside equipment and processors of an interlocking are replicated. The central control function is a ROM-based generic program which polls TFM's and the signalman's control panel, receiving telegrams which report the state of the railway to control and sending commands to set trackside equipment to appropriate safe states. Details of the SSI system, including the hardware redundancy and safety validation strategies, have been published elsewhere [1], [2].

The central control maintains in RAM an image of the area which it controls, updating this and using it to construct safe output telegrams to trackside and control panel. It accesses a geographic database which describes the area controlled : essentially a set of incidence relations such as incidence of tracks and points on the route approaching a signal from its various sighting points, the incidence of tracks and points on overlaps down route from a signal, etc.. British Rail Research have developed a set of software tools to support the production, checking and testing of such geographic databases, and are carrying out research into techniques to automate the process [3]. In keeping with the current consensus on best practice in engineering safety critical systems, formal methods and

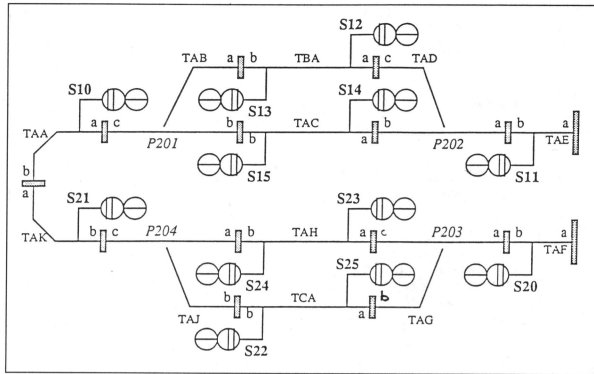

Figure 1 :A signalling area

mechanized proof of safety are being used. We report here some results of a study of the *behavioural correctness* of geographic data, based on a finite state automaton model of interlocking.

The object on which this study of interlocking behaviour focuses is the image in the SSI of a signalling area. It is a dynamic object, changing as routes are set and cleared, as trains move from one track section to another, as points are moved, as trackside equipment fails. The state transitions of this image are data-driven, because the generic polling program of SSI consults its area-specific geographic database in computing a next-state and an output telegram. In this context, when we say that the geographic data of an area is behaviourally correct, we mean that the dynamical evolution of the SSI image of the railway is constrained to pass only through states which are safe, whatever input streams arrive from the trackside and the signalman's panel.

For those unfamiliar with signalling terminology, we give below two examples of geographic data selected from the 55 lines of data needed to describe the signalling area of Fig.1 to an interlocking. From the so-called route-request data, the datum ***Q10B** which determines whether to allow a request from the signalman's panel for the

setting of route R10B (from signal S10 over points P201 and track sections TAB and TAC to signal S14) is:

*Q10B if P201 cnf, UAB-AC f, UAC-AB f
         then R10B s, P201 cn, UAB-CB l,
         UAC-BA l

whilst from the so-called points-free-to-move data, the datum ***P201N** which determines whether it is safe to allow points P201 to move normal (that is, to the straight through position, rather than to the left) is:

***P201N TAB c, UAB-AC f, UAB-CA f **

The route request ***Q10B** says (in geographic data language[1]) that if the points P201 are controlled normal or are free to move normal and if subroute over track TAB from b to c is free (that is, not locked for another opposing route) and if the subroute over TAC from a to b is also free, then, in the SSI image of the railway, set route R10B, control P201 to the normal position and lock subroutes over TAB from c to b and over TAC from b to a. This " if TEST then COMMAND " sentence bars the setting of the requested route if there are opposing subroutes over the same track already locked for passage of another train. The points free to move data is a simple test invoked by the P201 cfn clause in the route request datum. Its effect is to test the SSI image of track section TAB containing points P201 : if it is clear of trains, and the subroutes over it from a to c and from c to a requiring a reverse setting of P201 are free (that is, not locked for an approaching train), then the test succeeds and the request which invoked it is granted by the interlocking.

The general form of the logicals in data is " if TEST_TREE then COMMAND_TREE ", and these can readily be translated into operations on the states of a VDM module [5] or a Z schema [6] - to provide a denotational semantics for state transitions and output generation of an interlocking. We are not concerned here with the details of this semantics. They simply provide a foundation for our proof studies, and give a guarantee of the consistency of data-types in the specification of the model of SSI described below.

THE MODEL AND ITS SAFETY INVARIANTS

After initialization, the SSI image of the railway evolves in response to received inputs in the form of panel requests and telegrams from the trackside. Its behaviour is fully specified as a finite state machine of the Mealy type [4] by three sets and two functions:-

- a set S of states, whose members s_0, s_1,... are all possible SSI images of the railway;
- an input alphabet A , whose members are all possible inputs a_1, a_2,... each a being a pair whose first term is an input telegram and whose second term is either a panel request or nil;
- an output alphabet B , whose members are all possible output telegrams b_1,b_2,... prepared by the SSI and sent to the trackside;
- a next-state function ν mapping

  $(a, s) \mapsto \nu(a, s)$, the new state at the end of the polling cycle beginning in state s and processing the pair a;
- an output function ω mapping

  $(a, s) \mapsto \omega(a, s)$, the output of the cycle beginning in state s and receiving the pair a .

The next-state and output functions are determined by the generic SSI polling and the geographic data of an area. These functions in turn determine the *behaviour* of an interlocking: that is *both* the

state sequences

$$(s_N) = (s_0, s_1, s_2, \ldots , s_N, \ldots)$$

and the output sequences

$$(b_N) = (b_1, b_2, b_3, \ldots , b_N, \ldots)$$

produced by the system beginning in a prescribed state s_0 and evolving in response to arbitrary input sequences

$$(a_N) = (a_1, a_2, a_3, \ldots , a_N, \ldots) .$$

The state of the Mealy machine is a function from the set of *elements* of the railway to the set of *values* which such elements may take. Elements include both the physical components of the area (track-sections, points, signals...) and the control elements which figure on the signalling panel and appear in the geographic data (routes, subroutes, overlaps...). The values which an element may take vary : a route may take values 'set' or 'unset'; points have a more complex set of values depending on whether they are 'controlled', 'detected', 'free-to-move' in one of the two directions 'normal' and 'reverse'; track-sections have state values indicating whether trackside equipment last reported them 'occupied' or 'clear'.

Broad analysis of the safety principles underlying historical signalling practice has revealed two families of safety-related predicates of state. The first family, $[P_1, P_2, \ldots P_M]$, are predicates referring only to next state of the interlocking, and the second family, $[Q_1, Q_2, \ldots Q_N]$, are predicates which also refer to SSI outputs to trackside. Some examples from the first family are:

$P_1(a, s)$ that if in state s a sub-route or sub-overlap incident on any track is locked, then on receipt of an input a, unless it becomes free in $\nu(a, s)$, no other sub-route or sub-overlap over the same track is locked in the state $\nu(a, s)$;

$P_2(a, s)$ that if any route passes over certain points which in state s are controlled against it and not free to move, then in the state $\nu(a, s)$ that route is not set.

These predicates denote the notions that conflicting subroutes are not set over the same track, that points may not be moved against an approaching train, and so on.

The predicates depending on output are exemplified by:-

$Q_1(a, s)$ that if, on receipt of input a, in state $\nu(a, s)$ any signal is red, then $\omega(a, s)$ commands the trackside module of the signal to light the red lamp and put out the yellow and green lamps;

$Q_2(a, s)$ that if, on receipt of input a, in state $\nu(a, s)$ any point is controlled normal, then $\omega(a, s)$ commands the trackside module to activate the hydraulic valve for the normal direction and deactivate the valve for the reverse direction.

These capture the notion that the output command issued by an interlocking does not command any of the trackside equipment into an unsafe setting.

The invariants of state which bear on safety are expressible in terms of the above predicates:

$$\text{safe}(s) \quad\equiv \forall a \bullet P_1(a,s) \land P_2(a,s) \ldots \land P_M(a,s),$$

$$\text{safe\_output}(s) \equiv \forall a \bullet Q_1(a,s) \land Q_2(a,s) \ldots \land Q_N(a,s).$$

These invariants can be defined pointwise on evolutionary sequences of states:

$$\text{safe}((s_N)) \quad\equiv \forall N \bullet \text{safe}(s_N) \quad ;$$

$$\text{safe\_output}((s_N)) \equiv \forall N \bullet \text{safe\_output}(s_N)$$

- to capture the notion that a sequence (s_N) *evolves safely*. Then behavioural correctness can be formulated using these invariants, together with input sequences (a_N), and SSI responses (s_N) and (b_N):-

$$\text{SAFE} \equiv \forall (a_N) \bullet \text{safe}((s_N)) \land$$

$$\text{safe\_output}((s_N)).$$

The property SAFE is that of safe evolution under all possible input sequences.

In order to prove that SAFE is true of an SSI, one must consider the states which are accessible from a given start

don't need this!

s_0, and the predicate

$$\text{accessible}(s_0,s) \equiv (s=s_0) \lor \exists s_1 \bullet \exists a \bullet$$

$$s=\nu(a, s_1) \land \text{accessible}(s_0,s_1)$$

is useful. The formal proof obligation may be stated therewith as

$$(\text{safe}(s_0) \land \text{safe\_output}(s_0)) \qquad \land$$

$$(\text{accessible}(s_0,s)) \to (\forall a \bullet$$

$$\text{safe}(\nu(a,s)) \land \text{safe\_output}(\nu(a, s)))$$

$\vdash$ SAFE.

Less formally, the claim of safety for all evolutionary paths from s_0 is validated by proving two things known as *inductive start* and *inductive step*. The *start* is that the initial state and its output are safe. The *step* is that if a state is accessible, then any next state and its output are safe. Such induction principles have been identified by the VDM community, for example, as the standard means to reason about sequences or other recursive data types [5].

SAFETY TRANSITIVE EVOLUTION

The approach to interlocking safety which signalling safety principles attempt to embody is one of safe initialization and a design intended to ensure that safe states cannot evolve into unsafe ones. We capture this notion in a formal property which may be called *safety-transitivity*. An interlocking is called <u>safety-transitive</u> if and only if

$$\forall s \bullet \quad \text{safe}(s) \land \text{safe\_output}(s) \quad \to$$

$$\text{safe}(\nu(s, a)) \land \text{safe\_output}(\nu(a, s)),$$

or less formally, if and only if the safety of a precursor state is passed on to any immediate successor state.

SAFETY-TRANSITIVE is a stronger property than SAFE. On the one hand it is possible that in an interlocking whose accessible states are all safe, there are some safe but inaccessible states with unsafe successors. On the other hand, a safety-transitive interlocking can be proved safe:

<u>Transitivity Lemma.</u> In a safety-transitive automaton, all states

accessible from a safe state are safe and output safely.

Proof: Let $\mathbf{safe(s_1)} \wedge \mathbf{safe\_output(s_1)}$ and let $\mathbf{s_{N+1}}$ be accessible from $\mathbf{s_1}$ in the sense that there is a finite sequence of inputs inking $\mathbf{s_1}$ to $\mathbf{s_{N+1}}$:

$$\mathbf{s_2 = \nu(a_1, s_1)}, \; \mathbf{s_3 = \nu(a_2, s_2)}, \; \ldots$$

$$\mathbf{s_{K+1} = \nu(s_K, a_K)}, \; \ldots, \; \mathbf{s_{N+1} = \nu(s_N, a_N)}.$$

Then one can reason inductively that for any N, every state in such a sequence is safe and has safe outputs. The inductive start is to infer from $\mathbf{safe(s_1)} \wedge \mathbf{safe\_output(s_1)}$ by safety-transitivity that $\mathbf{safe(s_2)} \wedge \mathbf{safe\_output(s_2)}$. Then the inductive step is to infer from $\mathbf{safe(s_K)} \wedge \mathbf{safe\_output(s_K)}$ by safety-transitivity that $\mathbf{safe(s_{K+1})} \wedge \mathbf{safe\_output(s_{K+1})}$. ∎

From the lemma, it follows immediately that all states accessible from a safe start-up $\mathbf{s_0}$ are safe and have safe outputs. It is a little surprising that the proof obligation SAFETY_TRANSITIVITY is easier to discharge than the obligation SAFE, even though the latter is the weaker. The reason is that the obligation SAFE has the greater syntactic complexity, though this is concealed above in the very compact recursive definition of accessibility. The recursion actually specifies a large disjunction of states accessible from a start $\mathbf{s_0}$. This is important when such large disjunctions are put to most types of general-purpose mechanical proof assistant: the assistant "falls over" the combinatorially explosive tableau or search tree needed to deal with a large signalling area. The mechanization of safety reasoning, already described by Atkinson and Cunningham in the general context of Modal Action Logic [7], is now under examination by practioners of HOL,OBJ,CCS, and the availability of lemmas and concepts like the above – which can reduce the complexity of proof goals – will increase the applicability of mechanically-assisted proof.

Besides being easier to prove than the weaker "accessibility implies safety", the safety-transitivity concept has another advantage. It turns out that proof of safety-transitivity not only guarantees that accessibility implies safety, but also guarantees the robustness against maintenance-induced initialization faults of an interlocking.

The reason: safe states which are not accessible after a correct initialization might be reached in a SAFE SSI due to error of initialization, and later evolve to an unsafe state, but this impossible in a SAFETY_TRANSITIVE system – for any initial state passing the inductive start test must evolve safely, by the transitivity lemma.

SAFETY CONCEPTS AND GALOIS THEORY

Transitivity is a very simple safety-related concept whose usefulness in the management of proof obligation is indicated above. There are probably others waiting to be defined, and we end this note with a sketch of the possible role of formal concept analysis (FCA) in discovering what these might be. FCA or *Begriffsanalyse*[8] is founded on a pre-existing branch of algebra : Galois theory. It was developed by Wille as a tool for the automatic extraction concepts from data and it operates with a so-called Galois connection : an incidence relation $I \subseteq G \times M$ which represents the incidence of certain objects from set G on features from set M. One can use such a connection to pass between subsets $A \subseteq G$ and $B \subseteq M$:

$$\forall A \subseteq G \bullet A' \equiv \{m \in M \; | \forall g \in A \bullet (g,m) \in I\}$$

$$\forall B \subseteq M \bullet B' \equiv \{g \in G \; | \forall m \in B \bullet (g,m) \in I\}.$$

The result of passing twice in this way from a set S to another set S'' in the same superset (G or M) as S is called *closure*, and S'' is known as the closure of S.

It is easy to show that $\mathbf{A \subseteq A''}$ and $\mathbf{B \subseteq B''}$. The sets of the form $\mathbf{A''}$ are sets of objects which have all the features shared by objects in A, and represent the *extension* of a concept. Those of the form $\mathbf{B''}$ represent sets of features shared by all objects which share the features in B, and represent the *intension* of a concept. For some particular subsets of objects and features, it happens that $\mathbf{A = A''}$ and $\mathbf{B = B''}$ – in such cases Wille declares that the extension-intension pair (A,B) is a *concept* for connection I. FCA is concerned with the enumerating and ordering of such concepts. It is very widely applied to extract hierarchies of concepts automatically from large and complex databases.

In this study of behaviour of automata, the objects are sequences of inputs to

Simpler: $sf(s) \triangleq safe(s) \wedge safe\text{-}output(s)$

$safe \triangleq \forall s. \; accessible(s_0, s) \Rightarrow safe(s)$

$safety\text{-}transitive \triangleq \forall s. \; safe(s) \wedge \forall s'. \; \nu(s,a)=s' \Rightarrow safe(s')$

133

an interlocking and the features are the safe states. An input sequence is connected to a state if that state evolves safely under the action of that sequence. Subsets of input sequences are models of the railway environment. Practically, there are several classes of environment to be considered: the largest is one in which no restrictions are placed on the patterns of occupancy of track sections by trains, and the smallest is one in which trains only move from one track to a connected track without jumping to more remote tracks in the area and in which all drivers always see, understand and obey all speed limits and all signals.

The Galois connection I corresponding to safe evolution of an interlocking has the following properties:

- in a safety-transitive system, any safe state evolves safely, hence is connected by I to any input sequence;
- in any system which can be safely initialized, there is at least one input sequence under which the initial state evolves safely (for example, one corresponding to trains, points and lights remaining as they are and no panel requests being made).

Taking the case of a safety-transitive system with at least one safe initial state, these properties - which are not true of all Galois connections - imply the following property T of the associated Galois connection:

$$\left. \begin{array}{l} \forall \ g \in G \bullet \exists \ m \in M \bullet (g,m) \in I \\ \forall \ m \in M \bullet \exists \ g \in G \bullet (g,m) \in I \end{array} \right\} \quad \ldots T$$

The property T is sufficient to prove the highly non-trivial

Theorem (of topological closure). Any Galois connection with property T has closure operations satisfying:

$$\varnothing_G'' = \varnothing_G \text{ and dually } \varnothing_M'' = \varnothing_M ;$$

$$\forall A_1, A_2 \subseteq G \bullet \quad A_1'' \cup A_2'' = (A_1 \cup A_2)'' ,$$

and dually for B's from M.

The long but elementary proof of this theorem is available in full detail from the authors. The result says that the closed sets in G and M constitute a topology. In topology, there are many well-founded theorems about dense sets which enable one to infer, from a proof that a certain property holds for a set A, that the same property also holds for the larger set A''. For example, if A is a set of input sequences for which it has been proved that certain initialization procedures produce states which evolve safely under inputs from A, then the same procedures can safely be used when the environment behaves so as to produce inputs from the less restrictive A''.

The above theorem makes such reasoning available to safety proof, and this will be elaborated in subsequent papers. More generally, we suggest that notions such as FCA can make for closer and fruitful contact between the two cultures of mechanized proof axiomatics, and the more ancient culture of certain well-founded branches of mathematics.

REFERENCES

[1] A.H.Cribbens, *Solid State Interlocking (SSI): an integrated electronic signalling system for mainline railways*, Proc.IEE **134(3)**,pp 148-158, 1987.

[2] R.C.Short, *Software Validation for a Railway Signalling System*, SAFECOMP83 Conference Proceedings, Cambridge (UK), 1983.

[3] A.H.Cribbens and I.H.Mitchell, *The Application of Advanced Computing Techniques to the Generation and checking of SSI Data*, Railway Engineers' Forum Meeting, London (UK), 1991, and to appear in Proc.IRSE, 1992.

[4] J.Hartmanis and R.E. Stearns, *Algebraic Structure Theory of Sequential Machines*, Prentice-Hall,N.J. (USA), 1966.

[5] C.B.Jones, *Systematic Software Development Using VDM*, Prentice-Hall International(UK),1990.

[6] J.M.Spivey, *The Z notation: A reference Manual*, Prentice-Hall International(UK),1985.

[7] W.Atkinson and J.Cunningham, *Proving properties of a safety-critical system in FOREST*, Software Eng.J. **6(2)**,pp 41-50,1991.

[8] R.Wille, *Bedeutungen von Begriffs-verbänden*,in B.Ganter, R.Wille and K.E.Wolff (editors),*Beiträge zur Begriffsanalyse*, pp 161-211, B.I. Wissenschaftsverlag (Germany), 1987.

USING PETRI NETS FOR SAFETY ANALYSIS OF UNMANNED METRO SYSTEM

M. EL KOURSI & P. OZELLO
INRETS-CRESTA
20, rue elisée Reclus 59650 Villeneuve d'Ascq, France.
TEL : (33) 20 43 83 24
FAX : (33) 20 43 83 59

Abstract

In unmanned transportation systems, the certification of the control/command equipments is a technical process based on rigourous methods taking into account precise and detailed objectives. In France, for a number of new automated transport systems, INRETS has been in charge of this certification process as an authorized body, appointed by the Ministry of Transport. Such process intends to assess that the system design satisfies initially defined safety objectives. INRETS-CRESTA has developed a tool based on Petri nets and a methodology for applying this tool. The principle is to examine and eventually to complete the safety study achieved by the constructor, by coupling and simulating a functional model with environment model. In this paper we describe how this tool is used to specify safety functions and to demonstrate their safety. This method is illustrated by an example of application to the VAL automated system.

Key words: certification, safety, Petri nets, simulation, guided transport systems.

Introduction

The process of unmanned transportation systems certification intends to attest that the system design satisfies initially defined safety objectives. In parallel with the system life cycle adopted by manufacturer, the duly authorized body performs the certification life cycle. In the different safety validation steps the authorized body uses different method to find out, in the earliest hour, the unsafe situations which could occur during different phases of the system life. It checks that the Preliminary Hazard Analysis has taken into account all the particularities of the system and its degraded modes of operation. The functions dedicated to prevent each hazard are to be clearly defined. This verification continues throughout from the equipment specification (internal and external) to the final product. To improve the certification process, INRETS-CRESTA has developed a tool based on Petri nets and their application methodology.

Such a tool has been used to help the team in charge of the certification process of the VAL system of Lille, of the ORLY-VAL of Paris and of MAGGALY system of Lyon. It also has been used to analyse a critical software function of the VAL Chicago Automatic Train Protection (ATP).

In this paper we describe how Petri nets are used :

-	to analyse, by modeling, the specification of the safety functions in order to check the completeness and consistency of the system specification;

-	to check, by simulation, the correctness of the safety criteria attached to each safety function.

We give here under just an informal and synthetic recall of Petri nets definition:

A Petri net is an oriented bipartite graph. Places are represented by circles and transitions by bars. Places and transitions are joined by oriented arcs. The values of the input function are associated with each arc joining a place with a transition. The output function values are associated with the arcs joining a transition with a place. Moreover with each transition is associated a condition which corresponds to a logic or numerical information.

Safety analysis approach

The safety analysis of unmanned transportation systems is generally achieved by a top-down decomposition which allows to attach safety criteria to each functional entity, which should be satisfied by the corresponding equipment.

The manufacturers approach tends to prove the correctness of the specification, design and realisation of all the components. Our approach tries to find that components specification doesn't correspond to the requirement specification and design according to a safety criterion.

This approach can be decomposed into six phases:

- to identify the safety functions of the Automatic Train Protection (ATP) system and of their close environment,

- to identify the safety criteria attached to the safety function,

- to model each function and its environment in order to detect an incompleteness or an inconsistency in the specification,

- starting from the models to simulate environment and safety function in order to examine the dynamic behaviour of the function and check that the safety criteria are satisfied,

- to introduce failures in the model in order to check protection reactions,

- to link and simulate the set of the model functions and the model of environment to verify their interfaces and check that the global safety criteria are satisfied.

The specification model used to achieve safety analysis is divided into three parts. The first part is the environment model, in the broad sense,

which integrates the different steps of trains movement. Each state of the model corresponds to a signal activation. The second part corresponds to the interface between the environment model and the ATP model. The third model corresponds to the ATP specification (fig 1).

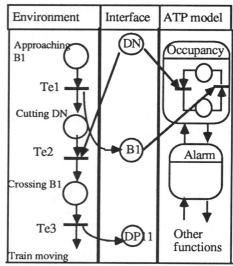

Fig 1 : modeling principle of an ATP.

We are illustrating our approach by an example of a transport system with a fixed blocks anticollision protection such as the VAL system (fig 2). The principle of such a system is that the track is divided into blocks. For each block, the safety is achieved by a **block logic** which determines the occupancy, the release and the alarm.

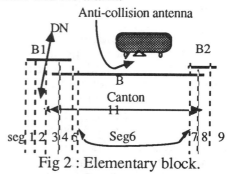

Fig 2 : Elementary block.

This block logic uses the information delivered by a set of loops which receive a signal from anti-collision antenna implemented on board the train. Normally, the train transmits a signal into the fixed loops on the track. The loops activation indicates the trains presence. So in figure 2, B1 allows the detection of a train entering a block. B is used to maintain the occupancy block information and B2 loop informs that the train is leaving the block. Moreover detection barriers based on infrared beams are provided on some place of the track. This detection barriers called DN (infrared barrier) delivers a low pulse at the passage of a train.

The **environment model** (Fig 3) represents a simple train driving along the block. The seg1, seg2, seg3, seg4, seg5, seg6, seg8, seg 9 denote the different train positions and correspond respectively to the train approaching B1 (loop), crossing B1, cutting DN (infrared barrier), crossing B (loop), release DN, release B1, crossing B2 , release B and release B2. Similarly, transitions Te1 to Te8 denote the events of signals activation of the loops.

When a transition is fired, the mark is put in the next place of the environment and of the interface model (Fig3).

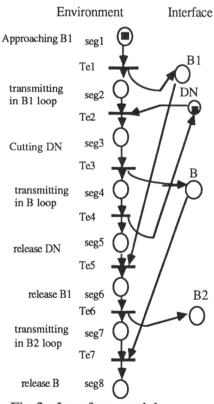

Fig 3 : Interface model.

The **model of interface**, will be integrated in the model environment. The firing of a transition of the environment model places a mark in the corresponding place of the interface model. This mark may be consulted or used by the

equipment model. For instance, the firing of Te1 puts a mark in the B1 interface place. A mark in B1 place indicates that the train anti-collision antenna activates the B1 loop [mark = activation, no mark = no activation].

Also the interface model may be deconnected from the environment model by using the synchronization possibilities of transitions. It is possible to synchronize the Ti (Transition interface) with Te (Transition environment). In the figure 4, the Ti-emision-B1 transition is synchronized with Te1. The firing of Ti-emission-B1 is not enabled before the firing of Te1.

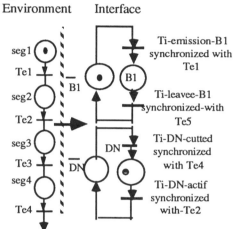

Fig 4 : interface model synchronized with environment model.

Automatic Train Protection (ATP) equipment model

In the equipment model, we proceed to a decomposition of the safety function into a set of subfunctions. At each subfunction is attached a set of safety criteria. These criteria are a result of SSHA (SubSystem Hazard Analysis). To each criterion, we associate an undesirable marking of the model. Each Petri net model of the subfunctions does not exceed 10 places and 10 transitions, in order to facilitate the analysis.

Consider our example of a logic block which is decomposed into two subfunctions:

- occupancy and release model,
- alarm model.

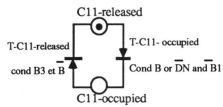

Fig 5 : Block occupancy model

If we look at the figure 5, the occupancy state of the block is intuitively equivalent to the B loop receiving a permanent signal from the train (anti-collision antenna). The designer must take into account the antenna failures. When the train cuts the DN (Infrared barrier) without transmitting a signal to B loop, the block must be declared occupied. These conditions are implemented in the condition of the T-C11-occupancy transition. The block is declared as released when the train leaves sequentially B and B2 loops.

The alarm model (fig 6) can be coupled with the occupancy model. It must generate an alarm if the train interrupt the transmission into the B loop while the occupancy place in the model hold a mark. This condition is implemented in the T-alarm transition.

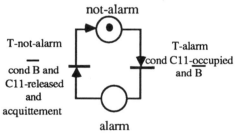

Fig 6: Block alarm model

The different conditions associated to the transitions associate loops signals and the states of some places from the models (environment, interface and ATP model).

Adding failures in the model

The failures can be modelled in the Petri nets. They correspond to the loss of a mark or to the generation of a spurious mark. In the model, the add failures will be obtained by different ways:

- addition or deletion of transitions,

- alteration of the transition condition for simulating the occurrence of an untimely remote control,

- addition or deletion of arcs.

For instance, the deletion of the arc between the Te3 transition of the environment model and B place of the interface model simulates the absence of train transmission into B1 loop. In this case, we check in the ATP model that the alarm model reacts correctly and puts the mark into the alarm place.

Model operation

We have developed a tool called "SIMPAR" which allows to calculate a set of reachable states in the direct and reverse way from any initial state.

Reachable graph

The direct reachable graph can be used to check if the set of undesirable marking (safety criteria) is reached from an initial state by a legal sequence of transitions firing.

The backward reachable graph allows to determine from an undesirable state the different ways which are the origin of this undesirable marking. The backward reachable graph shows if the model can generate these undesirable states.

Factual simulation

In unmanned transportation systems, remote controls are necessary to improve the operation of the system. Unfortunately, hazardous situations may result from an incorrect use of certain remote controls. For instance the initialization remote control can cancel certain safety alarms such as a call for emergency evacuation.

We can act on the model evolution by modifying a condition which enables the firing of a transition. The user can introduce an untimely remote control in the transitions predicate in order to evaluate the hazards resulting from such a remote control.

It's possible to simulate step by step the evolution of the Petri nets marking and choose the time where we can introduce failures or untimely remote controls.

Sequential execution of the different models.

It is always necessary to execute the different tasks in a defined order. Generally this order corresponds to the cyclic system behaviour. Each task can be modelled by a Petri net. In this case, we use the place called "macro-place". Each macro-place represents a Petri net model describing a subfunction. When the "macro-place" is marked the associated Petri net evolves until a stable marking is reached and puts the mark in the next macro-place. Sequentially the mark moves from one macro-place to another.

Validation approach

Individually, each subfunction is validated according to its specification. We check that the model corresponds to the specification and safeguards a set of safety criteria.

We validate a nominal function of the system. Then the model is submitted to aggressive scenarios by introducing failures of equipment, spurious remote controls and some particular operating modes.

Safety criteria and undesirable marking link.

Firstly, We look for the set of undesirable marking and check if these marks may occur in the nominal configuration.

For instance:
C10 is a criterion which stipulates that *a train without transmitter must be detected in the block entrance.*
At this criterion, we attach an Undesirable Marking UM10.

UM10 := [Not(DN), Not(B1), C11-released]

This marking describes the following situation:
-        in the environment model and interface model, the DN (infrared barrier)

is cut by a train which is not transmitting in the B loop. This case is described in the interface model by the DN and B1 places which are not marked. In the normal case, the train transmits in the B1 loop before cutting the DN barrier.

-        in the ATP model, the occupancy place is not marked.

We check that this marking is never reached in the normal sequence of transitions firing. and if we introduce failures to obtain this marking, we check that the corresponding alarm is set.

Conclusion
We have exposed the different ways to use Petri nets to examine and eventually to complete the safety study achieved by the constructor. The use of Petri nets allows to analyse properties such as safety and to help in determining a possible sequence of failures which can lead to accidents. The first benefit of the use of Petri nets is to understand exactly and criticize the manufacturer's specification of the safety functions. The second is the possibility of showing the eventually dangerous configurations.

References

M. EL KOURSI (1987) "Application des réseaux de Petri à commande-contrôle de processus en sécurité"
APII, 1987, N°21.
B.FAYOLLE & M. ELKOURSI (1991) "Spécification et Validation fonctionnelle des automatismes de sécurité", RTS, N° 33, 1992.
B.LETRUNG (1986) "Analyse de sécurité du logiciel par réseau de Petri"
INRETS, CR/A86.50, janvier 1986.
B.LETRUNG (1989) "Approval procedures for automatic equipment of unmanned metro system IFAC, CCCT'89 Paris.

VITAL CODED PROCESSOR AND SAFETY RELATED SOFTWARE DESIGN

P. Chapront

GEC ALSTHOM, Division Transport, Direction des Systemes de Signalisation, 33 rue des Bateliers 93404 Saint-Ouen, France

Abstract : the context of vital coded processor is recalled. Constraints of safety critical software are described, and a presentation of formal methods is made. The B-method is described with more detail on specification and design. Corresponding tools are mentioned. Some results obtained in application are given. Production of software for the vital coded processor is described and the link with B-method is made. Conclusions of GEC ALSTHOM experience are given.

Keywords : Safety. Software development. Failure detection. Error compensation. Formal languages. Software tools.

INTRODUCTION

Between 1981 and 1985 a consortium of French railway manufacturers [1] working for SNCF and RATP designed and realised the new train control system SACEM, which was installed on the line A of the rapid transit network of PARIS. Due to the requested performances, this system was based on microcomputers, which handle all functions, many of which being safety critical.

The originality of the solution is a systematic use of information redundancy to ensure fail safe behaviour. A single processor is in charge of the data processing and the way in which each information is encoded allows the detection of erroneous data, whatever the cause of the error. This is explained with much more details in other papers.

Of course, though it should be the case in many other solutions, the proof of correctness of the software had to be obtained. Like any software we can split its lifecycle in four phases :
a) Specification,
b) Design,
c) Production,
d) Execution in operation.

The vital coded processor technique guarantees the safety through the phases c) and d). The software correctness studies must therefore be concentrated on phases a) and b), since the final object code will be executed on a vital coded processor. Confidence in the software correctness is obtained by using formal specification and design. Automatic production of ADA code provides an elegant solution to the low level programming of the special routines needed by the vital coded processor.

THE SPECIFICATION OF SAFETY CRITICAL SOFTWARE

Functional Specification

As it is always the case when we have to solve a real word problem, the first step is to obtain a perfect understanding of it, and to be able to express it in clear and unambiguous terms. A way to reach this understanding is to perform a structured functional analysis and submit resulting information to the various concerned specialists, including the customers operation teams.

The language used must be as structured as

---

[1] GEC ALSTHOM, CSEE TRANSPORT, MATRA TRANSPORT

possible to avoid ambiguities and ensure consistency, but at the same time be easily learnt and understood by non specialists. We choose to perform this functional analysis using SADT to structure the process, finite state machine to describe dynamic behaviour and comments in natural language to supply complementary information.

A CASE tool, named ASA [2], removes the burden of drawing diagrams and provides coherence and consistency checking facilities.

Such a model is of course an activity oriented functional model because it expresses what must be done, which is the main concern of the customers. Data aspects are, of course, taken in account, but remain on a secondary level. It is well known that a software design mapped on a functional breakdown is not very good : the variables associated with data must often be global and side effects are nearly unavoidable. Moreover it is often very difficult to modify the functionalities without extensive software changes. The specification must therefore be reorganised into a data oriented structure.

Formal specification

To produce the data oriented model and ensure its fundamental qualities we use a mathematical language, with predetermined notations. This is the formal specification. Of course the basic information will be extracted from the functional model, but the structure of the new model is completely different, as the borders between the various objects are drawn around the basic data and not around the actions. So, we shall have to check that the formal model reflects correctly the problem to solve. This is an important issue of the method.

---

[2] Supplied by VERILOG

[3] JR Abrial was also involved in Z development

THE MODEL ORIENTED B_METHOD

Specification

Software engineering methods based on mathematics fall into two categories : algebraic and model approach. VDM is the pioneer in the second category (Jones 86). Z is another model approach technique, developed at OXFORD (Spivey 88). The B development methodology, due to J.R. Abrial[3](Abrial 92), supports the design of large specifications and program constructions. The mathematical model behind this methodology is an extension of the original Zermelo set theory. The "programming" notation is a subset of the specification notations.

The method is centred on the concept of abstract machine. A software system of any size can always considered as a box containing some data which can be read or modified by some "buttons" which trigger internal operations. The set of the internal data value forms the state of this machine. The operations are used to animate the model, while the relationship between the data and their internal properties constitute the invariant of the machine. The role of the operations is to modify the state of the abstract machine, within the limits of the invariant.

The specification of an operation is the description of the properties of the changes it performs. To express these properties, methods such as VDM and Z use logic statements which express the relationship between the values of the data before the operation takes place and the values the corresponding data will have just after. In the B-method this relationship is expressed by establishing the textual substitution implied by the operation, which have to be made for all the free occurrences of the data, in all the formulas in which they appear (mainly in the invariant).

The substitution in a formula P in which a data "n" has free occurrences may be noted :
$[n:=E]P$
where E is a set theoretic term, and this can be read as " E is substituted for n in P".

And as far as the invariant preservation is concerned we have to prove that :
$I => [S]I$
where S is a substitution and => the sign of logical

implication.

This simple notion of substitution must be generalized to other cases which mainly are :
-The multiple substitution
[x1, x2,...,xn := E1, E2,...,En]P
in which the n set theoretic terms E1...En may replace simultaneously all the free occurrences in P of the n distinct variables x1...xn.

-The preconditioned substitution
P|S
where the substitution S in constrained by the satisfaction of the predicate P. Preconditions ensure feasibility.

-The bounded choice substitution
S[]T
where one or the other of the two substitutions S or T may be used. This introduces a bounded non determinism.

-The guarded substitution
P==>S
where the substitution S is performed under the assumption P.

-The unbounded non deterministic substitution
@z.S
where the substitution S, which contains the variable z which does not appears anywhere in the invariant can be used whatever the value of z.

These various concepts allows to specify any real world problem. The internal coherence can be verified by checking that the initialisation (which guarantee that the model is not empty), establishes the invariant, and that other operations preserve it.
By nature the functionalities are mainly expressed in the invariant and also in the possible preconditions of the operations.

Of course large system have to be split into smaller ones. Provided the data can be divided in disjoint sub-collections, the division is possible and the sub-models can be separately established and proven. These sub-models are combined afterwards. Of course the external model cannot directly modify the variables of internal sub-models. Naturally the progressive comprehension of the system goes from its heart towards its external boundaries. It is a bottom-up construction and therefore requires a perfect understanding of the functionalities.

For an easier manipulation of the concepts, some "syntactic sugar" is provided by replacing symbolic mathematical notations with a simple pseudo-programming language. For example

P|S is written PRE P THEN S END. The use of such a language allows to avoid elementary mistakes and facilitates subsequent refinements.

Examples of real applications in the railway industry

This method has been used to specify several railway applications. The first one was the re-specification of the SACEM system. The B-method was then used to specify and design the CALCUTTA metro ATP, and the KVS train control system.

In this last example, the main abstract machine is divided into five sub-models which encapsulate the major objects of the application. Each submodel is itself divided in several smaller models, structured in several layers. The maximum level of layers is five and the total number of abstract machines is 72. The complete specification totals about 10000 lines in B_language. It involves about 1000 proofs.

Proofs of coherence. The tools.

As previously said, the use of proofs is an important feature of the method. These proofs concern :
-the verification of internal coherence : initialisation, invariant preservation, feasibility,
-the correct use of the data, through the various levels of abstract machines : visibility, respect of information hiding,
-the global consistency.

It is of course not possible to do this by hand. Tools must therefore be used in order to :
-control the proper use of the language,
-elaborate the various lemmas which must be proven (so called proof obligations),
-prove them automatically, using a library of basic rules, or interactively; in this case the user defines the proof strategy and includes new rules.
All these tools, which are also used in the design phase, are built around a central tool : the B-tool[4] (Abrial 91). The B-tool is a formula manipulator and provides the necessary rewriting and simplifications.

---

[4] The B-tool was developed by J.R Abrial and the other tools are produced by BP Research with the collaboration of GEC ALSTHOM.

The formal design

The design is a step by step process. Each abstract machine will be replaced by a new one, called a refinement of it, which yields comparable results, from an external point of view.
The refinements concern data and operations.
Data refinement is introduced via changes of variables. The object of these changes is to reduce the non-determinism. Of course proof of consistency between the refinement and its specification must be done.
Operations refinement concerns the breakdown of the operations into smaller components. This introduces new layers with simpler operations. During this work, parallel substitutions are replaced by sequential statements, and the classic notion of loops is introduced. Proofs of consistency are also mandatory.

The number of proof obligations increases very quickly with the number of conditional substitutions involved by the operations. The tools allow to simplify substitutions using symbolic evaluation. Tautologies and contradictions are detected and removed.

The last step of refinement is the translation of the lower formal description produced in B-language into a classical programming language. In fact we use a subset of the ADA language. This source code can then be compiled to produce the executable program. The translation is automatic.

To continue our example, the refinement of the KVS specification resulted in 12000 lines of B_langage, and involved about 5000 proof obligations. The translation into ADA produced 16000 lines of ADA code.

Surprisingly, the executable code was efficient in terms of execution time and memory space. At the same time the program worked right immediately and integration with hardware was very easy.

THE SOFTWARE FOR THE VITAL CODED PROCESSOR

Programming

We recall that, in the vital coded processor technology, each time a statement is executed on a variable, some special manipulation must be made on the check field associated with this variable. Each time a test or a loop is written, some special procedures must be called to ensure adequate operation of the program during its execution.
These additional procedures appear in a library of subprogram containing the so-called "elementary operations".

When programming by hand, the programmer must select the operation from the library, depending of the program context. A mistake at this stage has no unsafe consequences, but makes the execution of the program impossible, and looking for such a mistake is quite time consuming.

Several features of ADA (overloading of identifiers, generics, library management) takes most of the burden off the programmer, while enhancing the readability of the program. The automatic production of the source code eliminates all errors in variables and procedures manipulation.

The last task consist in computing the tables of constants used to compensate the various check variables, each time an alternative is closed or a loop is released. This work is done by a special tool called MPC-ADA.

The MPC-ADA tool

The MPC-ADA tool is used after the source ADA program has been produced. This tool :
-detects and signals misuses of the vital coded processor, in case of programming by hand,
-introduces automatically the special procedure calls associated with tests and loops,
-calculates, by symbolic execution, the modifications which will be made during real execution of the program on the signature of each data, in each path of the program,
-determines the points of the program where compensation of signatures must be made, and the associated values,
-builds the so-called compensation-tables.
To produce these results, the MPC-ADA tool
-analyses the source code and builds the syntactic tree of the program,
-uses symbolic calculus to determine the optimal size of compensation-tables, with the associated points,
-performs the symbolic execution to calculate the value, and generates the tables.

Note that the errors in the tool or in the compiler can be ignored at this stage. Such errors will be completely equivalent to hardware failure in the program memory (errors during compilation) or in the data memory (error in the compensation-tables). These errors will be detected by their effects on the output signatures with the same coverage rate as the equivalent hardware failures. The vital coded processor technique therefore ensures safety during production and execution of the program.

CONCLUSION

From the end of the SACEM project onward, GEC ALSTHOM has gained an extensive experience of safety critical programming, using both formal method and vital coded processor implementation.

These constitute two complementary aspects of the subject, ensuring software correctness and safe execution. Using the vital coded processor technology eliminates the need for any time consuming hardware safety analyses. The formal method has proven to be very efficient, both in the design process as during validation process. The teams can concentrate their efforts on understanding the problem, as the design process guarantees the production of a program which
-satisfies its specification
-works immediately
-is efficient

The various tools allows to build an efficient, readable and traceable documentation, available for assessment.

The efficiency of the formal B-method encourages us to extend its application to non critical software, after adequate training of our software engineer teams.

REFERENCES

Jones C., (1986), Systematic software development using VDM, *Prentice-Hall*

Spivey J.M., (1988), Understanding Z: a language and its formal semantics, *Cambridge University Press*

Abrial J.R., (1992), The B method, *book to appear*

Abrial J.R., (1991), The B reference manual, *Edinburgh Portable Compilers, 17 Alva Street, Edinburgh, EH2 4PH, U.K.*

VITAL PROCESSING BY SINGLE CODED UNIT

ABSTRACT

Author : M. Jean MARTIN

MATRA TRANSPORT
48 à 56 rue Barbès - BP 531
92542 MONTROUGE Cedex
FRANCE
Phone : (33-1) 49 65 73 42
Fax : (33-1) 49 65 70 93

Matra Transport designs urban transportation systems ; the driverless VAL system operating in LILLE since 83 is an example of Matra Transport innovation process.

The topic of the proposed presentation is focused on the vital computer operating in PARIS and MEXICO :

- vital code approach leading to a single processor unit : how the code detects errors and why a single coded processor may be safe and more flexible than redundant architectures
- vital code implementation and software generation process : how real time, code generation and checking are held
- hardware interfaces with signalling fail safe environment : how interfaces are managed with and between vital computers.

This vital computer is now used in all our new developments, CHICAGO O'HARE VAL and MAGGALY systems will be operated in 92 with this technology. Our various Automatic Train Protections and Interlocking Logics will be roughly described as well as their operating figures.

1   VITAL SINGLE PROCESSOR UNIT

This new safety concept has already been introduced during the VIENNA IFAC conference which was held in December 89. This new IFAC meeting offers the opportunity to overlook seven years of intensive use and several implementations.

At first, let us review main characteristics of the coding and interface technics.

Starting from the fact that a vital data transmission is easier to obtain by coding than repeating, MATRA-TRANSPORT proposed in the early eighties to RATP and SNCF, an extrapolation of transmission technics to data processing.

As no exhaustive model of degraded mode was available for microprocessors and peripheral components, the code objective was defined against random failures. Data processing was analysed apart from hardware in order to define what kind of integrity the code had to protect.

Based on a code associated with each processed variable, it has two principal objectives :

- It detects calculation error in the process
- It detects if the real-time computed sequence of instructions is in concordance with the programmed sequence.

This approach allows to reach a safety level which does not depend on the complexity and on the technology of hardware but which depends on the size of the redundancy (number of bits used for coding).

2   PROTECTION AGAINST OPERATION ERRORS

How operation result errors are detected by the arithmetic code ?

A processed variable is represented by a coded value X which is composed of a functional field and a code or control field.

The coded information X is structured as follows :

N_f bits	k bits
functional field	code or control field

According to the design of this structure, there are $2^{N_f + k}$ possible values. Only 2^{N_f} of these values are correct. They correspond to all possible functional values.

In these conditions, the probability of undetected error is :

$$Pi = \frac{2\,Nf}{2\,Nf + k} = \frac{1}{2^k}$$

This value is directly linked with the safety level of the system because it represents the probability of undetected error. Theoretically, this safety level can be as high as possible by choosing the adapted size of the coded field k.

A coded information X will be implemented by $(x, -r_{kx})$ using two different machine memories :

> r_{kx} is the rest of the Euclidian division of $2^k x$ by A. ($r_{kx} = 2^k x$ MOD A)
>
> A is an integer called the key of the code
>
> k is chosen in order to reach $2^k > A$
>
> the number $2^k x - r_{kx}$ is a multiple of the integer A

A simple example allows the understanding of the principle of a calculation error detection. Let $X = Y + Z$, the result of the addition of the coded variables Y and Z.

> - the functional field of the result will contain : $x = y + z$ by adding the two functional fields
> - the control field will contain : $- r_k (y+z)$ by adding $- r_{ky}$ with $- r_{kz}$
> - if the addition is processed without any error, the number $2^k (y+z) - r_k (y+z)$ will be a multiple of the integer A.

Then a calculation error will be detected by the loss of the property of divisibility by A.

3 PROTECTION AGAINST OPERAND, OPERATOR AND REFRESHING ERRORS

How the predetermined signature concept detects operand and operator errors ?

A predetermined value B_X which is called static signature and which is associated to X identity is added to the control field of X.

X becomes ($2^k x$, $- r_{kx} + B_x$)

A simple example allows the understanding of the detection of operand and operator errors. Let $X = Y + Z$, the coded result of the addition of the coded variables Y and Z.

The following cases can occur :

> A- The addition is correctly processed and the coded value X contains :
>
> $2^k (y+z) - r_{k(y+z)} + F_{plus} (B_Y, B_Z)$
>
> Where F_{plus} (By, Bz) is the signature of the operation Y + Z .
> $F_{plus} (B_Y, B_Z) = B_Y + B_Z$
>
> B- There is an operand error : T is used instead of Y.
>
> The coded value contains :
>
> $2^k (t+z) - r_{k(t+z)} + B_T + B_Z$
>
> The error will be detected if $B_T \neq B_Y$
>
> C- There is an operator error and "op" is used instead of "+". The coded value then contains :
>
> $2^k (y \text{ op } z) - r_{k(y \text{ op } z)} + F_{op} (B_Y, B_Z)$

This example shows how predetermined signature allows operand and operator errors detection :

> In the cases B or C, the signature of the result $[(B_T + B_Z)$ or $F_{op} (B_Y, B_Z)]$ is not equal to the predetermined signature $B_Y + B_Z$.
>
> The detection efficiency relies on the signature distribution (at random between $\emptyset$ and A-1).

The refreshing errors are detected by another variable which is called the dynamic signature (or date) and which gives a temporal validity to each variable of the cyclic process.

Finally, the structure of the coded variable is :

$$X = 2^k x - r_{kx} + B_x + D$$

    functional   control

    field   field

4   VERIFICATION PRINCIPLE

The validity of any information of the programme is the verification of a characteristic property.

For a coded data X, the characteristic property is the congruence (modulo A) to a predetermined Bx. In order to check the validity of any information X of the programme, we have to substract the date, divide by A and compare the value obtained to the predetermined Bx.

In fact, this verification is not realised after each elementary operations but only each cycle of the process. The processor generates a global digital sequence composed of signature key variables which have been used in the process and the result of vital output self-checks.

This sequence is compared to a predetermined sequence. When a difference occurs between the two sequences, all outputs of the vital processor are desactivated and the processor has to be reinitialised, or a standby processor may take over.

Predetermination of the final signatures has to deal with real-time optional executions : after a test with a conditional branch, data signatures evolve differently according to the chosen branch. The coded data signatures are adjusted at the convergence of branches, so that the same values are obtained independently of the programme choice : this requires the use of predetermined data compensation tables that enable the modification of variable signatures in accordance with programme flow choices.

5   HARDWARE ORGANISATION OF VITAL CODED PROCESSOR

However, in an automatic train control, both safety approaches, fail-safe and coded exist :

- coding principles ensures safety when the components used for processing or transmission cannot be, because of their complexity, analysed with an intrinsic fail safe approach (microprocessor, bus, buffer, data transmission channel)
- intrinsic fail safe principles ensures safety of relays or power devices

The general hardware organisation is based, in current applications, upon the use of a 680X0 microprocessor type.

The principal functions are : coding of fail-safe inputs delivered by sensors, coded data processing of (microprocessor) and output decoding.

Coding fail-safe inputs

The coding of fail-safe logical inputs, in order to obtain coded stream at the microprocessor input, is carried out by input fail safe encoders that provide a specific signature for each high level input.

Processing coded DATA

The same microprocessor processes both functional and control field.

The microprocessor generates the functional control outputs and a global calculated signature. This computed signature constitutes an input of the dynamic controller.

Decoding coded outputs

The global signature stream generated by the processor is compared, by a fail safe dynamic controller, with the predetermined signature (the predetermined signature is included in the dynamic controller's PROM). The dynamic controller provides the energy to all vital output in case of identity of the two sequences. In case of error, the energy supply is disabled and all vital outputs are forced in a restrictive state.

6   SOFTWARE GENERATION PROCESS

The coded source file (writen in Modula II) will be :

- compiled in order to generate the machine code,
- analysed by the software tool which "pre-computes" all static signatures and determines the compensation tables that may be used by the program.

7   APPLICATIONS OF THIS TECHNOLOGY

Since the first researchs in the early eighties supported by RATP and SNCF, all new MATRA-TRANSPORT systems are developped with this technology.

SACEM

The aim of this first system, is to improve the throughput of an existing metro line (RER Line A). The performance is obtained by :

- signalling track occupancy in the cab instead of the track-side (the track-side signalling is cancelled when an equipped train approaches the area)
- subdividing platform track circuits to improve train detection accuracy in the critical headway zone

Two main constraints were established :

- the revenue service had to be maintained during installation and test
- the operation of equipped and non equipped trains must be possible at any moment

In each station, a ground based vital equipment gathers the signalling information to be transmitted to the trains, and cancels the signal in front of equipped trains. In each train, the on-board vital computer locates the train on the network, thanks to beacons and tachometer, and controls three times per second that the maximum possible speed is not overtaken.

400 microprocessors, compute several time per seconds the 15000 real-time coded instructions in PARIS Line A or MEXICO Line A.

In PARIS, more than 800 000 passengers are carried on this line every day.

220 m long trains may reach a 2 minutes headway (including 50 seconds station dwelling time).

MAGGALY

The aim of this system is to operate a new large capacity metro line without any attendant on board.

Special consideration has been focused on availability :

- train detection availibility implies that it could not be held by track circuits any more : train detection and protection are managed according to "moving block" principles : each train sends its position to the station based equipment which gives back the next train position.

- fault tolerant architecture had to be used : automatic commutation between two computers is provided during operations, it implies to get sure that no diverging computing between redundant equipment could lead to an unsafe operation.

Ten vital ground based equipments manage track occupancy for 36 dedicated trains. All revenue and storage operations are driverless. Minimum headway : 90 seconds (with 25 seconds dwelling time in station). Revenue service in September 92.

CHICAGO O'HARE AIRPORT VAL SYSTEM

This application of the VAL system uses a vital computer to ensure the ground based logic : train tracking, switches controls, train movement authorizations and traction power supply control.

Each station is equipped with a vital computer, a special control center equipment transmits operator vital orders, and manages general emergency functions.

The system is designed for a 24 hours service a day : all tracks can be operated in both way of circulation, "hot" redundancy is provided for all revenue service track operations. All revenue and storage operations are driverless. Revenue service is sheduled at the end of 1992.

KVIM/KVBP

This system will mix two types of train control : a "SACEM-like" system (absolute location of the train on the network and continous transmission from track to the trains), with a "distance to go" system (spread beacons transmitting the available track downstream).

This combination will allow powerful operations in the urban area (short headway) and up-graded sub-urban operations (based on an existing ground based system).

This SNCF requirement is focused on the PARIS RER Line C network which spreads on a very large area of the PARIS suburbs.

METEOR

The main characteristics of this future system (1997) are :

- mix driverless equipped trains with manually drived unequipped trains : special consideration must be paid to passenger evacuation in case of driverless train, which involves that no confusion is allowed between equipped and non equipped trains

- ensure passager safety in station with platform doors : this protection is operating with the VAL in LILLE since 1983

- improve passager safety by transmitting real time video images of the train cabins towards the Central Control Room.

ASTREE

This system, using cellular transmission between trains and ground based equipments, is designed to equip intercity lines.

It relies on absolute location of the train on the network, continous transmission between track and trains, moving block, various sensors (doppler, tachometer, beacons..).

MATRA-TRANSPORT is delivering onboard vital computers to SNCF in order to reach the safety level required for that equipment.

8   CONCLUSION

This technic has proven it may fit many real time softwares which don't need to deal with real time data bases or response time lower than 100 ms.

The development process is completely under control : these various applications using the vital coded processor rose the quality standard of the tools and user guides, the allowed software structures are rather simple and common (IF..THEN..ELSE, WHILE..DO,...).

Development is now focused on response time. MATRA is working on a dedicated processor and a faster dynamic controller, to improve performances and enlarge the possible applications of this fail safetechnology.

GLOSSARY

RATP : Régie Autonome des Transports Parisiens

SNCF : Société Nationale des Chemins de fer Français

ASTREE - ODOMETRIC SAFETY CONTROL UNIT

Philippe STEPHAN - Olivier DIEUDONNE

Electricity and Command Control Department - TECHNICATOME
BP 34000 - 13791 AIX-EN-PROVENCE CEDEX 3 - FRANCE

Abstract. The Odometric Safety Control Unit is a system installed aboard every train which supplies this train with highly accurate position and speed data. The system was designed in two phases: a feasibility study (definition of the measurement and processing architecture) and the development of prototypes. The Odometric Safety Control Unit includes radars, a phonic wheel and repositioning beacons. This structure can be adapted for all the rolling stock and railroad network. The heart of the Odometric Safety Control Unit consists of a safety-oriented computer designed by TECHNICATOME. It is the result of 10 years of experience in the field of digital command-control systems piloting nuclear reactors. Basically, it is structured around a monoprocessor and a dual software; its unpredictable failure rate is 10^{-9} failures/hour. This performance can be achieved owing to a coherent and complementary set of hardware and software techniques which are implemented according to a pre-defined technology. The safety demonstration is based on the automatic fault-injection technique applied to the computer (hardware and software). Millions of failures were studied during fault-injection campaigns for which TECHNICATOME developed a specific methodology and special tools.

Keywords. Safety - Redundancy -Railways - Position control - Speed control - Nuclear Reactors - Real time computer systems - Kalman Filter.

PRESENTATION OF THE ASTREE PROJECT

The French National Railways (SNCF) ASTREE Project aims at replacing the current signalling system existing along railroads (associated with train sensors by track circuits), by a system based on quite different principles : each train can reliably and continuously determine its position along the railroads. The train exchanges data with the control center which knows the position and speed of trains, manages them according to safety rules and in order to ensure a fluid traffic, and sends them appropriate instructions. The *ODO Safety Control Unit* installed aboard trains provides them with continuous speed and position data: speed data is exploited in real time on the train for speed control purposes; position data is exploited mainly by fixed stations to manage relative train motions. The relative position of a train is defined with respect to a reference point used in common with the controlcenter; this common reference point changes according to train motions.

EXPECTED PERFORMANCE

The *ODO Safety Control Unit* shall provide the following data at all times:
- Position of the mobile with an accuracy better than 20 meters with an output error probability rate (o.e.p.r) less than 10^{-9}/hr.
- Speed with an accuracy better than 10 km/hr in safety conditions (associated with an o.e..p.r. less than 10^{-9}/hr) and 2 km/hr + 2% for traffic management (with an o.e.p.r. less than 10^{-3}/hr).
The reliability objective for *ODO Safety Control Unit*'s missions is 5000 hrs with nominal performance. In case of sensor failure, the accuracy of output data can be degraded but not output data fail-safeness. The reliability objective for the *ODO Safety Control Unit*'s missions is 50 000 hrs with minimum performance (before total odometric loss requiring visual navigation).

153

The *ODO Safety Control Unit* has to take into consideration the diversity of the rolling stock, of the network and climatic conditions.

DEVELOPMENT
PROCEDURE

The *ODO Safety Control Unit* was developed in two phases which consisted in a Feasibility Study and the Development of Entrainable Prototypes.

Feasibility Study

The objective of this phase was to define the architecture of the *ODO Safety Control Unit*'s system and the architecture of its measurement processing algorithms. The Feasibility Study consisted of analyzing a number of sensors' operating and inoperating characteristics, then of defining the related algorithms after a first selection was made. The study proper involved the ideal simulation of potential sensors (static performance, statistics, major functional failure modes), the detailed simulation of the *ODO Safety Control Unit*'s behavior during a mission and according to sensors' performance, the occurrence of failures and the organization of associated processings, and the execution of system and safety studies. Theoretical analyses were compared to actual recordings of measurements made on test railroad cars belonging to the SNCF. Then, these actual measurements were input in the processing algorithms loaded on the *ODO Safety Control Unit*'s simulator to check their adequation. The *ODO Safety Control Unit*'s simulator was described in ADA. It corresponds to approximately 12 000 lines of the code and is operated from a UNIX work station (see Fig. 1).

Development of Prototypes

It includes the development of safety-oriented computer prototypes at the SNCF format and of the *ODO Safety Control Unit*'s application software; then it also includes the development of a validation environment for the *ODO Safety Control Unit*, used for integrated software setting operations up to tests on site. In its comprehensive version, it integrates the *ODO Safety Control Unit*'s simulator during acceptance phases at the factory. Accordingly, it makes it possible to prepare complex mission profiles, to simulate sensor failures, and to use automatic tools for the reduction of simulator output data. An assistance environment aboard trains is useful for final settings, punctual diagnosis and performance analysis. Five prototypes are supplied to the SNCF which can therefore carry out performance tests over long time periods (two prototypes) and functional tests in safety conditions, *ASTREE*, in the scope of the "Safety-oriented Test" (three prototypes).

MEASUREMENT
PRINCIPLES ADOPTED

Measurement

The Feasibility Study demonstrated that the basic sensor which best met the requirements is the Doppler effect radar. This measurement, which is not safety-oriented when unique and unprocessed, must be consolidated by another equivalent measurement. The principle of functional redundancy which implies the use of another type of sensor (locked phonic wheel, accelerometer, etc.) or status data, was generally rejected since it rapidly led to a complex measurement architecture, or implied considering an excessive amount of data concerning the mobile or the railroads, and in all cases involved an increase of recurrent costs. The studies demonstrated that specified objectives could be reached by simply using an architecture based on physical redundancy and appropriate algorithms. A locked phonic wheel is used to detect possible motions at very low speed.

Repositioning

Since errors concerning the travelled distance accumulate, repositioning is carried out at regular intervals as the train passes by hyperfrequency beacons which are secured onto the railroad. The beacons are identified individually and distances between them are announced by the control center. These distances depend on the accuracy level required for traffic management. Safety is ensured in all cases. The principles defined above allow the adaptation of the system to the entire rolling stock, without any special requirement concerning the railroad.

Processing

The use of standard sensors led to the implementation of intrinsec measurement verification techniques (pre-processings), of value comparison techniques (vote), and of filtering techniques (Kalman filter) to reach the safety and availability objectives while complying with nominal accuracy objectives. The *ODO Safety Control Unit* currently uses three radars, one beacon reader and one phonic wheel (see Fig. 2). Specific triggered tests are implemented to detect hidden potential sensor failures. These processings are operated by the safety-oriented processing unit described below.

NOMINAL AND DEGRADED OPERATING MODES

The *ODO Safety Control Unit* operates in nominal mode when three or only two radars are serviceable. In predicted mode, which is limited in time, one single radar supplies a validated measurement. This second case makes it possible to overcome transient measurement errors if one radar has already failed. As a complement to the nominal mode, two "degraded" functional modes were defined to extend the operationability of the system. The principle adopted (see Fig. 3) admits a degraded accuracy of measurements while maintaining safety performance. Mode D1 corresponds to the loss of redundancy (failure of 2 radars out of three) and makes validation possible when passing by beacons. Mode D2 corresponds to the loss of any repositioning possibility when passing by beacons and leads to a progressive degradation until the next repositioning.

SAFETY-ORIENTED COMPUTERS - GENERAL DESIGN PRINCIPLES

Recall of objectives

TECHNICATOME safety-oriented computers are designed to meet major safety requirements pertaining to entrained applications. The main objectives are:
- *High intrinsic reliability*: approximately 50 000 hrs for the computer in severe environmental conditions,
- *Unpredictable failure probability rate* less than 10^{-9}/hr for the computer,
- *High computing power* (> 2 Mips in safety conditions).
TECHNICATOME applied these principles for TNFPs* mostly used for the control/monitoring of Nuclear Steam Supply Systems and CSGs*, a

version of which forms the heart of the *ODO Safety Control Unit*'s computer. (TNFP* : Traducteurs Numériques pour Fonctions de Protection, *digital translators for protection functions*; CGS*: Carte Sécuritaire de Gestion, *safety-oriented management card*).

Processing unit architecture - Principles

To avoid unpredictable failures, the general following principles are adopted concerning the processing unit architecture: monoprocessor hardware, duplex software, use of standard components. These principles are implemented under the following conditions: time dual software structure, monitoring and sequencing systems, one vote hardware system, design principles preventing any latency of failure. These conditions must be applied in a consistent manner in order to reach the safety objective (10^{-9} unpredictable failures/hr). Experience shows that these safety-oriented principles do not significantly compromise the usual performance of the processing unit: the extra cost for the hardware (reliability/dimensions/consumption) is limited to 15% compared with a non safety-oriented unit. The processing unit performance is 50% of that of a non safety-oriented unit. The use of standard components makes it possible to reach the industrial perenniality objectives pertaining to these fields of application.

"Dual time" structure

In order to detect potential hardware failures, the processing software is doubled to achieve dual processing. Specific conditions are implemented to de-correlate software processing using hardware equipment: duplication of memory resources associated with vital functions, logic segregation of resources through the addressing systems and control of access, use of specific structures for simplex resources such as interrupts. During the design phase, the software selected is either of twin-check type or dissymmetrical, depending on cases. The alternative is chosen according to application requirements. It must be noted that in a dual structure, the maximum effort for the implementation of a dissymmetrical structure must be made during the specification phase and, during the design phase, by taking the constraints imposed by the target system into consideration. As regards these two points, the introduction of an actual diversity is often much more difficult to achieve.

Sequence monitoring

Sequence monitoring is considered with special attention during software and hardware design: systematic data updating at short repetition period, monitoring of software operation during elementary procedure chaining, development of a cyclic software and specific management of interrupts, use of two clocks and safe watchdogs. Specific measures are taken to guarantee their operation.

Voter

A hardware voter is used systematically for safety-oriented information. According to the needs, it consists of a dynamic logic failsafe voter including a sequence check (acting on computer outputs) and of an analog data digital voter (ODO Safety Control Unit) applied to certain intermediate data and final values. Voter operation is independent of the microprocessor.

Hardware design with no latency of failures

All hardware watch systems are either failsafe or controlled. They have full control on the processing unit. Identically, all major components (ROM, RAM, microprocessor, etc.) are subjected to cyclic redundancy checks to avoid potential latent failures of sub-assemblies that are not activated at a given time (protection against latent failure propagation). As a complement, our experience led us to implement individual instruction checks through associated Hamming codings. This measure complements the ROM periodical check.

SOFTWARE ENVIRONMENT

For the development of safety-oriented software, TECHNICATOME uses a methodology which is backed by a software workshop and which is based on the maximum use of standard tools and methods (Teamwork[1], Keyone[2], CMF[3], etc.). They cover all development phases from software specification up to validation, configuration management. All real-time management and safety functions of CSG software form a "basic function library" linked with application software via automatic tools.

HARDWARE ARCHITECTURE PRESENTATION

General layout (see Fig.4)

The CSG is a single monoprocessor card. All resources are located on the card and communications with the exterior are achieved by means of asynchronous series links, a "slow series safety-oriented bus" which provides for communications with interface cards while guaranteeing the non-introduction of common modes (redundant interfaces), a slow bus in parallel for non safety-oriented utilities (for example: displays).

Basic resources

In its standard version, the card includes the following resources:
- 68020-68882 at 20 MHz,
- PROM-readable codes (base up to 256 KB),
- Series links RS232 (base up to 6),
- 2 slow buses.

Safety ASIC

Most hardware watch functions (dynamic watchdogs, specific address decodings, bus access control circuits, etc.) as well as certain functional utilities (timers, etc.) of the CSG card are grouped in an ASIC-type component. Thus, the card MTBF is considerably increased. It must be noted that this ASIC is not dedicated to a given microprocessor but can be associated with most 16- or 32-bits microprocessors.

PARTICULARIZATION OF THE PROCESSING UNITS

The policy developed in the field of safety-oriented processing units consists of making a "solution" package available: failsafe ASIC, base library, development/validation methodology. CSG cards can be adapted to the special features of applications, including processing resources as well as mechanical packaging and hardening. The *ODO Safety Control Unit* computer CSG card is at the Double Europe format extended with stiffeners. A version at Simple Europe format with stiffeners and thermal drains is currently being analyzed.

PROCESSING UNIT SAFETY DEMONSTRATION

For every application, the use of the CSG card is backed by a global methodology based on the computer conformity proving, and on the evaluation of the processing unit unpredictable failure rate.

Conformity proving

The key points of this methodology are as follows: implementation of the Quality Plan in compliance with usual critical application standards (D0178, CEI880, etc.); implementation of a software workshop supporting this methodology, the automatic test and replay of the various tests executed, and the implementation of an independent structure to carry out functional acceptances.

Evaluating the processing unit unpredictable failure rate

The existence of an unpredictable failure rate has been evidenced since 1984 by the fault injection technique. This principle is based on the simulation of hardware failures on a Central Processing Unit equipped with the operational software and functionally active. Its behavior is observed when in presence of injected faults intended to evaluate the following indicators: unsecure rate (percentage of failures which resulted in a potentially dangerous action of the computer), Detection Rate (percentage of failures detected by the computer). The unpredicatable failure rate of the computer is determined by the failure rate of the computer (depending on component types and environments) and the unsecure failure (or detection) indicator. The injection of faults is controlled automatically during test campaigns carried out over several weeks which allow to study several millions of failures on a Central Processing Unit. TECHNICATOME has been implementing this procedure for more than 7 years now, and has a methodology and specific tools to conduct test campaigns.

DEVELOPMENT OF SAFETY-ORIENTED COMPUTERS HISTORY

The main steps of this development are the following:

Generation 1 - 1984/1990 - TNFP Computer
1984 - On nuclear reactor Land Prototype (PAT), putting into service of 8 pre-series computers in view of concept validation. These computers control the reactor "safety injection". They have been operating 24 hours a day since.
1989 - On consideration of this experiment, integration of 50 computers on a nuclear reactor; these computers execute all reactor safety actions (10^6 cumulated running hours).
1990 - development of the TSAR system ["ARIANE" launcher destruction remote control (ground station)].
1991 - Integration on board the new-generation nuclear submarine of a command/control system basically using TNFP computers.

Generation 2 - 1989/ ... - Central Processing Unit CSG card
1989/1990 - Design studies concerning Generation 2 safety-oriented computers. Definition of CSG and safety-oriented ASIC.
1991 - Development of the CSG card, the heart of new safety-oriented computers. Validation of the CSG prototype : 4th quarter 1991.
1992 - Production of a CSG pre-series for qualification and development of the "ODO Safety Control Unit" ASTREE computer.

CONCLUSION

The ODO Safety Control Unit is a high-performance safety-oriented system installed aboard trains. The structured chaining of design and test phases, and the implementation of homogeneous safety-oriented hardware and software techniques, have made it possible to reach specified objectives while optimizing system architecture and recurrent costs. The demonstration of product conformity is based on a coherent set of design studies and tests, in particular as regards the fault injection technique applied to the operational computer.

1. Teamwork is a registered trademark of CADRE TECHNOLOGIES
2. Keyone is a registered trademark of LPS.
3. CMF is a registered trademark of EXPERTWARE.

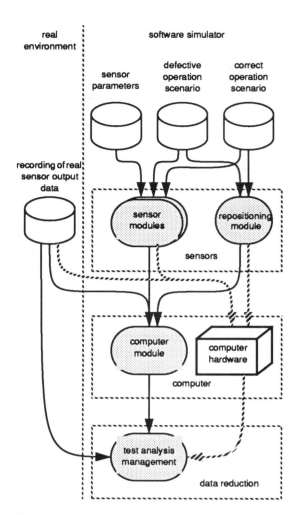

Fig. 1 : Simulator structure

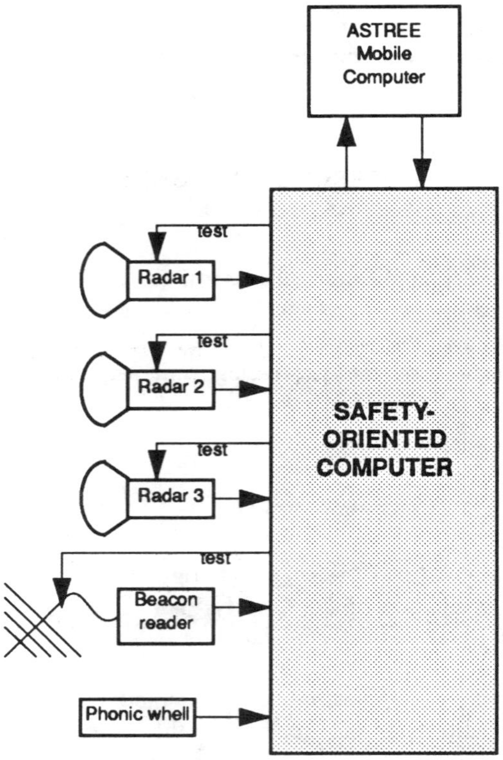

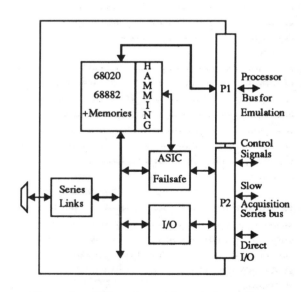

Fig. 2 : Hardware architecture

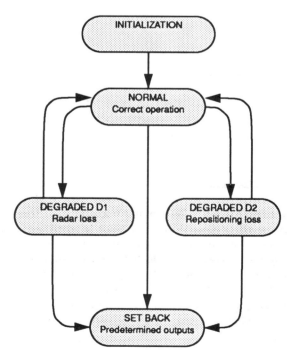

Fig. 3 : Operating modes

Fig. 4 : CSG - Functional layout (Double Europe Version)

TESTING OF A COMPUTER BASED INTERLOCKING SOFTWARE: METHODOLOGY AND ENVIRONMENT.

Abbaneo C., Biondi G., Ferrando M., Mongardi G.

ANSALDO TRASPORTI s.p.a., via dei Pescatori 35, GENOVA-ITALY

Abstract: Ansaldo Trasporti Computer Based Interlocking System "ACC" is based on multiprocessor architecture and software developed with safety criteria.

It achieves the same levels of safety and availability as relay interlocking.

Safety and availability are fundamental attributes of dependability requirements for the ACC system; they are assured by the following fault avoidance and fault tolerance techniques:
- development methodology (Structured Analysis and Design),
- independent Verification & Validation (V&V) methodology,
- fault-detection techniques,
- software diversity for the three sections of TMR developed by different teams using different languages,
- software voting of results.

This paper discusses in some detail:
- adopted V&V methodology,
- V&V environment.

V&V activities are carried out during the whole software development cycle ("Step by Step V&V"), in parallel with the project team activities.

V&V activities are conducted separately from software development activities by an independent group. This organization increases the V&V efficiency to avoid repeating specification misconception during V&V phases.

Software tools have been especially developed for V&V activities.

Data related with errors found during the different V&V phases and data logged during the first period of ACC real service will be examined.

Keywords: Railway interlocking, vital architecture, dependability, safety, reliability, Verification & Validation, Functional Coverage, Development Cycle, Functional and Structural Testing.

INTRODUCTION

ACC general requirements can be briefly defined as the main features of dependability - i.e. safety and availability - as well as modularity, maintainability, diagnosticability and configurability.

In order to fulfill the above requirements and in view of the characteristics and requirements of the systems to be controlled - such as lay-out, mechanical and electro-mechanical installation conditions, areas available for installation, connection cable economic requirements - a distributed type of architecture was designed for the ACC, whereby processing nodes are redundant, operate on the grounds of comparison and majority voting criteria, and are interconnected by means of a communication network ensuring fail-safe data exchange.

As far as fault-avoidance is concerned, the design principles and employed implementation techniques ensure to a reasonable extent avoidance of design errors both in hardware and software:
- the project was organized and planned according to the International Standards applicable;
- a Quality Assurance Plan was drawn up in compliance with the relevant International Standards;
- a specific methodology relevant to design, verification and validation was defined and approved both for hardware and software; a team of engineers was appointed for the verification and approval, fully independent of the team in charge of the design;
- a complete system testing plan was drawn up, also defining an ACC testing environment with

testing tools.

The ACC consists of two subsystems that independently perform vital and non vital functions respectively (see Fig.1).

The vital section consists of a central unit - Safety Nucleous (NS) - and of a peripheral section, consisting of a number of peripheral Units, whose number depends on the size of the controlled station; such posts are connected by means of a fail-safe communication system using a custom- designed protocol.

The NS controls an operator interface consisting of functional key- boards and synoptic panels to be used by the traffic controller to interact with the system and send the commands required for traffic management in the station.

For the NS an architecture based on three parallel connected computer sections was adopted, to create a "2-out-of-3" majority logic (triple modular redundancy - TMR) with a fail-safe external hardware device detecting any disagreement of a section; when such a disagreement is detected, the section is cut off from the configuration (Exclusion Logic - LE).

The TMR configuration with safety exclusion logic adopted in the central post combines the safety characteristics of "two-out-of-two" systems with the availability resulting from the redundancy already present in the system; in the case of faults in a unit, the LE cuts off the unit in disagreement so that a further fault in one of the two units which are still operating cannot be summed up to the first and cause majority error.

The three NS sections independently perform the same functions.
The software architecture and operating environment are exactly the same.
Diversity has been adopted, however, for the development of application software modules running in the three NS sections, that implement interlocking safety logic, route selection and operator interface functions.

The software of the NS, apart from the application programs, also includes modules for the execution of diagnostic testing of all hardware components, and the control of the correct operation of the actual application programs.

For the Trackside Peripheral Units (TPU) a vital architecture (2-out-of-2) was adopted, equipped with fail-safe hardware circuits that force the TPU outputs into a safe status,in the case of discrepancy between the two units.

THE METHODOLOGY OF VERIFICATION AND VALIDATION

The correctness and reliability of the software are made by the application of formal and rigorous methods both for development and verification and validation.

The methodology of V&V generally adopted for the ACC design is of the "step-by-step" type (6,7).

The activity of V&V is carried out during the complete cycle of software development in parallel to the design activity; it is not an activity added on at the end, but rather a more diversified activity, in which each part of the product development corresponds to an adequate verification and validation action.

This allows for the timely identification of any errors made during the design and development phases; consequently:

- an error occurring in a development cycle phase cannot have any effect on a successive phase, since it is corrected immediately;
- the correction of errors is facilitated, with a

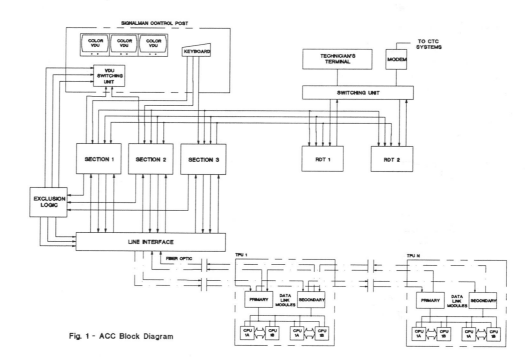

Fig. 1 - ACC Block Diagram

160

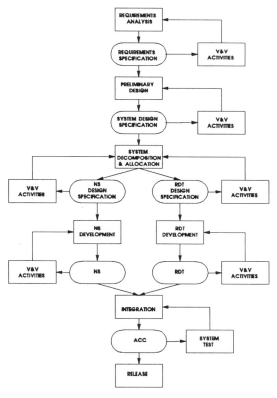

Fig. 2 - ACC Development Cycle

The V&V methodology adopted required the complete separation of the design group from the V&V group. This system of organization increased the effectiveness of the verification and validation since:

- erroneous interpretations of problems or requirements, made during the development, are not repeated in the verification phase,
- the objective of the V&V, that is the exposure of errors, is more easily achieved if the persons do not have to revise their own work.

THE ACTIVITIES OF V&V

The development cycle adopted for the software of the ACC design is described in detail in Fig. 2: the activities for the design group and the V&V group are shown for each phase, together with the documents produced.

A "diversity" technique is adopted for the functions of safety subsystem, that is by the use of three different programs, one for each computer, which carry out the same functions. From the functional specification three design specifications and three codes are produced, and for each of these three V&V activities are independently carried out (see Fig. 3).

The V&V methods and techniques adopted for the ACC project differ according to the phases into which the development cycle are subdivided.

The following paragraphs describe for each phase the choices made, the documents produced, the procedures followed during the course of the activities, and the tools developed to support the activity.

V&V of Requirements Specification

The V&V activity of the requirements specification consists of a "revision", intended as a series of criticisms of the document, with the aim of:

- verifying that the specification contains all the parts established during the phase of standards definition,
- points out the inconsistencies between different requirements,
- highlights imprecisions, unsatisfied references,

consequent reduction of the probability of introducing further errors.

This results in a higher level of confidence in the accuracy of the system, together with reduction in the time and cost of development.

The adoption of the verification and validation methodology described also allows for achieving a higher overall quality and reliability of the final software product, since the documentation produced is verified at every phase of the development, resulting in a product which is easy to maintain and modify.

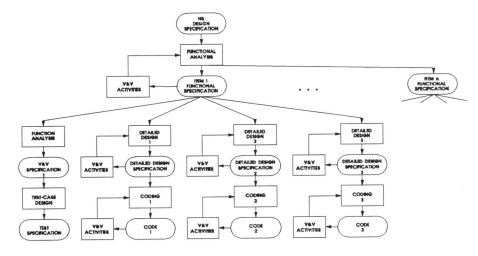

Fig. 3 - NS Development

incompletion,
- classify and analyze each requirement having regard to its characteristics,
- distinguish between functional requirements and quality functions,
- check the verifiability of requirements, or rather the possibility of their implementation.

After defining the requirements to be verified a "verification matrix" will be drawn up, indicating the chapter or paragraph of the subsequent documents where each software requirement is repeated or specified in order to follow the evolution and assist in the verification.

V&V of Technical Specifications

The Technical Specifications of the System and of the Subsystems constitute the initial concrete form of the product requirements and indicate in general the replies and solutions which will be adopted during development. These are also the references for the entire process of Quality Assurance of the system.

A first aspect of the verification of the Technical Specification is to specify the software requirements covered by the general solutions adopted.
A second aspect of the V&V of the Technical Specifications concerns the verification and validation of their functional analysis; this analysis is described both informally, in everyday language, and technically, in the "Structured Analysis" (SA).

The V&V for this part of these Specifications is, therefore, based on checking the text of the Specification and the description of the system given by the two models, that is:
1. a model of the data transformation, composed of:
   - Data Flow Diagrams (DFDs),
   - logic description of the changes (textual or using tables);
2. a dynamic model, composed of:
   - State Transition Diagrams (STDs).

This type of verification allows for an evaluation of system feasibility from an operational viewpoint: in fact, relations between subsystems, possible critical connections, other as yet hidden details required by the system, are shown here.

The matrix of requirements drawn up in the previous phase is updated, verifying that all the requirements of the Technical Specification have been satisfied.

V&V of Functional Specifications of Software Elements

Each Functional Specification is verified in comparison with the Subsystems Technical Specification.
The Decision Table Tool (8), based on the Decision Table described in literature (9), is used in order to validate and control the correctness and reliability of the project.

Using these guidelines, the entire specification is rewritten, permitting a rigorous control and pointing out any incompleteness or ambiguities caused by the use of everyday language. This method requires the taking into account of all combinations of input outlined in the specifications, and a description of the subsequent behavior of the system. The method also shows up any unscheduled input combinations or those for which no follow-up action has been specified.

The sequence of states which makes up the software is validated by means of State Transition Diagrams. The State Transition Diagrams indicate any impossible or "deadlock" conditions and allow the control of the uniformity of treatment of sequence analogue behavior.
The State Transition Diagrams are used both for the design phase and the verification phase: they are, however, produced independently by the design group and the V&V group, and any comparison between them can be a further means of verification.

V&V of Design Specifications

Each Design Specification is verified with regard to the corresponding Functional Specification by means of a careful check of each document.

The methodology of design adopted for the ACC is the "Composite Design" (12, 15); this methodology, mainly oriented towards modularity, is seen as the answer to the problem of difficulties and high implementation and maintenance costs of large systems.

The main objective is to divide the program into modules with a well defined function, which are as far as possible independent between themselves, in order to increase the quality of the software in terms of: reliability, ease of maintenance, ease in making modifications, and testability.

The V&V of the Design Specification verifies:
- that the design has been made following the methodology established during the phase of standards definition,
- that the "quality" requirements have been met,
- that the fault-tolerance techniques required for each software item have been adopted.

V&V and Testing of Code

The V&V of code of each program consists of:
- the assurance that each module has performed its specified function with regard to flow and input and output data,
- the assurance that the coding of each module has been carried out, according to the established programming techniques,
- the testing activity.

For the first two activities a comparison is made of the Design Specifications with the code tabulation.

The methods most frequently used for the testing of industrial software are (11, 13, 14):
- functional testing (black box testing)
- structural testing (white box testing).

The functional testing views the software as a "black box" without knowing the internal structure.
The scope of this approach is to find the circumstances in which the program does not behave according

to the specifications.

The structural testing is based on the analysis of the internal structure of the program, both for the representation of the data and the flow control.

Both methods have their limits:
- The functional testing is tied to the correctness of the functional specifications, from which all the data is taken for the tests ("test case"), leading to the possibility of an abstract idea of the functions, and not revealing their functional details.
- The structural testing does not guarantee that the program carries out the correct specified functions, it may detect the presence of errors, but not the omission of implementation of functions.

The testing of the ACC project adopted a prevalently functional type of approach, since it was considered more suitable for the system to be tested. Each NS program is structured with the minimum quantity of codes feasible, unchanging for different system configurations, used in the application of a series of data tables which permit the implementation of the program function.
In this case the operation of all the program paths would reveal the correct application of each type of table, but risks not checking many functions and severely limiting the effectiveness of the test.

It is, therefore, still necessary to face up to the limits in functional testing, as previously defined: the assurance of the correctness of the Functional Specifications is reached by means of the revision of the same specifications with the final user with regard to the applied functions, and by means of their verification and finalization in the Complete Decision Table and State Transition Diagrams. With regard to the lack of analysis of the functional details, it has been decided to combine the functional testing with a subsequent valuation as to how many and which parts of the program will be subjected to the functional test-case.

If the required objectives are not reached after this valuation, further functional test-cases will be instituted, with the aim of testing the components not already covered.

Test-cases selection. Exhaustive testing, which tests all the possible combinations of input data of a program, is considered impossible (9,10), and the choice of the test-cases therefore becomes the key to effective testing.

There remains the problem of establishing a method of selecting the test-cases so that the operation of the test ensures the highest probability of revealing any errors. The criteria chosen are:
- subdividing the input data into classes so that the assumption can be made that the execution of the test with a value of the class is equivalent to the execution with any other value of the same class; such classes are defined as "equivalence classes" (9,13);
- select a representative value for each equivalence class between the limiting values of the same class ("Boundary Value Analysis").

The choice of the test-cases for the V&V of the ACC project is made using the Complete Decision Tables.

This method of formalization of the functional specifications allows for a rigorous method in the construction of the test-cases, in addition to the verification of its coherence and completeness.
The general principle for the construction of the test-cases, starting from the Complete Decisions Table, is that of providing a test-case for each vertical input combination ("rule"), with the corresponding results attained being shown in the table.

Coverage criteria. The measurement of coverage is defined as the ratio between the portion of the software which has been tested compared to the total software to be tested.

With reference to the two methods of testing previously described, functional and structural testing, two steps can be identified (9):
- the functional coverage, given the ratio between the number of functions tested in comparison with the total quantity,
- the structural coverage, given the ratio between the number of components tested in comparison with the total quantity. The components examined may be the instructions, branches or paths.

The examination of the structural coverage takes into consideration one class of components, calls up the program whose data puts into effect the operation of the component, and with suitable instruments checks that the component has been examined.

The examination of the functional coverage takes into consideration the functions of the program described by the Functional Specification and uses the actual program with data that implement the execution of each single function.

Using the Complete Decision Table the grade of functional coverage is given by the ratio between the "rules" already implemented and those still to be put in operation.

The objectives of the coverage of testing for the ACC project are as follows:
- execute the test-case taken from the Complete Decision Table until the established functional coverage is obtained, that is the execution of all "rules" of all of the tables;
- calculate the structural coverage obtained (percentage of branches feasible) by means of functional testing;
- arrange additional test-cases to exercise the branches that remain unexplored.

The procedures adopted combine the objectives of functional and structural testing, testing all the functions that the software must execute and checking all the parts of the software at least once.

VERIFICATION AND VALIDATION ENVIRONMENT

For verification and validation of system operation and of software components, after the choice of methods to be adopted, dedicated software tools

Fig. 4 - V&V RESULTS FOR "DISPATCHER CONTROL POST"

Version of Functional Specification	1.0	2.0	2.1	2.2	3.0	3.1	3.2	3.3	4.0	4.1	4.2	5.0
N. report	36	51	44	31	15	16	8	9	8	5	1	6
Designed Test-case				905				810				1010
Executed Test-case				755				513				676
N. SPR (Software Problem Report)				48				21				13
Functional coverage (executed t./designed t.)				0,83				0,63				0,67
SPR/functional coverage				57,8				33,3				19,4

were designed and implemented to support or perform the required activities, accounting for an integrated V&V environment and fulfilling the specifications of the ACC system.

The above-mentioned tools are as follows:
- Decision Table Tool for the verification and validation of functional specifications
- Test-Case Specification Tool, for test case generation
- Test Driver, for test execution
- Flagger, for program instrumentation
- Simulator.

The Decision Table Tool (DTT) is based on the Complete Decision Table (DT) formalism in order to:
- formalize software functional specifications, so as to make verification and approval easier;
- identify and select functional test cases;
- guarantee that a given function is fully covered by Test-Cases and prevent Test-Case redundancy.

Test-case Specification Tool (TST) is a software tool for the construction of test documentation ("test specifications").
TST derives individual test-cases from Complete Decision Tables; it allows for controls between the number of test-cases constructed and those envisaged by the tables, and for easier means of modification and updating of the test-cases with regard to the tables.

The Test Driver (TED) allows guided execution of tests, including automatic recording of all the operations carried out by the operator, as well as of test results, so as to allow any test campaign, and the controls between the results obtained and those still to be executed, to be subsequently automatically repeated.
The use of TED does not modify the program being tested with the addition of useful instructions or commands.
TED was designed so as to allow simultaneous control of the TMR three sections. This allows both designers in the debugging stage and inspectors in the testing stage to interact with and verify the behavior of any software element, or of the entire NS software system on all three NS sections at the same time.

The Flagger is used to insert assertion statements in specific points of the programming code. Once a test campaign has been carried out, execution of these statements makes it possible to evaluate the obtained coverage, in terms of percentage of code branches.

DTT and TST were developed and run in a DEC-VMS environment. TED and Flagger run on a MODIAC unit.

The plant simulator is a software tool capable of real time simulating the controlled process.
It can be customized to the features of a given station or of a section of the railway line including more than one station; it simulates the behavior of field devices, thus providing the ACC with their status and position controls and reacting to commands originating from ACC or from its own operator interface.
Moreover, by varying the free/occupied status of track circuits, it can move trains on to the simulated yard. Lastly, it can also simulate all the typical field devices abnormal operations.

RESULTS

The data presented refers to the V&V activity used for an element of the Safety Unit chosen as a significant example: the "Dispatcher Control Post" which is used to obtain and check the operator imposed controls and their relevant displays.

With regard to the pattern of the failures, the data relating to site testing at the Genoa-Bolzaneto railway station have been analyzed.

This choice was based on the fact that the data obtained during testing does not allow a timely evaluation of the pattern of failures: the test-cases executed during the testing activity are made up in such a way as to try out all the functions of the program, but the sequence used does not reflect the user's circumstances, as happens with site testing.

The data collected during the V&V activity for the documents (Fig. 4 shows an example for the functional specification of the "dispatcher control post" software element) show a rapid decrease in modifications required over three or four versions. The reversals of the trend correspond to the issue of versions of the documents requested by the user that require functional modifications.

The three test series carried out for the "dispatcher control post" software element show a reduction of about 50% in errors in each successive test series.

This percentage of residual errors can be attributed to the modifications made to the code between one test series and another, due to modifications to the functional specifications (see Fig. 5).

Site testing began on September 1, 1991, and is still underway; the pattern of failures has been evaluated for the period from the 1st September 1991 to 30th April 1992 (see Fig. 6). During this period 36 failures were noted, of which 22 (see Fig. 7) were due to the software; of this last number two types of failure were found (the classification of types of errors is shown in Fig. 8):

- failures due to errors in configuration, that is errors in the compilation of data base which represent current practice (category "CO"),
- failure due to software errors, including coding errors, and errors in the interpretation of the specifications (category "SW").

Fig. 5

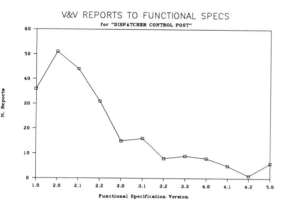

V&V REPORTS TO FUNCTIONAL SPECS
for "DISPATCHER CONTROL POST"

Fig. 6

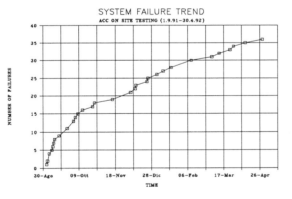

SYSTEM FAILURE TREND
ACC ON SITE TESTING (1.9.91–30.4.92)

Fig. 7

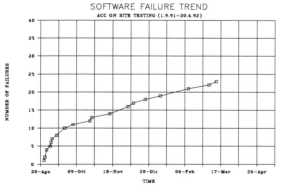

SOFTWARE FAILURE TREND
ACC ON SITE TESTING (1.9.91–30.4.92)

Fig. 8

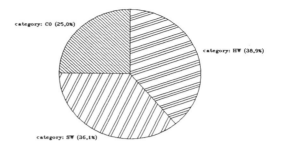

SYSTEM FAILURES
ACC ON SITE TESTING (1.9.91–30.4.92)

category: CO (25,0%)

category: HW (38,9%)

category: SW (36,1%)

REFERENCES

1. "Verification and Validation for Safety Parameter Display System", NSAC 39, 1981

2. "Guideline for Verification and Validation of Safety related Software", EWICS TC7 333, 1983

3. R. Dunn, "Software Defect Removal", McGraw-Hill Book Co.

4. B.W. Boehm, "Seven Basic Principles of Software Engineering", SW Engineering Techniques, INFOTEC State of the Art Report, 1977.

5. T. Thayer, M. Lipow, E. Nelson, "Software Reliability", TRW System and Energy.

6. M.S. Fujii, "Independent Verification of Highly Reliable Software", COMPSAC 77.

7. M.S. Deutsch, "Software Verification & Validation", Prentice-Hall Series of Software Engineering, 1982.

8. A.M. Traverso, "A Tool for Specification Analysis: Complete Decision Tables", SAFECOMP 85.

9. G.J. Myers, "The Art of Software Testing", Wiley & Sons, NY, 1979.

10. Goodenough, Gerhart, "Forward a Theory of Test Data selection", IEEE Transaction of Software Engineering, 1975.

11. "Software Validation, Verification and Testing Techniques and Tool Reference Guide", NBS Special Publication 500-93, 1982.

12. E. Yourdon, L. Constantine, "Structured Design", Prentice-Hall, 1979.

13. S. Klim, "Systematic Software Testing for Microcomputer System", Elektronic Centralen.

14. E.F. Miller, "Structural Techniques of Program Validation", COMPCON 74.

15. G.J. Myers, "Reliable Software through Composite Design", Van Nostrand Reinhold Company.

16. A. Avizienis, "The N-Version Approach to Fault-Tolerant Software", IEEE Trans. on Sw Engineering, December 1985.

Practical Experience with Safety Assessment of a System for Automatic Train Control

Tor Stålhane, Ph.D.,
Johan Fredrik Lindeberg,
SINTEF DELAB, 7034 Trondheim, Norway

Abstract.
The paper describes the models, testing and assessments done for an automatic train control system (ATC). The reliability and safety of the system is assessed by combining data from the quality assurance activities performed during the project and the acceptance test run before installation. The data are combined through a Bayesian framework.
In order to have an independent assessment of the reliability, we have also estimated the total number of errors and the number of errors remaining in the system. The number of remaining errors are "converted" to a MTTF via a table based on experience. This MTTF is, however, used for auxiliary assessment only.
The paper concludes that the system can be put into operation under certain conditions

Keywords: Software engineering; Reliability; Quality control; Bayes methods;

INTRODUCTION.

This paper describes the work done at DELAB during the development and commissioning of a system for automatic train control (ATC). We will give a short description of the system, the strategies chosen for verification and validation and the models chosen by DELAB in order to assess the safety and reliability that was achieved. Finally, we draw some conclusions and try to point out some consequences for further work in the area.

SYSTEM DESCRIPTION.

The delivery consists of two systems, called system 1 and system 2. They are developed by different companies and will be installed in two different parts of the railway network.

System 1 consists of a single computer, partly duplicated hardware interface and dual channel software. It consists of a total of 70 KLOC and is written in a PLM-like language.

System 2 consists of a duplicated computer, partly duplicated hardware interfaces and single-channel software. It consists of 15 KLOC and is written in assembler. The data used for reliability and safety assessment are from this system. Thus, our conclusions are at the present relevant for system 2 only.

Both systems are made from the same customer's specification. The functionality and man-machine interface are the same for both systems.

The following simple diagram shows the main parts of the ATC system.

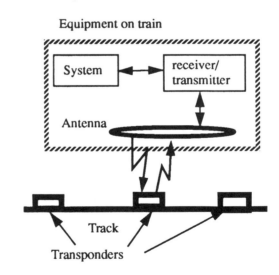

Figur 1 Simple system block diagram.

The ATC systems considered in this paper contains both operational and safety functions in the same computer.

TESTING STRATEGY.

The final testing is done in two steps. These steps are shown in fig. 2 and 3 below.

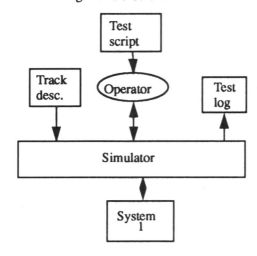

Figur 2 Step one: Build a basis for comparison in step 2. This set-up is also used for single system test.

When we have built the test log from the track description plus the test script for system 1, we use this test log as a basis for comparison when testing system 2.

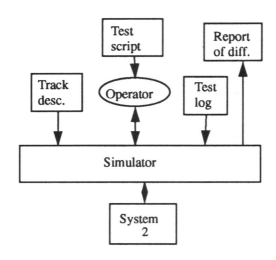

Figur 3 Step two: Testing system 2 and comparing with results form system 1.

If any differences are observed, the reasons for these are tracked down and will probably lead to changes to either system 1 or system 2. In some cases, however, the specification must be changed or enhanced

Supplier 1 tests each software channel separately before they are installed together with the comparator software in the target computer. Neither of the channels are exhaustively tested.

Supplier 2 tests the software against a complete one channel implementation, written i Ada, in a back-to-back configuration. This methods is comparable to a dual-channel solution provided that we achieve nearly exhaustive testing relative to the perceived input space.

In all cases, the test operator is an experienced engineer. For most of the test cases he can rely on the alarms build into the simulator. When necessary, he can resort to visual inspection of the test log and the behaviour of the (simulated) train.

The testing of each system has been done with 800 test scenarios. The tests have been fed to the systems via the test scripts as shown in figures 2 to 4. Each passing of (a set of) track transponders is considered as an atomic test case. The 800 test scenarios contain a total of ca. 150 000 atomic test cases. Each test scenario is combined with 15 different train speed profiles, thus bringing the total number of atomic test cases up to 150 000. As a comparison, it should be noted that the railway in question is 10 000 km. long and has 15 000 transponder sets. The customer has estimated the test compression factor to be more than 10. Due to this, the customer consider that the 150 000 atomic test cases corresponds to normal operation for a period of 15 years.

RELIABILITY VS. SAFETY.

For the project at hand, we will focus on reliability rather than safety. In order to defend this rather heretical stance, we argue as follows:

Compare two control systems Z1 and Z2 with their respective reliability R1 and R2. Z1 will be fail-safe while Z2 is not. For most systems it will follow that Z1 will be less reliable than Z2. Let the reliability of the total system, with the control system turned off, be R0.

What separates the system under consideration here from some other safety critical systems, is that the system must keep on operating even if the computer control system fails and turns itself off. Thus, any fail-to-safe action leaves us not in a safe state, but in a state with a much higher risk than before.

Thus, for control systems which are part of systems that can not be stopped in case of a failure or any other stoppage, high reliability may be more important than the fail-to-safe property. We consider the ATC systems to be systems of this type.

MODELS FOR RELIABILITY AND SAFETY PREDICTIONS.

For a system such as the one we are considering in this paper, we need to use all available information. Just a simple reliability estimate, based on testing is not enough. This has the following implications:

- We must use a Bayesian approach for the reliability where the prior is constructed from the total set of quality assurance activities during development

- We must gather supporting evidence by estimating the number of errors in the software; both the total number of errors and the number of errors remaining after release

- We must look at alternate ways to do reliability estimation. In our case we have focused on alternative ways of estimating the MTTF

We will discuss each of the selected approaches in one of the following subsections.

Reliability. For reliability, we have chosen to use the checklists made by Soisteman and Ragsdale (1985) to construct a Beta prior for the reliability. The method is straightforward, see for instance Stålhane (1991).

The number of tests and failures from the V&V, simulation and field tests can be used to improve on the prior in a straightforward manner. If we let the subscripts v, s and f denote the results pertaining to V&V, simulation and field tests respectively, and further more let the number of test be denoted by Y while the number of failures is denoted by X, we can write:

$$\hat{R}_0 = 1 - \frac{\beta + X_v + X_s + X_f}{\alpha + \beta + Y_v + Y_s + Y_f}$$

It is also straightforward to find the lower bound for this estimate once we have decided on a confidence level for our reliability estimate.

The reliability estimates developed from the prior can be considered to be valid for the whole system. The improved estimates are, however, depending on the quality of the sampling done when selecting test cases.

Safety. We will define software safety (S) as follows:

S = P(system will not fail in a dangerous way)

We will denote the probability of being in a dangerous way by P_{danger}. By some simple manipulation we can then change the definition of safety to:

$$\hat{S} = 1 - (1 - \hat{R}) \hat{P}_{danger}$$

A dangerous failure can further more be described as a combination of two events as follows:

- The control system is in a potential safety critical state. The probability of being in such a state is denoted by P_{d1}

- The train is in a potentially dangerous state where a safety critical failure can lead to an accident. The train's probability of being in such a state is denoted P_{d2}

The safety can then be written as:

$$S = 1 - (1 - R) P_{d1} P_{d2}$$

Mean Time To Failure. When the system "settles down" to a steady, low failure rate, we can write the connection between reliability and MTTF as:

$$MTTF = -\frac{T}{\ln(R)}$$

We can thus compare two reliability estimates stemming from two different methods. If they agree to the same order of magnitude, this will give us increased confidence in the reliability estimates.

Number of Errors. Under the assumption that all errors have the same probability of being discovered, we can use the capture - recapture technique to estimate the number of errors. The following results are taken from Rudner (1977):

$$\hat{N}_{rem} = \frac{s \cdot t}{\max\{c, 0.5\}}$$

N is the initial number of errors, s is the number of errors found by the first debugger, t is the number of errors found by the second debugger and c is the number of seeded errors found by the second debugger. See also figure 5. The total number of errors - N_0 - is estimated as:

$$\hat{N}_0 = \hat{N}_{rem} + (s + t - c)$$

As mentioned above, the capture - recapture model builds on the assumption that all errors have the same probability of being found during testing. This will, however, not be the case for most software systems. In particular, there exist some errors with a high probability of being found. These will be found in the first round by both parties and thus make the first c (common errors) much too high. For this reason, it may be wise to ignore the first N_0 estimate, since its value will be much too low.

In our case, we have not seeded errors into the system. We have instead used the following approach:

1. The customer run his test set and note all errors.

2. Only the number of errors found (s) is reported back to the project group, not how or where they were found. The errors found here is considered to be seeded.

3. The project group has to make their own tests and corrections. The number of errors found by the test team is t.

If we uses a confidence interval of 90%, we can now compute the upper (u) and lower (l) limits of this interval as follows:

$$\hat{N}_{u,l} = \hat{N} \left(1 + \frac{1.35}{c} \pm 1.64 \sqrt{\frac{1}{c} - \frac{0.68}{c^2}} \right)$$

This result holds under the assumption that c is normally distributed for any fixed N.

For a Bayesian approach on the number of errors we have selected the non-parametric Bayesian estimate as developed by Colombo et al (1988). If we let the subscripts prior, post and obs denote prior, posterior and observations respectively, the non-parametric Bayes estimator is:

$$F_{post}(.) = \frac{n}{n+m} F_{prior}(.) + \frac{m}{n+m} F_{obs}(.)$$

The two constant m and n are the subjective and observed number of observations respectively. n - the subjective count - is a measure of our confidence in the prior.

MTTF Based on Error Density. There exists estimates for MTTF based on the observed or estimated error density. For our work, we will use the table below, published by C. Jones and quoted by M. Brooks (1982).

Table 1: MTTF based on Errors / KLOC

Error density	MTTF estimate
> 30	1 minute
20 - 30	4 - 5 minutes
10 - 20	1 hour
5 - 10	several hours
2 - 5	24 hours
1 - 2	several days
0.5 - 1	1 month

Table 1: MTTF based on Errors / KLOC

Error density	MTTF estimate
< 0.01	indefinite

These estimates should be taken with some grains of salt (quantum satis) but they seems to be in some agreement with common computer experience. Note also that the MTTF's in the table are only valid for "common operations", which we have equated with "normal operations".

With the caveats above in mind, we can compare this MTTF estimate against the one computed previously and see if the two results are in the same ball park.

There is, however, another way to use the N estimate:

• large N estimate indicates that the quality assurance activities in the project have not been good enough

• small N estimates indicates that the development has been under adequate quality control throughout the project

In order to carry this approach any further, we need to consider what is meant by a large or small N. In a report published by the RADC, McCall et al (1987) have given the following number for an acceptable error density in process control systems.:

$$\text{Number of errors} / (KLOC) = 1.8$$

A commonly used rule of thumb is that the number of errors found during operation is 10% of the number of errors found during integration and system tests. In this case, we would get an operational error density of 0.18 errors per 1000 lines of code. This is in agreement with the experience that we need less than 0.2 errors per 1000 lines of code in order to have software that is reliable enough to be released to the users. This observation is confirmed by S.J. Keene (1992) who has gathered information on the software written for the NASA space shuttle. This software has never failed in operation and its fault density is estimated to 0.11 faults per KLOC. We will use the rule that:

• N > 1.8 errors per KLOC => low confidence

• N < 1.8 errors per KLOC => high confidence

RELIABILITY AND SAFETY ESTIMATES.
The model of Soisteman and Ragsdale. By use of the standard check lists that are defined by Soisteman and Ragsdale, we have computed estimates of the reliability of the system based on the quality assurance activities performed during development. We found the following values:
Rworst = 0.9932, Rnominal = 0.9934

and thus $\sigma = 0.0002$. In order to include personnel uncertainties in the standard deviation estimate, we will base our Beta prior on a σ-value of 0.0004. See Stålhane (1991) for a discussion of prior distributions form this model. This gives us that R a priori is Beta(88.27, 0.45) distributed.

In the prior used for this evaluation, the effect of all tests done inside the project is included in the Beta prior. We will thus only include the results of the final test suite here. In the final test, a total of 150 000 atomic tests (transponder passing) were executed. None of these failed and our final reliability estimate based on the Soisteman and Ragsdale's model is thus $R = 1 - 3.0*10^{-6}$. This gives us a MTTF of circa 3.3 years.

We are, however, more interested in the safety. In order to compute this value, we must have an estimate for P_{danger}. The customer estimates the two probability components used to find P_{danger} as 10^{-3} and $2*10^{-2}$ respectively. This gives us $P_{danger} = 2*10^{-5}$.

Let the average number of transponder passages per train per year be denoted by PT - 10^5 - and the total number of trains be TR. In our case TR is 1000. The expected number of accidents per year - E(AC) - is then given as

$$E(AC) = TR \cdot PT \cdot (1 - R) \cdot P_{d1} \cdot P_{d2}$$

By inserting the estimates for the system under consideration, we get that the expected number of accidents per year is 0.006. The system is expected to be in operation for 10 years and the expected number of accidents over this period is thus 0.06, which is considered acceptable.

In order to have a proper perspective on the reliability number, the following data, published by Det norske Veritas, are of interest:

Table 2: Accident probabilities per year and unit for some means of transportation

Accident type	Probability
Total ship wreck per year	$0.6*10^{-2}$
Death of a North American per year (all causes)	$5.5*10^{-3}$
Fatal car accident in a Canadian city per year	$5*10^{-4}$
Aeroplane crash per year	$2.8*10^{-6}$
Safety critical failure for the ATC II per year	$6.0*10^{-6}$

We can conclude form this table that the ATC system has a safety critical failure rate which is only twice as high as that of the crash probability of an aeroplane and that is more than 100 times as safe as a private car in a Canadian city.

The Capture - Recapture model. The customer and the producer has both tested the system. The test cases can be considered to be independent. The table below shows the test results. The derived estimates are shown in fig. 5:

Table 3: Errors found for System 2

no.	Producer	Customer	Common
1	25	36	17
2	29	30	11
3	23	21	13
4	0 - 1	0 - 2	0

The effect of a too high first c is value is clearly seen.

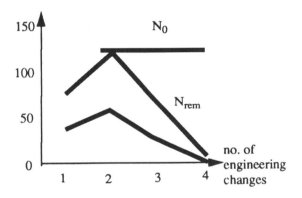

Figur 4 Estimates for N_0 and N_{rem} as functions of the number of engineering changes

The subjective estimate for N_0 made by the quality assurance personnel is N0 = 150. We have chosen to give the estimate based on capture - recapture four times as much weight as the subjective estimates. Thus, we find that:

$$N_0^* = \frac{4}{5}125 + \frac{1}{5}150 \approx 130$$

For the number of remaining errors, the same team has given an estimate of 15 errors. In the same way as above, we find:

$$N_{rem}^* = \frac{4}{5}4 + \frac{1}{5}15 \approx 6$$

The size of the system is 15 KLOC. This gives an errors density of 8.7. This is way above our limit of 1.80 and we can thus not have confidence in the system's quality on the basis of its error density.

The main reason for this high error density is most likely that the systems functional specification has been changed three times during development, in one case in a quite drastic manner. Such changes do not inspire confidence.

The number of remaining errors is less than 6. Thus the density of remaining errors is less than 0.40 errors per KLOC. This is four times as much as S.J. Keen (1992) observed for the NASA Space Shuttle software. If we use the table of C. Jones we find that this corresponds to a MTTF of a little more than a month.

CONCLUSIONS.

The conclusion is split into two parts. Part one is concerned with general experience deducted form the ATC project, while part two is concerned with our recommendations to the customer concerning the ATC-II system.

General recommendations. We make the following recommendations concerning methods:

- The model of Soisteman and Ragsdale plus test information is well suited to make reliability assessments

- When using the capture - recapture technique for estimation of error content, it is important to beware of the effect of the errors with a over-average probability of being found by both parties

- When using statistical methods for reliability assessment, it is of paramount importance that the statistician is employed in the process of defining test data, test procedures and failure data collection.

Recommendations concerning ATC II. We have chosen to recommend that the system is put into operation. The reasons for this are that:

- The reliability and safety assessments are sufficiently good

- Even though the number of remaining errors is high, we believe that the remaining errors have a low probability.

Our acceptance thus hinge on the representativeness of the tests. The customer and the producers must cooperate in order to make sure that no new operational states appear due to changes in placement of transponders, signalling lights or operational proce-

dures. Under this condition, the test data are representative for the operational profile and the system can be considered to be safe.

REFERENCES.

Soisteman, E.C. and Ragsdale, K.B., (1985) Impact of Hardware/Software Faults on Systems Reliability. Procedures for Use of Methodology, Rome AirDevelopment Centre, Griffis Air Force base, NY. RADC-TR-85-228, vol. II (of two)

Stålhane, T., (1991). The Balancing of Quality Assurance Against Validation Activities, SAFECOMP'91, Johan F. Lindeberg (ed.). IFAC Symposia Series, 1991, Number 8.

Rudner, B. (1977). Seeding/Tagging Estimation of Software Errors: Models and Estimates. Rome Air Development Centre, Griffis Air Force base, NY. RADC-TR-77-15,

Colombo, A.G., Constantini, D. and Jaarsna,R.J. (1988). Bayes Nonparametric Estimation of Time-dependent Failure Rate, IEEE Transactions on Reliability, vol. R-34 no. 2, June 1988

Brooks, M. (1982). Reliability: One Part of Software Quality. Presented at the SINTOM seminar at Sundvolden in1982

McCall, J., Randall, W., Bowen, C.,McKelvey, N., Senn, R. Morris, J.,Hecht., H., Fenwick, S., Yates, P., Hecht, M., Vienneau, R., (1987). Methodology for Software Reliability Prediction. Rome Air Development Centre, Griffis Air Force base, NY. RADC-TR-87-171, vol. II (of two).

Keene, S.J., Assuring Software Safety. Presented at the Annual Reliability and Maintainability Symposium, 1992

FAULT-TOLERANT MULTIPROCESSOR FOR EMBEDDED PROCESS CONTROL

T. T. Siegrist

Computer Architecture Group, Computer Science Department, ABB Research Center, Baden, Switzerland

Abstract. Workby operation of two multiprocessors implements either integer (safe) or persistent (available) process control systems on the same hardware platform. A tight, pair-wise synchronization allows an early failure detection and a fast switch-over, as required by time-critical plants. The fault-tolerant computer uses off-the-shelf hardware with special features. An additional component, the Update and Synchronization Unit, highly supports the workby operation. The extension of a standard operating system hides redundancy from the user as far as possible, thereby easing the transfer of an application from a single system to the fault-tolerant system. A prototype has been built with components developed and used by a major company for protection and substation control systems.
This contribution describes the operating principle and the main design decisions.

Keywords. Safety; system integrity; redundancy; multiprocessing systems; industrial control; process control;

1. INTRODUCTION

Fault-tolerant systems traditionally appear in highly safety-related applications (aerospace, nuclear power plants, railway interlocking, automatic train control etc.) and applications that require high availability (power transmission/distribution, telephone exchange, computer centers etc.). Maehle (1988), Kirrmann (1987b), and Nelson (1990) present a good survey of such systems. At one end of the spectrum we find the systems with fault-tolerance mechanism solely implemented in hardware (e.g. AXE-10, VAXft 3000) at the other end the pure software solutions (e.g. SIFT). For these very high dependability goals the customer can afford specific developments.
In most industrial applications of process control systems we do not encounter fault-tolerant systems. But as the number of elements for controlling the process increases, engineers start puzzling about the reliability of their systems. Very soon "Fault-Tolerance" appears to them to be the solution to the their problem. But as they can not afford to develop and maintain a special product line for fault-tolerant applications, they look for a way to upgrade their systems. For these cases we must look for a wisely balanced hardware/software solution.
The approach presented in this paper allows to extend an ordinary process control system to a fault-tolerant one with only additional hardware and with small impact on the application software.

The basic conceptual work that led to this approach was carried out by H. Kirrmann and can be gathered from his thesis (Kirrmann, 1987a), which also includes a compilation of general terms and methods in the domain "Fault-Tolerance".

2. GOALS AND REQUIREMENTS

Our work shall increase the dependability of a process control system using standard elements. We shall mainly focus on hardware dependability, but we shall also keep software dependability in our minds.
The behaviour of our process control system should be
– persistent (keeps up functionality in spite of faults)
or
– integer (does not output false data to the controlled plant).
The requirements for a fault-tolerant process control system for industrial applications are (Kirrmann, 1987a):
1) To keep low the cost of the system used in non fault-tolerant applications, redundancy must be additive. A few additional elements should allow the introduction of fault-tolerance.
2) To meet different dependability goals, the system must be able to mix different degrees of redundancy for each hardware and software element.
3) If we add elements to a system, we lower its reliability i.e. it will produce more faults. To really gain overall availability, we must provide on-line repair.
4) Fault-tolerance should be made as transparent to the application as possible. The hardware or a special software layer should handle redundancy.
5) The system still has to meet real-time requirements. The response to an event must occur within a defined time.

3. APPROACH

3.1. Basic Configurations

With the following two basic configurations we can achieve the required behaviour of our fault-tolerant system:

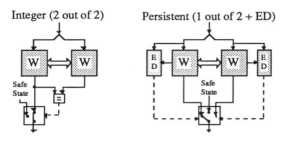

Fig. 3.1. Basic configurations

The core of both configurations is a duplex system consisting of two identical systems. The input either comes from redundant sensors or will be duplicated by a spreader. By choosing different output connections, we select the behaviour of the system:

integer: A comparator continuously checks the two output data streams and puts the process into a safe state in case of a disagreement.

persistent: A switch connects one of the two systems to the process. To be able to choose the correctly working one, additional information is necessary. An error detection logic supplies a status signal.

3.2. Workby

The core duplex system has to produce identical output data streams (in time and value) for integer operation and keep its two halves in the same states for persistent operation. A <u>workby</u> duplex system fulfils the latter two conditions. The notion "workby" means that the two systems process identical data at the identical times. (exact definition of the notion "identical" see section 4.1.).

A workby duplex system updates the states of its parts implicitly. This has the following advantages:
- It can handle applications with a huge amount of data representing the state.
- The application programmer does not need to identify data representing the state.
- The switch-over may take place at any point of program execution.
- The switch-over can be much faster because the roll-back / roll-forward phase is avoided.

3.3. Error Detection

The workby duplex system offers error detection through periodic comparison of intermediate values. The user may choose the appropriate level of error detection by selecting the values to be checked. Moreover hardware supervision and plausibility checks in the software provide system dependent status information.

At first glance error detection is only needed to select the properly working system when persistent behaviour is required. Integer behaviour is solely based on the safe output comparator with shut-down switch. But error detection might be mandatory to achieve higher degrees of integer behaviour, too. The German test house "TÜV" prescribes that the redundant hardware and software have

to be diversified for safety-related applications of the first degree (Hölscher, 1984).

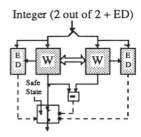

Fig. 3.2. Integer system with error detection

Enhancing the level of error detection may easily double the amount of additional hard- and software needed for fault-tolerance. Such a system would look quite like a triple-modular-redundancy (TMR) system with diversified hard- and software but the way diversity is introduced is much more promising. Instead of providing twice or three times the same functionality in different ways, we should prefer to use one part for doing the work and the other(s) for checking the result. This checking should rely on a separate specification defining error conditions.

This paper does not cover the construction of diversified software of the above kind.

3.4. Teaching of a Repaired System

The teaching of a system after a repair or even only after a transient fault is a huge problem in workby operation. As we do not want to force the application programmer to identify the data representing the state of his application, the running system must update the repaired one with all the data it has stored. The amount of this data is usually very large. Because the running system has to keep on controlling the process, it may only be stopped for a short period and its processing power may only be lowered as far as it can still meet the real-time response requirements.

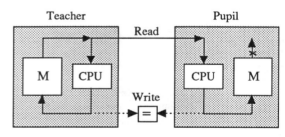

Fig. 3.3. Principle of teaching

During teaching the correctly working system ("teacher") and the repaired system ("pupil") operate in workby. The teacher controls the process.

Updating the pupil's state comprises two parts:
1) The state must be copied from the teacher to the pupil in a systematic way in order to complete teaching in a finite time. The duplex system copies the state in the background (when there is processing power available). This first part is called the <u>explicit</u> update of the state.
2) Because his state is initially invalid, the pupil reads all state data from the teacher's memory. By writing changes of the state into his own memory, pupil prevents the state already explicitly copied from becoming obsolete. This second part is called the <u>implicit</u> update of the state.

4. SYSTEM MODEL

To describe our system in a more formal way, we make use of the specification method first introduced by Tom DeMarco (1978) and the extensions by Hatley and Pirbhai (1987).
We also have to define some extensions to be able to express the fault-tolerant properties of our system.

4.1. Fault-Tolerance Extensions

One of the requirements is the mixture of different levels of redundancy. In our system there are two of these levels for the components:

simplex: no redundancy, only one component
duplex: one additional component with the same function

For duplex components we define two levels of exactness in fulfilling the same function:

Identical: Two processes are identical if all corresponding input data, input control signals, subprocesses and the control specifications are identical.
Two primitive processes (processes of the lowest level) are identical if all corresponding input data and the process specifications are identical.
Control and process specifications are static and have to match each other exactly to be identical.
Two store or context components are identical if the data or control signals which produce their contents are identical. If there are multiple producers of the contents, all of them must be identical.
Data or control signals consist of discrete values which are transmitted at discrete moments in time. For the data or control signals to be identical, their discrete values must match each other exactly and the transmission must take place at the same moment in time. The core element determines and forces this identity in time of the two systems (see sections 5.2.2./4.).

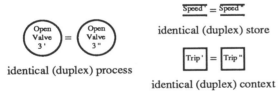

identical (duplex) process

identical (duplex) store

identical (duplex) context

Fig. 4.1. Representation of identical components

Identical processes produce identical output data and control signals.
Similar: All components which can not meet the above requirements for identity must be considered similar (representation sign: ≈). Some processes can or should not be identical (e.g. AD-converters, terminal drivers). A process may contain both similar and identical subprocesses (representation sign: ≅). To determine the identity properties of its outputs, we have to check the producing subprocesses.

4.2. Context

The context is the boundary between the system and the environment. The context diagrams specify the top level of our duplex system. Context inputs and outputs may be simplex or duplex components.
Typically all duplex context inputs are similar only because the environment can not produce identical data or control signals.

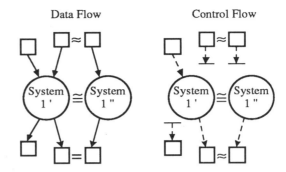

Fig. 4.2. Context diagrams of a duplex system

4.3. Concurrent Processes

Two processes are called concurrent if they can be active at the same time. The distinction of "real" concurrency (running at the same time) and "pseudo" concurrency (ready at the same time to run) is a property of the implementation and not of the system model. Communication between concurrent processes is another source of similarity. If producing and consuming of data or a control signal do not occur in the same order in the two systems, the identity of the data or control signal is lost.

4.4. Achieving and Preserving Identity

Because the duplex system is capable of checking the identity of its components and thereby ensuring a high level of error detection, we should avoid similarity as far as possible.
To enable data and control flows between processes of different identity and concurrency properties, we have to set up communication rules:

1) Data or control flow from a similar to an identical process, producer and consumer can be either sequential or concurrent:
The consuming identical process must eliminate the difference of the data or control signal and make it identical. We call this operation "Matching". Matching requires knowledge about the application. We therefore must leave it to the user of our system. The user should check whether the difference does not exceed a defined limit in order to improve error detection.

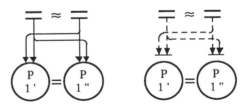

Fig. 4.3. Matching of similar data or control signals

The duplex system already contains a matching algorithm for a special kind of similar control signals. On appearance of either of the two parts of this similar control signal a duplex process is activated. The user may then retrieve the information in which system the control signal appeared and apply his/her own matching algorithm.

2) Data or control flow between two concurrent, identical processes:
Data and control signals must always flow through

stores from one concurrent process to another because concurrent processes can be active at the same time but do not need to be. Special communication procedures maintain the same order of producing and consuming in the two systems. The communication may comprise synchronization of the producer and the consumer.

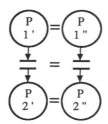

Fig. 4.5. Communication between concurrent, identical processes

3) Only identical processes may spread data or control signals from one system to the other. Similar or simplex processes may only consume/produce data or control signals from/for components in the same system. This rules prevents propagation of errors.

If we follow all of the above mentioned rules for communication within the duplex system, its implementation will be an easy task. The next chapter will describe the allocation of processes to hardware and software elements.

5. SYSTEM IMPLEMENTATION

Although we are describing a process control system that is in use today and extensions to it that we built as a prototype, we only want to point out the features our approach is based on. This should simplify the transfer of the presented approach to other process control systems.

5.1. Multiprocessor

The considered multiprocessor architecture consists of a few elements only. The processor element is an independent computer system containing all resources to run a process control application. The I/O element (input/output) is the interface to the process for more complex input/output data. The backplane bus finally offers communication between the elements.

5.1.1. Processor element. The processor element itself is split into different units (Fig. 5.1.):
- CPU (Central Processing Unit): It can be any kind of CPU that runs the chosen kernel (see section 5.1.4.) and that fulfils the following assumptions:
  - The CPU has to admit a certain synchronization between its execution unit (executes the instructions) and its bus interface unit (runs bus cycles on the local bus). An interrupt generated during a read bus cycle must be handled right after the execution of the corresponding instruction.
  - The CPU must be capable of masking all interrupts except one special interrupt. The remaining interrupts can still be monitored by reading a register.
- Local I/O: The processor element may have a process interface on board. This interface usually is a serial communication controller that provides a connection to a host for monitoring, debugging or up-/downloading purposes.

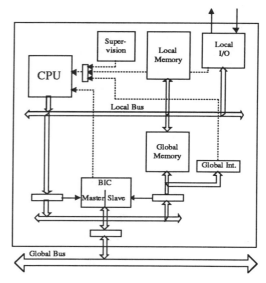

Fig. 5.1. Processor element

- Local Memory: The processor element keeps the program code and the local data in the local memory.
- Global Memory: The elements of a multiprocessor use global, shared memory for the communication between each other (accessed via the global bus). The access to the own global memory via the local bus accelerates the communication.
  The global memory consists of a logical and a geographical part. These parts are accessed via a logical respectively a geographical global bus transfer (see section 5.1.3.).
  To implement teaching mode (see section 3.4.), the processor element has to keep (part of) its state in the logical global memory. It requires local access (for normal mode) and global access (for teaching mode) to this memory.
- Global Interrupts: Interrupt transfers on the global bus are converted into local interrupts and sent to the CPU.
- Global Bus Interface: A bus interface controller (BIC) converts the bus cycles on the local bus into bus transfers on the global bus and vice versa. This controller combines a master interface and a slave interface.
- Supervision: Hardware supervision circuits (e.g. hardware/software-timeouts, power monitors) provide error detection of the lowest level.

5.1.2. I/O element. We distinguish two kinds of I/O-Elements:
- Simple I/O-Elements only include a slave interface to the global bus and a portion of geographical global memory where they put/take their data in/from.
- Advanced I/O-elements are processor elements with a process interface mounted as subprint. They must be treated in the same manner as processor elements with local I/O.

5.1.3. Global bus. The global bus is the most important non additional part of the system. To allow synchronization of two multiprocessors, it introduces some special features usually not found in backplane busses:
- The global bus is a multi-master bus i.e. more than one element with a master interface may control it. The result of the arbitration which selected a master among other competitors for the bus must be available on the bus. A special element connected to

176

the bus may delay the termination of the arbitration or prevent the arbitration winner from taking control of the bus. If it does not agree with the result it can reject it and force a new arbitration.

- An element connected to the bus can delay the termination of a data transfer and send an error message to the master if it does not agree with the content of the data transfer. The error message produces an interrupt on the master element.
- An element connected to the bus can identify two types of transfer by the address:
  - logical transfer: An address subspace may be allocated to each element by software configuration according to its logical meaning.
  - geographical transfer: An address subspace is allocated to each element by hardware configuration according to its geographical location. In particular the two systems have distinct geographical address subspaces.
- Master elements may send interrupts to other elements.
- The bus comprises a watchdog line giving information about the status of the corresponding system.

We must take into account these features when transferring the approach to another process control system.

5.1.4. Operating system.
In our prototype implementation we have chosen VRTX[1] as operating system because it is in use in one of our target process control systems. VRTX represents a real-time kernel suitable for an embedded single processor system. The system calls we mainly use, deal with:

- task management
- task synchronization[2]
- inter-task communication
- interrupt handlers

By building a notification mechanism on global interrupts we can add on some features of a multiprocessor operating system.

5.1.5. Mapping the model to the implementation.
Context inputs and outputs correspond to sensors and actors resp. in the terminology of embedded systems. Hardware elements which independently perform a certain job (e.g. internal timers, simple or local I/O-elements, AD-converters, DMA-controllers) implement concurrent processes. The software elements which implement concurrent processes are called "tasks" and "interrupt handlers" in the terminology of our operating system. System calls, local and global interrupts are components of the control flow. Stores in the data or control flow between concurrent processes must be located in the global memory, i.e. accessible through the global bus.

5.2. Duplex Multiprocessor

A multiprocessor can be extended to a duplex multiprocessor by duplication of the hardware and adding two new types of elements to it, the USU (see below) and the output connection (see section 3.1.). The application engineer may specify for each element if it is duplicated and if not in which system it is

---

[1] VRTX is a registered trademark of Hunter & Ready, Inc.
[2] Here 'synchronization' has its original meaning of establishing a relation between producer and consumer

situated. He may tailor his system according to his dependability requirements.

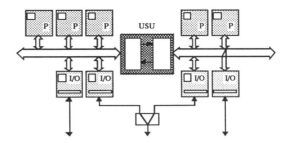

Fig. 5.2. Duplex multiprocessor

5.2.1. Update and Synchronization Unit (USU).
The USU is the heart of the duplex multiprocessor. It provides communication between the two systems and synchronization of them on the level of the global bus. The USU consists of two identical modules. The two modules are interconnected with a bidirectional link. This link can either be parallel for connection within the same cabinet or serial for longer distances. Dividing the USU in two modules wards off higher dependability requirements for this element. There is only one additional requirement: A module must always be able to separate from the other module in case of a failure in the latter.

A USU module includes three major units: one controls the arbitration, one controls the data transfers, and the last one grants access to the USU itself.

5.2.2. Operation modes.
The USU utilizes the special features of the global bus (see section 5.1.3.) to provide the following operation modes:

- Disconnected: The USU is completely passive. The two systems are separated.

If the USU is active, each (duplex) processor element may select asynchronous or synchronous mode:

- Asynchronous: The USU is acting as a global arbiter over the two busses. Each processor element may gain control over both busses. It only has access to the other system via a geographical transfer. Logical transfers are limited to the system where the processor element is sited.

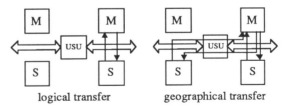

logical transfer   geographical transfer

Fig. 5.3. Asynchronous mode

- Synchronous: The USU only grants global bus access to a processor element in one system when its partner also competes for the bus. When this duplex processor then gains control over the bus the USU synchronizes its data transfers.

In a logical transfer the duplex processor communicates with another duplex element, each processor element accessing its corresponding element. The USU only checks whether the address and the data transmitted are equal on both sides.

In a geographical transfer the processor pair communicates with only one element at a time. The USU can tell from the address on what side the accessed element is located. It copies the data from one side to the other in read transfers whereas in write transfers it only checks them.

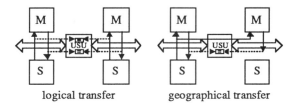

logical transfer   geographical transfer

Fig. 5.4. Synchronous mode

In teaching mode the USU must copy the data read in a logical transfer from the pupil's side to the teacher's side.

The error handling of USU obeys the principle that no error in one of its two modules or in the system in which it is sited may impair the correct operation of the other module or the other system. In case of an error at least one module of USU is able to recover the correct state and provide useful information about the cause of the error for the processor element involved.

5.2.3. Fault-tolerant operating system. As we must leave the application unchanged as far as possible, we need to define an interface to it. The process control system includes an operating system so we should use its interface for this purpose. We can enhance the operating system to a fault-tolerant one by adding a layer while leaving the interface unchanged.

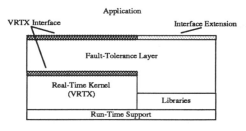

Fig. 5.5. Structure of the fault-tolerant operating system

Because the operating system does not provide all the services we need, we must specify an interface extension. The additional system calls deal with:

– not synchronized communication between hardware/software elements on the same/different processor elements through shared variables. This kind of communication is used for cyclic processing in real-time applications.
– global semaphores for global resource management.
– interrupt handler installation, enabling and disabling interrupts.
– configuration of the fault-tolerant system.

Transferring software from simplex to a duplex system mainly consists of employing the procedures of our interface extension for all communication through shared variables.

5.2.4. Mapping the model to the implementation. The USU is the element which determines the identity property defined in the system model (see section 4.1.). Identity becomes only visible when the data or the control signal is transferred through the global bus (control signals are transferred as data). The USU forces the two corresponding moments of data transfers in the two systems to appear as one identical moment in time. It checks whether the two identical transfers occur

within a predetermined time interval, and whether the values of the data transferred match each other exactly.

6. CONCLUSIONS

The presented approach provides a generic platform for both safety-related and high availability process control applications. An extension to a well-known specification method enables the application engineer to describe the properties of his fault-tolerant system with different levels of redundancy. Preserving the interface to the operating system facilitates the transfer of existing applications to this generic platform. A precompiler may perform this transfer of parts which do not require application-specific know-how. The workby operation achieved in this way has two main advantages: fast switch-over and rigorous identity checking of intermediate values. Hard- and software contain additional error detection mechanisms.

For safety-related applications of the highest degree this platform can only be a basis. Therefore future activities will have to deal with the improvement of the error handling and the construction of diversified software.

7. REFERENCES

Hatley, D.J. and I.A. Pirbhai (1987). Strategies for Real-Time Specification. Dorset House Publishing, New York.

Hölscher, H. and J. Rader (1984). Mikrocomputer in der Sicherheitstechnik. TÜV Rheinland, Köln.

Kirrmann, H.D. (1987a). A Method for the Design of Embedded Fault-Tolerant Computers for Process Control and a Design Example, Ph. D. Thesis. Swiss Federal Institute of Technology, Zurich.

Kirrmann, H.D. (1987b). Fault Tolerance in Process Control. IEEE Micro, October, 27 - 50.

Maehle, E. (1988). Architektur fehlertoleranter Systeme. Informationstechnik, 3/88, 169 - 179

De Marco, T. (1978). Structured Analysis and System Specification. Prentice-Hall, Englewood Cliffs, N.J..

Nelson, V.P. (1990). Fault-Tolerant Computing Fundamental Concepts. IEEE Computer, July, 19 - 25.

CERTIFICATION OF DIGITAL SYSTEMS IN COMMERCIAL AVIONICS APPLICATIONS

A. Cook.

Systems Engineer, British Aerospace Airbus Limited.
PO Box 77, Bristol BS99 7AR, England.
Tel: (0272) 365930. Telex: 44163. Fax: (0272) 364344.

Abstract. Systems controlling the flight of commercial aircraft are traditionally hydro-mechanical or analogue electro-mechanical. The procedures to gain approval for flight of a large passenger carrying aircraft, by regulatory authorites (Certification), are described in respect of such systems. The principles underlying the certification procedures are identified and described. The evolutionary approach adopted in the introduction of digital electronic equipment to commercial aircraft is then reviewed. The application of these, previously identified, principles to digital electronic systems is discussed and extension to the principles described where necessary.

Future avionics systems architectures are proposed which will rely on logical rather than physical partitioning. Methods for demonstrating that such systems comply with airworthiness regulations are discussed.

Keywords. Digital systems, Redundancy, Reliability, Safety, Software development, Type certification.

TYPE CERTIFICATION

Type Certification of commercial transport aircraft ensures that the design of an aircraft type, or variant, complies with a set of requirements imposed by national airworthiness authorities. Individual systems and components are not certified in their own right. The impact of a system on the safety of the aircraft is assessed by consideration of the aircraft function it provides or affects. The type certification process deals with the complete design and function of the aircraft. There are therefore no specific requirements for certification of electronic equipment or software. The equipment must satisfy the requirements of the aircraft function it provides or affects, the technology employed in the implementation dictates the means of compliance to be used.

REGULATIONS AND AUTHORITIES

The certification of Aircraft developed in the U.K. is regulated by the Civil Aviation Authority. The code of requirements currently applied, by the CAA, to all new aircraft projects, were formulated by the Joint Aviation Authorities (JAA). The JAA consist of the national airworthiness authorities of nineteen member states who have agreed a common set of airworthiness regulations. Large passenger carrying aircraft must comply with Joint Airworthiness Requirement 25 (JAR 25). This regulation was originally based on the U.S. Federal Aviation Regulation 25 (FAR 25). Subsequent changes to the regulation have been harmonized with FAR 25 to ease certification of European designed aircraft destined for U.S. operators and vice versa. The JAA have also agreed requirements applicable to engine design, light aircraft and helicopters.

JAR 25 places requirements on the structure of the aircraft, its flight characteristics, its resistance to environmental damage or interference, provision of warning devices and safety equipment and the performance of systems and equipment. To achieve type certification, the aircraft design must comply with every paragraph in JAR 25, unless it can be shown that the paragraph is not applicable to the particular aircraft. Interpretation of the requirements and acceptable means of compliance are provided by the JAA in Advisory Circulars (ACs) and Advisory Material Joint (AMJs). The means of compliance described in ACs and AMJs are not mandatory, a manufacturer may elect to propose an alternative means of compliance but must convince the authorities of its validity. The basis for certification of the aircraft is defined in the early stages of the project. Discussions take place between the Airworthiness Authority and the aircraft manufacturer. The paragraphs of the regulations applicable to every component or system are identified and means of compliance are agreed. Where previously untried technology is to be employed, or normal means of compliance are not applicable the, Airworthiness Authority may raise a Certification Review Item (CRI) with the manufacturer. Manufacturers respond to CRIs by proposing a special means of compliance or specifying a course of action to address the issue.

SYSTEM REQUIREMENTS

Any system must satisfy requirements of the regulations specific to the functions affected. In addition, and if no other paragraph is applicable, the system must satisfy the requirements of JAR 25 paragraph 1309 - `Equipment, Systems and Installations'. This paragraph is particularly important for avionics equipment. The paragraph places requirements on the design of systems. Fundamentally a system essential to the continued safe flight and landing must be designed to perform its function under any foreseeable operating conditions, other systems providing non-essential services must be shown to be neither a source of danger in themselves or be liable to jeopardize the proper functioning of any essential service. The system should be designed so that:-

(i) The occurrence of any failure condition which would prevent the continued safe flight and landing of the aircraft is extremely improbable

(ii) The occurrence of any failure condition which would reduce the capability of the aeroplane or the ability of the crew to deal with adverse operating conditions is improbable.

Compliance with these requirements is shown by analysis and, where necessary, by ground, flight or simulator tests. The paragraph makes additional requirements concerning crew warning devices and loads on power supplies.

SAFETY ANALYSIS

The form of analysis acceptable as a means of compliance is described in AMJ 25.1309. The AMJ makes the following definition of a Failure Condition:

"The effect on the aeroplane and its occupants, both direct and consequential caused or contributed to by one or more failures, considering relevant adverse operational or environmental conditions."

Failure Conditions are classified according to their severity as follows:

MINOR Failure Conditions do not significantly reduce aeroplane safety, and involve crew actions well within their capabilities.

MAJOR Failure Conditions reduce the capability of the aeroplane or the ability of the crew to cope with adverse operating conditions to the extent that there would be, for example, a significant reduction in safety margins or functional capabilities, a significant increase in crew workload or in conditions impairing crew efficiency, or discomfort to occupants, possibly including injuries.

HAZARDOUS Failure Conditions reduce the capability of the aeroplane or the ability of the crew to cope with adverse operating conditions to the extent that there would be:

i) A large reduction in safety margins or functional capabilities

ii) Physical distress or higher workload such that the flight crew cannot be relied upon to perform their tasks accurately or completely or

iii) Serious or fatal injury to a relatively small number of occupants

CATASTROPHIC Failure Conditions prevent continued safe flight and landing

FUNCTIONAL HAZARD ASSESSMENT

A functional hazard assessment should be performed on the system. This assessment is a systematic, comprehensive examination of a system's functions to identify potential failure conditions, which the system can cause or contribute to, and to classify them according to the above scale. If the Functional Hazard Assessment shows that system mal-functions cannot result in worse than Minor Failure Conditions, or affect other airworthiness related functions no further safety analysis is necessary to show compliance with JAR 25.1309. The Functional Hazard Assessment is qualitative and based on operational experience and engineering judgement. Knowledge of failure conditions and their severity enable precautions to be taken in design.

QUALITATIVE AND QUANTITATIVE ASSESSMENT

Failure conditions which are major, hazardous or catastrophic are subject to further analysis. Analysis may be quantitative or qualitative depending on the severity of the failure condition or the nature of the system. A quantitative analysis of failures is required for complex systems, where novel technology is to be introduced or if any failure conditions would be catastrophic. The following qualitative probability terms are defined by AMJ 25.1309:

MINOR failure conditions may be probable

MAJOR failure conditions should be no more than improbable (Remote)

HAZARDOUS failure conditions should be no more

than improbable (extremely remote)

CATASTROPHIC failure conditions should be no more than extremely improbable

Qualitative analysis is based on operational experience and engineering judgement. Design appraisals and data gained from previous experience with similar systems may be employed. Systematic analysis methods such as failure modes and effects analysis and dependence analysis are used to demonstrate that common mode failures cannot occur and that redundancy exists in complex systems where required.

Quantitative analysis employs the systematic analysis methods of failure modes and effects analysis and either fault tree analysis or dependence analysis. The analysis is used to establish numerical probabilities for each failure condition identified in the functional hazard assessment and ensure that the probability is appropriate to the severity of the failure condition. Numerical probabilities are defined to describe the qualitative probability terms :

Probable Failure Conditions are those having a probability of 1×10^{-5} per flight hour or worse

Improbable (Remote) Failure Conditions are those having a probability between 1×10^{-5} and 1×10^{-7} per flight hour

Improbable (Extremely Remote) Failure Conditions are those having a probability between 1×10^{-7} and 1×10^{-9} per flight hour

Extremely Improbable Failure Conditions are those having a probability of 1×10^{-9} per flight hour or better.

ANALYSIS TECHNIQUES

Failure modes and effects analysis considers the effects of failure modes of individual components on the system. Numerical probabilities of each failure mode occurring can be obtained from manufacturers data or previous experience.

Fault Tree analysis and Dependence Analysis are graphical methods which relate the identified failure conditions of the system to the individual component failures identified in the Failure Modes and Effects Analysis. Dependence Diagrams consider which failure modes must not occur to preclude each failure condition. Fault Tree Analysis consider which failures must occur to cause each failure condition. In a quantitative analysis the diagrams are used to calculate the probability of occurrence of failure conditions based on the combined probabilities of contributory failure modes.

INTRODUCTION OF NEW TECHNOLOGY

The techniques recommended in AMJ 25.1309 are applicable to all traditional technologies used in aircraft system eg. hydraulics, mechanical linkages and analogue electronics. New technologies have been subjected to the same techniques, generally a quantitative analysis being required. This means that a substantial amount of experience of a technology is required before it can be employed in any function which may have hazardous or major failure conditions. Innovative technologies are only introduced to aircraft after they have been proven in non safety related applications in other industries. Experience is gained in aviation by introducing the technology in the implementation of non-critical functions or functions where a reversionary back-up, using traditional technology, can be easily implemented. This evolutionary approach was adopted in the introduction of digital electronics. The first application of airborne digital electronics was in flight recording systems, later the technology was applied to digital engine controls and secondary flight controls, the most recent aircraft designs employ full digital control of the flight surfaces with a minimal mechanical back-up.

DIGITAL TECHNOLOGY AND SOFTWARE

It has been possible to gather data relating to the components employed in the design of digital hardware, enabling assessment of designs to be made by normal methods of analysis. Software has however provided a more challenging problem. Failures in software are systematic errors arising in the design or implementation, it is also unrealistic to completely test a piece of software of even moderate complexity. Software is generally written specifically for a system with little re-use in other systems. For these reasons assessments of the probability of software failures cannot be made. Attempts to model software reliability have not achieved a high degree of success [Littlewood 87]. AMJ 25.1309 acknowledges these problems and analysis of software is precluded from the normal means of compliance with JAR 25.1309. Instead it is recommended that the software development is controlled and assessed according to the guidelines defined in the document RTCA DO-178A/EUROCAE ED-12A (undergoing review, shortly to be re-issued as RTCA DO-178B/EUROCAE ED-12B).

DO-178A describes a life-cycle for development of software and describes the verification and validation activities necessary at each life cycle step. The extent of the verification and validation effort depends on the software level. Software levels are determined by consideration of the most severe failure condition associated with the system. DO-178A defines three software levels:

Level 1 is associated with systems whose worst failure condition would be catastrophic (Critical functions)

Level 2 is associated with systems whose worst failure condition would be major/hazardous (Essential functions)

Level 3 is associated with systems whose worst failure condition would be minor (Non-essential functions)

A CRI raised by the JAA for certification of the Airbus A330/340 clarifies the distinction between major and hazardous failures conditions by introducing software level 2A and 2B respectively. It may be possible to assign a lower software level if it can be demonstrated that the system is protected by back-ups using dissimilar technology.

By application of the principles recommended in AMJ 25.1309, for safe design of systems, and the application of guidelines laid down in DO-178A, it has been possible to gain Type Certification of aircraft such as the Airbus A320. The A320 employs digital systems to control the operation of all its flight surfaces. Redundant processing resources with appropriate physical separation are employed to protect against common mode failures, dissimilarity ensures that the system is not vulnerable to common mode software failures.

FUTURE SYSTEMS

Future avionics systems are being investigated which provide aircraft functions through a standardised computing facility. The computing facility has a distributed modular architecture. Standard cabinets contain Line Replaceable Modules (LRM). LRMs are either power supply modules, processing modules or bus bridges. Communications between modules within a cabinet are handled by a back-plane data-bus which conforms to the emerging standard ARINC 659. The bus bridge module handles input and output to and from the cabinet by making a connection between the internal ARINC 659 bus and the external ARINC 629. The ARINC 629 data-bus is a serial, controller-less, multiple-access data-bus. The ARINC 629 bus provides inter-cabinet communications, and communications between cabinets, actuators and sensors. Some actuators, known as Smart Actuators, interface directly to the ARINC 629 bus and contain their own control loop processing. Smart sensors may have their own ARINC 629 interface. Conventional sensors are connected to Remote Data Concentrators which multiplex data from a number of sensors and provide an interface to ARINC 629. The architecture of such a system is shown in illustration 1. The system's functionality is provided by software applications running on the processing modules under the control of an operating system. The perceived advantages of this type of system are:

(i) Reduce airframe manufacturing complexity by reduction of wiring

(ii) Reduction in airframe weight

(iii) Reduce design costs by evolving a standard approach to design of avionics

(iv) Reduce procurement costs by using standard hardware and software components and therefore increasing competition amongst suppliers

(v) Reduce maintenance costs by standardisation of many components and reduction of number of wires through airframe

(vi) Increase in safety margins by provision of greater redundancy of processing resources.

Such a system however raises many issues for Type Certification of the aircraft. Every function provided by the system must comply with the regulations applicable to that function. The functions must also satisfy the requirements of JAR 25.1309 in terms of probability of failure conditions. It must be possible to demonstrate by analysis that failure of one function will not have an adverse effect on other functions and that failure of an individual component will not cause common-mode failure of several functions.

In such a system physical boundaries between functions have largely been removed, all cabinets can communicate freely and software providing different functions can be co-located on processors. The physical isolation of systems regarded as essential for the identification and prevention of points of common mode failure will be removed. Great reliance is placed on the integrity of software to provide independence of functions.

It is unlikely that a system can be immediately introduced which provides the whole of an aircraft's avionic functionality. Instead an evolutionary approach to its introduction will have to be followed, to gain experience with the concepts and to obtain the approval of the regulatory authorities. Initial implementations will only involve a selected group of functions whose loss or mal-function would have only a limited impact on the safe operation of the aircraft.

More critical functions may be implemented using the modular components. However the allocation of functions to processors and the communications between processors may be restricted to provide physical separation of functions. This separation makes the system more amenable to the form of analysis used to demonstrate compliance with JAR 25.1309.

The primary objectives of implementing such systems are to enable the use of diverse components and shared resources. Provision of redundancy and dissimilarity is not therefore a problem.

However difficulty will arise in proving by analysis that

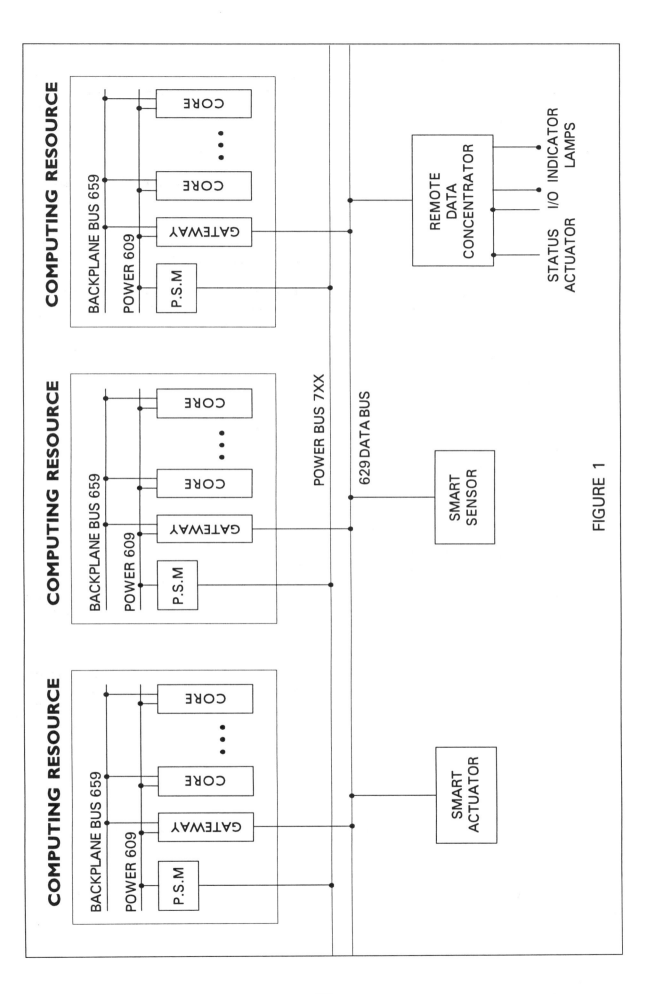

FIGURE 1

functions are independent ie. cannot adversely affect other functions. In any implementation it will be essential that applications software can be mapped to particular processors and the memory limits of each application must be deterministically controlled. It is then possible to judge the effect of loss of any particular module or cabinet, on the functionality of the aircraft, in a safety analysis. Decisions can then be taken on physical location of cabinets, routing of busses and distribution of power. These concerns are vitally important to protect against common mode failure resulting from physical damage to the aircraft. Redundant versions of the same application must not be located in the same cabinet if failure of the application will result in loss of a critical or essential function.

Because increased reliance is placed on software, review of methods of development and analysis must take place. Methods to analyze the complexity of software must be adopted, for example software fault tree analysis [Leveson 83], to identify failure conditions which could arise as a result of failures within software. It is unlikely that numerical probabilities for failure of software can be obtained with any degree of accuracy. However identification of failure conditions within software will assist with the safe implementation of the software. The operating system will control several applications, being responsible for management of memory and scheduling of applications. It is essential that the behaviour of the operating system is deterministic, it must therefore be simple and capable of being analysed. The technique of N-Version programming, traditionally employed to provide fault tolerance in software, may be applied to the operating system and applications. Where this technique is employed analysis must demonstrate that true diversity is obtained ie. diverse versions of an application run under diverse versions of the operating system.

CONCLUSIONS

Aircraft are certificated as a whole. Systems providing aircraft functions must be demonstrated to provide that function with an inverse relationship between probability of loss of function and severity of effect on the aircraft and its occupants. New technology or complex systems can only be introduced to aircraft in an evolutionary manner. This approach has been adopted in the introduction of digital electronics to aircraft. Currently it is not possible to perform quantitative analysis on software and so standards have been introduced to control the development of software to assure a product of appropriate quality.

Future systems are proposed which involve modular components and integration of aircraft functions. Such systems can only be introduced if they can be demonstrated to be as safe as existing systems. The introduction of this type of system will therefore be evolutionary in order to gain experience and data. Safety analysis can

only be successfully carried out if applications providing functions can be mapped to individual processors allowing assessment of the fault tolerant properties of the system to be made. In the future the reliance placed on software means that new methods of analysis of critical software components must be introduced.

REFERENCES

Joint Aviation Authorities. Joint Airworthiness Requirement 25

Littlewood. B (1987) How Good are Software Reliability Predictions. Software Reliability, Achievement and Assessment Blackwell Scientific Press

RTCA/EUROCAE RTCA DO-178A/EUROCAE ED 12A - Software Considerations in Airborne Systems and Equipment Certification

Leveson. N & Harvey P.R. (1983) Analyzing Software Safety, IEEE Transactions on Software Engineering, Vol. SE-9 No. 5 Sept 83

THE CODED MICROPROCESSOR CERTIFICATION

Ozello Patrick
INRETS-CRESTA   2 Avenue Malleret Joinville 94114 Arcueil, France

Abstract. In France, the coded microprocessor is certified as a fail-safe component. It is increasingly used in Automatic Train Protection in the guided transport systems. The safety operation of coded microprocessor is based on the information redundancy concept using an error-detecting codes. This redundancy allows a high level of protection against all types of microprocessor failures, as well as against compiler errors.
Two coded microprocessor types have been certified by French Duly Authorised Body :
 - the first one uses a separable code with two fields : 32 bits of data information and 48 bits of check word. It was certified in 1989 and used in the protection of ligne A of the Paris RER express metro and of the POMA system in Laon.
 - the second one differs from the first by the check word length which is 31 bits. A new certification has been necessary for this second type which will be used in the MAGGALY (Metro Automatique à Grand Gabarit de Lyon) system in the line D.
Other applications will be put into service shortly in the track-side equipment of the VAL (Vehicule Automatic Leger) in Chicago (fullfilling many operational features: two-way operation, shuttle and run around) and also in the Channel Fixed Link signaling system.
In this paper we present a brief introduction to the coded microprocessor principles and explain the main steps of safety proof which have been necessary to certify this component according a safety objective. The error detection capabilities using an arithmetic code and signature technique as well as the assessment of the probability of an undetected error will be presented. We also describe the certification process and organization.

Key words : Coded microprocessor, safety, certification, error detection codes, railways.

1. INTRODUCTION

The signaling system for guided way means of transport has become more complex these last years and thus requires the use of microprocessors. The use of microprocessors to perform functions of train protection, like speed monitoring or interlocking raises two major problems:

1   software safety: protection against programming or specification errors.

2   hardware safety: protection against hardware failure (dormant or not) of the microprocessor cards.
The coded monoprocessor is a solution to the second problem. Other solutions have been largely used, like the biprocessor with voter in the aviation or nuclear fields, where safety and availability requirements are very high (Rouquet and Traverse 86), (ElKoursi and Stuparu 90).
The coded monoprocessor performs by itself a high level of safety, and may be used in parallel with another to achieve high availability.
The principle of the coded monoprocessor consists in coding all the variables of the program, the code is chosen in such a way that any deviation from the source program gives way to an "out of code" word which will trigger the dynamic controller. This last controller, designed with fail-safe technique, shuts off the supply power at the vital outputs.

The coded monoprocessor has been developped in the frame of the SACEM project for the line A of the Regional Express Metro in Paris (George 90). This system has been put into revenue service in 1988. Each train is equipped with one coded monoprocessor and the trackside equipment are redundand for the purpose of availability.

The cable-car system Poma in Laon (Gourdon 87), with cabin capacity of 20 persons, and with a through-put of 800 persons/hour has been also equipped with Automatic Train Protection based on the coded monoprocessor, on board and on the trackside.

In the following paragraph, we shall describe the certification approach used by the Duly Authorised Body for the certification of the coded monoprocessor.

The third paragraph recalls the principle of the coded monoprocessor: the coding of the variables, the controlling of the code, and the signature predetermination.

The fourth paragraph introduces the main steps of the demonstration of the coded monoprocessor.

2. CERTIFICATION APPROACH BY THE DULY AUTHORISED BODY

In march 1987, that is 15 months before the revenue service of the line, the French Transportation Ministry created the National Safety Commission whose members are experts from different administrations: Rail Authority, Metro Authority, Atomic Energy, Aviation and INRETS. The last members are representatives of the government. On certain points, the commission had secured the help of external experts from university.

The purpose of the commission is to analyse the adopted principles and the overall approach to obtain safety : the operation RATP was in charge of producing the proof of safety of the system SACEM.

The commission had paid particular attention to the new features enhancing the safety :
- The principle of the coded monoprocessor and the safety demonstration ;
- The design and validation of the critical software ;
- The consistency between the cab signaling and the classical track side signaling. The safety demonstration of the coded monoprocessor in the 48 bits version was scrutinized by the commission. The dossier was constituted of:
- The contractor demonstration (in fact the contractor is a set of manufacturers MATRA TRANSPORT, ALSTHOM, CSEE) ;
- a report from the CNRS ;
- and a complementary study by the RATP.

After more than one year of hard work, the commission approved the SACEM system in general, and the 48 bits code monoprocessor in particular. This approval has allowed the revenue service in July 1988.

3.SUMMING UP OF THE CODED MONOPROCESSOR PRINCIPLE

The principle of the coded monoprocessor has been presented in (Martin 89) and (Forin 89).
We briefly remind here this principle: Every variable X of the software is composed of two fields (xf, xc) :
- a field xf significant of the actual value of this variable X. The type may be boolean or integer ;
- a field xc called "control part" of X.
The pair (xf, xc) is considered in this way to be the encoded variable X.

The program instructions must be designed to deal with encoded variables, that is, they use only inputs in the encoded form and issue output in the encoded form. So, a library of elementary operations called OPELEM, substituting the classical operations has been created.

3.1 The code used.

The used code is in fact constituted of three types of codes intimately mixed, in order to detect four classes of errors :

-1- an arithmetic code with key A which is a prime integer, used to detect computing errors (error of carry over, error of shift,...). The code (xf, xc) of the variable X is a word of the code if and only if the following equality is true:

$$2^k xf + xc \equiv 0 \ (\text{modulo } A) \text{ , where k is a fixed integer.}$$

In the SACEM monoprocessor, the key A is a prime integer filling 48 bits ($A \approx 10^{14}$), the control field fills also 48 bits, after scaling if needed.

- 2 - a signature part to detect addressing errors (operand error, operator error, variables confusion). To each of the variables X is associated an integer Bx, called signature of X, independent from the value xf of X. This signature is superimposed on the arithmetic code mentioned above. In this way, X = (xf, xc) is a word of the code if and only if the following equality is true :

$$2^k xf + xc \equiv Bx \ (\text{modulo } A) .$$

The signatures of the input variables are chosen by the programmer. In fact it is recommended to choose it randomly among the integers in the range of 1 to A-1.

The signatures of the intermediate variables and of the outputs are determined by the input signatures and the operations performed. We shall give as example the "add" operation; the "if then else" instruction is described in (Forin 89). Furthermore, we can compute with the help of a tool named signatures predetermination, the signatures of all the outputs of the program, these last being independent of the value of the inputs and of the execution paths followed.

- 3- a timing code to detect dating error (unwanted storage, incorrect number of loops...). Every processing cycle, or more generally every indentation of loop is characterized by its proper date D. This date is incremented at every loop. The date is inserted in the coding of every variable and the final definition of the code is the following:

The code (xf, xc) of a variable X, at the time D, is a word of the code if and only if the following equality is true:

$$2^k xf + xc \equiv Bx + D \ (\text{modulo } A) .$$

- 4 - Finally, to protect against certain sequencing or branching errors, a special global variable has been added, called "tracer". The use of the tracer will be explicited in the example of the "if then else" instruction (Martin and all 90). This tracer is updated after every instruction and can be computed by the predetermination tool.

3.2 Characteristics of the OPELEM
(elementary operations).

The OPELEM must have the following characteristics :
- process coded variables at the input
- produce coded outputs
- maintain the code, i.e. if the inputs (tracer included) of an elementary operation are words of the code, then the outputs must be words of the code (tracer included). This characteristic requires that the signatures of the outputs can be precalculated. In other words, that means that for any operator $Z := Op(X1,..., Xn)$, there does exist a function Fop such that $Bz = Fop(BX1, ... , BXn)$, where BXi is the signature of the variable Xi.

3.3. The validity of the processing

Thanks to the characteristic of the OPELEM to maintain the code, it is guaranteed that the processing of coded input will give output in the code.

Inversely, if one or some of the variables are out of code, the system will fall in a safe state, by putting all the outputs in a safe state.

For technical reasons, there will be no control after each instruction. Only a final control is triggered at the end of the program on the quantity G, called final signature $G = Tr + G1 + ... Gk - k*D$ where Tr is the tracer and $Gi = 2^k sif + sic = BSi + D$ where $Si = (sif, sic)$ is a safety related output.

The final signature G and the date D are sent to a dynamic controller designed in fail safe technique, called CKDYN. The CKDYN pulls out the date from G and then compares G-D to the signature B of the program. This signature is a constant which has been precalculated by the signature precalculating tool and stored in the Read-Only-Memory of the dynamic controller.
If the CKDYN detects a deviation of G-D from B, then it means that G is out of the code. The controller cuts off the supply power of the output S and hence all the outputs S1, ... , Sk are in the safe state.

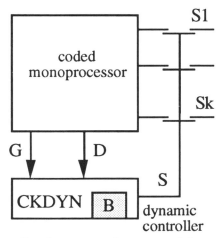

fig 1. processing control by the dynamic controller

We give now an example of the OPELEM library : the "add" operation of two coded variables.

3.4. Addition of two coded variables

$Z := ADD(X . Y)$

Let $X = (xf, xc)$ and $Y = (yf, yc)$ two coded variables. The add algorithm of the coded monoprocessor is :

$$zf = xf + yf$$
$$zc = xc + yc - D \quad \text{(D is the actual date)}$$

We verify that the addition algorithm maintains the code, by demonstrating that if X and Y are words of the code, then Z belongs to the code. For this purpose we demonstrate that there exists a signature Bz independent of zf such that

$$2^k zf + zc \equiv Bz + D \quad \text{(modulo A)}.$$

$$
\begin{aligned}
2^k zf + zc &\equiv 2^k(xf + yf) + (xc + yc - D) \\
&\equiv 2^k xf + xc + 2^k yf + yc - D \\
&\equiv Bx + D + By + D - D \\
&\equiv Bx + By + D .
\end{aligned}
$$

In defining Bz as $Bz = Bx + By$, it is clear that
$$2^k zf + zc \equiv Bz + D .$$

3.5. The coding of the safety related inputs.

All the inputs to the coded monoprocessor must be coded. For this purpose, electronic cards, designed in fail-safe technique, transform the boolean inputs into coded and dated variables.

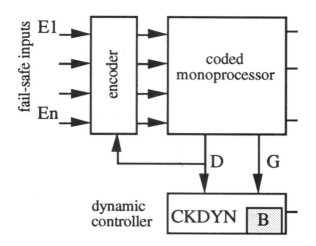

fig 2. inputs encoding

3.6. Signature precalculation tool.

This tool proceeds from the source program and the signatures of the input variables. Thanks to the characteristic of the OPELEM to maintain the code, the tool calculates the signature of all intermediate variables and the final signature G to be sent to the CKDYN controller, as well as all the compensation tables used where branching or looping takes place. These compensation tables are then included in the compiled software by a linker in order to get an executable program.

4. MAIN STEPS IN THE SAFETY DEMONSTRATION OF THE CODED MONOPROCESSOR

The demonstration proceeds from three requirements: it is to be probabilistic, independent of microprocessor type and without initial assumptions about the error models. They are explained below:
- the safety requirements are given in terms of wrong-sided failure rate: the National Commission of SACEM has approved a global catastrophe rate of

10^{-9}/hour . train.

This global rate is decomposed into individual rates which are allocated to different components of the system. This approach requires a probabilistic demonstration for each component. The coded monoprocessor fits very well this requirement, thanks to the mathematical properties of the code.
- The contractor has looked for a demonstration independent of microprocessor type in order to avoid renewing the demonstration in case of a technology change.
- the third requirement comes from the fact that it is impossible to list exhaustively all the consequences and the probability of a failure occurrence in the execution of the instruction. This abstraction from error models gives birth to the notion of an "a

priori" probability, which will be defined in the paragraph 4.2.a.

The safety demonstration is composed of two main parts. Part one is the analysis of the residual scenarios. We show in this part that any error by the microprocessor or combination of errors, is detectable using the coding technique defined in §3.1. In part two, we caculate the probability Pnd of non detection of an error. We have explained in §3.3 that a control is only made at each cycle end. An error occurring during execution can thus affect negatively other variables ant yet be compensated before being controlled. The calculation of Pnd is made in two steps:

a) first we assume that a coding control is made for each variable after each instruction. Let P1 be the probability of non detection of an error under this assumption.

b) secondly, we calculate the probability P2 of error compensation after N instructions, given that P variables were out of code before the execution of the N instructions.

Without going into details, we show in the next two paragraphs, the methods used for this demonstration.

4.1. First part - Residual scenarios analysis.

The scope of the residual scenarios analysis is to show that every error, or combination of errors, is detectable by the coding technique defined in § 3.1. We have explained that the code is a superimposition of three types of code and one "tracer", each of these is bound to detect a particular class of error. The matter is to know if there exists other classes of errors which will not be detectable by the code

$$2^k xf + xc \equiv Bx + D \ (\text{modulo } A).$$

It has been admitted that there are only four classes of errors which may occur in a microprocessor :

- computing or operator error ;
- addressing error (operand, operator, shift error) ;
- memorizing error ;
- sequencing error.

So, it has been demonstrated that any single error is detectable by the code, taking into account the algorithm of the OPELEM which handles the coded variables, and also that some constraints must be taken into account by the programmer. The method of analysis is the Failure Modes and Effects Analysis, usually used in analysing electronic cards, but adapted to software. This analysis has shown that some combinations of errors are not detectable. In this case, we proceed to the evaluation of the occurrence probability. These combinations are very complex and the corresponding probabilities are far lower than the objective allocated to the monoprocessor.

4.2. Second part: determination of the probability of non-detection of an error.

4.2.a. First step.

We make the hypothesis that each coded variable is controlled after each instruction. An error E transforms a coded variable X in $X' = X + E$ with $X' \neq X$.

The error E is undetectable if and only if X' is a word of the code, i.e. if and only if

$$2^k x'f + x'c \equiv Bx + D \pmod{A}.$$

In the case of coded data transmission in a transmission channel, the determination of the probability to detect an error E in a message X is possible if the error model is known, that is, the occurrence probability $Px(E)$ in the message X. The probability of non detection is then given by:

$$Pnd(X) = \sum_{E \in Ex} (X+E).Px(E)$$ where Ex is the set of undetectable errors by the code.

The knowledge of $Px(E)$ derives from the characteristics of the transmission channel and the disturbance coming from the environment.

In the case of the coded monoprocessor, it has not been possible to determine $Px(E)$ because the failure mode and the probability of occurrence are not known. Nevertheless, some error models have been considered and the corresponding non-detection probabilities have been calculated. For example, one may quote the model $Px(E) = p^k (1 - p)^{n-k}$ where k is the Hamming weight of E and $P \in [0, 1]$ the bit error rate.

To define the non-detection probability independent of the error model, we have used the notion of "a priori" probability, which considers that the designer has chosen the words of the code in a random way. Hence the calculation of the "a priori" probability of non detection, results from the following reasoning:

Let Cx be a set of pair (cf, cc) chosen randomly in a set M of all possible pairs (cf, cc) containing : $\dfrac{\text{element number of M}}{A}$ elements. Hence, for any word $X' = (x'f, x'c)$ of M, the probability to get $x' \in Cx$ equals :

$$P = \frac{\text{element number of Cx}}{\text{element number of M}} = \frac{1}{A}$$

In the following lines, let Ωx be the set of words used in the coded monoprocessor :

$$\Omega x = \{ (cf , cc) \text{ such that}$$
$$2^k cf + cc \ / \ Bx + D \pmod{A} \}.$$

If Ωx is taken as a set of words Cx randomly chosen and this must be justified then the result may be expressed in the following formulation:

For all $X' = X + E$, the probability for X' to be a word of the code ($X' \in \Omega x$) is $P1 = 1/A$.

In other words : whatever the result of error E on the variable X may be, the probability for E to be undetectable by the coded monoprocessor is 1/A.

It remains to justify that all the words of Ωx are actually randomly chosen. First, the element number of Ωx is

$\dfrac{\text{element number of M}}{A}$ where A is the key of the code. The random character of the words has been justified in comparing the distribution of the arithmetic weight of the words in Ωx with the distribution of the words in Cx, which have been effectively chosen in a random manner.

4.2.b. Second step.

We evaluate here the probability of error compensation.

When one or more of the coded variables are erroneous during the processing, the final signature G sent to the CKDYN at the end of the program is itself positioned by an error, and the error Eg on G is expressed by a polynomial in term of m variables $E_g = Q (E_1 , E_2 , \dots , E_m)$. This characteristic proceeds from the design of the OPELEM.

This polynomial is null in $(0 , 0 , \dots , 0)$, i.e. $Q(0 , 0 , \dots , 0) = 0$; and the coefficients of Q are dependent of the number of instructions performed between the moment of occurrence of the error and the delivery of the signature G. We demonstrate (Ozello 89), under the hypothesis that the coefficients of the polynomial Q are random, that for any error $E \neq (0 , 0 , \dots , 0)$ the probability P2 of non detection is $P2 = 1/A$.

Hence, the loss of the detection ability due to eventual compensation is 1/A and the total probability of non detection of the coded monoprocessor is

$$Pnd = P1 + P2 = 2/A.$$

Remark. The hypothesis concerning the equiprobability of the coefficients of the polynomial Q is questionable. Mr Forin has shown in (Forin 88) that the longer the software, the greater the probability to have a polynomial identically nul. Nevertheless, for a program of less than 10000 lines, this effect is negligible.

5 CONCLUSION.

The safety demonstration of the coded monoprocessor has been investigated and accepted by the Safety National Commission. The coded monoprocessor is now used in many dedicated guide way means of transport such as Automatic Train Protection, in onboard and way-side equipment.

Researchs are being carried out in order to enhance the processing time and improve tools to implement software.

RÉFÉRENCES

ElKoursi M. and Stuparu A. (1990) Etude comparative des architectures microprogrammées utilisées dans les applications de sécurité. INRETS CR/A-90-41.

Forin P. Principe du processeur code . Application à SACEM. 1988

Forin P. Vital coded microprocessor principles and application for various transit systems. CCCT'89 IFAC Paris 1989.

Georges J. P. Principes et fonctionnement du Système d'Aide à l'Exploitation et à la Maintenance SACEM. Revue Générale des chemins de fer N°6 Juin 90.

Gourdon M. Les systèmes POMA 2000. Colloque AFCET 1987.

Martin J. and Wartski S. Vital coded processor: the new safety for transit system. IFAC IFIP Vienne December 1989.

Martin J. and Wartski S. and Galivel C. Le processeur codé: un nouveau concept appliqué à la sécurité des systèmes de transports. Revue Générale des chemins de fer N°6 Juin 90.

Ozello P. Monoprocesseur codé, étude de la propagation des erreurs jusqu'à la signature finale INRETS CR/A-89-96 1989.

Rouquet J.C. and Traverse P.J. Safe and reliable computing onboard the Airbus and ATR aircraft. IFAC , Sarlat France 1986.

SAFETY CASE STRUCTURE: ISSUES RELATED TO CERTIFICATION OF AVIONICS SYSTEMS

Benita M Hall

Avionics Systems Engineer, British Aerospace (Airbus Ltd)
New Technical Centre, Centre 9 - Location C1
Dept B67-02, Filton House, Bristol, BS99 7AR, UK

Abstract. The intention of this paper is to identify an appropriate form for argument representation and to establish a basis for modelling systems and their operational environment.

A structure of a safety case will be given for an aircraft system, which could be used as part of the process for obtaining certification for an aircraft type. This will consist of a complete, high level overview and description of the structure and inter-dependencies of a safety case.

The description of this structure will be given using the concepts of a Safety Argument Manager (SAM) tool. SAM is a generic tool with a general purpose framework for safety argumentation, which will be tailored to a range of application domains and development standards within the domain of the certification of commercial aircraft systems.

One main objective of the SAM project is to produce improved tool support to aid representation and consistency checking of safety arguments, and to provide improved techniques for certifying complex systems upon large-scale aircraft.

Keywords. Safety, Modeling, Management System, Safety Argument Management, Avionic System Certification

INTRODUCTION

Airworthiness requirements and their associated advisory material define safety assessment as a means of demonstrating that an aircraft system is safe. These safety assessments are currently carried out using classical techniques such as fault tree or dependence diagrams, sometimes assisted by graphical computer tools. The safety assessments look at hardware failures only and make no attempt to address software errors. The techniques used presently will become increasingly difficult to manage if systems become more complex or if the assessment is required to include software.

This paper describes a computer based technique which could be used to manage the safety assessment process for very complex systems. The technique is illustrated by taking examples which are currently treated using classical (manual) techniques and showing how the proposed technique can then be used to express the arguments in a manner which may then be automated.

A structure of a safety case is given for an individual aircraft system, which could be used as part of the process of obtaining certification for an aircraft type. The term safety case is used to mean:

. the complete set of evidence produced (by one organisation) to convince some authority that a complete operational system/systems is safe to deploy (for its intended use).

This structure will be described using the concepts of the Safety Argument Manager (SAM) tool. The purposes of doing this are to explain the structure of safety cases and to assess the relevance of the SAM concepts.

A complete, albeit high level, overview and description of the structure and inter-dependencies of the safety case will be given.

There are three main strands to the safety case as it relates to aircraft systems:

. establishment of the process by which aircraft systems will be assessed;
. assessment of the systems;
. demonstration to the airworthiness authorities that the

safety case is acceptable.

These three strands form the top level substructure of the overall safety case.

Prior to presenting an example of the safety case structure, some limitations of current approaches to the handling and management of safety cases will be outlined, followed by a description of SAM and its primary concepts.

It is intended that this will give an insight into the difficulties of the production and management of safety cases, and an outline of one proposed approach to addressing these difficulties.

LIMITATIONS OF
CURRENT APPROACHES

In almost all cases achievement and assessment of safety requires a multi-disciplinary approach, perhaps involving mechanical, electrical and software engineers and human factors experts, including psychologists. Some of the limitations of current approaches arise from the difficulties of identifying interactions between different disciplines, although many arise from other causes such as system complexity and the difficulty of placing a boundary around the factors/issues relevant to the safety argument.

A major source of problems arises from assumptions that are made in system development and assessment. If the assumptions were stated explicitly then it would become possible to assess their validity. A more serious problem is that many assumptions are never made explicit so their validity, and consistency with other assumptions, cannot be assessed. A computerised tool cannot automatically derive assumptions but it can help to draw attention to the absence of assumptions and/or justification for assumptions. An example where rigorous justification of assumptions is required is in assessing the independence of failure modes in redundant systems.

A strongly related issue is completeness. Many arguments are incomplete in that some of the stages of the argument structure are missing. These omissions may reflect implicit assumptions. Completeness is a problem but automated support will help build a broader database which will minimise omissions.

A further practical problem is inconsistency between arguments and/or assumptions. Inconsistent arguments can lead to erroneous conclusions and the failure to make assumptions explicit will increase the likelihood of inconsistency. Automated support for argumentation gives the opportunity to check, at least some aspects of, argument consistency.

There are many examples where failure, or even the expected behaviour, of some part of a system or its environment has caused an unexpected failure in another part of the system. In many cases these problems arise because experts in one discipline fail to take into account important characteristics of the system on which they are working. Again automation should enable cross-checks to be made between arguments relating to different disciplines, eg. to see if all consequential failure modes have been taken into account.

Automation is not a panacea. None of the above problems can ever be completely avoided, mainly because they involve reasoning about the `real world' (McDermid, 1991). SAM will alleviate the above problems by making safety arguments easier to inspect and by facilitating analysis of the validity of individual arguments and the inter-relationships between arguments.

OBJECTIVES AND HIGH
LEVEL REQUIREMENTS

McDermid (1992) expounds the functionality and the different scenarios of SAM. For the purposes of this paper, high-level objectives and requirements will now be outlined.

The primary objective for SAM is that it should facilitate the production of complete system safety arguments (safety cases) which are of higher quality than is normally achieved in current practice. Important objectives are:

.SAM will make safety arguments more visible, thus facilitating informed human assessment of argument quality;

.SAM will automate some aspects of safety analysis eg. fault tree analyses or reliability calculations, and thus improve the completeness and accuracy of arguments;

.SAM will have automated mechanisms for linking to other tools;

.SAM's mechanisms for ensuring update when imported should reduce the risk of error in maintaining an evolving safety argument.

These basic objectives lead on to a number of high level requirements.

SAM will support:

.creation, modification, browsing and printing of arguments including the ability to follow complex argument chains;

.sophisticated argument manipulations such as identifying the consequences of change, and help to generate summaries of complex argument structures;

.the development, modification, printing and browsing of system models, and linking these models to arguments;

.importation of supporting evidence from other tools, spanning the whole development process, to provide basic data on which the arguments depend;
.links to simulators, particularly to provide information to drive simulators and incorporating the resulting information as supporting evidence.

These requirements capture the current notion of the basic functionality required of SAM.

When using SAM, three different aspects of a safety case, and the relationships between them are available. These aspects are:

.documents - presented as hypertext, including diagrams, formal arguments, explanatory text, etc;
.models - representing the system and its operational environment, and perhaps its development and evaluation environments;.arguments - formalised representations of chains of reasoning.

These three components of a safety case can be developed in any order and can evolve together.

There are multiple facets of a safety case and SAM must support work on these facets in any order, and give the user the ability to change between facets, translate between views of the safety cases, and support the development of high quality documents, relating the case to other system documentation in a traceable way.

PRIMARY CONCEPTS OF SAM

Primarily by using the term safety case we mean:
.the complete set of evidence produced to convince some authority that a complete operational system is safe to deploy.

In various industries other terms are used for this collection of evidence, eg. certification case and hazard log, but the concepts seems to be broadly applicable. Although we use the term `safety case' in the singular there is no implication that this is a single document. It represents the totality of information produced in whatever form, eg documents, databases, etc.

In defining the structure of a safety case there are five primary concepts that are currently supported by SAM. We discuss each one in turn, starting with the most fundamental, the concept of a `goal'. The other concepts are : context, strategy, solution and system model.

Goal

The most important idea underlying the structuring of a

safety case is that we are trying to satisfy some overall goal, eg to show that the system is safe. Further, to satisfy this overall goal we have to satisfy a number of sub-goals, eg showing that particular subsystems are safe. Thus a goal is:
.some objective which has to be achieved, eg.
- demonstrating that an aircraft is safe;
- demonstrating that an aircraft will not hit the ground;

It is also important to note that a goal is not:
.a document, although satisfaction of a goal may be recorded in a document;
.an activity, although one or several activities may be undertaken in achieving a goal, or the solutions to several goals may be the by-product of one activity.

Goals are particularly important as they provide the primary structure for the safety case. As implied above, goals are decomposed hierarchically, that is one goal can have several sub-goals, and those sub-goals have their own sub-goals. Goals do not exist in isolation, they are only meaningful as part of a context.

Context

In order to understand how to satisfy a goal, we need to understand the context in which that goal is articulated. Thus a context is:
.the information necessary to allow a goal to be unambiguously interpreted;
Typically we expect a context to have three components:
.a `scope' - the range of situations, or classes of systems, for which the goal applies;
.a set of `constraints' - factors that constrain or guide the way in which the goal will be met and which usually are outside the control of those who are developing the safety case:
.a set of `assumptions' - factors that constrain or guide the way in which the goal will be met but which are within the control of those who are developing the system or safety case.

In practice the scope may be a set of aircraft types, the constraints will include statutory requirements, eg international standards imposed by certification bodies, and assumptions may be aspects of the design strategy, or policy, chosen to make design and certification simpler.

Strategy

A goal can usually be satisfied in more than one way. The way in which a goal is intended to be satisfied is determined by the strategy. Thus a strategy is:
.a set of rules or guidelines which govern or influence the activities undertaken in order to satisfy the goal;
Often the strategy will identify the set of immediate sub-goals. Thus the decision to analyse a system on a functional basis, rather than in terms of its physical structure, would be an example of a strategy.

Solution

Although the goals provide the structure to the safety case it is the set of solutions which show that the system is safe. Thus a solution is:
.a means of showing that the goal has been satisfied;
Taking the examples in section 4.1, example solutions might be:
.demonstrating that an aircraft is safe - analysis of structures, systems and performance;
.proving that a theorem is true - a proof, or a reference to a paper or a book in which the theorem is proved.

Solutions may take any form, but one of the central theses of the SAM project is that there is a general form for arguments, based on the work of the English philosopher, Stephen Toulmin (Toulmin 1958), which can be used to help structure and present solutions. Toulmin divides the constituents of a single argument step into six parts:

CLAIMS are the statements we wish to justify;

DATA are the grounds we produce when asked to show what we are basing our claim on. This can be experimental observations, common knowledge, statistics, personal testimony or previously established claims;

WARRANTS are step-authorising statements, eg laws of nature, legal principles, rules of thumb, engineering formulae and inference rules;

BACKING is general information providing reasons for trusting the warrant, eg that it is based on well-tried and trusted statistical principles;

QUALIFIERS are modal terms which record the degree of certainty a warrant allows;

REBUTTALS are specific circumstances in which the argument will not hold.

In principle arguments presented in this canonical form would have all these components but, in practice, many are often omitted, eg it is quite common to omit backing for warrants from commonly used theories such as reliability theory. In the example of aircraft systems certification rebuttals and qualifiers will not be used.

At detailed levels in a safety case the solution may be quite complex, eg the complete FMEA for a system. At higher levels the solutions will tend to be summaries, eg asserting that the current goal has been met as all the sub-goals have been met. Thus the top levels of the argument structure can be thought of as providing `indices' into the detail of the safety case.

System Model

The other four parts of the safety case, but most notably the goal and solution, will need to refer to parts of the artefact which we wish to show to be safe. We refer not to the artefact itself, but to a suitable model. Thus the system model is:

.a set of problem domain entities necessary to articulate the goal and safety case, eg:

- a definition of the set of systems on an aircraft;

- the identification of zones on an aircraft;

- the identification of failure modes which might affect a particular system.

It should be noted that, although the term system model is used it potentially has a much broader scope than an aircraft system, eg. brakes and steering control system. For example we would probably wish to include organisations such as the Airworthiness Authorities and documents which form part of the safety case in the system model.

The system model is useful for consistency checking as, for example, in principle, we can automatically check that a solution which is intended to relate to every failure mode affecting a system does cover all failure modes, as defined in the model. In this case the faults may be identified by means of the context referring to the appropriate sub-part of the model. Thus the system model forms the basis on top of which the overall safety case is built, and against which it can be checked.

In many circumstances some parts of the model have to be produced before it is possible to start solving the goal, and some further parts are produced in satisfying the goal. An example here might be the definition of zones on an aircraft which must exist before a zonal analysis can be undertaken and a zonal failure mode summary. In our example we will treat documents which form part of the safety case as part of the system model, and we also limit our decription of the model to those items which are pertinent to a particular goal.

AN AIRCRAFT SAFETY CASE

We have now produced the conceptual framework necessary to allow us to outline the top levels of a safety case for an aircraft. The `systems' side of the safety case is dealt with in significant detail although, in principle, it would be possible to provide this level of detail for the structures and performance part of the case. The goal structure is presented in terms of levels, eg. level 1,2-6. Documentation that is produced as part of the safety case will be included as part of the system model of each goal.

Goal Structure

In order to clarify the structure of the safety case, an overview of the safety case structure is now given.

GOAL DESCRIPTION

0 Produce Safe, Certificated and Economically Viable Aircraft
1 Define the Aircraft
1.1 *Define the Aircraft systems
1.2 Define the Aircraft Structures
1.3 Define Aircarft Performance Limits
2 Agree Certification bases and deviations from Rules
2.1 Agree System/Equipment Certification Plans
2.2 Define Assessment Rules for Structures
2.3 Define Assessment Rules for Performance Limits
3 *Assess Aircraft Systems
3.1 Assess individual systems
3.1.1 Do Functional Hazard Analysis (FHA) for each system function
3.1.2 Define Zonal Rules for each system in a zone
3.1.3 Define installation rules for each system in a zone
3.1.4 Analysis as determined by Means of Compliance (MOC)
3.1.2.1 Do Zonal Safety Analysis
4 Assess Aircraft Structures
5 Assess Aircraft Performance Limits
6 Produce Safety Case

* This goal is iterated over the set of systems.

Top Level Goal

The top level goal is concerned with the safety of the complete aircraft. As an example of the goal structure, an outline of the top level goal will be given here. A complete list of the goals and their associated strategies, solutions and system models have been published as an internal British Aerospace document (Hall, SDF/B67/Gen/61/1603, 1992).

GOAL 0: Produce Safe, Certificated and Economically Viable Aircraft
CONTEXT:
Scope Commercial Aircraft > 12,500 kgs
Cconstraints: Safe Acceptable Risk accident statistics
legal liability
cost of accident
Certified JARs & FARs (there are others, but these are normally based on JARs & FARs)
CRIs, Special Conditions
Viable Market Demand for aircraft type
Cost complexity, re-use and technology
Timescale
Assumptions: Operating conditions for aircraft, eg typical flight profiles;
Cost of Ownership parameters
STRATEGY: IN PARALLEL: Negotiate assessment process with Airworthiness Authorities (AA) and Airbus Industrie (AI) (goal 2)
Demonstrate compliance with AA requirements for systems, structures and performance (goals 3,4 and 5)
FOLLOWED BY: Formal Certification (`signing off'

safety case) (goal 6)
SOLUTION: Overall aircraft assessment, including individual systems assessments, and conclusions of AA and Airlines discussions - summary of lower level arguments.
CLAIM Aircraft is certificated and is safe and viable
DATA 1 Safety assessment procedures agreed with AI and AA (goal 2)
DATA 2 Safety assessment process completed for all systems on the Aircraft showing compliance with the AA requirements (goal 3)
WARRANT Assessment of all systems, structures and performance, to procedures agreed with the AAs and AI, subject to independent checks by the AAs, yields a safe and certificated aircraft
BACKING Accepted practice in the industry and with the AAs
SYSTEM MODEL: INITIALLY: No model of the aircraft required for this level, but some model of enterprises (roles and responsibilities, etc) might be appropriate to ensure that all relevant standards are adhered to, that properly authorised individuals sign off safety cases
FINALLY: Safety Case, Type Certificate and a Certificate of Airworthiness produced as a result of the process of satisfying the above goal.

Most of the above should be self-explanatory. The constraint to size of aircraft is important as different airworthiness requirements apply to smaller aircraft.

The argument here can be thought of as `pure' summary, in that all it does is draw overall conclusions about safety from the main analyses. However it is important as it defines the topics of interest in the remainder of the safety case. Note that goals 3, 4 and 5 represent the `real' safety case whereas goal 6 is largely procedural (but vital), and goals 1 and 2 are concerned with establishing the lower level contexts for assessment.

The remainder of the goal structure is concerned primarily with the way in which goal 3 is satisfied.

ANALYSIS AND COMMENTARY

This paper has been restricted to the top level of the safety case, therefore substantial parts of the structure have been omitted. However it should serve to illustrate the use and utility of the SAM concepts.

Structure of the Case

The structure of the safety case reveals the graphical representation and textual support. Three levels of the safety case were identified in section 1 of this paper, although, the ordering of the list remains unclear. However, the purpose of the structure is to provide some means of navigation through the safety case, in terms of illustrating the overall strategy.

STRENGTHS AND WEAKNESSES OF THE STRUCTURE

In this instance SAM is being used in support of the certification process for avionics systems. It can be used as a source of information about the safety case and the associated system, which can then be checked and assessed by the Certification authorities.

The structure of the safety case enables visibility and clarity of the safety arguments, and also provides the ability to show validity of arguments and inter-relationships between arguments. Weaknesses of the structure relate to the fact that it is not explicit how the solution to a specific goal relates to its sub-goals and associated solutions; there are no means to ensure that the solution does satisfy the goal; there are no means to show that the claims in a specific solution are relevant to the goal, and also the criteria for judging the solutions is not explicit.

It should be clear from the above discussion that the overall structure of an aircraft safety case is very complex and, to some degree, has been `forced' onto a tree structure. However the issues addressed by each goal are conceptually different, and this still seems to be a good way of decomposing the safety case. What has been made explicit is the difficulty of managing the case because of the inter-connections between the arguments.

CONCLUSIONS

The problem of developing safety cases has been discussed in fairly broad terms, but focused on the ideas of a particular experimental tool, known as SAM. It is accepted that there already exist a number of valuable safety analysis tools, however, these focus on particular problems or techniques, eg Fault-tree analysis, Failure Modes and Effects Analyses (FMEA). SAM should provide a co-ordinating and integrating framework for complete safety cases in a way which builds on the strength of current tools, and supplements them by managing their interactions and dependencies.

SAM differs from the above mentioned tools by providing a framework with which a safety case can be structured by decomposing goals and sub-goals. Each goal can be satisfied by argument fragments (solutions) in a local context which follow a strategy. This paper has attempted to show that there is a need for a tool and a methodology to support the overall structuring and management of the complete safety case.

The main objective of this paper was to identify an appropriate form for argument representation of safety cases, and to establish a basis for the modelling of systems and their operational environments: this paper has illustrated a potential mechanism to manage safety cases.

REFERENCES

Hall, B.M. SDF/B67/Gen/61/1603 (1992). Aircraft Safety Assessment - Overall Safety Case Structure. British Aerospace Internal Document.

Leveson, N.G. (1986). Software Safety: Why, What and How. Computing Surveys, Vol. 18

McDermid, J.A. (1991). SAM - A Tool for Supporting Reasoning about Safety: Objectives, Requirements and Operational Concept. University of York: SAM/02

McDermid, J.A. (1992). Safety Cases and Safety Arguments. CSR Paper

Toulmin, S (1958). The Uses of Arguments. Cambridge University Press.

FAULT DIAGNOSIS OF A BATCH OF MICROPROCESSORS

Jianwen HUANG*

Jiangsu Institute of Technology, Zhenjiang, Jiangsu, China

René DAVID

Laboratoire d'Automatique de Grenoble, BP 46, 38402 Saint-Martin-d'Hères, France
E-mail: david@lag.grenet.fr.

Abstract. A batch of 50 circuits (microprocessors MC 6800) has been tested through several methods, by engineers working at the CEA : a randomly generated test sequence has detected more faulty circuits than test sequences generated in a deterministic way by different approaches. In order to identify what faults were detected by a random test sequence, while there were not detected by a deterministic sequence, a diagnosis of the faulty circuits has been performed. This paper presents the results of the fault diagnosis, and it is explained why the random test has been more efficient.

Key words. Detection; fault diagnosis; random test; deterministic test; microprocessors.

1 INTRODUCTION

Studies are done in France at the CEA (Commissariat à l'Energie Atomique), for measuring the effect of low irradiation on the microprocessors (Gérard, 1983; Laviron, 1989). The aim is to know the behaviour of the circuits which are installed in a nuclear plant. There are mainly two kinds of experiments. First kind: some tens of microprocessors (identical and functioning correctly) are placed in an enclosure with a low level irradiation rate. After a certain time, these microprocessors are taken out from the enclosure and tested. In this way, the proportion of the circuits becoming faulty in some defined experimental conditions is estimated. Second kind of experiment: only one microprocessor is placed in an enclosure as mentioned above. A tester, outside the enclosure and connected to the circuit, tests it periodically. We thus estimate the moment when the circuit becomes faulty.

In these experiments, *the tester is an essential measurement tool* (Gérard, 1983]). It "decides" if a circuit is correct or not in the first kind of experiments, and when a microprocessor becomes faulty in the second kind.

The test of a digital circuits consists of sending an input sequence, known as *test sequence*, and observing the output sequence. In the general case where the circuit is sequential, the set of test vectors in the test sequence is not enough to characterize this sequence: their order are important for testing some faults.

There are essentially two approaches to design a test sequence. The first one, known as *deterministic,* consists in making faults hypotheses, then to construct a sequence of input vectors which can test these faults. If the circuit is relatively simple, we can make the hypotheses taking into account the structure of the circuit (such as stuck-at-0, stuck-at-1, bridging fault...). If the circuit is complex, generally the user can only consider the faults at the functional level (such as an instruction or operation which is not executed, or incorrectly executed...). The second approach, known as *random*, consist in applying a sequence of vectors which are randomly drawn among the possible input vectors (abiding by the specification of the manufacturer). Then no fault hypothesis is necessary for constructing a random test sequence. In most cases, the random test vectors are equiprobable.

The observation of the output sequence may be a comparison of the output sequence of the circuit under test with the output sequence of a reference circuit (which may be either recorded or generated in real-time by applying the same input sequence to both the circuit under test and the reference circuit). The signature analyse can also be used. The signature is a compact function of the output sequence, which is generally obtained with a linear feedback shift register (Frohwerk, 1977). This avoids the use of a real reference circuit for comparison. The probability that a faulty circuit gives a fault-free signature can be neglected is the shift register is long enough. The signature analyse technique can be used with any test sequence, provided that it is reproducible.

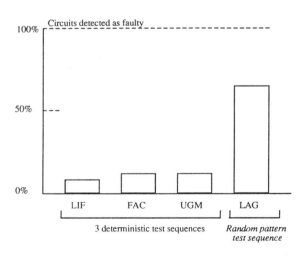

Fig. 1. Results obtained by the CEA
on a batch of 50 microprocessors MC 6800

The engineers of CEA (in Valduc) have used several kinds of test methods. Since 1984, a random tester for testing microprocessor MC 6800 has been used. The tester was made to provide their needs (i.e. to perform the two kinds of experiments previously explained) by the Laboratoire d'Automatique de Grenoble (Fuentes, 1984). It is based on previous works of this laboratory (Thévenod-Fosse, 1983; Fédi, 1984; David, 1984; Fédi, 1986) . It uses the signature analyse technique.

* This work was done when she was visiting the Laboratoire d'Automatique de Grenoble.

In 1989, the engineers of CEA (from Valduc and Fontenay-aux-Roses) have published comparative experimental results about the fault detection of some circuits. For a batch of 50 microprocessors MC 6800, three determinist test sequences and one random test sequence have been used.

Figure 1 extracted from (Lavion, 1989) presents the summary of the results. The test sequences called LIF, FAC and UGM are deterministic. The test sequence called LAG is a random one.

LIF contains about 50 bytes.
FAC contains 2 K bytes.
UGM contains about 60 K bytes. It is based on functional faults hypotheses. However the data are random. For example : when the addition of the numbers in registers R_1 and R_2 is tested, the operands put into theses registers are random (Bellon, 1985).
LAG is the test sequence generated by a random tester mentioned above.

Figure 1 shows that for this batch of MC 6800:
1) the random test sequence has detected more faulty circuits than the other test sequences (this phenomenon had already been observed under other occasions (David, 1984; Deneux, 1984));
2) the number of circuits detected as faulty by the deterministic test sequences do not increase very much when the length of the sequence is greater (the length of the test sequence UGM is about 30 times as the length of FAC and about 1200 times as the length of LIF).

It was interesting to know why these results were obtained. The first question coming to mind is : are the *suspicious* circuits (we shall use this word for the circuits detected as faulty by the random pattern test sequence, and detected as fault-free by the deterministic test sequences) really faulty ? If the answer is "yes" the second question is : what kinds of faults are detected by the random pattern test sequence, while none of the three other test sequences have detected them ? In order to answer these questions, a fault diagnosis has been performed. This paper presents the results of the fault diagnosis (in the functional meaning, not physical) performed on the batch of 50 microprocessors (Huang, 1990).

2 BASIC DATA

Before presenting the diagnosis, it is useful to recall the main features of the concerned circuit, and to give some indications about the manner that the random test sequence is designed.

2.1 The MC 6800 (Motorola, 1979; Thomson, 1984)

Since the test consists in observing the outputs when the inputs are activated, we must know what the inputs and the outputs are. This is illustrated in Fig. 2.

The *inputs* of this circuit are the following ones.
a) A 8-bit data bus (bidirectional).
b) 6 control lines: RESET, HALT, IRQ (interruption request), NMI (non maskable interruption),TSC (tri-state control), DBE (data bus enable).
c) 2 clocks (opposite phases) noted Φ_1 and Φ_2 (a period corresponds to a cycle).

The *outputs* of this circuit are the following ones.
a) A 16-bit address bus.
b) 3 state lines: R/W (read/write), VMA (valid memory address), BA (bus available).
c) The data bus when the microprocessor is in the reading state.

There are mainly 4 types of *instructions*: arithmetic operations, logic operations, transfer and branching. These instructions use various addressing modes (Motorola, 1979; Thomson, 1984), and there are 197 different operation codes. Each operation code is coded with 8 bits, so there are 59 invalid code among the 256 possible values (i.e. for these 59 operation code, the function is not specified by the manufacturer). Every instruction needs a given number of data (0, 1 or 2), and is executed in a given number of clock cycles.

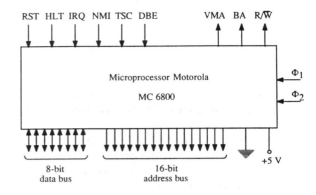

Fig. 2. Inputs and outputs of the MC 6800.

2.2 Random test sequence

Some features useful for understanding this paper are presented here. For more details, the reader is refered to (Fédi, 1984) or (David, 1984).

The clock inputs are those specified by the manufacturer. It remains 14 inputs to consider, the 8 bits of the data bus and the 6 control lines.

A possible test strategy consists in applying, at each clock cycle, any 14-bit random vector (Timoc, 1983). But this strategy presents a great drawback: the test sequence may be incompatible with the specification of the manufacturer. It could lead to the conclusion that the circuit is faulty, although it has a behaviour different of the reference only for some case which is out of the specifications (invalid code for example).

The approach which has been used in our laboratory in Grenoble (David, 1984; Fuentes, 1984) is different. The test sequence abides to the manufacturer's specifications. That is to say that the test sequence which is applied to the microprocessor (random instructions with random data) is syntactically correct.

Data bus. At each clock cycle, a byte is randomly drawn. The microprocessor can read it if it needs it, and if it is waiting for an operation code the byte is drawn among the valid operation codes only.

Commands. The input DBE is connected to the clock Φ_2. At every cycle a random drawing is performed for each of the other control lines. When a control has been drawn, it is maintained a number of clock cycles according to the user's manual. The occurrence probability of a command should be small, in order to avoid interrupting the "normal work" of the microprocessor frequently.

Initialization. It is a deterministic sequence, putting the inside registers in a defined state, which is applied to the microprocessor before the actual test sequence.

In practise, the test sequences are pseudo-random. Their statistical properties are very near a pure random sequence, but the former is reproducible.

3 DIAGNOSIS

For this batch of 50 circuits, the authors did not have any information about the circuits, but only the indication of Fig. 1. They did not know what circuits were found as faulty by the four test sequences. A circuit found as fault-free by all the test sequences, not belonging to this batch, is considered to be the reference circuit.

3.1 Development of the study

As posed in Section 1, the first question is : are the suspicious circuits really faulty?

We insist that if the random tester works properly (any out-of-order tester could give aberrant results), the suspicious circuits are really faulty. In effect, as pointed out in Section 2.2, the test sequence respects the constraints of the manufacturer. Therefore, if a circuit is detected as faulty by such a test, it means that there is a behaviour of the circuit under test (compatible with the specifications) which is different from the behaviour of the reference circuit.

The first experiments have been done with the random tester built by X. Fédi in 1983 (Fédi, 1984; David, 1984). A same test sequence was applied to the 50 circuits, which have been classify into several groups. The test length (number of instructions) when the first error is detected defines a group. Then the prime diagnosis was performed by varying the probability of the instructions and commands and observing the responses of the circuits by a logic analyser (Fédi, 1984; Hewlett, 1980). From these experiments, some hypotheses of faults were deduced which have guided the next experiments.

The actual diagnosis experiments were done on the logic circuits test system GR115 (Genrad) at the Centre Inter-Universitaire de Micro-Electronique de Grenoble (CIME). Short test sequences have been specially designed to verify if some faults (assumed from the prime experiments). This appoach has been efficient.

3.2 GR115 tester (Genrad, 1988a and b; Bouvier, 1989)

The logic circuits test system *GR115 VLSI Tester* allows testing of any kind of integrated logic circuit. It works under UNIX system. This tester includes a computer with a central unit 68 000, a keyboard, a printer, an hard disc, etc.

The GR115 system needs two kinds of informations for testing a circuit (Genrad, 1988a and b). These informations correspond to files which are prepared by the user: a file *XX.par* which indicates some parameters given by the circuit manufacturer, and a file *XX.tpp* (test pattern process) which defines the test sequence. The file *XX.tpp* produces a file *XX.vtt* (vector truth table). It is then possible to modify some parts of this table from the keyboard.

The file *XX.par*, which corresponds to the microprocesor MC 6800 and which is independent of the test sequence, was previously performed by the Laboratoire de Génie Informatique de Grenoble (LGI). The files *XX.tpp* correspond to the applied test sequences which will be shortly presented in Section 3.3 and 3.4.

When a test sequence has been recorded, the corresponding output sequence, for a fault-free circuit, can be obtained by two ways: either by simulation or by learning thanks to a reference circuit. The second method has been used. When the system is performing a test, a generator applies the successive input vectors and the circuit responses are recorded at each cycle, simultaneously on all the pins, then the obtained values are compared with the correct values.

3.3 Diagnosis results

The test sequences which have been used were designed in order to bring to the fore some faults which are assumed to be present (Section 3.1). Let us first present the results which have been obtained, before giving an example of test sequence (Section 3.4).

The faults observed in the circuits in the batch are shown in Table 1. There are 9 faults named f_1, f_2,...f_9. Some of them are very easy to observe. For example, the fault f_2: the RESET which is carried out in the initialization sequence should put the hexadecimal value *FFFE* on the address bus; but if the fault is present the value is *FFFF*. Some faults are difficult to be observed, such as f_6 and f_9 which will be discussed later.

The circuits are numbered from 1 to 50. Table 2 indicates the faults which are observed in such and such circuit. For example, faults f_2 and f_3 are in circuit n° 34, and fault f_6 is in circuits n° 1, 5, 23, etc. For each of the faulty circuit, we have diagnosed 1 or 2 faults. It does not mean that there are not any other faults in these circuits, but this is not important for our purpose.

TABLE 1. Definition of the observed faults

The values in PC (Program Counter) and the instruction codes are expressed in hexadecimal.

f_1 Add. 0 stuck-at-*1* (i.e. address line # 0 stuck-at-*1*).

f_2 When the instructions of the initialization sequence are executed, PC = *FFFF*.

f_3 Add. 3 stuck-at-*1*.

f_4 Add. 8 stuck-at-*1*.

f_5 During the first cycle of RESET, the VMA line is in tri-state instead of having level *H*.

f_6 If RESET occurs during an instruction JSR (*BD* or *AD*) or BSR (*8D*), then the change of line R/W from level *L* to level *H* is delayed of one cycle.

f_7 When the temperature of the circuit increases, the circuit does not work correctly. A fault detection occurs at an undefinite time. This is not a hard fault.

f_8 When instruction PUSH B (*37*) is executed, levels *H* are written on all the bits of the data bus, instead of the expected value.

f_9 This fault is connected with fault f_6. If instruction STS (indexed mode, *AF*) or STS (extended mode, *BF*) is executed, after a faulty output due to f_6 appeared, all the bits of the data bus have the level *H* instead of the expected value (which is the value in the stack pointer, SP).

TABLE 2. Diagnosis results

Circuits numbers	Faults in the circuits
35	f_1 and f_2
34	f_2 and f_3
2	f_4
22	f_5
1, 5, 23, 24, 25, 30, 43, 47, 48, 49, 50	f_6
3, 4, 6, 9, 10, 13, 14, 15, 16, 17, 18, 19, 20, 21, 26, 27, 28, 40, 46	f_6 and f_9
31	f_7
29	f_8
7, 8, 11, 12, 32, 33, 36, 37, 38, 39, 41, 42, 44, 45	fault-free

3.4 The test sequences

For diagnosing the faults, 6 sequences have been used. These sequences and the faults detected by each of them are given in Table 3. R. Velazco (LGI), had already programmed a test sequence for the circuit MC 6800 on the tester GR115. This sequence is called /velazco/pcr. The sequence which is called *Initialization* is the initialization of the sequence /velazco/pcr (i.e. its beginning) slighty modified. The four other sequences (*Lag1, Lag2, Lag3, Lag 4*) have been specially designed in order to point out the faults assumed to be present. Each of them must be preceded by the sequence *Initialization*. One of them will be detailed.

Table 4 presents the concatenated sequence *Initialization.Lag 3*. The sequence *Initialization* contains 23 cycles numbered from 0 to 22, and the sequence *Lag 3* contains 34 clock cycles numbered from 23 to 56. The initialization sequence consists essentially to put known values in the registers. For example instruction LDS *CCCC* (cycles 14 to 16) puts the hexadecimal value *CCCC* in the stack pointer (the symbols which are useful only for the machine in order to understand assembly language have been omitted for clarity).

TABLE 3. Faults detected by the various test sequences

Sequences	Faults detected
Initialization	f_1, f_2, f_3, f_4
Lag 1	f_5
Lag 2	f_8
Lag 3	f_6, f_9
Lag 4	f_6, f_9
/velasco/ pcr	f_1, f_2, f_3, f_4, f_7, f_8

As it has already be said the sequence *Lag 3* allows bringing to the fore some faults.

Exhibition of fault f_6. Fault f_6 is presented in Table 1. The sequence *Lag 3* contains an instruction JSR (starting at cycle 27), and a RESET is applied during its execution (from cycle 32). From the specifications (Motorola, 1979; Thomson, 1984), the R/W line should change from the low level, *L*, to the high level, *H*, at cycle 34, and keep this level for some time. When a circuit is affected by the fault f_6 its changes to level *H* at cycle 35.

What is read on the screen at cycle 34 is shown in Table 5. The low level and high level are respectively noted *0* and *1* for the inputs and *L* and *H* for the outputs. The last input/output column (before the dot) corresponds to the R/W line. One should have *H* but we have *L* (which is underlined in order to show that this is an incorrect value).

TABLE 4. A test sequence: Initialisation followed by Lag 3.

	Cycle	RESET	HALT	Instructions	States
		Control lines			
Initialization (cycles 0 to 22)	0	0	1		
	1	0	1		
	.	.	.		Add. = FFFE
	7	0	1		VMA = L , R/W = H
	8	1	1		
	9	1	1		
	10	1	1		VMA = H , R/W = H
	11	1	1	LDX 3333	
	12	1	1		PC = 0000
	13	1	1		Index Reg. = 3333
	14	1	1	LDS CCCC	
	15	1	1		
	16	1	1		SP = CCCC
	17	1	1	LDA B 55	
	18	1	1		ACC B = 55
	19	1	1	LDA A AA	
	20	1	1		ACC A = AA
	21	1	1	TAP	
	22	1	1		CCR = AA
Lag 3 (cycles 23 to 56)	23	1	0	NOP (01)	
	24	1	0		
	25	1	0		
	26	1	0		
	27	1	1	JSR (extended) (BD)	
	28	1	1		
	29	1	1		
	30	1	1		
	31	1	1		
	32	0	1		
	33	0	1		
Detection of f_6 *	34	0	1		
	35	0	1		
	36	0	1		
	37	0	1		
	38	0	1	NOP	
	43	0	1		
	44	1	1	STS (extended) (BF)	
	50	1	1		
Detection of f_9 *	51	1	1		
Detection of f_9 *	52	1	1		
	56	.	.	STOP	

TABLE 5. What is read on the screen.

Cycle 34, correct microprocessor	/0 11 1 1 11 0 00010001 HHHHHHHHLLLLLLLL L	H./
Cycle 34, with fault f_6	/0 11 1 1 11 0 00010001 HHHHHHHHLLLLLLLL L	L./
Cycle 51, correct microprocessor	/1 11 1 1 11 0 HHLLHHLL LLLHLLLHLLLHLLLH H	L./
Cycle 52, correct microprocessor	/1 11 1 1 11 0 HHLLHHLL LLLHLLLHLLLHLLLH H	L./
Cycle 51, with fault f_9	/1 11 1 1 11 0 HH̲H̲H̲H̲H̲H̲ LLLHLLLHLLLHLLLH H	L./
Cycle 52, with fault f_9	/1 11 1 1 11 0 HH̲H̲H̲H̲H̲H̲ LLLHLLLHLLLHLLLH H	L./

The 8 first values are $\overline{RESET}$, $\phi 1$, $\phi 2$, DBE, HALT, $\overline{IRQ}$, $\overline{NMI}$, TSC.
Then we have the 8 bits of the data bus, from d7 to d0, then the 16 bits of the address bus from ad15 to ad 0, and finally VMA, R/W, and BA. The . means non significant (corresponds to the bus availability). The // show the beginning and the end of the line.

Exhibition of fault f_9. Fault f_9 is presented in Table 1. The sequence *Lag 3* contains an instruction STS (starting at cycle 44). From the specifications, the microprocessor should be in the reading state at cycles 51 and 52, and the value on the data bus should be the value of the stack pointer (low weight byte at cycle 51 and hight weight byte at cycle 52). Since the value *CCCC* was put in this register, one should have *HHLLHHLL* on the data bus at both cycles (the binary coding *HHLL* corresponds to the hexadecimal value *C*).

What is read on the screen at cycles 51 and 52 is shown in Table 5. The bundle of 8 bits about the middle of the line corresponds to the data bus. In the reading state the value are presented as *0*'s and *1*'s, and in the writing state the value are presented as *L*'s and *H*'s. The faulty *H*'s are underlined.

4 CONCLUDING REMARKS

The results in Table 2 are coherent with those obtained by CEA shown in Fig. 1, as far as the proportion of fault-free circuits is concerned. Some of the circuits affected by the fault f_6 and eventually the fault f_9, may be affected by an additional fault which has not been diagnosed, and which may have been detected by a deterministic test.

It is clear that the faults which are detected by the random test sequence, and have not been detected by the 3 deterministic test sequences used by the CEA, are relative to the asynchronous control signals (RESET, more precisely). As a matter of fact, in a deterministic sequence, *the control inputs are applied at certain moments, but we cannot test their effect in all the possible cases*. For illustrating this idea, let us consider a very simple circuit.

Figure 3 presents a D flip-flop whose working is as follows. When a rising edge of the clock C occurs, the output Q takes the value of the input D (and the output $\overline{Q}$ has always the Boolean value complementary to Q). The values of Q and $\overline{Q}$ remain unchanged up to the next rising edge of the clock C. This is the basic working of this flip-flop. It is a synchronous working. There are two additional inputs S and R (S for Set and R for Reset) whose working is asynchronous. When R = 1 (i.e. $\overline{R} = 0$), the output Q takes the value 0, independently of C. When S = 1 (i.e. $\overline{S} = 0$), the output Q takes the value 1, independently of C. The manufacturer does not consider the case where S = 1 and R = 1 at the same time (Sescosem, 1975).

A possible test sequence is illustrated in Fig. 4. The first impulse on R puts the flip-flop in a known state (this is not a test of the correct working of R since the state of the flip-flop when it is powered on is unknown). Then the impulses on S and R test the correct working of these inputs. Finally it is verified that the synchronous behaviour corresponds to the specifications. This a functional test since it is designed without precise hypothesis about the faults which may affect the circuit. This test sequence may appear as satisfactory, however it does not detect the stuck-at-1 fault which is shown in Fig. 3. As a matter of fact, this fault can produce a faulty behaviour only when the clock C has the value 1. In order to be sure of the correct working of the inputs S and R, it would be necessary to test them in all the possible cases: they should be tested for various values of C and D, and even the sequence of these inputs changings should be taken into account.

Now, let us transpose this idea to the microprocessor. The inputs RESET, HALT, etc. are asynchronous signals, which

200

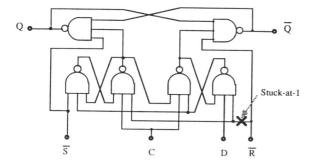

Fig. 3. D flip-flop with asynchronous S and R.

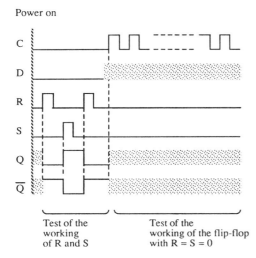

Fig. 4. Test of the D flip-flop in Fig. 3.

Acknowledgement

The authors are very grateful to X. Fédi, R. Velazco, J.-P. Acquadro and the technical group of the Laboratoire d'Automatique de Grenoble, who were very helpful, to the engineers working in CIME who have supplied the VLSI Tester and the guidance, and to the CEA who posed the questions and supported this study.

Bibliography

BELLON, C., E. KOLOKITHAS, R. VELAZCO (1985). Le Système GAPT : une chaîne de test pour microprocesseurs, *L'Onde Electrique*, Vol. 65, n°6/99, 99-109.

BOUVIER, G. (1989). *Test de Circuits Intégrés*, Tecnical Report CIME.

DAVID, R., X. FEDI , P.THEVENOD-FOSSE (1984). Test aléatoire de microprocesseurs : étude théorique et expérimentations, *Technique et Science Informatiques*, Vol.3, n°6, 421-433.

DENEUX, H., P.THEVENOD-FOSSE (1984). Test aléatoire de circuits développés par le CNET / CNS, *4th Int. Conf. on Reliability and Maintenance*, Perros-Guirec (F).

FEDI, X. (1984). *Etude expérimentale du test aléatoire de microprocesseurs*, Thèse de Docteur-Ingénieur, INP Grenoble.

FEDI, X., R. DAVID (1986). Some Experimental Results from Random Testing of Microprocessors, *IEEE Trans. on Inst. & Measurement*, Vol. IM-35, 78-86.

FROHWERK, R. A. (1977). Signature Analysis : A New Digital Field Service Method, *Hewlett Packard J.*, May, 2-8.

FUENTES, A., R. DAVID (1984). *Testeur aléatoire pour MC 6800. Descriptif technique et notice d'utilisation*, Rapport final du contrat LAG / CEA Valduc, Oct..

GENRAD (1988a). *Component Test Systems GR 1xx. Operator's Guide*, Version 2.0.

GENRAD (1988b). *Component Test Systems GR 1xx. Programmer's Guide*, Version 2.0.

GERARD, G., M. RAETH, A. LAVIRON (1983). *Sensibilité des microprocesseurs aux rayonnements. Importance de la méthode de test*, Commissariat à l'Energie Atomique, Report SRSC n° 173, .

HEWLETT PACKARD (1980). *1615 A Logic Analyzer. Operating and Service Manual*.

HUANG, J.W., R. DAVID (1990). *Diagnostic de fautes dans un lot de microprocesseurs MC 6800*, Contract Report n°662.248 S, Sept..

JACOMINO, M., W. ISSA, R. DAVID (1992). *Méthode statistique de prédiction de fautes*, Technical Report LAG 92-01.

LAVIRON, A., G. GERARD, T.Y. HENRY (1989). Effects of Low Irradiation Dose Rates on Microprocessors to Simulate Operation in Nuclear Installation. A Safety Approach, *OPERA*, Lyon.

MOTOROLA Data Book (1989). *Microcomputer Components. Systems on Silicon*.

SESCOSEM (Thomson CSF) (1975). Circuits intégrés logiques TTL.

THEVENOD-FOSSE, P. (1983). *Test aléatoire des microprocesseurs 8 bits. Application au Motorola 6800*, Thèse de Doctorat d'Etat, INP Grenoble.

THOMSON Semiconductors (1984). *Microprocessor and Peripher!cal Data Book*.

TIMOC, O., F. STOTT, K. WICKMAN, L.HESS (1983). Adaptive Self-Test for a Microprocessor, *Int. Test Conf.*,701-703.

can modify the behaviour of the circuit at any moment. Testing their correct behaviour in all the possible cases cannot reasonably be considered, then is not contemplated in the deterministic methods. However some faults show themself only in very particular conditions. For example, fault f_6 produces a faulty behaviour only in the condition that RESET arrives when the instruction JSR or BSR is executed (similar behaviours have already been observed (David, 1984)). If a random test sequence is applied (as described in Section 2.2), the probability that this particular condition occurs is not nil: if the test length is long enough, this particular condition will appear sooner or later, i.e., sooner or later the fault will be detected.

In short, *only specified behaviours* have to be tested (see Section 2.2 and the case R = S = 1 in this section), but *all the behaviours corresponding to the the specifications* must be tested when there are not any information about the faults in the circuits. This is practically impossible because there are too many possible behaviour sequences, but one can come up to this result with a long enough random test sequence.

The following strategy could be contemplated: 1) apply a very long random test in order to find the faulty circuits; 2) diagnoses the faults actually in the circuits; 3) thanks to this information, design a deterministic test sequence able to detect all these faults. Now a question arises: given the fault distribution in the circuits which have already been tested (and diagnosed) what can we predict about the faults in the circuits which have not yet be tested ? This is a current reseach (Jacomino, 1992).

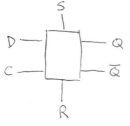

A D flip-flop

201

A VERSATILE MONITORING SYSTEM FOR DISTRIBUTED REAL–TIME SYSTEMS

Ulrich Schmid, Stefan Stöckler
Technical University of Vienna, Department of Automation 183/1
Treitlstraße 3, A–1040 Vienna
Phone: 0043–222/58801–8189, Fax 0043–222/563260
E–Mail: s@auto.tuwien.ac.at, stoe@auto.tuwien.ac.at

Abstract. This paper surveys the potential capabilities of monitoring of (distributed) real–time systems and presents some major issues of our actual monitoring system implementation VTA (Versatile Timing Analyzer). First, monitoring is identified as an efficient way to provide theoretical research with realistic (timing–)information concerning the actual stimuli the controlling system of a real–time system has to cope with. Moreover, there are certain specification checking applications, which regard requirements engineering, and last but not least there are several important monitoring applications within the testing area. We elaborate on the design issues resulting from such applications and provide a short architectural summary of the prototype version of the VTA currently being under development at our department.

Keywords. real–time computer systems, distributed computer systems, event driven monitoring, hybrid monitoring, timing analysis.

1. INTRODUCTION

Monitoring of computer systems is undoubtedly a powerful and well–established tool in traditional computer performance engineering. However, new and very much more important applications of monitoring systems have been found in the field of distributed systems' development: It became apparent very soon that traditional (breakpoint–based) debugging approaches do not lend themselves to a suitable extension for parallel systems, so novel techniques were needed and eventually developed. The most important one, commonly referred to as *event based debugging*, uses a monitoring system to observe and record the internal activities of the system under study. The recorded information is used afterwards for data analysis or replay techniques; see McDowell and Helmbold (1989) for a very complete survey.

Dealing with *distributed real–time systems* adds an additional level of complexity to the whole problem. Since any malfunction of the *controlling system* of a critical real–time application (e.g., a nuclear power plant or an aircraft) might cause a severe environmental damage due to unpredictable actions of the *controlled system*, it is of vital importance that not only the logical, but also the timing correctness of its controlling actions (i.e, real–time computations) is verified rigorously. Such timing issues, however, are almost totally neglected by the traditional research on distributed debugging.

For that reason, we are currently developing a flexible monitoring system (the *Versatile Timing Analyzer VTA*[1]) which is capable of performing timing analysis in distributed real–time systems. The research activities are located at the Department of Automation at the TU Vienna and started in the mid of 1991. This paper surveys the basic conceptual and design ideas of the VTA and is outlined as follows: Section 2 provides the aims and the scope of the application of the VTA, Section 3 is devoted to a survey of the major conceptual and design principles. Finally, Section 4 contains a short description of the architecture of the prototype actually developed.

2. AIMS AND SCOPE OF THE VTA

Applications of the VTA may be found both in scientific research and in practical real–time systems engineering. Actually, it is possible to use the VTA for

- **Monitoring environmental behavior**
  The whole idea of developing the VTA has been stimulated by some of our theoretical research on deadline–meeting properties of *event driven real–time systems* (cf. Drmota and Schmid 1991, for example). To be more specific, in order to develop suitable *environmental models* (describing the behaviour of a controlled system) for such real–time systems, there is a need for proving a model against real

[1] This research is supported by the Austrian Fund for Support of Scientific Research, Grant P8390–PHY.

environmental conditions. In addition, for such a model to be applied in practice, it is necessary to determine certain characteristic parameters (e.g., distributions of sensor data interarrival times) by means of a monitoring of an existing system.

A related practical application of the VTA arises in the context of specification checking: Since there is a certain danger to build a real−time system upon a wrong environmental specification, a continuous monitoring of the environmental behavior is invaluable in order to decrease the risk of a failure due to a specification error.

- **Monitoring system operation**
  Another very important application of the VTA, especially for today's "industrial standard real−time systems"[1] is to use it as a test tool. To be more specific, a continuous monitoring of multiple quantities allows to

  ○ *Check the timing behavior of the controlling system with respect to deadline meeting properties,*
  ○ *Supervise the internal (timing) behavior of the controlling system,*
  ○ *Check the resource utilization of system resources.*

Note that, in opposition to the research purposes mentioned in the previous item, there is an immediate applicability of the VTA within this area!

Despite the fact that the VTA provides some debugging support based on data analysis techniques (cf. McDowell and Helmbold 1989), too, it is important to notice that the major design relies on the basic assumption of a *carefully designed* and *logically fault−free real−time system* to be monitored. Though it would be perfectly reasonable to build a system capable of both powerful debugging and (subsequent) timing analysis, we feel that such an approach calls for elaborate replay techniques (cf. Tsai and others 1990 or LeBlanc and Mellor−Crummey 1987, for example). This, however, would divert us too much from our primary intentions and problems.

The following two issues make the VTA approach feasible:

- **The problem of monitoring a carefully designed real−time system may be reduced to the problem of monitoring the controlling system only.**
  The controlling system of a carefully designed real−time system should perform *process health monitoring* of the controlled

system as a part of its normal operation. This requires that the controlling system is provided with any necessary information (i.e., sensor data) to perform that task. Thus, the problem of monitoring a real−time system may be reduced to the problem of monitoring the controlling computer system (subsequently called *target system*), including its environmental interface, of course.

- **A carefully designed and logically fault−free real−time system permits the monitoring system to be intrusive up to a certain extent.**
  Essentially, the VTA relies on a *hybrid monitoring* approach (cf. Haban and Wybranietz 1990) based on a light−weight software instrumentation, i.e., a few statements inserted into the target software, in conjunction with a dedicated monitoring hardware for subsequent processing. Though the instrumentation causes an execution delay of a few microseconds only, one has to account for that intrusion. However, the assumption above implies

  ○ *Race−free target software*
  Race conditions within the target system are to be prevented explicitly; for example, assumptions concerning the ordering of events must be made in accordance with Lamport's happened before relation (see Lamport 1978). If that point is maintained, then it is possible to delay the execution of arbitrary tasks without endangering the task synchronization of the system.

  ○ *Timing reserves*
  For a real−time system being carefully designed, it is evidently necessary to provide certain slack times for time-critical computations, i.e., deadlines must be met with a certain "security reserve". Therefore, it is should be possible to delay even real−time computations up to a certain extent without missing a deadline.

In summary, the "Heisenberg effect" caused by the VTA should not alter the general real−time behavior of the target system. Note that the intrusiveness must be as low as possible since the overhead of several instrumentations (can) add up!

3. CONCEPTUAL AND DESIGN ISSUES OF THE VTA

As already mentioned, the most of the existing work on monitoring of distributed sys-

---

[1] The quotation is due to the fact that there is usually very few real−time in applications based on the widespreadly used real−time kernels like pSOS, VRTX or os9.

tems is devoted to the debugging context. Nevertheless, a close inspection of the literature reveals that some of the proposed techniques are, to some extent, well-suited to our needs, too. A short categorization of the research appropriate for our purposes looks as follows:

- **Theory**
  Some researchers deal with a general theoretical framework, i.e., the development of a formal model (event action model) for the process of monitoring of distributed systems (cf. Marinescu and others 1990).

- **Instrumentational issues**
  A considerable amount of research elaborates on the advantages/disadvantages of different instrumentation concepts. The essentials are: *Hardware* monitoring (cf. Tsai and others 1990) is non-intrusive but inflexible and difficult with respect to information abstraction, pure *software* approaches (cf. Aral and Gertner 1988) are unacceptable intrusive but offer a great flexibility regarding the instrumentation, and well-balanced *hybrid* techniques (cf. Haban and Wybranietz 1990) allow the combination of the advantages of both hardware and software monitoring (to a certain extent, of course).

- **Data abstraction**
  In order to reduce the enormous amount of data produced by the instrumentation and to provide only meaningful information to the user of the monitoring system, it is evidently necessary to employ certain methods which generate high-level information out of the low-level data stream. Many existing monitoring systems rely on a certain *Event Definition Language* (see Bates and Wileden 1983) for data abstraction; the research of Snodgrass (1988), however, shows that the problem is admissible to a (conceptual) relational data base modeling as well.

- **Real-time systems**
  Restricting the scope to (performance-) monitoring of real-time systems, the number of existing papers dwindles rapidly. For uniprocessor systems, there are some rather straightforward approaches (see Schrott and Tempelmeier 1983) and some (even commercially available) systems employing ICE-based techniques (cf. Föckler and Rüssing 1989), which provide very limited capabilities only. A noticeable exception is the (replay-based) debugging tool for multitasking systems developed by Tsai and others (1990), where elaborate hardware monitoring techniques are used in order to provide non-intrusiveness. Even worse is the situation if monitoring of distributed real-time systems is considered: Bhatt and others (1987) deal with a monitor for a special testbed for real-time systems development, and Tokuda and colleagues (1989) use a software monitor integrated within their real-time kernel ARTS.

Our VTA relies – like the most of the existing monitoring systems – on the *event action model* developed by Marinescu and others (1990), which is built upon user-programmable monitoring *actions* triggered by the occurrence of *events*. Basically, there are two classes of events: primitive and compound events. *Primitive events* are characterized by the occurrence of a simple, "local" change of state of the target system; the two most important ones are

- **Statement events**
  Generally speaking, a user performing monitoring is interested in situations where a significant change of state within the target system occurs. Such situations, however, are usually reflected by the execution of certain parts of the target software which are responsible for handling the particular case. For that reason, the VTA supports the runtime-setting of arbitrary events to be generated on the execution of a particular statement within the target software, with the option of simultaneously extracting certain software-related information (memory contents, i.e., variables).

- **Environmental events**
  In order to improve the monitoring systems' view of the controlled system, it is necessary to provide an additional access to the environmental interface at hardware level. Otherwise, it would be impossible to account for delays introduced by the target interface hardware. For that reason, it is possible to connect certain taps into the environmental I/O lines at the electrical level, which are sensed in order to generate certain environmental events.

Using such primitive ("microscopic") events, it is possible to construct higher-level *compound events* representing "global" changes of state of the target system. Such compound events are "macroscopic" in the sense that they are characterized by a certain "sequence" of (primitive) events; for example, the compound event (A or B) occurs when either the event A or the event B occurs.

The programmable *actions* to be executed by the monitoring system at the occurrence of an event provide the basis upon which various *measurement methods* may be built; simple examples are the measurement of the probability (i.e., sampling) distribution concerning the time between two different events (*intervals*) or the number of occurrences of an event during an interval.

Note that the specification requirements for primitive events and compound events or actions differ considerable. The specification of primitive events is highly dependent on the particular target system. For example, one has to define which particular statement within the target software should cause a statement event and which variables are to be extracted. On the other hand, the specification of compound events and actions is – in a certain sense – independent from the particular target system. At this level, the VTA deals with "abstract" events optionally carrying some additional information, and with actions triggered by the occurrence of events, which constitute a certain measurement method. It is evidently not necessary to consider the connection to the target system any more.

This conceptual general background has to be combined with elaborate provisions regarding flexibility and user–friendliness. Note that the latter is inevitable in order to deal with currently unknown or evolving requirements which are likely to arise in any of the applications of the VTA mentioned in Section 2. Providing such capabilities imply

- **Support of different target hardware**
  The VTA supports target systems consisting of several (possibly different) shared memory multiprocessor nodes, which are interconnected via a certain network. A single target node may consist of several different processors coupled via a certain bus. The VTA does not impose any restriction to the processor architecture: pipelining, caches and memory management units are supported transparently. In addition, there are no restrictions regarding how the controlled system (i.e., sensors and actors) is electrically connected to the target system; e.g., by dedicated I/O–lines or field–busses.

- **Support of different target software**
  The VTA supports target systems running different operating systems at different processors, taking care of the related impact on application software (i.e., task structure, memory resident or disked modules, ...) as well. Some very important issues concern the software development tool chain supported; therefore, we will treat this point separately (see *flexible views*).

- **Plug–in monitoring**
  In order to investigate a certain target system with the VTA, all what is needed is to plug–in a monitoring hardware into the bus of the target nodes of interest, to connect some electrical taps to desired

environmental I/O lines, and to start monitoring. Though arbitrary and numerous monitoring activities may be specified at runtime, there is no need for recompiling or relinking/reloading the target software. In addition, it should not be necessary to provide a special monitoring support during the development of the target system.

- **Flexible measurement methods**
  The VTA provides the user with an elaborate object oriented specification language (GOLD MINE), which facilitates the task of building powerful yet simple to use measurement and display methods; a key issue is the *reusability* of existing methods in order to derive new ones.

- **Flexible Views**
  One of major features of the VTA, however, is the capability of the monitoring system to *adapt to the views of the user* (developer) of a target system, instead of forcing the user to adapt to the views the monitoring system provides.

The development of real–time systems, like any other software development, usually relies on a certain tool chain supporting the software life cycle. Consider, for example, the traditional tool chain consisting of a CASE system, certain high–level language compilers, a linker, and a debugger. The developers of a particular target system are naturally bound to view their product according to the abstractions the tool chain provided to them: e.g., a *functional decomposition* including the environmental interface at the upper level, a certain *task map view* showing the task and IPC structure of the system, certain *high–level language programs* constituting the software implementation, and finally the architecture of the underlying *operating system and hardware*.

Forcing the user of the VTA (which is usually a developer, of course) to transform that intimate knowledge into an abstraction dictated by the monitor would surely prohibit the full utilization, even the acceptance, of the system. Thus, a much better approach relies on a powerful *basic system* in conjunction with a certain set of (vendor– or even user–supplied) *views* tailored to the specific abstractions a particular tool chain provides. For example, the lowest level of abstraction, namely operating system and hardware, is adopted by the *system view*, which comprises simple events relying on machine instructions, target memory addresses, and operating system calls. Above, there are usually *high level language views* dealing with simple events relying on source code statements, variables, and (symbolic) operating system calls. Additional views are conceivable, which adopt to even higher-level design abstractions provided by CASE systems, e.g., task maps or event-action modeling and functional decomposition.

Anyway, it should be easy to implement and integrate new views supporting a specific tool chain without changing the basic system of the VTA. It is obvious that such requirements call for an elaborate development support based on software reusability techniques within the VTA.

The conceptual issues mentioned so far led us to a design of the VTA relying on the following functional decomposition: The *basic system* of the VTA consists of three major subsystems, namely the

- **GOLD MINE tool set**
  This subsystem consists of a number of tools for managing GOLD MINE specifications, including a (graphical) editor/browser, a compiler and a librarian tool for managing compiled specifications.

- **Target subsystem**
  This subsystem is responsible for all target-related activities of the VTA and consists of 3 parts, the

  o *GOLD MINE runtime system*, which performs all actions necessary for "enabling" events and monitoring activities by "plugging" the appropriate compiled GOLD MINE specifications into the event recognizer.
  o *Primitive event management*, which is responsible for setting primitive events into the target system (at the system level of memory addresses) and to collect the stream of primitive event occurrences from the target system.
  o *Event recognizer*, which generates ("enabled") compound events and executes monitoring actions at the occurrence of events. Its operation is controlled by the GOLD MINE runtime system and actually driven by the primitive event stream from the target system. Note that the event recognizer is fully distributed!

- **I/O Subsystem**
  This subsystem constitutes the basic human interface of the VTA. It consists of the

  o *Controlling I/O subsystem*, which provides basic mechanisms for handling windows dedicated to the controlling of the operation of the VTA.
  o *Analysis I/O subsystem*, which is responsible for handling windows for displaying and manipulating monitoring data. The essential difference to the controlling I/O subsystem described above lies in the fact that GOLD MINE actions may interact with analysis windows but not with controlling ones.

Note that both subsystems use a display manager, which actually controls the display and input devices of the VTA.

That basic system of the VTA is supplemented by a set of (layered) *views*, as already mentioned. A view has the following responsibilities:

- **Simple Event Management**
  Each level of abstraction provides a set of "elementary" events, which we call *simple events*. Note that simple events and primitive events denote different categories: Though simple events of some low-level views (e.g., the system or a high-level language view) may coincide with the primitive events (appropriately specified), it is possible to conceive higher-level views where simple events are built upon several primitive events actually constituting a certain compound event.

  However, it is important to notice that the primitive event functionality of a high level view has to be built upon the services of the lower level views. Similar to the well-known layer model for computer networks, where only the lowest level physical layer has an actual connection to its peer, it is the primitive event management of the basic system which actually maintains the monitoring connections to the target system; any higher level primitive event management uses virtual monitoring connections only!

- **Compound event and action management**
  Currently, there is no need for a view-specific compound event management, but it might be in the future. At the moment, a "dummy manager" simply passes through the capabilities of the GOLD MINE runtime system.

- **Controlling I/O Interface**
  This interface uses the mechanisms offered by the controlling I/O part of the input/output subsystem in order to provide the user with a human interface (HI) which is as close as possible to the HI of the corresponding tool of the development tool chain. For example, the source code display/browser of a high level language view should provide the same "look and feel" as the symbolic debugger of the tool chain the user of the VTA is familiar with.

- **Analysis I/O Interface**
  Similar to the compound event management, there is currently no need for a view–specific compound event management. At the moment, a "dummy interface" simply passes through the capabilities of the analysis I/O subsystem.

4. ARCHITECTURE OF THE PROTOTYPE OF THE VTA

The prototype version currently being under development is designed for target systems consisting of several VME bus based multiprocessor nodes connected via an arbitrary network. The flexible design of the VTA relies on a set of *support packages*, which provide the necessary support for different VME CPU boards (Force CPU–6, CPU–30) and operating systems (pSOS+). The views actually under development are tailored to the Microtec C tool chain in conjunction with SCG's symbolic cross debugger XRAY+.

The VTA system itself consists of a single UNIX workstation *VTA host* and several *VTA targets*, which are connected via an independent *VTA ethernet* network:

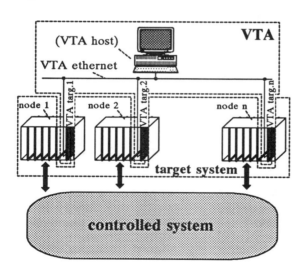

For each target node, there is a single dedicated VTA target (actually a Force CPU–30 board) additionally plugged into the VME bus, which performs the monitoring activities concerning the processors of that node. Together, the VTA–Targets are responsible for the collection and recognition of the events signaled via the target instrumentation. The VTA host provides the human interface for the whole VTA system. By means of the sophisticated multi window environment a user may specify events to be monitored, activate and deactivate monitoring functions, and direct the analysis and the display of traced data.

References

Aral Z., I. Gertner (1988), High level debugging in Parasight, *Proc. ACM SIGPLAN and SIGOPS Workshop on Par. and Distr. Debugging*, May 1988, 151–162.

Bates P., J.C. Wileden (1983), High–level debugging of distributed systems: The behavioral abstraction approach, *J. Syst. Software*, 3, 255–264.

Bhatt D., A. Ghonami, R. Ramanujan (1987), An instrumented testbed for real–time distributed systems development, *Proc. IEEE Real–Time Syst. Symp., December 1987*, 241–250.

Drmota M., U. Schmid (1991), Exponential limiting distributions in queuing systems with deadlines, to appear in *SIAM J. Appl. Math*.

Föckler W., N. Rüssing (1989), Aktuelle Probleme und Lösungen zur Leistungsanalyse von modernen Rechensystemen mit Hardware–Meßwerkzeugen, *Proc. GI/ITG Fachtagung Mess., Modell. und Bew. von Rechensyst. und Netzen, Sept. 1989*, 39–50.

Haban D., D.A. Wybranietz (1990), A hybrid monitor for behavior and performance analysis of distributed systems, *IEEE Trans. Soft. Eng., vol. 16, no. 2*, 197–211.

Lamport L. (1978), Time, clocks and the ordering of events in a distributed system, *Comm. ACM, vol. 21, no. 7*, 558–565.

LeBlanc T.J., J.M. Mellor–Crummey (1987), Debugging parallel programs with instant replay, *IEEE Trans. Comput., vol. C–36, no. 4*, 471–482.

Marinescu D.C., J.E. Lumpp jr., T.L. Casavant, H.J. Siegel (1990), Models for monitoring and debugging tools for parallel and distributed software, *J. Par. Distr. Comput., no. 9*, 171–184.

McDowell C.E., D.P. Helmbold (1989), Debugging concurrent programs, *ACM Comput. Surv., vol. 21, no. 4*, 593–622.

Schrott G., T. Tempelmeier (1983), Monitoring of real–time systems by a separate processor, *Proc. IFAC/IFIP Workshop on Real–Time Processing, March 1983*, 69–79.

Snodgrass R. (1988), A relational approach to monitoring complex systems, *ACM Trans. Comput. Syst., vol. 6, no. 2*, 157–196.

Tsai J.J.P., K. Fang, H. Chen, Y. Bi (1990), A noninterference monitoring and replay mechanism for real–time software testing, *IEEE Trans. Soft. Eng., vol. 16, no. 8*, 897–916.

Tokuda H., M. Kotera, C.W. Mercer (1989), A real–time monitor for a distributed real–time operation system, *Proc. ACM SIGPLAN SIGOPS Workshop Parall. Distrib. Debugging, January 1989*, 68–77.

ON STATIC ANALYSIS OF DEADLOCKS
IN TRANSPUTER NETWORKS

Algirdas Pakštas*

Department of Software Engineering for Distributed Computer Systems, Institute of
Mathematics and Informatics, Akademijos 4, LT-2600 Vilnius, Lithuania
UNIT/NTH-IDT, N-7034, Trondheim, Norway, Algirdas.Pakstas@idt.unit.no

Danutė Paketūraitė

Department of Software Engineering for Distributed Computer Systems, Institute of Mathematics and Informatics, Akademijos 4, LT-2600 Vilnius, Lithuania,
danute@ma-mii.lt.su

Abstract. One of the most important problem, which arised during the creation of distributed software configurations (DSCs) for parallel systems and distributed computer control systems (DCCS), is deadlocks between interacting processes. Deadlocks are the subject of research, because their influence on normal computer systems behaviour is obvious. In the DCCS-oriented software development system ALADDIN/LAMP during DSC debugging and maintenance the problem of deadlocks elimination also was faced. Programming language OCCAM was designed for development of DSCs runing on the transputer networks. This paper deals with the problem of DCCS software components operation reliability increasing by means of deadlock analysis and elimination. As the most important OCCAM language features as the approach to ALADDIN/LAMP tools extention for deadlocks analysis in OCCAM-written DSCs are presented.

Keywords. Parallel processing; Distributed software configurations; Software operation reliability; Deadlocks; OCCAM; Software tools

INTRODUCTION

One of the most important problem, which arised during the creation of distributed software configurations (DSC) for parallel systems and distributed computer control systems (DCCS), is deadlocks between interacting processes (see Isloor (1980), Zöbel (1983)).

As was discovered in Pakštas (1987; 1989b; 1990) during DSC debugging and maintenance in the DCCS-oriented software development system ALADDIN/LAMP (see Pakštas(1989a; 1991a)) the problem of deadlocks elimination also was faced. Concerning the operation of ALADDIN/LAMP system tools the interests in deadlock problems are the following:

- automated DSCs production (building) from

the prepared components requires the guarantee of DSC correct operation;

- deadlocks can arise and should be eliminated in the debugging phase of DSC development.

In this work we'll use the folowing deadlock definition which is formed on the basis of Pakštas(1989a): *"The deadlock arises when all processes (two or more) of the same group sending the messages are infinitely blocked and can not be executed without special system interactions because of waiting messages from the processes of this group"*.

At present there are a number of methods for deadlocks' prevention, avoidance and detection-repairing (see Isloor (1980), Zöbel (1983)). Very often deadlock detection methods are based on *"wait-for-graph"* costructing and searching for cycles in this graph (see Menasce(1979), Sugihara(1984)). The similar

*This work was partially funded by NTNF. Dr.Algirdas Pakštas now with IDT NTH as NTNF post-doctoral research fellow.

method for static deadlocks analysis was also adopted in the ALADDIN/LAMP system tools (see Pakštas(1989d)).

Programming language OCCAM was designed for development of DSCs runing on transputer networks. According to the OCCAM-language semantics presented by Jones(1987) and Barett(1992) the processes can interact via channels by messages sending. And naturally deadlocks problem was also faced (see Agaronian(1990), Surridge(1990), Talia(1990), Waring(1990)). The present article considers an approach to the deadlocks analysis in the transputer networks when DSCs are written in OCCAM.

OCCAM LANGUAGE AND DEADLOCKS FEATURES

An OCCAM program comprises the collection of processes that can be executed in a serial or parallel fashion (see Jones(1987) and Barett(1992)). OCCAM defines the basic processes to be assignement process, input process and output process.

Higher-level processes are built of these building blocks using OCCAM constructs. The most common constructs are:

- SEQ – for the sequental processes execution;

- PAR – for the parallel processes execution.

Other constructs exist; for example, for allowing to replicate process a specified number of times.

Processes can be nested within processes, forming a hierarchical processes structure. Data can be declared local to processes.

Input and output processes operate via OCCAM channels and provide the synchronised interprocess communication between concurrent processes. The channel is used to pass data from one concurrent process to another.

Rules for OCCAM programs writting differs from other current programming languages. An OCCAM program comprises a set of logical strings. They can be divided into several physical strings, in this case, new physical strings are written in the lines following the first line, indented by two or more spaces. This applies for composed processes as well.

According to the proposed definition, the deadlock arises as a result of infinite waiting for the messages. In OCCAM-programs we have 3 typical cases:

1. **Incorrect interprocess protocol.** Process A completed the data passing to the process B, but didn't inform about it, and as result the process B waits for messages and blocks the other processes that are interconnected with him. This case is typical not only for transputer networks, but also for other types of distributed systems.

2. **Incorrect process-coordinator implementation.** If the "process-coordinator" haven't the possibility to accept more than one message from coordinated processes, then the other messages will be lost. The processes, that sent "lost" messages, will wait infinitely for confirmation and will block other processes. This case is typical for OCCAM-language, when variable value is assigned from several channels in parallel.

3. **Incorrect external environment ("human inspired deadlocks").** This special kind of deadlocks arises as result of deadlock cycle closing via external non-mashinery environment, i.e. when humans are also active processes in distributed system (terminal I/O, manual switching, etc.).

THE EXAMPLE OF SMALL DSC IN OCCAM

The adopted approach will be illustrated with the DSC example (see Fig. 1 from Talia(1990)). The DSC has three processes that are executed in parallel:

- `Producer`;

- `Buffer`;

- `Consumer`.

The process `Producer` produces the messages and sends them via the channel `prod` to the process

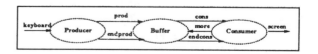

Fig. 1. An example of distributed software configuration with process `Buffer` which has limited size

```
PROC BoundedBuffer
    (CHAN OF BYTE producer, consumer,
     CHAN OF ANY endprod, endcons, more)
[10]BYTE buffer  :
INT in, out      :
BOOL termination :
BYTE any         :
SEQ
  in := 0
  out := 0
  termination := FALSE
  WHILE NOT (termination)
    SEQ
      ALT
        (in<(out+10))&producer?buffer[in REM 10]
          in := in + 1
        (out < in) & more ? any
          SEQ
            consumer ! buffer [out REM 10]
            out := out + 1
        (out = in) & endprod ? any
          SEQ
            more ? any
            endcons ! any
            termination := TRUE
:
```

Fig. 2. An OCCAM-program fragment with
limited size **Buffer** process

Buffer up to filling this process buffer, afterwards
sends the message about the completed reception
via the channel **endprod**.

The process **Buffer** has limited size buffer - till
10 one byte messages (see Fig. 2). The process
Consumer receives these messages via the channel **cons** and sends to the screen via the channel
screen. The requests for following messages are
sent via the channel **more**. When all messages
are passed, the process **Buffer** informs about this
process **Consumer** via the channel **endcons**.

Under the possible deadlocks classification presented in Section above in this example can occur
cases 1 and 3. Case 2 wasn't presented.

MODEL OF VIRTUAL DIS-
TRIBUTED SOFTWARE
CONFIGURATION WITH
INFORMATION-TRANS-
PORT PORTS

Proposed approach to deadlocks analysis in
OCCAM-programs is based on the model of virtual distributed software configuration (VDSC)
with information-transport ports (ITPs) as interconnecting servers. The model was initially proposed for the distributed computer control systems development by means of the AL-
ADDIN/LAMP system tools.

VDSC is a quadruplet

$$VDSC = < Blk_i, Rapr_i, ITP_j, CS >,$$

where Blk_i - program blocks, $Rapr_i$ - program
blocks requirements for the hardware or software
using, ITP_j - information-transport ports of the
i-th program block, CS - communication scheme
which defines the topological structure of the links
between ITPs, $i = 1...NB$ (NB - the number of
program blocks in DCCS) and $j = 0...NP$ (NP -
the number of ports in DCCS).

The CS is presented by directed graph CS =
(PORTS, LINKS).

$$PORTS = < ITP_i | i = 1...NP >,$$
$$LINKS = < (ITP_i, ITP_j) |$$
$$ITP_i := ITP_j, i, j = 1...NP >,$$

where NP is total number of ITPs. An expression like "$ITP_i := ITP_j$" designates that ITP_i
receives messages from ITP_j, i.e. that these ITPs
are linked.

Such VDSC representation is directly mapped
to ALADDIN language syntax and semantics.
More details about this model are presented in
Pakštas(1991a). For a practical VDSC use the
fact that all links between ITPs are defined in CS
is very important. Therefore, the VDSC description can be used as the data for the statical analysis of potential deadlocks.

SCHEME   OF   USING
OCCAM-ORIENTED
TOOLS

An approach to ALADDIN/LAMP tools extention for OCCAM-written DSCs handling is shown
in Fig. 3 where the following subsystems are
shown:

- OSE (OCCAM-Oriented Structure Editor);

- OSX (OCCAM Structure eXtractor);

- translator of system architect's language AL-
  ADDIN/OOB;

- DLA (Deadlock Locator and Analyser).

**The OCCAM-Oriented Structure Editor
OSE** (see Pakštas(1992)) is helpful tool for program writing in OCCAM-2, because it provides
faster program development and supports program structure.

The OCCAM Structure eXtractor OSX has the following functions:

1. *OCCAM-programs analysis, interconnected processes and used channels names extraction.* The OCCAM syntax analyser for OSX is under implementation by means of grammar-based technique as described in Pakštas (1989c; 1991b). Unfortunately, as OCCAM specifics result, we found some difficulties in construction of non-ambiguous LALR(1)-grammar for OCCAM-2 language. It was independently confirmed also by Polkinghorne(1989).

   It should be noted that only this analysis and extraction functions of OSX are language-depended. Other two functions are universal.

2. *ITPs interconnection scheme reconstruction.* According to virtual DSC model each channel in the OCCAM-program is associated with two information-transport ports that belong to the different processes. In the used example for the processes **Buffer** and **Consumer** the channel **cons** is mapped into the 2 ports: output ITP **Buffer.cons** and input ITP **Consumer.cons**.

3. *ALADDIN-written VDSC description preparation* (example is shown in Fig. 4). Neither information about distributed hardware configuration nor assignments of program blocks on workstations are presented here.

   It's easy to see that LINK-operators contain all information which is necessary for potential wait-for-graph constructing. For the more deep analysis and OCCAM-programs simulation (for example, by Petri nets, as in Agaronian(1990)) all necessary information presented in OCCAM-programs leaves in their ALADDIN-descriptions. For example, the input ITP **Buffer.prod** has limited queue length which is equal to the buffer array size as defined in the OCCAM-program (Fig. 2).

The ALADDIN/OOB translator task is to build DSC using already existing components and to prepare the data for DLA (a list of interconnected ports according to LINK-operators, see example in Fig. 5). This list also can be prepared manually according to available unformal specifications.

Deadlock locator and analyser DLA (see Pakštas(1989d)) uses recursive algorithm for search of cycles in potential wait-for-graph. This graph is constructed of the two parts:

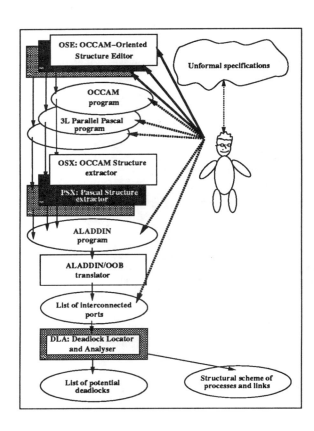

Fig. 3. OCCAM-oriented extention of ALADDIN/LAMP tools

```
-- software components
BLOCK Producer;     -- BLOCK description
                    -- PORT descriptions
  PORT keyboard (EXTERNAL_IN; ... );
                               END PORT;
  PORT prod (OUT; FORMAT = BYTE;
       SIZE = 1; QUEUE = 1);  END PORT;
  PORT endprod (OUT; ... );   END PORT;
END BLOCK;
BLOCK Buffer;
  PORT prod (IN; FORMAT = BYTE;
       SIZE = 1; QUEUE = 10); END PORT;
  PORT endprod (IN; ... );    END PORT;
  PORT cons (OUT; ... );      END PORT;
  PORT more (IN; ... );       END PORT;
  PORT endcons (OUT; ... );   END PORT;
END BLOCK;
BLOCK Consumer;
  PORT cons (IN; FORMAT = BYTE;
       SIZE = 1; QUEUE = 1);  END PORT;
  PORT more (OUT; ... );      END PORT;
  PORT endcons (IN; ... );    END PORT;
  PORT screen (EXTERNAL_OUT; ... );
                               END PORT;
END BLOCK;
-- scheme of interconnections
LINK (Producer.prod => Buffer.prod)
LINK (Producer.endprod => Buffer.endprod)
LINK (Buffer.cons => Consumer.cons)
LINK (Buffer.endcons => Consumer.endcons)
LINK (Consumer.more => Buffer.more)
```

Fig. 4. A fragment of ALADDIN-program corresponding to DSC with limited size **Buffer** process

```
# PORTS = 12,    # EXTERNAL LINKS = 5
OUTPUT:          INPUT:
Producer.prod    Buffer.prod
Producer.endprod Buffer.endprod
Buffer.cons      Consumer.cons
Buffer.endcons   Consumer.endcons
Consumer.more    Buffer.more
```

Fig. 5. The example of DLA input data file
format

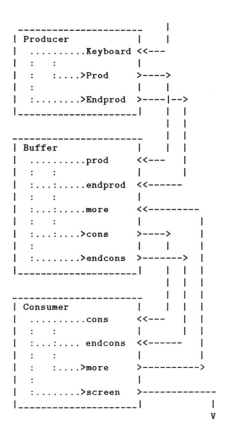

Fig. 7. Structural scheme of DCS processes and
their interconnections

external (according to interconnection scheme CS described in ALADDIN-program by LINK-operators) and internal (derived from the same original information taking into account semantics of process-to-ITP calls, i.e. "internal links").

Cycle search algorithm is used from Lipski(1982). This recursive algoritm is based on the search into the depth of a graph. Each new node met in the search is allocated in the stack, presented by the array STACK, and is removed from the stack after using it. Obviously, the stack always contains a succession of nodes from the considered node V to the root.

DLA outputs potential deadlocks list (see example in Fig. 6) and structural scheme of processes interconnection (pseudographical, see example in Fig. 7). In the Fig. 7 program blocks are shown as rectangles, output and input ITPs are marked by symbols ">" and "<". The lines like "..." mean the "internal port connections" that DLA adds to the interconnections list according to the principle "all inputs with all outputs". The lines "---" mean external links between ITPs that belong to different blocks.

Human inspired deadlocks can be analysed according to corresponding ITPs parameters **external-in** and **external-out** (see Fig. 4). This possibility is optional and should be defined before running DLA.

```
# PORTS = 12, # ALL LINKS = 17

LIST OF POTENTIAL DEADLOCKS:
1. Consumer.more Buffer.more Buffer.cons
Consumer.cons Consumer.more
2. Buffer.endcons Consumer.endcons
Consumer.more Buffer.more Buffer.endcons
```

Fig. 6. The list of potential deadlocks

CONCLUSIONS

OCCAM language features that are the most important for deadlocks analysis were shown in the paper. The model of virtual DSC was used as a basis for deadlock analysis approach forming. The Deadlock Locator and Analyser DLA and OCCAM Structure Extractor OSX were offered as helpful tools for reliable OCCAM-based DSC development, because they provide faster DSC checking and support the visualization of program structure.

DLA and OSX implementations for IBM PC under MS-DOS were developed as components of integrated OCCAM programming environment including structure editor, compiler, debugger, deadlock analyser and process configurator.

DLA can be used not only for OCCAM but for other parallel and object-oriented languages too. All what is necessary - to develop corresponding structure extractor for the new target language (PSX for Pascal, etc., see Fig. 3).

DLA and OSX can be useful also as components of reverse engineering technology.

ACKNOWLEDGEMENTS

We're very thankful to Silvano Balemi (Automatic Control Laboratory, ETH-Zentrum, Switzerland, balemi@aut.ethz.ch) who developed beautiful set of style files for LaTeX that allow to save a lot of time and energy for technical preparation of Camera-Ready-Copy according to IFAC requirements.

REFERENCES

Agaronian, A. et al. (1990). *Simulation of OCCAM-programs with Petri nets.* Institute of Informatics Problems, Moscow. (Preprint in Russian).

Barett, G. (1992). *OCCAM-3 Reference Manual.* INMOS Limited.

Isloor, S. and T.A. Marsland (1980). The deadlock problem: An overview. *Computer, 13*, 58–78.

Jones, G. (1987). *Programming in occam.* Prentice-Hall.

Lipski, W. (1982). *Kombinatoryka dla programistow.* Wydawnictwa Naukowo-Techniczne Warszawa. (In Polish).

Menasce, D. and R.R. Muntz (1979). Locking and deadlock detection in distributed data base. *IEEE Trans. on Software Eng., SE-5*, 195–202.

Pakštas, A. (1987). Programming support of reserving and handling deadlock and other exceptional situations in distributed systems. In *FTSD-10, Proc. 10th Int. Conf. on Fault-Tolerant Systems and Diagnostics.* Varna, Bulgaria. pp. 142–147.

Pakštas, A. (1989a). *Distributed Software Configurations: Analysis and Development.* Mokslas, Vilnius. (in Russian).

Pakštas, A. (1989b). Exceptional situations mechanism for interaction environment. In *FTSD-12: Proc. 12th Inter. Conf. on Fault-Tolerant Systems and Diagnostics.* Prague, Czechoslovakia. p. 357.

Pakštas, A., R. Meidutė and G. Stradalov (1989c). A software system for parser constructing with full-screen debugging facilities. In *System Sciences X, Inter. Conf. on Systems Sciences.* Wroclaw, Poland. p. 145.

Pakštas, A. and D. Paketūraitė (1989d). DLA: Locator and analyser of deadlocks in distributed software configurations. In *FTSD-13, Proc. 13th International Conference on Fault-Tolerant Systems and Diagnostics.* Varna, Bulgaria. pp. 171–176.

Pakštas, A. (1990). Methods and algorithms of distributed deadlock detection for DCCS on-line diagnostic subsystem. *Technical Diagnostics'90: Proc. 7th IMECO TC 10 Symp. on Technical Diagnostics.* Helsinki, Finland.

Pakštas, A. (1991a). Architecture, organization and building of distributed software configurations for the microcomputer control network. In Jaakso, U. and V.I.Utkin (Ed.) *Automatic Control. World congress 1990. "In the Service of Mankind". Proceedings of the 11th Triennial World Congress of the International Federation of Automatic Control, August 1990, Tallinn, Estonia*, Vol.4. Pergamon Press, Oxford, UK. pp. 123-128.

Pakštas, A. and N.V. Zolotarev (1991b). *Syntax-oriented Components of Distributed Systems: Development and Debugging Tools on the Basis of Formal Descriptions.* Nauka, Moscow. (in Russian).

Pakštas, A. and A. Tamkevičius (1992). OSE: OCCAM-Oriented Structure Editor (preliminary version). In *Proc. 3rd Nordic Workshop on Programming Environment Research.* Tampere, Finland.

Polkinghorne, P. (1989). README file for OCCAM.YACC file set. Moderated news group comp.sources.misc, vol. 7, GEC Hirst Research Centre, (pjmp@uk.co.gec-rl-hrc or ...!mcvax!ukc!hrc63!pjmp).

Sugihara, K., T. Kikuno and N. Yoshida (1984). Deadlock detection and recovery in distributed database systems. *Systems, Computers, Controls. Scripta Electronica Japonica, 15*, 48–56.

Surridge, M. (1990). A topology independent, minimal memory, deadlock-free, general message passing harness. EMS Report: Software Migration Aids for Transputer Systems (Contract Extension) Dept. of Electronics and Computer Science, University of Southampton. The SERC/DTI Initiative in the Engineering Applications of Transputers. P15.

Talia, D. (1990). Notes on termination of Occam processes. *Sigplan Notices, 25*, 17–24.

Waring, L. (1990). A general purpose communications shell for a network of transputers. *Microprocessing and Microprogramming, 29*, 107–119.

Zöbel, D. (1983). The deadlock problem: A classifying bibliography. *SIGOPS Operating Systems Rev., 17*, 6–15.

/home/selje/pakstas/papers/occam-deadlocks-safecomp92.tex   May 29, 1992

AN ADAPTIVE APPROACH TO DESIGNING ANTIVIRUS SYSTEMS

M.A.Titov
International Center of Computer Science & Electronics, 19 Presnensky val, Moscow, Russia

A.G.Ivanov, G.K.Moskatov
Central Research Institute "Center", 11a Sadovaya-Kudrinskaya, Moscow, Russia

Abstract   *We propose a concept of Virus Tolerant Machine. The concept is based on Le Chatelier-Brown principle. We introduce the notion of a movable equilibrium state (virus-free state) of a computer system. Then we describe a multilevel model of Virus Tolerant Machine. We present seven adaptive antivirus algorithms. Discussion is illustrated by application of some adaptive algorithms.*

Keywords *Virus Tolerant Machine; classification; feedback; adaptive algorithm; coding; debugging.*

1.State of the Art

Antivirus methods now in use (Cohen,1988; Pozzo; Gaj) are valid if no software modifications are allowed. There are several critical items for resourse-shared computer systems in which software may be modified by programmers. Provider has to re-immunize, re-encrypt modified software after modification session. For how long may this session last? How much time can a provider afford to antivirus prevention and/or repair? How many viruses can exist in a system for a still safe computing? There are no answers up to the moment. More than that, well-known formalizations of viruses (Adleman; Cohen, 1989; Gleissner) are not enough to formulate task to antivirus systems designers. Relativization of abstract theory and formalization of design limitations and aids are necessary.

2. New Contribution

Our approach is based on the application of Le Chatelier-Brown principle to the design of inherently safe adaptive control systems (Moskatov; Maiorov). For better comprehension of the contents let us outline our view on computer viruses.

2.1. Definitions and designations

Let a description of an automaton be a set of symbols. Consider an environment in which there are automata able to produce other automata from their descriptions. (Note, an executing program under any operating system may be considered as an automaton with its descriptions in external storage, e.g. executable disk file . And on the other hand, protein is an automaton produced from its DNA/RNA-description.)

We perceive a virus as an automaton which can inject its description into other automata descriptions so that an automaton produced from modified description (infected automaton) reproduces a given virus behaviour.

(An infected automaton can have partial recursive computable characteristic function (Adleman). Besides this it can have non-recursive one. A self-copying program can be virus (Cohen,1989). However there are examples of self-copying programs which are not viruses.)

We classify viruses with the following essential signs :

a1. a way of structure modifications within an infected automaton;
a2. a kind of change of characteristic computable function of corresponding attacked automaton ;
a3. an infection intensity ;
a4. a degree of concealment ;
a5. an infected levels list (in hierarchical systems);
a6. an ability to recognize a previous infection.

Let us use signature *a1a2a3a4a5a6* to denote virus class. (We may omit some signs which are not vitally important .) Denote that if a vurus Substitutes a piece of an attacked automaton description for the virus description, then *a1* becomes S. If a virus Inserts its own description code into an attacked automaton description then *a1* is I. There are prefix- (denote p), suffix- (denote s) and kernel- (denote k) viruses for von Neumann machines. E.g., Sp -virus means *prefix substituting virus.*

If an infected computable function is union of uninfected and virus functions then *a2* becomes A (Adding virus). Otherwise, *a2* becomes S (Superseding virus). It isn't difficult to prove that IA-virus increases space and time-complexity function of the attacked automaton.

a3 denotes supreme value of derivative of integral sign of an infection process. (This integral sign was introduced by W.Gleissner.) Since it isn't possible to construct Virus Proof Machine (Cohen,1989), consider henceforth any collision of the system : attempts to corrupt program resources and detections of corruptions. All this detected collisions per time is the collision intensity (approximately evaluated) including the virus intensity value.

For the explanation of *a4* and *a5* terms, let's take "bird's eye view" on hierarchical systems . There are numerous computer systems for which term level is essential. It may be security level in Bell-laPadula/Biba models, layer in the ISO network model. It may also be a level in ordinary sense, e.g. for MS-DOS IBM PC environment the lowest level is hardware, second one is BIOS, next one is DOS, next one is AutoLISP software, etc. Assume that we can enumerate all levels in a given computer system. Thus *a4* becomes C if a virus uses *i*-level and does not use resourses of other levels (with numbers not equal *i*) or uses them by evasion of allowed procedures and remaining invisible for system provider. *a4* is equal pC (nC) for partially concealed (non-concealed) viruses (respectively). Note, that total intelligent tracing of executing program can detect C-viruses, but this is not an effective way.

Let *a5* be "m-n" if virus infects **m** higher levels, entry level and **n** lower levels. If **m** and **n** are not equal null then it would be suitable if adjacent levels would check each other and refresh corrupted ones.

Now let's introduce initial design limitations:
- Random time of repair must be strictly less than the given value introduced into specifications;
- User's effective time must be much longer than provider's;
- Availability of virus-free state[1] must be close to 1;
- Infection intensity must not exceed the given limit.

2.2. A Multilevel Virus Tolerant Machine

Let us consider a multilevel model (Titov) of a Virus Tolerant Machine. The proposed general scheme of a level is presented in Fig. Each level contains a single collisions' register (1) and a single autodebugger[2] (2) with interrupter (3) and specifications' register (4).

Collisions' register locks the level execution for some time when frequency of collisions exceeds the known limit. A level is able to

---

[1] If we don't observe collisions during the known time interval then we call this state a virus-free state. This is a movable equilibrium state of a non-stationary computer system.

[2] We use term *autodebugger* (or, briefly, *debugger*) to denote an automatic debugger.

inspect adjacent levels behaviour. If the level's delay exceeds the known value, the lower level is able to regenerate the former level. The lowest level (hardware) isn't liable to modification. Level *i+1* can be created only by level *i* . Created level's autodebugger is being switched on. Father is sending the rights list to his child's debugger. If .the .rights are conflicting then the debugger can deny them and switch off itself.

There are also other possible elements in the proposed model (Fig.) :
(5) - generator(s) of programs;
(6) - an I /O mediator;
(7) - a reconfigurator of processes ((8) is (4)'s duplicate) ;
(9) - a frequency analyzer of modification patterns;
(10) - a modifications pool;
(11) - general files (descriptions) pool;
(12) - swapped processes pool;
(13) - antivirus scanning processes;
(14) - processes with mutual integrity checking;
(15) - virus patterns pool;
(16) - any processes, not mentioned above.

Elements of the model are connected by information channels (17) and signal and/or control lines (18, 19, 20, 21) into several feedback loops. An interlevel interface is also provided (22,23). Interconnection between different levels having the same father are being implemented in conformity with the rights received by the levels' creation. Descriptions of automata are stored in a pool (11) separately from environment of automata operation. The pool of a level is isolated from the pool of another level. Thus only the father (as another level) can touch the pool of the son directly during the son's creation. The frequency and duration of internal and external inspections, number of scanning processes and their activity time, frequency and depth of (7)'s external cyphering, as well as immunization and camouflage power of (5) - all these are controlled by adaptive algorithms. Briefly, the frequency and duration of antivirus processing increase when the intensity of collisions increases. The first two decrease when the system moves up to the virus-free state.

2.3. Adaptive algorithms

Seven algorithms are proposed:
- an adaptive antivirus scanning algorithm (including processes reconfiguration within the given level);
- an adaptive algorithm of external run-time cyphering;
- an adaptive algorithm of processes mutual integrity checking;
- an adaptive algorithm of immunization;
- an adaptive algorithm of object coding variation;
- an adaptive algorithm of autodebugging;
- an adaptive algorithm of external reconfiguration (i.e. level-to-level interaction).

Let us consider them in more detail.

Scanning

Designations
$k_1, ..., k_6$ - coefficients of reaction;
w_1, w_2 - transfer functions ;

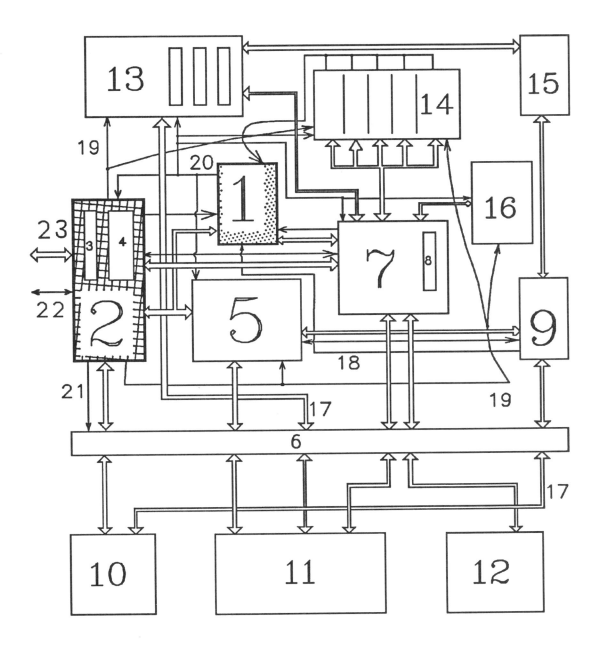

Fig. General scheme of a Virus Tolerant Machine level

T_{max} - a given time-limit of waiting process (time-out);

N_{max} - a given number-limit of scanning descriptions per process activity period;

m   - a number of executable descrip- tions in the pool (11);

ΔN - a current number-limit of scanning descriptions for actual process;

ΔT - current time-out for actual process;

N_{st} - a number of steps of tracing new scanning process;

$Name_i$ - name of description with $number_i$;
Random - function generator of random number;
N_p - a number of executing antivirus scanning processes ;
Sum - work variable.

Initial state
N_p : 1
$Name_i$: arbitrary
ΔN : 1
ΔT : T_{max}

— Antivirus scanning process
Step 1.
Check ΔN descriptions starting with $Name_i$;
Sum : = 0 ;
If virus description is detected ,
   then   {
     Sum : = Sum + k_1;
     Restore infected description;
     Inform about collisions. }
  else   Sum : = Sum - 1

Step 2 . $\Delta N := \Delta N + Sum \cdot (k_1 + \dfrac{k_2 \cdot Sum}{\Delta T + 1})$;

    If $\Delta N < 1$ then $\Delta N := 0$
Step 3. $\Delta T := \Delta T - (Sum \cdot (k_3 + (k_4 \cdot Sum)))$;
    If $\Delta T > T_{max}$ then   {
      If $N_p \neq 1$ then Terminate the process
          else $\Delta T := T_{max}$ } ;
    If $\Delta T < 0$ then $\Delta T := 0$
Step 4. If $\Delta N > N_{max}$ then {
   Create the process with identical rights,
   values and Entry point being Step1 ;
   $\Delta T := 0$;
   $\Delta N := N_{max}$ }
Step 5. If $\Delta N = Random(m)$ then
   $\Delta N := m$ — Random switch
Step 6. Wait ΔT
Step 7. $i := Random(m)$;
   Go to Step 1

— processes reconfigurator (fragment)
Entry 1.
If Input = Create
  then { Check integrity of the process-initiator:
  If initiator is corrupted then restore it
  If N_p is maximal then Swap non-antivirus
                          process ;
  Generate new process with given parameters
  and place it in service queue ;
  $N_p := N_p + 1$ }
If Input = Terminate then   {
   Terminate the process ;
   $N_p := N_p - 1$ }
Entry 2.
If there is a process in service queue then {
   Trace the process for the N_{st} steps :
     If there is a collision then   {
   $N_{st} := N_{st} + (k_5 \cdot w_1)$;
   Terminate the process   }
                         else   {
   $N_{st} := N_{st} - (k_6 \cdot w_2)$;
   If $N_{st} < 0$ then $N_{st} := 0$ }   }

Above mentioned scanning algorithm performs parametric adaptation which transforms into structural one when the parameters reach the given limits.

External run-time cyphering

The algorithm   implements   the procedure
Load & Execute .

Initial state   Flag = — 1

Step 1. Flag : = Flag + 1
Step 2. Load description, and Save initial state and the loaded code
Step 3. If Flag = 0 then Decrypt description
Step 4. If Flag = 1 then   {
  Encrypt description;
  Write the encrypted description into the pool (11) ;
  Refresh the decrypted description (program)}
Step 5. Trace ($N_{st} \cdot (Flag + 1)$) steps of the program so that :
  If illegal instruction takes place or the other rights are broken   then   {
   Restore initial state and the loaded code;
   Stop tracing ;
   If Flag = 2 then   {
      Flag : = — 1 ;
      Go to Step 6 }
               else Go to Step 1   }
                        else   {
  Flag : = — 1 ;
  Continue the program execution without tracing }
Step 6. Analysis of errors

To implement procedure Load (without execution) it's enough in Step 5 to substitute the words "Trace ... steps" for "Check patterns", "illegal instruction takes place or ..." for "Checking is wrong" and delete the words "Stop tracing" and "Continue ...". By "Check patterns" we mean checking code sectors created by program generators (5) (e.g. , during compilation).

The weak spot of cyphering approach is that it's rather slow. It may be satisfactory (for the Ap -infection detection) to encrypt completely only description headers. The rest part of description must be encrypted partially. Problem of modification of patterns topology and of cypher keys would be solved easily when we would use parametric adaptive algorithm of cyphering. Frequency of keys modification F_c, density of cyphering D_c (ratio of sum of cyphered sectors length to the whole length of description) should be changed adaptively: the growth of collisions frequency is accompanied with greater values of F_c and D_c.

Processes mutual integrity checking

Processes (at the same level) may check each other in the following way. Processes described have access to each other, they check and repair code pieces of each other. When new such process is created, it sends its own code to partners and receives their patterns for further checking. The process that is terminated is removed from checking list.

Designations
$L1_i$ (l) - a list of the processes' numbers for checking by means of the i-th process;
l - length of the list ;
$L2_k$ - a list of the code pieces of the k-th process with Δl and Δt, where
Δl - lengths of the pieces ;
Δt - number of checks

Process i
For k from $L1_i$ (l)
   Check & Refresh the k-th process
   by using the $L2_k$ so that :

If There are collision then (else) {
increase (*decrease*) Δ *l*-lengths and
Δ *t*-times in L2$_k$ and length 1 of L1$_i$}
Continue ordinary execution

Immunization

Self-checking of automata must be performed
without tracing because a virus can inject its
executable code into tracing algorithm and
become invisible for the checker. It 's easier
to apply isomorphic coding algorithm depend-
ed on the computer system speed. Program
generators ought to have it and to be able
to embed it into object programs. This is
enough to forbid more than one execution
of such self-checking session to hinder
A-infection (See example).

Designation

$\longleftrightarrow$ - synchronization mechanism

For subsequent executions the debugging is
initiated at the known points.

External reconfiguration

Let ΔT be time interval between two inspections and P$_i$ be some polynomial. Let us
consider the following algorithm.

Entry. *Inspect* level i
If *min* < measured delay < *max*
  then $\Delta T := \Delta T \cdot P_1$

  else $\Delta T := \dfrac{\Delta T}{P_2}$

If $\Delta T \leq 0$ or Negative result of inspection
  is obtained then {
  Regenerate level i ;
  $\Delta T := T_{max}$ }
If $\Delta T > T_{max}$ then $\Delta T := T_{max}$
Sleep ΔT ;
Go to Entry

Checker 1   Debugger-Arbiter 2

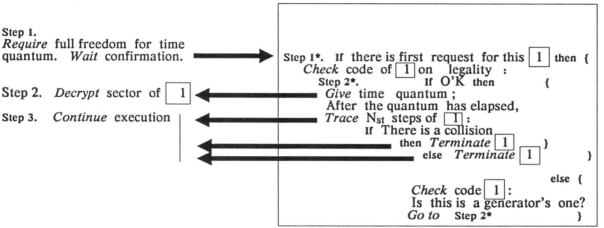

Step 1.
Require full freedom for time
quantum. *Wait* confirmation.

Step 2. *Decrypt* sector of 1

Step 3. *Continue* execution

Step 1*. If there is first request for this 1 then {
  Check code of 1 on legality :
  Step 2*. If O'K then   {
  Give time quantum ;
  After the quantum has elapsed,
  Trace N$_{st}$ steps of 1 :
  If There is a collision
        then *Terminate* 1 }
        else *Terminate* 1   }
                                        else {
  Check code 1 :
  Is this is a generator's one?
  Go to   Step 2*   }

Object coding variation

When description of an automaton has unique
code, virus automaton encounters more handi-
caps to recognize it. It means that on one
hand, program generator implementing an
algorithmic function (e.g., some partial recursive function) can produce a majority of different algorithms for this function. A trivial
way is the introduction of additional null or
debugger's instructions into the automaton
description. Here the adaptation takes the form
of increasing redundancy under agressive virus environment. On the other hand, a program can variate own code itself, e.g. in the
following way: *Decrypt* A then *Execute* A
then *Encrypt* A or by means of above mentioned code diffusion. This algorithm may be
self-learning.

Autodebugging

Obviously, *static execution tree* (SET) method
(Gaj) must be transformed into *dynamic execution tree* (DET) one. Debugging must be
self-learning. Suspicious instructions (conditional branches, modifications of executable
codes) must be saved in DET tables and substituted for debugging initiating ones. A new
program is emulated totally for the first time.

2.3. Registers' programming

Autodebugger

As it was mentioned above (see 2.2), a level's
debugger (2) checks the level's rights while
the level is being created. Besides this, debugger checks rights of the level during the
level's lifetime and can check rights of the
processes within the level. When a process
within a level (or another level) attempts to
add some processing to another process (or
to the level, resp.), or reconfigurator (7) is going to add one, debugger checks rights and
supplements this processing with new entry
initiating itself. An example follows.

Designations
Add   - code of additional processing;
DebInt(N$_{st}$) - code of debugger initiating with
                given tracing steps' number;
Old   - code of the process A;
Entry   - entry point of the process A;
Top (code) - function for locating the module
                code entry.

Initial state
There is request *Supplement the process A*

Check rights of the intercessor :
If O'K then   {
Lock the A ;
Add : = Catenation (DebInt(N_{st}) & Add);
Save Old and Top(Old) ;
 Old : = Catenation (Add & Old) ;
Entry : = Top (Old) ;
Unlock the A and *Inform* about modification}
       else *Deny* the request

<u>Initial state</u> Debugging initiated

Step 1. *Save* initial state
Step 2. *Trace* N_{st} steps of Old so that :
If there are collisions within Old   then   {
 If Stack , in which Old and Top(Old) are
   saved, is not empty
     Then   {
 Restore previously saved Old and Top(Old);
 Restore initial state ;
 Inform about collisions ;
 Go to Step 1 }
     else *Lock/Terminate* process/level and
     Inform   }

Collisions' register

There are two possible kinds of collision's register. The first of them is just an element with inertia which generates time of the level's locking. Let TL be time of locking and CF - collisions frequency.
Then TL = f (CF) , and if $CF_1 > CF_2$ then f(CF_1) > f(CF_2) . On the other hand, the register may be a more intelligent element. It may analize Nst , Fc, Dc and so on, optimize them and send them to inputs of elements connected with itself. Resume: increasing the N_{st}, N_p, F_c and the other parameters increases provider's time. This can (indirecly) increase the time of the level's inspection, that in its turn increases probability of the level's regeneration.

3. Simulation

The first two of the algorithms were initially implemented on IBM PC using MUMPS environment. It turned out that using an adaptive antivirus scanning algorithm (with effective time << total life cycle time) one can heal the computer system from apriori known viruses; the recovery period being approximately 40 times less than the virus operand time in the corresponding model of an unprotected computer system investigated by W.Gleissner.

Another observation is that an adaptive cyphering algorithm (as well as an adaptive scanner mentioned above) makes it possible to automate provider's corresponding activities (see "State of the Art").

All seven adaptive algorithms are being investigated in the Project of Ada compiler design.

4. Conclusion

The proposed model and algorithms are of course not perceived to be universal. Some of the model nodes and links as well as algorithms may be removed (simplified) or ,

contrary, made stronger; new elements, links and algorithms may be added. Input design limitations for a given environment make it possible for a designer to choose suitable architecture of the system. We have shown the way to design these systems in general. Authors hope to implement this approach in a new Ada compiler. The compiler must generate executable programs with inherently antiviral features (i.e., programs must acquire these features not by programming , but by compilation and interpretation). It is supposed to sutisfy provisional items of the Annex *Safety and Security* of the Ada 9X Project and , mainly, Revision Request RR-0644 : " Standard should specify time bounds/constraints for certain operations " (Ada 9X). Obviously, such an adaptive approach can help in designing more safe computer systems with respect to many other risks. We envisage two main directions of further research. These are : thorough investigation of initial design limitations and of the Model of Virus Tolerant Machine in more strict logical and mathematical terms; application of this approach to new real computer designs.

5. References

Ada 9X Project Office (1991). *Ada 9X Requirements Rationale.* Carnegie Mellon Univ., 158 pp.

Adleman, L.M. (1989). An Abstract Theory of Computer Viruses. In S.Goldwasser (Ed.). Advances in *Cryptology: CRYPTO'88* , Lecture Notes in Computer Science, N 403, Springer, Santa-Barbara, USA. pp. 354 - 374.

Cohen, F. (1988). On the Implications of Computer Viruses and Methods of Defense. *Computers & Security, 7,* 167-184.

Cohen, F. (1989). Computational aspects of Computer Viruses. *Computers & Security, 8,* 325-344.

Gaj, K., K.Gorski, R.Kossowski and others (1990). Methods of Protection against Computer Viruses . *Proceedings IFAC Symposium SAFECOMP'90,* UK, pp.43-48.

Gleissner W. (1989). A Mathematical theory for the Spread of Computer Viruses. *Computers & Security , 8,* 35-41.

Maiorov, A.V., G.K. Moskatov , G.P. Shibanov (1988). *Operating Safety of Automated Objects.* Mashinostroenie Publishers, Moscow, 264 pp.

Moskatov , G.K. (1992). The principle of Le Chatelier-Brown and its application to the synthesis of inherently safe adaptive control systems. *Safety Problems in Emergency Situations,* The Russian Academy of Science, 2, 55-77.

Pozzo, M., T.Gray (1987). An Approach to containing Computer Viruses. *Computers & Security, 6,* 321-331.

Titov, M.A. (1989). Organization principles of non-stationary immune computer systems. *Proceedings of the 1st International Conference on Nuclear Power Plants Safety and Personnel Training,* Obninsk Institute of Nuclear Power Engineering, USSR, pp.28-29.

OPERATING MSDOS IN A CONTROLLED ENVIRONMENT

R. Posch

Institute for Applied Information Processing and Communication Technology, Graz University of Technology, Austria

Abstract. Due to costs and performance PC architectures running MSDOS systems (IBM, 1986) are widespread. With the software platform available market is still growing. However from the point of view of security and operating systems concepts this architecture is all but outstanding. Most efforts to improve security have side effects on the compatibility. Starting with a secure state influence on security and integrity can only come from outside. Thus, keeping a computer system safe means control of external data and I/O operations.

The presented approach for keeping the system safe in a MSDOS environment is performed by introducing an alternate special file system with security and integrity features. It is based upon a reliable boot procedure as a crucial point in system. As experience with alternate file systems for other purposes exist the approach can be qualified as feasible. As a further side effect of the method presented, unattended periods can be controlled to a remarkable extent.

Keywords. File system security; MSDOS systems; password systems; access control; security domains.

INTRODUCTION

With MS-DOS systems a set of security measures to build a controlled system has to cover the following aspects.

(a) *Reliable boot:* It must ensured that only entitled personnel can turn on and use the system. The presented approach puts its weight on the term "and use" in the sense that the turning on of the system by intruders leads to an unusable file system. This demand imposes the need for *open* and *close* procedures for the file system. In addition to open and close passwords have to be implemented in a way that even disassembling and tracing would hide the password information. To be able to be used widely only software methods are considered.

(b) *Control of unattended periods:* The main concern is not information hiding by encryption but making sure that third parties can not manipulate data or programs. The method employed is a closing password and temporal preventive closing the file system for periods where updates are not performed. Manipulation during unattended periods thus can be detected in the temporal closed and quasi read only mode of a file system. The opened file system does not allow for changes unless it will be closed with the correct key. Reopen mechanisms give a tool for detecting threads.

(c) *Program consistency control:* The design of the whole system consists of several file systems forming the various security domains. It is therefore possible to

221

prevent a programmer from effectively reading and from manipulating data and on the other hand users can be prevented from write access to programs. This method also fulfills an essential maintenance demand.

(d) *Data consistency control:* Reopen mechanisms in connection with book keeping for released file blocks allows the implementation of a rollback as a recovery mechanism for a qualified user. Basically the mechanism for detecting violation can be used to recover from an unsafe state or from other erroneous situations. This operation is similar to the UNIX salvol operation.

Controlled operation is in many applications much more important than data secrecy. Therefore the concept concentrates on this first aspect not involving file encryption which would slow down the system extremely. However on a different level there are basically the same aspects to be solved.

ENSURING RELIABLE BOOT

Additional hardware could be used to server as a security token (Chaum D., Schaumüller-Bichl I.(ed), 1988). Such a method would be effective if encryption of actual data is done through this hardware device. Otherwise such devices like chipcards will have the effect that users will get a feeling of a higher security level.

In the presented solution reliable boot is reached by a "DEVICE" building the alternate file system. This device driver is from a certain point onwards depending on a password. The password is then used to get the crypto key for a file system. As a convolution like algorithm is used for this mapping from the password to the key hacking the code is not effective to get the password or the key and the password can furthermore be freely chosen. By some method the integrity of this device has to be ensured. Otherwise a fake device would kill security.

The basic problem is to introduce an executable element into a standard interface and to make it most probable that neither the password is tapped by extra code or a fake device nor the system is modified until the reliable boot device is started.

The presented solution uses the first "DEVICE" on the CONFIG.SYS level. The work of the driver for this device consists of identifying the booting person and building the alternate file

system. For this purpose it has to be assumed that the function of the driver is known by an intruder.

For the reliable boot this first driver is tailored during installation. It consists of k parts executed in a sequence. During installation these parts are shuffled according to a relatively large random number and to reduce the tracing attack the register assignment in each of these parts is shuffled as well. There are generally two keys used; the driver opening key which is built using an internal key1 and the user password, and the file key which is calculated from the user password, the environment signature and an internal key2. The starting sequence is always the "get user password and decrypt the driver" function. The following is a list of functions performed to retrieve the environment signature:

(i) Speed check. This is performed within limits to avoid internal tracings. The execution time of the whole driver code is measured during installation and a timing reference interval is used as a portion of the key.

(ii) Memory signature. The driver clears all memory that is not used during boot before it starts execution. The memory signature is also use to modify the key.

(iii) Stack check. Position and contents is used in an interrupt disabled or restricted mode.

(iv) Processor type validation. This is to avoid protected modes for outside tracers.

Self clear is performed after calculation of the file key.

If the user takes care that the system *never* crashes between the input of the password and the startup complete, this method is a rather safe boot procedure. The startup complete must be dependent on user data to avoid fake startups with password input. Since a crash in this period could as well be an attack any such crash has to be analyzed.

A FAT ENCRYPTION MECHANISM

Control of unattended periods and data consistency control is achieved by encrypting the file allocation table (FAT) and by random cluster allocation. Employing system states of the file system and transition functions as shown in figure 1 allows the implementation of these security features (Posch R., Welser M., 1991). The file control tables are kept twice in the system to enable rollback and check operations. All control tables are encrypted and the data itself is signed electronically when written. Since this encryption and decryption takes place mainly during open and close public key methods with higher processing amount can be afforded. In the presented approach RSA (Rivest R., Shamir A., Adlemann L., 1978) is used. In addition to the random cluster allocation a life cycle mechanism is applied so that in most cases clusters are assigned that have not been used during the actual session. This mechanism also enables for a checkpoint restart mechanism on a session basis.

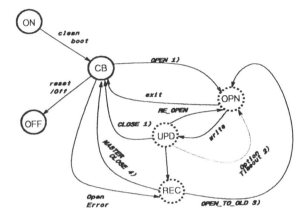

Figure 1: The security state diagram.

The system is started at the ON state. This state is tied to the reliable and clean boot by the mechanisms described. This way usage of bootable diskettes is no feasible circumvention of the mechanism.

The fat encryption has two main goals:

(A) No actual cluster of the file subsystem in discussion can be determined to be in use or to be free. Freed clusters are never cleared.

(B) Finding a piece of a file will not lead to subsequent pieces of the same file.

(C) Modification of data files cannot be effectively done. This is especially true when FAT encryption is combined with cluster signature when a write is performed.

While signature can be done using available mechanisms (Rivest R., 1992) and hashing functions, control table encryption has to be viewed more carefully. The main goal is that it should not result in much overhead in normal operation. Moreover it has to be taken into account that directories include the first cluster position. This means that finding a directory block

by chance would increase the probability of identifying small files. This effect is eliminated by adding to the encryption a remap function for the clusters. This method in term ensures random cluster allocation. Even if random cluster allocation cuts on file system speed most of this negative effect can be eliminated by standard caching products.

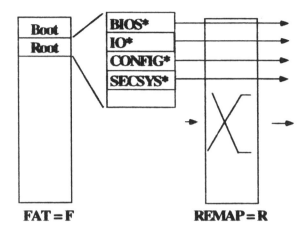

Figure 2 Remapping cluster entries.

The remap function is retrieved from the key. The FAT itself thus never contains actual cluster positions. The only exceptions are the boot files BIOS, IO, CONFIG and the security device itself (SECSYS). Building and usage of REMAP is shown in figure 3.

```
Install:
  (a) z0 = Δt from keyentries.
  (b) Build R =REMAP the z0 permutation of {0..#Clusters}
Close:
(F*,R*) = encipher(F,R,close_key)
Open:
  (F,R) = decipher(F*,R*,open_key)
```

Figure 3 Building and usage of REMAP.

SECURITY ISSUES

The presented mechanism is claimed to be secure in the term that it recognizes changes in the file system and prevents from reading data consistently. This security level is held as long as no intruder can hook up a Trojan horse during the boot phase and thus can tap on the password.

This security system can be overcome if one of the two following attacks are possible:

(A1) The bootstrap is faked until the password is keyed in and thus the key could eventually be tapped. This attack requires physical access and modification to the boot sequence in the first place. In the second place it requires deep program analysis since, by means of code shuffling and register functionality shuffling as well as by setting the processing environment as a part of the file key, it is extremely complicated to automatically and thus online tap on the key.

(A2) An external analysis with online data access is possible to retrieve the file key. It is suggested that it is not possible to install such a machinery.

As all the keys are long integers and as the user should be free to choose and manipulate the password to access the file system a special method is used to calculate the key from the password.

(i) $k_p = \alpha_1 \ldots \alpha_p$ are the digits keyed in by the user as password.

(ii) $k_p^* = \alpha_1^* \ldots \alpha_p^*$ is formed by omitting non significant bits.

(iii) e^* is built by concatenation of k_p^* k_p^{*2} k_p^{*j} to reach the length used for the key.

(iv) The final key k is formed by adding the processing environment signature to $e^* + k_m$ with k_m being the memory resident part of the key.

This procedure makes it possible for the user to choose any key desired and for the system to avoid storage of significant parts of the key.

CONCLUSION

Access to the MSDOS environment is achieved by a mixed password key system using public key encryption. Temper dedection is based on control table encryption. Program consistency control is done by generating different file systems in different security domains. This approach is much like partitioning a disk but is done at a higher level to get device independence. Thus also network oriented configurations could be serviced.

The presented security method has various side effects:

(a) It is easy to control R/W access to data and read only access to programs for normal users.

(b) It is an inherent capability of this method to hide application data from the programmer. This is an effect of asymmetric ciphering algorithms.

(c) Strict application of the method can be used to build a limited checkpoint restart mechanism.

The prevailing goal of the security system is to ensure integrity and prevent from consistent data access. Even if blocks of data can be read it cannot be determined whether these data blocks are actually relevant data or just lost or intentionally spread out.

REFERENCES

IBM (1986) Disk Operating System Technical Reference, IBM, March 1986

Chaum D., Schaumüller-Bichl I. (ed) (1988) Smart Card 2000: The future of IC Cards, Proc. IFIP WG 11.6, Laxenburg, Elsevier, Amsterdam.

Posch R., Welser M. (1991) A concepual View of MS-DOS File System Security; Report 294, Institutes for Information Processing Graz.

Rivest R., Shamir A., Adlemann L. (1978) A Method for Obtaining Digital Signatures and Public-Key Cryptosystems; Comm. of the ACM (Feb. 1978), 120-126.

Rivest R. (1992) The MD4 Message-Digest Algorithm; RFC 1320; MIT Lab. f. C.S. & RSA Data Sec. Inc. April 1992.

ARE WIDELY USED SECURITY SYSTEMS INADEQUATE?

G. Futschek, Chr. Weninger

Institute for Software Technology, Vienna University of Technology
A-1040 Vienna, Resselgasse 3, Austria

Abstract. The aim of any security system is the prevention of unauthorized access to or use of data or programs. To circumvent any security measure specific knowledge about the functionality of the attacked system is essential. Since the information on the functionality of popular and widely used computer systems is accessible, these systems are the primary target for security attacks. The usually higher effectiveness (e.g. cost, compatibility, reliability etc.) of widespread systems is decreased by loss of security. Consider e.g. the widespread PCs and the enormous security efforts that are required to prevent virus infection and to recover data. A dynamic model was created to calculate the correlation between security, effectiveness and the degree of distribution. It shows that it is better to provide specific security systems for each user, even if these systems are relatively simple, than to provide all users with a single very sophisticated system.

Keywords. data security, security systems, trusted systems, computer viruses, virus epidemology

INTRODUCTION

An extensive increase in system penetration indicates that there is no perfect software system to prevent such attacks. Therefore it is necessary to realize that only the efforts to penetrate these systems vary. Specific knowledge of protection measures is an obvious prerequisite to the security violation effort. The probability of successfully attacking a security system is usually higher for a widely used popular system than for a specific system used in few computers. Hence the question arises whether or not a sophisticated standard security system is preferable to rather simple but specifically designed systems.

Data stored in computers are threatened by the loss of

- data confidentiality
  = unauthorized access to information
- data integrity
  = unauthorized modification of information
- data availability
  = unauthorized impairment of system
    functionality

(Zentralstelle für Sicherheit in der Informationstechnik, 1989).

Several technical and organizational methods are applicable to prevent the loss or modification of data. Organizational procedures like

- training and informing employees
- forming a group of security specialists
- consulting independent specialists

are always necessary. They supplement technical measures like the

- use of security software (i.e. encrypting
    methods)
- use of biometric systems
    (i.e. finger prints, retina check)
- use of other electronic surveillance systems
    (i.e. chip-card based systems)

Most of these technical methods are very cost intensive, biometric systems in particular, so that only few people will derive benefit from them. Since the application of security software has evolved to become the most commonly used technique to protect data, it will be given special attention in this paper. First of all it has to be understood that there is no possibility, no matter what measures are applied, to build a system which is absolutely secure.

Unauthorized modification of protected data requires specific knowledge about the structure of the system protection mechanism. Hence, attacking a widely used popular system is more likely to succeed than trying to beat a specifically designed system. In the following we will come to the conclusion that applying a single highly sophisticated protection system for all users is not as effective as providing each user with a specific and even simple system.

A serious threat, of which PC users especially have become aware of recently, is caused by computer viruses. A virus is defined in Cohen (1987) as

'a program that can infect other programs by modifying them to include a possibly evolved copy of itself.'

Virus infection causes the loss of data integrity and data availability. Only the execution of an infected program can increase the number of infected programs or systems. In order to prevent virus infection, program modifications have to be detected as soon as possible. A security program that runs in the PC-Dos environment was developed by the authors, which is able to detect unauthorized modifications of data and programs (Weninger, 1991). A test of this system in a virus-infected environment showed its resistance against any security attack, but a good knowledge of the internal structure of this specific security system would make successful violations possible.

Assuming that a virus is intended to make use of a specific flaw in a protection mechanism (which means that the virus can only penetrate systems employing the same protection mechanism), it has to be realized that, if it was intended by the programmer of the virus to infect as many systems as possible, he would certainly have chosen to attack a widely used security system. If every user employs a specific security system, virus propagation will be almost impossible. The following models will describe the correlation between security, effectiveness and the degree of virus propagation.

UNRESTRICTED VIRUS
PROPAGATION

The basic model on virus propagation considers the number of infected and clean systems and the probability of virus infection.

x ...   rate of currently infected systems
        $(0 \leq x \leq 1)$
$1 - x$ rate of clean systems
a ...   probability of infection of a clean system

The rate of infected systems increases proportional to the probability that a clean system will become infected by exposure to an infected system. This result is the well known differential equation for unrestricted virus propagation (Solomon, 1990; Murray, 1989)

$$dx/dt = a (1 - x) x \qquad (1)$$

with the solution

$$x(t) = x_0 / (x_0 + (1 - x_0) e^{-at}) \qquad (2)$$

The rate of infected programs tends to 1 (the state when every system is infected) from every starting point $x_0 > 0$.

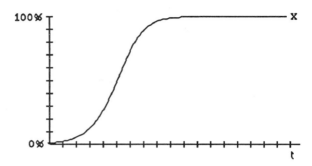

Fig. 1 Model (1), a = 0.1, x_0 = 0.01

If we assume that viruses are detected and removed from some systems, the virus propagation is reduced by a term which is proportional to x.

$$dx/dt = a (1 - x) x - e x \qquad (3)$$

e ...   probability of detection and removal

The function x(t) tends to 0, if $e \geq a$ (see Fig. 2). Otherwise x(t) tends to $1 - e/a$, so the probability that a system is clean tends to e/a (see Fig. 3).

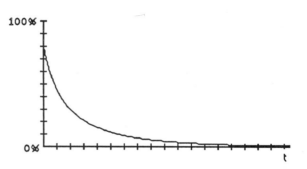

Fig. 2 Model (1), a = 0.05, e = 0.07, x_0 = 0.8
Countermeasures beat the virus infection

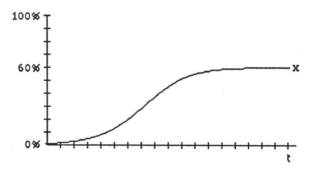

Fig. 3 Model (1), a = 0.1, e = 0.04, x_0 = 0.01
60% of all systems remain infected

226

USE OF A PERFECT PROTECTION SYSTEM

Now we assume that we use perfect protection systems, that make any virus infection impossible.

y ... rate of currently protected systems ($0 \leq y \leq 1$)
p ... probability of newly protecting an unprotected system

The infected and protected systems are disjoint ($0 \leq x \leq x + y \leq 1$).

$1 - x - y$ ... rate of not protected and clean systems

The increase of protected systems is proportional to the rate of infected systems x.

$$dy/dt = p\,x \qquad (4)$$

The number of protected systems y increases by the protection of not infected ($1 - x - y$) or infected systems.

$$p = d\,(1 - x - y) + e \qquad (5)$$

d ... probability of newly protecting a clean system
e ... probability of newly protecting an infected system

$$dx/dt = a\,(1 - x - y)\,x - e\,x \qquad (6)$$

$$dy/dt = d\,(1 - x - y)\,x + e\,x \qquad (7)$$

We assume that every time a system is newly protected all viruses are removed. Therefore the term $-e\,x$ is added to (6).

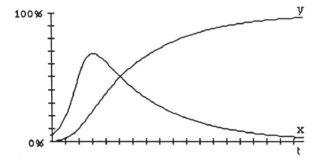

Fig. 4 Model (6, 7), $a = 0.2$, $d = 0.01$, $e = 0.02$
$x_0 = 0.05$, $y_0 = 0$

We see that all systems will be protected (y converges to 1 whenever $d > 0$ and $e > 0$ holds) and no virus will remain.

If we reduce the number of protected systems whenever the number of viruses decreases, we will get the following differential equation system:

$$dx/dt = a\,(1 - x - y)\,x - e\,x \qquad (8)$$

$$dy/dt = d\,(1 - x - y)\,x + e\,x - c\,(1 - x)\,y \qquad (9)$$

$c\,(1 - x)$ ... probability of removing a protection system

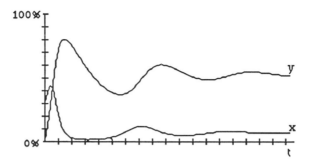

Fig. 5 Model (8, 9), $a = 0.5$, $c = 0.03$, $d = 0.02$
$e = 0.2$, $x_0 = 0.3$, $y_0 = 0$

The behavior of this system is similar to a predator-prey model. A decrease of the virus rate reduces the number of protection systems, so that the viruses can spread again, which increases the rate of protection systems again.

NOT PERFECT PROTECTION SYSTEMS

No virus protection system is perfect. If the virus knows the specific protection procedures it can circumvent the system or misuse the procedures for its own purpose. In order to model this situation, we add a third variable z and a factor b to model (8, 9).

z ... rate of protected but infected systems
b ... probability of infection of a protected system

Usually b has a smaller value than a. We have

$y - z$ ... rate of protected & clean systems
$x - z$ ... rate of not protected & infected systems
$1 - x - y - z$ ... rate of not protected&clean systems

$$dx/dt = a\,(1 - x - y - z)\,x + b\,(y - z)\,x - e\,(x - z) \qquad (10)$$

$$dy/dt = d\,(1 - x - y - z)\,x + e\,(x - z) - c\,(1 - x)\,y \qquad (11)$$

$$dz/dt = b\,(y - z)\,x \qquad (12)$$

Equation (12) says that z increases proportional to the probability that a protected and clean system becomes infected by exposure to an infected system. This amount must also be added to (10).

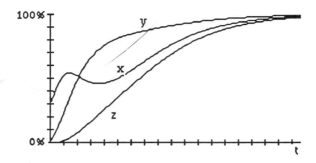

Fig. 6 Model (10-12), a = 0.2, b = 0.04, c = 0.01,
d = 0.02, e = 0.05, x_0 = 0.3, y_0 = 0, z_0 = 0

All protected systems become infected in this example. The existence of some infected systems increases automatically the number of protected & infected systems.

The use of a protection system may make the detection and removal of viruses easier, so that some of the protected & infected systems will become clean. This can be modeled by a term − f z which is added to (10) and (12).

f ... probability that a protected & infected system is cleaned

$$dx/dt = a(1-x-y-z)x + b(y-z)x - - e(x-z) - fz \qquad (13)$$

$$dy/dt = d(1-x-y-z)x + e(x-z) - - c(1-x)y \qquad (14)$$

$$dz/dt = b(y-z)x - fz \qquad (15)$$

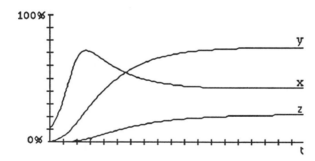

Fig. 7 Model (13-15), a = 0.2, b = 0.02, c = 0.01,
d = 0.01, e = 0.02, x_0 = 0.1, y_0 = 0, z_0 = 0

The behavior of this system is equivalent to the use of a widespread but not perfect protection system.

A widespread protection system is only sufficient, if it is perfect. Otherwise it can only slow down virus propagation.

DIFFERENT PROTECTION SYSTEMS

The basic idea: Every virus makes use of a specific flaw of a protection system in order to infect it.

Therefore a virus can only infect systems which use the same protection mechanism.

In the following we will try to find out to what extend the number of different protection systems that are used worldwide may influence the rate of infected systems.

We assume that there exists a variable number n of different protection systems and these protection mechanisms are equally distributed amongst all these systems. The rate of systems, that use the same protection mechanism corresponds to 1/n.

The rate of infected systems x is increased proportionally to the probability that a clean system gets infected by exposure to an infected system, which has the same protection mechanism. e x equals the part of infected systems, which introduce new protection mechanisms.

$$dx/dt = a(1-x)x/n - ex \qquad (16)$$

$$dn/dt = enx/(1-ex) \qquad (17)$$

Equation (17) can be calculated on the assumption that all protection mechanisms remain equally distributed. After the introduction of Δn new protection mechanisms we have a rate of $\Delta n/(n + \Delta n)$ of newly protected systems, which should be equal to ex. From $ex = \Delta n/(n + \Delta n)$ follows that $dn/dt = enx/(1 - ex)$.

For e = 0 we have a constant number n of protection systems and the model (16, 17) is reduced to model (1). So a constant number of not perfect protection systems leads in principle to the same drastic increase in virus infection as the unrestricted virus propagation.

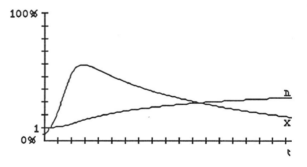

Fig. 8. Model (16, 17), a = 0.3, e = 0.08,
x_0 = 0.05, n_0 = 1

The rate of infected systems converges to 0 whenever the number of different protection systems exceeds a/e.

Now we assume that the use of many different protection mechanisms leads to an average reduction of the quality factor efficiency.

228

Efficient protection mechanisms are characterized by:
- highly reduced virus propagation
- high detection & removal rate

Instead of a constant probability of infection a, we use $(1 - h / n)$ a, which is minimal for $n = 1$ and tends to a for a high value of n.

The detection & removal rate is assumed to be g / n. This is a very defensive assumption. The efficiency of one system is n times higher than that of n systems

$(1 - h / n)$ a ... probability of infection
g / n ... probability of
              detection & removal

$$dx/dt = (1 - h / n) a (1 - x) x / n - e x$$
$$- (g / n) x \qquad (18)$$

$$dn/dt = e n x / (1 - e x) \qquad (19)$$

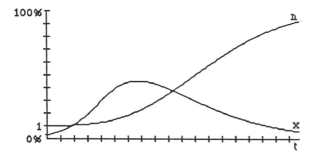

Fig. 9 Model (18, 19), $a = 0.3$, $e = 0.05$, $h = 0.5$, $g = 0.02$, $x_0 = 0.03$, $n_0 = 1$

Again all infected systems become clean, whenever the number of different protection systems becomes large enough.

CONCLUSION

The discussed models show that the use of many different protection systems can be more effective than the use of a single very sophisticated and efficient system. It is necessary to develop new and further develop existing protection systems or the battle against computer virus propagation will be lost.

REFERENCES

Cohen, F. (1987). Computer Viruses, Theory and Experiences. *Computer & Security, 6,* 22-35.
Futschek, G. (1991). Experiments with Self-Reproductive Logo Programs. *Proceedings of the 3rd European Logo Conference,* Parma.
Murray, J. D. (1989). *Mathematical Biology.* Springer.

Solomon, A. (1990). Epidemology and computer viruses. *Virus News International, 9,.*15-21.
Weninger, Chr. (1991). *Betrachtungen zur Virenproblematik und Implementierung des PC- Antivirenprogramms PROTECTOR (Germain).* Diplomarbeit, TU-Wien.
Zentralstelle für Sicherheit in der Informationstechnik (1989). *IT-Sicherheitskriterien - Kriterien zur Bewertung der Sicherheit von Systemen der Informationstechnik (IT).* Bundesanzeiger Verlagsges.mbH., Köln.

Propagating Temporal Demands into the Software Design to Support the Evaluation of Safety Critical Hard Real-Time Systems

R. Bareiss

Institute for Control Engineering and Industrial Automation

University of Stuttgart,

Pfaffenwaldring 47, D-7000 Stuttgart 80, Germany

Tel. ++49/711/6857312, FAX. ++49/711/6857302

Abstract: When developing safety critical hard real-time systems, there's a great need for powerful and practically usable analysing methods for supporting the evaluation and validation of the temporal behaviour of real-time systems, already on the level of the software design. In this contribution, one approach for reaching this aim is presented. It is based on a formal constraint propagation technique. The underlying idea is to derive the temporal relationships inside the software design on the basis of the environmentally motivated temporal constraints and the user-defined temporal system requirements. Thus, we get the temporal time constraints that have to be fulfilled by procedures implemented later on. Further, the calculated overall temporal behaviour can be visualized in a time diagram for validation and evaluation purposes.

Keywords: Safety, constraint propagation, temporal reasoning, time state machines embedded real-time systems.

1. Introduction

Compared to pure sequential systems, embedded hard real-time systems have to fulfill the following additional demands (see, e.g. [Laub89]):

- The computer for process control has to react on the inputs from the environment (the technical process) always right in time. Depending on the environment, right in time can mean the computer has to react within a range of milliseconds or microseconds.

- The control system has to react on simultaneously incoming events at virtually the same time. This demand implies parallelism.

From a temporal point of view, the computer for process control is totally subordinated to the temporal constraints from the environment.

Looking at real-time programming languages like ADA, PEARL, etc, the reflections of these real-time specific requirements can already be noticed. They provide concepts for parallel (or quasi parallel) execution, they include scheduling concepts, they provide concepts for defining programmable reactions on external events, etc. Finally we can conclude, that for supporting the realization of real-time systems, very powerful facilities at programming language level are already available.

In contradiction to that, the support of an engineer on his way to a *good and correct* design with respect to its temporal behaviour (especially in safety critical hard real-time applications) has not been addressed adequately, yet.

Of course there are many methods (and tools) intended to support the modeling of hard real-time systems, mostly based on (timed) petri nets (see, e.g. [PACE90, Mura89]) or extended state machines (see, e.g. [Ostr89, HaPi87, Ha et al 90]). But, regarding to the aspect of analyzing the temporal behaviour of the model there is a lack of practically usable formal methods, although there are several research activities in the domain of formal verification stressing particularly the real-time aspects (see, e.g. [MaPn83, MaPn92, Koym90, Ostr92, JaMo87]) and in the domain of timing analysis (see, e.g. [SaHo90, BeDi91]).

For evaluating the temporal behaviour of an embedded hard real-time system it is extremely helpful to know precisely, what are the *consequences of certain quantitative temporal requirements* on the planned and/or specified, low level and merely sequential procedures in the software design. There are two main facets:

- For designing the implementation of the procedures on a low level, it's extremely helpful to know the temporal intervals quantitatively, in which the procedures have to provide their solutions to make the entire system able to meet the hard external temporal constraints.

- Knowing *all* the temporal constraints in the software design that have to be met by the procedures implemented later on in order to meet the external temporal constraints even in worst case (at maximum work-load), an experienced software engineer is able to recognize possible bottlenecks. This kind .of evaluation activity could be supported by an adequate visualization technique, for instance, a timing diagram, illustrating completely the behaviour of the considered part of the real-time system at maximum work-load.

In this contribution we want to present a powerful approach to support the engineer in designing safety critical hard real-time systems and particularly, to support him in evaluating and validating the designed temporal behaviour. The presentation is structured as follows:

Section 2 describes the basic ideas and the global strategy of our approach. The presentation of the approach itself will be illustrated with an example. A general idea and a rough characterization of the example is given in section 3, combined with the example-related concrete definition of what we want to reach. This example is kept very small and easy to understand in order to enable the reader to focus his attention on the time propagation technique.

In section 4 the formal model of the already characterized real-time system will be introduced and discussed. This is done for illustration purposes of the formal method being the basis for the propagation technique and for having an example forming the basis for presenting the propagation technique. The propagation technique itself will be presented and discussed in section 5. Section 6 summarizes the results and the benefits of our approach.

2. Basic Idea and Strategy of the Approach

The basic idea of our approach consists of *calculating the temporal consequences of the user-defined temporal requirements and of the existing and not changeable temporal constraints of the environmental behaviour in the software design.* The time propagation technique is based on the following information:

- Formal specification of the quantitative temporal requirements on the embedded hard real-time system.

- Formal specification of the temporal behaviour of the controlled environmental technical process in a quantitative way, as it could be observed at the interface to the control computer. Or, if the behaviour of the controlled technical process is quite sophisticated (as in the example presented here), it may become necessary to specify the temporal behaviour of the whole controlled technical process.

- The detailed structuring of the software design on the lowest level without any quantitative timing information. It consists of control flow, data flow and information about parallelism and synchronization.

The aim of this approach can be summarized in the following two topics:

- Calculating the *whole amount of temporal* relationships inside the real-time system and particularly the adapting relationships inside the software design at maximum work load. This information forms the basis for visualizing the temporal behaviour in a time diagram and is useful at evaluating the temporal behaviour of the entire real-time system.

- Calculating the upper and lower time bounds in which the elementary, pure sequential functionalities (for instance procedures, functions, etc.) have to deliver their output parameters.

Figure 1 illustrates the integration of the constraint propagation technique into the process model and visualizes the strategy. In this Figure only the intermediate products being relevant for the constraint propagation algorithm are shown. The aspect of the temporal behaviour is stressed particularly.

The arrows show the information flow when using the constraint propagation approach.

Compared to verification-based techniques the underlying strategy of the propagation technique is construction-oriented and forward-directed. There's no need for explicit specification of the quantitative temporal behaviour in the software design that have to be verified 'post mortum', but they are deducted directly.

Compared to other approaches based on timing analysis assuring the correctness between the requirements and the software design regarding temporal aspects (see, e.g. [SaHo90, BeDi91, GMMP91]), the main characteristic of this strategy is that all time figures used are based on facts and not on estimated values. For instance:

- The temporal requirements on the entire hard real-time system represents directly the throughput of the real-time system. Therefore, these are either well-known or easy to obtain.

- The information processing inside the technical process is based on physical laws. Thus, the information processing is deterministic and the time required for the constraint propagation algorithm can be easily measured.

Another very important aspect of the time propagation algorithm is that it is decidable and needs no interaction for processing by the user. But because of lack of space in this contribution, this aspect of how to automate the propagation technique can't be mentioned at all.

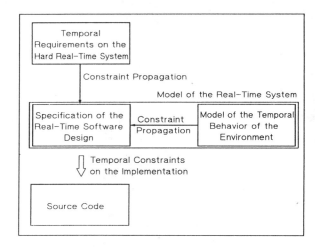

Figure 1: Integration of the propagation technique into the process model

3. Specifying the aim of the propagation technique more precisely at an example

For illustration purposes we want to apply the propagation technique to a part of a parcel distribution system. Figure 2 gives an overview of the entire system at it is existing in form of a real model at our institute.

The parcels are reaching the entry station via a conveying belt where a bar code reader reads their target address. Afterwards they are gliding through the binary-tree-structured distribution part with switching devices at the nodes. The task of the control system is to set the switches always right in time in a way that each parcel will reach its target.

To keep the example simple for illustrating the propagation technique, we just want to look at the part focused in Figure 3. It consists of the 'entry-track' into the distribution part (the part between 'ED' and 'SD1' denoted with 'track-1') and the first switching device.

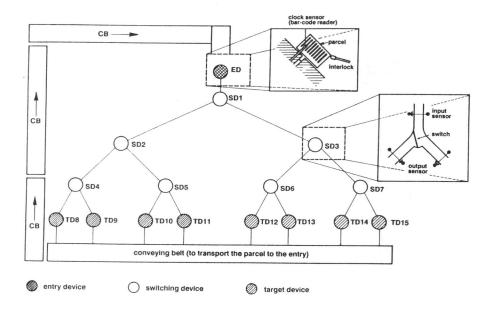

Figure 2: *Sketch of the parcel distribution system.*

232

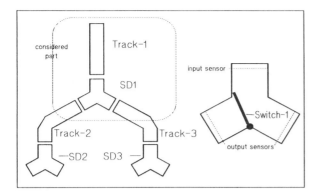

Figure 3: *Considered part of the parcel distribution system for illustrating the propagation technique.*

We further assume (for the sake of simplicity to keep the model presented in the next section as small as possible), that with the parcels' entering into 'track-1', the control system gets the target address of the entering parcel to calculate the position of the switch in the first switching device. This calculation and the positioning process of the switch have to be finished with recognizing the parcel at the 'input sensor' at 'switching-device-1'.

If we know the speed of the gliding parcel as well as the length of 'track-1' and the time for positioning the switch, we are able to calculate the *longest duration the procedure is allowed to consume* to calculate the position of the switch for each parcel. But this information is not enough. We are further interested in the *smallest duration* the procedure *must consume* to *keep the whole system running* regularly.

To deduce this duration, we're observing the special case of *maximum work-load*, that each time the parcel is leaving 'track-1' and entering the 'switching-device-1', the succeeding parcel enters 'track-1'. Now, if the procedure calculating the switch position for the currently entering parcel is too fast (maybe finished in 0,1 ms), the switch in the switching device possibly changes its position while the previous parcel hasn't left the switching device yet. This will cause a lock in the switching device and may lead (in reality) to damaged parcels.

4. The Specification Method, its Time Model and the Formal Model of the Application

On the one side, a specification method forms the basis of the propagation technique. On the other side, for the developer modeling a system and proceeding the evaluation, the specification method forms some kind of 'human user interface'. To satisfy both requirements, it has to be formal and - even for 'pure' practitioners - easy to understand and easy to apply. Therefore, the following strategy has been chosen:

We based our specification method for modeling hard real-time systems on easily understandable communicating state machines, substantiated the method with proper semantics and extended it with a suitable formal time model based on *interval semantics*. This time model was selected because of its exactness in modeling the temporal real world behaviour in contradiction to *point semantics*.

With modeling the temporal behaviour of a system using *point semantics* (see, e.g. [Ostr89, SaHo90, CLRT91]) you could refer times as points and as constant periods of time defined by the time difference between time points, respectively, like 'delay(10ms)' or like 'to provide a certain functionality 100ms are required'. But, if you want to describe any process unit in the real world in an exact and error-free way, this is a far to idealistic model. To do this you need an interval-based formalism providing a lower and upper bound to enclose the real temporal behaviour at modeling [Alle 83].

4.1 Basic Structures of the Specification Method

Figure 4 gives an overview of the horizontal structuring on the lowest hierarchy level of our model. The considered part of the real-time system is specified with four state processes presenting the behaviour as follows:

❑ 'Track-1' models the fact that a parcel may be on the track concerned or it may be empty.

❑ The behaviour of the 'switching device 1' (SD1) is modelled via the two state processes 'SD1' and 'Switch-1'. In analogy to 'Track-1' 'SD1' describes the fact that a parcel may be inside or outside the 'switching device 1'. 'Switch-1' models the behaviour of the switch inside switching device 1.

❑ 'Calculate Position Switch-1' describes the (very simple) software design.

As it could be seen in Figure 4, the symbolized state processes are linked with communication channels for information exchange, with signal exchange links and event links. The latter ones are used for defining a synchronization and a control flow between state processes.

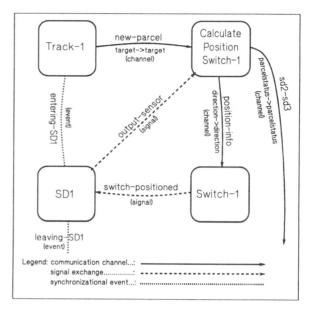

Figure 4: *Illustrating the horizontal structuring of the model including the communication and control flow between the state processes*

The specification of the 'local' temporal and functional behaviour inside the bubbles in Figure 4 is each based on one state machine. A state machine is defined by a directed graph with 'states' as nodes and 'transitions' as edges. Both elementary elements are characterized as follows:

Temporal behaviour of states and transitions:

❑ A state Sx represents a duration in time. This means, a state machine may remain in a state for a certain time.

Formally: $dur(Sx) \geq 0$ (duration for remaining in the state Sx is longer or equal 0) (1)

❑ A transition tx occurs at a time point. It has the character of an instantaneous event without any finite temporal duration.

Formally: $dur(tx) = 0$ (2)

Functional behaviour of states and transitions:

❑ At states we are differing between two types of states. There are 'active' and 'passive' states. While remaining in an 'active' state, some kind of 'information processing' takes place, for instance, the process of positioning the switch in the switching device from the left to the right position and vice versa. In contradiction to that, a 'passive' state is a pure 'waiting' state. 'Nothing' happens while remaining in this state.

At applying the modeling technique to specify a software design, an 'active' state is characterized by a reference on an elementary, pure sequential functionality, for instance, a procedure. This 'procedure' is processed while the state machine remains in the certain active state. After time of stay the list of parameters given back by the procedure has to be calculated. A passive state doesn't refer to a procedure.

❑ A transition denotes the passing from one state to the succeeding state. It occurs, when the logical AND-connection of the following optionally specifyable conditions are true:

- A specified logical condition is true
- The present time is inside the specified time interval
- The synchronizing event linked with the transition occurs
- The signals and information channels are ready to receive (the according sending event has already taken place)

With occurring a transition the 'process' of sending information and a signal is initiated.

The entire model of the considered part of the real-time system is visualized in Figure 5. In a first step, we only want to consider the aspects described by states and transitions.

The status of the entering track 'Track-1' is modelled by the states 'free' and 'Parcel-in-Track-1'. The state 'Parcel-in-Track-1' is an active one, because while 'track-1' remains in this state, the parcel is sliding and after a certain time it leaves 'Track-1'. At that time 'Track-1' passes into the waiting state 'free' again. 'SD1' has been modelled in analogy to 'Track-1' by a passive state 'free' and an active one 'Parcel-in-SD1'.

The model of 'Switch-1' needs some more explanation. To describe the complete functional and temporal behaviour of 'Switch-1', a state machine with the states 'left-hand-side' (passive), 'right-hand-side' (passive), 'turning-left' (active) and 'turning-right' (active) would have been necessary. But, for calculating the upper and lower time bounds within the procedure 'calc-pos-switch-1' has to deliver its parameters, only the aspect has to be considered, that in worst case the position of the switch has to be changed before each parcel reaches 'SD1'. Accordingly, 'Switch-1' can be modelled with a passive state 'positioned', describing the fact of either remaining at the left hand side or at the right hand side, and with an active state 'positioning', where the referred functionality 'changing' represents the turning to the left hand side or to the right hand side.

The software design is modelled by the state process 'Calculate Position Switch-1'. Its internal behaviour is defined by a passive state 'wait' and an active state 'calc-pos-switch-1' referring to the procedure of the same name for calculating the output variable 'direction' and 'parcel-status'. The first one is for positioning the switch of the switching device while the second variable denotes the software internal representation of the status of a certain parcel in the distribution system. Hence, we are just considering a part of the control software, the variable 'parcel-status' is not referred to any more in the specification in Figure 5.

4.2 Semantics of Communication, Signal Exchange and Synchronization

4.2.1 Looking at Synchronization

With linking two transitions in different state processes by one event label, we define, that these transitions have to occur simultaneously.

In the model this type of synchronization is used once to force that $t_{1.2}$ and $t_{3.1}$ are occurring simultaneously. The name of the linking event label is 'entering-SD1' (see Figure 4 and 5). 'entering-SD1' is used to model the fact, that with leaving the entering track, the parcel enters the switching device. Therewith the model represents the reality exactly, we define that the time point of leaving the entering track is the one of reaching the input sensor.

4.2.2 Discussing the Signal exchange

Signals are needed for the convenient expression of predecessor successor relationships in time between transitions in different state processes.

For instance, the important time constraint that the switch in switching device one must have finished positioning before the parcel is reaching this switching device, is expressed in our model with the signal 'switch-positioned'. It is sent at $t_{4.2}$ and it will be received at transition $t_{3.1}$. From a pure temporal point of view with this signal we define the fact, that the transition $t_{3.1}$ *must occur later or at the same time* as transition $t_{4.2}$. Formally:

❏   time point $(t_{3.1})$ ≥ time point $(t_{4.2})$ (3)

The second time constraint, that the calculation of the next switch position mustn't be finished before the previous parcel has left the switching device, is expressed by the signal 'output-sensor'.

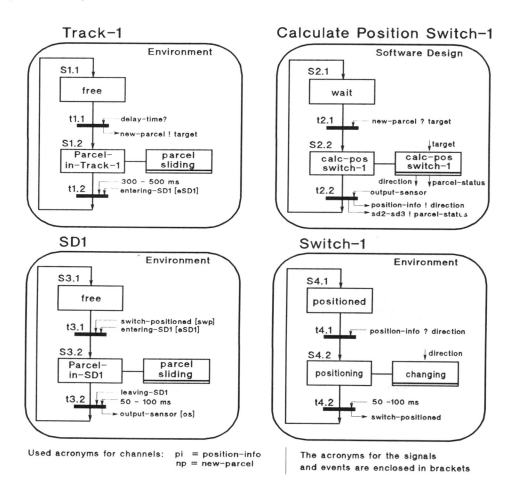

Used acronyms for channels: pi = position-info
                             np = new-parcel

The acronyms for the signals and events are enclosed in brackets

Figure 5: Specification of the internal behaviour of the state process

4.2.3 Looking at the Communication via Channels

Considered from a pure temporal point of view, a communication channel defines the same predecessor - successor relationship as a signal. For instance, with occurring transition $t_{2.2}$, the sending of the value of 'direction' via the channel 'position-info' is started. With occurring transition $t_{4.1}$ the receipt is finished. The information exchange happens between the *sending event* ($t_{2.2}$) and the *receiving event* ($t_{4.1}$).

The functional behaviour of a channel can be explained by the following virtual elementary operations:

1. With occurring of the sending event, a virtual operation is started that assigns the value of the process local variable of the sender to the channel. For instance:

   - position-info := direction$_{Calculate Position Switch-1}$ (4)

2. The content of the channel 'position-info' is assigned to the process local variable of the receiving process. For instance:

   - direction$_{Switch-1}$:= position-info   (5)

   Now, the transition $t_{4.1}$ is enabled to occur.

3. After occurring of the receiving event (with $t_{4.1}$), the channel has to be reset again.

The transfer of the parcel target to the computer and the information transfer back from the computer to control 'Switch-1' is modelled by the channels 'new-parcel' and 'position-info'.

4.3 Specifying Quantitative Temporal Behaviour

Because a transition represents an instant time point, it's a very suitable and exact 'anchor' for linking temporal requirements and constraints. To provide a maximum flexibility in specifying temporal requirements, we allow in our method the specification of *absolute* and *relative* time requirements. Both types of facilities can be used mixed in one specification.

For the considered example in Figure 5, only relative time requirements are needed. For instance, at $t_{1.2}$ the requirement 'rel-time = 300 - 500 ms' expresses, that for regular processing the transition must occur between 300 and 500 ms after entering the previous state $S_{1.2}$. It's a very similar concept as the one that can be found at time petri nets (see e.g. [BeDi91]).

Finally, one comment to the used unit 'ms': The time model is based on a *linear continuous time scale*. For regular processing, the propagation algorithm doesn't need a discrete time model (using 'ticks') as it's needed for many other formal correctness assuring methods, as for instance at that one, based on some kind of temporal logic (see e.g. [Ostr 89, Ostr92, Koym90]). Thus, the scaling of the numbers in the model in Figure 5 is completely arbitrarily. They are just introduced to the reader to provide a better feeling for the time relations in the real-time system. For the propagation algorithm they are completely irrelevant.

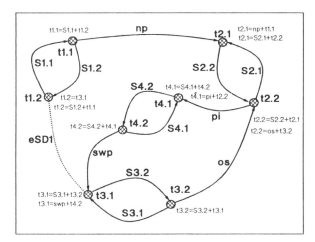

Figure 6: *Visualization of the specified temporal relationships in Figure 5*

5. The Propagation Technique

5.1 Step 1: Extracting the Specified Temporal Relations

A lot of time relations between transitions have been specified in the model in Figure 5 by state-transition sequences, by communication and signal links and by event labels. The resulting net of the temporal relationships is illustrated in Figure 6.

The graph was created by the following transformation:

❐ *Transitions* in Figure 5 become *nodes* in Figure 6. They represent the *time points* of the transitions' occurring.

❐ *States, communication channels* and *signal links* become *directed edges*. They represent *durations in time* and any kind of *'time consumer'*, respectively, for instance, the duration for processing the information exchange via a data channel.

❐ *Event labels* lead to *not directed edges* (see relation between $t_{1.2}$ and $t_{3.1}$).

The equations in Figure 6 define the temporal relations mathematically. For instance, '$t_{1.2} = S_{1.2} + t_{1.1}$' is the short form of the equation 'time point ($t_{1.2}$) = duration ($S_{1.2}$) + time point ($t_{1.1}$)'. It is interpreted in the following way: The time point of occurring $t_{1.2}$ can be calculated by adding the duration the state machine remains in the state $S_{1.1}$ and the time point the transition $t_{1.1}$ is occuring.

5.2 Step 2: Preparing the System of Equations for the Worst-Case Analysis

The equations in Figure 6 are describing the temporal behaviour of our example completely and correctly. It was easy to derive them directly from the specification. However, as a consequence of the sophisticated time model based on interval-semantics, the variable in the system of equations doesn't represent one single number but a 2-tuple (the upper and lower bound of an interval). Thus, the system of equations doesn't describe one solution but an infinite solution space and is therefore not solvable in the well known simple way.

To come to a simple solution being particularly suitable for the evaluation of the temporal behaviour of the entire real-time system, we first have to derive a further system of equations defining the outer time framework, in which the actual temporal behaviour of the real-time system will be enclosed, by referring to interval bounds. The extraction of the new system of equations is the task of the 'worst-case' analysis, forming the core in interval processing. But, the formal presumptions for operating the worst-case analysis are equations of the type as shown below:

$$\sum_{i=0}^{i=n} (\pm \, dur(S_i)) = k * 'cycle\text{-}time' \qquad (6)$$
$$\text{with } k = 0, 1, -1 \text{ and } n = 1, 2, 3, \ldots$$

In the equation 6 'cycle-time' (or in short 'cyc'; see below) denotes the duration of one system cycle.

Equations of that type can be derived from the system of equations describing the temporal behaviour of a cyclic system eliminating the transitions. A result of the continued elimination of transitions in the system of equations in Figure 6 is shown in Figure 7. It describes the temporal behaviour of our model in Figure 6 completely and linear independently by adding up pure relative durations without any references to the absolute time scale.

$S_{1.1} + S_{1.2} = cyc$	(7)
$S_{2.1} + S_{2.2} = cyc$	(8)
$S_{3.1} + S_{3.2} = cyc$	(9)
$S_{4.1} + S_{4.2} = cyc$	(10)
$S_{1.2} - swp - S_{4.2} - pi - S_{2.2} - np = 0$	(11)
$S_{1.1} + np + S_{2.2} - os - S_{3.2} = 0$	(12)

Figure 7: *System of equations describing the temporal behaviour of the model in Figure 6 in form of chained up durations.*

5.3 Step 3: The Worst-Case Analysis

Formally, during the worst-case analysis a system of equations in terms of intervals, like the one in Figure 7, has to be mapped into one in terms of bounds of intervals. The resulting system of equations is solvable, finally. A more detailed definition of the durations in time (S_x) is given in the following equation:

❐ $S_x = [S_{x/min}, S_{x/max}]$ (13)

In substance, the aim of this transformation is to get a system of equations defining the outer time framework, the actual temporal behaviour of the real-time system will be enclosed in. This new system of equations referring to the interval bounds will be derived by considering the most extreme cases of temporal behaviour, that can happen in the real-time system. The resulting new system of equations will also include the equations for calculating the wanted *smallest upper time bounds* and *largest lower time bounds*, that guarantees the satisfaction of all temporal requirements and constraints at any case, if the output parameters of the certain procedures are right in time.

For motivating the transformation we take into account what kind of functionality with what kind of temporal behaviour each variable represents and in what sequence these model-inherent 'functionalities' are chained up.

In our example we've used the following types of model-inherent functionalities with the following temporal behaviour under worst-case conditions:

❑ An *active state* in a state process *modelling the behaviour of an environmental part*, like $S_{1.2}$, $S_{3.2}$ and $S_{4.2}$.

These variable refer to the temporal behaviour of the technical process and form the framework of constraints in which the procedures have to proceed. They are not changeable by the software engineer and generally well-known or measurable and enclosed in an interval. In the system of equations in Figure 8 the certain variable are identified with the attribute 'TP' for 'technical process'.

❑ An *active state* in the *software design referring to a procedure* like $S_{2.2}$.

Generally, these are the sought after variable. In Figure 8 they are identified with the attribute 'PR' for 'procedure'.

❑ The variable $S_{1.1}$, $S_{2.1}$, $S_{3.1}$ and $S_{4.2}$ denote *pure waiting states* (identified with 'WA'). One criterion of the worst-case analysis is to assume *a smallest* duration for the *waiting states* to be able to offer the active states as much time as possible.

❑ The variable 'swp', 'np', 'pi' and 'os' are referring to channels or signals (identified in Figure 8 with 'CH'). Based on the very general definition of

■ $S_{channel} = [S_{channel/min}, S_{channel/max}]$ (14)

$S_{channel/min}$ identifies the smallest possible time, needed for the information transfer itself in best case, and $S_{channel/max}$ denotes the longest possible time, needed for the information transfer itself in worst case.

Because the varible 'cyc' forms the spine in calculating the time framework (e.g. system of equations in Figure 7), the duration of the system cycle at maximum load in worst case has to be calculated first. In this example, we assume as maximum load that at each time a parcel leaves 'Track-1' and enters 'SD1' a succeeding parcel enters 'Track-1' again. At maximum load the duration of remaining in the waiting state 'free' of 'Track-1' is zero ($S_{1.1/min} = 0$).

The calculation of the cycle time based on equation (7) in worst case at maximum load leads to solutions as follows:

❑ Because $S_{1.2}$ can not be influenced by the software engineer, we had to *assume the longest possible duration of $S_{1.2}$* for calculating the *shortest possible duration of system cycle which we can guarantee to the user*. Based on the following modified equation (7)

■ $S_{1.1/min} + S_{1.2/max} = cyc_{/max} \wedge S_{1.1/min} = 0$

we can calculate $cyc_{/max} = 500$ ms.

❑ For calculating the *shortest possible system cycle duration* we have to interpret equation (7) in a way as follows:

■ $S_{1.1/min} + S_{1.2/min} = cyc_{/min} \wedge S_{1.1/min} = 0$

This leads to $cyc_{/min} = 300$ ms and defines the strongest conditions for the time framework that have to be fulfilled by the procedures implemented later on.

As a second step of the worst case analysis we have to consider the remaining equations (no. 8 - 12) in the sense of how they will behave in the most extreme cases from a temporal point of view. The derived new system of equations to calculate the wanted temporal framework is shown in Figure 8.

$$S_{\underset{WA}{2.1/min}} + S_{\underset{PR}{2.2/max}} = cyc_{/min} \quad (15)$$

$$S_{\underset{WA}{3.1/min}} + S_{\underset{TP}{3.2/max}} = cyc_{/min} \quad (16)$$

$$S_{\underset{WA}{4.1/min}} + S_{\underset{TP}{4.2/max}} = cyc_{/min} \quad (17)$$

$$S_{\underset{TP}{1.2/min}} - swp_{\underset{CH}{/max}} - S_{\underset{TP}{4.2/max}} - pi_{\underset{CH}{/max}} \quad (18)$$

$$- S_{\underset{PR}{2.2/max}} - np_{\underset{CH}{/max}} = 0$$

$$S_{\underset{WA}{1.1/min}} + np_{\underset{CH}{/min}} + S_{\underset{PR}{2.2/min}} - os_{\underset{CH}{/max}} - S_{\underset{TP}{3.2/max}} = 0 \quad (19)$$

Figure 8: *System of equations describing all temporal relations of the real-time system at worst case.*

The reasoning of what means the 'most extreme cases' with respect to each equation is discussed in the following:

❑ Justification for the mapping leading to the equation (15):

A variable of type 'PR' is a sought after one. At equation (15) we argue, that if a procedure can satisfy an upper time bound being calculated based on the smallest cyclic time, the meeting of the global time requirements are guaranteed at any case.

❑ Justification for the mapping leading to the equations (16) and (17):

The calculateable variables $S_{3.1/min}$ and $S_{4.1/min}$ are needed for proving that the real-time system behaves absolutely deterministic. Therefore all variable values in the system of equations in Figure 7 have to be non-negative. (To get a feeling why this is so, please assume $S_{4.2/max} = 350$ ms and think about the resulting consequences in reality and in the model).

Furthermore, they are of interest when defining a part of the adapting temporal relations in the entire real-time system at worst case, for instance, to visualize them in a time diagram like in Figure 10.

❑ Justification for the mapping leading to the equation (18):

This equation defines the worst case combination of interval bounds leading to the *smallest* duration of the *upper interval bound* of the wanted variable of type 'PR'. Thus, satisfying the resulting time constraint by the procedure will lead to the fulfilling of all other time requirements and constraints under any circumstances.

❑ Justification for the mapping leading to the equation (19):

This equation defines the worst case combination of interval bounds leading to the *longest duration* regarding to the *lower interval bound* of the wanted variable $S_{2.2/min}$ of type 'PR'.

5.4 Step 4: Solution of the derived system of equations

Figure 9 provides an overview over the solution process of the system of equations. It summarizes the known variable, the already calculated time for a system cycle, the assumptions to reach a complete solution and the calculated solution in form of time figures.

Known variable:		
$S_{1.2} = [S_{1.2/min}, S_{1.2/max}] = [300, 500]$ ms		(20)
$S_{3.2} = [S_{3.2/min}, S_{3.2/max}] = [\ 50, 100]$ ms		(21)
$S_{4.2} = [S_{4.2/min}, S_{4.2/max}] = [\ 50, 100]$ ms		(22)
Assumption defining the maximum work load:		
$S_{1.1/min} = 0$ ms		(23)
Already calculated duration of the system cycle:		
$zyk = [zyk_{/min}, zyk_{/max}] = [300, 500\ ]$ ms		(24)
Further Assumptions:		
$os = [os_{/min}, os_{/max}] = [0, 0]$ ms		(25)
$swp = [swp_{/min}, swp_{/max}] = [0, 0]$ ms		(26)
$np = [np_{/min}, np_{/max}] = [0, 0]$ r 3		(27)
$pi = [pi_{/min}, pi_{/max}] = [0, 0]$ ms		(28)
Solution derived on system of equations in Figure 8:		
$S_{2.2} = [S_{2.2/min}, S_{2.2/max}] = [100, 200]$ ms		(29)
$S_{2.1/min} = 100$ ms		(30)
$S_{3.1/min} = 200$ ms		(31)
$S_{4.1/min} = 200$ ms		(32)

Figure 9: *Summary of the known (specified) variable, the assumed variable and the calculated solution based on the system of equations in Figure 8.*

Some final comments to the assumptions denoted with equation number (25) to (28).

The signals 'switch-positioned' and 'output-sensor' are pure virtual signals to specify the predecessor successor relations between certain transitions without the necessity of a representation in a possible realization. On that background these assumptions are obvious.

To justify the assumption that the time needed for communication over the channels is zero, we assume that the procedure 'calc-pos-switch-1' picks up its input parameters at the interface directly after starting and sends them back again at the last code statement before finishing. So in this example, the time needed for communication was added up to the time allowed for processing 'calc-pos-switch-1'. Because the communication time is related very closely to the time of starting and finishing the procedure, these simplification has nearly no effect on the exactness of our solution with respect to the reality.

5.5 Visualizing the Temporal Behaviour

Figure 10 provides an overview over the temporal behaviour of the entire real-time system at maximum work-load - that means $S_{1.1} = 0$ - and with all transitions describing the worst case.

Figure 10 shows the behaviour of all state processes and visualizes the synchronization, the signal exchange and the communication. The crosshatched boxes at active states show the time intervals in which each succeeding transitions are allowed to occur.

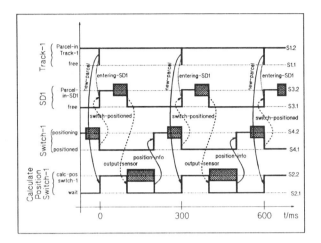

Figure 10: *Time diagram of the temporal behaviour of the real-time system.*

6. Summary: Results and Benefits

After the application of the constraint propagation algorithm the developer has obtained the total overview of all temporal relationships inside the entire real-time system. Figure 11 visualizes how the results could beneficially be used and which intermediate products are concerned.

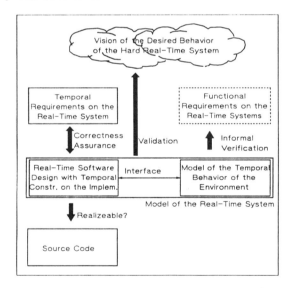

Figure 11: *Results after application of the constraint propagation algorithm*

Details:

☐ Because of the complete availability of all internal temporal relationships inside the real-time system (and of course inside the software design), the developer gets an idea of the actual parallelism at run-time. With this information and the time constraints that have to be met by the procedures, an experienced developer gets the chance to recognize possible performance bottlenecks in the software design already in the design phase. This means, he gets information about where to change the design to remove the bottleneck already on the level of the design phase and not only after the implementation is completed.

☐ With the knowledge of all *quantitative* temporal constraints that have to be met by the procedures and the knowledge about the actual concurrency, an experienced developer gets an idea of these functionalities that have to be implemented in a particularly efficient way (for instance in assembler).

☐ Through proper visualization of the quantitatively known temporal behaviour of the entire real-time system or parts of it at maximum work load, for instance in a time diagram, the developer can check if the real-time system behaves as expected. Hence, the results of the constraint propagation approach are also useful for validation and informal verification purposes.

☐ If there's a need to guarantee the meeting of the temporal requirements, for instance in applications with extremely high safety and reliability requirements, the constraint propagation algorithm could be seen as a first step. It assures formally that when the derived duration intervals are met by the implemented elementary pure sequential procedures, the user-defined requirements are met, too.

For the second step, the assurance of the meeting of the time constraints on the level of software design, the following two different strategies would be possible:

■ A very pragmatic approach is to test the meeting of the time constraints using run-time tests. If the time conditions are violated, a fail-safe procedure could be started. This approach assures the meeting of the time constraints in a very simple way since the real-time system works regularly.

■ A more theoretical founded approach is based on code analysis and schedulability analysis (see, e.g. [HaSt91]). Using this approach the proof of meeting the temporal constraints in the software design by the implementation is adduced.

References

[Alle 83]   Allen, J. F.: Maintaining Knowledge about Temporal Intervals, Communications of the ACM, Volume 26, Number 11, pp. 832 - 842, November 1983.

[BeDi 91]   Berthomieu, B. and Diaz, M.: Modeling and Verification of Time Dependent Systems Using Time Petri Nets, IEEE TRANS. ON SOFTWARE ENGINEERING, VOL 17, No. 3, 1991, pp. 259 - 273.

[CLRT 91]   Creusot, D., Lemoine, P., Roux, O., Trinquet, Y., Kung, A., Marbach, O. and Serrano-Morales, C.: Execution environment for ELECTRE applications, ESEC'91, Milan, Italy, October 91, Lecture Notes in Computer Science 550, Springer Verlag.

[GMMP 91]   Ghezzi, C., Mandrioli, D., Morasca and S., Pezzè: A Unified High-Level Petri Net Formalism for Time-Critical Systems, IEEE Trans. on Software Engineering, Vol. 17, No. 2, 1991, pp. 160-172.

[Ha et al 90]   Harel, D., Lachover, H., Naamad, A., Pnueli, A., Politi, M., Sherman, R., Shtull-Trauring, A. and Trakhtenbrot, M.: STATEMATE: A Working Environment for the Development of Complex Reactive Systems. IEEE Trans. on Software Engineering, Vol. 16, No. 4, April, 1990, pp. 403-413.

[HaPi 87]   Hatley, D. J. and Pirbhai, I.: Strategies for Real-Time System Specification, New York 1987, Dorset House

[HaSt 91]   Halang, W. A. and Stoyenko, A. D.: CONSTRUCTING PREDICTABLE REAL TIME SYSTEMS, Kluwer Academics Publishers, 1991.

[JaMo 87]   Jahanian, F. and Mok, A. K.-L.: A Graph-Theoretic Approach for Timing Analysis and its Implementation. IEEE Trans. on Computers. Vol. C-36, No. 8, August 1987

[Koym 90]   Koymans, R.: Specifying Real-Time Properties with Metric Temporal Logic, Real-Time Systems, 2, pp. 255-299, Kluwer Academic Publishers, Netherlands, 1990.

[Laub 89]   Lauber, R.: Forecasting Real-Time Behaviour During Software Design Using a Case Environment. The Journal of Real-Time Systems, 1(1), S. 61 - 76, 1989

[MaPn 83]   Manna, Z. and Pnueli, A.: Verification of concurrent programs: a temporal proof system. Technical report, Dept. of Computer Science, Stanford University, June 1983.

[MaPn 92]   Manna, Z., Pnueli, A.: The Temporal Logic of Reactive and Concurrent Systems, Springer Verlag, 1992.

[Mura 89]   Murata, T.: Petri Nets: Properties, Analysis and Applications, Proceedings of the IEEE, Vol 77, No. 4, April 1989, pp. 541-580.

[Ostr 89]   Ostroff, J. S.: Temporal Logic for Real-Time Systems. Research Studies Press LTD, (Taunton, Somerset, England), John Wiley & Sons INC., 1989.

[Ostr 92]   Ostroff, J.S.: A Verifier for Real-Time Properties. REAL-TIME SYSTEMS, Kluwer Academic Publishers, Vol 4, No 1, March 1992, pp. 5-35.

[PACE 90]   PACE User's Manual. Available from: GPP mbH, Kolpingring 18a, 8024 Oberhaching, Germany

[SaHo 90]   Sagoo, J. S. and Holding, D. J.: THE SPECIFICATION AND DESIGN OF HARD REAL-TIME SYSTEMS USING TIMED AND TEMPORAL PETRI NETS. Proc. of 16th EUROMICRO Symp. on Microprocessing and Microprogramming (EUROMICRO 90), Eds. Fay, D. and Mezalira, L., Amsterdam, August 27-30, 1990, pp. 389-396.

Integrity Prediction during Software Development

P.Hall, J.May,D.Nichol,K.Czachur and B.Kinch

Abstract A new approach to software development integrity prediction is proposed. The approach is intended to form the basis for a software tool to help project managers assess the quality of completed software development work. Integrities for intermediate products in the development lifecycle are predicted from measurements of integrity-related attributes of the development process and products. The software development lifecycle is modelled as sequences of atomic processes. The analysis only considers development stages after requirements capture and prior to code testing. Atomic processes are considered to comprise of design problems followed by design reviews. The same set of integrity-related attributes are associated with each atomic process. Differences between the atomic processes are modelled by the measured values for the attributes.

Integrity for a product of a development stage S is determined from the integrities of the processes within S and integrities of the processes and products of stages prior to S. The analysis contains simple probability arguments which are developed in the paper. In addition, a brief introduction to graphical probability models is given. It is suggested that GPMs provide the appropriate formalism to perform the key role of Bayesian updating in the analysis.

1 Introduction

High integrity systems are specified with required integrity levels. Before and during the development it is necessary to be able to predict the expected integrity in a manner similar to cost predictions. Currently we can only do this in the grossest manner, by having categorised particular methods and tools (and engineers) in terms of the integrity of the systems that they (are expected to) produce.

The FASGEP Project (Fault Analysis of the Software Generation Process) being carried out within the DTI Safety Critical Systems programme aims to predict the integrity of safety critical software based on a close examination of the activities performed within the development process. FASGEP aims to provide analysis techniques useful to process engineers [Madhavji & Schafer, 1991] and to project managers. This paper studies a measure of the integrity of the 'work-to-date' for a project - key information in safety-critical software development. The determination of the integrity of a particular development phase is based on the ability of the processes within that phase to prevent the introduction of unspecified features.

FASGEP is looking specifically at integrity predictions during the software development process, ie. after software requirements analysis and before code testing. The dynamic testing stages which occur in most software lifecycles after the coding stage are not considered as part of the predictive model. The role of the dynamic testing stages is to validate and calibrate the model as discussed in section 4.

FASGEP seeks to identify the conditions or mechanisms which characterise the introduction of faults, and thereby establish a means of monitoring the possibility of faults introduction throughout the software development process.

2 Modelling the software development process

The software development process is composed of those activities that are performed in the production of software. These activities are both technical and managerial.

To date a number of software development life-cycle models have been developed, including the Waterfall model, Evolutionary model, and the Spiral model. In general, these life-cycle models help us gain a better understanding of the software development process, which can result in improved quality and reliability, increased effectiveness of methods and tools, and reduced software development and maintenance costs, leading to increased customer and developer satisfaction.

The FASGEP project aims to build generic lifecycle models, and yet needs to be able to capture and exploit details of particular lifecycles, because we believe it is events at that level of detail which determine whether a system achieves high integrity or fails through the introduction of defects. Models such as the waterfall lifecycle model, useful for pedagogical reasons, do not contain sufficient detail to describe the engineering issues concerned with fault introduction. Instead, the FASGEP software development process model is composed of generic process components. These components are specific in nature, but have parameters which allow them to be tailored to specific processes, and they can be put together in different parallel and sequential ways to reflect the details of particular software lifecycles.

We have taken the view that any process within software development can be considered as a transformation on the products previous processes. Thus we start from a standard generic input-process-output atomic process model, which we term the 'fundamental model,' shown in figure 1. In general, many of these components will be associated with each activity typically undertaken in software development.

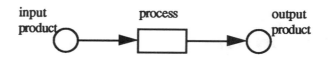

fig 1. The fundamental model

Initially in FASGEP, and for the purposes of this paper, the components will be composed in structures corresponding to the hierarchical software structure, as shown in figure 2.

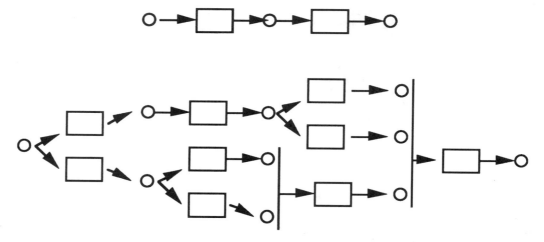

fig 2. Part of a lifecycle built from fundamental model components

In figure 2, two specifications (ie. design problems) for components are transformed by sequences of atomic design processes described by fundamental models (attributes not shown). Initially the design process proceeds by transformations of the single input products, each of which results in one or more subsidiary design problems. If the result of the transformation is several subsidiary design problems, the output product node has several branches emanating from it. When code is produced, integration-of-code processes occur with multiple inputs. In figure 2 integration processes are identified by vertical lines connecting their input products.

3 Probability models for the composition of integrity measures

There are two ways of deriving integrity statements for software. The standard method involves *direct measurements* of software reliability by statistical dynamic testing of the software code [Steel & Dugard, 1991] [Littlewood,1988]. The second approach treats integrity derivation as a *correlation* problem; attempting to discover a relationship between the integrity of a product P delivered during the development process and integrity-related attributes of the development process and products prior to delivery of P [Kitchenham & Walker, 1989]. This paper proposes a technique within the second (correlation) approach above. However, a relationship between the proposed technique and methods for direct measurement is also discussed (section 4).

A sub-branch of the direct measurement methods exploits the structure of software to compute software reliability from the reliabilities of its components [Mellor, 1992] [Littlewood, 1981] [Laprie &

Kanoun, 1992]. The probability model derived in this section is also based on software structure, but within the framework of the correlation approach to derivation of integrity statements.

The model described in this section predicts an integrity for software based on measurements of attributes of the software design and its development process. The particular integrity measure used is defined in definition 1.

Definition 1: an integrity measure for software design

Let S be a design product. The measure of integrity used in this paper is P(S|E), where E is the current collected evidence from all integrity-related measurements.

A design product is any physical document or code which is produced during software development.

There are two parts of the model. Firstly, a probability model based on design structure relates the integrities of products from separate development stages (section 3.1). Secondly, a graphical probability model is used to compose evidence from measurements of different integrity-related attributes within each atomic development process. The graphical models feed their results into the structural model.

3.1 A probability model of integrity based on software structure

The following analysis is based on the 'independent development assumption' given in definition 2.

Definition 2: Independent Development Assumption

If a node in the process graph emanates a set of processes $Y=\{\alpha_i : i \in 1..n\}$, the event 'faults have been introduced into the product produced by process α_j' is independent of the introduction of faults into products of other processes (ie. independent of the the event 'faults have been introduced into the products produced by one or more of the processes in set $Y - \alpha_j$').

In the following $P(\mathcal{A} | \mathcal{B})$ has its usual interpretation in conditional probability: the probability of occurrence of event $\mathcal{A}$ given that event $\mathcal{B}$ is known to have occurred [Casella & Berger, 1990]. Referring to a process model of the type shown in figure 2, let r be greater than the longest path to a node N. Let $out_N(r)$ represent the event that the output product associated with node N is correct ie. no errors have been introduced relative to the specification at the start of the process model. Let the event $in_N(r)$ be the event that all products associated with nodes with processes leading from them to N, are correct. Let $e^{N(r)}$ represent the collected evidence of all measurements of attributes made along all paths to N, and $e_{N(r)}$ represent the collected evidence of similar measurements made during the atomic process stage which leads to N. Define Γ as the set of ancestor nodes to N.

Then the integrity of the product associated with N is given by (1) and (2), which are derived in appendix A.

(1) $P(out_N(r) | e^{N(r)}) = P(\text{correct transformation from input of process pointing at N to product at N} | e_{N(r)})$.

$$\prod_{I \in \Gamma} P(out_I(r-1) | e^{I(r-1)})$$

(2) $P(out_X(y) | e^{(y)}) = \alpha_X$, where X is a node with no ancestors and α is either assumed to be 1 or computed from measurements of integrity attributes for the product associated with node X using a graphical probability model (section 3.2)

(1) and (2) offer a recurrence formula for computing the required integrity, with (2) as the bottoming-out condition. The values α_X and P(correct transformation from input of process pointing at N to product at N | $e_{N(r)}$) are computed using a graphical probability model as described in section 3.2.

3.2 Graphical probability models

Graphical probability models (GPM) [Lauritzen & Spiegelhalter, 1988], also known as causal nets [Pearl 1988], provide a means of building custom probability distributions for sets of random variables related by dependence assumptions. GPMs can be used to calculate the quantities required by the probability model of section 3.1, namely α_X in (2) and the first term on the right hand side of (1). A GPM is constructed for each required quantity.

A GPM is based on a Bayesian network [Pearl,1988] in which nodes contain variables. A variable takes discrete values. Some of the variables may naturally range over continuous values eg. integrity values. In this case the range must be divided into discrete intervals. The example in figure 3 illustrates a Bayesian network. This example is too simplistic to be of practical use, and is used for the purposes of illustration only.

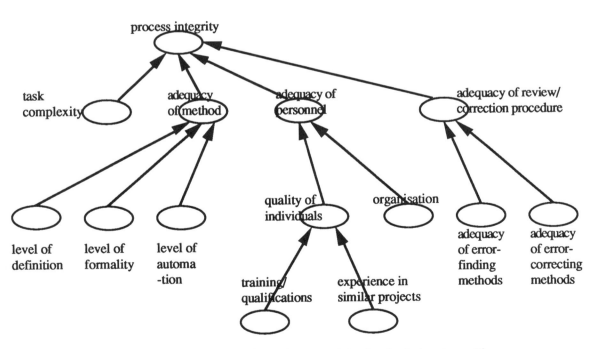

fig 3   A simple Bayesian network relating the output integrity of a design stage with integrity-related attributes of the design transformation process

241

The structure of the network (a tree in fig 3, but a directed acyclic graph in general) reflects conditional dependence assumptions regarding the variables at the network nodes. The general relationship between any Bayesian network structure and the dependence conditions it represents is given by Pearl [Pearl, 1988]. However, to illustrate the type of reasoning involved in building Bayesian networks a simple example will be taken. Suppose 'task complexity' (figure 3) was considered too vague, and consequently not measurable. One possible solution might be to treat task complexity as two separate items: 'task category' and 'task size.' Task size might be considered an independent measurement directly affecting integrity and be placed in the position of the task complexity node in figure 3. However, task category clearly affects the adequacy of the method and so must appear below that node in the tree of figure 3. In fact, a task category node should possibly point to 'level of definition','level of formality','level of automation' and 'experience in similar projects.'

The organisation of integrity-related attributes into a Bayesian network is a significant modelling problem. Valid dependency relationships amongst the variables must be established. Initially these relationships are engineering assumptions, made by the model-builders based on their knowledge and previous experience of the software development process under study. The validity of these assumptions can be tested using the usual approach of experimental science: by observing the accuracy of the model's predictions (see also section 4). In addition, it would be possible to check individual dependence assumptions made in a Bayesian network by statistical experiment.

The GPM requires certain a priori information to be specified in addition to the structure of the Bayesian network. In particular, the conditional probabilities of each variable conditioned on its parents is required. Conditional probabilities of greater complexity are not required; this is one of the great strengths of the GPM technique. The construction of Bayesian networks is treated in detail by Pearl [Pearl, 1988].

Once the network structure and prerequisite probability information is specified, algorithms are available which compute the joint distribution of the variables in the network. As evidence is obtained it is used by the algorithm to update this distribution. Work on these algorithms, and even implementations of them, already exist [Anderson et al, 1987] [Spiegelhalter,1989]. Evidence takes the form of measurements of the integrity-related attributes. A measurement can result in instantiation of a network variable with a single value. Alternatively, measurement could result in a prior distribution being associated with a variable (pearl, 1988]. In either case the effects are propagated throughout the network to produce a coherent posterior distribution of the network variables according to Bayesian probability theory.

3.3 Other work on correlation models in software integrity prediction

The COCOMO work [Boehm, 1981] on cost prediction for software development is an early example of 'correlation modelling' (see section 3.1). As part of the REQUEST project [Request, 1990] COQUAMO used correlation modelling to predict the quality of software development products [Kitchenham & Walker, 1989][Klim,1989]. The COQUAMO method used metrics

taken for a particular development project and compared them against target values ascertained from similar projects. Discrepancies between the measured values of the metrics and their target values were used to signal potential problems to project managers. In addition correlation modelling was used to compute attributes of interest from measured metrics. Statistical regression techniques were used to establish these models. Thus the purpose of the correlation models in COQUAMO was similar to the that of the probability model of this paper, namely to specify an attribute of interest in terms of more easily measured attributes.

The use of regression methods to define correlation models for software attributes has been further refined by the work on MERMAID [Kitchenham & Kirakowski, 1991]. Although the MERMAID approach has been used for cost prediction rather than quality prediction, similar principles apply. Comparison of GPM techniques with regression techniques is difficult, they are two very different approaches; it will be best achieved by use of the two techniques on the same projects. However, the following two points expose fundamental differences between the two :-

(i) Regression seeks linear relationship between attribute of interest and other attributes. GPMs does not assume functional relationships of any form, but can describe with functional relationships if necessary [Pearl,1988]. GPMs use assumptions of a different nature, namely conditional dependence assumptions amongst clusters of variables which are local to each other in the network. The theory of Bayesian nets is relatively new compared to regression techniques [Lauritzen & Spiegelhalter, 1990] [Casella & Berger, 1990], and was conceived to provide a powerful theory for analysis of causal relationships amongst variables [Lauritzen & Spiegelhalter, 1990, 1988] [Pearl, 1988]. Using the kind of argument which was used govern the addition of new attributes to figure 2, complex nets may be set up which incorporate much of the engineering knowledge of the process engineer within a formal framework. Further discussion of the special role of GPMs within probability and statistics is given by statisticians in comments listed after the landmark paper by Lauritzen and Spiegelhalter [Lauritzen & Spiegelhalter, 1990, 1988].

(ii) Both the MERMAID approach and GPMs are capable of producing a distribution for integrity variables. However, GPMs do not use a particular analytic form for the distribution of the integrity values.

4 On-going work within the FASGEP project

The five main areas of work which are relevant to this paper and are on-going within FASGEP are listed below.

(i) The derivation of probability models usually involves independence assumptions, and the model proposed in this paper depends on several such assumptions. Most are justified in a simple manner. The exception is the independent development assumption (definition 2 in section 3.1) which is employed in appendix A. If some of the design problems emanating from a node in a diagram such as figure 2 possessed similar characteristics, this assumption would be questionable. There are two approaches to this problem :-

1. relax the assumption in the cases where dependence exists;

2. design software so that the independence assumption is valid.

Approach 1 above requires quantification of the dependence, and is not discussed further in this paper, although (iv) below is relevant to this issue.

Approach 2 directly addresses one of the aims of the FASGEP project, namely to find methods of software design that facilitate subsequent integrity analysis for the software. Work has been done which raises doubts about the assumptions of independence used in multi-version programming [Knight & Leveson, 1986][Butler & Finelli,1991]. This suggests that design faults in similar design tasks cannot be made independent, even when different personnel are asked to solve the task in different ways. If this is true a good design (for integrity analysis) should use components which are very 'different in purpose' from each other. The precise meaning of 'different in purpose' is not clear, and is the subject of more research within the FASGEP project.

(ii) The efficacy of the correlation approach to integrity prediction relies on the availability of integrity-related attributes of the software development process and its associated products. Whilst the example in figure 2 is a simple illustration it is clear that, for example, the complexity of the design tasks within a stage is an attribute which cannot be ignored when considering the likelihood of error introduction [Kitchenam et al., 1990]. It follows that the study of metrics is integral to the correlation approach. For a review of current work on metrics see for example [Fenton, 1991]. An important issue in this respect is the level of detail to which the Bayesian networks are developed. For a given application, a more developed network should require less complex metrics at its leaf-nodes ie. metrics which attempt to measure simpler attributes of the development process and its products.

(iii) A model is validated by comparing its predictions against the behaviour of the system it models. For the probability model proposed in this paper validation requires observation of integrities for the various design products produced at the end of the process elements; from the top-level design products down to the code of the bottom-level design components. By studying the correspondence between the design products and the hierarchical structure of the software produced, it is hoped to produce dynamic testing strategies based on software structure which can directly measure the required design integrities. Such tests will allow the model to be calibrated as data from its application is gained.

(iv) Work within FASGEP aims to incorporate failure mode analysis, constructing complex networks to model specific error categories for the software development processes, and the software products themselves. Further extensions of the approach taken in this paper are also being investigated. In particular, work is currently under way to allow reviews and design corrections as separate process stages. This complicates the probability model but facilitates more detailed modelling of iterative development-review-correction processes.

(v) The collaborators within the FASGEP project will test the techniques presented in this paper, or subsequent developments of them, using data from new projects as they proceed. Dynamic testing of the software will be used to validate the techniques and calibrate the models used. The performance of the technique will be compared with other methods for predicting integrity during software development [Kitchenam & Walker,1989].

5 Conclusions

1. A new probability model for estimating the integrity of software development has been proposed. The upper level of the model is based on standard probabilistic reasoning.

2. A role for GPMs in software development integrity prediction has been identified. GPMs provide the lower levels of the probability model. Graphical probability models (GPMs) provide an extremely flexible method of reasoning under uncertainty. Figure 2 only provides a simple illustration. As demonstrated in section 3.3, GPMs represent a very different approach to the existing correlative models of software development integrity which use linear regression techniques to establish relationships between measurements (metrics).

3. Problems associated with the treatment of dependence relationships have to be faced in any solution to integrity prediction. The probability analysis in 1 and 2 above identify the crucial role of independence assumptions very precisely. In particular, the Independent Development Assumption (definition 2) is central to the presented analysis. The FASGEP project is concerned with development techniques which facilitate subsequent integrity analysis. With respect to this paper, software developmemt techniques which sanction the IDA are an important and intriguing area for future study.

4. Validation and calibration of the model will be facilitated by specifically focussed dynamic testing techniques.

Appendix A

This appendix derives a formula for the integrity of the development product D associated with a node N, conditional on all evidence (ie. all attribute measurements) E made up to the point in time at which D was completed. Some of the notation is explained in section 3.1, but in addition let $out_\Gamma(r-1)$ be the event that all products associated with nodes in Γ are correct. Similarly, define $e^{\Gamma(r-1)}$ to be all evidence measured for all processes on paths to nodes in Γ.

It is assumed that $P(out_N(r) \mid E) = P(out_N(r) \mid e^{N(r)})$.

(3) below is a straightforward application of $P(\mathcal{A} \& \mathcal{B}) = P(\mathcal{A} \mid \mathcal{B}) P(\mathcal{B})$, based on the fact that $out_N(r)$ <-> $in_N(r)$ & correct development within the atomic process leading to N (and where '<->' means 'is equivalent to').

$$(3) \qquad P(out_N(r) \mid e^{N(r)}) = P(in_N(r) \mid e^{N(r)}) \, P(out_N(r) \mid in_N(r) \, \& \, e^{N(r)})$$

Now $in_N(r) = out_\Gamma(r-1)$. Also $out_N(r)$, conditional on $in_N(r)$, can be considered independent of all evidence $e^{\Gamma(r-1)}$ collected before the nodes in Γ in the network (since all of the impact of that evidence is obtained via evidence '$in_N(r)$'). Note that $e^{N(r)} = e^{\Gamma(r-1)} \cup e_{N(r)}$, and therefore (4) follows.

$$\text{(4)} \quad P(out_N(r) \mid e^{N(r)}) = P(out_\Gamma(r-1) \mid e^{N(r)}) \, P(out_N(r) \mid in_N(r) \, \& \, e_{N(r)})$$

A further reasonable independence assumption states that $out_\Gamma(r-1)$ does not depend on evidence collected after its outputs have been produced. (5) follows.

$$\text{(5)} \quad P(out_N(r) \mid e^{N(r)}) = P(out_\Gamma(r-1) \mid e^{\Gamma(r-1)}) \, P(out_N(r) \mid in_N(r) \, \& \, e_{N(r)})$$

Using the independent development assumption (definition 2) produces (6).

$$\text{(6)} \quad P(out_N(r) \mid e^{N(r)}) = \prod_{I \in \Gamma} P(out_I(r-1) \mid e^{I(r-1)}) . P(out_N(r) \mid in_N(r) \, \& \, e_{N(r)})$$

In section 3.1, equation (1) is simply a restatement of (6), and (2) states that the integrity of the first stage under consideration in the lifecycle is obtained directly by some other analysis (as explained in sections 3.1 and 3.2).

References

Anderson,S.K., Jensen,F.V., and Olesen,K.G. "The HUGIN core - preliminary considerations on systems for fast manipulations of probabilities," in *Proceedings of Workshop on Inductive Reasoning: Managing Empirical Information in AI-systems*, Riso National Laboratory, Roskilde, Denmark. April 1987

Boehm,B.W. Software Engineering Economics. Prentice Hall, New Jersey 1981

Butler,R.W. and Finelli,G.B. "The Infeasibility of Experimental Quantification of Life-Critical Software Reliability," in *Procs. ACM SIGSOFT '91 Conference on Software for Critical Systems*, New Orleans,Louisiana. Dec 4-6 1991

Casella,G. and Berger,R.L. *Statistical Inference*. Wadsworth & Brooks/Cole 1990

Fenton ,N. Software Metrics a Rigourous Approach. Chapman & Hall 1991

Kitchenham,B.A. and Walker,J.G. "A Quantitative Approach to Monitoring Software Development." *Software Engineering Journal*, Jan 1989

Kitchenham,B.A., Pickard,L.M. and Linkman S.J. "An Evaluation of some Design Metrics." *Software Engineering Journal*, Jan 1990

Kitchenham,B.A. and Kirakowski,J. "The MERMAID Approach to Software Cost Estimation," in *ESPRIT'90*, Kluwer Academic Press 1991

Klim,S. "Overview of COQUAMO - a Constructive Quality Model." REQUEST report R1.8.15. Aug 1989.

Knight,J.C. and Leveson,N.G. "An Experimental Evaluation of the Assumptions of Independence in Multiversion Programming." *IEEE trans. on Software Engineering*, v12 n1, Jan 1986

Laprie,J-C. and Kanoun,K. "X-ware Reliability and Availability Modelling." *IEEE trans. on Software Engineering*, v18 n2, Feb 1992

Lauritzen,S.L. and Spiegelhalter,D.J. "Local Computations with Probabilities on Graphical Structures and Their Application to Expert Systems," *J. Royal Statistical Society B*, v50 n2, 1988. Alternative reference (same title) : in *Readings in Uncertain Reasoning*, Eds. Shafer,G. and Pearl,J. Morgan Kaufmann, San Mateo, California 1990

Littlewood,B. "Software Reliability Model for Modular Program Structure." *IEEE trans. on Reliability*, v R-30 1981

Littlewood,B. "Forecasting Software Reliability," in *Software Reliability Modelling and Identification*, Ed. Bittanti,S. Springer Verlag, Berlin 1988

Madhavji,N.H. and Schaffer,B. "Prism - Methodology and Process-Oriented Environment."*IEEE trans. on Software Engineering*, v17 n2, Dec 1991

Mellor,P. "Modular Structured Software Reliability Modelling in Practice," paper from 4th European Workshop on Dependable Computing, Prague, 8-10th April 1992

Pearl,J. *Probabilistic Reasoning in Intelligent Systems: Networks of Plausible Inference*. Morgan Kaufmann, San Mateo, California 1988

Request. "REQUEST Final Report." Dec 1990

Sommerville,I. Software Engineering (fourth edition). Addison-Wesley 1992

Spiegelhalter,D.J. "Fast Algorithms for Probabilistic Reasoning in Influence Diagrams with Applications in Genetics and Expert Systems," in *Influence Diagrams*, Eds. Barlow,R. et al. Wiley, Chichester 1989.

Steel,D.A. and Dugard,P.I. "Modelling Software Reliability in Practice." Bulletin of the Institute of Mathematics and its Applications, v28 n3, March 1992

CONSIDERATIONS ABOUT AN AXIOMATIC BASIS FOR SOFTWARE CONTROL FLOW MEASURES

J. Brummer

Gesellschaft für Anlagen- und Reaktorsicherheit (GRS) mbH, Forschungsgelände, D-8046 Garching, Germany

Abstract. The fundamentals for software complexity measures, defined on
control flow skeletons of programs, are studied. The domain of program
control flows is precisely introduced and numerically prepared. Program
trees are translated into sequences of natural numbers with symmetric appearance.
Control flow measures are not constructed according to intuitive suggestions about "good measurement", they are introduced from a pure mathematical
point of view: The conditions for control flow measures are stated as formal axioms. A mapping from the class of control flows to the natural numbers is called a valid control flow measure, if it harmonizes with the
algebraic structure (additivity) and respects the natural order on the
class of control flows (monotonicity).
Finally, based upon this foundation, it is proved that the set of control
flow measures is not empty and contains a "canonical" prototype.

Keywords. Software complexity, control flow measures, axioms of measurement, additivity, monotonicity.

I. INTRODUCTION

Many propositions exist for reflecting upon
the quality of software programs by simple
numerical measures: A metric profile should
give a close insight into the quality and
applicability of the software product. The
difficulty is to find syntactical equivalents for quality attributes or to determine what kind of quality feature (i.e. testability, maintainabilty, understandabili-
ty, etc.) is adressed or even covered by a
special complexity measure.

A possibility to compare software measures
is suggested by Weyuker (1988): There software measures have to fulfill certain properties of well-definedness, i. e. the intuitive requirements for measures are gathered and formulated as a catalog of
axioms. On this basis it is proved that
some well-known and wide-spread measures
violate essential prerequisites for complexity measures.

In this report an axiomatic basis for the
construction and comparison for a special
class of software measures will be developed: For those that evaluate the control
flow of a program. Due to the restricted
view of programs not all of the conditions
in Weyuker (1988) have to be considered,
some of them are carried over, possibly in
a stronger version, while others are weake-
ned or even omitted.

The fundamentals of control flow measures,
their domain and values, are introduced in
section II. For measuring the control flow
complexity of programs we do not need the
full information of program texts, we only
have to observe the language constructs
ruling the control flow. The control flow
constructs are extracted from program texts
(control flow trees) and a transformation
of control flows into sequences of natural
numbers is performed. With this representation the numerical treatment, the overview
of the class of control flows and the analysis of control flow mappings is facilitated.

In section III the conditions for control
flow measures are motivated and brought
into an axiomatic form. Two domain axioms
lay down the distribution of complexity
values over the range of natural numbers.
They reflect the "coarseness" and "fine-
ness" of regular measures. Two other axioms
relate to the operations for generating
control flow sequences (concatenation and
nesting): An algebraic axiom demands the
(additive) respectation of concatenation, a
monotonicity axiom directs the attention to
the "natural" order on the set of program
control flows.

It is shown in section IV that the set of
control flow measures (control flow mappings satisfying the stated axioms) has an
infinite number of elements. A special ex-
ponent of this set is presented which, in a

sense, is the smallest one and can be regarded as a "canonical" control flow measure.

Section V summaries the main results of the report. A comparison with other well-known control flow measures reveals their deficits in satisfying the elementary requirements. The restriction of the results to the valuation of control flow skeletons is mentioned again, nevertheless the transfer of the methodology to other types of software complexity measuring is stressed.

II. BASIC DEFINITIONS: CONTROL FLOW LANGUAGE AND CONTROL FLOW MAPPINGS

First we have to come to an applicable definition of what programs are in our context. We restrict ourselves to the ´kernel´ of any well-structered ALGOL-like languages: to while-programs built up of assignments, if-then-else statements and while-loops (Manna, 1974). Since we are only looking at control flows, we can abstract from the internal details of the program statements and fix only the syntactical items of the language that regulate its control flow.

The smallest unit of this control flow language is the indivisible assignment statement neglecting its internal structure. The construction of complexer programs is provided by the recursive application of two operators:

- concatenation of programs (building sequential blocks)

- nesting of programs by if- or while-branches.

This control flow language ignores the single statement constituents, the variables as well as the arithmetic and boolean terms. Only the description of the possible paths through program execution is retained.

This process of abstraction from concrete program texts to control flow extracts is demonstrated by a small example, a program for the greatest common divisor (GCD) of two natural numbers m and n:

```
x   :=    m
y   :=    n
while    x  ≠  y
         do
         while    x > y
                  do x  :=    x - y
         while    x < y
                  do y  :=    y - x
z   :=    x
```

The control flow of this original program may be presented as control flow tree by extracting and hierarchically ordering

branches (whiles) and by a left to right node ordering of sequential blocks. In Fig.1 the control flow tree of the GCD-example is given, where the tree nodes, representing the single program statements, are inscribed with the corresponding statement´s type (assignment or branch).

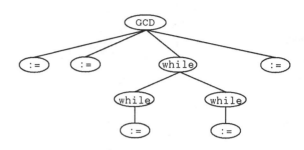

Fig.1: Tree representation of GCD-program

It is well-known that these control flow trees can be equivalently represented as balanced sequences of right and left brakkets. Similar to the recursive definition of while-programs, the class of control flows can be recursively defined as Regular Parenthesis Expressions (RPE):

( )   is a Regular Parenthesis Expression (representing a simple assignment statementor a branching-frame),

if   a and b   RPEs, then   (*)

ab   is regular   (concatenation rule)   and

(a)   is regular   (hierarchical or branching rule)

Applying these linearization rules the tree of Fig.1 can be transformed to

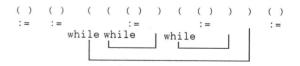

Obviously, these Regular Parenthesis Expressions correspond to the control flow structures of programs, and the aim of control flow measures is to evaluate these linear expressions in terms of difficulty and complexity.

In order to get a better platform for the numerical manipulation and evaluation of such Regular Parenthesis Expressions, it is useful to translate these strings into corresponding sequences of natural numbers. The algorithm for this translation is based on the principle "number of open brackets".

Algorithm ("in-/decreasing brackets
        counting"):
If $k_1, \ldots, k_n$ is a RPE ($k_i \in \{(,)\}$)
then a sequence of natural numbers
$a_1, \ldots, a_n$ is defined by   (i=2,...,n)

$$a_i := \atop (a_1 := 1) \begin{cases} a_{i-1} & \text{for } k_i \neq k_{i-1} \\ a_{i-1} + 1 & \text{for } k_i = k_{i-1} = "(" \\ a_{i-1} - 1 & \text{for } k_i = k_{i-1} = ")" \end{cases}$$

With this transformation a natural number
is assigned to each bracket. These sequences of natural numbers, standing for control flows, are constructed in a way which
preserves the symmetrical peculiarity of the
RPEs (a left open bracket has a corresponding right one): Each number in a sequence
has a corresponding one at the same level.

One can easily state the following properties of control flow number sequences:

i) $a_1 = a_n = 1$, $a_i > 0$ for
   $1 \leq i \leq n$, n is an even number.

ii) $| a_i - a_{i-1} | \leq 1$ for $2 \leq i \leq n$
iii) (symmetrical balance of numbers):
For each $1 \leq h \leq \max \{a_1, \ldots, a_n\}$ and
for the associated partial sequence
$a_{h_1}, \ldots, a_{h_m}$ ($a_{h_j} = h$; j=1,...,m) the
following is true:
$m \geq 2$ is even and $h_{i+1} - h_i \geq 0$ always is
even (i=1,...,m-1), i.e. $a_{h_{2k-1}}$ and $a_{h_{2k}}$
(k=1,..,m/2) are corresponding numbers.

According to the given algorithm our GCD
program from Fig.1 is represented by the
sequence

    1 1 1 1 1 2 3 3 2 2 3 3 2 1 1 1 .

We then introduce a symbol I for the smallest possible control flow unit "1 1" (assignment or branching frame) and substitute
it into the sequence:

    I I 1 2 3 3 2 2 3 3 2 1 I

(see also Fig.2 illustrating this profile).

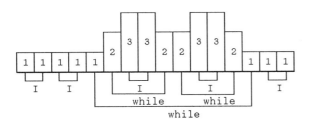

Fig.2: Control flow profile of GCD-program

Summarizing the methods of control flow
extraction just described, all the prerequisites for a precise definition of con-

trol flow measures are present (see also
Fig.3):

A control flow measure is a mapping defined on the class **P** of control flow
number sequences into the range of natural numbers, which fulfills certain conditions.

In the next section these conditions are
gathered and formalized as axioms.

Programs $\xrightarrow[\text{extract}]{}$ control flows P $\xrightarrow[\text{measure}]{}$ |N

(full texts)   (trees
                   RPEs
                     number sequences)

Fig.3: Definition of control flow measures

III. AXIOMATIC BASE FOR CONTROL FLOW
     MEASURES

In Weyuker (1988) an axiomatic base for
general complexity measures is presented:
In order to compare different models of
measurement, intuitive suggestions and requirements of range diversity and monotonicity are brought into an axiomatic form.
For a complexity measure M, the following
axioms must hold (see Weyuker, 1988):

1) $\exists$ a, b $\in$ **P** with $M(a) \neq M(a)$

2) $M^{-1}(n) := \{a \in \mathbf{P} : M(a) = n\}$ is finite
                $\forall n \in$ |N

3) $\exists$ a, b $\in$ **P** with $M(a) = M(b)$

4) $\exists$ a, b $\in$ **P** with a $\equiv$ b (semantical
   equivalence) and $M(a) \neq M(b)$
5) $\forall$ a, b : $M(a) \leq M(a;b)$ and $M(b) \leq M(a;b)$
6) $\exists$ a, b, c with $M(a) = M(b)$ and $M(a;c) \neq M(b;c)$

7) $\exists$ a, b , where b is permutation
   (of statements) of a and $M(a) \neq M(b)$
8) If a and b are only different in names
   of variables, then $M(a) = M(b)$
9) $\exists$ a, b with $M(a) + M(b) < M(a;b)$

In this context A und B are the syntactical
forms of software programs (after extraction from the full program texts) and the
operator ";" is solely the sequential connector of programs (i.e. simple concatenation). Other program construction principles, like nestings and hierarchical rules,
are not taken into account here.

This list of axioms is formulated according
to generally accepted requirements for the
construction of program measures. Nevertheless, this combinatin of axioms has some
significant weaknesses: (a) The requirements are not mutually independent (for
example, axiom 2 implies axiom 1), (b) some
axioms cannot be verified in a purely syntactical environment (for number 4 the specifications of programs have to be compared) and (c) some are irrelevant with re-

gard to control flow measures (e.g. number 8 is always true for control flow measures because of their abstraction from data structures).

In the remainder of this report we shall

- develop a system of axioms covering the above set of requirements 1 to 9; the new axioms are formulated according to the algebraic structure and natural order on the class of control flows $\mathbf{P}$ (III.1 to III.3) and

- characterize the models for the stated axioms, more precisely: We shall show that valid control flow measures do exist, even a "smallest" one (IV).

III.1 Domain axioms

Two axioms taken directly from the above list regulate the domain partition and the range of values for control flow measures. First, a control flow measure m should not be too "coarse", i.e. a measure is not sensitive enough if it divides all programs into only a few complexity classes:

(a) $m^{-1}(n)$ is finite $\forall\, n \in |N$

This axiom (see number 2 above) guarantees that control flow measures are not constant (axiom 1 above). Furthermore, the measure m is not bounded from above: For every program there is another one with a higher degree of control flow complexity. These two statements follow immediately from this axiom (a) and the fact that there is an infinite number of control flow sequences in $\mathbf{P}$. The sizes of program complexities exceed every limit.

A further axiom prevents an excessive splitting of program evaluation:

(b) m is not injective,
     i.e. $\exists\, P_1 \neq P_2$ in P with $m(P_1) = m(P_2)$

This condition is necessary if we do not want a excessively "fine" measure which assigns to every program its own complexity number.

The axioms (a) and (b) are intuitively given and classify the domain and regulate the scale and range of complexity measures. Evidently they comprise the conditions 1, 2 and 3 in the above list. Considering that there is an infinite number of syntactical versions of a semantically equivalent program (doubling an assignment statement again and again), then condition 4 is additionally covered.

III.2 The "Theorem of Construction" and an algebraic axiom

Up to now we have not considered any internal structure in the class of control flows $\mathbf{P}$ and it has not been necessary to associate the control flow complexity measures with a given operation on $\mathbf{P}$. Repeating conditions 5, 6 and 9 from above, one can see that they are formulated with regard to a connection of programs, in relation to an operation on $\mathbf{P}$.

It seems to be useful to consider not only the concatenation of programs, but to enlarge program operation to include hierarchical nesting: First, because the control flow of programs is constructed by concatenation as well as by nesting of program units. Second, because then the replacement of single statements by complexer units is included (note the technique of subroutines, or the idea of top-down development).

We define a nesting operation on $\mathbf{P}$ which also covers concatenation as a special case (as "nesting one after another"). It will be demonstrated that this operation is fundamental for the whole class $\mathbf{P}$: All elements can be constructed by applying the operation on a generating unit (see the "Theorem of Construction" below).

For
$$a = a_1, \ldots, a_n \in \mathbf{P},$$
$$b = b_1, \ldots, b_m \in \mathbf{P} \text{ and } k \in |N \text{ define}$$

$$c = c_1, \ldots, c_{n+m} = a +_k b :=$$

$$\left. \begin{array}{l} c_1, \ldots, c_m = b_1, \ldots, b_m \\ c_{m+1}, \ldots, c_{m+n} = a_1, \ldots, a_n \end{array} \right\} k = 0$$

$$\left. \begin{array}{l} c_1, \ldots, c_n = a_1, \ldots, a_n \\ c_{n+1}, \ldots, c_{n+m} = b_1, \ldots, b_m \end{array} \right\} k \geq n$$

and for $1 \leq k < n$

$$c_1, \ldots, c_k = a_1, \ldots, a_k$$

$$c_{k+1} = b_1 + \left| \begin{array}{ll} \min(a_k, a_{k+1}) & \text{for } a_k \neq a_{k+1} \\ \min(a_k, a_{k+1}) & \text{for } a_k = a_{k+1} \\ & k \text{ odd} \end{array} \right.$$

$$c_{k+m} = b_m + \left| \min(a_k, a_{k+1}) - 1 \text{ for } a_k = a_{k+1} \right.$$
$$k \text{ even}$$

$$c_{k+m+1}, \ldots, c_{m+n} = a_{k+1}, \ldots, a_n$$

This operation is - as one can easily see by computation and comparison - the numerical equivalent for the recursive definition of the RPEs (*). In particular, the concatenation ba is simulated by k = 0 , the concatenation ab by $k \geq n$, the hierarchical arrangement (nesting) by $1 \leq k < n$.

It should be noted that the operation is not commutative and not associative. Nevertheless it enables the generation of the entire class of all possible program control flows $\mathbf{P}$ as the following theorem demonstrates.

248

"Theorem of Construction":
I is a generating element in $\mathbf{P}$, i.e.
for each $a \in \mathbf{P}$ there is a finite sequence
of operations generating a:

$$a = I \ +_{k_1} \ I \ +_{k_2} \ \cdot \ \cdot \ \cdot \ +_{k_m} \ I$$

Proof (by natural induction):

Let $a = a_1, \ . \ . \ . \ , a_n$ (n is even !);

Induction base n = 2: $a = I$

Induction step n-2 $\rightarrow$ n:

There is a maximum level $h(\in |N) \geq a_i$,
$1 \leq i \leq n$, and $a_{k+1} = h$ for the first time
$(k \geq 0)$. Then $a_{k+2} = h$ is valid and, with
the definition of $+_k$ ($a_k = h-1$, see above
property ii of control flow sequences),

$$\underline{a_1, \ . \ . \ . \ , a_k, a_{k+3}, \ . \ . \ . \ , a_n} \ +_k \ I = a$$

Induction Hypothesis

Evidently, there are several ways to combine "a" with the fundamental element I ($+_k$
is not associative), but the generating
sequence always has the same length:

Corollary: Every generating sequence for
$a = a_1, \ . \ . \ . \ , a_n$ consists of n/2
summands.

Proof: With the definition of $+_k$ the
following is always true:
$$a = b_1, \ . \ . \ . \ , b_1 \ +_k \ c_1, \ . \ . \ . \ , c_m$$
$$\Rightarrow \ l + m = n$$

Here the question arises, how a control
flow complexity measure should be connected
to this operational structure on $\mathbf{P}$, especially how to respect the "Theorem of Construction". At first glance, considering
the generating sequences, one may try a
homomorphism axiom and require the additivity of all control flow measures m:

$$m(a \ +_k \ b) = m(a) + m(b) \quad \forall \ a, b \in P$$

But this requirement would imply (as an
immediate consequence of the "Theorem of
Construction") that there is essentially
only one control flow measure

$$m*(a) = n/2 \ \times \ m*(I),$$

where n is the length of the control flow
sequence. With the norm $m*(I) = 1$ one
can conclude that the unique mapping re-
specting the additivity requirement is the
"measure of statement count".

But is the demand for unrestricted additivity a reasonable requirement for control
flow complexity? Additivity, independent of
the nesting position, means that concatenation as well as the hierarchical nesting of

programs are treated and weighted in the
same manner.

From an intuitive point of view, the mixing
of "external" concatenation and "internal"
nesting is not desirable. The additivity
should be restricted solely to the "independent connection", i.e. the concatenation
of control flows (with a norm for the unit
element I):

(c) $m(I) = 1$,
    $m(a + b) = m(a) + m(b)$
    for the concatenation of programs a
    and b $\in \mathbf{P}$

This axiom is accompanied by the idea that
the complexity measure of purely sequential
programs should be composed in the simplest
way, i.e additively, from its constituting
parts (blocks).

Roughly following up the argumentation for
the concatenation homomorphism, the inequality

$$m(a \ +_k \ b) \ > \ m(a) + m(b),$$
$$1 \ \leq \ k \ < \ n \qquad (**)$$

must be valid for the operation $+_k$.

This requirement turns out to be too vague
and does not allow a unique determination
of measures with the stated properties.
Therefore, a stronger condition must be
formulated which implies the inequality
(**) and is oriented according to the natural structure of the class $\mathbf{P}$.

III.3 Axiom of Order and Monotonicity
       Property

A complexity measure introduces an order, a
quantity relationship, on the class of control flows $\mathbf{P}$: "a is smaller than b" if
$m (a) \ \leq \ m(b)$. But there is already a natural order on $\mathbf{P}$, given by

$$a \leq b :\Leftrightarrow \exists \text{ partial sequence } b_{i_1}, \ . \ . \ . \ , b_{i_n}$$
$$\text{in b with } a_j \ \leq b_{i_j}; \quad j = 1, \ldots, n$$

This order is based on the idea that a program a is smaller than another program b,
if a is a subpart of b. It seems reasonable
that a valid control flow complexity measure should harmonize with this natural order
("<" is defined by $a < b :\Leftrightarrow a \ \leq \ b$ and
$a \neq b$):

(d) $a \ < \ b \quad \Rightarrow \quad m(a) \ < \ m(b)$

It can easily be shown that this monotonicity axiom for control flow measures implies the above inequality relation for the
nesting operation (**):

From $a \ +_k \ b \ > \ a \ +_l \ b$, if $1 \leq k < n$ and
l=0 or $l \geq n$, it follows

$$m(a \ +_k \ b) \ > \ m(a \ +_1 \ b) \ =_{(c)} \ m(a) \ + \ m(b)$$

It is worth mentioning that this last axiom is stronger than all similar statements and includes axiom (a):

From the properties i) to iii) for the control flow number sequences (see above) it follows: For every even number $k \in |N$, there is a finite number of profiles in **P** with length k. For these elements it is true that

$$m(a) \ \geq \ \tfrac{1}{2} \cdot k \qquad \text{(axiom (c)!)} \ .$$

For $n \in |N$, let k be even and $k > 2n$. Then, the number of elements in **P** with length at most k is finite and all programs of length greater than k have measure

$$m(a) \ \geq \ \tfrac{1}{2} \cdot k \ > \ \tfrac{1}{2} \cdot 2n \ = \ n$$

IV. THE "INTEGRAL MEASURE"

In the axioms (a), (b), (c) and (d) the structural properties of **P** are interpreted as requirements for a control flow measure. Until now, it has not been decided if a mapping **P** → $|N$ actually exists that satisfies the stated axioms. Such a model may be called a valid control flow measure. A further question arises: Is there any "canonical" measure with particular properties that should be preferred to the others ?

We shall introduce a model for the axioms, the "integral measure", and subsequently prove its special rank in the class of control flow measures. Consider the mapping **P** → $|N$

$$m^{(1)} \ : \ (a_1, \ . \ . \ . \ , a_n) \ \mapsto \ \tfrac{1}{2} \cdot \sum_{i=1}^{n} a_i \ .$$

The factor ½ is caused by the norm $m^{(1)} \ (\ I \ ) = 1$ for the generating element. It can easily be seen that this mapping is a measure (a mapping satisfying the axioms) and computes the "integral" of the control flow profile $a_1, \ . \ . \ . \ , a_n$ combining the length of a program with its depth (nesting level).

Surely, the "integral measure" $m^{(1)}$ is not the only measure for the axioms (a) to (d). For example, all k-power mappings $(k \in |N \ )$

$$m^{(k)} (a) \ := \ \tfrac{1}{2} \cdot \sum_{i=1}^{n} (a_i)^k$$

are valid measures. But, the measure $m^{(1)}$ has a special position in the set of control flow measures as the smallest one.

Theorem: The "integral measure" $m^{(1)}$ is smaller than every other measure μ with respect to the axioms (a) to (d):

$$m^{(1)} (a) \ \leq \ \mu (a) \qquad \forall \ a \in \mathbf{P}$$

Proof:
i) For each valid measure μ,

  $a = a_1, \ . \ . \ . \ , a_n \in \mathbf{P}$ and $0 \leq k \leq n$ it is valid $(a_0 := 0)$

$$\mu(a \ +_k \ I) \ \geq \ \mu(a) \ + \ \min(a_k, a_{k+1}) \ + \ 1$$

because: for $\text{minim} := \min(a_k, a_{k+1})$ every $1 \leq j \leq \text{minim}$ can be found in the sequence $a_1, \ . \ . \ . \ , a_n$ (i.e., there is $a_{i_j} = j$ in $a_1, \ . \ . \ . \ , a_n$ for every j).
Consider the sequence

$$
\begin{array}{ccccc}
a_{i_1} & < & a_{i_2} & < \ . \ . \ . \ < & a_{i_{\min}} \ ; \\
\| & & \| & & \| \\
1 & & 2 & & \min
\end{array}
$$

now, it follows

$$a \ +_0 \ I \ < \ a \ +_{i_1} \ I \ < \ . \ . \ . \ < \ a \ +_{i_{\min}} I$$
$$\underset{(d)}{\Rightarrow} \quad \mu(a +_k I) \ > \ \mu(a) \ + \ \text{minim} \ + \ 1$$

ii) For $m^{(1)}$, $a = a_1, \ . \ . \ . \ , a_n$, $b = b_1, \ . \ . \ . \ , b_t \in \mathbf{P}$, $k \in |N$ and $a_k \neq a_{k+1}$

$$m^{(1)}(a \ +_k \ b) \ =$$
$$m^{(1)}(a) \ + \ m^{(1)}(b) \ + \ \min(a_k, a_{k+1}) \cdot (t/2)$$

is an immediate consequence of the definition of $+_k$ and of the measure $m^{(1)}$

iii) By Induction over the length n of a
  Induction base: $\mu(I) \ = \ 1 \ = \ m^{(1)}(a)$
  Induction step: $a = a_1, \ . \ . \ . \ , a_{n+2}$;
  the "Theorem of Construction" states that there is $\hat{a} = \hat{a}_1, \ . \ . \ . \ , \hat{a}_n \in \mathbf{P}$ and $k \in |N$ with $a_k \neq a_{k+1}$ and $\hat{a} \ +_k \ I = a$
  (else, if $a_1 = \ . \ . \ . \ = a_{n+2} = 1$, apply the additivity axiom (c)) ; then

$$\mu(a) \ = \ \mu(\hat{a} \ +_k \ I) \ \underset{i)}{\geq}$$
$$\mu(\hat{a}) \ + \ \min(\hat{a}_k, \hat{a}_{k+1}) \ + \ 1 \ \underset{\text{Ind. Hypoth.}}{\geq}$$
$$m^{(1)}(\hat{a}) \ + \ \min(\hat{a}_k, \hat{a}_{k+1}) \ + \ 1 \ \underset{ii)}{=}$$
$$m^{(1)}(\hat{a} \ +_k \ I) \ = \ m^{(1)}(a)$$

V. SUMMARY AND FUTURE WORK

In the previous sections we presented a survey of the fundamentals for control flow measures. First, the domain of program control flows was precisely introduced and numerically prepared. Abstract program trees were translated into sequences of natural numbers with symmetric appearance.

Next, the conditions for control flow measures were stated as formal axioms. A mapping $P \rightarrow |N$ is a valid control flow measure, if it harmonizes with the constructive connection (homomorphism) and if it respects the natural order on P (monotonicity). Finally, based upon this foundation, it was proved that the set of control flow measures is not empty and contains a "canonical" prototype.

This prototype was not constructed according to intuitive suggestions about "good measurement", it was introduced from a pure mathematical point of view: If one accepts the formal conditions (a) to (d), then this "integral measure" can be derived as a particular (smallest) model. Compared with other well-known measures for control flows, it lacks their defects:

- The "measure of statement count" considers the length of a program, but neglects the depth (violates axiom (d)).

- The cyclomatic number of McCabe (1976) counts the increasing steps of a control flow profile, but neglects the length of a program (violates axioms (c) and (d)).

- The nesting level alone (Piwowarski, 1982) does not consider the length and violates axiom (c).

It should be noted that for a control flow skeleton an abstraction from the original program has to be established. The control function of each statement is taken exclusively into account. The internal structure of a statement, the different variables and the syntactic complexity of arithmetical or boolean expression building the assignment and branching statements are ignored.

The meaning of a program (its semantics) is influenced by and based upon these language features. One must consider the control flow as only one aspect (perhaps not the most important one) of the quality analysis of computer software. In order to come to a further and comprehensive estimation of program complexity, the "micro-structure"

of program statements must be taken into account.

Supplementing control flow measuring, suitable scales and quantifiers for the operational variety and data flow of a program must be offered. For example, the studies in Weyuker (1988) have yielded that such well-known concepts as Halstead's operationality count (Halstead, 1977) and the data flow measure, given by Oviedo (1980), have serious defects and do not fulfill relevant conditions for program measures.

As explained above for control flows, also for data flow and operationality measures a three step development is desirable:

- A precise definition of domain and range, usually a numerical abstraction from the full syntactical program structure.

- A list of requirements, usually in the form of axiomatic conditions.

- A characterization of the models for the axioms and, if possible, a particular representative.

VI. REFERENCES

Weyuker, E. J. (1988). Evaluating Software Complexity Measures. IEEE Trans. Software Engineering, vol. SE-14, no. 9.

McCabe, T. J. (1976). A Complexity Measure. IEEE Trans. Software Engineering, vol. SE-2, no. 4.

Piwowarski, P. (1982). A Nesting Level Complexity Measure. SIGPLAN Notices, vol. 17, no. 9.

Halstead, M. H. (1977). Elements in Software Science. Elsevier North-Holland, New York.

Oviedo, E. I. (1980). Control Flow, Data Flow and Program Complexity. In Proc. IEEE COMPSAC, Chicago, IL.

Manna, Z. (1974). Mathematical Theory of Computation. McGraw-Hill Computer Science Series.

A FRAMEWORK TO SUPPORT DECISIONS ON APPROPRIATE SECURITY MEASURES

Kurt Bauknecht
Institut für Informatik, Universität Zürich-Irchel,
Winterthurerstrasse 190, CH-8057 Zürich
phone: +1-2574311; fax: +1-3630035

Christine Strauß
Institut für Betriebswirtschaftslehre, Universität Wien
Brünner Straße 72, A-1200 Wien
phone: +1-392647511; fax: +1-392647504

Abstract Security is the result of various decision processes on different organizational levels. While the achievement of an overall security level is a corporate-wide task, there are on each corporate level different aspects, various priorities, views, and interests which can help and influence the decision process of the involved managers.
The intention of this paper is to introduce a framework which suggests the kind of information needed on different management levels to prepare and coordinate high-quality security decisions. We will focus on the choice, collection, and preparation of the relevant information as processes which can influence a security decision in a significant way. Furthermore some tools and methods suitable to prepare and present these informations are briefly discussed and compared. The usefulness of the proposed framework will be demonstrated by the example of Network Security Management in an Open System.

Keywords security framework, security in Open Systems, system integrity, standard, modeling, data acquisition, data handling

INTRODUCTION

Security is a widely used and rather fuzzy term. We therefore define security as "..the result of various security measures. Security is to be understood as a continuum which has gradual distinction. Total security is a hypothetic ideal state. The state of security of a defined system increases with decreasing risk potential" (Strauß, 1991). Based on this very general definition we can define security in the field of information technology: a secure system is one that is shown to satisfy the required security properties with the desired assurance. These properties may refer to confidentiality, integrity, availability or any combination of these three categories (Thomson, Lee, and coworkers, 1988).

Terminology

We will use in this paper several terms which need to be defined. **Security requirements** are functional or performance properties placed on a system in order to assure a desired level of security. There are at least three "classic" categories of security requirements[1] that need further definition: **Confidentiality** is the state of a system when data are protected from unauthorized disclosure. Confidentiality focuses on the

---

[1] Parker (1991) suggests an integration of security purposes by mandatory evaluation of five (instead of three) requirements. He suggests the separate evaluation of authenticity (which is up to now part of integrity) and the separate evaluation of usefulness (which is up to now part of availability). This mandatory evaluation has to happen in information systems on five levels of abstraction: level of information, level of application, level of operating system, level of hardware and user level.

access mode class of "observation", that includes reading, viewing, printing, or knowing of the existence of an asset. **Integrity** is the state of a system when data has only been transformed in an intended way. Integrity focuses on the access mode class of "alteration", such as writing, changing, altering status, and deleting. **Availability** is the state of a system where the services and the functions of the system will not be denied to legitimate users but performed within an acceptable period of time.

To develop and establish appropriate methodologies in the field of security, security architectures, frameworks, models, and techniques are needed. Furthermore confidential systems require that the data used are classified and the users of the system are cleared. The **classification** maps data onto a given schema according to the sensitivity of data, sensitivity of an application, and/or sensitivity of the location at which the data and application will be used. The classification might be descriptive (e.g. "unclassified", "restricted", "confidential", "secret", and "top secret", see Department of Defense, 1985) or simply a numbered set of classes (e.g. the functionality classes F1 to F5 or the assurance levels Q0 to Q7 in the IT-Security Criteria (German Information Security Agency, 1989)). **Clearance** is the level of trustworthiness of a user.

A **security architecture** describes generic security services and security mechanisms as well as the necessary functions of security management within a certain system architecture. A **framework** is a generic solution for specific security requirements (e.g. authentication, integrity, access control). It ensures consistency in the security enhancements by providing a modular composition. A **security model** applies the various concepts developed in the framework to specific parts of an architecture and details how and when mechanisms and framework elements are combined. **Techniques** finally provide building blocks and appropriate tools for a specific implementation.

A specific security policy for information technology evolves from a **corporations' general security policy** which manifests the risk appreciation of the company's decision makers. The **specific security policy** is based on results from an applied risk analysis and is a statement indicating the goals of the intended security effort. It determines a set of rules that constrain the decision process for security management. The **quality of the decision process** for security management depends essentially on the quality of the requirements. There are several criteria to assess requirements for quality. Figure 1 shows the mentioned elements of a security-related decision model and their interrelation.

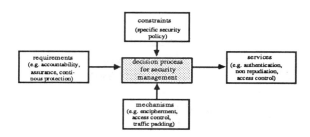

Fig. 1 Interrelation between elements of a security related decision model

A **security measure** can be a device, an organizational step, a rule, a software, a procedure or any activity that supports security. The security measure includes all activities which help to integrate the chosen measure into the specific environment. **Security services** are based on implemented security mechanisms and provide support to protect assets. A security **mechanism** is an algorithm for realizing a specified functionality.

DEVELOPMENT OF A FRAMEWORK FOR SELECTING APPROPRIATE SECURITY SERVICES

In the second part of the paper we will first give an overview on security relevant activities in the context of an organizational hierarchy. Then the framework to prepare and coordinate high-quality security decisions will be introduced and discussed. As it is one of the goals of a framework to show possible embedding in specific architectures, an integration of the framework into security system management will be shown. The third part will then demonstrate an application of the suggested framework by an example of Network Security Management in an Open System.

Security within an organization depends on various security relevant activities that are carried out by people assuming different responsibilities in the company. To perform these activities they need appropriate information. Figure 2 gives a survey over the various activities, maps them to an organizational hierarchy, and lists typical information required.

Level	Activity	Information required
top management	- define a corporations' general security policy	objectives of the organization, general management goals, culture, strategies, laws, regulations etc.
staff/line department	- define a specific security policy - perform risk analysis	corporations' general security policy architectures, models, framworks etc. general security policy, standards, statistics, check-lists etc.
	- select measures	specific security policy, standards, evaluation techniques etc.
	- implement measures - verify measures	product descriptions, documentation etc. documentations, assumptions and results of risk analysis etc.
operative	- apply security measures	user instructions

Fig. 2 Organizational context for security relevant activities

To reach a desired security level in an organization the security relevant actions have to be consistent over the different levels. This requires that top management give the initial impulse and direction by defining a **corporations' general security policy**. The security policy goals given by the top management in the form of long-term and company-wide binding standards must be in line with general management goals. In order to ensure the long term validity of these standards, as well as to justify their derivation, it is advisable to make available the methods how to determine theses standards rather than just to give the values themselves. The following list, which is not exhaustive at all, gives examples of what a carefully designed security policy should contain:
- Parameters used as basis for risk assessment
- Parameters used as basis for classification of risks
- Methodology for cost evaluation of security measures

- Criteria for selection of favourable security measures
- Financing policy
- Rules for delegation
- Delimitation of competence (see Bauknecht, Strauss 1990).

To derive a case oriented **specific security policy** one needs results from a sound, preliminary risk analysis. There are various techniques to perform risk analysis but it goes beyond the scope of this paper to discuss them in detail. Therefore we will restrict our deliberations on a pattern that underlies most risk analysis procedures. The basic idea is to identify sources and targets of threats and to evaluate possible or probable damage. Figure 3 depicts this basic pattern and uses as an instance the expected value of damage as an evaluation of risk. A basic problem consists in the quantification of qualitative aspects.

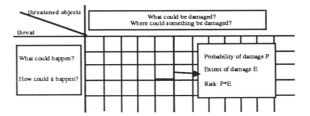

Fig. 3 Basic pattern of risk analysis

Depending on the result of the risk analysis and the corporations' general security policy procedures for selecting appropriate security measures need to be defined and categorised. As there are usually several requirements their priorities must be determined. If the requirements cannot be weighted explicitly at least a simple ranking should be made, Delphi-techniques being useful to achieve this.
Finally the quality of the requirements should be examined, according to quality criteria as completeness, consistency, correctness, feasibility, necessity, traceability, and verification (Pfleeger, 1991).

Figure 4 depicts the components which influence the selection process for the necessary security service which allows to guarantee and maintain the required security.

Fig. 4 A Framework for Selecting
        Appropriate Security Services

The representation and integration of the framework into Security System Management is shown in Figure 5. The Security Management System is supported by the Security Management Information Base (SMIB) which might be implemented as a database or a full expert system.

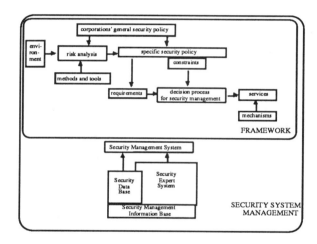

Fig. 5 Integrated Security System
        Management using a Framework for
        Decision Processes

The organizational chart of Fig. 2 shows that there is a great amount of information to be maintained but only a small part of it is needed at a time. There are many different people involved in security activities and they only need selected information and they have according to their activities different views. The quality of a company´s overall security activities being very dependent on the degree of tuning all security-measures it is quite obvious that a security expert system could efficiently support the security management system.

An expert system has several advantages over a pure security data base:

- In security the risk analysis is essential. There are various methods to perform a calculus of uncertainty, and the quality of the estimated value of damage depends very much on statistics about comparable situations. An expert system could support both the experts' selection of methods for risk assessment and the interpretation of results.
- An inference engine - the core of an expert system - is a rule based system which is stable and less critical to environmental changes.
- Furthermore the results of implemented security measures can better be evaluated as former results are preserved and will influence consecutive actions.

SECURITY MANAGEMENT IN OPEN COMMUNICATION NETWORKS

Security Policy

Many organizations depend today heavily on reliable communications systems and their operations would be severely disturbed by networks which cannot guarantee the necessary level of trustworthy operations. The corporations' general security policy therefore has to pay special attention to the importance of the security of a communication system. Extensive risk analysis has to cope with potential threats and their consequences to the system functions.

The specific security policy, a set of laws, rules, and practices that regulate how the organization manages, protects, and distributes sensitive information has then to define appropriate rules which allow to guarantee the requested security level of the communication system. These rules will give feasible solutions to questions like:

- how data communication in Open Systems is protected against eavesdropping on data exchange
- how the interrelationship between two domains is managed and administered
- how security audit trail information has to be collected and where it has to be directed to

The policy being rather guideline than a strict implementation of instructions says what has to be achieved whilst the "how" is dependent on the specific environment and the available mechanisms.

Selection of services and mechanisms

Both users and operators of communication networks have manifold requirements for system security. Amongst the major services are authentication, access control, confidentiality, integrity, and non-repudiation. The implementation of these services is realized by various mechanisms the most important covering encipherment, digital signature, access control, data integrity, authentication, traffic padding, routing control, and notarization. Figure 6 shows the relationship between services and mechanisms and indicates meaningful combinations.

SERVICE / MECHANISM	Encipherment	Digital Signature	Access Control	Data Integrity	Authentication Exchange	Traffic Padding	Routing Control	Notarization
Peer Entity Authentication	Y	Y	.	.	Y	.	.	.
Data Origin Authentication	Y	Y	.	.	.	.	.	.
Access Control Service	.	.	Y	.	.	.	.	.
Connection Confidentiality	Y	.	.	.	.	.	Y	.
Connetionless Confidentiality	Y	.	.	.	.	.	Y	.
Selevtive Fiel Confidentiality	Y	.	.	.	.	.	.	.
Traffic Flow Confidentiality	Y	.	.	.	.	Y	Y	.
Connection Integrity with Recovery	Y	.	.	Y	.	.	.	.
Connection Integrity without Recovery	Y	.	.	Y	.	.	.	.
Selective Field Connection Integrity	Y	.	.	Y	.	.	.	.
Connectionless Integrity	Y	Y	.	Y	.	.	.	.
Selective Field Connectionless Integrity	Y	Y	.	Y	.	.	.	.
Non Repudiation, Origin	.	Y	.	Y	.	.	.	.
Non Repudiation, Delivery	.	Y	.	Y	.	.	.	Y

Fig. 6 Services and mechanisms supporting security management in open communication networks.

Security Management

Security management being part of the overall management of an open communication system has to collect and present the relevant data necessary to control the performance of the implemented security services and mechanisms. It has to demon-

strate how the defined security levels are reached.

The OSI (Open System Interconnect) security management is based on a Security Management Information Base (SMIB) which holds all information relevant to guarantee the requested overall system security. The OSI security management distinguishes three categories of security management
- system security management
- security services management
- security mechanism management
In addition every participating subsystem may also maintain its own local information base and perform security management specific to the local situation (Fig. 7).

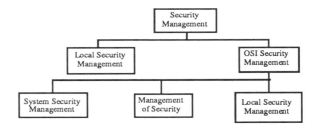

Fig. 7 Areas of security management in an open communication system (Ruland, 1990).

While the system security management deals with the all over security aspects in the open communication system it is the duty of services and the mechanisms management to assure the requested security for services and mechanisms. (For details see ISO 7498 (2) and ISO 7498 (4)).

Literature

Bauknecht, K. and C. Strauss (1990). Portfolio techniques to support risk management and security. *Proceedings IFIP TC-11, Sixth International Conference and Exhibition on Information Security.*

Department of Defense (1985). *Department of Defense Trusted Computer System Evaluation. Criteria*, DOD 5200.28 STD, Library No. S225.711.

Garbe, K. (1990). Sicherheitsstandards für offene Kommunikationssysteme. *PIK, 13*, 139-145.

German Information Security Agency (1989). *IT Security Criteria - Criteria for the Evaluation of Trustworthiness of Information Technology (IT) Systems.* Bundesanzeiger Verlagsges. mbH, Köln.

ISO 7498(2). Open Systems Interconnection. Part 2: Security Architecture.

ISO 7498(4). Open Systems Interconnection. Part 4: Management Framework.

Parker, D.B. (1991). Neuformulierung der Grundlagen der Informationssicherheit, *Datenschutz und Datensicherung 11/91*, pp. 557.

Pfleeger, S.L. (1991). A framework for security requirements, *Computers & Security, 10*, 515-523.

Ruland, C. (1990). Sicherheit und Sicherheitsmanagement in offenen Kommunikationssystemen. *DATACOM, NOV*, 202-213.

Strauss, C. (1991). *Informatik-Sicherheitsmanagement - Eine Herausforderung für die Unternehmensführung.* Teubner Verlag, Stuttgart.

Thomson, B., E.S. Lee, P.I.P. Boulton, M. Stumm and D.M. Lewis (1988). *A Trusted Network Architecture.* Computer Systems Research Institute, University of Toronto.

SECURITY POLICIES FOR DATABASES

G. Pernul

Institute of Statistics & Computer Science, University of Vienna,
Liebigg. 4/3-4, A-1010 Vienna.

A M. Tjoa

Institute of Statistics & Computer Science, University of Vienna,
Liebigg. 4/3-4, A-1010 Vienna.
Research Institute for Applied Knowledge Processing, University of Linz

Abstract. This paper discusses advantages and disadvantages of security policies for databases. While database security will be defined by using a broader perspective main attention is given to access control models preventing a database from unauthorized disclosure or modification of information. In addition to Discretionary and Mandatory Security which are identified as requirements for the higher security classes of evaluation criterias, Adapted Mandatory Security, the Clark and Wilson Model and the Personal Knowledge Approach will be discussed.

Keywords. Database management systems, Computer security, Information storage systems, Modeling, Models.

INTRODUCTION

It is widely recognized that information stored in databases is often of important economic value to an enterprise or to the public. Indeed, many databases or portion of databases are so crucial that its corruption or destruction (malicious or accidental) could endanger the economic functioning of the enterprise or even human life.

Database security is concerned with ensuring the secrecy, integrity, and availability of data stored in a database while with safety all actions are meant that protect against faults or malicious system behavior that could endanger human lifes, property, the environment, or a nation. Denning (1989) has shown that security generally supports safety and that both topics are closely related. This paper takes more a security perspective by discussing advantages and disadvantages of different database security policies.

The security features of the database management system (DBMS) enforce the security requirements and can be classified into the following categories:

(1) *Identification, Authentication, Audit.* Usually, before getting access to the database each user has to identify itself to the computer system. Authentication is a way to verify the identity of a user at log-on time. Auditing is the examination of all security relevant events by a process or person that was not responsible for causing the event.

(2) *Authorization.* Authorization is the specification of a set of rules about who has what type of access to what information. Authorization policies govern the disclosure and modification of information.

(3) *Integrity, Consistency.* Integrity constraints are rules that define the correct state of a database during database operations and therefore can protect against malicious modification of information.

In this paper we take not such a broad perspective of database security and are mainly focused on authorization policies. This is legitimate because identification, authentication and auditing normally fall within the scope of the underlying operating system and database integrity and consistency are subject of the close related topic of semantic data modeling or dependent on the physical design of the DBMS software.

Computer security is currently subject of many national and international standardization work. The best known are the Orange Book (1985) of the US National Computer Security Center and some national proposals that have extended it. For example, see the German Criteria (1989), the

259

Canadian Criteria (1991), or the proposal of the EC, the EC Criteria (1991). Relevant for database security is the interpretation of the Orange Book for databases, the so called Purple Book (1990). Based on the Orange Book the Purple Book has developed a metric with which DBMSs can be evaluated for security. It consists of a number of levels ranging from A1 to D, and for each level a list of requirements that are necessary for systems trying to achieve that level of security. The Purple Book requirements tend to focus on secrecy of information as well as unauthorized and improper modification of information. As identified above unauthorized disclosure and modification fall into the scope of access control policies. The following of this paper contains a comparative study of the most relevant security models for databases covering access control strategies by taking a critical point of view.

DATABASE SECURITY MODELS

Most security models implemented in commercial DBMS products are based on Discretionary Access Controls (DAC). As it will be shown DAC is only of limited use in systems that are used for security critical applications. More restrictive is data protection in multilevel secure DBMSs that in addition to DAC support Mandatory Access Controls (MAC). Based on the requirements of the Purple Book systems trying to be classified at levels C1 and C2 have to provide discretionary protection of their data, systems at level B1 in addition to DAC have to support MAC and systems at levels B2 or above have to provide increasing assurance by assigning security labels to physical devices, supporting trusted recovery or should be proved with formal methods of being free of covert information channels. In addition to academic prototypes (for example, see SeaView (Denning and colleagues, 1988, Lunt and colleagues, 1990), LDV (Stachour and Thuraisingham, 1990), or ASD-Views (Garvey and Wu, 1988) several commercial system builders (Ingres, Oracle, Sybase, Trudata, to name a few) are busy building prototypes or have already announced or introduced systems meeting the higher evaluation criteria. Mandatory policies were originally developed for data protection in military systems and although they are very effective it has turned out that they cannot be applied as they are for data protection in civil applications. This resulted in further development and in the Adapted Mandatory Access Control (*AMAC*) model which is fine-tuned for the use as a database security model in civil applications meeting high security requirements. *AMAC* is not the only proposal as the underlying security policy for civil databases. In the remainder of this paper we will also discuss the Clark and Wilson model that is based on the concept of well-formed transactions and the Personal Knowledge Approach that is mainly concerned with the privacy aspect of information.

THE DISCRETIONARY MODEL

Discretionary security models are based on the concepts of a set of *security objects O,* a set of *security subjects S*, a set of *access privileges T* defining what kind of access a subject has to a certain object, and in order to represent content-based access rules a set of *predicates P*. Applied to relational databases O is a finite set of values $\{o_1,...,o_n\}$ representing relational schemas, S is a finite set of potential subjects $\{s_1...s_m\}$ representing users, groups of them, or transactions operating on behalf of users. Access types are the set of database operations such as select, insert, delete, update, execute, grant, or revoke and predicate $p \in P$ defines the *view* of subject $s \in S$ on object $o \in O$. The tuple $<o,s,t,p>$ is called *access rule* and a function f is defined to determine if an *authorization f(o,s,t,p)* is true or false:

$$f: O \times S \times T \times P \rightarrow (True, False).$$

For any $<o,s,t,p>$, if $f(o,s,t,p)$ evaluates into *True,* then subject s has authorization t to access object o within the range defined by predicate p.

An important property of discretionary security models is the support of the principle of *delegation of rights* where a right is the (o,t,p)-portion of the access rule. A subject s_i who holds the right (o_i, t_i, p_i) may be allowed to delegate that right to another subject s_j $(i \neq j)$. For a more detailed discussion of discretionary controls see Fernandez and colleagues (1981) and for open research questions and recent developments see Lunt (1991).

Discretionary models suffer from four major drawbacks when applied as a security policy to databases. In particular we see the following limitations:

(1) *Users enforce the security policy.* DAC is based on the concept of ownership of information. DAC systems assign the ownership of information to the creator of the data items in the database and allow the creator subject to grant access to other users. This has the disadvantage that the burden of enforcing the security policy of the enterprise is in the responsibility of the users themselves and cannot be controlled by the enterprise without involving high costs.

(2) *Cascading authorization.* If two or more subjects have the privilege of granting or revoking certain access rules to other subjects this may lead to cascading revocation chains. As an example consider subjects s_1, s_2, s_3 and access rule (s_1,o,t,p). Subject s_2 receives the privilege (o,t,p)

from s_1 and grants the access rule to s_3. Later, s_1 grants (o,t,p) again to s_3 but s_2 revokes (o,t,p) from s_3 because of some reason. The effect of these operations is that s_3 still has the authorization (from s_1) to access object o by satisfying predicate p and using privilege t even if subject s_2 has revoked it. This has the consequence that subject s_2 is not aware of the fact that authorization (s_3, o,t,p) is still in effect.

(3) *Subject of Trojan Horse attacks.* A Trojan Horse (which is a malicious software that tricks a user without his/her knowledge into performing certain actions he/she is not aware of) can be used to grant a certain right (o,t,p) of subject s_i on to s_j $(i \neq j)$ without the knowledge of subject s_i. Any program which runs on behalf of a subject with the subjects identity acts with the subjects identity and therefore has all of the DAC access rights of the subjects processes. If a program contains a Trojan Horse with the functionality of granting access rules on to other users this cannot be restricted by discretionary access control methods.

(4) *View update problems.* In most relational DBMSs DAC is implemented by using the concept of database *views*. This has the advantage of being very flexible to support the subjects with different views and to automatically filter out data a subject is not authorized to access but has the disadvantage that not all data is updateable through certain views.

THE MANDATORY MODEL

While discretionary models are more concerned with defining, modeling, and enforcing access to information mandatory security models are in addition concerned with the *flow of information* within a system. Mandatory security requires that security objects are assigned to certain security classes represented by a label and the label for an object is called its *classification* while a label for a subject its *clearance*. The classification represents the sensitivity of the labeled data while the clearance of a subject its trustworthiness to not disclose sensitive information to others. A security label consists of two components: a hierarchical set of sensitivity levels (for example: top_secret > secret > confidential > unclassified) and a non hierarchical set of categories, representing classes of object types of the universe of discourse. Clearance and classification levels are totally ordered resulting security labels are only partially ordered - thus, some subjects and objects are not comparable in the class lattice. We say, security class c_1 is comparable with and *dominates* ($\geq$) c_2 if the sensitivity level of c_1 is greater than or equal to that of c_2 and the categories in c_1 contain those in c_2.

Mandatory access control requirements are based on the Bell-LaPadula security paradigm (Bell and LaPadula, 1976) and formalized by two rules. The first protects the information of the database from unauthorized disclosure, and the second protects data from contamination or unauthorized modification by restricting the information flow from *high* to *low*er trusted subjects.

(1) Subject s is allowed to read data item d if

$$clear(s) \geq class(d).$$

(2) Subject s is allowed to write data if

$$class(d) = clear(s).$$

Mandatory security leads to multilevel databases because the relations may appear different to users with different clearances. This is, because not all clearances may authorize the subjects to all data or in the case of cover stories are supported may not authorize them to the proper data. Since the above rules are mandatory and enforced by the database management system automatically, the system compares the assigned security classes of the subject and the referenced objects for each read and write access and thus, can protect against Trojan Horse attacks. Moreover, instead of leaving the burden of enforcing the security policy of the enterprise at the users side it is possible to introduce a security administrator with the responsibility to carefully analyze the sensitivity of the objects and the trustworthiness of the subjects and to assign corresponding labels. For a more detailed discussion of MAC and the multilevel database model see Jajodia and Sandhu (1991).

Although being more restrictive than DAC models MAC are only of limited use when applied to civil databases. In particular we see the following limitations:

(1) *Granularity of security object.* It is not yet agreed about what should the granularity of labeled data be. Proposals range from protecting whole databases, to protect files, to protect relations, attributes, or even certain attribute values. Careful labeling is necessary because otherwise it could lead to inconsistent or incomplete label assignments.

(2) *Automated Labeling.* As databases usually contain a large collection of data, serve many users and labeled data is often not available manual labeling may result in an almost endless process.

(3) *N-eyes-principle.* Many business rules require that certain office tasks need to be carried out by two or more persons (four-eyes-principle). As an example consider subjects s_1, s_2 with $clear(s_1) > clear(s_2)$, data item d with $class(d) = clear(s_2)$ and the business rule that writing of s_2 on d needs the approval of s_1. Following Bell-LaPadula's write-access rule would require the same level of

clearance for s_1 and s_2 and this is inadequate for many database applications.

THE ADAPTED MANDATORY SECURITY MODEL

Adapted mandatory security falls into the class of *role-based* security models. Each potential user of the database performs a role in the organization and based on his/her role is cleared to perform certain database operations. The *AMAC* model does not only support access controls but is also a design environment for multilevel secure databases that are designed for implementation in DBMSs supporting DAC and MAC. The technique consists of high-level data and security modeling using entity-relationship (ER) techniques, a transformation policy from ER-schemas into multilevel secure relations, a decomposition approach for the construction of single level fragments from multilevel base relations, a supporting policy for the automated labeling of security objects and subjects, and a security enforcement by using database triggers. The following phases of design for security critical databases by using *AMAC* can be identified:

(1) *Requirements Analysis and Conceptual Design.* Based on the role they perform in the organization the potential users of the database can be classified into different groups. For different roles data and security requirements may differ significantly. The ER model (Chen, 1976) and its variants serve as an almost defacto standard for conceptual database design and have been extended in *AMAC* by Pernul and Tjoa (1991) to model and describe security requirements. The security and data requirements of each role performed in the organization are described by individual ER-schemas and form the *view* of each user group on the enterprise data. Please note, here a view describes all data, security requirements, and functions users performing a certain role in the organization are aware of while a view in the DAC based models can be seen as a window for the users to the stored data. In order to arrive at a conceptualization of the whole database as seen from the viewpoint of the enterprise *AMAC* uses view integration techniques.

(2) *Logical Design.* In order to implement the conceptual schema into a DBMS a transformation from the ER-schema into the data model supported by the DBMS in use is necessary. This step is only needed because todays DBMSs are not powerful enough to capture all semantics of the ER-model. *AMAC* contains general rules for the translation of ER-schemas into the multilevel relational data model. Output of the transformation process is a set of *relational schemas, global dependencies* defined between

schemas, and a *set of views* describing access rules on relational schemas.

(3) *Decomposition of multilevel schemas.* In order to enforce the security requirements a structured decomposition of multilevel relations into single level fragments is necessary. Structured decomposition is based on the definition of *overlapping, isolated,* and *connected* views and results into a set of fragments, called *fragmentation schema.* Let fragment F be the intersection of views V_1 and V_2 $(V_1 \cap V_2 \neq \{\})$. In this case the decomposition results in a fragmentation schema $FS = \{F_p..., F_n\}$ and V_p, V_2 are defined over a set of fragments from FS $(V_1 \rightarrow \{F_p...F_j\}; V_2 \rightarrow \{F_p...F_k\})$. A fragment $F_i \in FS$ is *valid* if for any view V

$$(\not\exists F_i' \subset F_i)\ (V \rightarrow F_i',\ V \not\rightarrow (F_i)).$$

Let fragment F be $(V_i \cap V_j)$ then F represents the largest area of the database to which two groups of users with the same level of clearance (with respect to F) have common access. If $F = (V_i \setminus V_j)$, then F is only accessible by users having view V_i as their interface to the database. In this case, F represents data which is not contained in V_j and therefore not accessible for the corresponding user set. From a security point of view, fragment $(V_i \setminus V_j)$ should be separated from fragment $(V_j \setminus V_i)$ and fragment $(V_i \cap V_j)$ even if all fragments belong to the same relation. The construction of V_i and V_j should be done by providing multilevel relations in a way that only the necessary fragments should be combined to construct the different views. For a more detailed discussion and for necessary consistency criterias in fragmentation schemas consult Pernul and Luef (1991).

(4) *Support of automated security labeling.* Structured decomposition produces from a multilevel database schema a set of disjoint fragments. In *AMAC* the granularity of the security object is a *fragment* and of the security subject a *view.* Automated labeling is based on the following assumption: The more the number of views accessing a particular fragment, the lower is the sensitivity of the contained data and is the level of classification that needs to be provided for the fragment. This assumption seems to be valid because a fragment that is accessed by many views will not contain sensitive information and at the other side, a fragment that is accessed by only few views can be classified as high sensitive. Views are ordered based on the number of fragments they access and on the assigned classifications for the fragments. In general, a view needs a label that allows the corresponding users to access all fragments the view is defined over. *Class(F)* applies to the fragmental schema F as well as to all attribute names and type definitions for the schema. *Clear(V)* applies to all transactions executing on behalf of V and classifications and clearances are stored in catalog relations.

(5) *Security Enforcement.* In *AMAC* fragments are physically stored by using a general purpose DBMS while catalog relations are placed in a TCB. Security is enforced by using *trigger mechanisms* that are supported by many commercial DBMS products. Triggers are hidden rules that can be fired (activated) if a fragment is effected by certain database operations. In databases security critical are the select (read access), the insert, delete, and update (write accesses) commands. In *AMAC select-triggers* are used to route queries to the proper fragments, *insert-triggers* are responsible to decompose tuples and to insert corresponding sub-tuples into proper fragments, and *update-* and *delete-triggers* are responsible for protecting against unauthorized modification by restricting information flow from *high* to *low* in cases that could lead to an undesired information transfer. For a more detailed discussion on security enforcement by using triggers in *AMAC* see Pernul (1992).

In comparison to MAC, *AMAC* has the following advantages which make the model a good basis as a global security model for databases: (1) Supports all phases of the design of a secure database. ⇐∃‡ Uniform labeling by using fragments as the granularity of the security object is possible. Furthermore, a supporting policy to derive single level fragments from multilevel base relations is provided. (3) Automated labeling leads to candidate security labels that can be refined by a human security administrator if necessary. (4) By using triggers security enforcement can be fine-tuned to meet the security requirements. For example, n-eyes-principle may be supported in some applications and not supported in others.

THE CLARK AND WILSON MODEL

Similar to *AMAC* this security approach is also role-based. It was first summarized and compared to MAC by Clark and Wilson (1987). The approach consists of three basic principles: there are security subjects, (constraint) security objects, and a set of well-formed transactions. Users are restricted to execute only a certain set of transactions permitted to them and each transaction operates on an assigned set of data objects only. We interpret this approach as follows:

(1) *Security subjects are assigned to roles.* Each business role is mapped into a database function and ideally at a given time a particular user is playing only one role. A database function corresponds to a set of (well-formed) transactions that are necessary for the users acting in the role. In this model it is essential to state which user is acting in what role at what time and for each role what transactions are necessary to be carried out.

(2) *Well-formed transactions.* A well-formed transaction operates on an assigned set of data and needs to be formally verified that all relevant security and integrity properties are satisfied. In addition it should provide logging and atomacy and serializability of resulting subtransactions in a way that concurrency and recovery mechanisms can be established. It is important to note, that in this model the data items referenced by the transactions are not specified by the user operating the transaction. Instead, data items are assigned depending on the role the user is acting in.

(3) *Separation of duty.* This principle requires that each set of users being assigned a specific set of responsibilities based on the role of the user in the organization. The only way to access the data in the database is through an assigned set of well-formed transactions specific to the role each of the users play. In those cases where a user requires additional information, another user (which is cleared at a higher level) acting in a separate role has to use a well-formed transaction from the transaction domain of the role he is acting in to grant the user temporary permission to execute a larger set of well-formed transactions.

The Clark and Wilson model has gained wide attention in recent years. However, although it looks very promising at a first glance, we believe a detailed and thoroughly investigation is still missing because major questions are not solved in Clark and Wilson (1987). In particular, the authors only address as potential threats to the security of a system the penetration of data by authorized users, unauthorized actions by authorized users, and abuse of privileges by authorized users. As identified at the beginning of this paper these are only a subset of the necessary functionality of the required access control features of a DBMS.

THE PERSONAL KNOWLEDGE APPROACH

The personal knowledge approach, developed by Biskup and Brüggemann (1988, 1989), is focused on protecting the privacy of individuals stored in a database or information system and serves as the underlying security paradigm of the prototype DBMS Doris (Biskup and Brüggemann, 1991). The main goal of this model is to meet the right of humans for *informational self-determination* as requested in Constitutional Laws of many countries. In this context, privacy can be summarized as the basic right for an individual to choose which elements of his/her private life may be disclosed. The personal knowledge approach is built around the concept of a *person* and its *knowledge*. Each person represented in the database knows everything about itself and if he/she wants to know something about someone else that person must be asked. To achieve this goal, the personal knowledge approach combines techniques of relational databases, object oriented programming, and capability based operating systems. More technically it is based on the following constructs:

(1) *Persons*. Persons either represent information about individuals stored in the database or are the users of the database. Each person is characterized by its *personal knowledge*. Technically, a person is seen as an *encapsulated object* that 'knows' anything about itself (its application domain) and about its relationships to other persons known to the system. This are the only two components of 'personal knowledge' and for any person it is not permitted to remember permanently anything else. Within the system each person is uniquely identified by a surrogate.

(2) *Acquaintances*. Persons are acquainted with other persons. The set of acquaintances of a person describes the environment of that person and is the set of objects with which the person is allowed to communicate. Communication is performed by means of *messages* that may be sent from a person to its acquaintances for querying about their personal knowledge or for asking to perform an operation, for example, to update their knowledge. Acquaintances of a person are represented in the knowledge body of the corresponding person object by their surrogate.

(3) *Roles and authorities*. Depending on the authority of the sender the receiver of a message may react in different ways. The authority of a person with respect to an acquaintance is based on the role the person is currently acting in. While the set of acquaintances of a person may change dynamically authorities and roles are statically declared in the system.

(4) *Remembrance*. Each person remembers the messages that it is sending or receiving. This is established by adding all information about recent queries and updates together with the authorities available at that time to the 'knowledge' of the sender and receiver person. Based on this information auditing can be performed and all transactions can be traced by just asking originator of affected persons.

Security (privacy) enforcement based on the personal knowledge approach is based on two independent features. First, after login each user is assigned as instance of a person object type and thus holds individually received acquaintances and statically assigned authorities on roles. Second, if the user executes a query or an update operation the query is automatically modified such that resulting messages are only sent to the acquaintances of the person. Summarizing, the personal knowledge approach is fine-tuned to

meet the requirements of informational self-determination. Thus, its main advantage as the underlying security paradigm for databases are applications in which information about humans not available to the public is kept; for example, hospital information systems or databases containing census data.

CONCLUSION

In this paper we have discussed five different approaches how to model and express database security. The discretionary security approach may be the first choice if a high degree of trust is not necessary. Keeping the responsibility to enforce a security policy at the users side is only adequate if potential threats against security will not result into considerable damage. Mandatory security models offer the most powerful protection mechanisms against unauthorized disclosure and modification of information but are only of limited use if security levels are not available. Implementing mandatory security into a DBMS brings a lot of overhead. A fundamental property of databases is the fact that an event of reality is represented in the database only once. This needs not be true for multilevel systems because reality may be seen at each security level differently. This has the effect that consistency and integrity mechanisms available for general purpose DBMSs need to be changed or extended. Moreover, mandatory security does not offer any design guidelines that aid a human designer in arriving at a satisfactory database design. We believe that this is one of the strongest points of the adapted mandatory security model. This model offers a comprehensive design environment for secure databases and the level of trust in the security features of the database can be fine-tuned based on the requirements of the application. The Clark and Wilson model is an interesting alternative because security enforcement is delegated to the application programs. But what if the application programer is not trusted, can we then rely on 'well-formed' transactions? The approach of personal knowledge seems to work very well if only authorized database users should be restricted from performing unauthorized actions but does not address disclosure or modification of information by unauthorized database users. However, we believe that object-oriented concepts (for example, the property of object encapsulation) as used in this model are very close to the 'nature' of hidden personal knowledge and role specific behavior of individuals.

All five approaches originate from emphasizing different goals. In a nutshell, discretionary models try to assign *privileges*, mandatory models try to keep *secrets*, adapted mandatory models offer different *degrees of security*, the Clark and Wilson approach guards security by *well-formed transactions*, and the approach of personal knowledge is focused on the constitutional right of *informational self-determination*. We feel that database security needs to deal with all aspects discussed above even if the degree of a goal may vary among different applications.

A future direction in the field of secure database development is the implementation of computerized tools that support the various phases of system design. The *AMAC* model identifies five phases for the design of a secure database and offers guidelines for the quality of the output produced in each phase. Most activities in *AMAC* can be automated making this model the first choice as the underlying methodology for a computerized design tool for the development of secure databases.

Acknowledgement. This work is supported by the Austrian-Spanish Scientific and Technical Cooperation Agreement.

REFERENCES

Bell, D. E. and LaPadula, L. J. (1976). Secure Computer System: Unified Exposition and Multics Interpretation. *Technical Report MTR-2997*. MITRE Corp. Bedford, Mass.

Biskup, J. and Brüggemann, H. H. (1988). The Personal Model of Data: Towards a Privacy-Oriented Information System. *Computers & Security, Vol. 7,* North Holland (Elsevier) 1988.

Biskup, J. and Brüggemann, H. H. (1989). The Personal Model of Data: Towards a Privacy Oriented Information System. *Proc. of the 5th Int'l. Conf. on Data Engineering (DE)*, 348-355, IEEE Computer Society Press.

Biskup, J. and Brüggemann, H. H. (1991). Das datenschutzorientierte Informationssystem DORIS: Stand der Entwicklung und Ausblick, *Proc. 2. GI-Fachtagung "Verläßliche Informationssysteme.",* 146-158. Informatik-Fachberichte 271, Springer Verlag. (In German).

Canadian Criteria (1991). The Canadian Trusted Computer Product Evaluation Criteria. Canadian System Security Centre.

Chen, P. P. (1976) The Entity-Relationship Model - Towards a unified view of data. *ACM Trans. Database Systems (ToDS)*, Vol.1, No. 1, 9 - 36.

Clark, D. D., Wilson, D. R. (1987). A Comparison of Commercial and Military Computer Security Policies. *Proc. IEEE Symposium on Research in Security and Privacy.*

Denning, D. E., Lunt T. F., Schell, R. R., Shockley, W. R., Heckaman, M. (1988). The SeaView Security Model. *Proc. IEEE Symposium on Research in Security and Privacy*, 218-233.

Denning, D. E. (1989. Secure Databases and Safety: Some Unexpected Conflicts. In: *Safe and Secure Computing Systems*. (T. Anderson, ed.). 101-111. Blackwell Scientific Publications.

EC Criteria (1991). Information Technology Security Evaluation Criteria (ITSEC). Provisional Harmonised Criteria, Commission of the European Communities, Brussels.

Fernandez, E. B., Summers, R. C. and Wood, C. (1981). *Database Security and Integrity*. Addison-Wesley.

Garvey, C. and Wu, A. (1988). ASD_Views. *Proc. IEEE Symposium on Research in Security and Privacy*, 85-95.

German Criteria (1989). IT Security Criteria. Criteria for the Evaluation of Trustworthiness of Information Technology (IT) Systems. German Information Security Agency.

Jajodia, S. and Sandhu, R. S. (1991). Toward a Multilevel Secure Relational Data Model. *Proc. ACM Int'l. Conf. on Management of Data (SIGMOD)*, 50-59.

Lunt, T. F., Denning, D., Schell, R. R., Heckman, M., Shockley, W. R. (1990). The SeaView Security Model. *IEEE Trans. on Software Engineering (TOSE)*, 593-607. Vol. 16, No. 6.

Lunt, T. F. (1991). Security in Database Systems: A Researcher's View. *2nd German Confernce on Computer Security*.

Orange Book (1985). Trusted Computer Systems Evaluation Criteria. *US National Computer Security Center*.

Pernul, G. Luef, G. (1991). A Multilevel Secure Relational Data Model Based on Views. *Proc. 7th Annual Computer Security Application Conference*, 166-177. IEEE Computer Society Press.

Pernul, G., Tjoa, A M. (1991). A View Integration Approach for the Design of Multilevel Secure Databases. *Proc. 10th Int'l. Conf. on the Entity-Relationship Approach*, San Mateo, CA.

Pernul, G. (1992). Update Propagation in Multilevel Secure AMAC Schemata. *Submitted for Publication*.

Purple Book (1990). Trusted Database Management Interpretation of the Trusted Computer System Evaluation Criteria. *US National Computer Security Center*.

Stachour, P. D. and Thuraisingham, M. B. (1990). Design of LDV: A multilevel secure relational database management system. *IEEE Trans. on Knowledge and Data Engineering (TKDE)*, 190-209. Vol. 2, No. 2.

CONCEPT OF A SECURITY CONTROL CENTER

Johann Fichtner Cornelia Persy

Siemens AG Otto-Hahn-Ring 6 D-8000 Munich 83

ABSTRACT Up to this point, research methods for enhancing computer security have concentrated on *offline* risk management. Only few attempts emphasize *online* risk management adapting to the rapidly changing threats of complex distributed systems. The security manager of such a distributed system requires online support for assessing the actual risks and for selecting and implementing cost effective security measures.

Our paper describes the concept of a *security control center* that will execute online risk management effectively. The security control center applies mathematical models for the refinement of information obtained from two major sources: risk relevant data already available in the system and judgements from human experts. This refined information provides the basis for risk assessment models which in turn deliver input for decision support models. We called our approach of loosely coupled modeling *open modeling*. In addition, a comfortable user interface with graphic representation to support the security manager is essential.

KEYWORDS control systems, IT systems, modeling, risk management, safety, security

I. INTRODUCTION

A major part of computer security deals with threats that aim at data. Originating from the military needs, threats against the confidentiality of data were particularly emphasized. This direction is significant in today's security criteria catalogs (TCSEC 1985, ITSEC 1991) for secure Information Technology (IT) systems. In addition to requiring the confidentiality of data, the integrity and availability of data have pulled up to equal importance in computer security.

In recent years we observed a shift within the computer security community from a data oriented approach to a process oriented approach. In particular, the *risk management* process is defined as:

- estimating potential losses due to the use of or dependence upon IT systems (often referred to as risk analysis)

- analyzing potential threats and system vulnerabilities that contribute to loss estimates

- selecting and implementing cost effective safeguards that reduce costs to an acceptable level (Katzke 1991)

These goals seem to be widley agreed upon (Fites, Kratz, and Brebner 1989; Katzke 1991). Still a point of discussion is: what are the necessary methods and tools to adequately support risk management? The annual 'Computer Security Risk Management Model Builders Workshop', initiated by NIST in 1988, is an excellent forum on the subject.

An overview over the existing relevant methods and tools in risk management (Fichtner, Persy 1992) shows their commonalities:

- only support offline risk management

- totally depend on the judgement of experts

- do not model internal relationships in IT systems

- do not use information already available in IT systems

In contrast, complex networked IT systems in safety and security critical applications demand *online* risk management to allow for detection of dynamic changes in the security status (e.g. hacking via the net, insider abuse of security privileges, loss of redundancy). Also, the relative ease of configuring modern distributed systems bears the danger of creating new security loopholes. These loopholes need to be detected immediately and not just during the next routinely scheduled *offline* risk analysis.

Online risk management cannot relay on ever present experts. The dependence on subjective judgements must be reduced to a minimum. Subjective judgements such as loss of prestige through security violations in a banking environment are vital and they remain valid long term. However, rapidly changing parameters should not depend on human expertise, e.g. changed probabilities for loss of service due to the failure of a redundant component.

The security manager, who is more an applications manager than an expert in analysis and assessment, must be relieved from these kinds of assessments. Preferably, a model-based risk analysis will derive automatically the correct values from simple facts.

Even in a simple form, the online risk management must already accomplish more than the offline risk management. An online risk management tool will only be accepted if the input effort for the relevant data is small. This means, information readily available in the system must be utilized, e.g. configuration data and perfomance data.

Thus in modern IT systems there is a need for a *security control center* that must provide the following properties:

- support online risk management
- keep subjective judgement to an absolute minimum
- model security properties of IT systems
- utilize information already available in IT systems

Our paper introduces the concept of such a security control center with the following features:

- display of security relevant *static* features and *dynamic* states of IT systems
- risk assessment via model-based utilization of available information
- selection and application of the necessary security measures

These tasks are not merely relevant for IT systems in a small scope. Risk management using model-based analysis in a security control center is a cross section approach for complex systems and networks, e.g. in energy production, public and private communication. This paper will concentrate on networked Unix systems that have gained increased importance also in safety critical applications.

II. ARCHITECTURE

The architecture figure gives an overview of the major components and the information flow among them within the security control center. We identified three key tasks performed by the security control center:

- system-to-control interface (software sensors, audit data, network information, effectors)
- refinement of information
- user dialogue

SYSTEM-TO-CONTROL INTERFACE

The system-to-control interface resolves two major tasks: First, the gathering of information that is performed in the three moduls, software sensors, audit data, and network management. And second, the carrying out of security measures that is accomplished through the software effectors module. The information necessary for the gathering part is collected automatically in the IT system. The user is largely relieved from this task. The information sources and the software effectors are described in detail:

Software Sensors

Software sensors are processes in IT systems that report periodically security relevant system data to the security control center. Of primary concern are: failures of hardware and software components (e.g. crash of the mail server), system loads (e.g. processors, storage media, network load), or structure of access rights (e.g. indirect access to other accounts via .rhosts). Statistics on the administration of access rights can be generated readily (e.g. percentage of files with access rights set readable for all). In complex networks intermediate storage and partial aggregation of sensor data is achieved through a hierarchical system observation facility (Hofstetter et al. 1990).

Audit Data

Secure IT systems write audit trail data of security critical actions (e.g. attempted login, success/failure of file access, switch user). The Orange Book (TCSEC 1985) requires auditing from the second lowest security class onward. Auditing was originally intended as part of accountability where actions affecting security can be traced to the responsible party. In our approach auditing is used for online risk assessment to counter security breaches timely and effectively. Even an average IT system can generate massive amounts of audit data. Mainframes record about 500k bytes per user and hour of audit data. Tools for analyzing audit data offline (Lunt 1988, Weiss and Baur 1990) already exist.

Network Management

According to the ISO definition network management covers the following areas:

- configuration management
- performance management
- fault management
- security management
- accounting management

In ISO security is defined narrowly. The security control center must also be informed about the configuration and fault management to perform a risk assessment. Presently, the standardization and development of network management is still in flux. The de facto standard Simple Network Management Protocol (SNMP) is defined at too low a level for the security control center and thus is only of limited use. In the future, network management will become an indispensable information source.

Software Effectors

Software effectors allow for the direct application of certain security measures. Easy examples are: scheduling automatic backups and adjusting configuration parameters. Complex measures (e.g. changing access rights) could be initiated by the security manager. This calls for a comfortable access mode to the existing administration tools. Certain organizational or constructional measures canr ot be carried out using effectors. Thus text editors (ranging from electronic notebooks to a complete set of prearranged forms) must be provided.

REFINEMENT OF INFORMATION

The format of the information available from a system is neither suitable for advising the security manager or building the basis for automatically generating counter measures. The amount of data and their unhandy presentation is one problem, another is that information has to be combined from various sources. The major task of the security control center is the compression, compilation, and enrichment of information. This is achieved with four functional units that are based on mathematical models.

Factual Models

Factual models are the starting block for the requirement, assessment, and decision models. Also, the results from factual models can be used directly by the security manager.

Factual models state objective facts. Examples are, the aggregation of loads in the past, the identification of trends, and the prediction of future loads, e.g. based on regression procedures. These models are used as new data arrive (e.g. sensor or audit data), or they are invoked from the user interface, or other models.

For the analysis of audit data it may be useful to look at sessions outside the normal working hours. In this case, a working hours model is invoked that tests for user activity of a particular session whether or not it was inside the normal working hours.

Requirement Models

Requirement models are built on factual models. They test if a security policy is enforced. A security policy is a set of operational rules that state, as a result of a risk evaluation, what is considered a reasonably secure mode of operation in a specific situation. Part of these rules could be: no sessions allowed outside normal working hours or dispatch of demanding jobs only if the system is lightly loaded.

Assessment Models

Because these rules are not always strictly enforcable, it is important to know the significance of deviations from the security policy. Deviations may be ranked in negligible, serious, and crucial. The decision is often based on a combination of rule violations. Ideally, the risk measures are expressed in monetary units. E.g. the distribution of 'number of failures of business processes per year' and 'duration of failure of a single business process' can be derived from the availability indicators of the system components (Meitner 1990). In this approach, a business process is a collection of individual activities, where only their collective consideration is useful (e.g. billing and printing of payroll). The risk measure for the expected damage per year is computed as follows:

E(total duration of failure of business processes per year) *

    hourly cost rate

Decision Models

These models support the cost/benefit analysis of potential security measures. A security measure is cost effective if the difference of the expected annual loss, with and without the security measure, is greater than the annual cost for the measure. Cost models for security measures are thus an important part of decision modeling. Catalogs of security measures and their appropriate application are included in decision models. Some actions can be triggered automatically without human intervention, yet, their scope is limited.

USER DIALOGUE

This interface allows for a comfortable information exchange between the security administrator and the security control center.

User Friendly Interface

The definition of the user interface is based on ergonomic dialogue features and includes corporate style guides (DIN 66234, SNI 1990). The major criteria are:

- suitability for the task
- self-descriptiveness

- controlability of the displays (e.g. amount, duration, speed)
- conformity with user expectation
- error robustness
- individualization (e.g. key board or mouse)
- learnability

These common requirements to an user interface are even more crucial for the security control center because the correct usage of the user dialogue must often be achieved in critical, and thus stressful, situations.

Flow of Information

A good part of all security relevant information can be extracted directly from the system. Yet, it is necessary for the security manager to input certain facts, requirements, and assessment data. These can be organizational relationships among users, current security requirements, judgements, and subjective probabilities. The user dialogue guides the input and checks for its completeness and plausibility.

The display of the current system status is comfortably devisable by the user. The graphic presentation of a network allows for zooming into detailed parts of the network. Every part or component can be associated with an individual display pattern. A graphic presentation is offered for availability, load, frequence of use, access rights, and rule violations.

Additional important features of the user interface are: automatic responses, warnings, and alarms indicating particular occurrences, like failure of a server, hacking, and exceeding certain load boundaries. The classification of these occurrences is configurable by the security manager. Categories are distinguishable in presentation (color, shape, acoustic signal), reaction required by the security manager (explicit confirmation), and accounting logfiles.

The security control center requires the security manager to react to alarms and provides concrete suggestions for applying counter measures. Ideally, the suggestions are specific to a point that they only need to be accepted or rejected. The use of certain counter measures, e.g. those automatically carried out using effectors, may require explicit acceptance or rejection. This means the security control center is operated either automatically or half-automatically. Because only part of the security measures can be carried out directly using effectors, the user dialogue provides an important component for interacting with other tools and thus allowing for more complex security measures.

The user interface is based on the de facto standards X Windows and OSF/Motif. Object oriented interaction using icons is provided where ever possible.

III. MODELING

Large technical systems supply a huge amount of basis information. The security manager is flooded with information that needs to be filtered and prioritized. During the design and configuration phase of a system often mathematical models are used for optimization. These or related models can be used in support of the risk management during operation. The goal is the refinement of information (compression, aggregation, extraction of valuable data from status data and model assumptions). The results have to be transformed into a useful representation. At times, a simple aggregation may be sufficient to achieve significant values. As an analogy, the aggregation of millions of transactions to a balance sheet allows for a diagnosis of a firm.

More elaborate models are also necessary:

- from statistics (e.g. linear regression, variance analysis, trend analysis)
- from operations research (e.g. queueing theory, renewal theory, reliability theory, Monte Carlo simulation)
- models of communication flow
- physical models (e.g. energy supply, emanation)

Individual models or methods are understood quite well. However, the integration of heterogenous models is still a problem. In principle, this can be achieved two ways, through closed modeling or open modeling.

CLOSED MODELING

This approach unites all aspects in a huge closed model. An extreme example is the so-called world models. Their disadvantages are:

- almost complete modeling of the system is required
- model assumptions are hard to understand
- final results are difficult to verify due to a lack of intermediate results
- not enough support for detailed decisions

In addition there are practical problems:

- development, enhancement, and adjustment to a specific system are very work intensive
- high usage of resources causes problems in online operation
- correctness of the implementation is difficult to verify

All these reasons discredit the approach of a closed modeling in a security control center.

OPEN MODELING

This alternative approach uses a class of loosely coupled models. The advantages are:

- extendability of the original approach (new models can be added, simple models can be replaced by more complex models)
- easy adoption to changes
- step-by-step increase of input and output

Open modeling is easier to use in online operation. It is also more practical for the user because already known models are realized in separate components and not buried under a huge complex model.

The coupling of models requires great care. This is done using shared data from the database (see architecture figure). After compression of the input (e.g. aggregated audit and sensor data) in the factual models the results are written into the database. These results together with requested factual data (e.g. asset values, threats and vulnerabilities, direct and consequential losses for typical loss events) can be accessed by the next models. These models in turn read the database

and write their results into it. New models can build on this construct.

The flow of control is distinguished into three parts:

- system under observation is the trigger: certain models will become active when system data arrive
- other models are the trigger: results from different models may be needed, or additional models need to be activated (internal alarms)
- security manager is the trigger: user dialogue may activate models

The individual models need to fulfill the following requirements:

- common modeling philosophy
- compatible model assumptions
- balanced modeling depth
- common input data (syntax and semantics) if possible
- common output data (syntax and semantics) if possible

This approach allows for complementary modeling, i.e. reaching similar conclusion using different paths and thus verifying the results. Alternate security scenarios can be applied and analyzed.

IV. CONCLUSION

The technique of complex distributed systems introduces serious security problems. The security risks involved demand a powerful online risk management. The responsible security manager must be supported by a security control center.

The security control center extracts from the system's inherent data (audit, sensor, and network management) the necessary information to perform a risk assessment and initiates the appropriate counter measures. Mathematical models are essential in describing the security relevant features of an IT system. Open modeling allows for the suitable application of loosely coupled models.

The online risk management is a cross section topic applicable to complex systems and networks, e.g. power generation or communication systems. A security control center is needed where ever security aspects must be treated in a unified approach.

ACKNOWLEDGEMENT

We would like to thank the members of the risk management project, Anja Hentschel, Hans Lindmeyr, and Frank Schalkowski, for their valuable contributions.

REFERENCES

DIN 66234 Teil 8. Bildschirmarbeitsplätze: Grundsätze ergonomischer Dialoggestaltung. February 1988.

Fichtner, J. and Persy, C. (1992). Risk Management für IT-Systeme - Übersicht über vorhandene Methoden und Werkzeuge. H. Lippold and P. Schmitz (Eds.): Sicherheit in netzgestützten Informationssystemen. Vieweg, Braunschweig.

Fites, P. E, Kratz, M. P. J. and Brebner, A. F. (1989). Control and Security of Computer Information Systems. Computer Science Press, Rockville, MD.

Hofstetter, I. et al. (1990). Implementation Specification for a Distributed System Observation Facility. Deliverable D1 of Subtask IV.2.1, Esprit Project COMANDOS.

ISO IEC 7498-4. Management Framework.

ITSEC (1991). Information Technology Security Evaluation Criteria. Provisional Harmonised Criteria. Office for Official Publications of the European Communities.

Katzke, S. W. (1991). A Framework for Computer Security Risk Management. B. J. Garrik and W. C. Gekler (Eds.), The Analysis, Communication, and Perception of Risk. Plenum Press, New York. pp. 361-473.

Lunt, T. F. (1988). Automated Audit Trail Analysis and Intrusion Detection: A Survey. Proceedings of the 11th National Computer Security Conference. October 1988, Washington D. C., pp. 65-73.

Meitner, H. (1991). Modellierung und Analyse von Ausfallrisiken in verteilten Informationssystemen. H. Lippold, P. Schmitz and H. Kersten (Eds.): Sicherheit in Informationssystemen. Vieweg, Braunschweig. pp. 75-87.

SNI (1990). Styleguide - Richtlinien zur Gestaltung von Benutzeroberflächen, V1.0, Siemens Nixdorf Informationssysteme.

TCSEC (1985). Trusted Computer System Evaluation Criteria. Department of Defense. DoD 5200.28-STD. December 1985.

Weiss, W. and Baur, A. (1990). Analysis of Audit and Protocol Data using Methods from Artificial Intelligence. Proceedings of the 13th National Computer Security Conference. October 1990, Washington D. C., pp. 109-114.

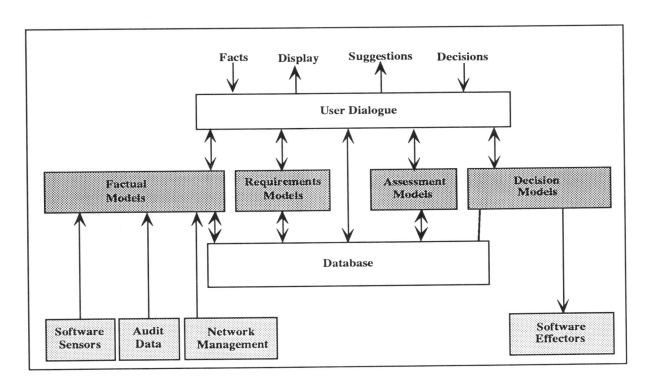

Architecture of the Security Control Center

MODELING USERS' BEHAVIOR AND THREATS FOR SECURITY

S. Castano   P. Samarati

Dipartimento di Scienze dell'Informazione
Università degli Studi di Milano
Via Comelico, 39/41
20135 - Milano - ITALY
e-mail: {castano, samarati}@imiucca.csi.unimi.it

Abstract. This paper describes a system for detecting security violations in a target system, preventing users from ending attacks, during system use. Detection is based on the hypothesis that a correlation exists between threats and anomalous behavior of the users. Detection is enforced by control rules using the fuzzy logic for evaluating the possibility that a user is attempting violations. Upon detection of suspicious and dangerous situations, the Security Administrator is alarmed.

Keywords. Auditing, Behavior, Fuzzy systems, Modeling, Monitoring, Safety, Security.

INTRODUCTION

Protection of information is usually enforced at the very moment of the access request, by access control mechanisms, that prevent unauthorized accesses to data. However, also when an access control mechanisms are used, violations can happen. For instance, authorized users can misuse of their privileges, or exploit existing system flaws for accessing protected data. To detect if the system has been violated, additional off-line controls (audit controls) are usually employed, for examining all the actions executed by users on the system. Such controls provide only a post-facto analysis, and a violation may be pointed out much time after its occurrence. Moreover, audit controls are very complex, due to the amount of data to be examined, and their completeness depends on both the completeness of the information recorded in the audit trail, and on the capability of the auditor(s) of finding suspicious actions and violations during analysis.

This paper describes a system able to detect security violations to a target system, based on the analysis and evaluation of user behavior during the system use. The system we propose controls violations attempted either by outsiders trying to penetrate the system or by insiders misusing of their privileges, by analyzing the audit trail.

The problem of enforcing audit systems based on user behavior has been already considered by researchers. Real-time expert systems that semantically enrich security mechanisms and enforce control rules for detecting security violations are proposed in [Bonfils 1987, Tener 1986]. In [Denning 1987] a threat detection system based on the hypothesis that security violations can be detected by monitoring the system activities involving abnormal usage of system is proposed. Metrics and statistical models are used to evaluate observed behaviors and to detect abnormal ones. The use of fuzzy logic is proposed in [Hoffman 1978] to off-line evaluate the protection level of a given system. In [Brignone 1986] the fuzzy logic is used to combine unauthorized user requests (assigned a weight) disconnecting the user when the combined weight of a sequence of requests exceeds a predefined threshold.

The system described in this paper detects threats, based on the hypothesis that a correlation exists between threats and anomalous behavior of the users. User behavior is defined as the collection of all actions initiated by the user. Our system proposes the use of control rules, defined embedding the knowledge about the correlation between anomalous actions and threats. Control rules use the fuzzy logic to evaluate the possibility that a user is attempting violations on the system. Upon detection of suspicious and dangerous situations an alarm is sent to the Security Administrator (SA). A prototype of the system has been developed using the Common Lisp programming language on a Sun 3/50 workstation [Carrettoni 1991].

The paper is organized as follows. In Sect.2 the system activities are described. In Sect.3 data acquisition and formalization activity is described. In Sect.4 the anomaly detection process is presented. In Sect.5 and in Sect. 6 the threat evaluation and the behavior update processes are described.

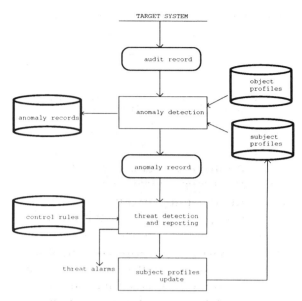

Fig. 1 Threat detection phases

SYSTEM ACTIVITIES

The system working is characterized by the following phases:

- <u>Acquisition and formalization</u> of the data concerning the target system environment (i.e., data concerning subjects and objects). Such activity is performed by the SA only the first time the system is used, to collect data about the protection requirements of the target system. During this phase the system defines the subject profiles and the object profiles used in the following phases for the detection process.
- User behavior analysis and <u>anomaly detection</u>. During this phase, the system analyzes behavior of the users, in form of audit records incoming from the target system, to detect anomalous actions, according to what is considered normal use of the system resources. Upon detection of anomalous actions, the systems defines anomaly records, for describing each detected anomaly.
- <u>Threat detection and reporting</u>. The system evaluates how much dangerous the anomalous behavior detected in the previous phase is. The evaluation is enforced by control rules, embedding the knowledge about the correlation between anomalous behavior and threats, i.e., what anomalous actions are symptomatic for which threats.
- <u>Subject profile update</u>. During this phase, the system determines the appropriate level of danger of each user, in order to reflect the level of danger reached during each session.

The first phase is done only the first time the system is used. Remaining phases constitute the threat detection activities (Fig. 1) always enforced by the system.

In the following sections each phase is described.

ACQUISITION AND FORMALIZATION

In order the system work correctly, data describing the target environment must be provided the first time the system is used. Such data describe the characteristics of the subjects and the objects of the system. Responsible for providing the data about the subjects and objects of the target system is the SA, who is concerned with the following activities:

• Definition of the legitimate users and definition of the classes of users, according to the activities performed and/or the roles played by the users (e.g., programmers, final users) [Bianchini 1990, Castano 1992].

• Definition of the objects, i.e., logical (e.g., relations, tuples) and physical (e.g., terminals, printers) resources to be protected, and definition of possible classes of objects. Objects classes are generally defined to group resources having similar protection requirements, reducing the quantity of data to be managed by the system. Moreover, the SA should specify what is considered normal use of the objects by users, i.e., what operations users and user classes can perform on objects, and under which time and location conditions they should be performed.

• Definition of additional anomalous behaviors (i.e., combinations of anomalous actions) related to specific threats of the system under control. Our system automatically defines the corresponding control rules, enriching the base set of control rules provided by the system (see sections "Threat detection and reporting" for the definition of control rules).

After collecting data about the target environment, the system formalizes data concerning subjects and objects, in form of subject and object profiles, i.e., data structures used by the system during the monitoring and detection phases.

Subject profiles

According to information provided by the SA about the users and user classes, our system automatically defines the corresponding subject profiles. Subjects are the users and user classes. We consider actions executed by a process, i.e., a program acting on behalf of a user, referred to the user who initiated the process.

A subject profile is a triple:

$< Subject\_id, Subject\_Class, User\_Weights>$

describing:
- the identifier of the subject;
- the class(es) the user belongs to;
- the "level of danger" actually reached by the user, i.e., how much dangerous the system considers the user, according to the type and the number of anomalous actions he/she executed in past sessions. In particular, User_Weights component of the triplet is a table of pairs:

$< rule\_id, weight>$

in which the first component identifies a given control rule (and, consequently, the threat the rule is referred to), and the second component is a real number expressing how much dangerous is the subject in reference to the threat detected by the rule. User weights are introduced to get flexibility in the application of the control rules. The more dangerous the subject is considered in reference to a given threat, the greater the corresponding weight becomes, and consequently the more restrict the rule behaves for that subject. User weights are updated at the end of each session. At the creation of the profile, the system automatically sets to one the User_Weights component, which is the default level of danger assigned to users.

Each subject profile is univocally identified by the Subject_id component.

Object profiles

Object profiles define what is considered normal use of the system, and are automatically fulfilled by the system according to information about the objects and object classes provided by the SA.

An object profile is a 5-uple:

$<Object\_id, Subject\_Class, Action, Time, Location>$

describing:

- the subject class allowed to access the object;
- the type of actions;
- the time and location conditions under which specified actions are considered normal for the object.

For an object (or object class) several object profiles can exist, describing different subject classes and/or types of actions. Each object profile is univocally identified by the Object_id, Subject_Class and Action components.

ANOMALY DETECTION

During this phase, the system analyzes the audit records incoming from the target system, for detecting the anomalous actions requested by the users.

Before describing how the anomaly detection is enforced, let us describe how the audit records and the anomaly records are defined.

Audit records

Audit records are generated by the target system. An audit record is created for both actions denied and granted, either those terminated and those aborted.

An audit record is a 6-uple:

$<Subject\_id, Action, Object\_id, Term\_Number,$
$Time\_Loc, Er\_Cod>$

whose components describe respectively:

- the subject requesting the action;
- the type of action requested;
- the object on which the action was requested;
- the time and location at which the action was requested;
- an error code (only for unauthorized and aborted actions), expressing the type of error associated with the request.

Some user requests can involve multiple objects. For example compiling a program implies to access three different objects: the source file in the read mode, the object file in the write mode and the compiler program in the execute mode. Our system requires every user action be split into elementary or single-object actions, involving only one object. For example, the compiling request is decomposed into three single-object actions seen above, and the corresponding audit records are generated. The task of defining audit records in the appropriate format is left to the target system. A filter can be added, which takes as input the audit records and translates them into the appropriate format.

Anomaly records

Anomaly records are generated upon observation of anomalous actions. An anomaly record is a 5-uple:

<Subject, Action, Object, Anomaly, Occ_Number>

describing:

- the subject of the action. Although the action is always requested by a single user, the subject field can be either a single user (subject_id), or a class of users (class identifier). Class identifiers are used to consider together all the operations performed by any member of the class, to point out global anomalous behavior of the class not referred to any particular user. Considering classes, actions performed by any member of the class are taken into consideration and concur in updating the record. The class "all" is predefined and denotes the set composed of every user of the system;
- operation requested (performed or attempted);
- object (class of objects) on which the action was requested. This component can refer to either a single object (object_id) or a class of objects (class identifier). Anomaly records referred to a class of objects point out threats involving the whole class. Then, actions executed on any object of the class are taken into consideration and concur in updating the record. The predefined class "all" denotes the set composed of all the objects of the system;
- reasons for which action was considered anomalous;
- how many times the anomaly involving the specific subject, object (or member belonging to them in case classes are specified), and action occurred.

Anomaly records are univocally identified by the Subject, Action, Object, and Anomaly components.

Depending on whether the subject and object components of the 5-uple are referred to single subjects and objects or to classes of them, we can control different situations. More precisely our system can control actions performed by: single subjects on single objects (Subject_id-Object_id), single subjects on class of objects (Subject_id-Class identifier), any subject belonging to a class on a single object (Class identifier-Object_id), a single subject on any object of the system (Subject_id - All), any subject on a given object (All-Object_id), a class of subjects on any object (Class identifier - All), by any subjects a class of objects (All - Class identifier), whichever subject on whichever object in the system (All-All).

The set of all the anomaly records defined by the system is stored in the anomaly record base.

Anomaly detection process

Each audit record incoming from the target system is analyzed, with the purpose of detecting anomalous actions. Anomalous actions include:

- actions denied by the access control mechanisms of the target system,
- actions granted by the access control mechanisms of the target system but aborted,
- actions granted by the target system access control mechanisms and fulfilled by the users, for which no object profile matching them can be found.

Upon detection of anomalous actions, the anomaly record base is updated, to record the new detected anomaly.

Depending on the anomalous action pointed out, two situation can occur:

- Update of the anomaly record base
  The anomalous action just detected is described by already existing anomaly record(s). In this case, existing anomaly record(s) is(are) updated, incrementing by one their Occ_Number component;

- Creation of a new anomaly record
  It is the first time the anomalous action is pointed out. New anomaly record(s) is(are) created, for describing the type of anomaly just detected. Occurrence_number field of the new anomaly record(s) is(are) initialized to one.

A single audit record can give origin to more than one update/insertion, depending on the different formats by which the information regarding the anomaly has to be described (e.g., if both user and class behavior is monitored, anomalous actions executed by single users lead to update/insertion of the anomaly records related to both the user and the user classes).

Any inserted/updated anomaly record is passed for the threat detection process.

THREAT DETECTION AND REPORTING

During this phase, each anomaly record passed is evaluated, to establish the level of danger of the threat related to the anomalous behavior pointed out.

Control rules are enforced to detect the threats acting in the system and evaluate how much dangerous the threats are, in reference also to the subjects involved. Control rules are defined embedding the knowledge about the correlation between anomalous behavior and threats, i.e., which is the user behavior that usually is shown by users attempting a threat.

As previously seen, the SA can specify, during the initial acquisition and formalization phase, anomalous behaviors related to threats typical of the environment to be protected. Our system provides to the definition of the corresponding control rules. Let us describe how control rules are defined.

Control rules

A control rule is composed of a set of triggers, a body and a weight_table.

<u>Triggers</u>. Patterns to be matched with the anomaly records passed for the evaluation. Satisfaction of one of them fires the rule.
It is described by a 5-uple:

$$<S_i, A_i, O_i, Ano_i, Occ>$$

where the first three components are variables matching, respectively:
- the subject involved in the event. It can represent a single subject or a class of subjects;
- the action in the anomaly records. It can be also a value, in which case only the anomaly records having that value match such components;
- the object involved in the event. It can represent a single object or a class of objects.

Remaining components of the 5-uple define respectively:
- the anomaly symptomatic for the threat,
- how many times the anomaly involving the specific elements of the 5-uple has been recorded.

Variables can be free (the trigger matches every anomaly record passed) or bound to some values, in which case the trigger matches the anomaly records satisfying the constraints.

<u>Body</u>. The body of the rule is composed of an antecedent and a consequent.

The <u>antecedent</u> is an AND/OR expression of patterns to be matched with the anomaly records passed for the evaluation. Patterns have the form:

$$(S_i, A_i, O_i, Ano_i, Occ)$$

where elements can be free or bound to some value. Other constraints can be put on the variables. The Occ field is always free. In the rule evaluation process the Occ field will be bound to the value of the occurrence field of the anomaly record matching the pattern.

An rule antecedent is satisfied whenever anomaly records matching the patterns exist, that satisfy the AND/OR expression. Some variables require the elements binding them to be the same.
For instance, in the expression:
$(S_i, "read", O_i, "Er\_Cod3", Occ_i)$ AND $(S_i, "write", O_i, "Er\_Cod3", Occ_j)$
the subject and the object of an anomaly record passed for the evaluation have to be the same, whereas the values of the occurrence fields in the two patterns can be different.

The consequent of a control rule states the actions to be executed when the antecedent is satisfied, and the situation represent a threat (i.e., the computed weight is greater than the threshold specified for that rule). Typically, such actions consist in sending messages and alarms to the SA.

<u>Weight table</u>. A weight table is a 7 column table. Tuples of the table have the form:

$$<Subj\_class, Obj\_class, Action, Anomaly, Occurrence, Weight, Threshold>$$

defining the weight to be assigned to each occurrence of an anomaly, in reference to the subject and object classes involved.

Given a value of the first four elements of the tuple, greater weights are assigned to greater occurrences of an anomalous action, expressing the membership function of the anomalous action to the fuzzy set representing the threat [Klir 1988]. Weights express how dangerous should the situation be considered, depending on the subject, object, action and anomaly involved, and on how many times the anomaly has been recorded. Weights range from 0 (the situation is considered no dangerous at all) to 1 (the system believes the situation to represent a threat in any case). Intermediate values give a measure of the level of danger of the situation per se, without considering the actual level of danger of the involved subjects. The real level of danger of such a situation is determined during the evaluation process, depending on the actual level of danger of the involved subjects (see next section for details).

Threshold component in the 7-uple specifies the value exceeding which leads to alarm generation. Default threshold is set to 1. Values less than 1 may be specified by the SA, forcing threat detection before users end the threat.

Threat detection process

Threat detection is a fuzzy logic based process. Upon reception of an anomaly record, control rule base is checked, firing every rule whose triggers match the anomaly record just passed.

When a rule is fired, its antecedent is evaluated. If the antecedent is not satisfied, no threat is pointed out. Let AR be an anomaly record passed for the evaluation. Satisfaction of an antecedent is established using the following conditions:
- the OR operator between two patterns is satisfied if at least one of them is satisfied, i.e., if AR matches at least one of the two patterns;

- the AND operator between two patterns is satisfied if both of them are satisfied, i.e., if AR satisfies both the patterns, or if AR satisfies at least one of them, and another anomaly record exists satisfying the other pattern.

The antecedent is satisfied if all the OR and all the AND operators included are satisfied, by AR and by the existing anomaly records. If more than one anomaly record satisfying the pattern exist, then the different cases are considered separately.

After the satisfaction of the antecedent, the values of the elements in the different patterns are bound. Let us call evaluation record a pattern bound to given values. Evaluation is enforced using the weight_table associated to the rule.

For each evaluation record, the tuple in the weight_table is selected having the same values of anomaly, action, occurrence components of the evaluation record, and having the subject_class and object_class components such that the subject and object of the evaluation record are member of them.

Weight of the selected tuple is multiplied by the weight of the user specified in evaluation record, related to the executed rule (selected from the User_Weights table of the corresponding subject profile). Let us call this value relative weight.

All the relative weights computed for the evaluation records of an antecedent are combined, replacing AND/OR operators with MIN/MAX operators respectively [Klir 1988]. The result is a numerical value, called global weight, expressing how much dangerous the observed anomalous behavior is. If the value is greater than the threshold specified in the selected tuple, the SA is alarmed, notifying the threat and the involved users.

SUBJECT PROFILES UPDATE

During this phase, the system provides to update, at the end of each user session, the subject profile of the users, to reflect the level of danger reached by users during the session. A new weight is computed for each threat in which the user has been involved during the session, preferably for the rules in which the global weight computed for the threat exceeds a predefined acceptance threshold (e.g., 0.5). This to prevent the system to behave too much strictly, forbidding the users to perform accidental mistakes and unauthorized actions.

For the selected rules, new user weights are computed considering the global weight each rule and the total number of occurrences of anomalous actions in which the user is involved. The quantity (global weight / total occurrences) is computed and summed up to the actual user weight associated to the rule in the subject profile. In such a way, the user is assigned a weight increasing with the number of anomalous actions he/she performed. So,

the more dangerous the user is considered in reference to a given threat, the greater the corresponding weight becomes, and consequently the more restrict the rule behaves for that user.

Update of the weights related to a class of users is done in the same way, considering the rules fired by anomalous behavior of each member of the class.

CONCLUSIONS

A system for detecting security threats during the system use has been presented in this paper. Detection is based on the hypothesis that a correlation exists between threats and anomalous behavior of the users, and is enforced by control rules using the fuzzy logic, preventing users from ending the threat. Upon detection of suspicious and dangerous situations, the Security Administrator is alarmed. Further research work is needed to complete the model of the system. In particular, criteria to automatically updating and controlling the user classes behavior are being studied, and rules for evaluating the global behavior of users are being developed, considering at the same time all the threats attempted by users.

Acknowledgements. Part of this work has been supported the Italian National Research Council Project "Sistemi Informatici e Calcolo Parallelo", L.R.C. INFOKIT. Discussions and common work with Prof. G. Martella is gratefully acknowledged.

REFERENCES

Bonfils, E., I. Mamadou, and S. Miranda, (1987). An Expert Data Security System (EDSS), BAOU research report n.52, University of Nizza

Bianchini M., G. Martella, P. Samarati, (1990). Un Sistema di Sicurezza per la Protezione dei Documenti nei Sistemi Informativi di Ufficio, in Proc. AICA Annual Conference, Bari, 907-933

Brignone, A. (1986). Fuzzy sets: an answer to evaluation of security systems?, in Proc. IFIP/Sec. 86, MonteCarlo

Carrettoni, F., S. Castano, G. Martella, and P.Samarati, (1991) "RETISS: a REal TIme Security System for threat detection using fuzzy logic", in Proc. 25th IEEE Int. Carnahan Conf. on Security Technology, Taiwan

Castano, S., and P. Samarati, (1992). An Object-Oriented Security Model for Office Environments, in Proc. 26th IEEE Int. Carnahan Conf. on Security Technology, Atlanta

Denning, D.E. (1987). An intrusion detection model, IEEE Trans. on Software Engineering, Vol.13, N.2, 222-232

Hoffman, L.J., E.H. Michelman, and D. Clements, (1978). SECURATE - Security evaluation and analysis using fuzzy metrics, in Proc. of the Nat. Computer Conference

Klir, G.J., and T.A. Folger, (1988). Fuzzy Sets, Uncertainty and Information, Prentice Hall, Englewood Cliffs, New Jersey 07632

Tener, W.T. (1986). Discovery: an expert system in the commercial data security environment, in Proc. IFIP/Sec. 86, Montecarlo

RELIABILITY EVALUATION OF COMMUNICATION NETWORKS

Mohamed El Khadiri and Gerardo Rubino

IRISA
Campus de Beaulieu, 35042 Rennes Cedex, FRANCE

Abstract. In the evaluation of the capacity of a communication network architecture to resist to the possible faults of some of its components, several reliability metrics are currently used. The evaluation of these metrics is in general a very costly task since most of them are, as algorithmic problems, classed in the NP–hard family. As a consequence, many different techniques have been proposed to solve them. We discuss here a promising class of methods called "factorization" and some of the implementation issues. An alternative approach to these exact techniques is to perform statistical estimations using a Monte Carlo simulation. It allows to deal with larger networks (having, say, hundreds of components) if the user accepts probabilistic answers. In the case of highly reliable networks, the standard Monte Carlo technique is also prohibitively expensive and variance reduction techniques must be used. We propose here a new Monte Carlo algorithm specifically designed to this context. For both approaches, exact and simulation algorithms, numerical results are provided allowing a comparison and giving an idea of the performances that can be expected.

Keywords. Network analysers, reliability, large-scale systems, Monte Carlo methods, graph theory, stochastic systems.

INTRODUCTION

Consider a communication network topology from the point of view of its reliability when some of its components may fail. Given the ("elementary") reliabilities of these components and the structure of the system, we want to quantify the behaviour of the entire network faced to these failures. It is then usual to model it by a graph corresponding to the network topology, whose components are weighted by their elementary reliabilities. The graph is then used to evaluate a global reliability metrics. This is a binary system, that is, components and the whole system can be in one out of two states: either working or failed, the reliability being the probability of the first event. Moreover, the states of the different components are assumed to be s-independent. This classical approach is used not only for the evaluation of communication networks but also, for instance, for block-diagram analysis of complex systems.

We assume that the graph is undirected (undirectionnal communication channels) and that nodes are perfect (that is, not subject to failures.) The standard reliability measures for the entire system consider a subset K of the set of nodes and define the probability R that the nodes in K can communicate. In graph terms, R is the probability that there is at least a path between any pair of nodes in K with all its lines working. The case of $K = \{s, t\}$ is the fundamental one in this context. It is also called the source-to-terminal or 2-terminal one, and we will concentrate on it in the paper, but the results presented here basically hold in the general case.

This problem (and other related reliability problems) has received considerable attention from the research community. See Locks and Satyarayana (1986) and Colbourn (1987) for many references. One of the reasons is that in the general case, the problems are in the #P-complete class, a family of NP-hard problems not known to be in NP (Ball, 1986). More specifically, exact techniques can only deal, in general, with "medium size" models (say with a few dozens of components) and in any case, the computational cost is high (see the numerical results given later.) To have an idea of the difficulties here, let us fix some notation. The graph modelling the network is $\mathcal{G} = (\mathcal{V}, \mathcal{E})$ where $\mathcal{V}$ is the set of vertices and $\mathcal{E}$ is the set of edges. Let us denote by N the number of nodes and by M the number of edges. The elementary reliability of edge e is r_e. Let us denote by $\{\pi_1, \ldots, \pi_{MP}\}$ the set of minpaths between nodes S and T in any given order. Let P_i denote the event "every line in the minpath π_i is working." From the independence assumption, we have $\Pr(P_i) = \prod_{e \in \pi_i} r_e$. The reliability R is the probability of the union of all P_i's. By Poincare's formula we have

$$R = \sum_{h=1}^{MP} (-1)^{h-1} \sum_{i_1 < i_2 < \cdots < i_h} \Pr(P_{i_1} . P_{i_2} . \cdots . P_{i_h})$$

This is even worse than complete state enumeration which considers the whole state space of size 2^M, since the previous formula contains $2^{MP} - 1$ terms. However, it can be shown that it leads to many terms being cancelled out. In Satyanarayana (1982) and in Satyanarayana and Prabhakar (1978), the authors give algorithms that generate only the resulting terms.

Another approach consists of applying the following transformation (disjoint products sum):

$$P_1 \cup P_2 \cup \cdots \cup P_{MP} =$$

$$P_1 \cup \overline{P}_1 . P_2 \cup \cdots \cup \overline{P}_1 . \overline{P}_2 . \ldots . \overline{P}_{MP-1} . P_{MP}$$

in which we denote by $\overline{P}_i$ the complement of P_i. This relation involves MP terms "only." However, they are much more complex and difficult to obtain. A well known example of a method based on this relation is the Abraham algorithm (Abraham, 1979). See also Ahmad (1982) and the "supercubes" algorithm in Marie and Rubino (1988). The generation of the MP minpaths between S and T is an expensive problem itself (it belongs to the #P-complete class) and the computation of the probability of each term in the disjoint products expansion is also expensive. The complexity of the 2-terminal reliability in the number of minpaths is still an open issue in the context of undirected graphs.

FACTORING ALGORITHMS

A different class of methods to compute exactly the reliability R is the family of factoring algorithms. They perform quite well and they are based on the following simple ideas. The contraction of edge $e = \{x, y\}$ of $\mathcal{G}$ consists of eliminating the line e and "merging" the two extremities x and y. The resulting graph is denoted by $\mathcal{G}_e^c$. The result of deleting line e is denoted by $\mathcal{G}_e^d$. Making explicit the dependency of R with respect to $\mathcal{G}$ and conditionning on the state of e, we have

$$R(\mathcal{G}) = r_e R(\mathcal{G}_e^c) + (1 - r_e) R(\mathcal{G}_e^d). \qquad (1)$$

Relation (1) says that we can reduce the problem of computing the reliability of $\mathcal{G}$ to the computation of the reliabilities of two smaller graphs,

$\mathcal{G}_e^c$ and $\mathcal{G}_e^d$. Of course, applying (1) recursively deals to a binary tree with $2^M - 1$ nodes (and 2^{M-1} leaves.) To diminish this combinatorial explosion, a simplification technique as, for instance, a series–parallel reduction, is performed before the recursive application of (1). These simplifications can be performed in polynomial time, which implies that the overhead is negligible with respect to the cost of the whole reliability algorithm. On the other side, the gain can be considerable. Let us recall that two edges are in S, T-series if they are adjacent and they have only one common vertex with degree two and different from S or T. A S, T-series reduction consists of replacing two edges in S, T-series by a single edge between the not shared vertices. It receives as its elementary reliability the product of the reliabilities of the previous ones. Two edges e_1, e_2 are in parallel if they have the same vertices and a parallel reduction consists of replacing them by a single edge between the same vertices. The reliability of the new edge is $r_{e_1} + r_{e_2} - r_{e_1} r_{e_2}$. These definitions extend immediately to more than 2 edges.

As deleting and contracting lead to smaller graphs, sooner or later simplifications will appear reducing the size of the constructed tree. To be more specific, let us formalize the method in the form of a recursive procedure.

```
procedure FACT(G)
    reduce(G,G');
    if bond(G') then
        return fiabBond(G');
    e := chooseEdge(G');
    return r[e]*FACT(G'_e^c)
        + (1 - r[e])*FACT(G'_e^d)
end procedure
```

The simplification is performed by the $reduce()$ procedure, where $\mathcal{G}'$ denotes the reduction of $\mathcal{G}$. A bond is a graph composed by a single line. The $bond(\mathcal{G})$ function returns **true** iff $\mathcal{G}$ is a bond and $fiabBond(\mathcal{G})$ returns the reliability of (the single edge of) the bond $\mathcal{G}$.

This is a family of algorithms basically for two reasons: First, the simplification procedure needs not to be the series–parallel reduction. For instance, in Wood (1985) a different technique (the so-called polygon–to–chain reduction) is considered. Second, for a given simplification method, the algorithm is "indexed" by the strategy used to choose the edge whose state will be used to condition on. This is a crucial point. Different strategies may lead to different numbers of nodes in the related binary tree constructed by the recursive algorithm. For instance, with series–parallel reductions, the optimal binary tree is obtained from *domination theory* in Satyanarayana and Chang (1983). Their main result states that if $\mathcal{G}$ is S,T-irreducible, S,T-coherent and if it is not a bond (S,T-coherent means that any edge of $\mathcal{G}$ belongs to a minpath between S and T), there exists an edge e such that both graphs $\mathcal{G}_e^c$ and $\mathcal{G}_e^d$ are S,T-coherent and if the *choose*() function in the algorithm selects such an edge, then the number of leaves of the corresponding binary tree is minimal. This number of leaves is an important invariant of the graph, called *domination* and denoted by $D_{S,T} = D_{S,T}(\mathcal{G})$. It can be defined independently, for instance, as the absolute value of the difference between the number of S,T-formations with an odd number of minpaths and the number of S,T-formations with an even number of minpaths (a S,T-formation is a set of minpaths between S and T such us the union of all their edges is $\mathcal{E}$.) An important property of this invariant is that for any edge e, $D_{S,T}(\mathcal{G}) = D_{S,T}(\mathcal{G}_e^c) + D_{S,T}(\mathcal{G}_e^d)$. The authors also give practical insights into the implementation of such a strategy showing that it can be based on the decomposition into triconnected components. See also Wood (1986) for a discussion on the subject. Hopcroft and Tarjan (1973) give a $O(M)$ method to split a graph into its triconnected components. The implementation of their algorithm is a hard task and to our knowledge, there is no report on numerical results of a factoring algorithm corresponding to this optimal version. For instance, Resende (1988) proposes a $O(M^2)$ choice technique procedure and Page and Perry (1988) select randomly the edge used to condition on.

We implemented the optimal selection strategy and we present here some numerical results. Consider first complete graphs, that is, graphs with an edge between every pair of vertices. For n nodes, the complete graph is usually denoted by K_n and it has $n(n - 1)/2$ lines. The following table gives the evolution of the computer time when n increses and the corresponding number of leaves in any optimal tree.

Real networks designs have more sparse structures. Figure 1 shows a topology corresponding better with communication networks. In real architectures, there is more irregular and, in general, sparse configurations. The analysis of this graph takes about 7 hrs on a Sun-4 workstation. Observe that this computational cost does not depend on the value of the elementary reliabilities, in contrast with Monte Carlo techniques as we will see in the next section. Table 2 gives some numerical results of the factoring algorithm on this graph.

All the reported experiences say that, in general,

n	$L = D_{S,T}$	CPU time
8	720	3.5 secs
9	⁻5040	24.8 secs
10	40320	199.1 secs
11	362880	1784.0 secs
12	3628800	17747.9 secs

Table 1: The number L of leaves in the factorization binary tree and the executing time in seconds (Sun-4) of the factoring algorithm of Satyanarayana and Chang (1983) as a function of the number of vertices of the complete graph K_n. The domination of K_n is $D_{S,T}(K_n) = (n - 2)!$.

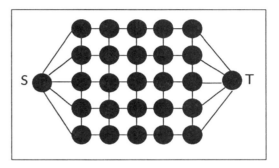

Figure 1: Regular topology used for tests (mean degree = 3.7.)

in the class of exact methods, factorisation performs fast. Our experiments confirm this. Another important property of factoring algorithms is that they need a storage of about $O(M^2)$ (recall that M is the number of edges) since the stack used to implement the recursive procedure has, at most, size M. In contrast, boolean techniques usually need to start from the set of minpaths (or mincuts) which are exponential in number, as a function of the size of the graph.

MONTE CARLO TECHNIQUES

Let us denote by X_e the random variable (r.v.) "state of edge e" with value 1 if e is working and 0 otherwise. To simplify the presentation, we denote by $\{1, 2, \ldots, M\}$ the set $\mathcal{E}$ of edges. We denote by $X = (X_1, \ldots, X_M)$ the system state random vector and by Φ the "structure function" defined by 1 if the network operates when its state is X, 0 otherwise. We have $R = \Pr(\Phi(X) = 1) = \mathrm{E}(\Phi(X))$. The random vector X defines a subgraph $\mathcal{G}(X)$ of $\mathcal{G}$ with the same node set and the edges e such that $X_e = 1$. Then, R is the probability that S and T are connected in $\mathcal{G}(X)$.

The estimation of the reliability R by the standard Monte Carlo method consists of generating s-independent samples $X^{(1)}, \ldots, X^{(N)}$ of X and

r	R
0.8	$1 - 5.89 \times 10^{-03}$
0.9	$1 - 1.12 \times 10^{-04}$
0.95	$1 - 2.60 \times 10^{-06}$
0.99	$1 - 6.41 \times 10^{-10}$
0.995	$1 - 1.94 \times 10^{-11}$
0.997	$1 - 1.49 \times 10^{-12}$
0.999	$1 - 5.87 \times 10^{-15}$

Table 2: Network reliability R when all the elementary reliabilities are equal to r, for different values of r, corresponding to the topology in Figure 1 (results of the factoring algorithm).

estimating the unknown parameter R by the unbiased estimator

$$\widehat{R} = \frac{1}{N} \sum_{i=1}^{N} \Phi(X^{(i)}).$$

The variance of this estimator is

$$\mathrm{V}(\widehat{R}) = \frac{R(1 - R)}{N}$$

and it is estimated by the unbiased estimator

$$\widehat{V} = \frac{\widehat{R}(1 - \widehat{R})}{N - 1}.$$

To implement this experiment on a computer (to simulate it), we use a pseudo-random version of each variable X_e and a depth-first search procedure to decide if nodes S and T are connected in the resulting pseudo-random subgraph of $\mathcal{G}$.

The experiments show that the time spent in the depth-first search procedure is very small compared to the time needed to generate each sample vector. For each sample of X, the generator of pseudo-random numbers will be called M times and it is clear that the time spent in this task does not depend on the topology of the model nor on the reliabilities of its edges. This can be improved considerably, by allowing the sampling to be made during the search task itself, which reduces the number of calls to the generator. We used this improved Monte Carlo procedure in El Khadiri and al. (1991), where numerical results illustrate the important obtained gains.

Consider now the case of very reliable networks (which is the usual situation.) For instance, assume that $R = 1 - 10^{-8}$ and that the computer experience consists of 10^7 trials. It can result in no system failure in the sample and might lead us to conclude that the network is perfect. To have a more formal view of this point, let us recall

a well known result of Bernstein: if $\alpha > 0$ and $0 < \varepsilon \leq R(1 - R)$, then

$$\Pr(|\widehat{R} - R| \geq \varepsilon) \leq \alpha$$

for any sample size N such that

$$N \geq \frac{9 \ln(\frac{2}{\alpha})}{8 \varepsilon^2}.$$

This shows that if the system is highly reliable, the standard Monte Carlo method requires a very large number of trials to give a good estimation of R. Table 3 gives an idea of the cost of evaluating the network of Figure 1.

r	$\widehat{R}$	ε	time
0.8	$1 - 6.12 \times 10^{-3}$	4.83×10^{-4}	37 sec
0.9	$1 - 1.20 \times 10^{-4}$	6.80×10^{-4}	34 sec
0.95	$1 - 2.77 \times 10^{-6}$	3.30×10^{-7}	7h 18 min

Table 3: Estimation $\widehat{R}$ of R, 5% half confidence interval length ε and execution time of the (improved) crude Monte-Carlo method, as a function of the common elementary reliability r of the edges of the network in Figure 1.

If we let $r = 0.99$, the value of R is so high that a crude Monte Carlo simulation will take years to give an accurate answer. We present here a new method for estimating the 2-terminal system reliability when all the lines are equally (and highly) reliable. It is based on the antithetic variates principle. The reader can see El Khadiri and Rubino (1992) for technical details about this method and Fishman(1986) and Kumamoto (1980) for previous work related to the use of antithetic variates in network reliability problems.

Let us denote by c the minimum cardinality cutset of the graph. This parameter can be computed by a preprocessing task in polynomial time. Let us denote by r the common elementary reliability of the lines, by $S = \{0, 1\}^M$ the space of vector states and by $\mathcal{O}_c$ the subset of S containing at most $c - 1$ components down. If we denote $R_c = \Pr(X \in \mathcal{O}_c)$, we have

$$R_c = \sum_{i=0}^{c-1} \frac{M!}{i!(M - i)!} r^{M-i} (1 - r)^i. \qquad (2)$$

Assume that $R_c \geq 0.5$ (which will always be the case in a highly reliable system.) We define the random vector W on S by

$$\Pr(W = x) = \Pr(X = x \mathbin{/} X \in \overline{\mathcal{O}_c}) \qquad (3)$$

The Bernouilli r.v. $\Phi(W)$ has success parameter $(R - R_c)/(1 - R_c)$.

Let us denote by L the value $\lfloor 1/(1 - R_c) \rfloor$ and split the interval $[0, L(1 - R_c)[$ into L sub-intervals $I_l = [(l-1)(1 - R_c), l(1 - R_c)[, \; l = 1, \ldots, L$. Let us define L r.v. Y_l, $l = 1, \ldots, L$, by

$$Y_l = \mathbf{1}_{\{U \notin I_l\}} + \Phi(W_l)\mathbf{1}_{\{U \in I_l\}} \qquad l = 1, ..., L \quad (4)$$

where U is a r.v. uniformly distributed on $[0, 1]$ and (W_l), $l = 1, \ldots, L$, are i.i.d r.v. distributed as W. Each variable Y_l is a Bernouilli r.v. distributed as $\Phi(X)$ and the algorithm uses it to estimate $E(\Phi(X)) = R$. In El Khadiri and Rubino (1992) we give the proofs of the claimed properties. In particular, we show that for each couple (l, l') we have $\mathrm{Cov}(Y_l, Y_{l'}) = -(1 - R)^2$.

The r.v. $\widehat{N}$ defined by

$$\widehat{N} = \frac{1}{L} \sum_{l=1}^{l=L} Y_l, \quad (5)$$

is an unbiaised estimator of R, with variance

$$\mathrm{V}(\widehat{N}) = \frac{R(1 - R)}{L} - \frac{(L - 1)(1 - R)^2}{L}. \quad (6)$$

Relation (6) implies that the estimator $\widehat{N}$ has a small variance than the standard estimator based on L independent samples of X and, consequently, it produces a more accurate technique to estimate R. Furthermore, the cost to generate the L samples is in the worst case the same to generate one sample by a standard method. In fact, when we generate an uniform pseudo-random number, if it belongs to the interval $[L(1 - R_c), 1[$ then all the Y_l's are in state 1; otherwise, there is only one interval I_l containing the generated number. In this case we generate a sample of W giving a state in $\overline{\mathcal{O}_c}$ and we perform a depth-first search to see if S and T are connected. The specific used procedure is described in El Khadiri and Rubino (1992).

To obtain at the same time an estimate of R and an estimate of the variance of the estimator we must use a s-ndependent sample $\widehat{N}_1, ..., \widehat{N}_B$ of the random variable $\widehat{N}$ and estimate R by means of $\widehat{R}_m$, defined by

$$\widehat{R}_m = \frac{1}{B} \sum_{b=1}^{B} \widehat{N}_b.$$

The variance of this estimator is

$$\mathrm{V}(\widehat{R}_m) = \frac{(1 - R)R}{BL} - \frac{(L - 1)(1 - R)^2}{BL}$$

and it can be estimated by the unbiased estimator

$$\widehat{V}_m = \frac{\sum_{b=1}^{B}(\widehat{N}_b - \widehat{R}_m)^2}{B(B - 1)}.$$

r	$\widehat{R}_m$	ε	time
0.95	$1 - 3.12 \times 10^{-6}$	8.83×10^{-07}	0.78 h
0.99	$1 - 8.33 \times 10^{-10}$	2.26×10^{-10}	0.45 h
0.995	$1 - 1.94 \times 10^{-11}$	1.20×10^{-11}	0.54 h
0.997	$1 - 2.38 \times 10^{-12}$	1.17×10^{-12}	0.51 h
0.999	$1 - 4.11 \times 10^{-15}$	3.04×10^{-15}	0.70 h

Table 4: Estimation $\widehat{R}$ of R, 5% half confidence interval length ε and execution time of the new Monte-Carlo method, as a function of the common elementary reliability r of the edges of the network in Figure 1.

Table 4 gives some results, always for the regular structure of Figure 1, when this algorithm is applied.

CONCLUSIONS

This work illustrate the problems that can arise when evaluating network reliability using exact techniques or Monte Carlo simulations. In the first case, we exhibit results of the factoring algorithm of Satyanarayana and Chang (1983), which is one of the most efficient known methods. To our knowledge, these are the first reported results of a complete implementation of the optimal version of this technique including the choice procedure in $O(M)$ using tri-connectivity theory. In the second, we propose a new variance reduction algorithm which performs very fast, designed for networks with highly reliable identical components.

REFERENCES

Abraham J.A. (1979). An improved algorithm for network reliability. IEEE Trans. on Reliab., R-28(1), 58–61.

Ahmad S. (1982). A simple technique for computing network reliability. IEEE Trans. Reliab., R-31(1).

Ball M.O. (1986). Computational complexity of network reliability analysis: an overview. IEEE Trans. Reliab., R-35(3).

Colbourn C.J. (1987). The Combinatorics of Network Reliability. Oxford University Press, New York.

El Khadiri M., Marie R. and Rubino G. (1991). Parallel estimation of 2-terminal network reliability by a crude Monte Carlo technique. In Baray M., Ozgüç B. editors, Sixth International Symposium on Computer and Information Sciences, 559–570, Antalya, Turkey.

El Khadiri M. and Rubino G. (1992). Efficient estimation of network reliability in the case of identical components. INRIA Research Report, Campus de Beaulieu, 35042 Rennes, France (to appear).

Fishman G.S. (1986). A comparison of four Monte Carlo methods for estimating the probability of s-t conectedness. IEEE Trans. Reliab., R-35(2).

Hopcroft J.E. and Tarjan R.E. (1973). Dividing a graph into triconnected components. SIAM J. Comput.

Kumamoto H., Tanaka K., Inoue K. and Henley E.G. (1980). Dagger-sampling Monte Carlo for system unavailability evaluation. IEEE Trans. Reliab., R-29(2).

Locks M.O. and Satyarayana A. editors (1986). Network reliability – the state of the art. IEEE Trans. Reliab., R-35(3).

Marie R. and Rubino G. (1988). Direct approaches to the 2-terminal reliability problem. In Orhun E., Gelembe E. and Başar E. editors, Third International Symposium on Computer and Information Sciences, 740–747, Ege University, Çeşme, Izmir, Turkey.

Page L.B. and Perry J.E. (1988). A practical implementation of the factoring theorem for network reliability. IEEE Trans. Reliab., 37(3), 259–267.

Resende L. (1988). Implementation of a factoring algorithm for reliability evaluation of undirected networks. IEEE Trans. Reliab., 37(5), 462–468.

Satyarayana A. (1982). A unified formula for the analysis of some network reliability problems. IEEE Trans. Reliab., R-31, 23–32.

Satyarayana A. and Chang M.K. (1983). Network reliability and the factoring theorem. Networks, 13.

Satyarayana A. and Prabhakar A. (1978). New topological formula and rapid algorithm for reliability analysis of complex networks. IEEE Trans. Reliab., R-27, 82–100.

Wood K. (1985). A factoring algorithm using polygon-to-chain reductions for computing k-terminal network reliability. Networks, 15, 173–190.

Wood K. (1986). Factoring algorithms for computing k-terminal network reliability. IEEE Trans. Reliab., R-35(3).

SAFETY ASSESSMENT OF COMPUTER SYSTEMS USING HAZOP AND AUDIT TECHNIQUES

M. F. Chudleigh
Cambridge Consultants Ltd, Science Park, Milton Road, Cambridge CB4 4DW

J. R. Catmur
Arthur D Little, Science Park, Milton Road, Cambridge CB4 4DW(on secondment to
TM Consult, Arturo Soria 92-V2, Madrid)

Abstract. Because of their many advantages the use of computer based systems is increasing
rapidly. The advantages have a price - complexity - and it is clear that increases in complexity
lead to increases in mistakes during system development. Such computer systems are being
used increasingly in situations where failure could affect safety adversely. A difficult area is to
decide on the most cost-effective way of assessing the safety of such systems. An approach
using HAZOP and management audit as key tools is effective. The traditional HAZOP, familiar
in the petrochemical industries, has been extended to explore the electronics and software
requiring knowledge of design techniques for safety critical hardware and software, knowledge
of the current and evolving standards, together with wide experience of the HAZOP
methodology. Typical results are described. Complementary to the HAZOP is a management
audit using case specific audit protocols and a small multi-disciplinary audit team. The
approach is considered applicable to all application areas.

Keywords. Safety; Hazard Analysis; Electronics; Software; Audit.

INTRODUCTION

The use of electronics and software in systems has
many advantages, including increased functionality,
increased flexibility and ease of use. Because of these
advantages their use is increasing dramatically,
including applications where failure could impact
safety adversely. For example, computer systems are
now widely used in transport systems. In cars, there
are many models with anti-lock braking and engine
management systems; on rail, much signalling is
computer controlled; in the air; automated systems are
beginning to be used to carry out functions
previously done by pilots.

Unfortunately, there is a price to be paid for the
advantages of computer systems: that price is the
potential for mistakes. The ease with which extra
functionality it may be added and more flexibility
built in often leads to systems which are overly
complex. During system design, the more complex
the design is, the more difficult it is to reason about it
logically and this difficulty leads to human mistakes
being made. The more mistakes that are made during
system design and implementation, the greater the
chance that those mistakes are not found. The
mistakes will remain latent until a particular set of
operating conditions triggers a system fault which
leads to failure. These failure modes are unpredictable
and some of them could compromise system safety.

Such failures are referred to as systematic in contrast
to random failures which arise from degradation
mechanisms in the hardware. Systematic failures
arise from mistakes at each phase of the system life:
quantifying systematic failure rates is difficult,
particularly when considering safety critical systems
where failures are rare events. It should be noted that
all software failures are systematic *but* not all
systematic failures are in software. It is the
complexity inherent in the system which governs its
propensity for systematic failures.

With safety critical systems a staged approach is
needed to establish the risk, use development
methods which match the required integrity, verify
and validate the system. Assessment of the process
and product is a necessary part of assuring the safety
of systems and the need for independent assessment is
brought out in new standards such as those from the
U.K. Ministry of Defence (MOD 1991a, 1991b) and
the International Electrotechnical Commission (IEC
1989a, 1989b).

This paper describes an approach to system
assessment that has proven to be cost effective for
the authors. The necessity for an overall systems
approach is discussed first, followed by descriptions
of two key tools that are used in many assessments,
these being Management Audit and Hazard and
Operability Study (HAZOP). Finally, some
conclusions are presented.

OVERALL SYSTEM-WIDE APPROACH

An overall systems approach is both natural and necessary. It is natural to approach any complex task in layers, obtaining the whole picture first and then investigating lower level areas of interest. It is necessary in order to constrain costs. Safety-critical software systems often takes tens of man-years to develop and put into operation. Doing a full rigorous validation of such systems is an equally time-consuming process. It is rumoured that independent validation of the protection system for the Ontario Hydro nuclear plant took 35 man years and a published paper (Guiho, Hennebert 1990) quotes 100 man years for the verification of a railway signalling system. Purchasers of safety critical systems who wish for an independent view of the safety of the system they are considering buying are, not surprisingly, often reluctant to make such a large investment. A further complication is that many systems pre-date the current standards activity and so cannot all be expected to match currently advocated rigorous standards. What is needed is a pragmatic approach which allows confidence in the integrity of the system to be built up and to identify areas of concern. A layered approach is good at identifying any areas of concern at a high level and guides any further analysis towards exploring those areas in more detail than the remainder.

It is necessary to consider the hardware and the total system design as well as the software within the system. The hardware, either mechanical, electronic or electrical are all prone to random faults and, in addition, are also prone to systematic failures in the same way as the software. Also, it is becoming more and more difficult to distinguish between hardware and software as this boundary has been blurred by new components. Even more important is the problem of overall system design. Our experience has been that it is unrealistic to assume that the system has been designed perfectly so that all systematic failures are within the software. Thus our safety assessments look at all the system: architecture, hardware and software in order to provide a full assessment.

MANAGEMENT AUDIT

A thorough management audit of the development process, including the products of the process is an extremely cost-effective route to establishing a view on the ability of the system to meet its objectives.

The Audit Process

A specific audit guide or protocol is drawn up for each audit because all developments are different and have particular characteristics requiring a specialist approach. This protocol is used to guide the progress of the audit and to record the work carried out.

The first days of the audit are primarily spent holding discussions with system development team members.

This enables the audit team rapidly to gain an overview of: the function and architecture of the system; the history of the project; the management structure; the procedures followed and the safety strategies employed.

Getting this understanding is an essential step in the audit process. The remainder of the safety audit is carried out using a layered approach. The first stage is to examine the documented Project and Quality Management Systems, and to ascertain their suitability for a safety-critical development of the nature under review. Each system or procedure is then tested, aiming to establish how well the team conformed to the documented procedures and how effective the procedures proved to be in practice. The key to this process is to examine in detail the documentation relating to a vertical slice through the system. This includes not only any formal documentation, but also meeting minutes, progress reports, error reports and other such documents as are available. Thus it is possible to gain insights into the actual sequence of events and to understand the areas where problems are most likely to arise.

Throughout the audit all actions undertaken are noted in working papers and cross referenced to the protocols. This ensures that all items are covered. Regular team meetings are held in which team members are expected to raise concerns, confirm the steps completed and generally check the progress of the audit.

Included in the protocol are references to various checklists which we have found useful in safety audits of many computer based systems. The checklists are developed from our own product development experience and collated from a variety of published sources. In general, these checklists are used once a section of the audit is completed so as to check that the coverage is complete. This ensures that the team is not constrained by the checklist into missing items of interest, but are also sure to cover the basic areas of concern covered by the checklists.

In addition to the checklists, the audits draw on recent draft standards such as those from the IEC (IEC 1989a, 1989b) and the UK Ministry of Defence (MOD 1991a, 1991b). Often these documents have been issued during or after the development of the system under study and hence would not necessarily have been available to guide the development. However, they nevertheless provide a useful view of current accepted best practice against which to measure a modern computer-based safety-critical development.

Experience to date has been that a small multi-disciplinary audit team of two or three is most effective. All team members should have knowledge of development methods for electronics and software, safety analysis, quality assurance and project management but it has been found important to have experts in high reliability electronic and software design as part of the team. Typical audits take about two weeks working on site with access to the development team and their documentation.

Audit Results

The results from the audit are presented as findings 'by exception'. Thus only deviations from expected good practice will be reported as findings. It is normal practice to discuss areas of concern with the development team as they arise so that additional information can be found or clarifications made to the audit team's understanding. The audit usually finishes with a presentation by the audit team of their findings and gives an opportunity for immediate feedback from the development team so that any such comments may be included in the audit report. Obviously, safety audits by their nature tend to be confidential so the examples of findings given below are merely to give a flavour of the issues examined during a typical audit.

Finding 1: Some of the standards and procedures manuals were not formally issued until the development was well underway, and it is not clear to what standards initial work was carried out.

Finding 2: The fault-tree analysis for board x is calculated in a confusing manner when combining probabilities through an AND gate. This approach has the potential to produce erroneous results if used elsewhere.

Finding 3: Static analysis included data flow and information flow analysis but did not include semantic analysis.

Finding 4: The checksum test used to detect EPROM faults could miss detecting faults in the more significant bits.

Finding 5: The y module is optimised for timing and so has some 'clever' assembler code not complying with structured programming principles.

Finding 6: A single point failure was identified in card p which the self-tests would not detect. This failure could lead to a safety failure.

The findings will usually identify some areas of concern where additional work is considered necessary to raise confidence in the approach taken. These are presented as recommendations.

Experience has been that audits go smoothly if both good documentation and knowledgeable personnel are available. It is possible, but much more difficult, to audit from the documentation only.

HAZARD AND OPERABILITY STUDY (HAZOP)

We have found the HAZOP a cost-effective method of carrying out a qualitative safety analysis, often in response to concerns raised during a management audit.

This section describes how a HAZOP may be used to explore potential hazards resulting from a computer system and covers the following areas:

> The traditional use of HAZOP in examining process plant to put the remainder of the section in context for those unfamiliar with the technique

> Extensions to the traditional approach to make HAZOP a powerful tool for exploring the hazards of computer systems.

> Some examples of the use of the approach

> The major advantages of the approach

What is a HAZOP?

The full name of HAZOP, Hazard and Operability Study, says a great deal about its purpose. It is to ensure both that necessary features are incorporated in a design to provide for safe operation and that features are avoided which could give undesirable outcomes (ie hazards). The technique was developed by ICI in the late 1960's and has grown to be well established in the petrochemical industries. An excellent introduction to the technique is given in (CIA, 1977).

In the process industries it is usual to describe plant designs in the form of Piping and Instrumentation Diagrams (P&IDs). The HAZOP is carried out by a team with the following members: team leader; team secretary; personnel who have detailed knowledge of operation of similar systems; personnel who have detailed knowledge of the design intent of the system; specific technical specialists as necessary.

The team should be small (4-8 people) and they work logically through the P & IDs, examining them critically for areas where deviations from normal operation can lead to an undesired action. For each deviation, the team asks "can it happen?" and if so, "would it cause a hazard?" (a hazard could be things such as a fire or release of toxic material). The team will consider what mitigating features there are to control the hazard (in the process industries these might be things such as relief valves, shutdown systems, alarms etc). To guide the process a series of guidewords and potential deviations are used. Thus for liquid in a pipe, a relevant guideword is "flow" and potential deviations are "high, low, no, reverse." For fluids another guideword is "pressure" with deviations "high, low". In theory, each guideword/deviations should be applied to each process line and vessel . In practice, an experienced team leader will judge the correct detail of questioning for each area. The results of the HAZOP may be presented in a number of ways: usually the team secretary inputs information directly into a portable computer during the study session. This presents results under the following headings:

Item number - a simple count of items logged from the beginning of the HAZOP

Equipment item - a description of the area of plant for which a deviation has been found

Guideword - such as temperature, pressure, flow etc.

Deviation - such as high, low etc.

Cause - the circumstances that could give rise to the deviation

Consequence/Implementation - the effect on the plant that the deviation might lead to

Indication/Protection - any feature that will either identify the deviation or mitigate it's effects (eg an alarm signal or a pressure relief valve).

Question/Recommendation - questions arise from items considered a potential hazard which cannot be resolved by the meeting. Recommendations are generally for changes to the design or particular actions to be taken during operation.

Answers/Comments - This allows the later insertion of answers to questions raised or notes which the team consider relevant to the design but are not questions or recommendations.

The first two items in Table 3 gives typical examples of HAZOP results from a petrochemical plant.

The very positive experience of Arthur D Little in using HAZOP has made it their technique of choice in carrying out hazard and risk studies in the petrochemical industry, both at the plant design stage and in assessments of existing plant. Because of similar hazard analysis requirements in a wide variety of other industries it has been natural to question whether HAZOP technique can be extended to domains other than process plant. Within Cambridge Consultants we had been working for many years on computer systems where safety was a factor and a dialogue began between the two groups, both based on the same site. It was obvious that many of the guidewords and deviations appropriate for process plant were not applicable to electronics and software, but was there a way of transferring the approach to this new area? The next section outlines our approach to the problem.

HAZOP Approach for Electronics and Software

We first extended the use of HAZOP to electro-mechanical systems by a suitable choice of

guidewords and deviations and then began to consider electronics and software. One of the main features of HAZOP is that it works from a pictorial representation (P&IDs) of the plant under consideration and thus for electronic designs there are obvious parallels with block diagrams and circuit diagrams. There is considerable uniformity in this pictorial representation of electronic designs across a variety of industries and so a transfer of HAZOP methodology appeared tractable. It is rather more difficult selecting an appropriate set of guidewords and deviations. Some of those found useful are given in Table 1.

TABLE 1 Selected HAZOP Guidewords and Deviations for Electronics

GUIDEWORD	DEVIATION
voltage	high
current	low
amplitude	none
power	loss
frequency	other

During HAZOP sessions on particular electronic designs it has proven necessary to use the HAZOP team intuition to identify additional guidewords and deviations specific to that design. The full set of guidewords and deviations is continually evolving and the methodology being refined.

With software architectures and designs there is far less uniformity in representation, with a few examples being the network diagrams of MASCOT (BSI, 1991), modular decompositions showing calling hierarchies, the dataflow diagrams of structured design (Yourdon, Constantine, 1979), (Hatley, Pirbhai, 1988) and the mathematically formal methods where there is no pictorial representation such as VDM (Jones, 1980). There are obvious advantages in the precision and lack of ambiguity of formal methods and recent standards rightly advocate their use in safety critical systems. However, most of the systems presented to us for assessment do not use formal methods and the current HAZOP approach has not yet been extended to software designs using formal methods where there may be no accompanying pictorial representation. Designs presented as structured designs have proven most straightforward to HAZOP as the data and control flows between processes have clear analogies with the pipes and process vessels of the petrochemical industry. Designs using network diagrams and calling hierarchies have also proven tractable to the HAZOP approach.

The set of guidewords and deviations is under

continual review. Table 2 shows some of those that have proven useful.

TABLE 2 Selected HAZOP Guidewords and Deviations for Software

GUIDEWORD	DEVIATION
data value control value	no incomplete incorrect stale (unchanging)
algorithm function	wrong sequence wrong specification wrong algorithmic derivation
data rate	too high too low no
comms protocol	corrupted transmission wrong prefix wrong handshake
timing (of actions)	too early too late too slow too fast out of sequence

At the moment we are exploring particular deviations associated with different data types and data structures.

For both electronics and software we have found that the traditional HAZOP team structure and general approach can be used without change. However, it has been found essential to have independent technical personnel who are experienced in safety critical system design as part of the HAZOP team. They use their experience to prompt for potential hazards in the design.

Some Examples of the Use of the HAZOP Approach

Some typical results from HAZOP sessions are shown in Table 3. To put the results fully in context it would be necessary to present the pictorial representation of the relevant designs. Unfortunately, this is not possible as nearly all of our assessment work is carried out in confidence and hence the examples given are merely to give an idea of the issues explored. As mentioned earlier, Items 1 and 2 are typical of a HAZOP in the petro-chemical industry. The remaining examples are typical of a HAZOP of a system containing electronics and software.

Once the HAZOP process is completed, the results are examined, structured and prioritised. Often, more detailed analysis of particular parts of the system will be recommended. The use of fault trees is a useful way of structuring the results and presenting them in an easy to follow manner.

The Advantages of the HAZOP Approach

The two main advantages of the HAZOP approach are:

it uses a team approach; and it promotes a layered approach to the system.

The team approach brings a variety of expertise and viewpoints onto a common problem. The discipline of focusing on hazard identification (rather than just looking for errors) leads to productive sessions and gratifyingly, there is rarely a defensive approach by the system designers and users. The fact that a team is involved means that there is much less impact to a mistake by one team member, in contrast to other techniques that are carried out by individuals. The presence of the team of key personnel associated with the system under assessment means that problem areas are brought immediately to their attention. Because the intent of the HAZOP is to identify hazards, not find errors, it is complementary to other activities of analysis and testing and to other team approaches of design reviews, walk throughs or inspections.

The layered approach, looking at the whole system first, allows a homing in to key issues based on the potential hazards and is very good at assessing system-wide implications. The approach of looking at symptoms and then the causes and consequences encourages exploration of non-obvious interactions, particularly of electronics and the software with the hardware, sensors, actuators and operators with which it interfaces. Bottom-up approaches, such as Failure Modes and Effects Analysis (FME), when carried out on their own must analyse every component to a similar level of detail which is time-consuming and because they are individual activities, potentially error-pone. In fact, the HAZOP is useful in guiding which are the most critical areas to concentrate on in any subsequent FMEA.

Finally, although this paper addresses assessment, it should be pointed out that a similar HAZOP approach is extremely effective at the conceptual design stage as a Hazard Analysis tool and also at the various subsequent levels of system decomposition. Doing hazard analysis at an early stage is mandated by emerging standards (MOD, 1991a), (IEC, 1989a) and we highly recommend the HAZOP approach.

CONCLUSION

This paper has shown that the complementary tools of Management Audit and HAZOP provide a pragmatic and cost-effective way forward to the assessment of safety-critical computer systems. It should be noted that the approach is qualitative and can serve only to increase confidence in the safety integrity of the assessed system (not give a guarantee that a particular level of integrity has been reached).

In some situations, this, together with existing operational experience may provide sufficient confidence. Where areas of concern have been identified, further analyses may be necessary to allow a judgement on the acceptability of those areas. However, where quantification of the probability of a safety failure is required then far more extensive analyses and testing are required, such as those described by Parnas, van Schouwen and Kuwan (1990) and Guiho and Hennebert (1990).

REFERENCES

BSI. (1991). Guide for a modular approach to software construction, operation and test (MASCOT). Draft for Development DD196.

CIA. (1987). A guide to hazard and operability studies, Chemical Industries Association Limited.

Guiho, G. and C. Hennebert. (1990). SACEM software validation. Proceedings of the 12th IEEE International Conference on Software Engineering.

Hatley, D. and I. Pirbhai. (1988). Strategies for real-time system specification. Dorset House.

IEC. (1989a). Functional safety of programmable electronic systems: generic aspects. Part I: general requirements. International electrotechnical commission.

IEC. (1989b). Software for computers in the application of industrial safety related systems. International electrotechnical commission.

Jones, C. B. (1980). Software development: a rigorous approach. Prentice Hall International.

MoD. (1991a). Interim defence standard 00-56. Hazard analysis and safety classification of the computer and programmable electronic system elements of defence equipment. UK Ministry of Defence.
MoD. (1991b). Interim defence standard 00-55. The procurement of safety critical software in defence equipment. Part 1: Requirements. Part 2: Guidance. UK Ministry of Defence.

Parnas, D.L., A. J. van Schouwen and Kwan S.P. (1990). Evaluation of safety-critical software. Communications of the ACM, Vol. 33, no4.

Yourdon, E. and L. Constantine. (1979). Structured design. Prentice Hall.

TABLE 3 Typical HAZOP Results

Item No	Equipment Item	Guideword	Deviation	Cause	Consequence/ Implication	Indication/ Protection	Question/ Recommendation	Answers/ Comments
1	Feed line to surge drum	Flow	No	Dead end of pipe after surge drum is permanently isolated	Possible enhanced corrosion due to collection of water	None	R1: Implement regular monitoring checks for corrision at dead ends	
2	Feed to deethanizer	Pressure	High	Valve left in manual mode. Emergency shut-down received and fails to close	Overpressure in line		R2: Remove handwheel from valve to increase reliability in emergency shut-down	
3	Module perform analysis 'p'	Data item x	Stale	Not cleared at beginning of module because of hardware fault in clear instruction, or skipped section of code	Could output previous value, thus failing to identify invalid analysis		Q3: Is there some other means of detecting this fault?	
4	Emergency shut-down signal ESD	Voltage	High	Failure of only one of gates k, l, m, n	ESD fails to operate		Q4: Does the FMEA of ESD output show that failure open of a single gate cannot lead to ESD failure?	
5	PROM a	Integrity	Low	Error in prodution or wrong PROM fitted to card	Critical parameters may be corrupted resulting in unsafe situation	Quailty procedure 1 gives rigorous procedure for programming and production of PROMs. TY-RAP holds in place but will not prevent deliberate attempt to remove	R5: Field replacement of PROMa should not be done without procedure to validate and re-test as associated cards	

TABLE 3 Contd. Typical HAZOP Results

6	PROM a		Corrupted	Overvoltage etc	May compromise integrity. Significant bit errors may not be detectable by checksum	Checksum	Q6: PROM a contains safety critical data. Are there checks to ensure that data is not corrupted?
7	Input band pass filter	Output frequency	High/low	Noise from external source	May not reject external noise and hence result in malfunction of safety critical system		Q7: Confirm that other frequency rejection is sensitive enough to reject noise?
8	Module search slide	Data: list of suspicious cells	Empty	Processing error	If empty in error could lead to safety failure		R8: Check consistency between number in list and count in header
9	Module capture image background intensity	Data: background intensity field	Too high/ too low/ random	Error in image processing hardware or software	Subsequent background corrected images will be corrupted leading to incorrect feature identification		Q9: Can this be checked for?

RISK PERCEPTIONS AND ACCEPTANCE OF COMPUTERS IN CRITICAL APPLICATIONS

A. Pasquini

ENEA - Via Anguillarese 301, Roma, Italy.

A. Rizzo

CNR Inst. of Psychology - Viale Marx 15, Roma, Italy.

Abstract This paper analyses some recent theories regarding risk and benefit perceptions, acceptance of new technologies and influence of people sociodemographic characteristics on these aspects. Then, it outlines the specific problems arising from the use of computers in safety-critical applications and the applicability of the previously mentioned studies to this domain. The study also analyses the possible effects on acceptance of some past incidents involving computer systems and of typical computer system malfunctions.

Keywords: computer applications, computer evaluation, industrial control, new technology acceptance, reliability, safety, risk perceptions, social and behavioural science.

INTRODUCTION

The interest in public reactions to technological development has been growing in the last 15 - 20 years. In particular, studies regarding the perceptions of the risk are increasing as a result of the growing opposition to some new technologies like nuclear power (Gardner, 1989; Williams, 1986).

Several experts believe that this opposition is due to a public overestimation of the risk induced by some technologies. In their opinion such overestimation comes from lack of technical knowledge, misinformation and irrationality (Kasper, 1980). It is well known the public tendency to emphasize the consequences of accidents rather than their probabilities of occurrence: technologies that can kill many people at once in a catastrophic accident are refused even if the accident has a very low probability of occurrence (Rayner, 1987).

Other experts emphasize that, in many cases, it is difficult to judge the accuracy and rationality of public perceptions since objective measures of the risk of new technologies do not exist (Otway, 1982). Indeed measures of the risk are based on complex analytic techniques (like failure mode and effect analysis and fault tree analysis) requiring a certain amount of subjective judgement by the experts that are using them (Shooman, 1986).

Use of digital control in safety-critical applications is a typical example of such technologies. Computers are increasingly used to control or support the control of nuclear and chemical processes, military and civilian aircraft, spacecraft and medical devices (Parnas, 1990). In all these applications a computer failure could produce severe consequences in terms of human lives, environmental impact or economical losses. There is no way to prove the attainment of the levels of reliability required in these applications, at least with the techniques existing today (Leveson, 1986).

This paper analyses in the second Section theories regarding risk and benefit perceptions, acceptance of new technologies and influence of people sociodemographic characteristics on these aspects. Then, in the third Section, it outlines the specific problems arising from the use of computers in safety-critical applications and, in the fourth Section, the implications of the previously mentioned studies for this domain.

RISK PERCEPTIONS AND ACCEPTANCE OF NEW TECHNOLOGIES

Risk is usually defined as the probability of an adverse event multiplied by the magnitude of its consequences and divided by time. Professionals tend to express the "magnitude" with the number of deaths the technology will cause; they then judge acceptability by weighting the technology risks and costs against its benefits usually measured in dollars (Wilson, 1979; Cohen, 1985).

Even if the given definition is useful to define risk at an engineeristic level, it is insufficient and misleading when dealing with people risk perceptions. People have a different conception of risk, with the magnitude of the consequences having much more importance than probability. In addition, the cost/benefit evaluation of a new technology do not follows a linear trend: people emphasize losses however they are expressed (money, human lives, environment integrity) and underestimate big benefits (Howard, 1968). Tversky and Kahnemann, on the basis of a set of experiments, proposed in Tversky (1981) a function that associates a subjective value to any quantity that can be lost or gained. This function is shown in fig. 1 and has been called value function. The bold line shows the subjective perceptions of costs and benefits while the tiny line shows objective costs and benefits. The tendency to emphasize losses and underestimate big benefits is clearly shown by the shape of the continuous line. It shows that a series of events having small benefits is perceived as more useful than a single event having the same total benefit. Likewise, several adverse events are considered worst than a single event having the same negative consequences. In addition, there is a constant tendency to overestimate losses.

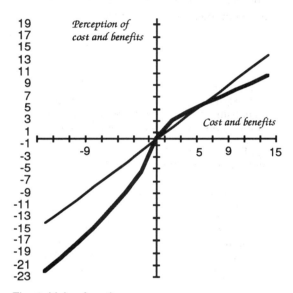

Fig. 1 Value function

People is also prone to a subjective perception of probability. A study on decision under risk (Kahneman, 1979) has shown the people tendency to overestimate low probabilities and underestimate intermediate and, especially, high probabilities. This tendency is shown in fig. 2. The bold line shows the subjective perception of probability in comparison with its real course (tiny line). The shape of the bold line, near zero, indicates that small probabilities are overestimated (this explains the success of lottery tickets). On the contrary, big probabilities are underestimated. This explains the people tendency to avoid risky events even if they have a very small probability of occurrence.

In addition to the mentioned factors, the acceptance of risky technologies is also affected by several qualitative characteristics

such as: the degree to which the risks of the technology are understood by professionals and the degree of apparent disagreement between them (Slovic, 1980); the kind of distribution of the technology benefits among population and people suffering the risk (Slovic, 1981); the importance of the technology for satisfying basic human needs, for example people frequently underestimate the risks induced by medicine (Gardner, 1989).

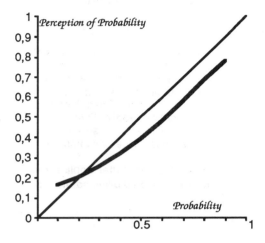

Fig. 2 Subjective perception of probability

Media have also a strong influence in public perceptions of risk. In a recent study by Bastide et al. (1989) a representative sample of 1000 individuals was asked to express his judged frequency of each of 30 mortality causes in the country. Comparison with the real frequency ranking showed that the most overestimated lethal events were clearly associated with dramatic and sensational events with high media coverage (motor vehicle accidents, industrial injuries etc.); while the most underestimated ones were common causes or less under media attention (disease, leisure and sports accidents etc.).

People sociodemographic characteristics are another factor that affects risk perceptions and acceptance of new technologies (Harding, 1984). Studies conducted in different countries leaded to similar results, showing that specific cultural and national contexts have little influence on those characteristics (Williams, 1986). In particular age, sex and level of income showed an effect on acceptance of new technologies: young people, women and low income or unemployed are more sensitive to technological risks, while people with a high level of education and income and residents of big cities minimize industrial sources of risk (Williams, 1986). These data show that a weak social position and lack of social relationship are clearly associated with a tendency to overestimate risks and suggest that risk perceptions are also affected by the sense of protection and self-assurance that the community inspire in its members. The effect of age can be explained with the well known tendency to emphasize the effect of the lethal events which are more likely to affect the group of age one belongs to. For example, young people are more sensitive to the possibility of accidents than those of disease or other natural causes of death.

In conclusions, the difference between the risk evaluation of the professionals and those of the population is not, or at least not only, due to lack of technical knowledge, misinformation and irrationality. People seem to include in their evaluation several not easily quantifiable factors, using a larger and more complex definition of risks, benefits and acceptability.

COMPUTERS IN CRITICAL APPLICATIONS

The enhanced flexibility and functionality of computer systems have led to their use in many new applications. They are replacing operators or analog devices in several safety critical systems. That is, in systems where their failure could produce severe consequences in terms of human lives, environmental impact or economical losses. Computers are now used to control chemical plants and nuclear reactors, medical devices, military and civilian aircraft.

But, within the engineering community, computers and especially software have still a reputation for being undependable and difficult to evaluate. Several surveys (Leveson, 1986; Parnas, 1985; Parnas, 1990) evidenced that computer systems are not reliable until a long period of operative usage, during which their software has failed and has been modified and corrected several times. Parnas (1990) reports of a survey from David Benson, professor of Computer Science at Washington State University. He looked for an example of a real-time system that operated adequately when used for the first time by people other than its developers. Only one software package (which was not a completely new software) satisfied this requirement. Even when computer systems have became relatively reliable, they frequently fail when the operating conditions change. A detailed analysis of the problems induced by software and of the differences between digital computers and analog devices can be found in (Parnas, 1990).

These considerations would entail the need of techniques to evaluate if computer systems are able to perform their functions in a specified use environment (Di Marco, 1989). But adequate and established techniques are available only for evaluation of the hardware (EWICS, 1988). On the contrary, techniques for evaluating software are still the subject of intensive research. From the seventies onwards, several models have been proposed to predict the reliability of software (Goel, 1985; Ramamoorthy, 1980; Yamada, 1985). They suggest a set of mathematical equations to estimate program performances such as reliability, number of remaining errors or Mean Time To Failure. Reliability growth models are the most widely used: they tend to estimate the reliability of software during testing by providing a measure of failure rates. At the present state of the art these models can be very useful for a first reliability estimation and as an aid for project management (EWICS, 1990).

But, software used in safety critical systems, is required to have a probability of failure ranging from 10-7 to 10-9 for 1 to 10 hour missions (Butler, 1991). There is no way that these levels of reliability can be measured with these models (Dunham, 1984; Leveson, 1986). They do not analyse the characteristics of the code and their assumptions are too far from the real software development conditions (Goel, 1985). In addition, the techniques used to estimate their parameters are not appropriate for software for critical applications: they require a failure history of the code and do not work for software which rarely fail during testing. The unsuitability of the statistical method for the quantification of critical software is analyzed in detail in (Butler, 1991; Dunham, 1986; Leveson, 1986).

COMPUTER ACCEPTANCE IN CRITICAL APPLICATIONS

An accident is usually defined as an unforeseen event, or series of events, leading to severe damages in terms of human lives, environmental impact or economical costs. Computer in itself is not a dangerous device: it does not directly causes damages, for example by exploding or catching fire. It can significantly contribute to accidents only if used to control potentially dangerous systems. In addition, in "popular belief", computers are still surrounded with a halo of infallibility. Friedman and Friedman (1989) investigated which are the major and the most frequently mentioned myths about computers as perceived by professionals in the area. The survey revealed that the most common and widely accepted myth is that computers are "magical" devices: they can do everything correctly without human intervention. This popular belief and the "lightness" (in terms of environmental impact, resource consumption and direct dangerousness) of the information technology favour the acceptance of computers reducing the perception of them as a risky technology.

People sociodemographic characteristics should affect computer acceptance in the same way they affect other new technologies. Even if there are not specific studies on this matter, we have seen that risk perceptions is influenced by the "feeling of security" that society as a whole procure to its members (Bastide, 1989) and this kind of influence is independent from the type of technology.

The described people tendency, rather in favour of digital technologies, could be compromised by a growing sequence of accidents caused by computer systems in recent years (Joyce,

1987; Neumann, 1991). Many of these accidents involved risks to the public and the environment or caused severe economical losses. Examples can be found in: space applications where the Phobos 1 and 2 computers caused the failure of the space missions (Hartley, 1989); communications with the well known AT&T crash (Kemp, 1990); medicine where a software fault in the computer-controlled radiation-therapy machine Therac 25 caused the over radiation and death of some cancer patients (Jacky, 1989); industrial and nuclear plant where a failure of the Crystal River nuclear reactor computer, controlling the process, caused radioactive water to be dumped on the floor of the reactor building (Marshall, 1980).

But, the accidents that have the strongest influence in computer acceptance are those with high media coverage or those affecting large amount of people. The effect of media has been analyzed in the second Section and Bynum (1991) reports the growing interest of the media for harmful computers malfunctions and computer viruses. The number of people affected by the consequences of a failure and its frequency are important, even if the consequences are not severe, because of the shape of the value function (several adverse events are considered worst than a single event having the same negative consequences) and because people are more sensitive to the risks of the technologies that already "hit" somebody close to them (Williams, 1986). From this point of view, frustration and economical loss incurred by individuals and businesses whose computers system have been infected by the Internet worm had a stronger influence than the consequences of more severe accidents.

Moreover a negative bias in the acceptance of computer tools in critical application is produced by both expert and mass media which stress the role of front-line event in accident reports. Yet deep investigation on major accidents revealed that behind the front-line events that triggered the disaster there were faulty socio-technical and organizational conditions (Perrow, 1984). The relevance of such factors can be understood though the framework for accident analysis put forward by Reason (1990). The framework moves from the distinction between Active failures and Latent failures.

Active failures are errors and violations that have an immediate and visible negative effect. They occur right before the accident. Usually, people and equipment involved in Active failures are active near to the outcomes of the man-machine system (e.g. pilots, control rooms operators etc.).

Latent failures are actions or decisions that produce conditions that may remain silent for a long time, until they combine with triggering conditions and then producing an accident. They are present in the system well before the onset of an accident sequence, and,

consequently, can facilitate the adoption of unsafe behavior. Latent Failures are also named, with a term borrowed from medicine, "resident pathogens" , which well illustrate their functioning. Indeed, they have to be considered analogous of inhabitant pathogens agents in the human body which combine with external factors to yield a disease.

From the analysis of severe accidents it arose that many of the events that had combined in producing the accident had previously made their appearance in isolation or in partial, not "explosive", combinations. But no risk had been perceived and in many cases their status were considered as normal. Suddenly, after the dramatic outcome, these Active failures became the relevant causal factors for both "expert" and mass-media.

Another factor that could negatively influence the acceptance of computers in critical applications is the present disagreement between computer experts. There is no common way to face the technical difficulties described in the previous Section. For example it is well known the strong debate in favour (Aviziens, 1985) or against software diversity (Knight, 1986; Knight, 1990; Shimeall, 1991). Even architectural solutions are subjected to similar disputes. Some computer scientists suggests to identify safety as a property separate from reliability and trustworthiness (Leveson, 1986; Knight, 1986). They propose to separate safety-critical code from other code in products used in safety critical applications. While other suggests to keep safety-critical software as small and simple as possible by moving any functions that are not safety critical to other computers (Parnas, 1986, 1990).

CONCLUSIONS

This paper presented the results of some studies on risk and benefit perceptions, acceptance of new technologies and influence of people sociodemographic characteristics on these aspects. Then it analyzed the acceptance of computers in critical applications in the light of these studies.

Computers are not yet perceived as source of risk even if used in potentially dangerous systems, but some recent accidents, media information (and sometimes misinformation) and controversies between experts could change this people attitude. Ethical values play a crucial role in people acceptance of new technologies, hence technical improvements in safety and reliability of the technology will not be sufficient to increase its acceptability. Responsible actions by experts in the field, growth of computer ethics and correct information to the public would be effective methods to keep people trust.

REFERENCES

Aviziens A. (1985). The n-version approach to fault-tolerant software. *IEEE Transactions on Software Eng.*, Vol. SE-11, No. 12, Dec. 1985.

Bastide S., J. P. Moatti, J. P. Pages and F. Fagnani (1989). Risk Perception and Social Acceptability of Technologies: The French Case. *Risk Analysis*, Vol. 9, No. 2, 1989.

Butler R. W. and G. B. Finelli (1991). The Infeasibility of Experimental Quantification of Life-Critical Software Reliability. *Proc. of the ACM SIGSOFT '91 Conference on Software for Critical Systems*, New Orleans, Louisiana, ACM Press, 1991.

Bynum T. W. (1991). Human Values and the Computer Science Curriculum. *Proc. of the 1991 National Conference on Computing and Values*, New Haven, 1991.

Cohen B. (1985). Criteria for Technology Acceptability. *Risk Analysis*, Vol. 5, No. 1-3, 1985.

Di Marco G. and A. Pasquini (1989). Safety Aspects of Computer Systems in Power Plants. In *Proc. of the IFAC Symposium on Power Systems and Power Plant Control*, Seoul, Korea, Aug. 1989.

Dunham J. R. (1984). Measuring Software Safety. In *Proc. of Compcon '84.*, Whashington D. C., IEEE Press, Sept. 1984.

Dunham J. R. (1986). Experiments in Software Reliability: Life-Critical Applications. *IEEE Transactions on Software Engineering*, Vol. SE-12, NO.1, January 1986.

EWICS (European Workshop on Industrial Computer Systems) TC7 (1988). Design and Production of Hardware for Safety Related Computer Systems. In F. Redmill (ed.), *Dependability of Critical Computer Systems 1*, Elsevier Science Publishers, 1988.

EWICS (European Workshop on Industrial Computer Systems) TC7 (1990). Prediction and Measurement of Software Reliability. In P. Bishop (ed.), *Dependability of Critical Computer Systems 3*, Elsevier Science Publisher, 1990.

Friedman H. H. and L. W. Firedman (1989). Myhts, Unethical Practices, Personnel Requirements: What Do Computers Industry Professionals Really Believe?. *The Journal of Systems and Software*, 10, 1989.

Gardner G. T. and L. C. Gould (1989). Public Perceptions of the Risks and Benefits of Technology. *Risk Analysis*, Vol. 9, No. 2, 1989.

Goel A. L. (1985). Software Reliability Models: Assumptions, Limitations, and Applicability. *IEEE Transactions on Software Engineering*, Vol. SE-11, NO. 12, Dec. 1985.

Harding C. and J. Eiser (1984). Characterising the Perceived Risks and Benefits of Some Health Issues. *Risk Analysis*, Vol. 4, No. 1, 1984.

Hartley R. (1989). Phobos 1 & 2 computer failures. *Science*, Vol. 245, 8 Sept. 1989.

Howard R. (1968). *Decision Analysis: Introductory Lectures on Choices under Uncertainty*, Addison-Wesley Publishing Co., 1968.

Jacky J. (1989). Programmed for Disaster, Software Errors that Imperil Lives. *The Sciences*, New York Academy of Sciences, Sept./Oct. 1989.

Joyce E. (1987). Software Bugs: A Matter of Life and Liability. *Datamation*, May 1987.

Kahneman D. and A Tversky (1979), Prospect Theory: An Analysis of Decisions under Risk. *Econometirca*, No. 47, March 1979.

Kasper R (1980). Perceptions of Risk and Their Effects on Decision Making. In R. Schwing and W. Albers (eds.), *Societal Risk Assessment: How Safe Is Safe Enough ?*, Plenum Press, New York, 1980.

Kemp D. H. (1990). AT&T Crash, 15 Jan. 1990: The Official Report. *ACM SIGSOFT*, Vol. 15, No. 2, Apr. 1990.

Knight J. C. and N. G. Leveson (1986). An experimental evaluation of the assumptions of independence in multiversion programming. *IEEE Transactions on Software Eng.*, Vol. SE-12, No. 1, Jan. 1986.

Knight J. C. and N. G. Leveson (1990). A reply to the criticisms of the Knight & Leveson experiment. *ACM SIGSOFT*, Jan. 1990.

Leveson N. G. (1986). Software Safety: Why, What and How. *Computing Surveys*, Vol. 18, No. 2, 1986.

Marshall E. (1980). NRC takes a second look at reactor design. *Science*, Vol. 207, 28 March 1980.

Neumann P. G. (1991). Illustrative Risks to the Public in the Use of Computer Systems and Related Technology (List of Risks Cases as of 4 Jan. 1991). *ACM SIGSOFT*, Vol. 16, No. 1, Jan. 1991.

Otway H. and D. Von Winterfeldt. Beyond Acceptable Risk: On the Social Acceptability of Technologies. *Policy Sciences*, No. 14, 1982.

Parnas D. (1985). Software Aspects of Strategic Defense Systems. *Communications of the ACM*, Vol. 28, No. 12, Dec. 1985.

Parnas D. and P. C. Clements (1986). A rational design process: How and why to fake it. *IEEE Transactions on Software Eng.*, Vol. SE-12, No. 2, Feb. 1986.

Parnas D., A. J. Van Schouwen and S. P. Kwan (1990). Evaluation of Safety Critical Software. *Communications of the ACM*, Vol. 33, No. 6, 1990.

Perrow C. (1984) *Normal accidents*. New York: Basic Book.

Ramamoorthy C. V. and F. B. Bastani (1980). Modeling of the Software Reliability

Growth Process. In *Proc. of the COMPSAC '80*, Chicago, IL, 1980.

Rayner S. and R. Cantor (1987). How Fair Is Safe Enough? The Cultural Approach to Societal Technology Choice. *Risk Analysis*, Vol. 7, No. 1, 1987.

Reason J. (1990) *Human error*. Camnbridge MA: CUP

Shimeall T. J. and N. G. Leveson (1991). An empirical comparison of software fault-tolerance and fault elimination. *IEEE Transactions on Software Eng.*, Vol. SE-17, No. 2, Feb. 1991.

Shooman M. L. (1986). *Probabilistic Reliability: An Engineering Approach*. Krieger, Malabar, FL, 1986.

Slovic P., B. Fischhoff and S. Lichtenstein (1980). Facts and Fears: Understanding Perceived Risk. In R. Schwing and W. Albers Jr. (eds.), *Societal Risk assessment: How Safe Is Safe Enough?*, Plenum, New York, 1980.

Slovic P., B. Fischhoff and S. Lichtenstein (1981). Characterizing Perceived Risk. In R. Kates and C. Hohenemser (eds.), *Technological Hazard Management*, Oelgeschlager, Gunn and Hain, Cambridge, 1981.

Tversky A. and D. Kahneman (1981). The Framing of Decisions and the Psychology of Choice. *Science*, No. 4481, 30 Jan. 1981.

Williams R. and S. Mills (eds.) (1986). Public Acceptance of New Technologies, Croom Helm, London, 1986.

Wilson R. (1979). Analyzing the daily risks of life. *Technology Review*, Feb. 1979.

Yamada S. and S. Osaki (1985). Software Reliability Growth Modeling: Models and Applications. *IEEE Trans. on Software Eng.*, Vol. SE-11, NO. 12, Dec. 1985.

COMBINING PROBABILISTIC AND DETERMINISTIC VERIFICATION EFFORTS

W.D.Ehrenberger
Fachbereich Angewandte Informatik und Mathematik
Fachhochschule
D - 6400 Fulda

Abstract. In many cases proofs and systematic testing on the one side and probabilistic testing on the other are applied during software verification. The paper derives overall risk figures for a software product based on the results of these tests and proofs. It uses the concept of stratified sampling. It is assumed that a risk consideration was made initially. Rules are given on how to apply supplementary verification, if first calculations show that the reliability target was not met.

Keywords. Software reliability, software safety, software verification, probabilistic testing, proving, stratified sampling, risk

INTRODUCTION

In many software projects reliability goals are given. These goals are just rough estimates of what a customer may tolerate or they are derived from careful analysis of the application. Sometimes they are mandated by rules. Normally these goals are proabilistic in their nature. Typically they require a certain upper limit for a

> failure probability per demand,
> failure rate,
> probability of survival during a
>   mission or
> risk

of the software product. In this paper the considerations are limited to the **risk** connected with the operation of the investigated software package. It is assumed that further reliability figures of interest can be derived from that. The notion of risk and its proper usage is particularly known from the studies [1,2].

On the other hand normally a mixture of probabilistic and deterministic verification methods is applied in verification projects. The deterministic methods usually comprise

> proofs and
> systematic tests.

Systematic testing is in many cases supported by tools that guarantee a certain test coverage.
Probabilistic methods are applied as

> probabilistic tests and
> use of operating experience.

Probabilistic testing usually is done on a test harness during system validation. Use of operating experience is normally made intuitively before pre existing software is employed, such as operating systems or other frequently used software parts; then the commonly known behaviour of that system is considered.

The purpose of this contribution is to show, how the differently gained results can be combined to one reliability figure. From that figure one may also derive any additionally needed verification efforts. In this way it is possible to minimise the verification efforts for a particular purpose. One may also derive statements about the effect of changes of the demand profile of the software; or of the effect of changes of its system reliability requirements. This paper is an extension of two earlier papers [3,4].

No particular assumptions are made on the development method employed or on the programming style used.

The next chapter shortly discusses possible outcomes of verification efforts. After that the concepts of risk and risk profile are introduced. They are connected with the overall system requirements. In order to facilitate the application of the described concept the necessary mathematical formulae are derived in this paper.

VERIFICATION METHODS

In this connection only four verification methods are considered: Proving, coverage/structural testing, probabilistic testing and use of operating experience.

Proving

Proving has been described in [5,6]. Here it is assumed that it demonstrates correctness of the treated software part. We do not consider the possibility of incorrect proofs. If necessary, one would need to apply the considerations on the use of probabilistic test results.

Systematic Testing

Systematic testing is considered here in only one way, namely testing the program according to its structure; in other words: glass box testing. Such tests concern in particular coverage tests, e.g. test of all individual:

        statements - C0,
        branches - C1,
        predicate terms in conditions - Cp,
        loops in minimum and maximum
                number of repetitions,
        pointers between each two connected
                elements,
        accessible data elements.

It is assumed that the outcome of each test case is correct.

Probabilistic Testing

It is assumed that any probabilistic tests are made as black box tests; i.e. that the test is made in order to detect malfunctions or failures of the software; the test is not designed to localise faults. It is further assumed that the rules for statistic tests are observed and that a failure probability per demand is derived from the test results connected with a level of confidence of 99% or 95%. The mathematical background is taken from the theory of probability or sampling, as e.g. described in [7] or any other book on statistics, probability or sampling theory.

Operating Experience

Operating experience is treated in the same way as the results from probabilistic testing. It is assumed that the observation of the operation period was ideal and that it allows to derive a failure probability per demand at the above mentioned level of confidence. A project on that topic is described in [8].

THE CONCEPT OF RISK

Risk is taken as the basic measure of reliability here. This is because tolerable limits of the risk connected to the operation of any software may form the political background for licensing. The term has proved to be useful for deriving the dangers of nuclear power during the risk studies performed for the plants of many countries. See e.g. [1,2].

In most cases it is reasonable to conceive the risk as a vector and to calculate its components independently. The following components and measures should be considered:

        - people killed
                instantly [number]
                in course of time [number]
        - people injured
                permanently [number]
                for a period of time [number]
        - times of illnesses [days]
        - polluted area
                [square kilometers times years]
        - loss of citizen rights (data
                security) [legal severity metric]
        - financial loss [money]

In many cases the expected value of the number of persons affected in one or the other of the components of the vector will be smaller than 1. In this case the related fraction shall be used.

The risk may be defined via probabilities or via frequencies. Sometimes the definition via frequencies leads to expressions that can be evaluated more conveniently. The tolerable risk should be evaluated for all components of the risk vector separately. In many cases it is sufficient to consider the risk connected with essential software parts only, since it is their failure that gives the most sensible contribution to the whole risk value. Another way is to restrict the consideration to the most important accidents or application scenarios.

If no event of a particular type occurs, the plant life time or a larger time period may be taken as a basis for the time and/or frequency to be considered.

The risk r connected with the operation of a program is defined as:

$$r_{total} = \sum_{all\ j} h_j\ X_j \qquad (1)$$

with:

X_j loss connected with event e_j.

h_j frequency of event e_j during the operation period.

It takes the measure of the component that is considered, e.g. numbers of lost human lifes or amount of lost money. The events are disjoint by their nature e_j.

Example 1:

A reactor core may cost $ 50 000 000.-, a main coolant pump $ 6 000 000.-. The frequency of loss of core

        h_{core} = 0.001 per year and

the frequency of loss of a pump

        h_{single_pump} = 0.005 per year;

Since four pumps are installed

        h_{all_pumps} = 0.02 per year; the risk

r = (50 000 + 120 000)$ per year.

A consideration similar to the example is necessary for the other possible losses and the other components of the risk vector. It is necessary for all accident scenarios.

The concept of risk allows to tolerate few "serious" program failures or, alternatively, many "small" failures.

The following more detailed considerations relate to the risk per program run. In this case it is more convenient to consider probabilities instead of frequencies. The total risk is subdivided into strata. In detail:

        K   number of types of demands to
                the program = number of stata
        j   index, j ε {1,...,K}, actual
                stratum considered
        X_j size of loss in case of
                program failure of type j
        n_j probability of demand of type j
        p_j probability of program
                failure in case of
                demand of type j
        X   total loss, connected with the
                program;
                per run

If the program runs m times during the operation period, the relationship of these sizes with formula (1) is:

$h_j = m\ p_j\ \Pi_j$. The risk from (1) is related to the risk r per run.

$$r = r_{total}/m = E(X) = \sum_{j=1}^{K} X_j\ \Pi_j\ p_j$$
$$= \sum_{j=1}^{K} r_j, \qquad (2)$$

with $r_j = X_i\ \Pi_j\ p_j$.

Reliability goals can be set by requirering

$$r <= r\hat{}, \text{ at a certain level of confidence } \alpha, \qquad (3)$$

$r\hat{}$ giving an acceptable upper risk limit. The following considerations show how this can be demonstrated.

The relative weight of a stratum is

$$g_j = \frac{X_j\ \Pi_j}{\sum_{i=1}^{K} X_i\ \Pi_i} \qquad (4)$$

g_j, relative stratum weight

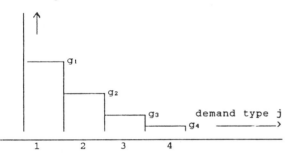

Figure 1: Stratification of input cases, risk profile

If the true loss is not known or if the strata as such cannot be identified clearly, a conservative estimate should be made.

We assume that the basic software verification method is probabilistic black box testing. In that method the test cases are selected proportional to the g_j. Then we get:

$$g_j\ p_j = \frac{X_j\ \Pi_j\ p_j}{\sum_{i=1}^{K} X_i\ \Pi_i}, \qquad (5)$$

probability of ((selection of stratum j) AND (failure))

$$\sum_{\text{all } j} g_j\ p_j = p_v$$

probability of ((selection of an arbitrary stratum) AND (failure)) = probability of failure per run

Using (5) and (2) we get a relationship between the risk and the failure probabibilty per run or demand:

$$p_v = \sum_{\text{all } j} g_j\ p_j = \sum_{\text{all } j} \frac{X_j\ \Pi_j\ p_j}{\sum_{\text{all } i} X_i\ \Pi_i} = \frac{r}{\sum_{\text{all } i} X_i\ \Pi_i} \qquad (6)$$

Let $p_v\hat{}$ denote an upper limit for p_v. The related confidence level be α. Formally:

$$p_v <= p_v\hat{} \text{ at the confidence level } \alpha. \quad (7)$$

Due to the proportionality between p_v and r as given by (6), a limit on p_v does also represent a limit on r. More clearly:

$$p_v <= p_v\hat{} \text{ at } \alpha$$
is equal to,
$$r <= r\hat{}, \text{ at } \alpha. \qquad (8)$$

Achievement of the reliability goal (3) can be demonstrated through demonstation of (7).

We are now looking for the number of necessary test runs to demonstrate (3). A test is made in order to do that. We consider in the following the relationship between p_v (or rather $p_v\hat{}$) and the number of runs.

We assume
   statistical independence between test runs,
   their distribution according to the risk profile,
   no occurring failure escapes observation,
   no failure occurs durnig n runs.

Due to the assumption of independence between runs one may state for n test runs:

$$(1 - p_v)^n$$
   probability of no failure in n runs

Because we require the confidence level α, we have to demand:

$$(1 - p_v)^n <= 1 - \alpha, \text{ or}$$

$$(1 - p_v\hat{})^n = 1 - \alpha$$

In other words:

$$n = \frac{\log(1-\alpha)}{\log(1 - p_v\hat{})} \qquad (9)$$

This leads to
$$n = 3/p_v\hat{} \qquad \text{for } \alpha = 95\%$$
   and
$$n = 4,6/p_v\hat{} \qquad \text{for } \alpha = 99\%$$

Consideration of (8) and substitution of (6) for $p_v\hat{}$ gives:

$$n = \frac{3}{r\hat{}} \sum_{\text{all } j} X_j\ \Pi_j \text{ for } \alpha = 95\% \quad (10)$$

$$n = \frac{4,6}{r\hat{}} \sum_{\text{all } j} X_j\ \Pi_j \text{ for } \alpha = 99\% \quad (11)$$

The main problem with these relationships is that the required n is very large in many practical cases. Therefore we consider the possibility of including other verification techniques as mentioned in chapter 2.

COMBINATION OF THE DIFFERENT VERIFICATION METHODS

During a particular project it is recommendable to make best possible use of all existing verification methods. This is also recommended in the standards [9,10]. They do, however, not give the mathemetical background of best selection among the methods, as it is suggested in this paper.

As a first step one has to map the individal software programs and program parts on the demands according to the risk profile of figure 1. This is important in order to make best use of the existing reliability statements. Most of the software parts will not be attributable to one specific stratum. In this case it is necessary to list them in all strata they influence.

Systematic Methods

In many applications one will be faced with software that is treated by systematic verification techniques beforehand in some of its parts. The verified **functions** can then be regarded as being **always** executed **correctly.** So the related failure probability is zero:

$$p_{syst\ part} = p_s = 0. \tag{12}$$

With $s \ \varepsilon \ \{1, \ldots, K\}$.

Systematic methods in this sense are proving and deterministic testing. We take for granted that proving leads always to the result (12), if applied. Systematic testing may lead to that in two respects as well:
1.) The test may be based on a careful analysis of the software, that derived the test cases that lead to an exhaustive test.
2.) The test may be done according to a coverage measure as mentioned above. Then a more detailed stratification of the involved stratum i is appropriate.
 stratum i1: functions according to coverage
 stratum i2: the rest of the functions.
The test makes statement (12) about the first stratum.

Of course analysis may find out in some cases that a test according to a coverage is already exhaustive in a certain respect.

Probabilistic Methods

Probabilistic methods should be applied to such functions only whose correctness has not been demonstrated systematically. The necessary test effort can then be calculated according to (9), (10) or (11).

If operating experience plays a role, (9), (10) and (11) are applicable as well. n

represents the observed demands to the program or program part or it can be calculated from the operation time.

In many cases the functions connected with a particular stratum are composed of different program parts. E.g. the functions of stratum i may contain

 operating system functions op_i
 functions of the run time system rs_i
 input functions in_i
 calculation functions cl_i
 output functions ot_i.

Obviously they are executed correctly if all parts are executed correctly. They are not, if one part fails. In other words

p_i = prob.of fail.(op_i OR rs_i OR in_i OR cl_i OR ot_i) <=
$p(op_i) + p(rs_i) + p(in_i) + p(cl_i) + p(ot_i)$

The "=" in the second line is an acceptable conservative approximation, since the sum of all pairs and triples etc of probabilities are normally very small. This is because the individual probabilities are quite small by themselves.

Example 2:

Operating system functions
 failure probability estimated from the operating experience of other users of the related computer, extremely low. $p(op) <= 10^{-10}$
Run time system functions
 failure probability estimated from the operating experience of other users of the related computer, very low. $p(ru) <= 10^{-8}$
Input functions
 tested with a large amount of test cases due to their extensive use for all functions of the program, $p(in) < 10^{-6}$
Output functions
 tested with a very large amount of test cases due to their extensive use for all functions of the program, $p(ot) < 10^{-6}$.
Calculation functions
 verified by proof, $p(cf) = 0$.
This leads to: $p_i = 2,0101 *10^{-6}$

Example 3:

The values for the failure probabilities of operating system, run time system and input/output functions are as above. The calculation functions have been subject to a systematic test with a tool. A C1 coverage was tested; no failure occurred. From similar applications it is known that in practice most demands do not exceed to what was tested by C1. There is, however, a portion of 1% of practical demands that may require a higher coverage, which was not tested. Therefore $p(cf) = 0,01$ is assumed.
 The conservative estimation of p_i leads to
 $p_i = 1,00020101 *10^{-2}$.
In many cases this figure may not be acceptable. To demonstrate that p_i is in fact smaller than mentioned would be possible in two ways:
1. By applying more than 300 test cases probabilistically to stratum i, according to the demand profile to that stratum; as

suggested by (9).
2. By applying an arbitrary number of probabilistic test cases to the related software part, that concern only the higher coverage. This would correspond to subdividing the demands into two strata: one corresponding to coverage C1 and another one corresponding to the rest.

In some cases the risk connected with program operation is equal for all strata. In this case the selection probabilities during operation play the role of the strata weights.

STRATEGY

It is reasonable to distinguish between projects that develop software and others that change software.

Software Developement

A project with high reliability requirements should be run as follows:

1. Evaluate the risk requirements.
2. Derive the risk strata.
3. Consider the already available software parts and assign them to the individual strata.
4. Develop the missing software parts according to the state of the art. Parts with involving high risk should
   - be kept as simple as possible
   - developed with great care
   - proved or analysed for exhaustive test.
5. Map the software parts on the risk profile. If no decoupling can be shown the related part shall be listed in all affected stata.
6. Calculate the risk.
7. Do subsequent verification at the parts with yet unacceptably high risk.
8. Calculate again.

In case of any doubt about the validity of a figure a conservative estimate shall be taken as the basis for the calculations.

Thereby it comes out that testing proportional to the risk profile leads to the minimum number of test cases required to demonstrate that the actual risk is below the acceptable one. In all practical cases there is the danger that the estimated risk profile deviates from the estimated one. Therefore:
The demonstrated risk should be well under the acceptable risk in order not to require immediate additional verification action in case that any change of the risk profile becomes apparent.

Change of the Risk Profile

It is very likely that during on-line operation the demand profile will turn out to be different from the originally assumed one. In the same way the size and the nature of losses in case of failure may change. Therefore:

During on line operation the demands to any computerised system with high reliability requirements should be monitored. The actual demand profile should be evaluated and compared to the originally assumed one. Deviations should be reported.

On the basis of such reports one should evaluate whether or not the derived figures of risk still do meet the overall system reliability requirements.

Should the newly-evaluated risks be unacceptably high, complementary verification actions should take place.
It is most likely that such new verification actions are needed in case of changes of the plant or of plant operation.

Example 4:

Before the beginning of plant operation a particular distribution of demands on its reactor core protection system was assumed over the various measuring channels. After two years operation time it turns out that power limiting demands via specific sensors happened more frequently than originally assumed.
Complementary verification should demonstrate that the originally derived figures of merit are still sufficient for showing that the actual risk is below the acceptable one.

During plant operation the operating experience with the employed software increases. If the system does not fail, the demonstrated software reliability is thereby increased automatically. **(If the demands on a system are rare, however, such as with shutdown systems, the increase of confidence in proper reaction is very low.)**

In case of software failure the follow-up procedures shall be similar to actions regarding conventional equipment, say machine tool equipment: Any serious program failure shall trigger the same actions as foreseen for conventional equipment with the same safety relevance.

Such actions will at least include careful investigation of the failure cause and proper remedial action. The problem with software, however, is that the detection of the underlying fault, the fault removal and the reverification use to be more time consuming than similar activities on conventional, say machine tool equipment.

Another question comes up due to the unavoidable changes of the software during plant operation. Here the same rules hold as for changes of conventional software.
After execution of the modification the new figures of merit should be calculated. If necessary, additional verification efforts should be carried out according to the rules for new software.

SUPPLEMENTARY REMARKS AND OUTLOOK

The above chapters have treated several aspects from an ideal point of view. In practical cases things are normally more complicated. Usually this results in more required test cases.

In the ideal case the number of test runs will be chosen **proportionally to the hight** of the individual strata according to figure 1. Test data selection will be such that each case of the selected statum will have equal chances of being selected.

However, due to technical reasons the test harness may be such that it is **too costly** to provide all input cases or input sequences with the required probability. In this case we may turn to a two stage sampling process. For details see [7].

ACKNOWLEDGEMENTS

I thank the Atomic Energy Control Board (AECB) of Canada and the Hessische Ministerium für Wissenschaft und Kunst (HMWK) for their support of the underlying investigations. Particular thanks are given to Dr.Kurt Asmis, AECB for his interest in the subject and Mr B. Krzykacz, GRS, Germany, for deriving essential parts of the mathematical background at the occasion of the publication [3]. I also thank Dr.F.Saglietti from GRS, for many helpful discussions and remarks.

REFERENCES

[1] N.C.Rasmussen
     Reactor Study - An Assessment of Accident Risks in US Commercial Nuclear Power Plants, USNRC, WASH 1400 (NUREG-75/014) October 1975

[2] Gesellschaft für Reaktorsicherheit
     Deutsche Risikostudie Kernkraftwerke, Verlag TÜV-Rheinland, 1989, ISBN 3-921059-67-4

[3] W.Ehrenberger and B.Krzykacz
     Probabilistic Testing
     in: Proceedings of the European Workshop on Industrial Computer Systems,
     Technical University of Graz, edited by V.H.Haase and W.J.Jaburek, April 1983

[4] W.Ehrenberger
     Probabilistic Techniques for Software Verification in Safety Applications of Computeriszed Process Control in Nuclear Power Plants
     IAEA-TECDOC-581, February 1991

[5] R.L.Baber
     The Spine of Software: Designing Provably Correct Software - Theory and Practice
     John Wiley & Sons Ldt, 1987, ISBN 0-471-91474-6

[6] I.M.O'Neill, D.C.Clutterbuck, P.F.Farrow, P.G.Summers and W.C.Dolman
     The Formal Verification of Safety Critical Assembly Code IFAC SAFECOMP '88, Pergamon Press

[7] H.Stenger
     Stichprobentheorie
     Physika Verlag Würzburg und Wien

[8] W.Ehrenberger, J.Märtz, G.Glöe and E.U.Mainka
     Reliability Evaluation of a Safety Related Operating System
     in Proceedings of SAFECOMP 85, Pergamon Press

[9] IEC Standard No 880
     Software in the Safety Systems of Nuclear Power Stations

International Electrotechnical Commission, 1987

[10] IEC SC65A(Secretariat)122 Version 1.0
     Software for Computers in the Application of Industrial Safety-Related Systems
     International Electrotechnical Commission
     Geneva 26th September 1991

TESTING KNOWLEDGE BASED SYSTEMS: A CASE STUDY AND IMPLICATIONS

P. Heino

Occupational Safety Engineering Laboratory
Technical Research Centre of Finland
P.O. Box 656, SF-33101 Tampere, Finland
E-mail Perttu_Heino@vtt.fi

H. Jaakkola

Information Technology (Pori)
Tampere University of Technology
P.O. Box 30, SF-28601 Pori, Finland
E-mail hj@cs.tut.fi

J. Tepandi

Department of Information Processing
Tallinn Technical University
Akadeemia tee 1, Tallinn EE0108, Estonia
E-mail tepandi@ti.ioc.ew.su

Abstract. Knowledge engineering and risk analysis have become
increasingly important for safety-related computer systems. The
first offers methods to cope with vague, uncertain, and badly
structured tasks, the second attempts to identify the extent and
likelihood of the consequences associated with hazards. The
methods and tools proposed in these approaches must themselves be
reliable. Based on a case study in testing a transnational
project - a knowledge based risk management system (KRM), the
authors analyze the impact of the specific features of knowledge
based systems on testing, propose a test design and
identification scheme for prototyping development, investigate
documentation, use of standards, and quality management in
knowledge based system projects, and consider tasks necessary to
improve the quality of development and use of risk analysis
software.

Keywords. Knowledge engineering; safety; quality control;
computer-aided system design; expert systems; software
engineering; standards; risk analysis.

INTRODUCTION

For safety-related computer systems, two
research and development approaches have
become increasingly important: knowledge
engineering and risk analysis. The first
offers methods to cope with the vague,
uncertain, and badly structured tasks, the
second attempts to identify the extent and
likelihood of the consequences associated
with hazards. The methods and tools
proposed in these approaches must
themselves be reliable.

Due to the specific features of knowledge
based systems (KBS), their high
reliability is not easy to achieve.
Therefore, the importance of verification,
validation, and testing of KBS has been
widely recognized. In a number of papers
and several books devoted to this topic,
promising methods and approaches have been
proposed (e.g., Ayel and Laurent, 1991;
Schildt and Retti, 1991). However, a few
empirical data concerning relevance of
these methods in real testing environment
is available.

The quality of safety models and methods
has been a subject of recent interest
(Britter, 1991; Rouhiainen, 1990; Suokas,
1988). Some other aspects of improving the
validity of safety analysis, such as
quality management and evaluation of the
model implementations, seem not to have
received sufficient attention. Meanwhile,
it is evaluated that the quality
management, testing, and validation of
software projects require more than 50% of
the overall software development effort
(GEC, 1986). Neglecting these empirical
data may lead to low quality
implementations of high quality models.

This paper attempts to aid in filling in
these gaps. Based on a case study in
testing a transnational project - a
knowledge based risk analysis and
management system (Heino and colleagues,
1992), the authors analyze testing,
validation, and quality management methods
that can be applied in knowledge
engineering and safety analysis. We
address the following questions: How
important are the specific features of KBS
for their testing? How to design and
maintain tests for prototyping
development? What are the quality
management problems for joint KBS

305

projects? What are the important quality issues to be considered in further development of software which has a role in the analysis and management of industrial risks, especially in the case of international collaboration? What issues of KBS quality management seem not adequately addressed in the current research?

THE CASE STUDY: A SYSTEM FOR THE INTELLIGENT USE AND COLLECTION OF SAFETY INFORMATION

When a new industrial system is designed, lots of information about it is created and collected in various documents. The use of modern CAD technology during the design makes it possible to create an object oriented description of the system, containing the physical structure of it and the characteristics of its components.

Safety and reliability analyses are carried out during the design using various methods. If the constructed fault trees and HAZOP tables etc. are documented with a computer, data bases with safety information are created. Later, when the system has been constructed and taken into use, new information is created when malfunctions are diagnosed and controlled. If the reporting of these occurrences is done with a computer, another data base with safety related information is created.

In addition to the above mentioned, there are also other sources of relevant information, for example standards, data bases (accidents, chemicals etc.), and experiences from other plants. The key idea of the KRM (Knowledge Based Risk Management) system is to make the use of safety information and experiences more efficient both during the design and the use of process plants.

KRM is a software package developed in a Nordic project with participants from Norway (Computas Expert Systems, Veritas), Sweden (Masic Ab) and Finland (VTT), and with good contacts to the Nordic chemical and petrochemical industry. The size of the project was 15 man-years.

KRM has two main objectives: analysis support and operator support. The analysis method included in the current version of KRM is Hazard and Operability Study (HAZOP). The purpose of HAZOP is to identify the possible deviations from the way the design is intended to operate and the hazards associated with these deviations. Deviations and their potential causes and consequences are the basic concepts in the knowledge based operator support methodology of KRM. In addition, items like means to detect the deviations, and operational instructions for disturbance situations can be utilized.

The internal knowledge representation framework of KRM is an object-oriented data model which serves the different modules of KRM. It contains a process description at the level of functional process units. The safety characteristics of the process are modelled with a complementary deviation model structure. The deviation model contains the necessary structures for storing HAZOP results and using them in disturbance analysis. The deviation model is linked to the process model by defining how the different deviations and causes can be detected in the modelled process using the available measurements, alarms and other indications.

Design and safety analysis - KRM-Hazop

In the KRM system, the safety data base is created using KRM-Hazop, the safety analysis support module of KRM. KRM-Hazop can be used by the analysis leader to plan the analysis. The leader has access to reported experience, such as results from previous analyses, and disturbance and accident reports. The resulting preliminary analysis can be used as an entry form for the analysis session members by filling in possible causes, consequences and actions for the studied deviations. A safety data base containing the HAZOP results is created by KRM-Hazop. The first version of the KRM system contains a module for transferring data from one commercial CAD system.

Compared to most of the commercial packages for HAZOP documentation, an advantage of KRM-HAZOP is that it creates a structured data base of HAZOP results. This data base can be seen as a safety model of the plant describing what are the potential hazards of different equipment and functions of the plant and what are the associated causes and consequences, what corrective actions should be taken during design and operation, and how the hazardous disturbances can be detected during plant operation.

Operator support - KRM disturbance analysis

The idea of the operator support part of KRM is to make safety analysis results available to operating personnel in a user-friendly form and to provide a tool for the recording of operating experiences. The operator support module of KRM is based on the use of safety information stored in the form of safety analysis results and disturbance reports. The user interface is a block diagram of the process. Usually, it is preferable that this block diagram looks similar to the display of the process control system. When the analysis of the current process state indicates that there are disturbances in the process, those process units which are supposed to be in abnormal state are coloured red in the diagram.

The analysis of disturbances (real or hypothetical) is based on the deviation graph display. The disturbance is matched to the set of deviations in the knowledge base, and the graph of the most relevant deviation is shown on the display. Potential causes of the disturbance are shown on the left side and potential consequences on the right side. Disturbances are reported during a special disturbance report input display. The information is filled in by making menu choices and typing additional information.

Pilot installations

The KRM system has been installed by the Finnish project group at two plants: Kemira fine chemicals plant and Neste oil refinery. In addition, a joint installation by the KRM partners was carried out at the Technical University of Lund, Sweden. Plant specific modifications were made to the system in each of the installations. The basic mechanism of disturbance analysis stayed still the same.

The installation of KRM to a heat transformer system in Lund was the first on-line installation of the system. The aim was to gain experience of the problems connected to the installation and use of the system. The Kemira KRM application was a quite restricted part from the fine chemicals plant including a reactor and its input lines. The aim was to focus on rare events related to major hazards. The application process at Neste oil refinery was a flare gas system collecting extra and leaking gases from a large area of refinery processes. It was found that the concepts and methodology of KRM disturbance analysis could be used also in this case which is not an ordinary safety problem but closer to an environmental one.

The Testing Project

Part of this system that was tested in the testing project (the target system) performs the disturbance analysis and display of the safety knowledge. The initial concerns of the testing project were correctness of the software and evaluation of the used software engineering principles. During the test plan development, the following areas of interest were specified:
- correctness of the software, including traceability, consistency, and completeness;
- the software engineering principles used in the user interface, file handling, and other functions;
  - reliability;
  - usability;
  - maintainability;
- planning the further development of KRM to a software product.

The quality characteristics not to be evaluated included functionality, efficiency, and portability.

THE IMPACT OF SPECIFIC FEATURES OF KBS ON TESTING

Specific features of KBS may be classified as:
- those associated with the paradigm of KBS (a focus on symbolic reasoning, use of heuristic knowledge, uncertain reasoning, integration of different kinds of knowledge, representation of knowledge on the different levels of abstraction, transparency);
- those associated with different knowledge representation mechanisms, such as rules, frames, or semantic networks;
- those associated with the KBS development (lack of complete specifications, prototyping, lack of standard development language or environment, difficulties of determining the quality of a solution).

It is well known that the features associated with knowledge representation strongly affect KBS validation, testing, and reliability (Ayel and Laurent, 1991; Schildt and Retti, 1991; Tepandi, 1991). In the current study, we have focused on the issues associated with symbolic reasoning and KBS development.

In a recent survey, O'Leary (1991) reports that about 50% of the KBS validation effort is accomplished by the development team (the expert and the knowledge engineers), about 20% - by a different expert, and only about 7,5% - by an independent validator (validation includes testing in this study). In traditional software development, independent testing is advocated due to many reasons, for example due to the developers' tendency to follow the same thinking patterns in construction and testing, or due to a human person's reluctance to critique one's own work (GEC, 1986; Myers, 1977; Pressman, 1987). At the same time, third-party testing requires highly qualified personnel and may take additional time, funding, or other resources. Besides, it is not clear whether the specific features of KBS introduce additional difficulties for testing and validation by an independent expert group. Here we address the last question.

From the test incidents reported, about 50% could be traced back to the specification problems and prototyping. About 7% of the incidents could be associated with environment, about 20% - with symbolic reasoning and transparency, about 10% - with difficulties in settling the transnational cooperation. The last number may not reflect the real situation, because many of the specification problems can probably be traced back to joint development. In some cases, these sources appeared simultaneously, so that in total the KBS specific features were the source of nearly three quarters of the incident reports. Our first conclusion is there-fore, that these features really did have a large impact on KBS development and testing.

At the same time, these features are not unique to KBS. Indeed, prototype development is often used in non-routine research and development projects; some kind of symbolic processing and use of explanatory facilities is characteristic for word processors and databases, and so on. Our next analysis shows that from the application point of view, about 40% of the incidents were specific to the target system. However, from the more general software engineering viewpoint, in nearly all cases the situations similar to those described in test incident reports could have occurred also in some other type of software (databases, spreadsheets, word processors, etc.).

For example, in one of the test incidents it was reported that after deleting a deviation it will disappear from the screen, but still impact the result of disturbance. This is specifically associated with the model of the process plant and the risk analysis method implemented in the target system. From the more general viewpoint, there exist different levels of abstraction in the system that must be consistent - a typical situation for databases. Or, if some elements on the process block diagram did not respond meaningfully to the user, this is associated with the model of the process plant implemented in the target system. Again, one can see the process diagram as a menu and require that all the menu elements should either respond or be marked as non-active. Of course, one must be cautious with the above type of reasoning - otherwise it is possible to conclude that all errors are similar. Associating generic test situations with the properties of the target system requires some background in testing and specific experience in dealing with similar type of software; specific KBS testing experience is desirable.

A TEST DESIGN AND IDENTIFICATION SCHEME FOR PROTOTYPING

In testing systems developed by proto-typing, it may be difficult to design and maintain the test cases. The situation is further complicated when changing quality criteria are to be evaluated using seve-ral sources of information. The following test design and identification scheme used in the case study may be recommended for its support to:
 - planning of the overall amount of test cases, as well as planning the number of test cases for different modes of testing;
 - compatibility with the representation of software factors, criteria, and metrics, thus allowing for a test design to evaluate these characteristics;
 - incremental test design taking into account the results of testing already performed;
 - flexibility in adding, modifying, and deleting test profiles, suites, and cases;
 - modifying the test design for the subsequent versions of software;
 - presenting test incident reports on different levels (individual reports for test cases, as well as more general reports concerning test suites on various levels).

As to the negative features of this scheme, so it does not support ordering of the tests. In general, the identifiers are not in alphabetical or numerical order. So it may be worthwhile in some cases to assign consecutive numbers to the cases after the final design has been performed.

The Test Design

The tests designed form a hierarchy. Here we will refer to an item on the first level of that hierarchy as '(test) profile', to an item on the lowest level - as 'test (case)', and to items on intermediate levels - as '(test) suite'.

Test profile determines the type of testing and the source of information for it. The following profiles were used in the case study: testing of the system as it was demonstrated to the testers, testing based on functional description of KRM, KRM system and user documentation based testing, KRM documentation review.

The hierarchy of test suites may be different for particular test profiles. For example, in the first profile two levels of test suites were used. The higher level identifies the functions, the lower level - the testing mode (normal work, boundary situations, erroneous work).

The idea of testing the system as it was demonstrated to the testers is as follows.

Typically, a system developed by prototyping is an innovative project, including a great deal of research. Therefore the most important concern may not be confirmance to the requirements - it may be more important that the implemented parts of the system were working and useful. We tried several functions based on the system "as it is", looking at specifications only when it is necessary.

Testing based on the functional description of KRM included all highest priority functions. The medium priority functions were tested, but a simplified level was sufficient. The lowest priority level was concerned only if there were resources left. Only the user documen-tation was utilized for test case cons-truction in the documentation based testing. The documentation review included checks of functional description, system documentation, and user documentation for completeness, consistency, and traceability.

This test design served twofold purpose. First, the tests had to enable the current testing activity; second, they had to be used in final testing. Therefore, a design description of tests was given even if it was known that these tests will not succeed with the current version of KRM, or if it was not possible to perform them due to test item restrictions or testing time limits. However, neither test case specifications nor incident reports were elaborated for such test cases.

The four test profiles designed comprised 17 higher-level test suites. The complexity of test cases varied from trivial (including one activity) to quite complex and time-consuming (including a sequence of activities). The first profile - testing of the system as it was demonstrated to the testers - included 10 higher-level suites and was elaborated in more detail. The test design for the case study presented here was not exhaustive. In particular, program-based testing was not considered in this testing project, according to the initial agreement.

The Test Identification

The test profiles, suites, and cases are identified in the following way. The first character of an identifier represents the test profile. Each level in the test suite hierarchy is identified by the concatenation of several characters with the upper level identifier. The individual test cases are distinguished by consecutive numbering or special identifiers. With an identifier N, the following documents and files may be associated:
 - a test specification <test_spec_general_id>-N;
 - a test incident report <test_incident_general_id>-N;
 - a test specification file <test_spec_file_general_id>-N;
 - a test incident file <test_incident_file_general_id>-N;
 - bitmap files <bitmap_file_general_id>-N-1.BMP, <bitmap_file_general_id>-N-2.BMP, etc. ;
 - other items, such as input-output data files, etc.

For example, the test case identifier

ADLE1 denotes test for demonstration ("as it is") - based testing (A), testing loading of the process diagram (DL), erroneous mode of work (E), test case 1. There were restrictions on the file name length, so the incident report KRM-TEST-VTT-009-ADLE1 for this test is kept in file T9ADLE1, and the corresponding bitmap - in file TADLE1.BMP. In the case of reports that describe incidents common to all DL tests, identifiers ADL1, ADL2,... can be used.

DOCUMENTATION, STANDARDS, AND QUALITY MANAGEMENT

Documentation and Standards

The ANSI/IEEE Std 730-1984 , IEEE Standard for Software Quality Assurance Plans, requires as a minimum the following documents:
(1) Software Requirements Specification
(2) Software Design Description
(3) Software Verification and Validation Plan
(4) Software Verification and Validation Report
(5) User Documentation.

It would be desirable to have those documents for software developed in joint KBS projects. However, this may be difficult in prototyping. In particular, in many cases it is not possible to make good documentation before the product is ready (Parnas and Clements, 1986). This may be even more characteristic of innovative software development where the product to be worked out is not properly understood before the implementation ("Prototype as a specification", or "How can I know what I think before I have programmed it"). In such cases, the following method may be recommended: Produce a revised specification, "Revision N" which includes a copy of "Revision N-1" as an Appendix. In Revision N, mark (by underlining, by side bar, or by indication in a separate section) those paragraphs where the new specification has been changed with respect to the previous revision. In this way, both a current specification and a history of its development are always available.

The ANSI/IEEE Std 829-1983, IEEE Standard for Software Test Documentation proved useful for KBS test documentation for this case study. It provides a structured framework of documents and topics, around which one can organize the ideas, plans, and results.

Some minor deficiencies in the standard were identified. In particular, the test-incident reports recommended by ANSI/IEEE (1983) provide a good structure for describing an incident as it occurred in testing, but the possibility of using this report for further monitoring and documenting the debugging and testing process in not supported. There is even no section to indicate whether the error has been corrected. Test-incident report forms proposed in (Bryan and Siegel, 1984; GEC, 1986) provide additional information on recommended solution, the necessary changes in modules, actions required to make the software operational, the status of the report and so on. However, the ANSI/IEEE (1983) seems to be better in describing the incident itself. The choice depends on how the test documentation will be used. It seems very reasonable that the test incident reports are utilized to support and manage the whole software testing and change process.

The incident form used in KRM testing combines the incident description according to the ANSI/IEEE (1983) and some further monitoring: error severity, actions proposed, actions taken.

Quality Management in Joint KBS Projects

The international cooperation is useful, but it may also introduce new problems - especially if the participants have troubles with fulfilling their promises. The following may be recommended:
 - every participant should have a quality management system that can be checked (certified);
 - when planning the cooperative project, it is desirable that the tasks of every contributing organization be assigned already in the requirements specification;
 - for such international cooperation, it is especially important to develop clear interface specifications, design "shortcuts" for the case the other participants are late, have common reviews, have good contacts with the future users, etc.;
 - it is important to plan sufficient resources for testing activities. For example, the GEC (1986) Software Engineering Handbook evaluates that Code and Unit Test take about 20%, Integration Test - about 25%, and Validation Test - about 15% of the overall project effort.

In particular, this case study has shown that especially for international cooperative projects it is desirable to develop some quality management plan. Various versions of such plans are available. However, the off-the-shelf quality management plans usually do not work - they must be tailored to the organization and its people. More importantly, everybody concerned should recognize the need for such a plan, and it must be followed. However, people tend to have difficulties with following standards and rules that exceed one or two pages. Therefore, introducing quality management plans should be done step by step - only when the current page of rules becomes a habit, it is possible to introduce the next one.

QUALITY OF SAFETY ANALYSIS SOFTWARE

There exist a lot of software for supporting the analysis and management of industrial risks. Besides new developments it should be made clear, how is the existing software used, what is its quality, and what are the quality requirements for future international projects. More specifically, the objectives of research and development in the area of quality of risk analysis software, its development, and adoption could be:
 - investigating adoption of risk analysis software, the efficiency of its use, factors affecting the efficiency, and measures to improve it;
 - developing a library of benchmark tasks based on experimental data for the

risk analysis software that would enable comparison of different software systems on the same problems;
- practical testing and validation of risk analysis software products;
- developing quality management policies for joint software projects, as well as methods for their implementation;
- investigating existing software safety analysis, testing, validation, and quality evaluation methods and tools, and if necessary, integrating them or developing new tools.

CONCLUSIONS

This study indicates that such specific features of KBS as focus on symbolic processing, transparency, prototyping, lack of detailed specifications, lack of standard development environment, really have a large impact on testing. The most important of these were prototyping and lack of detailed specifications. However, these features are not unique to KBS. Therefore, in the early phases of testing the correspondence of KBS to the software engineering practices and standards, it is necessary that the testers have general background in testing and specific experience in dealing with similar type of software; specific KBS testing experience is desirable.

We have also proposed a flexible test design and identification scheme for prototyping, analyzed the suitability of IEEE/ANSI (1983) standard for KBS testing, investigated quality management principles for joint KBS projects, and suggested the objectives of research and development in the area of quality of risk analysis software, its adoption, and development.

Such issues as KBS completeness, consistency, validation, and some others are specific to these systems and have received the attention they deserve. Still there are practical problems that seem not be investigated adequately, such as:
- the KBS technology transfer;
- applicability of the existing standards to the KBS development, verification, test, and validation;
- KBS quality factors, criteria, metrics, benchmarks, as well as applicability of ISO proposals for software quality characteristics, sub-characteristics and metrics to the KBS;
- quality criteria for and quality studies of the KBS environments.

ACKNOWLEDGEMENT

The authors are grateful to Veikko Rouhiainen and Cris Whetton for helpful discussions and suggestions.

REFERENCES

ANSI/IEEE (1983). Std 829-1983, IEEE Standard for Software Test Documentation.

ANSI/IEEE (1984). Std 730-1984 , IEEE Standard for Software Quality Assurance Plans.

Ayel, M. and Laurent, J.-P. (Eds.) (1991). Validation, Verification, and Test of Knowledge-Based Systems. Wiley, New York.

Britter, R. E. (1991). The Evaluation of Technical Models Used for Major-Accident Hazard Installations. Report to Commission of the European Communities Directorate General XII, Cambridge.

Bryan, W. and Siegel, S. (1984). Making Software Visible, Operational, and Maintainable in a Small Project Environment. IEEE Trans. Software Eng., vol. SE-10, no. 1, January 1984, pp. 59-67.

GEC (1986). Software Engineering Handbook. Prepared by General Electric Company. McGraw-Hill, New York.

Heino, P., Karvonen, I., Pettersen, T., Wennersten, R., and Andersen, T. (1992). Analysis and Monitoring of Hazards Using HAZOP-based Plant Safety Model. Reliability Engineering and System Safety (to be published).

O'Leary, D. E. (1991). Design, Development and Validation of Expert Systems: A Survey of Developers. In M. Ayel and J.-P. Laurent, (Eds.), Validation, Verification, and Test of Knowledge-Based Systems, Wiley, New York, pp. 3-19.

Myers, G. (1977). The Art of Software testing. Wiley, New York.

Parnas, D. L. and Clements, P. C. (1986). A Rational Design Process: How and Why to Fake It. IEEE Trans. Software Eng., vol. SE-12, no. 2, pp. 251-257.

Pressman, R. S. (1987). Software Engineering. A Practitioner's Approach. McGraw-Hill, New York.

Schildt, G. H. and Retti, J. (Eds.) (1991). Dependability of Artificial Intelligence Systems (DAISY 91). North-Holland, Amsterdam.

Rouhiainen, V. (1990). The Quality Assessment of Safety Analysis. Technical Research Centre of Finland, Publication No. 61.

Suokas, J. (1988). Evaluation of the Quality of Safety and Risk Analysis in the Chemical Industry. Risk Analysis, vol. 8, no. 4, pp. 581-591.

Tepandi, J. (1991). Expert System Reliability. In Y. Malmén and V. Rouhiainen (Eds.), Reliability and Safety of Processes and Manufacturing Systems, Elsevier Applied Science, London, 1991, pp. 137-148.

Wolfsberger, J. (1987). Space Station Hands NASA Its Biggest Software Task Yet. IEEE Software, November 1987, p. 95.

AN EXPERIMENTAL EVALUATION OF FORMAL TESTING AND STATISTICAL TESTING

B. Marre[2], P. Thévenod-Fosse[1], H. Waeselynck[1], P. Le Gall[2], Y. Crouzet[1]

[1] LAAS - CNRS, 7 Avenue du Colonel Roche, 31077 Toulouse Cedex, France
[2] L.R.I., URA CNRS 410, Université Paris-Sud, 91405 Orsay Cedex, France

Abstract. Functional testing from formal specification (or formal testing, for short) and statistical testing are the concern of quite different processes of designing test data sets. These differences are outlined, and their complementary features are analysed. Then, the paper reports on unit testing experiments performed on a program which is a piece of a software from the nuclear industry. Five test sets of each type have been automatically generated, and mutation analysis is used to assess their efficiency with respect to error detection. The 1345 mutants of the target program are killed by each of the 5 statistical test sets and by 3 formal test sets, the 2 other ones leaving alive only one and two mutants. These promising results encourage further investigation of integration testing, where both methods are expected to exhibit complementary efficiency with respect to actual faults.

Keywords. Software Testing, Formal Specification, Random Test data, Safety-critical Software, Experiments.

INTRODUCTION

In the present state of the art, the question of *how to select a test input set well-suited for revealing faults* still arises, due to the lack of an accurate software design fault model. Many test criteria, related to either the function or the structure of the software, have been proposed in the literature as guides for determining test cases (see e.g. Beizer, 1990). Each of them defines a proper set of subdomains of the input domain to be exercised during testing. Given a criterion, the most current type of test input generation is deterministic: input test sets are built by selecting one element from each subdomain involved in the set proper to the adopted criterion. Unfortunately, exercising only once each subdomain defined from such criteria is far from being enough to ensure that the corresponding test set is relevant to expose faults, since a real limitation of current criteria is their imperfect connection with faults.

This paper reports on two different methods for designing more relevant test cases. First, **functional testing from formal specification** – called **formal testing** in this paper, for short – aims at *defining pertinent functional criteria* under which exercising once each subdomain is sufficient. Test data are automatically selected from a *formal specification* of the software via selection strategies derived from

hypotheses tuned by the user of the system (Bernot, 1991b; Marre, 1991). The second approach, called **statistical testing**, is intended to *deal with imperfect criteria* that is, to derive test sets with a high fault revealing power, in spite of a tricky link between the adopted criterion and the faults. It consists in a *probabilistic generation of test data:* inputs are randomly generated according to a defined probability distribution on the input domain; both the distribution and the number of input data items being determined according to the adopted criterion (Thévenod, 1989, 1991a).

The next section outlines both testing methods, and examines their main complementary features. Then, the paper presents an experimental work performed on a **program** which is a piece of a software from the **nuclear industry**. Five test sets of each type have been experimented with, using mutation analysis (DeMillo, 1978) to assess their efficiency w.r.t. (with respect to) error detection. The experimental results involve a total of **1345 mutation faults**, seeded one by one in the original program source code. In the light of the results reported, both testing methods exhibit promising fault revealing powers. Because of their distinct underlying theoretical background, they should provide complementary test data sets: combining them becomes all the more interesting as there is no trusted design fault model.

COMPARISON OF FORMAL AND STATISTICAL TESTING

As outlined below, the two methods are the concern of quite different processes for designing test data.

Formal Testing

The motivation of this approach is that, providing that a formal specification of the program to be tested is available, it is possible to use the specification *to define black-box test criteria in a formal framework*. Such strategies allow us to test whether all the properties specified in the specification are actually dealt by the program. Test data selection is only guided by the structure of the specification: for each property expressed by a formula of the specification, test data are selected via strategies derived from hypotheses chosen by the user. Referring to these hypotheses offers the advantage to make explicit the relationship between testing and correctness.

General theoretical results are presented in (Bernot, 1991a, 1991b). We will only focus on the points which are relevant to the hereafter case study: the specifications are positive conditional algebraic specifications (Goguen, 1978). A specification is a pair $SP = (\Sigma, Ax)$; the signature Σ is a finite set S of *sort* (i.e. type) names plus a finite set of *operation* names with arity in S; the properties of the operations of Σ are defined by the set Ax of axioms of the form: $(v_1 = w_1 \& \dots \& v_n = w_n) \Rightarrow v = w$, where v_i, w_i, v and w are Σ-terms with typed variables.

Let P be the program to be tested which is supposed to implement a specification $SP = (\Sigma, Ax)$. Testing P w.r.t. SP is only possible if the semantics of P and SP are expressible in a common framework. As we are interested in dynamic testing, we have to execute P on a finite subset of its input domain and to interpret outputs w.r.t. SP. In order to consider P compatible with SP, we need first, to be able to compute the values of Σ-terms from P and secondly, to forbid that P handles "junk" values according to the operations. Indeed, if "junk" values existed, no test derived from SP could detect an error involving such a value. These two conditions mean that P implements all operations in Σ and exports only them, and will constitute the minimal hypothesis we do on a program to be tested: we say then that P defines a *finitely generated Σ-algebra*.

Let Exhaust be the set of all ground instances of the axioms obtained by replacing each variable by all ground terms of the same sort built from the operations in the signature. Each formula ϕ in Exhaust is a test which becomes *executable* when it is possible to check from P that ϕ is satisfied in P or not (in the first case, we have then $success_P(\phi)$). In practice, to decide if $success_P(t_1 = t_1' \& \dots \& t_n = t_n' \Rightarrow t = t')$, we need:

(i) first, to compute in P the values t_i^P, $t_i'^P$, t^P and t'^P denoted by the terms t_i, t_i', t and t';

(ii) then, to verify that whenever $(t_1^P =_P t_1'^P)$ and … and $(t_n^P =_P t_n'^P)$, we have also $(t^P =_P t'^P)$, where $=_P$ denotes a decision procedure of the equality in P.

Intuitively, we would say that assuming that P defines a finitely generated Σ-algebra, $success_P(Exhaust)$ is equivalent to the correction of P but, in general, the existence of the decision procedure $=_P$ is not guaranteed. Bernot (1991a) proposes a solution based on the notion of *observability*: for each observable sort s, P provides a correct procedure which decides if two terms of sort s are equal or not in P. Moreover, Bernot (1991a) has shown that it is useless to verify the conditional tests of Exhaust with a false precondition: this result precisely meets our intuition of the definition of $success_P$. Thus, we can define an exhaustive observational equational test data set EqExhaust as the set of all observational ground instances built on the *conclusions of the axioms* that validate the preconditions in the specification. Assuming that P satisfies some observational hypotheses, the success of EqExhaust is then equivalent to the correctness of P w.r.t. SP.

Unfortunately, EqExhaust is often infinite and we can only consider a finite subset of it. More precisely, in order to cover all properties of SP, we select, for each axiom ax of SP, a finite subset T_{ax} of the subset $EqExhaust_{ax}$ of EqExhaust corresponding to ax. When we select T_{ax}, we make the following selection hypothesis: $success_P(T_{ax}) \Rightarrow success_P(EqExhaust_{ax})$. Such hypotheses are usually left implicit. We prefer to bring them up since it seems sound first, to state hypotheses H and only after, to select a test set corresponding to them. We require both following properties for a relevant pair (H, T_{ax}) (such a pair is said *practicable*):

(i) under H, the test data set T_{ax} rejects all programs not validating ax (T_{ax} is *valid*), i.e.
$(H \& (success_P(T_{ax}))) \Rightarrow success_P(EqExhaust_{ax})$

(ii) under H, the test data set T_{ax} does not reject programs validating ax (T_{ax} is *unbiased*), i.e.
$(H \& (success_P(EqExhaust_{ax}))) \Rightarrow success_P(T_{ax})$

If (H, T_{ax}) is practicable and T_{ax} is finite, the success of T_{ax} is equivalent to the correctness of P w.r.t. ax. In order to exhibit relevant hypotheses, we do a decomposition based on a case analysis of the validity domain of ax (i.e. the domain where the preconditions of ax are satisfied in the specification). This case analysis is guided by the structure of the specification. This process of decomposition of subdomains may be refined w.r.t. the specification structure until the size of each subdomain may be considered as sufficiently small in order to only take one element per subdomain (uniformity hypothesis). The tool described in (Bernot, 1991b; Marre, 1991) allows the user to find automatically an element of each subdomain of validity: it uses unfolding methods based on equational logic programming with constraints. Decomposition by case analysis ensures that the user gets finite practicable pairs (H,T) where H combines the minimal hypotheses with uniformity hypotheses on each subdomain.

Statistical Testing

The motivation of statistical testing is *to deal with imperfect test criteria*, that is, to provide a method for determining test data sets with a high fault revealing power, in spite of a tricky link between the adopted criterion and the actual faults (Thévenod, 1991a). Since exercising only once each subdomain defined from an imperfect criterion is far from being enough to provide an efficient test set, an obvious improvement consists in exercising each subdomain several times. And for this, the probabilistic method for generating test inputs is a practical automatic means, the key to its effectiveness being the derivation of an appropriate probability distribution over the input domain. In particular, the generation of random test data based on a uniform distribution over the whole input domain (Duran, 1984; Hamlet, 1990), is not expected to be an efficient way to design test sets: revealing input data are unlikely to be uniformly distributed over the input domain. Actually, structural or functional criteria in current use do provide a relevant information on the product under test, and it can be expected that they are not strongly inadequate w.r.t. fault exposure (Thévenod, 1991b). Hence, the idea is to take advantage of this information and to compensate its imperfection by increasing the test size. Statistical testing is based on the theoretical framework recalled below (Thévenod, 1989), that induces a rigourous method for determining both an input distribution and a number of random test data items according to a given criterion.

Theoretical background. Given a criterion Ai, let S_{Ai} be the corresponding set of subdomains to be exercised. For example, the structural criterion "All-branches" requires that each program branch b_k be executed: this defines one subdomain k for each b_k, that gathers the input items executing b_k; then, Ai = "branches" $\Rightarrow S_{Ai} = \{k, \forall b_k \in B\}$, where B is the set of all the program branches.

Definition. A set T of N input data items covers a test criterion Ai with a probability q_N if each subdomain $\in S_{Ai}$ has a probability of at least q_N of being exercised during the N executions supplied by T. *q_N is the test quality w.r.t. Ai.*

Theorem. In the case of statistical testing, the test quality q_N and the number N of input cases are linked by the relation:
$(1-Pi)^N = 1-q_N$ with $Pi = \min \{p_k, k \in S_{Ai}\}$ (1)
p_k being the probability that a random input item exercises the subdomain k.

Relation (1) is easy to justify: since Pi is the probability per input case of exercising the least likely subdomain, each subdomain has a probability of at least $1 - (1-Pi)^N$ of being exercised by a test set of N random input cases. A practical consequence is that each subdomain $\in S_{Ai}$ is exercised several times on average. More precisely, relation (1) sets a link between the test quality and the expected number of times, denoted n, the least likely subdomain is exercised: $n \cong - \ln(1-q_N)$. For example, $n \cong 7$ for $q_N = 0.999$, and $n \cong 9$ for $q_N = 0.9999$.

Design of statistical testing. The method for determining a statistical test set T (input distribution and number N of random input data items) according to a given criterion Ai is based on the above theorem. Since the values p_k, and thus Pi, depend on the input distribution, it involves two steps (Thévenod, 1991a):

(i) *search for an input distribution* well-suited to rapidly exercise each subdomain $\in S_{Ai}$ in order to reduce the test size; or equivalently the distribution must let the value of Pi be as high as possible;

(ii) *assessment of the test size N* required to reach a target test quality q_N w.r.t. Ai, using the distribution previously defined and thus, the value Pi inferred from it; relation (2), deduced from relation (1), gives the minimum test size:
$N = \log (1-q_N) / \log (1-Pi)$ (2)

It is worth noting that the adopted criterion is used only for determining an input distribution and a test size, but not for selecting a priori a subset of input data items. Hence, one can reasonably think that the criterion adequacy w.r.t. actual faults should set a less acute problem in the case of random data generation. Actually, a meaningful link exists between fault exposure and statistical test data: from equation (1), any fault involving a failure probability $p \geq Pi$ per execution (according to the chosen input distribution) has a probability of at least q_N of being revealed by a set of N random inputs.

Structural and functional criteria. The above method has already been applied and experimented with, in both unit and module testing. At unit level, the adopted criteria were structural, based on the coverage of the control and data flow graph of the programs (Thévenod, 1991a). At module level, structural criteria being no more tractable due to the program sizes, Thévenod (1992) proposes functional criteria based on the coverage of behavior models – finite state machines, decision tables – deduced from informal specifications.

Complementary Features

Because of their distinct underlying theoretical background, one can expect that the two testing methods, formal and statistical, provide complementary – rather than competing – test data sets, that is, well-suited to expose faults of different kind. Hence, combining them becomes all the more interesting as there is no trusted design fault model. Indeed, although they begin both with a decomposition of the input domain into several subdomains, they differ from one another in the three main following points.

Subdomains originate from unrelated criteria, since based on different software models, namely: in the case of formal testing, an algebraic specification; in the case of statistical testing, either behavior models deduced from informal specifications, or program flow graphs, depending on the software complexity.

Provided with a set of subdomains, the methods support two distinct uses.

(i) For formal testing, decomposition may be as fine as wished w.r.t. the specification; applying uniformity hypotheses (and thus exercising only one element per subdomain) suffices when the specification is not too far from the program design. If it is not the case (i.e. unrelated structures), decomposition into subdomains can induce too strong uniformity hypotheses. On the other hand, faults connected to the program limits (special input items) must coincide with an explicit specification property, and consequently, they must normally appear as particular cases of the decomposition.

(ii) For statistical testing, a criteria is not considered as reliable enough; exercising only one element per subdomain is far too weak. So, increasing the test size by a probabilistic choice of several items from each subdomain aims to improve a non sufficiently sharp decomposition of the input domain. Yet, the risk of leaving extremal/special input values out is the main weakness of the approach, since these values remain, by essence, poorly catered with a random input generation, within reasonable testing time.

The oracle problem, i.e. that of how to determine the correct outputs which a program should return in responses to given input data (Weyuker, 1982), arises with any testing method, and it becomes crucial when numerous input data are concerned. Formal testing provides an oracle procedure as soon as the selected inputs/outputs are observable, while statistical testing does not.

EXPERIMENTAL FRAMEWORK

The whole experimental environment has already been presented in (Thévenod, 1991a), so that we only outline its main features.

Target Program

The target program, written in C language, is extracted from a nuclear reactor safety shutdown system. The whole module periodically scans the position of the reactor's control rods, and is composed of several functional units. The target program implements the **filtering unit**, that aims to check the validity of the measures acquired in order to eliminate doubtful ones. Its output results depend on both current and past values filtered. The size of the object code (separately compiled source code) amounts to 1133 bytes.

Target Fault Set

The target faults are **mutations** introduced in the source code (DeMillo, 1978). Three types of change are automatically performed by our mutant generator: 1) constant replacement; 2) symbol – scalar variable, array and structure reference, etc – replacement; 3) operator replacement; leading to an amount of 1345 mutants for the target program. A mutant is "killed" by a test data set if its output history differs from that of the original program. A **mutation score**, denoted $MS(T)$ for a test set T, is defined to be the fraction of non-equivalent mutants which are killed by T. $MS(T)$ is a number in the interval $[0, 1]$: a high score indicates that T is very efficient w.r.t. mutation fault exposure.

An acute question concerns the representativeness of a mutation score w.r.t. the *actual fault exposure power* of a test set, i.e. the representativeness of the mutations w.r.t. actual faults. The question is still an open issue. In the current state of the art, mutation analysis provides the only practical way to assess and compare the efficiency of various test sets on a large number of fault patterns. Assuming the *competent programmer hypothesis*, the changes introduced correspond to faults likely to be made during the coding phase. Hence, the mutation scores should provide a meaningful experimental metric, at least at the unit testing level addressed here.

Test Data Sets

Five test sets have been designed from each approach, in order to study eventual disparities within a category of sets. Both test sizes, although rather large for the (small) target program, are particularly justified in the case of safety-critical software.

Formal test sets. The sets F1, ..., F5 have been designed from a specification of the filtering unit defined with respect to the input data flow. A data flow of at least 6 inputs is needed to cover all the specified cases. The decomposition into subdomains is done by a case analysis on 30 axioms and applied only on the 2 last inputs of a data flow. This leads to 47 uniform subdomains (47 flows of 6 inputs, thus 282 input data). A 2 level decomposition seems to be a good compromise between the test size and the efficiency of the selected test data. The inputs and the expected corresponding outputs have been automatically generated by the tool (Marre, 1991).

Statistical test sets. The sets S1, ..., S5 have been designed from a structural analysis of the target program. The internal state of the filtering process is an explicit parameter of the program, in addition to the inputs and outputs defined for the functional unit, so that white box testing breaks the loop provided by the feedback. Hence, compared to the sets Fi, the sets Si involve supplementary input and output data. The input distribution is suited to cover the All-Paths criterion, and for a required test quality of $q_N = 0.9999$ the number of test data generated per set Si is N = 405 from relation (2).

EXPERIMENTAL RESULTS

Figure 1 displays the mutation scores supplied by each test set. Note that two scores are provided for the sets Fi, depending on whether the internal state of the filtering process is observed, or not.

These results must be compared with the previous ones related to the same program (Thévenod, 1991a, 1991b). Neither structural deterministic testing, nor uniform statistical testing were so efficient: two deterministic sets ensuring the coverage of "All-Paths" provided scores of 0.79 and 0.84; five uniform sets (of size N = 405) supplied scores ranging from 0.56 to 0.84.

Efficiency of Formal Testing

Mutations altering the internal state may need more than 6 consecutive inputs to be observable through the data flow outputs. This justifies the differences between the scores reached with and without observation of the internal state. This fact could be predicted since the size of 6 consecutive inputs is a lower bound to reach all the specified cases.

Additional observations on the internal state allow formal testing to kill almost every mutant still alive: only one mutant is not killed by the test data set F3, and one more by F4. Thus, formal testing provides almost perfect criteria (w.r.t. mutations). This is a very satisfactory result since there was a priori no reason for a functional test data set to reach a better coverage of structural faults than the "All-Paths" deterministic testing.

The single (resp. two) mutant(s) remaining alive for the set F3 (resp. F4) show(s) that the subdomain decomposition is not acute enough to ensure their exposure. Whether the internal state is observed or not, the five mutation scores reached by the sets Fi exhibit some disparity, which proves that uniformity hypotheses on subdomains are too strong in the present case. Hence the decomposition should be pushed further. However, this decomposition is intrinsically pertinent since one input item per subdomain suffices to kill almost every mutant. By comparison, the strongest structural criterion "All-Paths" clearly provides an insufficient partition.

Efficiency of Structural Statistical Testing

The perfect scores *MS(Si) = 1.0* are repeatedly observed for the five statistical sets Si, suggesting that the high fault revealing power is really due to the adequacy of the input distribution, and is not dependent of the particular values generated for the sets. All mutants are *rapidly killed*, far before the completion of the tests: actually, the final scores are practically obtained in the first third of each Si. On the contrary, a blind test based on a uniform sampling of the input domain is far from being adequate, as stated by the previous experiments involving uniform sets: poor final scores are supplied and great disparities are observed from one set to another. This provides evidence that the input distribution has a significant impact on the efficiency of random test data.

An input distribution ensuring a suitable probe of the source code of the program seems very adequate at the unit testing level addressed here. The information brought by the structural analysis is meaningful w.r.t. fault exposure, although not sufficient since the "All-Paths" deterministic sets fail to kill all the mutants and exhibit disparate mutation scores. During statistical testing, the imperfection of the criterion is compensated by the large number of test cases that the probabilistic approach allows to generate.

Actually, the whole experimental study on structural statistical testing involved four functional units of the software module – including the case studied in this paper – and a total amount of 2816 mutants: only 6

	1	2	3	4	5	controllability & observability
Formal Sets Fi	0.9703	0.9651	0.9688	0.9784	0.9703	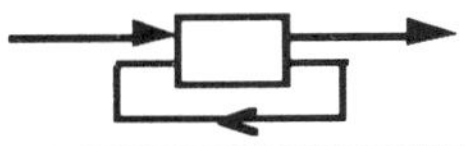
	1.0	1.0	0.9993	0.9985	1.0	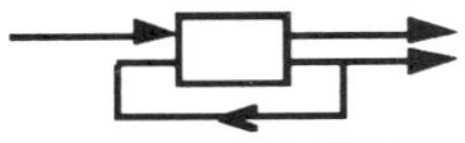
Statistical Sets Si	1.0 $\forall$ Si					

Fig. 1. Mutation scores.

were not killed by the structural statistical sets. These 6 mutants were changes affecting an array index, that can be revealed only by applying specific input patterns. Extremal/special values are, by essence, poorly catered for by statistical testing within reasonable testing times, and are more efficiently covered by deterministic test data specifically aimed at them.

CONCLUSION, FUTURE WORK

The efficiency of two testing methods has been exemplified by an experimental work conducted on a real program from the nuclear field. High mutation scores were observed: actually, formal test sets left alive only two of the entire set of 1345 mutants, and structural statistical test sets killed all of them. Neither "All-Paths" deterministic testing, nor uniform statistical testing achieved such a level of success. Hence, these first results clearly provide evidence that both formal testing and statistical testing can drastically enhance test stringency. Yet, this is at the expense of larger test sizes, but testing times remains reasonable at the unit level, and in any case is quite justified for safety-critical programs. They do not set a practical problem since: (i) in both methods, the generation of input data is automatically performed by tools; and (ii) formal testing provides an oracle procedure (as soon as the inputs/outputs are observable), that can also be used to solve the oracle problem remaining in the probabilistic approach.

This experimental study will be extended to **larger programs**. It is worth noting that the required test sizes will not be an increasing function of the software size and complexity: both methods consider adapted criteria for the module testing level (Bernot, 1991b; Thévenod, 1992).

In our mind, the ability of formal testing to cover extremal/special values, and the ability of statistical testing to compensate criteria imperfection (w.r.t. faults), justify a **simultaneous use of both techniques**. And even better, a promising approach could be a more elaborate testing method that merges both approaches. Indeed, a statistical testing strategy based on a decomposition built by selection according to formal testing would surely have the following advantages:

(i) the extremal input values are covered;

(ii) any remaining imperfection of the functional decomposition is compensated by the statistical selection.

ACKNOWLEDGEMENTS

It a pleasure to acknowledge Marie-Claude Gaudel and Gilles Bernot for their constant help during the elaboration of the algebraic specification used here.

This work has been partially supported by the PRC "Programmation et Outils pour l'Intelligence Artificielle", and by the CEC under ESPRIT Basic Research Action no. 3092 "Predictably Dependable Computing Systems (PDCS)".

REFERENCES

Beizer, B. (1990). *Software Testing Techniques*. 2nd ed. Van Nostrand Reinhold, New York.

Bernot, G. (1991a). Testing against formal specifications: a theoretical view. In *TAPSOFT CCPSD*, Springer-Verlag LNCS 494, Brighton. pp. 99-119.

Bernot, G., M-C. Gaudel, and B. Marre (1991b). Software testing based on formal specifications: a theory and a tool. *Software Engineering Journal, 6*, 387-405.

DeMillo, R. A., R. J. Lipton, and F. G. Sayward (1978). Hints on test data: help for the practicing programmer. *IEEE Computer Magazine, 11*, no. 4, 34-41.

Duran, J. W., and S. C. Ntafos (1984). An evaluation of random testing. *IEEE Transactions on Software Engineering, SE-10*, 438-444.

Goguen, J., J. Tatcher, and E. Wagner (1978). An initial algebra approach to the specification, correctness, and implementation of abstract data types. In Yeh (Ed.), *Current Trends in Programming Methodology*, Vol. 4, Prenctice Hall.

Hamlet, D., and R. Taylor (1990). Partition testing does not inspire confidence. *IEEE Transactions on Software Engineering, 16*, 1402-1411.

Marre, B. (1991). Toward automatic test data set selection using algebraic specifications and logic programming. In *8th Int. Conference on Logic Programming*, Logic Programming M.I.T. Press, Paris, 202-219.

Thévenod, P. (1989). Software validation by means of statistical testing: retrospect and future direction. *1st IFIP Working Conference on Dependable Computing for Critical Applications*, Santa Barbara, 15-22.

Thévenod, P., H. Waeselynck, and Y. Crouzet (1991a). An experimental study on software structural testing: deterministic versus random input generation. In *21st IEEE Symposium on Fault-Tolerant Computing*, Montreal, 410-417.

Thévenod, P., H. Waeselynck, and Y. Crouzet (1991b). Software structural testing: an evaluation of the efficiency of deterministic and random test data. LAAS Report 91.389.

Thévenod, P., and H. Waeselynck (1992). On functional statistical testing designed from software behavior models. To appear in *3rd IFIP Working Conference on Dependable Computing for Critical Applications*, Mondello.

Weyuker, E. J. (1982). On testing non-testable programs. *The Computer Journal, 25*, 465-470.

AUTHOR INDEX

KEYWORD INDEX